U.S. Foreign Policy in F

What is the long-term nature of American foreign policy? *U.S. Foreign Policy in Perspective* refutes the claim that it has varied considerably across time and space, arguing that key policies have been remarkably stable over the past hundred years, not in terms of ends but of means

Closely examining U.S. foreign policy, past and present, David Sylvan and Stephen Majeski draw on a wealth of historical and contemporary cases to show how the U.S. has had a "client state" empire for at least a century. They clearly illustrate how much of American policy revolves around acquiring clients, maintaining clients and engaging in hostile policies against enemies deemed to threaten them, representing a peculiarly American form of imperialism. They also reveal how clientilism informs apparently disparate activities in different geographical regions and operates via a specific range of policy instruments, showing predictable variation in the use of these instruments.

With a broad range of cases from U.S. policy in the Caribbean and Central America after the Spanish-American War, to the origins of the Marshall Plan and NATO, to economic bailouts and covert operations, and to military interventions in South Vietnam, Kosovo, and Iraq, this important book will be of great interest to students and researchers of U.S. foreign policy, security studies, history and international relations.

David Sylvan is Professor of International Relations and head of the Political Science Unit at the Graduate Institute of International and Development Studies, Geneva, Switzerland.

Stephen Majeski is Professor of Political Science and chair of the Department of Political Science at the University of Washington, Seattle, United States.

U.S. Foreign Policy in Perspective

Clients, enemies and empire

David Sylvan and Stephen Majeski

Routledge
Taylor & Francis Group

LONDON AND NEW YORK

First published 2009
by Routledge
2 Park Square, Milton Park, Abingdon, Oxon OX14 4RN

Simultaneously published in the USA and Canada
by Routledge
711 Third Avenue, New York, NY 10017

Routledge is an imprint of the Taylor & Francis Group, an informa business

Typeset in Times New Roman by
Taylor & Francis Books

British Library Cataloguing in Publication Data
A catalogue record for this book is available from the British Library

Library of Congress Cataloging in Publication Data
Sylvan, David, 1953-
  U.S. foreign policy in perspective : clients, enemies, and empire / David Sylvan and
Stephen Majeski.
    p. cm.
  Includes bibliographical references and index.
  1. United States–Foreign relations. 2. United States–Foreign relations–Philosophy. I.
Majeski, Stephen. II. Title.
  E183.7.S975 2009
  327.73–dc22
  2008041149

ISBN 10: 0-415-70134-1 (hbk)
ISBN 10: 0-415-70135-x (pbk)
ISBN 10: 0-203-79945-3 (ebk)

ISBN 13: 978-0-415-70134-1 (hbk)
ISBN 13: 978-0-415-70135-8 (pbk)
ISBN 13: 978-0-203-79945-1 (ebk)

To Irwin S. Sylvan and Sally v. Sylvan and to Sheila O'Brien

Contents

Figures

Tables

Preface

Early in the twenty-first century, United States foreign policy began to be talked about as having undergone major changes. Journalists and academics began to speculate that with the advent of the George W. Bush administration and its reaction to the events of 11 September 2001, the U.S. was now acting toward other countries in a way that was fundamentally different than in the past. Those differences included a more frequent resort to military force and a concomitant downgrading of diplomacy; a penchant for acting unilaterally rather than with allies or through multilateral institutions; and an ideological classification of countries into friends and foes, with the latter being combatted even if they did not pose a military threat to others. In short, whether this was seen as good or bad, the United States was said to have shifted to a fundamentally imperial stance toward the rest of the world.

These types of claims are misleading. On the one hand, they greatly exaggerate just how much U.S. foreign policy was militarized, or unilateralized, or ideologized, under Bush; on the other, they present past U.S. policy in a considerably more diplomatic, multilateral, and modest light than was in fact the case. Both criticisms are easy to demonstrate and we do so in the following pages. Specifically, we show how, from 1898 to the present, U.S. foreign policy has been fundamentally continuous, with the same types of routine and interventionary policies being opted for in similar situations. What this continuity involves is not an unchanging set of long-term goals but rather a small set of means, resorted to over and over as a means of taking on as clients certain states and supporting them, while at the same time actively opposing other states as enemies. In this sense, the book is both a detailed description of American foreign policy today and a history of how, within rigid limits, that policy evolved over the past eleven decades.

However, the broader question is why U.S. policy in fact changed as little as it did. To answer that question, we put forward a theory of how foreign policy gets made on three different time scales: day-to-day, when the problems dealt with involve the execution of existing policy; episodic, when that policy fails and has to be reevaluated; and epochal, when there is a sense that a historical turning point is at hand. To come up with this theory, we found that existing approaches to foreign policy analysis were of little use, mostly because they failed to take into account the details of how particular means were opted for in specific situations. Instead, we found that other intellectual traditions, namely cybernetics and organization theory, gave us the theoretical tools to explain the different types of policy continuity. Those explanations involve showing how policy is means-driven, through the availability of capabilities embedded in organizations, rather than spurred by any long-term goals or structural concerns.

To develop and test the theory, it was necessary to look closely at what precisely the U.S. was doing with regard to specific countries and at how the debates over what the U.S. should be doing unfolded in Washington. This meant that we had, as much as possible, to rely on primary source materials about the contours of U.S. policy, since secondary accounts were not always concerned with the same policy making issues as we were. It also meant that we had to amass a large number of cases of concrete U.S. policy making regarding specific countries, not only because continuity can only be demonstrated by showing that the same types of policies were opted for repeatedly over the course of more than a century, but because policy depended on the type of situation, and there were, by our count, some twenty-three of those. (There are, in fact, a small number of variables that generate those separate situations.) Although many of the cases are written up in the book, many others are simply mentioned, with full discussions of them being reserved for the book's website: www.us-foreign-policy-perspective.org

The theory we develop, the history we recount, and the description we put forward all point in the direction of the United States as possessing an empire of client states. That empire has been in existence for many decades and, we argue in the final chapter of the book, shows little signs of ending. Whether or not that is a good thing we leave to the reader to decide; although our views are easily discernible from the tone with which certain passages are written, this is a work of scholarship and not of advocacy.

We began our collaboration on this book in 2004, although it grew out of work we had done on U.S. military intervention over the preceding eight years, with that work in turn having its origins in a lengthy research project on U.S. foreign policy making with respect to Vietnam. Over the years, many of the ideas in this book were tried out on various colleagues, to whom we owe a debt of gratitude. Among those, we would single out Thomas Bernauer, Michael Byers, Lars-Erik Cederman, Michael Cox, Bruce Cumings, Richard Falk, Stephen Gill, Simon Hug, Anders Stephanson, and Donald Sylvan. Charles Kegley provided not only intellectual feedback but invaluable practical advice. Two other colleagues, alas now deceased, reacted to our ideas and were supportive: H. Bradford Westerfield and Hayward Alker. Hayward, in particular, kept up a drumbeat of suggestions, reactions, and "when will it be done" questions; we very much regret he never had a chance to read the book.

Colleagues and students at both our institutions also served as useful sounding boards. In Geneva, James Bevan, Thomas Biersteker, Andrew Clapham, Jussi Hanhimäki, Urs Luterbacher, Alexander Swoboda, and Charles Wyplosz each discussed one or more of the claims in the book with us. Students in The Foreign Policy of Great Power Intervention course and its predecessors read several of the chapters in draft form and reacted to them. In Seattle, comments, both formal and informal, came from Ellis Goldberg, Stephen Hansen, Brian Jones, George Lovell, Peter May, and Michael McCann; comments also came from the late Daniel Lev. Michael Ward not only reacted intellectually but was kind enough to produce the maps in Chapter 3. Students in several years' worth of courses on U.S. Foreign Policy read and commented on drafts of most of the chapters. Our respective institutions – the Graduate Institute of International and Development Studies, and the University of Washington – furnished support in various forms. Similarly, our research assistants – Navitri Ismaya Putri Guillaume and Christoph Pohlmann – were invaluable in tracking down information and constructing data sets.

Finally, our editor, Heidi Bagtazo of Routledge, was encouraging and patient beyond any reasonable expectations. Almost (but usefully, not quite) as patient were our families who, without ever coordinating their efforts, transmitted the same message for four years.

Abbreviations

ACRI	African Crisis Response Initiative
AFL-CIO	American Federation of Labor and Congress of Industrial Organizations
AID	U.S. Agency for International Development
ANZUS	Australia-New Zealand-United States Security Treaty
ARVN	Army of the Republic of [South] Vietnam
CAT	Civil Air Transport [CIA]
CIA	U.S Central Intelligence Agency
COCOM	Co-ordinating Committee for Multilateral Export Controls
DAC	Development Assistance Committee [OECD]
DDO	Directorate of Operations [CIA]
DEA	U.S. Drug Enforcement Administration
DSCA	Defense Security Cooperation Agency
ECA	Economic Cooperation Administration
ECOMOG	Economic Community of West African States Monitoring Group
ESF	Exchange Stabilization Fund
Ex-Im	U.S. Export-Import Bank
Fatah	Palestinian National Liberation Movement
FBI	U.S. Federal Bureau of Investigation
FMF	Foreign Military Financing
FMLN	Farabundo Martí Front for National Liberation [El Salvador]
FNLA	National Front for the Liberation of Angola
FY	Fiscal Year
G-8	Group of 8 Industrialized Countries [Canada, France, Germany, Italy, Japan, Russia, United Kingdom, United States; plus European Union]
GVN	Government of [South] Vietnam
IADB	Inter-American Development Bank
IAEA	International Atomic Energy Agency
IBRD	International Bank for Reconstruction and Development
IDA	International Development Association
ILEA	International Law Enforcement Academies
IMET	International Military Education and Training
IMF	International Monetary Fund
ISAF	International Security Assistance Force
JCET	Joint Combined Exchange Training
KGB	Committee for State Security [USSR]
Khalq-PDPA	People's Democratic Party of Afghanistan

KMT	Kuomintang: Chinese Nationalist Party
MAAG	Military Assistance Advisory Group.
MACV	Military Assistance Command, [South] Vietnam
MEK	Mujahedin-e-Khalq: People's Mujahedin of Iran
MI5	Military Intelligence, Section 5 [UK]
MI6	Secret Intelligence Service [UK]
MINUSTAH	United Nations Stabilization Mission in Haiti
MPLA	Popular Movement for the Liberation of Angola – Labor Party
MPRI	Military Professional Resources Incorporated
NATO	North Atlantic Treaty Organization
NSA	Anti-Communist National Salvation Army [China]
NSA	U.S. National Security Agency
NSC	National Security Council
OAS	Organization of American States
OECD	Organisation for Economic Co-operation and Development
OEEC	Organisation for European Economic Co-operation
OEF	Operation Enduring Freedom
OPC	Office of Policy Coordination
OPS	Office of Public Safety
OSCE	Organization for Security and Co-operation in Europe
OSO	Office of Special Operations
OSS	Office of Strategic Services
Pathet Lao	Land of Laos [communist movement]
PDF	Panama Defense Forces
PEJAK	Party for a Free Life in Kurdistan
PKI	Communist Party of Indonesia
PLAF	People's Liberation Armed Forces [South Vietnam]
PMC	Private Military Companies
RAF	Royal Air Force [UK]
ROK	Republic of [South] Korea
SAO	Security Assistance Office/Officer
SAVAK	*Sazeman-e Ettela'at va Amniyat-e Keshvar*: National Intelligence and Security Organization [Iran]
SEA	Southeast Asia
SEATO	Southeast Asia Treaty Organization
SOE	Special Operations Executive [UK]
SPG	Special Procedures Group
SPLA	Sudanese People's Liberation Army
SVN	South Vietnam
TFG	Transitional Federal Government of the Somali Republic
UAE	United Arab Emirates
UNITA	National Union for the Total Independence of Angola
UNMIL	United Nations Mission in Liberia
VC	Viet Cong: Vietnamese Communist army/soldiers
WMD	Weapons of Mass Destruction

1 Explaining the continuity of U.S. foreign policy

The 28th of September 2006 was an ordinary day for United States foreign policy. In Slovenia, the U.S. met with the other members of the North Atlantic Treaty Organization (NATO) about counterinsurgency operations in Afghanistan and peace enforcement in Kosovo. Meanwhile, in Washington, the State Department announced it was committing almost $40 million to six countries in Central America and the Caribbean to help them "enhance labor and environmental protection practices." Thousands of miles to the east, U.S. troops were engaged in combat operations in Iraq; still further east, U.S. military advisers continuing training Philippines battalions to "fight against insurgency and terrorism." At the same time, the Cuban government remained indignant over the decision of the U.S. to refuse its health minister a visa to attend the annual meeting in Washington of the Pan American Health Organization. Finally, the State Department's spokesman warned that "time [was] growing short" for there to be a "negotiated settlement" by which Iran would suspend enrichment of uranium.[1]

What these various U.S. policies had in common is that they were aimed at different problems faced by those in charge of the political and economic life of particular states. In some cases (the six countries in Central America and the Caribbean; Iraq and the Philippines), U.S. policy attempted to solve the problems of the states in question, either by furnishing resources or by taking over some of the tasks of the local actors. In another case, U.S. policy focused on involving third parties (here, other NATO members) as junior partners in solving the problems of one or more other states (Afghanistan and the likely future state of Kosovo). Elsewhere (Cuba, Iran), U.S. efforts were instead directed at creating problems for states, in some instances actually trying to bring about the overthrow of the regime. These cases can be multiplied many times over, not only in terms of U.S. actions but in terms of U.S. concerns; and it is no exaggeration to say that American policy is concentrated on maintenance of U.S. clients and hostility toward U.S. enemies. In August 2006, there were some 80 of the former and six of the latter (a few years before, there had been eight enemies).

This focus on clients and enemies is nothing new. Already, a full century before the policies described above, the United States was maintaining clients and acting against enemies. In 1906, the U.S.-backed government of Cuba was facing an insurgency and, after trying to cobble together a political solution, the U.S. finally proclaimed a provisional government, headed by Roosevelt's secretary of war and backed by U.S. troops. At the same time, the U.S. was arranging an emergency loan for the Dominican Republic and negotiating a treaty by which the president of the United States would appoint an administrator for the island's customs revenues. The U.S. was also growing increasingly exasperated with Nicaragua's policies toward its neighbors and would, a few years later, aid rebels in deposing the country's long-time leader. These stories, and others like them, can be repeated constantly, decade by decade, throughout the following hundred years, and there is no sign that they are becoming obsolete.[2]

Of course, U.S. foreign policy is and has been concerned with other issues beyond the maintenance of clients and hostility toward enemies. For decades, the U.S. has directed many of its actions at the creation and enhancement of a liberal economic order, one involving large numbers of minimally regulated commercial and financial transactions among private actors. The U.S. has also acted to foster its own security via a host of policies (including, critically, the possession of nuclear weapons and attempts to deter their use by others). In addition, the U.S. acts in various ways regarding the production and sale of narcotics, access to energy, and numerous other functional domains. What distinguishes these various types of policies from those concerned with clients and enemies is that the latter cut across the former. On the one hand, policy toward a given state may involve addressing problems of nuclear weapons transit, energy, port facilities, trade, and any number of other issue domains. On the other hand, policy making regarding functional issues has to be concretized as regards the political and economic situation of particular places: not only, say, energy production in general but building a pipeline across a specific country, providing particular investment incentives for pipeline investors, and training troops to protect that pipeline from potential attacks. For these reasons, a focus on resolving the problems faced by clients and exacerbating those faced by enemies captures much of the overall structuring of U.S. foreign policy, that is, how it is organized in such a way as to inform numerous specific policies in specific times and places. Put differently, our claim is that the U.S. has, for over a hundred years, resorted to the same set of activities: surveilling countries' domestic politics and economic policies, providing development assistance, coordinating with allies, selling weapons, running covert operations, carrying out overt acts of warfare.

How to explain this continuity? Why has the United States organized so much of its foreign policy, for over a century, around clients and enemies? Our answer is that the U.S. has a certain number of what we will call *policy instruments*: capabilities, embedded in particular organizations, for engaging in particular sequences of action. Policy making is instrument-driven: the U.S. spends much of its time devising programs to aid clients and hinder enemies because those are the competences it has. In this sense, policy is not driven by any overarching goals over and beyond those of helping clients and hurting enemies; instead, it is driven by the relatively limited set of means the U.S. has at its disposal. Policy making, as a process, is not a matter of trying to achieve long-term or structural goals by various means but of choosing a particular means that corresponds to whatever the immediate problem is faced by a client or presented by an enemy. Long-term, and indeed, intermediate, goals of various sorts are then, so to speak, pasted onto the means.

This argument, which we will develop abstractly in this chapter and then, with numerous historical examples, throughout the rest of the book, is obviously a far remove from the way in which U.S. foreign policy is normally presented. To see why, it is helpful to begin with a brief discussion of the more standard explanations for the continuity of U.S. policy. These are of three types: (1) those that posit certain goals which, it is claimed, U.S. leaders have pursued for over a century; (2) those that concentrate instead on the political culture of the United States and its elites' sense of mission; and (3) those that see the U.S. as simply one more powerful state driven by expansionist imperatives. Although these explanations are in many ways quite different from each other, they overlap in one important respect: that of ignoring policy instruments or at the least seeing them as of minor importance. In our view, this bias makes it impossible really to answer the question of why U.S. foreign policy has exhibited such striking continuity.

Explaining continuity: the problem with structural accounts

The most common account of why U.S. foreign policy has shown such strong continuity is that U.S. leaders have for over a century pursued an unchanging set of goals. Among those goals, the two most often mentioned are democracy and open markets: the claim is that the makers of U.S. policy have consistently tried to make other states democratic and their economies free market, whether by using marines and extending bank loans in Central America and the Caribbean in the early years of the twentieth century, or by similar means in Europe during and after World War I, or through a variety of overt and covert means in various parts of the world since the waning days of World War II. Of course, the argument continues, the U.S. has often been economically protectionist, just as it has often supported nondemocratic regimes, but such policies are, as one former ambassador to the United Nations put it, temporary compromises made to ward off the prospect of long-lasting illiberal systems. From this point of view, the U.S. acts more from ideological concerns than security-oriented ones, so that, for example, American policy makers' nearly 70-year long struggle with communism is explained not because communism posed a military threat to the U.S. but because it was the antithesis of the deepest American goals. Indeed, as several advocates of "grand strategy" have seen it, the U.S. has frequently pursued policies which were irrelevant, if not downright harmful, to its security because of its leaders' firm belief that the long-term prosperity and even survival of the U.S. as a liberal democracy depended on the world's being remade along American lines. The connection to clients and enemies is straightforward: the U.S. has faced a never-ending series of tasks, involving oversight, advice-giving, and frequent interventions to make sure that client states stayed on the right political and economic path and that enemies were at least overthrown, if not converted into clients.[3]

There are numerous variants of the democracy and open-markets arguments, depending on claims about the relative importance and mutual compatibility of the two goals, the extent to which these were conscious and long-term aims of U.S. leaders, and the significance of material interests as opposed to ideology in the formulation of particular policies. Nonetheless, there is a broad consensus among writers of various viewpoints that there is indeed an "American foreign policy tradition" based on open markets and the "liberal goal of democracy promotion" and which leads directly from John Hay's "Open Door" policy in China, through Wilson's war to "make the world safe for democracy," the Truman Doctrine and the Marshall Plan, and so on up to George W. Bush's intervention in Iraq and his war on terror. Indeed, it has been argued by some authors that even isolationism – the policy of "escape from a decadent Old World" – was still based on the "liberal impulse" that elevates democracy and open markets to the principal goals of United States policy. Note that this latter argument implies that U.S. foreign policy has been animated by the same goals not only since the end of the nineteenth century but far back into the days of pre-1898 isolation, perhaps even all the way to the dawn of the republic under Washington, Adams, and Jefferson.[4]

Of course, the fact that democracy and open markets are the most-often cited goals of U.S. foreign policy does not mean that they are the only goals ever put forward to explain that policy. Some authors, struck by the frequency with which U.S. officials have pursued nondemocratic or protectionist policies, or by just how often those officials have been violent, exclusionary, or dominating toward those not deemed worthy of democratic rule or free exchange, have instead argued that the U.S. is principally animated by the goal of security, understood in practice as countering other states or ideologies that do or could pose a threat. Clients would have to be defended against foreign and domestic enemies, either because their "loss" might endanger the U.S. at some future point or because the lack of a defensive effort would embolden enemies. Other authors, though, claim that U.S. policy toward many clients is motivated less by concern with U.S. security and more by a general goal of maintaining "stability," i.e., a pattern of regional and global power relationships that change slowly, if at all. Most U.S. efforts would in this case be directed at maintaining client states; enemy states would for the most part be dealt with by means of containment. Still other authors concentrate instead on economic goals that may have little or nothing to do with open markets: guaranteed access to resources such as oil; protection of major foreign holdings; captive markets for export or investment purposes. In these cases, clients would be aided because of their direct or anticipated economic utility, whereas enemies would normally be of less immediate concern.[5]

None of these most-cited long-term goals of U.S. foreign policy is in fact very good at helping to explain the continuity of that policy. One problem is that particular goals clearly conflict with each other – for example, stability may be interpreted as a warrant for backing dictatorial regimes – and there is nothing in the literature that sheds any light on which goals take precedence over which others under which circumstances. This problem is one aspect of an even more serious difficulty with goal-oriented explanations: they lack any sort of translation mechanism for determining what specific actions ought to be undertaken. A good case in point is the democracy goal discussed above. Even if we assume that U.S. leaders fervently wish to promote democracy in states around the world, that goal tells us nothing about what the U.S. will do in particular circumstances: will officials in Washington try to overthrow a nondemocratic regime, or conversely will they try to be close friends with it, hoping to convince the regime's top officials gradually to give up power to democratic institutions? If overthrow is the policy opted for, will the U.S. send in troops or simply content itself with condemnatory statements? If friendship is instead pursued, will the U.S. train the regime's armed forces, or instead try to bankroll particular politicians? And for all of these questions, when, and for how long, will these actions take place? In sum, long-term goals simply do not, and indeed cannot, translate convincingly into particular, country-specific policies; and for this reason, such goals are of little help in accounting for the continuity of U.S. foreign policy.[6]

An alternate argument about continuity in U.S. foreign policy is that it stems from something in the country's political culture. The approach here would concentrate not on long-term goals pursued for many years but on the way in which members of the U.S. foreign policy elite understand the world and see themselves as bound to act. Numerous authors, going back as far as Alexis de Tocqueville in the early nineteenth century, have argued along these lines, claiming that U.S. political culture is marked by a sense that the United States is an "exceptional" country with a mission to serve as a moral, and perhaps a political, leader in the world. Advocates of this sort of argument have a lengthy and apparently inexhaustible collection of speeches and writings to choose among, starting with the famous statement by John Winthrop in 1630 that "wee shall be as a Citty upon a Hill, the eies of all people are uppon us" and running through any number of nineteenth-century statements about "manifest destiny" and of twentieth-century presidents who spoke routinely of Americans as being "heirs of [the] first revolution," ready for "the role of defending freedom in its hour of maximum danger" and thus to "truly light the world." Given an outlook of this sort, officials could feel responsible for protecting client states and/or trying to rid the world of enemies. Note that these arguments do not necessarily presume that the United States is exceptional but simply that U.S. leaders feel they have a mission vis-à-vis other countries, if not the entire world. That mission may have religious roots, as in Winthrop's original statement, but it could also stem from a liberal political culture; from ingrained habits of expansion beyond a frontier; or from a sense of racial superiority.[7]

However, since there are numerous cases of threatened countries whom the U.S. clearly feels no responsibility to protect and of aggressive states against whom the U.S. does not intervene, theories that explain American foreign policy continuity by American political culture need to be refined. One common way of doing so is to notice that the U.S. appears to go through cycles of engagement abroad. During activist periods, U.S. officials act on behalf of clients and against enemies; during isolationist periods, by contrast, U.S. elites see the world as hopelessly fallen and unworthy of American attention. Even such "mood" theories, though, fail to solve the precedence and translation problems discussed above with respect to goals: for example, they say nothing about whether, in a period of isolationism, existing clients will be abandoned to their fate or if instead the sense of responsibility trumps that of being special; nor do they help in determining precisely how the U.S. will respond to an enemy state even in a period of involvement (e.g., will the policy be one of negotiation, quarantine, or direct overthrow?). In short, even if U.S. elites do feel a sense of responsibility stemming from something in the political culture, that feeling gives them little guidance about what they should do with respect to particular countries at particular times.[8]

The third, and final, standard argument about continuity in U.S. foreign policy brackets both long-term goals and political culture, highlighting instead the sheer growth in U.S. power. Whenever a country becomes populous and wealthy, the claim goes, its elites will tend to increase their military capabilities and expand abroad, annexing territory – or, as in the case of the United States, acquiring states as clients – and defending it against actual or potential enemies. The mechanisms behind this type of imperial expansion are varied, ranging from economic and political crises at home to bumping up against states seen as endangering present or future prospects; but all of these factors only can come into play for states whose power has increased considerably and whose elites see themselves as having no room for further growth under existing interstate arrangements. In the same way, whatever specific goals U.S. officials may have in mind are subordinate, in these kinds of explanations, to the structural factors that lead the U.S. to expand in the first place. Note that most such theories of imperial expansion are concerned with an initial leap abroad or a major jump in the extent and geographical scope of annexation or client acquisition; the routine maintenance of empires, including prolonged campaigns against enemies, is considered as mundane and not terribly interesting.[9]

However, using general theories of imperial expansion to account for the continuity of U.S. foreign policy is not much more convincing than is the case for theories based on long-term goals or political culture. One quite obvious problem is that, as we will see in Chapter 7, the United States was busily annexing territory belonging to others, including Western-style states, for many decades from its founding right up through the end of the nineteenth century; then, suddenly, annexation ended and the U.S. began operating through client states. To account for a century of clientilism by the same factors that are used to explain Roman or British territorial acquisition – or, for that matter, the U.S. expansion across North America – is unconvincing. A second problem is that the maintenance of annexed territory or client states is hardly a minor issue. As we will see later in this book, particularly in Chapter 5, client states are frequently beset by problems, and although U.S. policy makers usually expend considerable effort to defend them, on occasion, the decision is just to give up rather than to escalate. Theories which focus primarily on expansion are not good at dealing with the far more frequent cases of attempted client maintenance. Finally, as with the two other types of arguments, explanations of continuity as accounted for by imperial expansion shed no light on issues of precedence and translation: which states are acquired (or refused to be) as clients and when; what forms client maintenance takes; and what exactly to do against particular enemies at particular times.

None of the three standard approaches to understanding United States foreign policy comes even close to accounting for the continuity of that policy since the end of the nineteenth century: the fact that, decade after decade, U.S. actions have revolved around maintaining clients and combating enemies. The core problem, as we have seen, is that the prevailing explanations are structural in character – long-term goals, abiding political culture, core growth dynamics in power and resources – and as such are not well suited to address the medium-term and day-to-day issues of foreign policy. How are these structural factors to be translated into specific policies? If, somehow, that question is answered, then what to do if the translation of one structural factor is at odds with that of another? Unfortunately, the most commonly cited ways of thinking about U.S. foreign policy are of little use when it comes to explaining the striking, long-term continuity of that policy. Instead, we propose looking at what is common in routine policy: continuing use of the same policy instruments. To conceptualize those instruments, it is helpful to take a quick look at an alternate approach to policy-making, one based on the manipulation of existing action capabilities. This approach is what, for reasons that will become evident, we call cybernetic.

The cybernetic approach

In 1940, a mathematician named Norbert Wiener began work on what he called an "antiaircraft predictor," a combination of gun and aiming device that would fire at a place in the sky where an enemy airplane was predicted to be. The prediction was based on a statistical analysis of the evasive behavior the pilot had been engaging in during the preceding 10 seconds. Although it turned out that Wiener and his collaborators were never able to tune the predictor enough for it to be put into military use, they soon realized that their approach put human beings and machines on the same footing: on the one hand, the predictor's metal circuitry embodied the pilot's behavior; on the other hand, the pilot himself, "in attempting to force his dynamic craft to execute a useful manoeuver … behaves like a servo-mechanism," i.e., a mechanical device that automatically corrects errors in targeting or trajectory. When a person uses information about performance as a way of better accomplishing a task, this is "purposeful behavior," and exactly the same can be said of a machine employing "negative feedback" to "restrict outputs which would otherwise go beyond the goal." As Wiener put it, with deliberate provocation, "as objects of scientific enquiry, humans do not differ from machines."[10]

There are many implications of Wiener's position. First, the key to managing a purposeful system, whether human or inanimate, is error correction: how to design negative feedback loops so that mistakes are corrected rather than maintained or amplified. Whether we are building machines that mimic the "adaptive behavior" of kittens or communications channels that reduce errors in information transmission, success depends on how well the system can be steered on the basis of feedback. Wiener chose the Greek term "cybernetics" – steersmanship – to capture this key issue of design and control, and it was soon picked up by many other authors.[11]

Second, the process of designing well-functioning systems is itself cybernetic. When Wiener was working on the antiaircraft gun, he regularly attempted to improve the gun on the basis of its (limited) effectiveness after running various tests. These attempts at improvement included not only engineering changes but also seeking out flight data, hiring collaborators, and a host of other organizational activities. Indeed, organizations themselves can be designed with an eye to accomplishing particular tasks in a rapid and efficient manner, an insight that was developed by early management theorists. Both private business corporations and government agencies are, from this perspective, purposeful arrangements of purposeful activities; they are, in effect, machines for coordinating the activities of people.[12]

But what exactly are the purposeful activities of employees in an organization? To answer this question, it is helpful to return one last time to Wiener's antiaircraft gun. The gun was supposed to obtain information on where its target airplane was and where the last shell had been fired, record that information, perform a statistical calculation, use the results of that calculation to shift the aim of the gun, fire, and then, assuming that the shot missed, repeat the entire process. Similarly, the pilot of the plane, in performing evasive maneuvers, would repeat a set of actions beginning with where the last shot was relative to the aircraft. Both the gun and the pilot, in other words, were engaged in a recurring sequence of activities, with error correction as one or more parts of that sequence. The gun, of course, is constructed so as to accomplish a single task, and in the pursuit of that task, it engages in a single recurring sequence of activities. The pilot, though, can deliberately carry out multiple tasks, each with its own recurring activity sequence. By extension, organizations can have one or more purposes, each revolving around interlocking recurring sequences of intended activities by various persons.[13]

From this perspective, the relation of means to ends, and of immediate to longer-term goals, appears somewhat different than in the standard accounts of foreign policy. Any purposeful system is purposeful precisely because the recurring sequence of its activities – what it does, i.e., its means – incorporates and is governed by an error-correcting feedback mechanism. *The system's immediate goals, in other words, operate through its means.* Of course, those who use or design the system may have one or more long-term goals in mind, but they are, for the most part, add-ons to the purposeful system itself. Wiener and the U.S. military obviously wanted to win the war, and perhaps to usher in a new era of peaceful relations among democracies, but those goals had no bearing on the design and operation of the antiaircraft gun. Similarly, various U.S. presidents may have wanted to bolster American credibility or, later, to avoid humiliation, but the means chosen – counterinsurgency warfare through search-and-destroy missions, training and equipping of South Vietnamese armed forces, and supporting particular politicians in Saigon – had their own, built-in, immediate, and practical goals compatible with these and many other long-term goals. Indeed, policy making, as a practical activity, is heavily means-driven: should the U.S. negotiate, or cut off aid, or try to foment a coup, or engage in a bombing campaign? Of course, policy makers hope that accomplishing particular immediate goals will move them closer to achieving various long-term goals, but their only, very slight, influence over the latter is by opting for certain immediate goals rather than others.[14]

We said above that both individuals and organizations can have multiple purposes. To be sure, certain types of organizations may not survive if they do not achieve one particular goal, such as profit-making for a business corporation. Nonetheless, most organizations are not so limited and are characterized by multiple recurring sequences of purposeful activities. Often, these sequences are carried out by specialists who spend most of their working time engaging in particular sequential activities. Thus, for example, the military may have soldiers who specialize in combat training, others in intelligence, and so forth. Frequently, the capabilities for generating specific recurring sequences of purposeful activities are given a bureaucratic home within an organization; those capabilities, in a particular organization or part of an organization, are what we mean by *policy instruments*, such that the deployment of the instrument generates the corresponding sequences.[15] Hence, as we will see in Chapters 4, 5, and 6, U.S. foreign policy is marked by the development and continued existence of certain policy instruments, notably those concerned with the maintenance of client states and interventions against enemies.[16]

Policy instruments and missions

As we are using the term, policy instruments have built-in immediate goals whenever they are deployed: training a client's military, propagandizing against an enemy leader, and so forth. These immediate goals can be pursued in various times and places, and it is precisely in order to build up this capability that specific policy instruments are developed. However, the pursuit of these immediate goals will differ, at least slightly, from one context to another, depending on the specifics of the country and time. For example, budgetary assistance to a client state will vary not only by the specific policy instrument being employed (e.g., the Defense Department has "coalition support fund" reimbursement to a country's military, whereas the State Department has "economic support fund" payments for programs in health, education, job creation, and "democratic governance") but by the country and time in which the assistance occurs. Thus, a client state like Pakistan, whose regime the U.S. has seen since 2001 as endangered by insurgents, will be aided differently, even with the same policy instrument (e.g., the "Global Train-and-Equip program"), than a client state like Indonesia, where, for various reasons, funds are concentrated on naval interdiction; the latter, in turn, expanded from training naval personnel to track down terrorists to include anti-piracy training as well. We will call the immediate goal being pursued by the use of a specific policy instrument at a given time and place the *mission* of the policy. This now helps to characterize the basic issue dealt with in this book: when we say that there has been *continuity* in U.S. foreign policy for over a century, what we mean is that U.S. officials continue, decade after decade, to engage in the same types of missions to maintain clients and act in a hostile fashion against enemies.[17] Figure 1.1 schematically depicts the relation between policy instruments, sequences of activities, missions, and organizations.

By saying that there is continuity to U.S. foreign policy, we do not mean to imply that policy instruments have not changed in the past 100 years. Indeed they have, but in a highly constrained fashion (which is a principal reason for the persistence in types of foreign policy missions). When particular instruments turned out to be clumsy or inefficient, they were professionalized, typically by creating specialized bureaucracies within the U.S. government to replace what had been ad hoc policies carried out by business corporations or all-purpose organizations. This professionalization, as we will see throughout the book, is a major trend not only in the evolution of U.S. foreign policy but of the U.S. government more generally, one which mirrors the development of other modern states, particularly those with overseas empires. As a result, policy instruments which failed or worked poorly were improved on rather than scrapped. A second source of continuity is the proliferation of instruments across organizations. The United States has a number of ministries (referred to as "departments" in Washington), many of which enjoy strong budgetary support from congressional committees. Quite often, policy instruments are copied or cloned: an instrument in one department is constructed to carry out missions similar to those of an instrument in another department. This may occur either for reasons of success (whether from a desire to build on achievements or to get in on the glory) or of failure; it frequently involves the deliberate copying of procedures or the transfer of personnel; and it also is closely related to the process of client surveillance (see Chapter 2). Finally, even after policy instruments have become professionalized and have proliferated, they can still be adjusted to take into account changed situations in particular clients such as income growth or the development of narcotics trafficking. In all these ways, then, U.S. foreign policy can be strongly continuous in terms of missions while at the same time exhibiting some constrained change in policy instruments.[18]

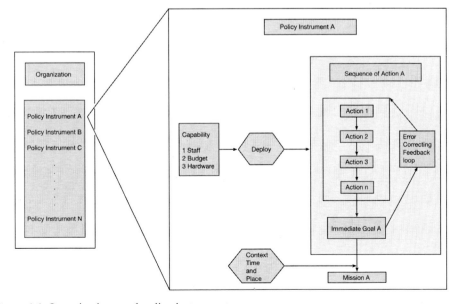

Figure 1.1 Organizations and policy instruments

Policy making as concrete problem solving

We have seen that policy instruments are purposeful, incorporating feedback in order to pursue missions. This implies, at a minimum, that failure to accomplish a mission is, for those who work in the organization as well as their superiors up to the highest levels, a problem. At a maximum, policy instruments may be employed in the first place because some situation is considered to be a problem. The latter may not be considered as grave or regime-threatening but it still is unsatisfactory for some set of policy makers. Of course, it is possible that inertia is sufficiently strong for policy instruments to continue being employed even after the situation is considered satisfactory, but in general this is not the case: at the very least, something about the situation can be improved and that explains the continued deployment of the instrument in question. Hence, both the day-to-day operation of a policy instrument and the resort to it are exercises in problem solving.

From a cybernetic perspective, problem solving in foreign policy is concrete and highly practical. To see this, let us focus on the second of the two issues above: how it is that a particular policy instrument is resorted to by a state in a given situation (see below for explanatory mechanisms). At first blush, we might imagine that this is primarily a matter of the state, or particular state officials, acting in an instrumentally rational fashion, in which they begin with a problem and choose among different policy instruments on the basis of which is most likely to succeed at, perhaps, the lowest cost. However, as has been understood for a long time, human beings lack the analytic capacities to scan over a wide range of alternatives and make fine-grained optimization decisions; under time pressure and with highly incomplete information, as is the case with most foreign policy problems, the idea that policy instruments could possibly be chosen in some sort of instrumentally rational fashion is illusory. It is for this reason that the great theorist of problem solving and organizations, Herbert Simon, discarded the notion of optimization and proposed instead what he called "satisficing": opting for alternatives which, if not optimal, were at least satisfactory. This opens the door to psychological processes in which perceptions, ideas, styles of thinking, role conceptions, psychodynamics, emotions, or small group processes lead policy makers to focus on, or at least strongly prefer, certain types of policy instruments over others. Numerous mechanisms involving these processes have been put forward, with attention being paid both to the criteria for preferring specific alternatives (e.g., reasoning analogically that because a given policy had worked well in the past, one similar to it is likely to work well in the future) and to the way those alternatives come to be considered in the first place (e.g., sequential search, in which options are assessed one at a time and the first satisfactory one chosen).[19]

There is no doubt that psychological processes are ubiquitous in problem solving, as in most other walks of life. However, foreign policy making is a particular sort of problem solving, some of whose most important features pose difficulties in glossing psychologically, as opposed to organizationally. One difficulty is that foreign policy making is multiple-actor, argumentative, and bureaucratized. Consider first the number of actors involved. Chess playing (one of Simon's favorite types of problem solving) is carried out by individuals but foreign policy making involves multiple actors: those reporting information, those presenting recommendations, and those culling the latter to a manageable number. The final decision might be up to a single person, such as a president or a general secretary, but at the very least, the policy options are already drastically limited and shaped well before the final act. Moreover, a leader cannot simply pluck decisions from thin air, if only because the decisions have to be implemented by others and thus be intelligible to them. This already presents a difficulty for psychological approaches because if multiple actors are involved and they have different modes of thought, perceptions, and emotions, then there has to be some type of mechanism for adjudicating among their different psychologies. Of course, patterns of thought or belief may be widely shared within a policy making unit and social-psychological pressures may silence those whose ideas are different, but this still begs the question of how multiple individuals' ideas about some novel situation would coincide, at least in the absence of communication among them.

One important type of communication is argumentation. When foreign policy is formulated, few officials simply say "we should do X"; instead, policy makers present elaborate arguments in favor of certain courses of action and against others. Certainly there are psychologically-rooted criteria which policy makers share for finding certain types of arguments more convincing than others, but when resisted, or indeed, even when communicated, the choice in favor of one position rather than another must itself be communicated verbally, as an argument. Similarly, social psychological phenomena such as groupthink are of little immediate relevance when constructing a written response to several conflicting memoranda, especially when the response is to some extent composed by cutting and pasting from the memos. This is all the more so because foreign policy options are written up (and, of course, executed) in a bureaucratic fashion: superiors order their subordinates to draft proposals and rebuttals and there is often considerable rivalry among officials from different bureaucracies. It is unclear how glossing these phenomena in terms of perceptions, reasoning styles, or emotions would shed much light.[20]

These various difficulties stem from a deeper one, namely that policy making is intensely practical. The multiple persons involved in policy making are arguing with each other, and working with the bureaucracy, about highly concrete situations. Both foreign policy problems and proposed solutions are specific: they pertain to a particular difficulty at a certain time and place (e.g., the military of country X is unable to stop village headmen from being assassinated, in spite of the combat training they are receiving from U.S. military advisers). To assume that means are matched to a specific problem by dint of some psychological criterion is to assume that the same kinds of translation difficulties that so bedevil standard explanations of policy continuity somehow magically disappear when it comes to policy making. Of course it is possible to translate problems and solutions into some type of abstract psychological categories, but in so doing, we open the door to matching other kinds of solutions to the same problem, and other kinds of problems to the same solution. Put differently: problem solving is highly concrete, having to do with particular policy instruments being used to carry out particular missions in particular places at particular times. Translating all this specificity into abstract psychological or other phenomena is at the very least complicated; instead, as we will now see, a cybernetic approach avoids these problems of translation.[21]

Dimensions of continuity

Thus far, the picture of foreign policy making that emerges from the cybernetic approach is as follows. Policy with regard to a given issue takes the form of one or more sequences (usually repeated) of purposeful activities, with error-correcting feedback loops being part of those sequences. Normally, the sequences occur as means-driven, deployed policy instruments, i.e., embedded organizational capabilities involving special-ists in those sequences. Certain types of missions – i.e., the immediate goals pursued by deploying an instrument at a particular time and place – tend to recur, and this is what we mean when we say that U.S. foreign policy has displayed great continuity for over a century. This continuity in fact has three dimensions: micro, meso, and macro. Micro-continuity is the recurring use of particular policy instruments in a given context, year-in, year-out. Meso-continuity is the recurring deployment of particular policy instruments in contexts where they had not previously been used. Macro-continuity is the recurring resort to particular policy instruments in very different historical settings.

Micro-continuity

In many places around the world, the United States has for numerous years been employing certain types of policy instruments: those with the mission of transferring economic resources, of aiding the local military, and of providing certain types of political support to the state's regime. These policy instruments have been developed over decades and, as we suggested above, have proliferated into variations across different organiza-tions. Chapter 4 describes the most commonly used of these instruments and how they are deployed routinely and in tandem as a way of maintaining the regimes – the arrangement of political and economic power – of the various states which the U.S. has for different reasons decided to support.

We saw above that policy instruments are deployed as a form of problem solving. This means that the recurring use of policy instruments for routine maintenance is of two sorts: situations where the problems have not been solved and those where they have. In both cases, as we discuss in Chapter 2, policy instruments are deployed in a context of an extensive U.S. bureaucratic presence, with detailed, day-to-day surveil-lance of the local situation and reporting of how well particular missions are being achieved. If they are not, then reporting to superiors will usually identify the proximate cause of the failure and suggestions for how to correct it. A mission may be described as not yet having succeeded but with trends in the right direction; in this case, the recommendation, logically, will be to continue the policy instrument's deployment. Alternatively, as is quite often the case, the problem may be ascribed to mistakes or inadequacies (including insufficient resources) in the use of the policy instrument, with the recommendation being to make administrative improvements, raise the budget, or increase the number of personnel assigned to the program. A third possibility is for the failure to be diagnosed as due to unforeseen circumstances; in this case, new programs may be called for (see below). Even in these situations, though, the problem at which the original mission was directed is usually seen as germane and so recommendations usually include the continued deployment of existing policy instruments.[22]

Much the same reasoning applies to the failure of policy instruments used in inter-ventionary situations, whether on behalf of regimes (Chapter 5) or against enemies (Chapter 6). Most of the time, policy instruments are continued with adjustments or given greater resources. This is true even in cases of escalation where radically new instru-ments are deemed necessary: existing instruments are continued, rather than scrapped. Only in rare circumstances, such as the complete collapse of a regime, are instruments terminated rather than continued.

What about cases of success? Here, the concreteness and practicality of policy instrument deployment come into play. Missions are not pursued in general: they pertain to specific issue domains and often are carried out in specific geographical regions in a country. Success in one domain and/or region is usually interpreted, at least in cases of routine maintenance, as evidence that the instrument should be expanded into others. For example, the foreign operations budget request for fiscal year 2009 includes the following phrases about Liberia: "support *completion* of the basic training"; "general access to basic education services will be *enhanced* through literacy and numeracy programs targeting over-age and out-of-school youth"; and "*continue* support to *expand* access to electricity in Monrovia and in rural areas." Although budgetary constraints can occasionally lead to cuts in or termination of successful programs, in general, missions which are deemed to succeed are rewarded rather than scaled down or ended. Only in the context of an intervention, i.e., where a client is seen as endangered or an enemy as needing to withdraw from a province or fall from power, is a successful policy instrument seen as superseded and thus as no longer in need of continuation.[23]

Meso-continuity

The issue of meso-continuity is the recurring deployment of particular policy instruments in contexts where they had not previously, or at least for a long time, been used. In Chapters 5 and 6, we address this issue at length, demonstrating that certain kinds of threats to regimes are always responded to by the U.S. deploying specific kinds of policy instruments and that certain kinds of situations involving enemy states evoke analogous responses from the U.S. This predictable connection between the type of situation in other countries and the type of U.S. response in fact holds for over a century, and Chapters 5 and 6 contain scores of examples of that connection. There are two types of cybernetic mechanisms which account for this policy making match between type of situation and type of policy instrument deployed.

The first mechanism is what we would call guided search. When U.S. officials report problems, whether in the pursuit of an existing mission or in the performance of a particular regime, they have to diagnose the cause of that problem and suggest a U.S. policy instrument whose use could solve it. The simplest possibility is regime insufficiency: in that case, policy recommenders look for a U.S. policy instrument whose mission resembles that which the regime is failing to accomplish.[24] Since in many cases, the officials who are surveilling the regime report on missions in which they themselves specialize (e.g., military attachés may file regular reports on the tactical combat skills of the host country's mid-level officers), there is little search on their part. A more complicated possibility arises when the problem is diagnosed as a new and unforeseen situation preventing an existing U.S. mission from succeeding. Since direct substitution of a U.S. policy instrument for a local one is impossible, search must instead try to find an instrument whose mission is the eradication or control of the diagnosed problem. There may be further limits on the search, such as geographical proximity or recent experience elsewhere.[25]

The second mechanism for matching policy instruments to types of situations is to begin with the former and then find a situation which, if only loosely, can be argued as appropriate to its use. This type of policy making, which we will call at-hand availability, occurs with some regularity, particularly as regards military instruments directed against enemies. A good example of this is the U.S. attack on the Taliban in Afghanistan in 2001 (see Chapter 6 for details). For some months, the CIA had been developing a plan to use its erstwhile allies, the Northern Alliance, in combat operations against Al Qaeda.

This would have involved a well-honed policy instrument: large cash payoffs to local warlords. The plan, which was in the process of being approved just before the attacks of 9/11, was, after the attacks, adjusted slightly to target the Taliban. Moreover, since the Taliban were far more numerous and better armed than Al Qaeda, two other instruments, used less than three years earlier in Kosovo, were added to the mix: Air Force bombing and special forces spotters.[26]

Macro-continuity

We have seen how cybernetic approaches help explain how foreign policy instruments in use continue to be employed as well as how specific types of situations are coupled repeatedly with specific types of policy instruments. Both of these dimensions of continuity presume that the places where instruments are deployed are easily classified by U.S. officials as either client states, i.e., those whose regimes should be maintained by the U.S., or as enemy states against whom the U.S. should be hostile. On this presumption, particular forms of micro- and meso-continuity follow in a simple cybernetic fashion (e.g., the success of a mission for clients in contexts of routine maintenance will be followed by expansion of the instrument into new domains or regions). However, as we discuss in Chapter 3, U.S. policy makers have been classifying states into clients and enemies since shortly after the Spanish-American War, in 1898. The world is a very different place now than it was then and a fundamental question is how, in different historical eras, the same type of classification can continue. (By extension, we can also ask what kinds of changes, if any, could lead to an end to this type of classification; see Chapter 7.)

To answer this question, it is useful to start by recalling that interaction between states can be either ad hoc or programmatic. The former was for centuries the only possibility: states would engage in diplomacy, fight, ally, conclude royal marriage contracts, and so forth, with each of these interactions understood as temporally limited. With the advent of specialized bureaucracies, it became possible for states to interact programmatically by engaging in recurring sequences of interlocking activities, such as a military training program (where one state would furnish the instructors and the other the trainees) or a joint weapons research project. Although most of these programs, which of course are carried out through the deployment of policy instruments, are of limited duration, they tend, as we saw above, to be renewed or shifted to cover related domains or regions. In addition, many of the programs are put together under the aegis of standing institutional arrangements, typically enshrined in non-time-limited treaties. Even policies of hostility can be made programmatic through the deployment of policy instruments (e.g., financial sanctions administered by the Treasury Department's Office of Assets Control).

We have mentioned several times that U.S. foreign policy displays strong continuity for over a century. This length of time is not simply a figure of speech: it corresponds to the period since the Spanish-American War, which, as we show in Chapter 7, ushered in a new foreign policy built around maintenance of client states and hostility to enemy states. That foreign policy, we will show, was deeply programmatic, involving the continued resort to, and renewal of, particular policy instruments. At first (Chapters 3, 4, 5), the U.S. had few instruments suited to various maintenance and hostility missions, and so there was a trial-and-error period during which existing instruments were adapted and new ones improvised, mostly for Central America and the Caribbean. By the early 1930s, most types of instruments had been developed. This in turn made it possible for the concrete problems of the 1940s in South America, Western Europe, and certain countries in Asia to be solved by adapting or scaling up existing policy instruments (see Chapter 4); subsequent waves of client acquisition were able to be addressed with even fewer changes in the range of those instruments. A similar, though less elaborated, trajectory can be seen with regard to policy instruments for carrying out hostile missions against enemy states (Chapter 6): the key decade is the 1940s, with the development of several instruments which would frequently be resorted to in subsequent decades.

The 1940s, of course, were the period of the cold war, and the extension of U.S. programmatic policy to other parts of the world took place in that context. Since the cold war ended, and indeed since the attacks of 9/11 and the advent of the so-called war on terror, the U.S. has continued its programmatic policies vis-à-vis clients and enemies. In effect, then, from a relatively early date, the U.S. evolved a programmatic way of interacting with other states, one with its own built-in dynamics of micro- and meso-continuity, which was first expanded to many additional states and then, in a presumably very different context, continued. There have thus been two vital moments of macro-continuity: the decade or so when policy instruments were adapted to deal programmatically with large numbers of states further away from home; and the post-cold war/post-9/11 periods when a full panoply of elaborated instruments has continued to be used for programmatic interaction with additional states as enemies, clients, or indeed potential clients.[27] We will address these two moments in Chapter 7, along with the initial organization of U.S. programmatic policy and its possible continuation in the future. For now, we will simply note that there are two cybernetic mechanisms that help to explain these moments of macro-continuity. One has to do with time pressure, the other with capabilities.

Many of the states for whom the U.S. initiated programs in the 1940s, and again in the 1990s and early 2000s, were seen by officials in Washington as having problems pertaining to an impending or just-concluded war. Although those problems were not considered so urgent that a solution was needed in 24 hours, they nonetheless were reported as potentially grave enough to necessitate some U.S. action sooner rather than later. Under these circumstances, policy making, as a guided search for a match between problems and solutions, naturally revolved around how existing U.S. capabilities could be deployed, though with some changes made in them. If instead an official had argued for putting together some type of policy from scratch, or for negotiating with the leaders who were considered the source of the problems, he or she would have been considered impractical. (Similar arguments apply to policies toward enemies.) Such a criticism, though, raises a more fundamental issue.

Why did policy makers in Washington consider that the actual or potential problems of countries thousands of miles from their borders should be responded to at all by the United States? One might imagine that U.S. officials were concerned about threats to U.S. security, although in fact the evidence of that concern is thin for most Western European countries in the late 1940s (see Chapter 3) and thinner still for many, more recent, instances of client acquisition or hostile action against enemy states. Indeed, if concerns about U.S. safety were preeminent, then American policy makers should arguably concentrate on Canada, Mexico, the Caribbean, and Central America, and abandon to their fate states bordering on U.S. enemies, instead of setting up various kinds of maintenance programs for those latter states.

The truer explanation, to use Thucydides' famous phrase, has to do with U.S. capabilities. As a populous, wealthy, and powerful state, the U.S. had the ability to develop various sorts of foreign policy instruments. By the initial months of World War II (and again, soon after the fall of the Berlin Wall, or the events of 9/11), it would have been disingenuous of U.S. officials simply to report on problems in other states as a pure news item, without any implication that the U.S. could do something about those problems. Indeed, for the president and his advisers to have failed to consider the policy instruments at their disposal would have been considered as an amoral act of selfishness or even as tacit support for Germany and Japan (or, after the Gulf War, for Iraq or Iran). This comes out quite clearly in Roosevelt's famous press conference about what would become the Lend-Lease program, in which he not only emphasized the defensive value of Britain to the U.S., but used the analogy of lending a neighbor a hose to fight a fire, characterizing it as help which the neighbor would then have "a gentleman's obligation to repay in kind."[28] By extension, the U.S., too, was a gentleman, whose capabilities (in this case, its capacities, not only as a great power, but as one with particular programmatic competences) imposed on it the obligation to use them to help other gentlemen. This practical ideology (see Chapter 7) is similar to the often-cited appeals to credibility that U.S. officials address to each other: if the U.S., as a superpower, can do something to help an actual or potential client, then not to do so will reflect badly on its position relative to both other clients and enemies. Thus, to put the point more abstractly, the development of U.S. policy instruments – its means, in the broadest sense of the term – led U.S. officials to use them in favor of some countries and against others. In other words, even the consideration of certain problems is to some degree a consequence of the development of means for solving them. Macro-continuity flows from micro- and meso-continuity.

Thus, we have seen that the cybernetic approach offers the possibility of explaining the continuity of U.S. foreign policy across several dimensions. In the rest of the book, we will focus on these explanations, expanding certain details of the mechanisms and providing dozens of examples of continuity drawn from the period from 1898 to the present. At the same time, we will also make a historical argument about the development of various U.S. policy instruments for different types of clients and enemies. In addition, we will give a detailed account of just how policy instruments work in a day-to-day sense as well as on exceptional occasions.

At various times in this chapter, we have used the term client state and have defined it informally. The concept of a client is at the heart of this book: it is the principal focus of most U.S. policy instruments, knitting them together and packaging problems and policy instruments deployed to solve those problems in country-specific terms. Other types of countries (notably enemies) exist and are significant, including in continuity terms, to U.S. foreign policy; but clients are, for many U.S. officials, the paradigm for the kind of role that all countries should occupy. Since, as we will see, client status is in important respects voluntary, the number, persistence, and policy significance of clients tell us much about U.S. dominance in the world over the past half-century or so. To get a better sense of these issues, we now turn to a detailed discussion of what it means to be a client state.

2 An empire of client states

We saw in Chapter 1 that the continuity of U.S. policy takes the form of resorting to the same policy instruments to solve country-specific problems. For the most part, these problems are domestic rather than international: a given country's regime is unpopular with its citizens, or is facing an economic crisis, or is incompetent in combating an insurgency. U.S. officials consider that such problems are in effect their problems; and that sense of responsibility, even if resented by the other country's leaders, is considered by them in turn as normal. This double perception gives us, in embryonic form, the basic concept of a client state and hence of what an empire of client states might look like.

Our aim in this chapter is to give a bird's eye view of such a U.S. empire. (The focus here is contemporary, although with the next chapters we will range over the 100-plus years of the empire.) We will begin with a general discussion of the concept of a client, a phenomenon which has lengthy historical roots. We then turn to the basic organizational arrangement of clientilism, American-style: the various agencies headquartered for the most part in the U.S., their local implantation abroad, and the linkages between them. Those linkages presuppose a continued activity of surveillance and reporting on the internal affairs of various countries; and this in turn gives us a more formal and precise definition of a client state. The relation between the U.S. and its client, we then argue, is a particular form of domination, namely, an empire, but there are of course other forms of empire, a topic which we briefly will discuss, along with a more general comparison between the U.S. and the client empires of other states. Finally, we end with a general list of all U.S. clients at the present day.

Clientilism in perspective

At least as far back as ancient Rome, powerful individuals have acted through a network of clients.[1] Typically, patrons would make gifts of money or, in some cases, of administrative appointments to their clients, who in turn would honor and support them. This even occurred in the army: Plutarch, for example, tells how Scipio lavishly distributed money to his own troops, thereby cementing their loyalty.[2] Many political systems have operated on a patron–client basis and it is by no means an extinct form of domestic or local governance, as bribery scandals in various countries attest. However, clientilism can also operate at the level of collectivities, such as states. For thousands of years, weak kingdoms would pledge loyalty to stronger ones in exchange for protection by the latter. This type of relationship persists even in an era of supposed U.S. dominance: a number of regional powers currently have networks of clients and any internet search engine will show just how prevalent the term is to this day.[3]

At the international level, patron–client relations work somewhat differently than within states. Typically, domestic patrons find it beneficial to have clients: they can achieve certain goals (notably political ones) with their support and thus have an incentive to increase the number of their clients up to some level. At the international level, as our discussion of cybernetics should make clear, things tend to be reversed. Organizations, we saw, tend first to adopt means rather than ends; when it comes to states, this implies that the benefits derived by patrons in their relations with clients are secondary, often quite diffuse, and at times even nonexistent, as compared with the relationship itself.

What, for example, does the United States gain from many of its small, poor client states? The majority of them do not have particularly valuable mineral resources, nor are they significant markets for U.S. exporters or investors. Of course, some states may be seen as occupying a strategic regional location, but, as we will discuss in the next chapter, arguments along these lines are often manufactured post hoc long after the state has been taken on as a client. The political benefits, if any, from clients of this sort are defensive: a concern that U.S. credibility might suffer if the state in question is not protected; or a worry that if the U.S. does not act, some other potential patron will step into the breach. Small wonder, then, that American officials, like their counterparts in other states, see many clients as more a burden than a benefit. As Lyndon Johnson put it about two U.S. clients,

> What the hell is Vietnam worth to me? What is Laos worth to me? What is it worth to this country? No, we've got a treaty but, hell, everybody else's got a treaty out there and they're not doing anything about it.[4]

For wealthier client states, the problem is reversed: the U.S. may well benefit, but there is no evidence that many of the clients are in any material sense aided by the relationship. This is obvious when it comes to economic issues, although even political benefits are somewhat aleatory. For example, American military allies such as Britain or France may well have felt protected by the U.S. during the cold war; since the collapse of the Soviet Union and the U.S. war in Iraq, however, the case is much more difficult to make. Arguably, most of the United States's wealthy European allies today feel more a sense of diffuse friendship with the American people and of general loyalty than of particular benefit. These sentiments are much less pronounced among poorer clients whether or not they are formal allies; often, clients in Asia and Latin America are resentful at their status.

Thus, if relations between the U.S. and many of its client states are not mutually beneficial, the nature of international clientilism is of necessity different than that of its domestic counterpart. The latter is a kind of exchange relationship; the former, though, is more a set of one-way commitments, mostly by the U.S. Why, then, would the United States undertake such commitments? To answer this question and to shed more light on the nature of international clientilism, let us take a look, per our discussion in Chapter 1, not at U.S. goals but at U.S. means. These means, concretely, are particular policy instruments which have been deployed frequently for over 100 years to solve problems with clients. We will discuss these instruments in detail in Chapters 4 through 6, but it is important first to understand how they are embedded in organizations whose form is tailor-made for reporting on and solving clients' problems. Indeed, organizational form helps explain, more abstractly, just what a client state empire is.

The organizational form of U.S. clientilism

The United States interacts with its clients through a set of twinned organizations: agencies headquartered usually in Washington, DC, and field offices of those agencies in the countries concerned. Such an institutional setup lends itself well to certain characteristic problem-reporting and-solving activities by U.S. officials. In order to get a sense of these activities, a brief organizational *tour d'horizon* is in order.

Headquarters

Surprising as this may be to some, the United States is one of the world's oldest continually functioning political systems.[5] Three of its organizations concerned with policy toward other countries – the State, War, and Treasury Departments – were created in the first months after the Constitution came into effect. Of these, State was the principal agency for foreign policy, and, because of both stringent budgetary limitations (the first secretary of state, Thomas Jefferson, had only four employees under him in New York) and of the then-standard practice (technically necessary, given the communications technology of the time) of delegating considerable authority to ambassadors and other officials posted abroad, policy making for decades revolved around correspondence between the State Department and its missions abroad.

Although the department grew, this country-specific focus remained. Thus, by the 1930s, when the number of personnel in Washington was around 900, the "great mass of reports and dispatches coming into the department daily from its field agents all over the world" was shunted in the first instance to six geographical divisions.[6] As of 2005, with up to 12,000 employees in Washington and around 20,000 overseas, the task of "integrating political, economic, global, and security issues into the United States' bilateral relationships" was carried out through six regional bureaus, each composed of a number of "country offices."[7]

The department also has a number of functional bureaus, currently ranging from economic issues to security, human rights, narcotics, population, and oceans. Some of these offices play an important role in policy making, but insofar as higher-level officials are confronted with problems, above all political or security problems, these will most of the time be country-specific. For example, successive U.S. administrations have been concerned about nuclear proliferation. Although part of the American effort has gone into the development of new rules, especially those dealing with inspections by the International Atomic Energy Agency, these efforts were spurred by concern over possible or actual proliferation in particular countries; and the major problems faced by policy makers in recent years had to do with the application of the new rules to certain states, notably Iran and North Korea. The same is also true of international economic policy. Trade liberalization, for instance, is a domain of general policy making and multilateral negotiations (not to mention no-holds barred domestic politics with different lobbying groups). However, much of the day-to-day negotiating work is bilateral, as are many of the problems that occasion new negotiating rounds and that stem from the adoption of new rules. In short, for most issue domains, the problems which the State Department attempts to solve are country-specific.

To put things in this way, though, is somewhat misleading, because it implies that the problems dealt with by State are either bilateral – how particular states interact with the U.S. – or concerned with the foreign policies of those states toward states other than the U.S. This is not true. For poorer countries, at least, the majority of problems (defined, informally, as situations serious enough to be dealt with by officials at the assistant secretary level or higher) for which the U.S. seeks solutions are domestic in nature: political difficulties for the government, such as popular discontent, a potential military coup, or a guerrilla insurgency; or economic difficulties, such as a serious budgetary shortfall or balance of payments crisis. For example, a recently published volume in the *Foreign Relations of the United States* series reproduces cables transmitted between the State Department and U.S. embassies in 16 different Latin American countries.[8] For each of those countries, the regime's domestic political problems make up at least half the cable traffic reported in the volume. In only five of the countries are bilateral issues (e.g., water, expropriation) or the regime's foreign policy even mentioned. We will return to this problem below; for now, note that it differentiates the country-specific nature of U.S. policy making from that inherent to all states' diplomacy.

What is true of the State Department is also true of other U.S. government agencies concerned with foreign policy. The CIA, for example, is organized to facilitate country-specific problem-solving. Practically from the beginning (see Chapters 5 and 6), the CIA's covert action arm was structured around the planning and execution of projects in particular states. This country-specific thrust continues today: the CIA's key directorate for implementing (and to some degree, developing) foreign policy, the National Clandestine Service, contains a number of "regional and transnational issues divisions"; so too does the analytical side of the CIA, its Directorate of Intelligence.[9] Similarly, the president's National Security Council (NSC) staff is divided into both issue and regional directorates, each headed by a "senior director."[10] The same is true of agencies focusing on economic and development policy: the Treasury Department (although more of its international affairs bureaus are functional than regional) and the U.S. Agency for International Development (AID).[11] It is worth noting that in all these organizations, the regional offices or bureaus report directly to a sub-cabinet-level official. This makes it easy for situations in specific countries to be transformed bureaucratically into foreign policy problems, much easier than if the flow of information passed first through functional or issue-specific offices.[12]

The picture that thus emerges is one in which U.S. foreign policy making regarding political and economic issues is organized around country-specific problems. It could be, of course, that this is simply a generalization of the State Department's administrative structure, with other agencies conforming to State's operating procedures. Thus, the Agency for International Development would have development projects in particular countries and have organizational arrangements designed to track those projects; similarly with various of the CIA's operational and intelligence activities; and so too for the NSC staff, which is tasked with the responsibility of coordinating policy making across agencies. Even the Treasury, which concerns itself more with general and multilateral issues than with particular countries, would find it convenient to organize country-specific policy making along geographical lines.

The connection between administrative structure and country-specificity suggests that the more an agency is organized geographically, the more it expects to deal with country-specific problems. A test of this proposition can be seen in a very different kind of bureaucracy, the Department of Defense. This is a far larger and more complex agency than the State Department, divided into an enormous military side – the uniformed armed services – and a still substantial civilian side.[13] The latter, in turn, includes International Security Affairs, which, as its informal label "the Pentagon's State

Department" suggests, has the task of aiding in the formulation of "international security and political-military policy for Africa, Asia-Pacific, Near-East and South Asia, and the Western Hemisphere."[14] Other, more operational, parts of the department are also organized geographically, such as the agency responsible for weapons sales and military training.[15] A similar geographical orientation also characterizes the Pentagon's "unified commands," which bring together units from the different branches of the military; and even though the contingency planning within the commands is more regional than country-specific, many of the details of that planning (e.g., liaison visits, joint exercises, military basing, and overflight privilege negotiations) have a strong country focus.[16]

It is tempting to imagine that the different foreign policy-making bureaucracies in Washington operate in separate, if not contradictory, ways. There is a kernel of truth to this claim, since there are clear differences of opinion among agencies and no small degree of competition between them. For example, for several decades, civilians in the State and Defense Departments have often been more apt to call for sending small detachments of troops than have the military, who fear ambiguous missions and growing numbers of casualties.[17] There are also infamous cases in which presidents have tried to bypass part or all of the bureaucracy.[18]

However, most problem-solving policies involve fairly extensive coordination between agencies.[19] Lower-level situations may be dealt with by a single organization, but when matters become important enough to necessitate involvement by higher-level policy makers, inter-agency consultation is the norm. A typical example is the response to the Moroccan request in the mid-1960s for military assistance to be increased.[20] Most cables from State on this issue show a pattern of clearances: the assistant secretary of state for African affairs and several of his subordinates; the deputy assistant secretary of state for politico-military affairs; plus officials from elsewhere in the State Department, the office of the assistant secretary of defense for international security affairs, and the Agency for International Development. Usually, cables were copied to the national security adviser at the White House and to various embassies in Europe and North Africa.

For major problems, both in crises and when time is less pressing, coordination goes much further. Typically, joint task forces are created, composed of representatives from different agencies and usually headed by a State Department official. These groupings will oversee policy toward specific countries and make numerous mid-level decisions. Top-level policy making, though, will often be hashed out in National Security Council meetings on the basis of papers which, wherever they may originate, will be cleared across agencies and coordinated at the level of the NSC staff.

Even when the policies in question involve covert activities, coordination is more the rule than the exception. We will discuss these operations and their control in some detail in Chapters 5 and 6, but for now, it is worth noting that most such operations are both approved and regularly overseen by different inter-agency groups. A case in point is the policy of aiding anti-Popular Movement for the Liberation of Angola (MPLA) groups in Angola in the mid-1970s. There was extensive coordination between the State Department, the CIA, and the NSC; at times the president himself was involved. Most, though not all, of the officials and bureaus involved were those whose responsibilities centered on African affairs.[21]

It thus appears that in Washington, the country-specific nature of much policy making permits problems to be dealt with across agencies in a reasonably coordinated fashion.

This does not mean that there is no inter-agency conflict or that country-specificity is the only means of facilitating coordination; but it does show how instinctively the U.S. grasps problems and tries to solve them in a country- rather than issue-specific way. In effect, the organizational structure of policy making is a kind of filter, or machine, for focusing on problems in countries.

The field

Each of the agencies we have discussed has a number of field offices whose purpose is to facilitate country-specific reporting and policy implementation. These offices are usually housed within the U.S. mission in the country: typically, but not always, an embassy. The chief of mission in a given country is considered the President's personal representative (and, not infrequently, may be nominated by the President because of political ties), a status which facilitates discussion of country-specific problems. It is important to understand that these missions are not made up simply of State Department diplomats and consular officials. Almost always, the U.S. staff of the mission includes personnel from other agencies, such as the Defense Department and AID. Frequently, there are several officials present from a given agency and at times (as we will see with military programs), the agency will have a fairly extensive field office. In this sense, a mission is a miniature version of the various foreign policy bureaucracies discussed above.

This structure creates a potential coordination problem. In principle, all U.S. government personnel in a country (with the partial exception of those under certain military commands, or reporting to other missions) are subject to the authority of the chief of mission. That authority, stemming from both Section 207 of the Foreign Service Act of 1980[22] and a letter written by the president to the ambassador upon the latter's taking office, may be exercised both directly and by organizational means. An example of the latter is the "country team," made up of the principal officers of the mission and headed by the chief of mission.[23] A country team, which typically meets several times a week,[24] has numerous domain-specific responsibilities, ranging from trade promotion to defense assistance; its principal function, though, is to integrate policies for the country as a whole. Such a task makes the country team a particularly apt instrument for advising on and implementing country-specific problems.

However, the formal authority exercised by the chief of mission (and, above him, by the secretary of state) is in practice often quite limited. In part, this is due to the multiple control channels by which mission officers report on their work and carry out orders. Minimally, mission officers from agencies other than State are responsible not only to the chief of mission but to authority back at their agency headquarters in Washington. For certain military officers in the mission, there is a third line of responsibility: to the commander of the unified command.[25] The chief of mission's formal authority is also limited by the range and technical complexity of the agencies and programs represented in the mission. For example, in many countries, the U.S. mission contains both defense attachés, who report to the Defense Intelligence Agency on matters pertaining to the military of the host country, and security assistance officers, who are in charge of arms transfers and training programs (we will return to these programs and their antecedents in Chapter 4).[26]

In spite of this proliferation and the inevitable bureaucratic rivalries it engenders, field offices in fact manage a common focus. They do so not so much through formal meetings and elaborated plans (though there are many of both) but, as we would expect cybernetically, through a problem-driven set of reporting and task assignment procedures. To see how this works, consider a particular U.S. mission, that in Bolivia in the mid-2000s. This of course was not exactly a typical U.S. mission since Bolivia was considered a key location in drug control efforts; but for this reason, the number of agencies represented was somewhat larger than elsewhere, and this gives a better sense of the "miniature Washington" aspect of field operations.

Persons listed in the embassy in La Paz as its principal officers included those responsible for political and economic affairs, consular affairs, economic aid, the Peace Corps, narcotics affairs, drug enforcement, security assistance, other defense issues, and, of course, the ambassador and deputy chief of mission; presumably, among these individuals, or unlisted, was the head of the CIA station.[27] Except for the ambassador and chief of mission, each of the above responsibilities involved supervising a number of employees. For example, security assistance in Bolivia was carried out under the immediate responsibility of the military group, which in 2004 had nine employees, a misleadingly low number, since the year before, over 2000 Bolivian troops and police were trained, almost all of them in the U.S., at some 30 separate locations.[28] Most of that training had to do with anti-narcotics efforts, and it is noteworthy that in 2004, the Drug Enforcement Administration (DEA) had no fewer than four offices in Bolivia.[29] Similarly, the largest of AID's economic aid programs in Bolivia was directed against narcotics.[30]

What Bolivia shows is that organizational fragmentation and empire-building can go hand in hand with a focus on a single problem, in this case, narcotics. Even if the different field agencies fail to coordinate their activities, the fact that each of them is supposed to be dealing with drug-related problems provides a built-in mechanism for inter-agency efforts. If, as we will contend below, an agency's reporting highlights the obstacles that prevent it from being successful, then, if only for crass bureaucratic motives, other agencies have incentives to try and tackle those obstacles. (Whether they succeed is another matter.) Inefficiency can be functional, even if this had nothing to do with the intentions behind setting up different field offices in Bolivia.[31]

Links with Washington

We have seen that both in Washington and in the field, policy making tends to focus on country-specific problems. This focus is sharpened yet further by the various links between Washington and the field. The most significant of these are the most routine: the day-to-day flow of written communications by which field offices report on the situation and what they are doing about it; and the responses – reactions, orders, directives – by agency headquarters to the messages from the field. In this enormous stream of communications, there are three mechanisms which have the effect of concentrating attention on particular problems. First, there is what we might call problem-filtering: ways of highlighting situations as problems so that they are more likely to be addressed. Although all communications from the embassy to State have the ambassador (or, if s/he is absent, the next in line) as the signatory, there are a number of ways to signal that the message concerns a problem which higher-ups should address: a cable can be marked with a time-urgency stamp; it can be copied to high-level officials (or even sent to them exclusively, using slugs such as "eyes only"); and it can be sent through certain channels (e.g., those of the CIA) deemed safer or more secure. The same applies, in reverse, for messages from State to the field. Although problem-filtering can be abused, such abuses are self-correcting, since whoever does so rapidly gains a reputation of crying wolf.

A second mechanism involves what could be called exception-monitoring. When a significant problem occurs, considerable pressure builds up for officials to show that they are helping to solve it. Requests will go out for information about what is being done and those who are not seen as being on the team are rapidly flagged and chastised, if not by their Washington superiors then by others to whom they report. Given that messages are often copied to multiple recipients, it is easy for individuals outside the agency to complain that a given official is being unhelpful. A famous example of this is the way in which the commander of the U.S. military assistance command in Vietnam, General Paul Harkins, was brought into line by his nominal superior, ambassador Henry Cabot Lodge. Harkins had favored working with the South Vietnamese president, Ngo Dinh Diem, who, by the autumn of 1963, was considered by most top U.S. policy makers as himself the problem. Lodge therefore initiated a campaign to force Harkins into line, telling him that:

> while it was true that the USG did not desire to initiate a coup, we had instructions from the highest levels not to thwart any change of government which gives promises of increasing the effectiveness of the military effort, insuring popular support to win the war, and improving working relations with the U.S. ... General Harkins expressed regret if he had inadvertently upset any delicate arrangements in progress and added that he would inform General Don that his remarks of 22 October did not convey official USG thinking.

Harkins was then bypassed in links between the embassy and the generals, as well as in situation reports sent to Washington.[32]

The third and most important mechanism for concentrating attention is what we call infinite focusing. Communications between Washington and the field are concerned above all with the success or failure of current policies: are they having the effect they are intended to have, and if not, why? This second question is important, since neither field operatives nor Washington policy makers can afford simply to give bland reports that policy is failing. Instead, they need to isolate particular factors blocking success and suggest ways that those impediments can be overcome. In effect, lack of success focuses communication on immediately proximate problems; success, on the other hand, permits longer-term issues to be addressed. A good example of infinite focusing can be seen in the Lodge cable quoted above. Up until the summer of 1963, the principal problem for the U.S. in South Vietnam was "the effectiveness of the military effort" against the insurgency. After the Diem regime used force to repress Buddhist protests, the military effort was seen as being hampered by the regime's lack of "popular support," a problem which in turn came to be seen as due to the South Vietnamese government's failure to improve its "working relations with the U.S." This problem was presented as impossible to resolve as long as the government was under the control of Diem and his brother, and so the policy then became one of trying to remove Diem from power. By opposing this policy, Harkins made himself the problem.

Infinite focusing is a classic cybernetic phenomenon. Long-term goals of course exist but they are of little direct relevance in policy making. The message flow highlights how things are going now and how they can be improved in the future: a focus on means, not on long-term ends. This, concretely, is one of the reasons why, even in a particular country over a short period of time, immediate goals and means can shift so drastically (for example, from a concern with rural insurgency to worries about whether generals would be able to pull off a coup). It also helps account for why policies are so country-specific: even if the problem at hand pertains to multiple countries, the communication flow between Washington and the field tends to highlight localized impediments.

In addition to the mechanisms of communication flow, other links also contribute to a policy making focus on country-specific problems. One is the regular visits paid to the field by higher-level officials. Assistant secretaries of state regularly tour the countries in "their" region, as do the generals and admirals in charge of unified commands. The heads of agencies also travel with some regularity, not only the secretary of state but also the secretary of defense, the AID administrator, and so on. These visits mobilize major efforts in the mission, and the expectation is that they will be preceded, accompanied, and followed, by briefing papers on the most pressing situations confronting each country on their itinerary. This is an invitation — indeed, an incitation – for both Washington agencies and their field offices to focus on a handful of overriding problems.

A final type of link, with effects similar to the first two, is the practice of employee rotation. The U.S. government, unlike its counterpart in other states, has a strong bias against officials spending their entire careers dealing with a single country. Hence, most operational employees (not analysts, but that is a different question) will rotate back and forth between Washington and the field, with their visits to the latter involving hopscotching from one country to the next. One result of this practice is that employees lack the knowledge to report on or respond to situations in real depth. Instead, they concentrate on how well current policies are working out, with their diagnoses of problems tending toward the immediate and the instrumental. Small wonder, then, that when top-level U.S. officials return from overseas visits, their reports are read so attentively: in the absence of real country specialists, cabinet secretaries and NSC advisers can in just a few days attain the status of expert.

Surveillance

Clientilism, as we have seen, is organizationally structured around country-specific problem-solving. This implies something quite distinctive about the phenomenon of international clientilism and the type of one-way commitments by which it is characterized. The explanation has to do with the kind of problems reported on and worried about: for most countries, those problems are domestic and revolve around the stability of the local regime. What U.S. officials are overwhelmingly concerned about in the majority of their clients is to make sure that the country's *regime* – the configuration of political and economic arrangements that give formal and informal power to certain types of actors – continues. Thus, whatever the regime is able or willing to do which might benefit the U.S. is distinctly secondary as compared with the basic fact of its maintenance in power.

There are several points worth noting about this argument. First, what the U.S. considers as an acceptable regime may differ widely from country to country as regards any number of issues; what matters is simply that the regime not lose power. For example, the U.S. backs democracies, dictatorships, and monarchies; free market economies and heavily interventionist welfare states; repressive states and liberal polities. As we will see in Chapter 6, there are certain types of regimes which are considered as enemies, but even in those cases, the issue is less the configuration of political and economic power in an absolute sense than it is of the regime's presumed alignment preferences. This is why, during the cold war, the U.S. could back (though not as a client) a single-party communist state (Yugoslavia); and why, today, an important U.S. client is a fundamentalist Islamic regime (Saudi Arabia). Of course, U.S. officials would prefer certain types of regimes to others, but such idealism is only translated into practice when a country's regime is no longer considered in even remote danger of falling.

This striking indifference may appear irrational. It is not. It stems from the fact that there are various motivations for taking on countries as clients (we will discuss these in the next chapter) and that those motivations have very little to do with a single over-arching ideology applied to every country. The variety of motivations means that whatever regime a country has at the moment of its becoming a client is, so to speak, "grandfathered" into the U.S. definition of what are acceptable and unacceptable regime types for that country. From a cybernetic point of view, this makes it easy to identify problems: whatever might overturn a regime, even when the likely alternative would seem to be closer to some U.S. ideal. This, as we will see in Chapter 5, is why the U.S. supports corrupt dictators who exercise state control over large parts of the economy against democrats who favor laissez-faire economic policies.

A second point worth noting has to do with the nature of the problems focused on by U.S. officials. They are condemned by the logic of their position to take an expansive view of threats to regime stability: not only insurgencies or massive protests or financial emergencies, but anything else which could plausibly be seen as weakening the regime and making more likely its fall. On the other hand, officials cannot simply construe any possible event as a potential problem, since they would risk being ridiculed as crying wolf every day. The solution to this dilemma, again, is cybernetic: to match events against prototypes, especially those already being used. During the cold war, for example, although protest marches might not in themselves have been seen as threatening to a regime, if the local communist party was identified as playing a significant role in the marches, this automatically set off alarm bells in Washington and the field.[33] Another example, showing how prototype matching works as regards both communists and the precedent of other countries (likely Iran under Mosaddeq), is British Guiana in 1962:

> I must tell you now that I have reached the conclusion that it is not possible for us to put up with an independent British Guiana under Jagan. We have had no real success in establishing a basis for understanding with him due in part to his grandiose expectations of economic aid. We have continued to receive disturbing reports of communist connections on the part of Jagan and persons closely associated with him. Partly reflective of ever growing concern over Cuba, public and Congressional opinion here is incensed at the thought of our dealing with Jagan. The Marxist-Leninist policy he professes parallels that of Castro which the OAS at the Punta del Este Conference declared incompatible with the Inter-American system. Current happenings in British Guiana indicate Jagan is not master of the situation at home without your support. There is some resemblance to the events of 1953. Thus, the continuation of Jagan in power is leading us to disaster in terms of the colony itself, strains on Anglo-American relations and difficulties for the Inter-American system.[34]

Policy makers also focus on other kinds of country-specific problems. These may be bilateral issues, such as disputes over tariffs or extradition requests; or about a country's foreign policy, such as its votes in the UN, or negotiations in the Organization of American States (OAS), or relations with third countries. However, although such other issues can, in any country, rise to the level of problems for U.S. policy makers, the stability of that country's regime is only considered a problem when the country is a U.S. client. American officials may display intense interest in the stability of any country's regime; but this does not mean that they consider threats to that stability as a problem that they have to solve. For example, the fall of Khrushchev in 1964 was closely followed in Washington; but as the U.S. felt no sense of responsibility for Khrushchev's position, his loss of power was not seen as a problem that needed addressing.[35]

Most of the time, U.S. clients are not seen as facing regime maintenance problems. In many cases, those problems were already solved; in other cases, the regime is considered sufficiently stable for such problems not to arise. This, however, does not mean that problems are considered as impossible: there could be an economic crisis, or an outbreak of political violence, or some other event which is seen as threatening the regime. Indeed, as we will discuss in Chapter 4, even in wealthy, stable countries, U.S. officials cannot exclude completely the possibility of something going wrong (as, for example, with the "Eurocommunism" scare in certain countries in Western Europe in the mid-1970s); and this means that countries never "graduate" from client status.

The procedural consequence of this lurking concern is surveillance. If regime instability is always a potential problem, then a principal task of U.S. field offices is to surveil clients. Hence the massive flow of information, not just about how programs are going, but how the situation is in general. In one sense, there is nothing new about this: diplomats have been surveilling events in other countries for centuries, at the very least. But in another sense, the kind of surveillance we are talking about goes well beyond traditional diplomatic tasks. Up to the nineteenth, and even the first few decades of the twentieth, century, diplomats kept track of what was going on in the countries to which they were accredited through conversations with a relatively small number of fairly highly placed individuals: the heads of state and government, the foreign minister, influential private citizens, and, of course, other diplomats. Defense attachés, who in many cases engaged in social interactions with other officers, would on occasion be permitted to attend military exercises. The only other regular source of information was newspapers and the occasional spy.[36] With embassies being tiny in size – typically under a half-dozen persons – such a limited range of reporting was all that could be expected.

With the expansion of the state and the advent of multi-agency missions, it became possible for reporting to take place across a wide range of issues and host government activities. Specialists on finance, or agriculture, or crime could, in carrying out their programmatic duties, report to Washington on detailed host country affairs taking place deep inside that country's state bureaucracy or, for that matter, non-state organizations. But for such reporting to occur, U.S. field officials had to be permitted such detailed and deep access. Hence, one of the peculiarities of international clientelism is that the host country acquiesces in this access. There may be great resentment by the client of this surveillance, all the more so if it results in advice from the U.S. to the client. Nonetheless, the central point remains: clients go along with U.S. surveillance and the concern for regime stability that both underlies the surveillance and is aided by it.

Of course, the proliferation of agencies and field offices is not restricted to the U.S. Most of the larger and wealthier states have such missions, even if the size of their

staffs and the sheer number of agencies is smaller than that of their American counterparts. For example, in 2004, there were almost 94,000 civilian employees of the U.S.
government stationed abroad in over 140 countries, with the Defense Department
employing over half of that number and, as we saw earlier, State some having 20,000.[37]
(To this should be added a large number of troops, even though this fluctuates by the
military situation.) By contrast, the United Kingdom's Foreign and Commonwealth
Office employed around 16,000 persons all told, both at home and abroad; most foreign UK diplomatic posts had four or fewer UK-based staff.[38]

In short, the evidence is that the U.S. surveils a considerably greater number of officials in its clients than do other states, that the surveillance covers a broader range of
activities, and that the surveillance is in a real sense more intrusive. This is blatantly
obvious on issues such as labor unions and drug enforcement; but it is also true of
more classically political issues. A case in point is the intense U.S. attention to the
details of constitutions, election laws, and voting rules. In recent years, such surveillance
has become common in states emerging from civil wars or holding their first contested
election, with advice-givers and observers ranging from international organizations
such as the UN, the OAS, and the Organization for Security and Co-operation in
Europe (OSCE) to nongovernmental organizations such as the Carter Center and the
International Crisis Group. Surveillance by the U.S., though, goes far beyond this, with
the concern being less the fairness of elections than the halo they cast on the client and
the likelihood of the regime surviving them.[39] As we will see in Chapter 5, U.S. concern
with elections in potentially endangered clients dates back over half a century, from
Italy in 1948 to Iraq in 2005.

A paradigmatic example of U.S. political surveillance is Uruguay in the 1960s. In
June of 1964, the assistant secretary of state for inter-American affairs, Thomas Mann,
was telephoned by President Johnson (who started the conversation by asking, "What are
our problems now? You got the Kubitschek problem in Brazil. What are the hot ones?
You got an election in Chile"); when the subject of Uruguay came up, Mann said, "we
have a lot of potential problems." A few minutes later, they returned to the question,
with Johnson asking, "now, what's the problem in Uruguay?" Mann answered:

> Well, Uruguay. They have this silly political system, Mr. President, where they've
> got five presidents of the country and, I think, it's seven mayors of Montevideo, the
> capital city, and it's a little tiny place, and graft and corruption is growing. They
> have an executive that's almost paralyzed because there isn't any one president. The
> people are beginning to talk about the need for strong leadership, but nobody's
> done anything about it yet. And in the meantime, their expenses are too high,
> they're paying too much, they're spending more than they're earning on social
> security and a number of other things, and just having a hell of a time making ends
> meet. And the result of this is a deterioration in confidence, the private sector is not
> investing in job-producing industries, and production is not going up. They actually
> had a slight decrease in their national GNP rate last year as compared with a fairly
> high birth rate, I think about two and a half per cent. And we are going to [sanitized]
> a skull session to see what it is we can do – because I see this one coming in some
> months ahead – and what it is we can do to get that economy rolling again. But
> when you have to work with five heads, a five-headed animal, a government, it isn't
> always very easy to do, because they don't, they fight like cats and dogs between
> themselves, they can't agree on anything. That's a major problem.[40]

The next day, Mann sent a telegram to the embassy in Montevideo, in which he speculated that "political reform" was "an essential ingredient of political stability" and asked whether the ambassador agreed "that there is a need for single executive and if so what are Colorado and Blanco groups prepared to do so that country can move in an orderly fashion ... while there is perhaps still time." Ten days later, Mann sent a letter to the ambassador, Wymberley Coerr, reiterating the point and encouraging him to "plant the idea with your close personal friends that maybe the democratic elements in Uruguay might like, on their own initiative, to begin thinking in terms of amending the constitution ... ." This occasioned a lengthy cable from Coerr analyzing the Uruguayan constitution and arguing for working through "politically constructive" Colorado candidates rather than speaking out publicly (which of course was not what Mann had suggested). Coerr finally gave in to Mann and both he and his successor as ambassador, Henry Hoyt, pushed constitutional and economic reforms through contacts with and pressures on high-level officials.[41]

What this example shows nicely is the intertwining of detailed observations and a concern for using those observations to stay ahead of the curve; it also shows just how much U.S. officials considered it their right to ask for information and give advice on fundamental questions of constitutional order and expected, at the very least, that the information would be provided and that the advice would be listened to. Moreover, the example also shows how policy makers from Johnson on down considered as a problem the lack of stability of the Uruguayan regime, a problem sufficiently serious to justify repeated political and economic intervention. If surveillance means continuously inspecting a wide range of activities to make sure that those activities are working out well, the kind of surveillance the U.S. engages in vis-à-vis its clients thus implies the potential for intervention to redress problems and the agreement of the client to this inspection and potential intervention. Such agreement, if characteristic of clientilistic relations, is different from other forms of surveillance.[42]

These reflections on organization and surveillance not only help to explain the curiously one-way nature of United States' commitments to its clients but also suggest a more comprehensive and formal definition of international clientilism. Specifically, a U.S. *client* is a state for which the maintenance of its regime (i.e., the configuration of political and economic arrangements that give formal and informal power to certain types of actors) is (1) considered by the U.S. government as a legitimate matter of concern which (2) is worth considerable political and, if need be, economic and military efforts, should the regime be seen as endangered. In addition, the dominant political forces in the state also (3) consider that characteristics (1) and (2) are themselves normal and legitimate.

As we are defining it, clientilism is above all a political relation between the U.S. and other states. That relation, to be sure, involves both political and economic arrangements within clients as well as the potential for economic measures to maintain those arrangements, but in the end, the relation is one of protection, not profit. U.S. firms may well have a significant presence in certain U.S. clients, whether as investors or exporters, and U.S. officials may well be interested in helping out those firms; but this is by no means necessary for clientilism. Many U.S. clients, such as South Korea or Jordan, assumed this status long before U.S. companies had any significant presence within their borders. Conversely, other states, in which U.S. firms are strongly present, are simply not U.S. clients (for example, South Africa or, until 1991, Kuwait).

Nor, in general, is it the case that the United States acquires states as clients because of their economic significance. There are numerous contexts in which client acquisition occurs (we will discuss these in the next chapter), but, except in rare circumstances, those contexts have little to do with private investments or trade. The same can be said of the general economic importance of certain countries. For example, as we will also see in Chapter 3, the timing and details of Germany and Japan's transformation into U.S. clients had much more to do with the need to work out adequate post-occupation arrangements (e.g., to maintain a U.S. troop presence) than with their regional economic importance. This is not to deny that economic motives were present; but it is to recall that there were multiple motives and that economic ends were secondary to the political means of regime maintenance.[43]

Clientilism and empire

In its emphasis on surveillance of the minutiae of day-to-day governance, international clientilism seems very much a throwback to some of the European colonial empires which flourished until the middle of the last century. The image that emerges is of something akin to British rule in India: a small number of British civil servants (seldom more than a thousand) administering a population that rose to 400 million. This was only possible because the British operated primarily through "inspecting," to use the contemporary term, an extensive Indian bureaucracy, 10 to 20 times larger.[44] Other parts of India (the so-called "princely states") preserved some measure of sovereignty and were administered through "indirect rule"; this was also true for "protected states" (e.g., Egypt, Zanzibar, the Malay States, Tonga) and later, with some modifications, for a number of African colonies (e.g., Nigeria, Tanganyika) and the "A" mandates granted by the League of Nations. The Dutch administered Indonesia similarly.[45]

Prior to the "new" imperialism of the late nineteenth century, Europeans operated far less bureaucratically.[46] In the Western Hemisphere, indigenous political elites were eliminated and replaced by settlers who increasingly governed themselves, with large expanses of territory subject only to thin and episodic control. In Africa and Asia, indigenous political groupings remained in power and European administration, as such, was restricted to port facilities and narrow strips of land. In these areas, European military power was at least as likely to be used against other European states as against local populations. In neither case did colonial administration involve surveillance, a fact not surprising since surveillance requires a cadre of professional and disinterested inspectors and none of the major European colonial powers developed a merit civil service until the nineteenth century. In this sense, both the U.S. client state system and European "new" imperialism were only possible in the context of a modern bureaucratic state.

There are, of course, significant differences between the "new" colonial empires and the U.S. network of clients. The most obvious one is that the U.S. deals with sovereign states enjoying full powers over both domestic and foreign affairs. Colonial officials were expected to give orders to their indigenous subordinates and routinely did; the subordinates usually had to obey. But although U.S. officials may expect their recommendations to be followed, there are no guarantees that clients will do so. In all colonies, including the most thinly governed ones, an army was present or within reach, officered by Europeans and with significant numbers of European enlisted men, and employed, often brutally, to put down rebellions. On the other hand, however important the U.S. may be for its clients in terms of potential or actual military support (including encadrement and perhaps combat), even the most extensive U.S. military presence would in principle have to be eliminated should the client so wish.[47] In short, without denying the enormous gap between the power of the U.S. and even the strongest of its clients, the fact that the latter are sovereign is of great importance.

Nonetheless, the similarities between the U.S. network of client states and European colonial empires are significant and go beyond the reliance on surveillance. Both ancient and modern empires, we can say, are arrangements in which one political unit continually constrains fundamental options of other, civically distinct, political units.[48] Here a bit of commentary is in order:

1 *Arrangements.* Empires are more than just interactions: they are deliberately structured relationships.
2 *Political unit.* Without denying either that some empires have been economically advantageous or that they may have deep economic roots, in the end, states, or dynasties, or some other kind of political organization must get involved.[49]
3 *Continuity.* When constraint is not continuous, we start shading over into spheres of influence or Great Power bullying or tribute-paying arrangements; imperial administrators are a means of providing this continuity.
4 *Constraints.* Subordinate units with some autonomy of action need not (although they can) be pushed in a particular direction; the point is to prevent certain outcomes.[50]
5 *Fundamental options.* Empires vary widely in what they ask of their subordinate units (e.g., a common religion; alignment against an enemy; labor for mines and plantations), but the reason they are both resisted so strongly and praised by propagandists so highly is that their demands bear on the most important aspects of rule.
6 *Civically distinct.* If subordinate units are so completely absorbed that their inhabitants enjoy the same civic rights as do persons in the imperial center, then de facto, the subordinate units cease to be ruled politically (this happened in Rome with the universalization of citizenship; and in the continental U.S. with statehood).
7 *Other ... political units.* There have to be at the minimum several such units (a state with only one subordinate does not have an empire) and the units have to have a political identity roughly on the same plane as that of the center (otherwise every state would be an empire, ruling over cities, counties, and other administrative units).

The U.S. network of client states fits every element of the above definition and is thus an empire. As we have seen, at the core of the empire is a particular arrangement: continual, agreed-on surveillance of client states' regimes in order to ensure their maintenance. Ideally, U.S. officials would like clients' regimes to maintain themselves in power; but they are ready for the U.S. to intervene politically, economically, or militarily if necessary. We will discuss this intervention, both on behalf of clients and against other states seen as enemies, in Chapters 5 and 6; but note for now that regime maintenance is a very distinct form of constraint. Even if a state resists or manipulates the U.S., even if it costs the U.S. dearly in lives and treasure, the state is very sharply limited as to which regimes it can have – at least without a major attempt by the U.S. to keep things in order.

The client state empire of the United States is neither the first nor the only such empire. In ancient times, the Peloponnesian League of the Spartans fell into this category, as did Roman arrangements with the Greek cities.[51] For some decades in the fourteenth century, Florence had a similar relationship with other Tuscan cities.[52] From 1945 until the fall of the Berlin Wall, the Soviet Union had a client state empire in central and eastern Europe; more recently, Russia has one with some of the former Soviet republics. In all of these cases, the patron maintained particular configurations of political and economic power-holding (i.e., regimes), notably who made decisions and who was loyal to whom.

More significantly, several U.S. clients themselves have networks of clients. This is notably the case for France and its former colonies in Africa, the French not only surveilling and providing military guarantees but indeed furnishing administrative personnel. It was also the case for Britain in parts of Asia and the Middle East; and still is true for some of the former British colonies in Africa.[53] For the United States, this type of two-level clientilism offers positive advantages, as the dangers and expenses of patronage can therefore be offloaded onto states which are reliable U.S. clients. Such delegation or decentralization is a distinctive feature of contemporary international relations and, as an imperial phenomenon, is something new.

In principle, there is nothing to prevent clientilism from extending to three, four, or even more levels. In practice, this is quite unlikely, given that most "second tier" clients are either former colonies of a Great Power or long-time clients of the U.S.; in neither case did they have the wherewithal to take on the maintenance of other regimes as an ongoing task. Thus, since even most regional powers such as Brazil or Nigeria would not have had the opportunity in the past to have clients of their own, the chances of a French or British client (say, Senegal or, in the past, Iraq) having clients are quite slim. Clients can of course be transferred from one patron to another; but as we will discuss below and in Chapter 3, such transfers do not involve more than two "levels." Interestingly, this same hierarchical "flatness" applies even more strongly to non-U.S. clients: states such as Russia and India have their own clients, but in only one instance can it be said that one of those clients had a client of its own.[54]

The subordinate quality of the French and British network of clients comes through in several ways. One pertains to the issue of client transfers. When France and Britain decolonized, many of their erstwhile colonies became U.S. clients (see Chapter 3); however, the reverse never took place. No U.S. client state was taken over as a client by France or Britain, even if, as in the case of Mobutu's Zaire, there were times when the French might have wished for such an outcome.

Another sign of French and British subordination has to do with the clearances given by the U.S. to its allies' interventions on behalf of their clients. One example of this is in 1958, when the U.S. gave permission and indeed shaped the British intervention in Jordan (we will discuss this example and the 1958 interventions more generally in the next three chapters); a more recent example concerns Operation Epervier (1986), when the French had to ask the U.S. for help in airlifting air defense batteries to the Chad government.[55]

A third indicator of the subordinate quality of British and French client networks is the lack of "insulation" of those networks from higher-level relations between the U.S and France and Britain. Thus, a primary instrument of French patronage in Africa, the CFA franc, was devalued due to strong pressure on France from the International Monetary Fund (IMF) and the World Bank. Similar pressures on the pound contributed to British withdrawal east of Suez.

These last examples point to another distinctive feature of the U.S. client state empire: its routine use of international organizations. There is nothing new about patrons using nonstate actors to maintain clients, from the chartered trading companies of the mercantilist era to private military organizations. Nor is there anything novel about states using other states to help them maintain clients. Where the U.S. client network is novel, though, is in its resort to international organizations, such as the IMF and World Bank, regional development banks, and the UN (along with its specialized agencies) itself. In Chapters 4 and 5, we will discuss the specific way in which some of these organizations act as "force multipliers"; for now, note simply that their broad membership and formal rule-based procedures permit U.S. clients to be supported by means which do not involve the financial burden and political onus of direct bilateral resource transfers.

One final point. The problems faced by clients are varied in the extreme but they include the actual or potential overthrow of regimes by forces which are deemed to be tools, or at the very least supporters, of certain states whom U.S. officials consider (with some circularity; see Chapter 6) as enemies of the United States. This is not unprecedented – other client empires have had their own enemies – but it is sufficiently common in U.S. policy to give that policy more of a security cast than was the case for many other client empires. Note in particular that it was not just a cold war phenomenon: U.S. officials identified enemies even before World War I, and they have continued to do so after the collapse of the Soviet Union.

In short, the U.S. network of client states is an empire which both resembles and differs from other empires, past and present. On the one hand, it is an arrangement of constraint very much like that of the British in the nineteenth century or indeed of ancient Rome. On the other hand, it operates in ways which are simultaneously more extensive in their intrusiveness (for example, concern with the types of crops farmers plant) and less identifiable as pertaining to the patron (for example, certain technical financial or military procedures) than that of other empires, be they client networks or direct rule. A sense of this combination of extensiveness and subtlety comes through if we look at a list of U.S. client states as of February 2005 (Table 2.1). (The rules for determining client state status are discussed in detail in the endnote to this paragraph.)[56]

Two features of this list stand out in sharp relief. The first is the sheer size of the U.S. client state empire. Over 40 percent of all states in the world are American clients and the U.S. has clients in every region, even if the number varies considerably from one region to another. The U.S. and its clients account for over two-thirds of the world's economic output and a similar proportion of its military strength. In fact, by most aggregate measures, the U.S. and its network of clients dominate the world; the one exception is population.

The other striking feature of the list of clients is its heterogeneity. U.S. clients run the gamut from highly populous countries to tiny islands; from wealthy countries to poverty-stricken ones; from long-standing allies to regimes recently installed by force of arms; and from peaceful lands to states beset by violent insurgencies. Not surprisingly, immediate U.S. goals vary widely from one client to another, even if for most countries, aid justifications and U.S. embassy web-sites contain these days a reference to the "global war on terrorism." This heterogeneity provides additional support for our basic argument: that the U.S. empire of client states is characterized not by a single, overarching policy aim (e.g., bringing democracy to the world), but by a consistent set of means, directed simply at maintaining regimes in power. We will discuss these means at length in Chapters 4 and 5.

The heterogeneity of U.S. clients – and, it must be said, the enormous geographical variation across regions – supports the arguments in Chapter 1 against explaining the continuity of U.S. foreign policy by single motives or long-term goals. For one, the

Table 2.1 U.S. clients as of February 2005

Clients	Nonclients	
Africa		
Ethiopia	Angola	Lesotho
Ghana	Benin	Madagascar
Liberia	Botswana	Malawi
	Burkina Faso	Mali
	Burundi	Mauritania
	Cameroon	Mauritius
	Cape Verde	Mozambique
	Central African Republic	Namibia
	Chad	Niger
	Comoros	Nigeria
	Congo (Dem. Republic)	Rwanda
	Congo	Sao Tome and
	(Republic)	Principe
	Côte d'Ivoire	Senegal
	Djibouti	Seychelles
	Equatorial Guinea	Sierra Leone
	Eritrea	South Africa
	Gabon	Swaziland
	Gambia	Tanzania
	Guinea	Togo
	Guinea-Bissau	Uganda
	Kenya	Zambia
		Zimbabwe

Total Countries in Region/Percent in Region

3–6.5%   43–93.5%

Total Population in Region/Percent in Region*

92,412,980–14%   567,541,804–86%

Total GDP (in Millions US \$) 2003/Percent in Region *

14,739–3.74%   378,953–96.26%

Clients		Nonclients
Western Hemisphere		
Antigua and Barbuda	Guyana	Cuba
Argentina	Haiti	
Bahamas	Honduras	
Barbados	Jamaica	
Belize	Mexico	
Bolivia	Nicaragua	
Brazil	Panama	
Canada	Paraguay	
Chile	Peru	
Colombia	Saint Kitts and Nevis	
Costa Rica	Saint Lucia	
Dominica	Saint Vincent/ Grenadines	
Dominican Republic	Suriname	
Ecuador	Trinidad and Tobago	
El Salvador	Uruguay	
Grenada	Venezuela	
Guatemala		

Table 2.1 (continued)

Clients		Nonclients	

Total Countries in Region/Percent in Region

33–97%   1–3%

Total Population in Region/Percent in Region

554,833,735–98%   11,299,000–2%

Total GDP (In Millions US $) 2003/Percent in Region

2,561,178–98.76%   32,130–1.24%

Europe

Austria	Poland	Albania	Lithuania
Bosnia and Herzegovina	Portugal	Andorra	Malta
Belgium	Spain	Belarus	Moldova
Denmark	Sweden	Bulgaria	Monaco
France	Turkey	Croatia	Romania
Germany	United Kingdom	Cyprus	Russia
Greece		Czech Republic	San Marino
Iceland		Estonia	Serbia and Montenegro
Italy		Finland	Slovakia
Luxembourg		Hungary	Slovenia
Macedonia		Ireland	Switzerland
Netherlands		Latvia	Ukraine
Norway		Liechtenstein	

Total Countries in Region/Percent in Region

19–43%   25–57%

Total Population in Region/Percent in Region

490,529,176–61.72%   304,277,492–38.28%

Total GDP (in Millions US $)/Percent in Region

10,863,917–87.63*   1,533,858–12.37%

Middle East and North Africa

Bahrain	Oman	Algeria	Sudan
Egypt	Qatar	Iran	Syria
Iraq	Saudi Arabia	Lebanon	Yemen
Israel	Tunisia	Libya	
Jordan	United Arab Emirates	Morocco	
Kuwait		Somalia	

Total Countries in Region/Percent in Region

11–55%   9–45%

Total Population in Region/Percent in Region

147,003,600–40.27%   218,124,000–59.73%

Total GDP (In Millions US $) 2003/Percent in Region

623,902–64.47%   34,380–35.53%

Table 2.1 (continued)

Clients		Nonclients	
Caucasus, Central Asia, and South Asia			
Afghanistan		Armenia	Kyrgyzstan
Pakistan		Azerbaijan	Maldives
		Bangladesh	Nepal
		Bhutan	Sri Lanka
		Georgia	Tajikistan
		India	Turkmenistan
		Kazakhstan	Uzbekistan

Total Countries in Region/Percent in Region

2–13%   14–87%

Total Population in Region/Percent in Region

177,205,008–11.83%   1,320,632,162–88.17%

Total GDP (in Millions US $) 2003/Percent in Region

73,415–9.03%   739,159–90.97%

East Asia and Oceania			
Australia	Singapore	Brunei Darussalam	Nauru
Indonesia	South Korea	Burma	North Korea
Japan	Taiwan	Cambodia	Papua New Guinea
Malaysia	Thailand	China	Samoa
Marshall Islands		East Timor	Solomon Islands
Micronesia		Fiji	Tonga
New Zealand		Kiribati	Vanuatu
Palau		Laos	Vietnam
Philippines		Mongolia	

Total Countries in Region/Percent in Region

13–43%   17–57%

Total Population in Region/Percent in Region

608,980,846–29.26%   1,471,790,809–70.74%

Total GDP (in Millions US $) 2003/Percent in Region

6,439,428–81.03%   1,507,521–18.97%

Total Countries Worldwide/Percent Worldwide

81–42.6%   109–57.4%

Total Population Worldwide/Percent Worldwide#

2,070,997,673–34.7%   3,893,665,267–65.3%

Total GDP (in millions US $) Worldwide/Percent Worldwide@

20,940,793–82.2%   4,535,441–17.8%

Sources: U.S. Department of State (2004c, 2005b), as per note 56.

Notes: * Most population and GDP figures from the September 2004 edition of the World Development Indicators database (World Bank 2008); some figures from the 2003 and 2004 editions of the U.S. Central Intelligence Agency (2005) Factbook; and from the April 2004 edition of the World Economic Outlook Database (International Monetary Fund 2008).

Excluding the population of the United States (including the U.S., percentages change to 38% and 62%).

@ Excluding the GDP of the United States (including the U.S., percentages change to 88% and 12%).

heterogeneity of U.S. clients points to multiple motives behind the acquisition of particular states as clients. Those motives have played out for over a hundred years – before, during, and after the cold war – and, second, they make it difficult to see the client acquisition process as reflective of some long-term goal of American policy. Instead, the list of clients should be seen as a kind of geological cut: different clients acquired at different historical moments for different reasons. What unites these states is the U.S. commitment to the maintenance of their regimes and their acquiescence in that commitment. This two-sided relationship is continuous, but it is particularly visible at certain key periods, one of which is the initial moment of acquisition.

3 Acquiring client states

Until the end of the nineteenth century, the United States had only a minor political presence outside of North America. Unlike European countries, it had no formal colonies; those territories it controlled were either uninhabited, such as Midway Island, or, for a few years, part of a joint protectorate, like Samoa. In the Caribbean, the U.S. had no preponderant role; and its relations with Liberia, a country founded by former American slaves, were far short of anything resembling client status. Within a few years, all this was to change. Even though it took a century for the U.S. to arrive at its current number of clients, the logic of a client empire and some of the principal contexts of acquiring those clients were well in place by the early 1900s.

In this chapter, we will give an overview of the U.S. client acquisition process. We will begin with a brief general discussion of the double nature of acquisition in general and how it structures the clientilism relationship thereafter. This leads us to a presentation of what we shall call acquisition contexts, isolating five distinct combinations of situations, motives, and programmatic means which led the U.S. to acquire particular states as clients. We will discuss each of these contexts in turn, providing examples from various historical eras from the late 1890s up to the present. Following that, we will give a historical account of U.S. client acquisition, emphasizing patterns found repeatedly in different decades. This accounts for the variety and heterogeneity of today's clients.

The nature of client acquisition

As we saw in Chapter 2, client states enjoy sovereignty, however nominal it may be in practice. This means that the basic arrangements of client status – surveillance, above all, but also U.S. efforts at client maintenance, perhaps by extraordinary means – must be agreed to by the client. Such agreement may be tacit most of the time, but when states first become clients, it has to be explicit. Monitoring or aid personnel such as military assistance groups cannot simply swoop in from the sky and begin working with mid-level officers, nor can money simply be given to a country's treasury. Arrangements have to be negotiated and the state in question has to agree to them.

The particular types of arrangements change over time. Early in the twentieth century, there was no panoply of economic aid programs, nor did the U.S. military have anywhere near the resources it currently enjoys. There was no CIA, no DEA, no array of agencies such as have now grown up. Nonetheless, as we will see, there were still ways by which monitoring could be carried out, resources transferred, and, more generally, regimes maintained. What was done then, as now, was for a treaty or executive agreement to be concluded with the U.S. Until recently, the vast majority of these arrangements were communicated publicly to the U.S. Congress, either to the Senate for ratification or at least notification, or to both houses for budgetary authorization.[1] This, incidentally, serves as an indicator of when client status began.[2]

Even when the arrangements were essentially forced on the new client, as was often the case in the Caribbean and Central America early in the 1900s, these arrangements had to be formally agreed to by local officials. The U.S. needed someone to work with, as well as to arrange what would decades later be known as an exit strategy. In other words, even if, in a number of early cases, the U.S. simply landed the marines in support of one faction, that landing was accompanied – always followed, and sometimes preceded – by formal, explicit accords signed with some source of (perhaps future, as in Panama) authority.

Of course, what is sauce for the goose is sauce for the gander: if clients have to agree to their status, so too does the United States. If the U.S. does not wish to take on the task of preserving a particular country's regime, then, no matter how much officials in that regime may wish for their incorporation in the empire, it will not occur. Often, in fact, U.S. officials turn down requests from would-be clients, either because the latter are deemed to be the responsibility of other patrons such as Britain or France, or because U.S. policy makers consider that there is no compelling reason to add these states as clients. Indeed, except for brief moments of imperial euphoria, U.S. leaders usually have considered themselves as reluctant to take on new clients. Other imperial powers in the past, notably Britain and ancient Rome, also considered themselves as forced into acquisition, and although this attitude is more than a bit hypocritical, it nonetheless needs to be kept in mind when looking at the highly uneven pace with which clients were acquired.

Since client status requires the consent of both the U.S. and the new client, a number of possibilities can hold for any nonclient at a given time. The U.S. can offer client status and the other state refuse; the latter can ask for client status and the U.S. refuse; the U.S. can fail to offer and the other state fail to ask; or finally, the U.S. can offer and the other state accept. Moreover, this last possibility may be realized only after a series of earlier possibilities have been played out: a request followed by a refusal (perhaps several times), then an offer followed by a refusal, and so forth.

The reason for this sort of dance is that to the United States, taking on a new client is not a trivial step. Should the client's regime be threatened, U.S. officials would feel obligated to try to defend that regime, perhaps by extraordinary means. Hence, those who are pushing for acquisition often have to confront skepticism, if not downright hostility, by certain agencies at the thought of taking on new responsibilities. For example, although the U.S. had military ties with Ethiopia since the late 1940s, including the Kagnew listening station in Asmara, and although both Emperor Haile Selasssie and the U.S. State Department were in favor of deepening those ties, the Defense Department repeatedly succeeded in blocking a more significant commitment on the grounds that Ethiopia was of "no strategic importance" to the U.S. Finally, in 1959–60, worry about Egypt's influence in the region, along with the communist inroads which would supposedly result, led DoD's objections to be overruled: the U.S. agreed to ship F-86 fighter aircraft to Haile Selassie, train and equip an entire division of his army, and state publicly its concern for "the security of Ethiopia." A few months later, when the emperor's own bodyguard tried to carry out a *coup d'état*, U.S. political and military officials in the mission strongly intervened to crush the rebels.[3]

Not all client acquisition involves such acrimony. In some cases, there is an early consensus in favor of acquiring a given state (or states) as clients. An example of this is the famous period in 1947 when the U.S. launched first the Truman Doctrine and then the Marshall Plan. As we will discuss below, these policies resulted in a significant number of client acquisitions, from Greece and Turkey to many of the countries in Western Europe. In spite of the enormous resources involved, and notwithstanding the typical and nasty infighting then occurring between different agencies of the government, there was "substantial consensus" on these policies by officials of those agencies.[4]

Whether acquisition is contested or consensual, its significance is the same: a sense in Washington that an important threshold has been crossed. Even if policy makers never use words like "client" or make legal distinctions between clients and nonclients, they nonetheless consider themselves as having extended their responsibilities when a state becomes a client. An example of this, worth noting precisely because it involved neither military bases nor a formal defense commitment, is the U.S. decision to increase significantly its aid to Jordan in the 1965–66 period. Prior to that point, the U.S. had sent the Sixth Fleet to signal support for the Hussein regime in 1957 and 1963, helped support a British airlift of commandos in 1958, and offered considerable economic and military aid beginning in 1959. U.S. policy was, in 1960, described as one of providing "support" to Jordan "lest without it the state collapse." But in 1965, the U.S. went further, transferring significant numbers of M-48 tanks, arranging for European aircraft, and, the next year, selling a squadron of A-4 Skyhawks and, on an emergency basis, airlifting additional military hardware to Amman. All of these actions were taken in the face of stiff Israeli and domestic U.S. protests; and as Nixon put it, the U.S. had thereby engaged its credibility, something that was demonstrated a few years later when the U.S. went to a nuclear alert and "decided to move with ground troops" into Jordan to repel a Syrian armored column that had entered the country.[5]

Given the potential significance of client status, it is not surprising that the acquisition process can be rather prolonged. On the one hand, the would-be client can request to be taken under the U.S. wing without that request being granted, at least for some time. Both Haile Selassie and Hussein, for example, had asked for a deeper relationship with the U.S. a number of years before it was granted. In some cases, the delay may be indefinite; this is what seems to have happened in Uganda and Morocco, or, more recently, in the Baltic republics (we will return to these latter later in this chapter). Refusals by the U.S. to acquire a client may be due to the sense that the state in question is someone else's responsibility, like the British or the French (in the case of Somalia in 1991, for example, the U.S. consulted both the British and the Italians, neither of whom had ruled the country for over 30 years); or to a feeling by American officials that the regime in question is either too shaky to be worth helping or not shaky enough to need help; or conversely, that the state does not fit readily into one of the acquisition categories discussed below; or that there are countervailing factors (e.g., proximity to another state) militating against such acquisition. Sometimes, what seems to be a smooth path toward a client relationship can be aborted when the leader upon whom the U.S. is counting is suddenly overthrown (this happened in Syria in 1949, for example, when the CIA-backed army chief of staff, Husni Zaim, was ousted and executed less than six months after he took power).[6]

On the other hand, the U.S. can extend an offer of client status to a state and have that offer declined. An example of this is Cambodia during the 1960s: in spite of U.S. exasperation with Sihanouk and his policy of quasi-neutrality, Washington would at first have been happy to have Cambodia as a U.S. client. Sihanouk, however, refused, and it was not until he was overthrown in 1970 that the United States became Cambodia's patron. Much the same happened with other states pursuing policies of non-alignment: Ghana under Nkrumah, Egypt under Nasser, Indonesia under Sukarno,

India under Nehru, and Burma under U Nu. As we shall see below, Cambodia-like switches took place in several of those states.

However, refusal by either side does not mean that the U.S. has no relations with the state in question. Once Washington establishes a new program (say, a certain kind of military aid), it can easily be transplanted well beyond the country or countries for whom it was intended. Thus, the U.S. has military ties with and provides economic assistance to dozens of countries which are not American clients. These relationships usually have a strong and often explicit political aim, and they may involve nontrivial amounts of money for years on end; at times (especially for relief purposes), far greater amounts than for many clients. Acquiring a client does not necessarily mean that the U.S. will spend large sums of money, at least most of the time; what it does mean is that the U.S. considers it has a new responsibility, one which may well involve significant commitments of treasure and even, under some circumstances, blood.

This commitment helps explain why, as we mentioned in Chapter 2, states do not "graduate" from client status. Even when the factors that led to a state's becoming a client have changed – for example, the state is no longer considered as facing a particular danger – the U.S. has no particular reason to renounce its commitment. Quite the contrary: since, by acquiring the client in the first place, U.S. officials saw themselves as having engaged American credibility, it would be a major blow to that credibility to decide that in some (perhaps unlikely) future crisis, the U.S. could not be counted on. Nor would it make sense to withdraw the U.S. commitment now if, in the event of a crisis, the U.S. would once more commit its prestige: this is tantamount to not renouncing the commitment in the first place.[7]

Of course, the client can decide to renounce its status. This, though, is a dangerous game. A state that really tried to scrap its U.S. umbrella would have to go well beyond closing U.S. military bases or restricting certain economic links: it would have to cut links to the military, disrupt the close surveillance of its performance, and otherwise pursue policies which make it clear that the U.S. would not be welcome to help out in the event of a crisis. These acts occur when there are revolutions or other types of regime changes; they obviously would be considered by the U.S. as a sign of hostility, and the U.S. would react by attempting if at all possible to overthrow that new regime (we will discuss this in Chapter 6).

In fact, most clients do not seriously contemplate drastic changes in their relation with the United States. They may well be resentful of the U.S. or feel that the Americans with whom they deal are crude and overbearing; but that is quite different from even imagining a break. This is not a matter of being scared but, as the definition of client status implies, of considering U.S. oversight and responsibility as normal. For example, France, a client whose U.S. reputation has, for decades, been one of prickliness and challenge, has always, even in the heyday of De Gaulle and Mitterrand, considered itself a loyal and faithful ally of the United States.[8] The reason for this acceptance of client status goes back to the moment of acquisition: a regime – that is, a configuration of political and economic arrangements that give formal and informal power to certain types of actors – that asks for or accepts U.S. patronage will have had considerable advantages over alternative power configurations; otherwise, the arrangement with the U.S. would not have been able to be consummated. Regimes can and do collapse, but barring such eventualities, there is no particular reason for them radically to transform themselves. Or, to paraphrase a well-known formulation: the U.S. developed its client state empire by invitation and this invitation has rarely been withdrawn.[9]

In principle, client acquisition takes place at a single moment in time: when both the U.S. and the other state have agreed on the new relationship. The U.S. may well have proposed client status long before the offer is accepted, just as the would-be client may have asked for this status long before the U.S. grants it; but only when both have signed on to the agreement can client status be said to have started. However, to us now, as outside observers, it is not always easy to pin down an exact date for a given state's acquisition as a client. Documents may remain classified and policy makers may be reluctant – or not find it necessary – to indicate explicitly their sense that an important commitment has been agreed to. This is why we have used multiple methods for identifying both current client status and the moment of acquisition.

Contexts of client acquisition

When the United States acquires a client, it does so in one of several distinct ways. Each of these ways is what we call a context of acquisition, a combination of the type of situation (what has happened and is deemed about to happen in that country and in that region), the range of immediate motives evoked by policy makers, and the focus and size of the principal programs and policies instituted at the moment of acquisition. These different elements fit together, so that even though particular features – especially programs – can span more than one context, they tend to recur in certain patterns.

The context in which a particular state becomes an American client has numerous implications for the subsequent relations between the U.S. and that state. If acquisition takes place in the context of U.S. military occupation, for example, initial U.S. involvement will tend to involve surveillance across many more issue areas than, say, when the context is one of tidying up a region after a war. Similarly, a state that becomes a client in the context of a dangerous enemy will find itself with a far larger and more focused U.S. military presence than in either of the above contexts. These implications help considerably in coding both the date and context of acquisition for particular clients.[10]

It is important to understand that contexts of acquisition involve more than simply particular motives. As we discussed in Chapter 1, there can be multiple motives associated with any given action, with policy makers often advancing contradictory goals one after the other. This does not mean that motives are unimportant but rather that they are part of a broader package which tends to be determined by the immediate problem policy makers face in a given country. In cybernetic terms, the reasoning is "last in/first out"; for example, when Japan was acquired as a client in 1952 (the date at which the peace treaty went into effect and the country regained full sovereignty), the immediate problem for U.S. policy makers was working out a post-occupation arrangement; the danger from China was less immediate, and the felt need to reorganize the East Asia and Oceania following on the end of World War II had to a great degree been pushed down in significance by the Korean War and the time elapsed since 1945.[11]

From the beginning of the U.S. client state empire to the present, there have been five contexts of acquisition. We will discuss each of them in the order of their first appearance.

Post-occupation

The oldest, and in some ways the simplest, context of acquisition is for states emerging from U.S. military occupation (see Table 3.1). This is a category covering

Table 3.1 Clients acquired: post-occupation

Client	Date acquired and duration of client status
Cuba	1902–1959
Italy	1945–present
Philippines	1946–present
South Korea	1948–present
West Germany (Germany)	1949–present
Japan	1952–present
Austria	1955–present
Grenada	1984–present
Marshall Islands	1986–present
Micronesia	1986–present
Palau	1994–present
Afghanistan	2001–present
Iraq	2004–present

Sources: Authors as per Chapter 2 note 56.

both states which were at one time U.S. colonies or possessions and those which the U.S. military were occupying in the aftermath of a war fought against that state or at the least on its soil. (In some cases, like the Philippines and Cuba, the second situation followed on the first.) Understandably, U.S. authorities do not wish their efforts to have been in vain; but just as clearly, local authorities who form the post-occupation regime will have been chosen for their cooperativeness with the Americans. The problem for both sides is to create or recreate a sovereign state, albeit one in which the U.S. can maintain a significant presence. There are various ways in which this circle can be squared, from large-scale aid packages to military training and basing arrangements.

In Cuba, for example, which had been occupied following the Spanish-American War in 1898, the basic instrument of clientilism was the Platt Amendment, passed by the Congress as a law in 1901 and then incorporated into the Cuban constitution. The amendment, named after the U.S. senator who introduced the bill but in fact drafted by the secretary of war, provided notably that the government of Cuba consented that "the United States may exercise the right to intervene for the preservation of Cuban independence [and] the maintenance of a government adequate for the protection of life, property, and individual liberty," and that the Cuban government would sell or lease to the U.S. land for naval stations (one of which, Guantánamo Bay, is notoriously still in operation). The Platt Amendment served as the legal basis for U.S. military inter-vention in Cuba no fewer than three times between 1906 and 1920; it was repealed in 1934, as part of Roosevelt's Good Neighbor policy, and replaced by more sophisticated means of regime maintenance centered around the Cuban military and its U.S.-backed strongman, Fulgencio Batista.[12]

Fast forward almost half a century, and the same pattern can be seen in the formal independence granted to the Philippines in 1946. The U.S. offered economic aid but demanded strict limits, to be assessed by the U.S. and the IMF, on Philippine government spending. Further surveillance mechanisms were set in place by the Bell Trade Act and other arrangements for guaranteeing that U.S. firms and investors would have the same rights as Filipino ones. In addition, the U.S. concluded a military assistance agreement with the Philippines, allowing a Military Assistance Advisory Group (MAAG) to advise, train, and equip local forces; and, as in Cuba, worked out extensive long-term basing rights guaranteeing use of up to 23 military bases.[13]

The transformation of Cuba and the Philippines from occupied lands to client states may be thought of as obsolete chapters from the heyday of colonialism. In fact, although instruments such as the Platt Amendment have long been retired from the toolbox of U.S. policymakers, the post-occupation context of acquisition is very much alive and well. Both Afghanistan and Iraq, occupied just over a century after the Spanish-American War, were acquired as clients in very much the same way as was Cuba: a pro-U.S. government put in place, electoral rules written to bind that and future governments, and arrangements made for a continued U.S. military presence.[14]

Of course, as the Philippines example shows, economic aid programs have been developed over the past half century to supplement post-occupation acquisition mechanisms. So too have multilateral institutions which can be used to reduce direct U.S. financial costs. As we will see in the next chapter, these economic means were first worked out immediately after World War II for both South Korea and the Philippines, as well as for certain countries in Western Europe, including France, the United Kingdom, and the U.S.-occupied states of Italy and Germany. But what distinguished the post-occupied states, wherever they were located, from other clients acquired at the same time was the strong emphasis on working out arrangements for the continued presence of U.S. troops. (The only exception to this was Austria, which because of its joint occupation with the USSR ended up neutralized.) In all of these post-occupation acquisitions, the U.S. maintained an extensive military presence for decades, including bases. Even at the end of 2004, with the cold war having ended over a decade earlier, this presence continued in Japan (36,000 troops and 7,000 civilians), Germany (76,000 troops and 16,000 civilians), Italy (13,000 troops and 2000 civilians), and South Korea (41,000 troops and 3,000 civilians); the U.S. also continues to occupy Guantánamo (700 troops and 300 civilians).[15] Of course, when the country in question is tiny, as in Grenada and certain Pacific states, the number of remaining post-occupation forces is correspondingly small and the extent of their stay is more limited.

Post-occupation acquisitions illustrate nicely a cybernetic feature of policy making which we have already discussed in Chapter 1: the way in which policy revolves around means rather than ends. Initially, the immediate problem faced by U.S. officials at the time of the formal end of occupation for each of these states was to find a way to combine independence with many of the features of occupation. Base and training arrangements, aid programs, and so forth could all be used to solve that problem, even if those means were adapted from other situations or represented modest revisions of the status quo ante in those new clients. But once the means were in place, it became possible to attach them to new ends. Thus, U.S. forces in South Korea originally were put there to receive the Japanese surrender; over the next few years, they served as a backstop for an anti-leftist counterinsurgency campaign by the South Korean government; and they were considered by Washington as an implicit brake on any efforts by the Seoul regime to invade North Korea. After the Korean War, U.S. forces were considered to serve a tripwire function against the North. Similarly, the U.S. base in Guantánamo, which was originally used as a coaling station and to surveil Cuba, was transformed into a symbol of U.S. opposition to the Castro regime after 1959 and, after 2001, to a detention facility for persons rounded up in the "war on terror." These and other examples show that it is important not to assume that current U.S. goals for its forces are the same as those which were germane at the time of the clients' acquisition.

Switching

By itself, post-occupation is not a context for acquiring client states unique only to the United States. Quite the reverse: as we saw in Chapter 2, other former colonial or imperial powers have worked out similar arrangements with their erstwhile possessions, including provisions for the stationing of their troops. But when we turn to the second context for acquisition, most of the similarities to other patrons vanish. This second context is switching, when a state which until then had been deemed by the U.S. to be an enemy undergoes a major change of its regime without being occupied by U.S. troops (see Table 3.2).

What exactly do we mean by "enemy"? For U.S. officials, an enemy is a nonclient whose regime is seen as choosing systematically to differ with the U.S. on key issues of foreign and domestic economic and political policy. Figure 3.1 shows, in chronological order, a list of enemies from the onset of the U.S. client state empire to early 2005.[16]

What this figure indicates is that enemies come in various ideological hues. Many, of course, are regimes seen during the cold war as dangerously close to domestic communists

Table 3.2 Clients acquired: switches

Client	Date acquired and duration of client status
Nicaragua	1910–1979
Iran (ex-Mossadeq)	1953–1979
Ghana	1966–present
Indonesia	1966–present
Egypt	1978–present
Cambodia	1970–1975
Nicaragua	1990–present
Suriname	1991–present
Ethiopia	1991–present

Sources: Authors as per Chapter 2 note 56.

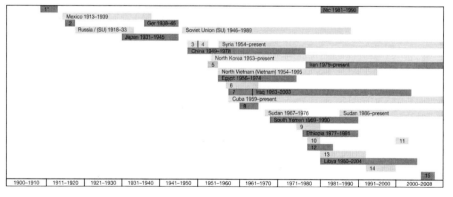

Figure 3.1 U.S. enemies post-1898
Source: Authors as per note 16.
Notes: * 1 – Nicaragua 1907–10, 2 – Germany 1915–18, 3 – Syria 1948–49, 4 – Syria 1949–51, 5 – Iran 1953, 6 – Indonesia, 1957–65, 7 – Iraq 1958–63, 8 – Ghana 1960–65, 9 – Cambodia 1975–79, 10 – Afghanistan, 1979, 11 – Afghanistan 2001, 12 – Grenada 1979–83, 13 – Suriname 1980–91, 14 – Yugoslavia 1992–2000, 15 – Somalia 2006–07

or the Soviet Union. But there are also Islamic regimes, fascist ones, local aggressors, and the very first one of all, a state which did not fit any of the above labels when the U.S. first categorized it as an enemy: Nicaragua (see Chapter 6).

In addition to their ideological dispersion, enemies also differ considerably by other standard criteria of friendship and disagreement. Enemies may be powerful or weak; strategically situated or located off the beaten path; and having had a lengthy history of relations with the U.S. or no prior relations at all. This implies that what triggers a particular state's being categorized as an enemy changes over time; the only feature shared by all these states is the view by the U.S. that they have chosen systematically to differ with it. (Note the word "chosen": states seen as having been dragooned into systematic policy differences with the U.S. are not considered as worrisome in their own right.) In fact, enemies seem to be categorized on a piecemeal basis, one at a time, as disagreements with particular states come to be seen as systematic.

Once a state is categorized as an enemy, it tends to remain in that category for quite a while. The U.S. organizes its policies toward that state around hostility to it so that new evidence against the enemy's undesirability tends not to be acted upon (even if the U.S. is not trying actively to overthrow the regime). Nonetheless, as we will see at the end of Chapter 6, enemies can be shifted out of that status, either by major changes in U.S. policy (by definition, these are quite rare), such as occurred when relations with Vietnam were normalized; or by an invasion of the enemy, such as occurred in some of the cases discussed above; or by a significant change of the enemy's regime. The context of switching pertains to this third possibility, whether or not the U.S. played an active role in the regime's overthrow: it welcomes and rewards successors to enemy regimes.[17]

This reward can take various forms. The classic example is Iran, where the CIA-sponsored overthrow of Prime Minister Mossadeq (see Chapter 6 for this and the other cases discussed in this section) – whose regime was considered an enemy because it was deemed as incapable of resisting local communists – in 1953 was followed in short order by the installation of an extensive aid and surveillance apparatus. The U.S. encouraged the new Zahedi government to ask for economic aid, responding quickly to the request by large increases in assistance, including training civil servants in each ministry. The CIA immediately began efforts to pull potentially dissident tribes into line behind the government and helped it set up a domestic propaganda program; the CIA also began to train Iran's intelligence forces. The armed forces, too, received new weapons and training, as did the gendarmerie.[18]

As mentioned above, there is evidence that a process similar to that in Iran was underway twice in Syria. The first time occurred in 1949, when Husni Zaim, installed by a CIA-aided coup, was welcomed with open arms by the United States. Evidence suggests that the U.S. was preparing to approve a large package of military and economic aid; however, Zaim was overthrown within half a year of his having taken power, thereby short-circuiting the process of Syria becoming an American client. A similar set of events took place in 1951, when Adib Shishakli dissolved parliament and established a military dictatorship; but once again, before an agreement with the U.S. could receive final approval, he too was overthrown.[19]

Another example of a switch is that of Ghana in 1966. The U.S. had been hostile to the regime of Kwame Nkrumah ever since he sided with Lumumba during the first Congo crisis. Although Kennedy tried for a rapprochement, he considered that his efforts were not reciprocated; ties then worsened under Johnson. When a U.S.-aided coup took place, the U.S. immediately released food aid and began to increase other kinds of aid, nearly quadrupling the figure from the preceding year; the new regime also asked for advice in a number of ministries, which the U.S. provided.[20] A similar process took place in Cambodia in 1970, when Prince Sihanouk, to whom U.S. officials had been hostile for years because of his unwillingness to cooperate fully in their fight against Vietnamese communism and North Vietnam in particular, was overthrown by his army chief of staff, General Lon Nol. The U.S., whose role in the coup is unclear, moved immediately to reward the new regime; although Congress, at that point scared of new U.S. commitments in Indochina and angry at Nixon's "incursion" into Cambodia, resisted an aid program, it eventually fell into line in early 1971. From then until the fall of Phnom Penh, the U.S. played a dominant role, furnishing extensive aid, advice, and surveillance, not to mention engaging in direct bombing on behalf of the regime.[21] Closer to home, the U.S. also took on Suriname as a client in 1991, when the military regime of Desi Bouterse, which the Reagan administration had proposed overthrowing, was gradually replaced by a civilian, democratic regime considerably more favorable to private capital. The U.S. responded by starting a program of economic assistance (the Netherlands restored its aid flows, which were considerably larger), by establishing a protégé relationship with key officers in the military, and by backing strongly the new regime against its domestic rivals.[22]

Another example of acquisition in the context of a switch concerns Indonesia. When Sukarno, who had become an obsession for U.S. policy makers, was ousted from power between October 1965 and March 1966, the U.S. reacted positively, increasing food aid, helping renegotiate Indonesia's debts, and setting up a longer-term package of both bilateral and multilateral economic assistance. The figures are eloquent: bilateral economic grants and loans, which had declined to $6.4 million in fiscal year (FY) 1965, increased to $23.8 million in FY 1966, to $57.4 million in FY 1967, to $94.8 million in FY 1968, and to $234.2 million in FY 1969; on top of this, the U.S. was able to persuade Japan and other donors, including multilateral organizations, to increase their aid sharply. A few years after the coup, the U.S. resumed military aid and rapidly increased it to levels triple what it had been, developing close relations with the Indonesian military. In 1969, and again in 1975, major Indonesian decisions – to avoid a referendum in West Irian and to invade East Timor – were cleared with U.S. presidents.[23]

Finally, one of the most important U.S. clients, at least if judged by the quantity of U.S. aid that flows to it every year, was acquired in a context of switching. This is Egypt, which had been considered by U.S. officials as an enemy since the mid-1950s. When Sadat succeeded to the presidency on Nasser's death, he began reshaping the regime. Pan-Arab and socialist officials were purged, economic policy was shifted in the direction of private investments, Soviet technicians were evicted, and, even before the Camp David accords, agreements were reached with Israel. These changes were amply rewarded by the United States. Economic aid, which for several years had hovered around zero, went within a few years to over $1 billion annually. A few years later, military aid followed suit. Since then, Egypt has been one of the top recipients of U.S. aid, usually ending up second only to Israel in total grants and loans. These figures are in fact the tip of the iceberg, since the U.S. also works closely with key Egyptian ministries, notably in the economic and security fields.[24]

The switching cases we have discussed above all occurred in the context of the cold war. However, the definition of switching has nothing to do with a particular ideological struggle: the first U.S. enemy, Nicaragua, was acquired as a U.S. client following the overthrow of the country's president and his successor by rebels operating with conspicuous U.S. military and diplomatic support. The Taft administration sent a financial envoy to take over the country's finances, even drafting the letter requesting U.S. support that was to be sent by the new president. Two years later, when Nicaraguan concessions for U.S. loans proved unpopular enough to spark a rebellion, the U.S. sent several thousand marines to fight against the rebels.[25]

Most switching acquisitions concern states which had never in the past been clients of the United States. However, given the significance of client status, we might well expect not only that the U.S. would take very hard the "loss" of a client but that it would welcome with open arms the overthrow of an enemy regime in a state which had earlier been a client. This occurred in Nicaragua decades after the first switch, when, after a lengthy U.S.-backed war against the Sandinista regime, the latter was turned out of office in elections, an event followed immediately by a close U.S. embrace. This same type of sequence also occurred in Ethiopia, which, as we saw, was a client from the late 1950s until a few years after the fall of Haile Selassie. When the Marxist regime headed by Mengistu Haile Mariam had been ousted by an armed coalition, the U.S. responded with an enormous jump in economic aid, giving sums far greater than during the heyday of Haile Selassie. Legislative restrictions on nonemergency aid were also lifted and diplomatic relations quickly upgraded. Once again, just as in the 1960s, Ethiopia was being described as "the key to U.S. security interests" in the region and the U.S. developed close links with various ministries. The implications of this, should there be future regime changes in Iran or Cuba, are clear.[26]

Danger

One of the most frequent claims made by U.S. officials when acquiring a new client is that the state in question faces some kind of danger. The immediate source of the danger is usually internal – political opposition, often armed – but to American policy makers, such domestic foes are more than likely to be linked to an external enemy state. Thus, during the cold war, shaky regimes facing some sort of leftist opposition were seen as being the potential prey, if not the overt target, of the Soviet Union, China, Cuba, or some other communist enemy. Since the Islamic revolution in Iran and, more recently, since the attacks on 11 September 2001, various Islamic opposition groups have been seen by U.S. officials as, at the very least, operating in tandem with one or more enemy states.

In these kinds of situations, the reaction by U.S. officials is to offer client status to states with regimes whom they consider endangered, whether or not those regimes have already asked for this status (see Table 3.3). The recipients of these offers are patronless or newly independent states located in the same region as a dangerous enemy, or in whom a dangerous enemy is deemed to have shown interest. Whether outside observers would concur in these judgments is irrelevant: what matters is that American policy makers believe that an enemy poses a danger to a particular regime. That belief, rather than any characteristics of the state or regime deemed to be endangered, is what is controlling.

Cybernetically, this context of acquisition is therefore as mechanical as are the post-occupation and switching ones. U.S. officials do not need to engage in complicated evaluations of potential clients or rank their various foreign policy interests; instead, they need simply to extend the policies they are already carrying out against that enemy, namely, by helping out the putative target of that enemy. A classic, indeed canonical, example of this is the U.S. acquisition of Greece as a client state in 1947. Greece had

Table 3.3 Clients acquired: danger

Client	Date acquired and duration of client status
China	1943–1949
Greece	1947–present
Turkey	1947–present
Thailand	1950–present
Taiwan	1950–present
Pakistan	1954–present
South Vietnam	1955–1975
Lebanon	1957–1984
Ethiopia	1959–1977
Jamaica	1963–present
Trinidad and Tobago	1963–present
Congo (Zaire)	1963–1997
Laos	1964–1975
Jordan	1965–present
Tunisia	1967–present
Malaysia	1977–present
Singapore	1977–present
Barbados	1980–present
Saint Lucia	1981–present
Saint Vincent and the Grenadines	1981–present
Dominica	1981–present
Antigua and Barbuda	1981–present
Belize	1982–present
Saint Kitts and Nevis	1984–present
Bosnia	1996–present
Macedonia	1996–present

Sources: Authors as per Chapter 2 note 56.

been a British client since the middle of World War II; even before that war ended, Britain had faced off against the Greek communists. Soon, a full-fledged civil war broke out, with Britain aiding the royalist side politically and financially. The U.S., which had been helping the British more generally, contributed a $25 million loan to the royalist government at the start of 1946.

After fighting resumed in late 1946, U.S. officials grew increasingly alarmed. They believed that the Soviet Union was behind the Greek communists, seeing Greece as simply the latest battleground in the ongoing struggle between the U.S. and the U.S.S.R. Mid-level officials in Washington began studying how to furnish direct military aid to the Greek government. When the British finally informed the U.S. officially that they would have to withdraw their troops and eliminate their financial commitment to Greece (and Turkey, as well), American policy makers were ready. Within a few days, a plan had been drafted to send economic and military aid to Greece and Turkey. Congress, duly frightened at the idea of Greece as a rotten apple infecting the rest of the barrel, approved Truman's aid request; the first shipment of weapons arrived in August 1947. This, however, was not enough, and the U.S. Military Advisory Group pushed through an increase in Greek forces and began to have its personnel give operational advice to army units down to the division level. (Even these means were insufficient, and for several months in late 1947 and early 1948, there was serious discussion of sending U.S. combat troops to Greece; see the discussion on the book's website.)[27]

The transformation of Greece into a U.S. client state reveals several interesting features of the danger context of acquisition. To start with, U.S. officials perceived Greece to be facing a danger that was both external and regional. External, because it was considered inconceivable that the Greek communists could even aim at an insurgency, much less have any hope of it succeeding, without a green light from the Kremlin and, as a corollary of that approval, cross-border support from what were considered Soviet puppets on Greece's borders. The danger to the Greek regime was also considered regional: it was thought as far back as 1945 that Stalin had decided to go after the eastern Mediterranean, and this is one reason why Turkey was lumped together with Greece, in spite of the complete absence of any internal insurgency in the former.[28]

The danger deemed to be faced by Greece was hardly that of imminent collapse. U.S. officials, keeping tabs on how the British were doing, saw a problem that was medium-term rather than immediate; their response, though couched in strong terms, was hardly one of panic. This sense of slow-motion menace was what led the U.S. to explore ways of sending financial and military aid to the Greeks even before the British announcement. Only many months after the Truman Doctrine was announced did some U.S. officials perceive an acute danger in Greece.

Even the initial perception of the royalist regime as endangered was to some degree a matter of expectations. Already, by the end of 1945, U.S. policy toward the Soviet Union was shifting, with those advocating a harder line gaining the ascendancy. The Near East (Iran and Turkey, in particular) was seen as a region in which the Soviets were on the move and Truman and his advisers consciously stiffened their policy there. Greece, categorized as part of the region and having a communist party already opposed by the British, was therefore tracked with particular closeness, with special attention being paid to the Greek army's performance. This is not to deny the latter's very real incompetence, but it is to say that the U.S. policy apparatus was already being focused on regional problems capable, in principle, of being solved by means that the U.S. already was developing (i.e., economic and military aid). Cybernetically, U.S. foreign policy was geared to a sensitivity to responding to dangerous enemies by acquiring states with endangered regimes as clients.

Which regimes were endangered? Consider the eastern Mediterranean in 1945. Most of the countries there either were not yet fully independent (for example, Egypt), or were already seen as present or likely future satellites of the Soviet Union (for example, Bulgaria). Only a handful of countries were left, and of those, two (Iran and Turkey) bordered on the U.S.S.R. and a third (Greece) had an active communist movement. Not surprisingly, all three of those states were seen by U.S. officials as actually or potentially endangered; in two of them (Greece and Turkey), the British announced that they were pulling out, leading U.S. officials to fear that they would be without protection. Hence, in spite of the enormous differences between the two countries, Greece was twinned in both time and space with Turkey as states with endangered regimes.

The Greek case is not unique. We count 26 cases of client acquisition in the context of danger, with the same characteristics – the focus on an external enemy even in instances of strong internal opposition, the regional and temporal clumping, and the focusing of the foreign policy apparatus on reporting certain kind of problems for which there were institutional means – surfacing over and over. These cases cover a long time period and are found in every corner of the globe; significantly, they are not restricted only to communist enemies during the cold war. For example, in 1957, two states were deemed by Washington to be endangered, not by communism, but by Egypt. One of these, Lebanon, became a U.S. client; the other, Jordan, although aided in 1957 and subsequently by the U.S., was considered a British responsibility then and was not taken under the American wing until several years later.

The U.S. view of Egypt as a dangerous enemy took several years to develop. When Nasser and his military colleagues overthrew King Farouk, U.S. policy makers were on balance pleased. The CIA at the least was informed of the coup in advance, having met with Nasser beforehand; and after the coup, the U.S. aided Nasser both openly and covertly. However, when Nasser decided to purchase weapons from the Soviet Union, the U.S. soured on him, responding by withdrawing its offer to finance the Aswan Dam, contemplating covert action to overthrow him, and looking for ways to counter his influence in other Arab countries. One way of doing this was via the Eisenhower Doctrine:

> [the U.S.would] cooperate with and assist any nation or group of nations in the general area of the Middle East in the development of economic strength dedicated to the maintenance of national independence ... [and] undertake in the same region programs of military assistance and cooperation with any nation or group of nations which desires such aid.

In addition, the U.S. would employ its armed forces to "protect the territorial integrity and political independence of such nations, requesting such aid, against overt armed aggression from any nation controlled by International Communism."[29]

Several states asked for Eisenhower Doctrine protection. One was Lebanon, which since 1951 had had an aid agreement with the United States. The U.S. resisted deepening its links until 1957, when both the American ambassador in Beirut and the Lebanese foreign minister argued that Syria and Egypt were subverting the Lebanese regime and, in essence, serving as a conduit for Soviet influence in the region. Washington's response was swift: an initial offer of $10 million in economic aid and another $2.7 million in military aid; considerably more military aid in the second half of 1957; covert support (including cash handouts) for the regime in the 1957 elections, to counter Egyptian and Syrian "interference"; and the formulating of "operational plans" for the country that same year. Some months later, as we will see in Chapter 5, the U.S. ended up sending troops to support the regime.[30]

The same year that Lebanon became a client, Jordan asked to become one. As we saw above, the U.S. did not grant this request, mostly because Jordan was considered as still under British protection, but also because it was considered by Dulles as having "never been a viable state." (The British view was similar, Macmillan referring to Jordan as a "tuppenny ha'penny place. It is worth nothing, but nothing.") The U.S. therefore aided the Jordanian regime both directly and, via the British, indirectly, but did not take over completely from the British until the 1960s. However, as we would expect from the context of danger, Jordan was twinned with Lebanon in both U.S. and British eyes, a perception reiterated by both Eisenhower and Macmillan in July 1958, when each country sent troops to its own client.[31]

It is tempting to view this history of client acquisitions as an exercise in cynicism, with U.S., Lebanese, and Jordanian officials busily assuring each other that the source of domestic opposition to unpopular regimes lay in Egypt, and that Egypt in turn served as a conduit for Soviet pressure. However, all the evidence points to these beliefs being genuinely held – at least by U.S. officials. Eisenhower readily admitted that many

U.S. clients were corrupt and genuinely unpopular but saw the Arab public as beguiled by Nasser, who in turn, even if not a communist himself, was nonetheless playing into Soviet hands. Similar statements can be found by Truman and most post-World War II presidents. This was all the more reason to acquire as clients such states: if a regime's danger was exacerbated by its own incompetence, then it was even more vital for the United States to start overseeing and correcting that regime's performance. It should also be noted that U.S. concern over Egypt continued past the height of the Eisenhower Doctrine. As we mentioned above, Ethiopia was acquired as a client in 1959 because of grave concern over Egyptian inroads in the region. Some years later, Tunisia also made the transition from friend to client, when the U.S., deciding that it made sense to construct a "professional military force" that could hold off an attack (from Egypt, most of all, but there were also concerns about Algeria) long enough for help to arrive, worked out a five-year plan of training and military equipment (including F-86 fighter jets, as well as arms transfers from Turkey) and began getting much more heavily involved in economic development issues.[32]

Both the cases of Greece and Turkey, and of Lebanon and Jordan, concerned regions in which the U.S., at the time of acquisition, did not have a massive military presence. The Sixth Fleet, of course, could be and was sent as a means of projecting power, but the firepower readily available there in those years was considerably less than that at U.S. disposal elsewhere. By contrast, in the Caribbean, the situation was and is very different. Barring some kind of new Cuban missile crisis, the U.S. has overwhelming dominance throughout the region. We might expect, then, that American policy makers would not seriously consider Caribbean states as endangered, at least not enough to take any special measures. In fact, though, client acquisition in the context of danger is remarkably similar in the Caribbean to that in other areas.

There were no fewer than four enemies in the Caribbean region about whom U.S. officials were exercised in the late 1970s and early 1980s. One was Cuba, which had been a U.S. bête noire since 1959. Recently, Cuba had sent troops thousands of miles away to Angola and Ethiopia, and so U.S. leaders once again considered it as obviously dangerous close to home. The second enemy was the Sandinista regime in Nicaragua, which had overthrown the dictator whose family had been a pillar of U.S. policy in the region for almost half a century. Unlike Cuba, which both the Ford and Carter administrations considered as a dangerous enemy, there was disagreement between Democrats and Republicans over just how active the Sandinistas were in the region; nonetheless, there was general agreement that the mere example of the revolution, with the U.S. being apparently unable to maintain its client in power, was an encouragement to other revolutionaries in the area. The third enemy, which we have already discussed, was Suriname, although U.S. concern over the Bouterse regime did not grow until the early 1980s.[33]

The fourth enemy was simultaneously the smallest and the most worrisome for what it represented in the Caribbean. This was Grenada, an island of 100,000 people which had gained its independence from Britain in 1974. In March 1979, a few months before the Sandinistas took power in Nicaragua, a *coup d'état* occurred in Grenada and a leftist regime came to power. Within a month, relations had worsened, with the new government importing arms from Cuba and the U.S. ambassador for the region warning against this and similar moves. By May, the U.S. was isolating Grenada while expanding economic aid to other Caribbean and neighboring nations. During the next year and a half, those states – all of which had been British colonies – concluded agreements for the U.S. to train their militaries. Meanwhile, with strong U.S. support, these countries were establishing a Regional Security System. By the start of 1981, five states had become U.S. clients; two more assumed this status in the next few years, when they became independent. Interestingly, even though neither Grenada nor Nicaragua have been U.S. enemies for some time now (see Chapter 6), the U.S. still has military bases in three of the seven states which became clients in the danger context of the late 1970s; and all but one of those states have recently concluded agreements with the U.S. military on logistics and/or the status of U.S. forces.[34]

As Table 3.3 shows, most of the cases of client acquisition in a context of danger took place during the cold war. The earliest case, that of China, was directed at Japan, but the Nationalist regime did next to nothing against Japan and used its U.S. assistance – with the knowledge and grudging acquiescence of Washington – to prepare for the next round of fighting against its principal enemy, the Communists.[35] For decades after that, the context of danger had to do either with regimes considered to be communist, or close to communists, or naive about communism, or likely to give way to communism.[36] Even Nasser's Egypt, which U.S. policy makers saw as a threat because of its pan-Arabism and which they recognized was not in the slightest a communist regime, was seen as overly willing to cooperate with the Soviet Union and, at critical moments, as semi-unified with an avowedly leftist regime, that of Syria.

Yet there is nothing in the definition of enemies mandating that only those on the political left can be considered as dangerous. We pointed out above that the list of U.S. enemies spans a broad ideological spectrum; certainly some nonleftist regimes could be seen as posing a threat to states which are not as yet clients. Why then is there not always a one-to-one correspondence between the appearance of a new enemy and the acquisition of new clients deemed to be endangered by that enemy? One reason is that not all enemies are deemed to be dangerous. By the mid-1920s, the Soviet Union was not considered as likely to subvert anyone and this is one of the reasons which led Franklin Roosevelt to give it diplomatic recognition a few years later (see Chapter 6). The same can be said of Ghana throughout the time it was an enemy; or of Vietnam in the early 1990s; or, more controversially, of Cuba in the past five years or so (the fact that Cuba is still considered an enemy does not mean that U.S. officials still see it as dangerous to other states).

The other reason that the appearance of a new enemy does not automatically translate into the acquisition of new endangered clients is that, even when the enemy may be considered to pose a threat of invasion or subversion, it could be that there are no states in its region still available for new acquisition. For example, the second U.S. enemy after the Spanish-American War was Mexico. This status began shortly after the Mexican Revolution broke out, with Woodrow Wilson going so far as to seize the port city of Veracruz and to lift the arms embargo he had imposed on the Huerta regime's principal opposition (see Chapter 6). For another quarter of a century, Mexico was intermittently described as an ideological danger and a potential source of subversion. However, by 1913, when Mexico was first categorized as an enemy, the United States had already acquired as clients most of the independent states in the Caribbean and half of those in Central America, and was on an active path toward acquiring the rest (see below). Mexico thus had no independent effect, as an enemy, on the acquisition of new clients in the region.[37]

After the end of the cold war, enemies continued to appear. Yet what we can call the Mexican situation recurred: the states that these enemies were perceived to endanger were either already U.S. clients when the enemy emerged or else were out of bounds for other reasons. For example, both Afghanistan under the Taliban and Iraq under Saddam Hussein were U.S. enemies during or after the 1990s (Iraq, of course, had been an enemy for decades before that). The states Iraq threatened were by then already either U.S. clients (e.g., Israel and the Arab states along the Persian Gulf; we will discuss these in the next sections) or enemies (Syria, Iran) whose regimes the U.S. had no interest in protecting. However dangerous the Taliban may have been to neighboring states, the same reasoning applies: those states were either already U.S. clients (e.g., Pakistan, which of course was friendly to the Taliban), or U.S. enemies (e.g., Iran), or former Soviet republics (e.g., Uzbekistan) whom it was considered impolitic to acquire as clients. A quick glance at a map shows that the same can be said of other enemies today: there are no states left in their regions available for acquisition as U.S. clients.

In order for new states to be acquired as clients in a context of danger, new enemies would have to appear in a region with numerous states still available for acquisition. This is what happened in the early 1990s in the Balkan area. When Yugoslavia began disintegrating a decade or so after Tito's death, the first instinct of U.S. policy makers was that all of this was irrelevant to them, that in the words of then-Secretary of State James Baker, "We don't have a dog in this fight." However, by late 1992, the U.S. had begun to focus on Serbia as the aggressor in the area. Bush issued a declaration around Christmas that "in the event of conflict in Kosovo caused by Serbian action, the United States will be prepared to employ military force against Serbians in Kosovo and in Serbia proper." This perception soon hardened: shortly afterward, when Clinton came into office, he sent his secretary of state to Europe to explore the possibilities of air strikes against Serb-supported forces in the newly proclaimed state of Bosnia-Herzegovina.[38]

Identifying Serbia as an enemy was not an abstract exercise. U.S. officials opposed the Milošević regime because it was a danger to some of the other former Yugoslav republics (Slovenia, which had successfully resisted Serbia in a 10-day war in 1991, was no longer seen as endangered by 1993). One of those republics, Croatia, was problematic, since it was also seen as aggressive and as having a regime of neo-fascist tendencies. Two other republics, though, were perceived by U.S. officials as innocent victims of Serbia. The first of those states, Bosnia-Herzegovina, was viewed as having earlier been a model of ethnic tolerance; when Clinton was campaigning for the presidency in 1992, he already attacked Bush for maintaining an arms embargo on Bosnia and not using air power in its defense. The corresponding proposal, called "lift [the embargo] and strike [the Bosnian Serbs]," was pushed by Clinton for months after he became president. Eventually, the policy was carried out, first by indirect means (forming a federation between Bosnia and Croatia; having a private company [Military Professional Resources Incorporated, MPRI: see Chapter 5] run by retired U.S. generals train the Croatian army; turning a blind eye to Muslim states' arms shipments to Bosnia), then by direct ones (a NATO bombing campaign against the Bosnian Serbs, in conjunction with a Croat and Bosnian ground offensive). Following the Dayton Accords, which brought an end to fighting in Croatia and Bosnia, the U.S. concluded a defense arrangement with Bosnia, contracted with MPRI to do additional Bosnian training, sent its own forces to Bosnia to participate in a peacekeeping force, and drastically increased the amount of economic and reconstruction aid it provided.[39]

The other republic identified as an innocent victim – in this case, an innocent potential victim – was Macedonia. By 1992, fighting had occurred in Slovenia, Croatia, and Bosnia-Herzegovina; although Milošević did not have claims on Macedonia, the Serbian province of Kosovo, with a population that was 90 percent ethnic Albanian, bordered on Macedonia and the fear was that any fighting in Kosovo would spill over the border. This is why Bush warned Milošević in late 1992, and why, a half year later, Clinton decided to send U.S. troops to Macedonia as part of a United Nations border patrol force. In 1994, the U.S. formally recognized Macedonia and began stepping up the amount of aid it gave. After Dayton, the relationship became much deeper and moved into one of patron and client: the two countries signed defense agreements, MPRI began to carry out training, the U.S. gave strong backing to the Gligorov regime, and, for several years before and after the Kosovo war (Chapter 6), the U.S. stationed troops in Macedonia as part of a larger NATO force.[40]

The Bosnian and Macedonian cases show clearly that the United States can acquire clients in a context of danger which has nothing to do with the cold war. This suggests that if the appearance of future enemies prompts the U.S. to acquire additional clients, it is most likely to happen in a region with a significant number of available states. The region with by far the largest number of such states is Africa. Up until now, African enemies have either been seen as not dangerous to other states in the region (this was the case with Ghana) or as endangering only states that were not available, such as French clients (this was the case with Libya, for example, which was seen as endangering Chad. The U.S. eagerly assisted France in intervening in Chad against the Libyans; see Chapters 2 and 5).[41] However, there are a number of African states which are patronless and if the U.S. sees a new enemy in Africa, it could acquire other clients nearby. A policy instrument capable of facilitating these acquisitions, the Pentagon's African Command, was created in 2007.

A note on alliances

One of the interesting aspects of the danger acquisitions is that none of them involved a formal military alliance with the United States. Certainly Greece and Turkey have for decades been members of NATO but in fact concern over aggression or subversion from the Soviet Union led them to become U.S. clients two years before NATO was even created. Similarly, fear of communism in Asia led Thailand to be acquired as a client in 1950, four years before the (less binding, compared with NATO) Southeast Asia Collective Defense Treaty was signed; Pakistan, too, moved to client status some months before the Southeast Asian Treaty (recall that in those years, Pakistan included what is now Bangladesh, and therefore bordered Southeast Asia). Taiwan also became a client several years before it concluded a (now-abrogated) mutual defense treaty with the United States.[42] By our reckoning, all of these states remain U.S. clients, even though several of the formal military alliances they once had with the U.S. are no longer in force. In short, a U.S. commitment to protect endangered regimes can be and has been undertaken without regard to whether the latter are counted as allies, in the technical sense of the term.

This suggests in turn that when the U.S. does conclude formal alliances, it has little to do with a sense that these pacts are a way of fending off danger. For example, such multilateral alliances as the Rio Treaty, the North Atlantic Treaty, the ANZUS Pact, and the Southeast Asia Collective Defense Treaty were signed with states which either already were U.S. clients or which were not considered to be in danger. The same goes for bilateral defense pacts with the Philippines, Japan, South Korea, and, as we saw, Taiwan. These arrangements were important both as ways of providing a framework for practical military arrangements and for their symbolic value; but they took too long to negotiate and were too contextually undifferentiated to have been considered as an adequate response to whatever danger might have existed.

A canonical example of this is the North Atlantic Treaty. Its immediate origins date to early 1948, when Britain, France, and the Benelux countries concluded the Brussels Pact. Significantly, this took place nine months after the launching of the Marshall Plan, which, as we shall argue in the next section, was the vehicle by which Western European countries became U.S. clients. Several months after the Brussels Pact was signed, the U.S. entered into talks with the Pact members. By the end of 1948, these had led to a draft treaty; and over the next few months, while the treaty was refined, it was arranged for Canada and additional Marshall Plan countries – Denmark, Iceland, Italy, Norway, and Portugal – to be invited to sign the treaty as well. By the summer of 1949, the treaty was ratified and a bill introduced for setting up a military assistance program for the new allies. The North Atlantic Council then began to meet and set up committees and other machinery for the running of the alliance. However, it was only in October 1950, several months after the Korean War broke out, that a real organization was created, with a commanding general and a commitment of U.S. troops.[43]

This rather leisurely sequence of events suggests strongly that the U.S. did not negotiate the North Atlantic Treaty as a response to some sense that the treaty signatories were endangered. Certainly there was concern over the strength of the Communist Party in France and Italy, and Acheson made it clear that the North Atlantic Treaty could provide a basis for armed intervention in the event of a coup in those countries. This concern, however, did not apply to most of the other states with whom the treaty was negotiated (indeed, one high-level official was reported to oppose the inclusion of Denmark and Norway as a provocation to the Soviet Union); moreover, the states the U.S. had seen as actively endangered, Greece and Turkey, were not admitted to NATO until 1952. Up until the Korean War, U.S. leaders simply were not worried about military threats from the U.S.S.R. The famous March 1948 telegram by the U.S. chief of the military government in Germany that war with the Soviet Union could come with "dramatic suddenness" turns out to have been a budgetary maneuver rather than reflecting a belief that the situation on the ground was different. During the Senate hearings on the treaty the next year, no leading official thought that NATO would serve as a response to a Soviet military danger. Instead, the treaty was seen as having other purposes, from reassuring Western European countries about Germany to helping foster economic integration.[44]

NATO, then, was not a means of acquiring clients in a context of danger. Its members were already clients at the time the North Atlantic Treaty was being negotiated; they had been acquired, as we shall see below, in a context that was not one of danger; and there is considerable evidence that the architects of the treaty were not worried about the ostensible threat posed by the Soviet Union. If we fast forward now to the mid-1990s, much the same pattern emerges in NATO enlargement. Much to the chagrin of certain conservatives, the two waves of enlargement did not occur because high-level policy makers perceived new members as endangered and NATO as a way of responding to that danger. Rather, enlargement was undertaken first and foremost as a way of keeping NATO together, then as a way of maintaining a U.S. military presence in Europe while integrating former Warsaw Pact countries and Soviet republics, and finally as a means of providing a multilateral force that could assist the U.S. in future military tasks.[45]

It therefore follows that the mere fact of becoming a new member of NATO does not necessarily mean that the state in question became an American client. Thus, the first post-cold war wave of NATO expansion saw three countries – the Czech Republic, Hungary, and Poland – added to NATO, but only one of them became a client. The U.S. established a military training program with Poland a number of years before accession; it extended a massive loan of almost $4 billion to buy F-16 fighter jets and deepen "military-to-military interactions"; and the range of its cooperative arrangements with Poland and the language it used in describing them was much closer to that of long-standing NATO allies than to either Hungary or the Czech Republic. By the same token, none of the countries – including the Baltic states – admitted in the second post-cold war wave of NATO expansion became a U.S. client.[46]

NATO is not the only formal alliance unconnected to client acquisition. Another example is the Southeast Asia Treaty Organization (SEATO), established at Manila in 1954. Ostensibly, the purpose of this organization was to protect members or other states in the region from both "aggression or armed attack" and other, unspecified, threats; but in fact, the U.S. had already made commitments to all the signatories before – in most cases, several years before – the treaty had even begun to be negotiated. Since the treaty's provisions were noticeably weaker than the North Atlantic Treaty (the latter committed each state "to assist the Party or Parties so attacked"; the former only to "act to meet the common danger") and since no real organization was ever created analogous to NATO, SEATO's value to the one state in the region – South Vietnam – acquired as a client the next year was nothing over and above the massive aid that Washington immediately began pouring into Saigon.[47] The founding of SEATO was more a symbolic gesture than a way of extending U.S. protection to endangered states.

A similar story can be told about the Inter-American Treaty of Reciprocal Assistance, the so-called Rio Pact. This alliance, signed in 1947, was concluded between the United States and states in Latin America, all of whom were already U.S. clients. Significantly, as we shall see below, the U.S. had concluded staff agreements with the militaries of all but one of those clients in 1940 and during the World War II years had significantly deepened those ties. In the case of Central America and certain Caribbean states, the client relationship went back decades before that. The significance of the Rio Pact was that it provided a legal basis for maintaining on a formal and multilateral basis the various arrangements that the U.S. had worked out with Latin American countries during the war. This comes through clearly in the pact's reference to the Act of Chapultepec, a resolution agreed to in 1945, before the war had ended, which called on its signatories to conclude a treaty specifying procedures for hemispheric military solidarity.

At first blush, the ANZUS pact seems to have had something more to do with endangered clients than did the United States's other multilateral alliances. By our coding, neither Australia nor New Zealand was a client before the treaty was signed in 1951 and the pact immediately led to fairly extensive military cooperation. However, there is little evidence that the U.S. perceived Australia and New Zealand to be endangered. Our impression is rather that this was a kind of postwar tidying-up operation, such as the U.S. was doing elsewhere (see below). Interestingly, the negotiation of ANZUS and the Japanese peace treaty led to jealousy on the part of the Philippines, which, although already a U.S. client, insisted on a bilateral defense treaty of its own that same year. Other bilateral defense treaties were also concluded with states which were already U.S. clients (South Korea in 1953, Taiwan in 1954, and Japan in 1960, extending the treaty of 1951), not because the treaties were needed to ward off danger, but for reasons of symbolism and coordination.[48]

Formal military alliances thus have little to do one way or the other with client acquisition. By the same reasoning, military bases also have no particular relevance to whether or not a state is a client. Many U.S. clients, of course, have U.S. bases located on their territory; in some cases, such as Germany, there were at one point literally hundreds of such bases. We saw above that if a client was acquired in a post-occupation context, it is more than likely to have numerous bases. However, states can perfectly well host U.S. bases as a purely instrumental arrangement: as a favor, or as a commercial proposition, or as a hoped-for, but not guaranteed, means of attracting future U.S. support. Ethiopia, as we saw, provides one example of this kind of limited contractual link: the U.S. paid Haile Selassie for the Kagnew facility but did not, for a number of years, go beyond and take on the regime as a client. Haile Selassie, of course, claimed that he was endangered, but this argument was not accepted until years after Kagnew was set up.

Similar hands-off basing arrangements pertain to other countries. One is Libya, in which, for several decades, the U.S. had a massive air base, but without taking on the regime of King Idris as a client. Another is Morocco, in which the U.S., although cooperating with King Hassan, always eschewed the role of patron. In the early 2000s, a similar relationship seems to have developed with several of the Central Asian republics: the U.S. obtained bases and provided some resources for the regimes of those states, but without developing the close relationships it had with clients. In these cases, the U.S. appeared to defer to Russia.

Prewar / postwar planning

The most important context of acquisition, at least if judged by the number of states which became clients in that context, has to do with the planning process that precedes and follows wars (see Table 3.4). In both cases, U.S. officials seek to organize entire regions, taking the states in those regions in hand and setting up procedures so that things run smoothly. When war is impending, this looks something like the danger context of acquisition we have already discussed, although with two important differences: first, that the region in question may not at all be perceived as exposed to any significant danger; and second, that instead of focusing efforts on a small number (often, as we saw, a pair) of states seen as particularly threatened, planning takes place for all the states of the region, no matter what their characteristics may be.

A good example of prewar planning is the arrangements the U.S. developed for South America in the first two years of World War II. Immediately after the war broke out, the U.S. set up patrolling arrangements for the Atlantic with countries in Latin America; in some cases, this involved opening ports to U.S. naval vessels. After the fall of France and the Low Countries, a foreign ministers meeting laid out language that invited military cooperation. The U.S. had already moved in this direction, sending military missions throughout Latin America in 1939 and 1940. Those missions had two tasks: to see that similar missions from Axis nations were dismissed, and to work out staff agreements in which the U.S. would offer defense assistance mostly in exchange for aid in the transit of U.S. forces. These agreements, which were concluded by the end of 1940 with every Latin American state except for Argentina, led to close cooperation, especially in the areas of training and arms procurement, with the militaries of those states.

Table 3.4 Clients acquired: pre-/post-war planning

Client	Date acquired and duration of client status
Panama	1903–present
Dominican Republic	1905–present
Honduras	1911–present
Haiti	1915–present
Costa Rica	1919–present
Guatemala	1920–present
El Salvador	1922–present
Mexico	1940–present
Colombia	1940–present
Venezuela	1940–present
Bolivia	1940–present
Ecuador	1940–present
Peru	1940–present
Chile	1940 present
Paraguay	1940–present
Uruguay	1940–present
Brazil	1940–present
Canada	1941–present
Liberia	1942–present
Argentina	1946–present
France	1948–present
United Kingdom	1948–present
Belgium	1948–present
Netherlands	1948–present
Luxembourg	1948–present
Denmark	1948–present
Norway	1948–present
Iceland	1948–present
Portugal	1948–present
Sweden	1948–present
Australia	1951–present
New Zealand	1951–present
Spain	1953–present
Kuwait	1991–present
Bahrain	1991–present
Oman	1992–present
Qatar	1992–present
United Arab Emirates	1994–present

Sources: Authors as per Chapter 2 note 56.

In addition, the U.S. also worked out numerous economic and financial agreements with Latin American countries. These accords involved both state and private activities, ranging from maritime cooperation to development finance and coffee marketing. The Export-Import Bank vastly increased its lending to Latin America. Arrangements were made for production and purchase of various metal exports. And significantly, in August of 1940, the U.S. set up a new agency to handle inter-American affairs, with a wealthy private businessman, Nelson Rockefeller, named as its first "coordinator."[49]

Several points should be noted about this prewar planning example. First, neither the U.S. nor the Latin American states perceived any real danger from the Axis powers. This is not to say that there were not moments of panic, notably after the attack on

Pearl Harbor (which took place after the most important arrangements had been worked out), but in general, the problem that was being addressed was the possibility, indeed, the likelihood, of future U.S. participation in the war. That participation would be far away from Latin America, even if areas such as the northeast of Brazil would be useful staging grounds for transatlantic crossings. Hemispheric leaders wanted to make certain that the United States would have access to raw materials and bases and, not coincidentally, that there would be no significant political distractions in particular Latin American countries.

Second, the arrangements applied to the entire region. U.S. planning encompassed both existing clients in Central America and the Caribbean, as well as the South American countries, which, in spite of U.S. economic dominance, had not yet been taken under Washington's wing. Among the new clients swept up in this planning exercise was Mexico, a U.S. enemy for a quarter of a century. We saw above how the U.S. had intervened militarily in Mexico in 1913; in subsequent years, the possibility of intervention arose again. Although relations improved under Hoover, the Cardenas presidency in Mexico led to renewed tensions, expropriating first land held by U.S. citizens and then, in 1938, British and U.S. oil companies. These disputes were nonetheless smoothed over, due in no small part to pressure from the War Department that Mexico should be incorporated into hemispheric war planning.[50]

Third, region-wide prewar planning also led to the acquisition of two non-Latin American countries as clients. One was Canada, which until then had kept some distance from the United States. In the summer of 1940, when it looked as if Britain might fall, the U.S. and Canada approved a contingency plan which, in essence, replaced the British fleet with that of the U.S. and subordinated Canadian military forces to American ones. By the spring of 1941, the situation for Britain was less worrisome and a new plan, giving less control to the U.S., was put together for when Washington would enter the war. At the same time, the Hyde Park Declaration by Roosevelt and the Canadian prime minister brought Canada's economy under U.S. oversight as regards defense purchases and raw materials imports. This involved, among other measures, the initiation of Canadian economic and diplomatic ties with different Latin American countries.[51]

The other client acquired as part of the prewar hemispheric planning process was, paradoxically, a country not even located in the Western Hemisphere. Liberia had been founded as a settlement in the early nineteenth century by freed U.S. slaves. In 1847, it became an independent state, with recognition following over the next two decades. In the early 1900s, after the U.S. had worked out financial supervisory relationships with the Dominican Republic, it tried to set up similar arrangements with other states (see below), one of whom was Liberia. On several occasions between 1912 and 1924, the U.S. tried and failed to establish a clientilistic relationship with Liberia, including both financial control and U.S. direction of the military. The attempts continued up through the 1930s, at State Department behest, with the Firestone Rubber Company. Always, arrangements fell apart because of either U.S. or Liberian reticence. But when war seemed imminent, these obstacles fell away. Liberia was not only a producer of rubber, an important commodity for any number of military products, but it was situated conveniently partway between the northeast of Brazil and the areas of North Africa in which the U.S. would be fighting. Accordingly, the U.S. concluded a defense arrangement with Liberia in 1942 which resulted in road construction, a deepwater harbor, and an international airport. The next year, two symbolic events occurred: Liberia declared the U.S. dollar as legal tender and none other than Franklin Roosevelt himself stopped for lunch at the new airport on his way back from Casablanca.[52]

Prewar planning thus led to the acquisition of all the Western Hemisphere (plus one African) states which were not already clients. Or, to be correct, all but one Western Hemisphere state, because Argentina refused to enter into a staff agreement with the United States. Relations remained at arm's length, with Argentina not even breaking relations with the Axis until 1944 and with Colonel Juan Perón, who would soon emerge as president, declaring that Argentina was indifferent as to whether the Allies or the Axis won the war. The U.S. put strong pressure on the regime, and although this led to a grudging declaration of war in 1945, it backfired, with the Argentinean electorate backing Perón rather than his nemesis, the U.S. diplomat Spruille Braden. Eventually, conservative pressure in the U.S. led Truman to ease relations with Argentina in 1946, with the latter quickly entering into the web of agreements the U.S. had spun with its neighbors in the preceding seven years.[53]

World War II was an exceptional event from a planning point of view, because, even though Roosevelt intended clearly that the U.S. enter the war, over two years elapsed between its outbreak in Europe and the attack on Pearl Harbor. This gave the U.S. considerable time to plan for entry into the war. By contrast, most other wars fought by the U.S. either took place with little or no planning (e.g., the Korean War) or else did not appear to high level officials as if they would in the end involve the United States (e.g., World War I). The one partial exception to this is the second war the U.S. fought against Iraq, in 2003. This war, which we will discuss with other cases of hostile intervention in Chapter 6, was planned well before it began. On 21 November 2001, when military operations were still proceeding in Afghanistan, Bush ordered his secretary of defense and his general in charge of Central Command (the same general running the war in Afghanistan) to start planning for a war in Iraq. Over the next 16 months, the U.S. worked out detailed overflight and basing arrangements for the war, with American forces being built up in no fewer than eight countries. However, all of those countries were already U.S. clients at the time, most of them containing U.S. bases for at least a decade prior to the war, and so planning for the second Iraq war did not lead to any new client acquisitions.[54]

It might be expected that postwar planning would differ from prewar planning in major ways. The latter, perhaps, might be more militarily focused than the former, since the problem at hand before a war is obviously how the war will be fought, whereas when the war is over, any number of other issues can come to the fore. In fact, though, both types of planning cover a wide variety of issues. We saw above that the arrangements the U.S. worked out for the Western Hemisphere were not restricted to military matters but also covered finance, commerce, and even economic development. Moreover, by dint of working out these particular arrangements, the U.S. strengthened regimes, if not with respect to public opinion then at least vis-à-vis important economic and military actors. In this sense, when the U.S. acquired a client as preparation for a war, it made a commitment on far more than simply military matters.

Much the same is true of postwar planning. Whenever the U.S. fought a war, it found itself with an increased presence – military, of course, but also economic – in the region. What was to become of that presence? Even if it was decided to liquidate all or most of it, as in effect the U.S. Senate chose to do after World War I (via its rejection of the League of Nations and its failure to ratify a security treaty with France), this would require some thought about the region's future and some coordination, however minimal, with the states concerned. But in fact, U.S. officials were not usually so divided and most of the time, there was a sense that the war's investment in blood and treasure could not simply be written off, and that arrangements had to be made to prevent future wars of that sort, or at the least, to prepare for them more adequately. Those arrangements, even if they aimed at the maintenance of regimes, could not only be military in nature.[55]

The best known of these arrangements is the relationship worked out between the United States and Western Europe after the end of World War II. Although, in the last years of the war, the U.S. had engaged in general planning for the postwar period – notably through the creation of the Bretton Woods agencies and the United Nations – planning for Western Europe as a particular region had mostly lagged behind. American officials quickly found themselves with a series of country-specific or regional problems. Great Britain, for example, was in dire financial shape after the termination of Lend-Lease aid in August 1945; the British asked the U.S. for a $6 billion grant and after hard bargaining finally settled for a $3.75 billion loan (disbursed in fiscal year 1947) tied to numerous economic concessions made to the United States. France, too, received nearly $1.5 billion in credits during the preceding year to address its economic difficulties and deflate political pressure from the French Communist Party. Italy, where the Communist Party was also powerful, received over $400 million during the same period. Other European states asked for smaller amounts of aid, some receiving it, but very much on an ad hoc basis.

However, these financial difficulties paled compared with the region-wide problems which had emerged by 1947. European export industries had been badly damaged by the war and simply were not earning enough dollars to finance the imports needed for recovery. This risked a major recession, if not worse, which would have grave effects on both the U.S. economy and the legitimacy of governments throughout Western Europe. In addition, the temptation would be great for the Europeans to enter into bilateral trade or barter arrangements as a way of circumventing the dollar shortage; this would destroy U.S. hopes for a liberal and multilateral trade and payment system.

In addition, there were other related regional problems. One concerned the present and future role of Germany: how, if at all, it was to be rebuilt, what its borders would be, and what its place would be relative to the rest of Europe. Another problem was to sort out the links, if any, that would exist between an increasingly Soviet-controlled Eastern Europe and the countries of Western Europe, not to mention bolstering the latter relative to the Soviet Union. Still another problem was to respond to the various pleas for U.S. action that arrived regularly from countries throughout the region.

To Truman and his advisers, these various problems were connected. They stemmed from the devastation of World War II, the fact that the old order had been destroyed and that nothing had yet come around to replace it. As Will Clayton, the under-secretary of state for economic affairs, put it, "It is now obvious that we have grossly underestimated the destruction to the European economy by the war. ... Europe is steadily deteriorating" and needed U.S. dollars "based on a European plan"; although other nations could help, "[t]he United States must run this show." Thus was born the Marshall Plan.[56]

From the perspective of patron–client relations, the significance of the Marshall Plan resides less in the quantity of resources it transferred – some $13 billion over four years (over $90 billion in 2008 dollars) – than in the broad range of responsibilities the U.S. assumed and the surveillance and control mechanisms it set up with the Europeans. To administer the Marshall Plan, the U.S. set up an Economic Cooperation Administration

(ECA), headed by an administrator who was responsible directly to the President. In each recipient country, a special ECA mission was established, headed by a chief who ranked second only to the chief of the U.S. diplomatic mission in that country. Aid was allocated and coordinated through a multilateral mechanism, the successor of which still exists as the Organisation for Economic Co-operation and Development (OECD); in this way, the U.S. gave a powerful boost to what would become decades of European integration efforts.

The U.S. insisted that for aid to be disbursed, each recipient state had to sign a bilateral agreement in which it pledged to the U.S. that it would undertake various economic policies and furnish reports to the U.S. on the progress of the program. In addition, most of the Plan recipients were required to set up so-called counterpart funds, an amount of money, in their own currency, equivalent to the dollars they received. Ninety-five percent of those funds could be spent by the recipient governments for projects to which the U.S. agreed. This gave an enormous power of oversight and control to the U.S. The remaining 5 percent of counterpart funds were deeded over to the U.S. for whichever purposes it saw fit. A significant portion of those funds were channeled by the ECA directly to the Office of Policy Coordination (OPC), the then-autonomous part of the CIA responsible for carrying out covert political (and military) actions. In this way, the Marshall Plan became, in effect, the funding mechanism for the secret side of the political maintenance of Western European regimes and, not coincidentally, for the hostile interventions undertaken by OPC in Eastern Europe (see Chapters 5 and 6).[57]

The main post-World War II planning process revolved around the Marshall Plan. However, when the U.S. began planning for the end of its occupation of Japan, considerable agitation arose among several states in East Asia and Oceania, in part because the draft peace treaty closed the door on reparations and in part because the U.S. envisaged concluding a defense arrangement with Japan. One of the disgruntled states, the Philippines, was already a U.S. client; another, Taiwan, would soon become one (when, after the outbreak of the Korean War, the Seventh Fleet was ordered to block a Chinese invasion); and a third, Burma, had already resisted U.S. blandishments. That left Australia and New Zealand, states beside whom the U.S. had fought in World War II and toward whom there was considerable sympathy. Neither Australia nor New Zealand had anywhere near the economic problems of most European countries (though Australia did ask for, and receive, a development loan from the World Bank, then, as now, controlled by the U.S.), nor did they, or the U.S., consider themselves threatened by invasion or subversion. Their concern was rather that their military forces would be called on in future efforts but that, lacking some kind of formal military-to-military ties with the U.S., they would in essence be voiceless. Originally, Australia had asked for a more equal role in Washington; but after elections in 1949, the new government in Canberra scaled down its request to a more asymmetrical type of link. The U.S., not wishing to offend its wartime allies, was now willing to oblige. The result was the ANZUS pact of 1951, accompanied by U.S. bilateral mutual defense agreements with each state (Australia in 1951 before ANZUS, New Zealand in 1952).[58]

From the perspective of client state acquisition, the final act of the post-World War II planning context involved Spain. Even more than Argentina, Spain was in bad odor with the U.S. in 1945, with the possibility of an intervention to overthrow the Franco regime having been discussed from time to time. Both Truman and the leaders of Britain and other states detested Franco; thus Spain was not invited to participate in the Marshall Plan or in the formation of NATO. But just as the State Department gave way over

Argentina, so Truman did over Spain. Starting in 1948, the Pentagon showed increased interest in the prospect of naval and air bases in Spain. Conservative forces in Congress inserted economic aid for Spain in 1950, and again 1951. Finally, Truman surrendered, sending two military missions to Spain in 1951 to survey base possibilities and open talks with the Franco regime. In 1953, a deal was struck, going well beyond military bases: the U.S. entered into close military and economic ties with Spain, the same type of arrangements it had earlier concluded with the other countries of Western Europe. With this, the U.S. post-World War II efforts in Europe and Oceania were complete.[59]

The most recent cases of client acquisition in the context of postwar planning are those of the Persian Gulf states after the first U.S.-Iraq war. Prior to the war, the U.S. had highly differentiated relations with those states, extending from having air and naval facilities in some states (Bahrain and Oman) to more distant relations with others (Kuwait). Up through the 1980s, Britain had an important role with all of the states, either because of treaty relationships with them and subsequent military ties (weapons, training, or encadrement) or because it had helped in a counterinsurgency war (in Oman). The U.S. military presence increased during the Iran-Iraq war, but still on an ad hoc and differentiated basis. After the end of hostilities in 1991, the U.S. decided that this disorganization could no longer continue. It negotiated close military ties with each of the Gulf states, providing not only for bases (often very large-scale ones) and military headquarters but for training, arms sales (some of them enormous, such as an $8 billion contract with the U.A.E.), and joint exercises. These arrangements turned out to have been useful for U.S. military action against Iraq over the next 12 years; they also were used for other patrols in the region and could of course be used in any military engagement with Iran.[60]

By 1991, the U.S. had considerable practice in postwar planning. As we saw above, the situation was somewhat different in the post-World War II period, not only because of the immense scale and devastation of the war but also because U.S. policy makers had not yet developed the policy instruments appropriate for dealing with states which were already highly industrialized and which had democratic and well-functioning governments. If we go farther back in time, to the first case of postwar planning, we see that the policy instruments then available to U.S. officials were even more limited; however enthusiastic they may or may not have been about acquiring client states, there was inevitably a period of trial and error. Hence, a progression: the first U.S.-Iraq War led to clients being acquired in three years; after World War II, it took eight years (six if Spain is seen as an exception); and after the Spanish-American War, it took 24 years. This earliest case is fascinating, because we can see the working out of an entire new policy.

When the "splendid little war" was over, less than four months after it had begun, U.S. officials soon felt as if they had unfinished business. Cuba was occupied, supposedly in transition to self-rule. Puerto Rico had been annexed and was almost immediately forgotten. The Philippines were taken over as a colony, though only after a loud and clamorous debate; and U.S. forces there soon found themselves in the midst of a violent counterinsurgency campaign. This, however, did not exhaust the difficulties. The U.S. had flexed its muscles in the Caribbean; what now was to become of the rest of the area? The immediate problem stemmed from the experience of the war with Spain. It had taken one of the navy's battleships over two months to travel around Cape Horn and arrive in Florida for the impending invasion of Cuba. This was unacceptable and the issue of an isthmian canal now moved to the top of the agenda. In the end, after numerous sordid maneuvers and with much connivance by the U.S., Colombia's northern province

of Panama was detached and proclaimed an independent country. Eleven days later, a
treaty had been neg   ᵈ with the U.S. for a canal. The Senate, holding its nose at the
impropriety, was   ˉˉˉˉvelt to ratify the treaty and let him "dig the
Panama Canal an   ˉᵈ " What resulted was a state bisected
by a swath of U.ˢ   ⁻ in defense of that canal, to
act "at all times

Several mont   p going to war in
1898 (apart fr   of a fear that the
counterinsurge   Cuban rebels would
either drag or   aos the likely result
whatever hap   . Other states in the
area were al   to seize power. Both
these rebell   to repress them were
financed b   pay foreign (European
and U.S.)   intervene militarily, in
effect rec   cidentally, posing what
Washing   ᵢ. Thus, the general task,
as Roos   attitude of protection and
regulati   od of the Caribbean."[62]
How   ng the marines, something
the U   which was implied in both
the F   Treaty. Roosevelt had no
obje   as the "duty" of a "civilized
nati   e too blunt to be of much use
exc   e flexible and nuanced means,
in   countries' finances. Typically,
th   concerned and someone else –
p   .S. government – to appoint a
f   country's customs facilities, and
                                                         ution that had already been tried
                                                        r countries in the Near East. Of
                                                       llers would have to be backed by
                                                      be necessary.[63]
                                                    igly and with numerous starts and
                                                   er of 1904, an arbitration award in
                                                  that led to an agreement (negotiated
                                                 avy commander) on a customs recei-
                                                ified as a treaty in 1907, but already in
                                               t to formulate his "corollary" to the
                                              le for intervention in the region. In the
                                             et unratified treaty as a "modus vivendi"
                                            economist who had earlier worked on
                                           y (later absorbed into Oklahoma) and an
                                          s service in the Philippines.[64]
                                         an important model to Washington policy
                                        omething like it in mind when he used the
                                       s secretary of state had prepared Dominican-
                                      s and was drafting plans along the same lines

for Guatemala and Liberia. This continued under the next president, Wilson, with slightly different plans (a contract between a U.S. bank and a foreign government, sponsored by the U.S. government) being made for Mexico, China, Guatemala, and other countries; most of those plans fell through, however. Still another variant, this time involving "voluntary" relationships with professional financial advisers (usually nominated by the State Department), was developed for other Latin American countries in the 1920s. However, in the absence of other political and military ties, financial arrangements in those years, even if agreed to by both sides, could only open the possibility for acquiring a client; full consummation would take more effort.[65]

Around the time the Dominican arrangement was being worked out, the U.S. began focusing on Central America. The instability Roosevelt had complained of was patently obvious: in 1906, El Salvador, supported overtly by Honduras and covertly, it was said, by Nicaragua (then an enemy) and Mexico, invaded Guatemala. Roosevelt called for mediation and with Mexican help held a peace conference on a U.S. naval vessel off the coast of El Salvador. A peace treaty was concluded, was then broken the next year, and finally, in 1907, a general Central American conference was held in Washington. None of these diplomatic actions led to any kind of lasting stability and so the U.S. looked for other, more direct ways of making sure that order would be preserved. One opportunity presented itself in Nicaragua (discussed above as a switch), followed, the year later, by a second opportunity in Honduras. A U.S. entrepreneur in the banana business, Samuel Zemurray (known widely as Sam the Banana Man), had significant investments in Honduras and feared that a new government might turn against him. He financed an expedition out of New Orleans with a former Honduran president and various soldiers of fortune. The U.S. in effect aided the rebels militarily and diplomatically to take over (one soldier of fortune became the U.S. consul; Zemurray later became commander in chief of the Honduran army). Interestingly, the deposed president, in a bid to save himself, had already tried to work out a U.S. financial oversight arrangement.[66]

What the Honduran case shows is that the United States, in spite of wanting to organize the Central American and Caribbean area to prevent instability, was limited in its means of doing so. Nothing like the Marshall Plan then existed and U.S. officials had first to invent new policy instruments, then look for places in which those instruments could be employed. Financial controls, because they so obviously smacked of colonialism, would, again unlike the Marshall Plan, be resisted by the states to whom they were offered. This meant that they could only be pushed through in situations of crisis, such as a rebellion (with the U.S. using its military force on one side or the other) or a financial panic. Viewed from Washington, such crises were highly likely but they were impossible to predict, and this, besides whatever residual anti-imperial reluctance still existed, meant that post-Spanish-American War clients would be acquired in random spurts.

This pattern of initial offer, followed by refusal and then, after a crisis, by no-nonsense acquisition can be seen in the next several Caribbean and Central American cases. The first was Haiti. In 1913, the U.S. unsuccessfully offered to buy land for a naval base; the following year, to set up Dominican-style financial controls. When a change of government occurred in Haiti, the U.S. pressed the financial plan as a condition for recognition. This, too, was rejected and Washington began contemplating the use of "force as may be necessary to compel a supervision." Finally, in July 1915, the marines landed to "cure the anarchy and disorder" in Haiti. The U.S. admiral in charge supervised an election, forced the Haitians to cede control over customs and other financial affairs, wrote a new constitution, and, when the legislature balked at approving it, turned them out at gunpoint and whipped through a plebiscite.[67]

In 1919, it was Costa Rica's turn. Controversy had been brewing for several years about contracts for oil exploration, with the U.S. applying pressure to ensure that only firms approved by the State Department be given concessions. When the Costa Rican president, who had come to power in a *coup d'état*, refused, the U.S. withheld recognition and began applying financial and diplomatic pressure on the regime. Eventually, the president fled, his brother (who was war minister) resigned and was assassinated, and his successor, in the face of open U.S. disapproval, also stepped down. The new government reopened the oil contracts and, for good measure, practically dismantled the country's military to prevent future coups. Several years later, the government accepted a loan with judicial officers of the U.S. as final arbiters.[68]

The process continued in the remaining Central American countries. In Guatemala, as we saw, the U.S. had earlier tried but failed to set up a Dominican-style customs arrangement; although the government did try and satisfy U.S. desires on petroleum concessions and also solicited advice from a U.S. expert on currency reform. A new opportunity presented itself in 1920, when the long-time dictator began imprisoning opponents. The U.S., in what would become a standard policy in numerous countries for decades to come, lectured the president on his behavior and extracted a public promise that he would no longer act in this way. When the promise was broken, the legislature, controlled by the president's partisans, deposed him on the grounds that he had become "insane" and appointed a successor. The U.S. then brokered a solution to the crisis, as it would do for other political crises in the next decade. In the meantime, intense discussions took place between the U.S. and the new government about a loan with the standard controls. None of these worked out, in each case because the State Department refused to give its unambiguous approval, which the Guatemalans were looking for. Eventually, plans for a loan were dropped and Guatemala set up a new currency pegged 1:1 to the dollar.[69]

The final state to be acquired as a client was El Salvador, a country in which the U.S. economic presence was proportionally smaller than anywhere else in the region. This was a state with a cohesive political elite, passing power from one leader to the next without either rebellions or *coups d'état*; thus from the U.S. perspective, the country was stable. A crack appeared in 1921, when the Salvadoran government faced a financial crisis and appeared as if it might fall. It asked the U.S. minister and the leading U.S. businessman in Central America to arrange a loan, with the understanding that some kind of financial controls would be instituted (they included a clause specifying that if a dispute arose, the U.S. secretary of state would refer the issue to the chief justice of the U.S. Supreme Court). After considerable haggling, mostly involving disputes between the U.S. government and New York banks, the loan went through. A U.S. banking official, approved by the State Department, served as fiscal representative and played an important role in the country's financial administration. Several years later, the U.S. began to play an overtly political role in the country's presidential politics, trying unsuccessfully to oust a military dictator and then serving as the contact point for both his opponents and supporters.[70]

El Salvador closes the post-1898 acquisition context, which by our count runs for 24 years. It is reasonable to ask if client acquisitions so many years after the Spanish-American War can really be said to be instances of the same context and indeed if it makes sense to use the word "planning" to describe what happened. On our view, the answer is yes, not because there was some sort of master plan hatched by McKinley or Roosevelt but because the basic problem governing client acquisition was clear to U.S. policy makers as far back as 1903, or perhaps even 1901, when the Platt Amendment was voted on. As we saw, the concern for every president since McKinley was to stabilize the region, finding a way of heading off overt conflicts of the sort the U.S. fought against Spain. The general outline of a solution was clear to Roosevelt, as to all his successors: to use U.S. power to keep each country in the region on an even keel.

To implement this solution, successive policy instruments were employed: first, the use of marines in a kind of constitutionally sanctioned role; then, when that turned out to be too costly, the setting up of financial receiverships; and finally, when those were not accepted, a combination of armed intervention, diplomatic pressures, and loans. As each instrument was developed, U.S. policy makers envisaged using it widely throughout the region; thus the U.S. laid postwar plans for Central America and the Caribbean no fewer than three times. The starts and stops were not due primarily to hesitation on the part of U.S. officials or to some difficulty in coming to grips with an imperial role; rather, they were cybernetic and diplomatic, stemming from the difficulties of developing new policies and organizational means of carrying them out and of getting those policies accepted by the intended clients.

In this sense, the U.S. task in later pre- or postwar periods was facilitated considerably by two factors. The first was the invention of new forms of client maintenance and surveillance mechanisms, such as military staff arrangements and economic and military aid (see Chapter 4). These policy instruments, when put in place in specific states, provided concrete ways for the U.S. to take responsibility for maintaining regimes and thus could be used as means for client acquisition. In addition, although the details of any specific program had to be worked out with each recipient government, there was nonetheless a general template to be applied. By contrast, when bank loan arrangements were being worked out before World War II, they had to be arranged anew through separate bank consortia, with different creditors being satisfied, in each country.

The second facilitating factor was the development of what we might call a common practical ideology (see Chapter 7). By 1940, when military staff arrangements were being worked out for the Western Hemisphere, there was remarkably little resistance to them by Latin American states, including some highly nationalistic ones. The same consensus could be seen in Western Europe and Oceania after World War II, as was also the case in the Gulf states after the first U.S.-Iraq War. This is a far cry from the reticence, if not downright hostility, shown by certain Central American and Caribbean governments to U.S. proposals early in the century.

Special access

The four contexts of client acquisition we have discussed so far all involved a decision by U.S. officials based on the client's situation at that moment: was it emerging from U.S. occupation, or switching sides to the U.S., or endangered, or in a region connected with U.S. pre- or postwar planning? A small number of states, however, were acquired because of the history of their – or their predecessors' – involvement with the U.S. prior to the moment of acquisition (see Table 3.5). Because of that history, those states had special access to Washington policy makers, whether through domestic lobbying or relationships begun prior to independence. The problem faced by U.S. officials in these cases was

Table 3.5 Clients acquired: special access

Client	Date acquired and duration of client status
Hawaii	1893–1898
Israel	1948–present
Saudi Arabia	1953–present
Guyana	1966–present
Bahamas	1985–present
Poland	1998–present

Sources: Authors as per Chapter 2 note 56.

how to satisfy the obligations entailed by a preexisting relationship when the situation had changed; the answer was to restructure the relationship in patron–client terms.

Perhaps the classic example of acquisition in a context of special access is that of Israel. After World War II, U.S. public opinion began to move strongly in the direction of establishing a Jewish state in some or all of the British Palestine Mandate. Politicians of both main parties responded to this, partly as a means of attracting Jewish votes in particular constituencies and partly out of more general electoral and policy concerns. Thus, in 1947, the U.S. supported a UN plan for partitioning Palestine into a Jewish and an Arab state; the next year, Truman overrode strenuous objections by the State Department to recognize the new state of Israel 11 minutes after it was proclaimed; and by late 1948, it was clear that whoever was elected as president in November would make sure that a large loan was granted to the new state. In addition, U.S. tax law indirectly underwrote private contributions to Israel. On the military side of things, even though the U.S. maintained an arms embargo on Israel in the early part of its independence, Washington did little to stop arms imports from elsewhere as well as military training by supposedly private citizens. Also, and quite early on, the two states worked out a close intelligence relationship.[71]

More than these specific arrangements, the diplomatic record shows an extremely tight relationship between Israel and the U.S. from the earliest moments. The two states talked with each other informally even before independence and there was an ease of access from the very beginning. More importantly, even during tense confrontations over specific issues, there was an evident presumption on both sides that the U.S. would always be a backstop for Israel. Thus, although it is of course true that the U.S. since the 1960s entered into far a more direct military relationship with Israel than had been the case in the years immediately following independence, the relationship fit the definition of patron and client from the very start.[72]

Another state which became a client in the context of a situation similar to that of Israel is Poland. Once again, the issue was not simply one of voters concentrated in certain states but of a broad consensus on the part of U.S. politicians that the Poles really merited a preferential arrangement. From the early days of Truman's presidency to the short-lived thaws when first Gomulka and then Gierek liberalized Communist rule after domestic unrest, U.S. leaders consistently saw Poland as "heroic" and themselves as "old friends." In 1980, when the Solidarity trade union movement appeared on the scene, it was aided overtly by the American AFL-CIO, covertly by the CIA, and, via diplomacy at the interstate level, by the White House and the State Department. After the end of Communist rule and the fall of the Berlin Wall, the U.S. expanded its ties with Poland, especially, as we saw above, in the military field; it now is described by the State Department as a "key ally" of the United States.[73]

Both Israel and Poland became clients because a consensus by U.S. politicians on the deserving qualities of both countries' populations provided those countries' leaders with special access to U.S. policy makers, who in turn were able to respond with offers of client status. Several other countries also were able to obtain this access but not because their populations were seen as specially deserving. Rather, there was already an active U.S. interest in those countries so that when the opportunity presented itself, policy makers thought it logical to ratify that relation by means of available policy instruments.

The Bahamas is a good example of this type of special access. For decades before its independence from Britain in 1973, the Bahamas had close governmental ties with the United States as well as extensive economic and tourist links. Not surprisingly, given that the two countries are only 45 miles apart at their closest point, a number of defense arrangements were worked out in the colonial era, including naval facilities, guided missile proving grounds, and navigation stations. After independence, those treaties remained in force and new ones were added, including a military training agreement, several important anti-narcotics arrangements, and cooperation to reform the Bahamian judiciary. It should be noted that 30,000 U.S. citizens are resident in the Bahamas and so one U.S. goal is to maintain stability as a means of ensuring their safety.[74]

Another country in the region with whom there was a relationship that predated its independence is Guyana. By the early 1960s as we saw in Chapter 2 (British Guiana), U.S. policy makers were greatly concerned that the prime minister of the colony, Cheddi Jagan, was either a communist or insufficiently hostile to communism. As a result, the U.S. tried to prevent Jagan from being prime minister when the British granted independence, both by pressuring the British to delay independence and to rig the electoral system so that he would not be able to form a new government; and by subsidizing his opponents in the trade unions (this was done by the CIA and the AFL-CIO, both of whom underwrote three violent general strikes) and in opposition political parties (see Chapter 5). The policy succeeded and when the British finally left, it was with an anti-Jagan politician, Forbes Burnham, safely in power. Even before formal independence, the U.S. immediately moved to establish client-like ties with the Burnham regime, granting economic aid and giving detailed political advice. After independence, the aid program expanded, including roadbuilding and significant amounts of food aid; there were also grants to anti-Jagan activists; no fewer than three meetings between Burnham and the U.S. president, Lyndon Johnson; and discussions on how to increase votes for Burnham's party by means of immigration and other measures and whether this would be more effective than sending Jagan into exile.[75]

The earliest example of a client acquired in the context of special access – indeed, the first client ever acquired by the United States – is Hawaii. This was an independent kingdom which had the unfortunate experience of attracting large numbers of American missionaries, who soon began occupying important high-level positions in the government. By the late nineteenth century, there were also extensive U.S. investments in sugar and other crops, as well as frequent naval visits. In early 1893, U.S. citizens, hoping for annexation by Washington, overthrew the queen and set up a provisional government, which was immediately recognized by the United States. Soon, however, a staunchly anti-annexationist Democratic president had been inaugurated and so the provisional government transformed itself into a republic with a constitution similar to that of the U.S. This situation lasted for four years, when, in the midst of the Spanish-American War, Congress finally voted to annex the republic.

From its inception, the new republic was a client state of the U.S. The coup of 1893 was aided by U.S. military threats against both the queen's government and restive Japanese laborers. In the early days, the provisional government was under the control of the admiral in charge of U.S. forces in the Pacific; and except for a three-month period in 1894, U.S. warships were present continually after 1893. The Japanese and the British were warned against interfering in Hawaii. In Washington, a sugar tariff was imposed, which had the effect of binding Hawaii even more closely to the U.S. Throughout this time, there was frequent contact between officials of the two governments; on grounds of citizenship, strategy, and social standing, the planters and descendants of the missionaries who ran the Hawaiian republic had special access to Washington.[76]

A final example of special access has to do with the one country in which natural resources were so significant that U.S. officials were led to establish connections at an early date, ties which created a subsequent presumption in favor of client status. This was Saudi Arabia, with whom the U.S. had ties going back to the 1930s. Those ties revolved around the petroleum industry and as the years went by, the U.S. government did everything it could to facilitate that connection. Thus, in World War II, the U.S. extended Lend-Lease aid to Saudi Arabia, even though the kingdom was not a belligerent. A few years later, the Truman Administration waived antitrust laws to permit a consortium of U.S. companies to finance a pipeline for carrying Saudi crude. In 1950, the U.S. government indirectly subsidized additional payments to the Saudi regime by ruling that royalties paid by oil companies would be eligible for a tax credit. Two years later, as he was leaving office, Truman instructed the Justice Department to terminate antitrust proceedings against five of the largest oil companies.[77]

To U.S. officials, it was obvious that Saudi Arabia was of great importance to the U.S. However, it took several years before that understanding would be transformed into a patron–client relation. This process began with signs of direct presidential interest in the kingdom: a face-to-face meeting between Franklin Roosevelt and King Ibn Saud in 1945; and letters from Truman and Eisenhower to the king, reaffirming U.S. concern for the territorial integrity and independence of Saudi Arabia and, more generally, the position of the U.S. as a "true friend" of the kingdom. However to the Saudis, this was not enough and they pressed for military aid and training agreements both as a way of getting weapons and so that the Saudi Arabian military would have close ties with its U.S. counterparts. The Pentagon resisted those ties at first, trying to make the arrangement purely one of shipping arms in payment for use of the Dhahran airfield. In the end, Eisenhower overrode the Defense Department. The resulting contacts had important implications for Saudi internal security, which henceforth became an explicit U.S. goal; it also opened the door to increased government-to-government contacts in other areas.[78]

These various cases of client acquisition in the context of special access illustrate yet again the dominance of means over ends in U.S. policy making. Each special access case involves the formalization of a relationship that had already existed, even though the goals U.S. officials were pursuing differed considerably from one case to the next (e.g., righting a wrong, obtaining oil, guarding against leftist rule). The important point for policy makers is that it was possible to make an explicit commitment, via different policy instruments, and that this commitment could serve multiple purposes. When debate took place (over Israel, Hawaii, and Saudi Arabia), it was precisely over whether or not there should be such a formalized commitment, not on the general thrust of U.S. policy toward the place in question.

Historical patterns of client acquisition

The United States has been acquiring client states for over a century. As we have seen, there are a handful of contexts in which these acquisitions occur, with a correspondingly limited number of policy instruments for carrying out the acquisition. In fact, as we will discuss in the following chapters, those instruments shift over time, with new ones being invented and certain older ones (though not all) being retired. Viewed more generally, though, what can be said about U.S. client acquisitions since 1898?

To answer this question, we can bring together all the cases of acquisition and array them over time (see Figure 3.2). This chart shows, for five-year periods, how many clients were acquired in the contexts of danger, of prewar/postwar planning, and of post-occupation, switches, and special access combined. Of course, by itself, these raw numbers only tell part of the story since we have not bothered to distinguish between clients which were subsequently "lost" and those which have kept this status to the present day; moreover, we have counted all cases of acquisition the same, whether the state in question is a tiny island or a wealthy and populous country.

The first pattern is one we already discussed: the sheer number of cases of acquisition in the context of prewar/postwar planning as compared with danger, and of the latter as compared with everything else. The largest number of U.S. clients were acquired because of a war that was about to take place or had just ended; the second largest number were acquired as a response to dangers perceived to emanate from one or more enemies. Neither switching nor post-occupation became extinct as contexts of acquisition (think of Afghanistan and Iraq), but there were far fewer such cases after the cold war than before. Add to this pattern another which we have already discussed, namely, the speeding up of planning acquisitions – the fact that they now occur in a few years, as opposed to around two decades in earlier eras – and the picture that emerges is one in which, if another war were to occur in a region with few clients, we might expect a rapid wave of acquisitions.

Figure 3.2 indicates that only three wars accounted for all the planning acquisitions, or in other words, some half of all total acquisitions. These wars – the Spanish-American

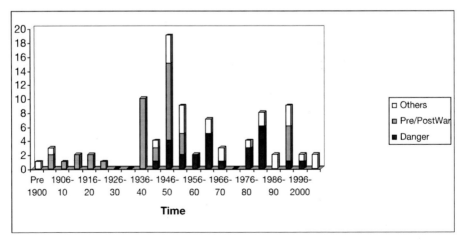

Figure 3.2 Client acquisition by context
Source: Authors as per Chapter 2 note 56.

War, World War II, and the first U.S.-Iraq War – significantly increased the number of U.S. clients. None of the other wars the U.S. fought – World War I, the Korean and Vietnam Wars, or the Kosovo or second U.S.-Iraq wars – led to acquisitions in the context of planning. By contrast, acquisitions in the context of danger are more spread out in time, occurring in most of the five-year periods since World War II. But since it is presumably difficult, if not impossible, to predict either when and where the next planning-inducing war will occur, or when and who the next dangerous enemy will be, the only thing that can be said about these two patterns is that they give little guidance for the future.

☐ US Client States
☐ Non Client States

Figure 3.3 Clients, 1940
Source: Authors as per Chapter 2, note 56.

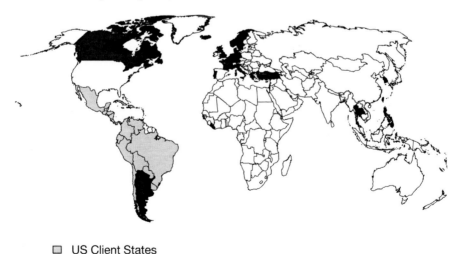

☐ US Client States
■ New Client States

Figure 3.4 Clients, 1950
Source: Authors as per Chapter 2, note 56.

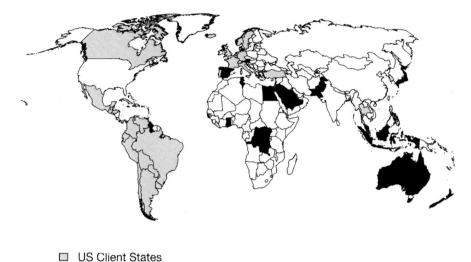

☐ US Client States
■ New Client States

Figure 3.5 Clients, 1980
Source: Authors as per Chapter 2, note 56.

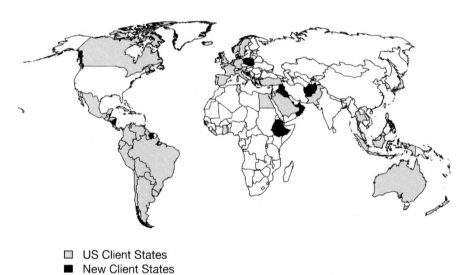

☐ US Client States
■ New Client States

Figure 3.6 Clients, 2005
Source: Authors as per Chapter 2, note 56.

The U.S. has acquired client states, in different contexts, for more than a century. Certainly World War II and the cold war were significant, but the pattern of acquisition both predates these events by almost 40 years and seems to have continued long after they both were only memories. In short, once the U.S. learned how to acquire clients, it never gave up the habit. Client acquisition became a means to multiple ends.

Nor is the pattern much clearer when it comes to geography. Figures 3.3–3.6 show the geographical spread of clients over time.[79] The earliest clients were in the U.S.

"backyard" of the Caribbean and Central America; though neither Canada nor Mexico was acquired until the eve of World War II. At that moment, a second wave of acquisition took place, with the rest of the independent states in the Western Hemisphere being added. A few years later, Western Europe and parts of East Asia and Oceania dropped into the basket. At that point, there ceased to be large geographical concentrations for a number of years except for a blip in the Middle East and North Africa. Suddenly, with the end of the Vietnam War, the U.S. swooped up a new set of Caribbean states; then, a decade later, the Persian Gulf states were added. Local dangers arose from time to time; enemies were occupied or switched back to the U.S. side; and every so often, a state was acquired through special access.

In one sense, the maps show what the late Stephen Ambrose called a "rise to globalism."[80] However, if we recall that it took decades for the U.S. to acquire as clients even its immediate northern and southern neighbors, whereas the U.S was active diplomatically and militarily in both Asia and Europe even before it had acquired all of the Central American states as clients, the picture seems a bit more complicated. Nor is it a matter of ideas catching up with power: Theodore Roosevelt proselytized for empire when the number of U.S. clients could be counted on the fingers of one hand. Rather, the story the maps tell is the coming together of organizational means and a permissive international environment, one in which the day-to-day experience of being a U.S. client was ready to hand for Washington and attractive to many regimes around the world. In other words, once the policy instruments had been developed, the specific location and timing of new client acquisitions were to a great degree random. To see this more clearly, let us now turn to the development of those policy instruments and the practices of routine client maintenance.

4 The routine maintenance of client states

At the beginning of 2008, the United States had a total of 81 clients around the world. However, the number of clients acquired by the U.S. since 1898 was higher: 92. The difference can be explained by the fact that some clients were "lost," although they might in fact have subsequently been reacquired. Most U.S. client states, though, have remained in that status without interruption, in the majority of cases, for over half a century.[1] To officials in Washington, this fact is anything but automatic: since many clients have faced problems which at least threatened to endanger their regimes, the U.S. has devoted considerable time and attention to maintaining them. Just how important those efforts were is an open question; but there is no doubt that both the U.S. and the clients believe that U.S. policies have an effect.

There are two types of policies the United States undertakes toward routine maintenance of its clients. The first pertains to economically deprived countries, seen by the U.S. as lacking the resources to solve potential regime-threatening problems on their own. For Washington, the challenges facing the regimes in these clients stem in the end from insufficient financial resources, whether because the countries are not (yet) wealthy or because they are still recovering from a war. Hence, the U.S. either has to supply the money needed to carry out various activities, or to provide directly the goods and services seen as important. (Those services, as we already pointed out in Chapter 2, include technical and political advice.)

To carry out these transfers, programs are needed. Some of these we have already mentioned in the chapter on client acquisitions, but they represent only a portion of the full range of maintenance activities. As a general rule, resource transfer programs are first tried out on an ad hoc basis for one or a handful of client states; then they take on regular organizational form, with annual budgets and professional staffs. From time to time, they change form, if officials decide that existing approaches are inadequate in some way. The result, as we will see in the next section, is a combination of persistent functions and proliferating programs.

Resource transfer programs provide built-in facilities for surveillance and advice. If, for example, a development project is being funded by AID, or soldiers are trained in the use of a new weapons system, or cocaine spraying is paid for by a narcotics control grant, the U.S. officials engaged in these activities will of necessity be overseeing the performance of their host-country contacts. Inevitably, they will also be giving advice, not only on the matter at hand but on more general issues as well. When added to other forms of oversight and advice by the ambassador and various subordinates, the result is that the U.S. occupies a significant place in many of the regime's activities, both vital and mundane.

The second type of policies undertaken by the U.S. concerns countries which are not considered economically deprived. In these cases, the issue is not one of inadequate financial resources but of maintaining regimes as valuable junior partners in an entire range of U.S. activities, including maintenance of economically deprived U.S. clients and opposition to U.S. enemies. This requires other sorts of policies, ranging from coordination of economic assistance and arms sales to cooperation in a host of domains, especially military. Some cooperative arrangements themselves involve the development of weapons systems; others involve joint military exercises and other military-to-military contact. Liaison also extends to political action against U.S. enemies. These links, if somewhat less one-sided than toward resource-poor clients, are in many ways even closer. The issue is not whether the state in question always follows Washington's advice; rather, the point is to maintain the regime as a particular type of political and economic actor.

Many of the above policies involve formal, ongoing programs analogous to those constructed for poorer client states. Some programs are the direct outgrowth of cooperative arrangements developed during more impecunious times. Others were worked out in an extensive and rapidly growing series of individual bilateral or multilateral arrangements in a number of domains. In all cases, the programs involve surveillance and an extensive U.S. presence, although, since the host country is not the recipient of largesse and the particular form of cooperation is often quite technical, there tends to be less nationalist resentment at the U.S. role. As we will discuss below, these arrangements are not only helpful to Washington in policy terms but quite lucrative as well.

Note that both types of client maintenance activities revolve around regular, ongoing programs administered by professional bureaucrats. This is why we have used the word "routine": to signify that U.S. efforts to maintain particular regimes are not exceptional, do not involve high-level policy making, and are for the most part a matter of regular organizational procedures. These obviously are not as dramatic as the interventionary forms of maintenance we will discuss in the next chapter – no late night White House meetings, no sending of troops or emergency loans – but they are no less important for their mundane nature. Most of the time, for most client states, U.S. policy is precisely the planning and executing of routine maintenance.

Our aim in this chapter is to give an overall sense of the two types of client maintenance activities. We will begin with a historical overview, describing how the major programs for each type of maintenance began, have been transformed, and have proliferated. For Washington, there is, ideally, a transition of clients from economically deprived to junior partner and we will discuss just how that transition occurs, as well as when and why it does not. Finally, we will discuss some of the overall trends in in resource flows as well as the continuing differences between clients and nonclients, given that many programs originally developed for the former are now being carried out in the latter as well.

Historical trends in client maintenance programs

We saw in Chapter 3 that for the first half century or so of the U.S. client state empire, practically all of the clients were from Latin America or, in the context of post-war recovery, Western Europe. In other words, the thrust of U.S. policy for decades was to invent ways of transferring resources to states considered as (temporarily or for a long time to come) economically deprived. For this reason, we will begin our historical walk-through with a discussion of the major programs developed to maintain regimes incapable of supporting various financial burdens.

Maintenance of economically deprived clients

It is convenient to divide U.S. transfers in cash or kind into three categories: (1) economic assistance of various sorts; (2) military assistance (including training); and (3) political assistance. There are, in fact, considerable overlaps between these categories, but for various bureaucratic and political reasons, they tend to be kept apart organizationally.

Economic assistance

Almost from the beginning, U.S. policy makers faced the problem of finding ways for their client states to maintain minimal levels of government spending. If civil servants and soldiers were not paid, a crisis could easily result. However, in the early 1900s, most states, especially in the Caribbean and Central America, had limited tax structures and relied for their revenues primarily on customs receipts. Since exports, and therefore the source of foreign exchange for imports, were overwhelmingly agricultural and mineral products, this meant that government revenues were hostage to swings in commodity prices.

In an era of limited U.S. government, there was little that Washington could do directly about this structural problem. We will see in Chapter 5 that in situations of dire emergency, New York banks could be sweet-talked into loans, at times with U.S. government oversight; on rare occasions, Congress itself approved grants. Such reactions, though, were certainly not a matter of routine maintenance. The only policy instrument falling into that category up through the early 1930s was the employment of U.S. experts to run parts or all of a country's financial bureaucracy. (We discussed this briefly in Chapter 3 in the context of planning for client acquisition in the Dominican Republic and elsewhere.) However, financial experts were hardly a panacea, since, whatever their efficiency and degree of acceptance, they had to work within the existing structure of the economy. This meant, in effect, that economic problems would have to be contained by military means: the use of marines and local constabularies (see below).

The first real means of providing ongoing financial resources came about in the early days of the New Deal, with the creation of the Export-Import Bank (Ex-Im). This was originally designed to help U.S. exporters trade with the Soviet Union and (via a second bank) Cuba; but in 1935, the Bank's mandate was broadened. Rapidly, lending focused on Latin America, with the scope of the loans widening: first to state agencies (often with strong backing from the State Department); then to public works; then to central banks, agricultural diversification, industrial projects, and, during World War II, the development of strategic materials. Whatever their technical merits, many of these and subsequent decisions were made at the explicit behest of the State Department. Ex-Im's geographic scope soon went beyond Latin America, being used for postwar reconstruction in Europe, China, and elsewhere (including Israel). By 1953, the Bank was lending to 48 countries, many for development projects; the comparable figures in the mid-2000s ranged from 69 to 79. Other Ex-Im-like agencies were subsequently created in 1971 and 1981.[2]

However, even before the end of World War II, it became apparent that the Export-Import Bank, too, had its limits. Its regulations restricted it to loans where there was a reasonable assurance of repayment; in addition, it also faced political constraints on its capitalization. As a result, U.S. policy makers created two new instruments to transfer financial resources to other countries. The first of these was the array of multilateral lending institutions which began with the World Bank; the second was the creation of a set of programs with the explicit purpose of aiding in reconstruction and development.

In 1944, at the Mount Washington Hotel in Bretton Woods, New Hampshire, delegates from some 44 states created two institutions. One, the International Monetary Fund (IMF), had been the object of intense discussions between the United States and the United Kingdom; the other, the International Bank for Reconstruction and Development (IBRD; also known as the World Bank, although it now includes other units), was somewhat of an afterthought, seen primarily as a means of getting European nations back on their feet so that the multilateral transactions dealt with by the Fund would not be stillborn. Development financing was originally viewed as a secondary and long-term task, though at Latin American insistence, it was upgraded in importance.

If there were any doubts, it rapidly became clear that the World Bank (and, as we will see, the IMF) would be an important way for the U.S. to aid states it considered to be in need of financial resources. Both the IMF and the World Bank were placed in Washington, DC, literally across the street from each other and just a stone's throw from the White House and the Treasury. Every president of the World Bank has been a U.S. citizen; the U.S. contribution to the Bank – and thus its voting power on loans – is bigger than that of any other country. This American dominance served to orient the Bank's lending, especially in its early days, toward U.S. clients and away from states whom the U.S. did not wish to help. Thus, during the first decade of its loans, the Bank lent money to ten U.S. clients in Europe, fifteen in Latin America and the Caribbean, and six in the rest of the world (including Australia and Japan); only seven nonclients were assisted, five of whom were former British colonies. States linked to the Soviet Union, like Poland, were politely rebuffed. Even after the U.S. ceased to provide the bulk of the Bank's capital, this pattern of lending continued.[3]

Since multilateral aid via the World Bank meant that other countries, in effect, were helping to pay for financial transfers to U.S. clients, the U.S. found it useful to support spinoffs and regional versions of the World Bank. In 1956, the Bank's members set up the International Finance Corporation to finance private sector development; in 1960, the International Development Association (IDA) was created, again by the Bank, to provide long-term, interest-free loans and grants to the poorest countries. The U.S. plays a dominant role in both of these institutions, casting over 60 percent of the IDA's weighted votes. In addition, various regional development banks were set up: the Inter-American Development Bank (IADB) in 1959 (also headquartered in Washington); the African Development Bank in 1964; the Asian Development Bank in 1966; and the European Bank for Reconstruction and Development in 1991. The U.S. is a founding member of each of these banks, with voting power ranging up to 30 percent.[4]

By emphasizing U.S. dominance in multilateral lending institutions, we do not mean to suggest that those institutions are mere puppets of Washington. The reality is more complex and more interesting. Development banks spread the costs of financial transfers to a number of countries, thereby relieving the U.S. of the sole burden. Their multi-lateral, and potentially universal, character means that they also provide political legitimacy for both the loans they make and those they reject. Those decisions, by dint of their technical qualities, appear as less overtly political than if they had been made openly in the U.S. government. Thus, the banks do not have to be simple transmission belts from Washington to serve U.S. interests.

Nonetheless, the United States does exert considerable pressure on the banks. Congress, for one, passes numerous laws specifying how U.S. representatives should vote on particular types of loans. High level U.S. policy makers regularly talk to top officials in the banks. This biases the banks in favor of lending to U.S. clients and, of equal importance, against lending to states currently out of favor with the U.S. A classic example of this latter possibility is the U.S. campaign against Chile in the early 1970s. After a Marxist candidate, Salvador Allende, had been elected and inaugurated in 1970 in the face of considerable efforts by the U.S. to influence the election and then to prevent Allende from taking office (this will be discussed in Chapter 5), U.S. policy makers resolved to punish Chile economically, to "make the economy scream." Nixon ordered that the U.S. bring "a maximum feasible influence to bear in international financial institutions to limit credit or other financing assistance to Chile." Thus, the U.S. "Executive Director of the Inter-American Development Bank understands that he will remain uninstructed until further notice on pending loans to Chile. ... this will effectively bar approval of the loans." The State Department also prepared "orientation questions" for World Bank staff members visiting Chile to raise "but without the hand of the U.S. Government showing in the process." Shortly after Allende took office, new loans from both the IADB and the IBRD ceased; a few months after he was killed in a *coup d'état*, the loans resumed.[5]

The U.S. derives great benefit from the World Bank. Its apparently technical criteria for lending are satisfiable in principle by any loan recipient; this makes the Bank politically advantageous to the U.S. but also limits the extent to which its loans can be targeted on specific countries, especially for more diffuse purposes. Hence, the Bank, and multilateral lending institutions more generally, complement rather than substitute for bilateral assistance programs. But as we saw above, the Export-Import Bank is itself too limited to serve as a broad source of financial resources. By 1947 this was clear: the demands on Ex-Im were far greater than it could satisfy; the World Bank was just starting up and itself had insufficient funds for reconstruction on the massive scale that was becoming necessary; and ad hoc arrangements, such as the $3.75 billion loan to Great Britain we discussed in the preceding chapter, were obviously impossible to work out on a case-by-case basis, with congressional approval, every year. What was needed was another kind of policy instrument.

What the U.S. opted for was a series of economic aid programs, administered by agencies whose task it was to disburse congressionally authorized funds every year. The first try, as we saw in Chapter 3, was the Marshall Plan. Whatever the virtues of this program, with its ingenious counterpart funds scheme, it suffered from an important failing: the only states eligible for funding were in Europe. Aid to China, for example, was tucked into the Marshall Plan legislation as a separate title; the Plan's administering organization, the Economic Cooperation Administration, also was tasked by Truman to disburse economic aid to South Korea. Thus, a few years later, a new law was passed: the Mutual Security Act of 1951. This set up an Agency to provide economic aid and technical assistance (the provision of equipment and advice) to any country in the world, provided that the president certify that this would "strengthen the security of the United States." Military aid would also be provided and the recipient was supposed to "take all reasonable measures which may be needed to develop its defense capabilities." Over the next few years, additional Mutual Security legislation was passed creating other forms of aid: development assistance, security assistance (i.e., financial transfers to relieve budget pressure occasioned by military spending), loan funds, and so forth.

However, the basic structure remained, with economic aid being fitted into a more general security relationship.[6]

By 1961, this kind of explicit link between economic and military aid had come to be seen as counterproductive. Latin America, for example, was considered underfunded simply because, up until the Cuban Revolution, the countries of the region were not perceived as facing an imminent security threat. Presumably, the same situation would arise with the newly independent states of Africa. In the Middle East, the problem was the reverse: economic aid was seen as having too many strings attached. Furthermore, if economic assistance depended on the security situation, then the amounts granted could fluctuate wildly from year to year, making planning impossible. In addition, a number of new types of economic assistance had been introduced over the preceding decade and it was felt that aid policy was becoming fragmented. Hence, a new law was passed, the Foreign Assistance Act of 1961. It dealt with fragmentation by mandating the creation of a new organization for economic development assistance, the Agency for International Development (AID). More importantly, the Foreign Assistance Act set up machinery for providing annual economic assistance "on a basis of long-range continuity" to countries anywhere, irrespective of the nature of those countries' military ties with the U.S. – or so the theory went (obviously, the U.S. did not fund its enemies; and the amounts transferred depended on the mood in Congress, which of course had something to do with the political and military situation in specific countries). Hence, for the first time ever, the U.S. had an instrument for transferring financial resources to its neediest clients on a regular basis. Although the Foreign Assistance Act of 1961 was often amended, it has never been replaced by new legislation and AID is still the principal agency in charge of routine financial maintenance.[7]

Today, the U.S. has at its disposal a series of policy instruments for day-to-day financial resource transfers. Chief among them are various types of concessional bilateral assistance administered by AID, both those applicable to all countries and those aimed at particular states (e.g., former communist countries). Ex-Im continues to exist and provides nonconcessional loans and loan guarantees, as do its sister agencies in the areas of investment and trade. The World Bank and regional development banks also serve as a source of funds. Thus, the history of routine financial maintenance is one of inventing policy instruments, refining and subdividing them, and then adding new instruments to begin the cycle once more. Note that earlier instruments do not disappear: instead, as we would expect cybernetically, they are maintained and updated.

Military assistance

In routine situations, there are essentially two ways in which a cash-poor country can be aided militarily. One is by supplying weapons; the other, by providing training. Obviously, there is a strong relationship between the two forms of assistance: many weapons systems are complex and require training if they are to be used. This is particularly true of larger and more complicated weapons systems, such as fighter jets. However, training can also occur in tactics, civil-military relations, and other subjects; and weapons can be furnished to armed forces already well-versed in their use. For this reason, even if the ideal type of military assistance involves both training and weapons, we should expect that the historical record will show separate origins for each component.

The earliest form of military training concerns the ad hoc arrangements worked out in order for the marines to leave some of the countries in Central America and the

Caribbean in which they had intervened. Often, the marines had disbanded or considerably weakened the national armies of these countries. Thus, it was necessary for new armed forces to be established, competent enough to put down future challenges to the regime and with political views that would not lead to their being aligned with factions opposed to the U.S. Typically, a National Guard or other kind of constabulary was created, with the officers and regular soldiers being trained in battle tactics and other military operations; small arms might also be provided, although the cost of these was low enough to be borne even by the client states. An example of this is in Nicaragua, where a formal agreement setting up a National Guard was signed with the U.S. in 1927. Once a rebellion by Augusto Sandino had been contained and the National Guard's marine instructors were satisfied the Guard could hold its own in future operations, the marines departed. Not long afterward, the Guard's commanding officer, Anastasio Somoza, arranged for Sandino to be assassinated; he then forced the country's president to resign and rigged elections to become the president himself. Similar post-marine arrangements, with similar outcomes (a military dictatorship later on, although the U.S. piously disapproved of this) were worked out in the Dominican Republic, Haiti, and Cuba.[8]

As a way of constructing a lower-profile system of indirect rule, the National Guard approach was efficient. However, it was very much a one-time policy: once the constabularies were created, they were on their own, with no U.S. material support. The U.S. made provisions to "detail officers and enlisted men" of its armed forces to "assist" the governments of Latin American and Caribbean countries (as we saw, there was also an abortive attempt to do this in Liberia), but without aid in cash or in weapons, and in the absence of local armed opposition such as had been the case prior to the marines' interventions, there was little incentive to take up the offer. This was truly the era of low-overhead empire: U.S. client regimes were maintained by their National Guard or army (in many cases, the armed forces ran the regime), Ex-Im bank credits and occasional economic advice, and, of course, the knowledge that if things seriously went wrong, the U.S. would step in directly.[9]

With the coming of World War II, the U.S. military began training and advising beyond Central America and the Caribbean. We have already discussed the prewar planning process by which the U.S. established military missions in Mexico and the countries of South America (see Chapter 3); by the time of Pearl Harbor, there were over 100 advisers in every country of Latin America. Over the next few years, the U.S. sent military advisers to Saudi Arabia, China, and Iran. This continued after the war, with advisers first in the Philippines, then in Greece and Turkey, and then in South Korea.[10]

This expansion had much to do with the emerging U.S. policy of supplying weapons to the armed forces of other countries. The principal program for this during the war was Lend-Lease, by which the U.S. gave or lent munitions (almost $50 billion worth) to "the government of any country whose defense the President deems vital to the defense of the United States." At the behest of Congress, Truman terminated Lend-Lease abruptly when fighting ended for all but two countries: China and Saudi Arabia. This created a bureaucratic problem because the military had become convinced that arms transfers and the coordination and training that accompanied them were a useful policy instrument for the U.S., especially in Latin America: they enhanced U.S. influence both directly and, by reducing arms imports from other suppliers, indirectly. Truman was persuaded and asked Congress to pass an Inter-American Military Cooperation Act but for various reasons, including financial concerns, State Department resistance to fueling an arms race, and the sense that with the worsening cold war, other areas were more vital, the legislation was never enacted.[11]

Instead, the U.S. carried out a series of ad hoc weapons transfer arrangements. Legislation was passed for the Philippines in 1946; then, in 1947, for Greece and Turkey; and in 1948 for China. When the U.S. Army withdrew its occupation forces from South Korea, it arranged to transfer weapons to the newly created Korean army. Elsewhere, sales of weapons were made under the Surplus Property Act of 1944 for some countries in Latin America and Europe (including Sweden; a small credit was also authorized for Iran). Truman also acted (without legislative authority) to transfer non-surplus arms to Italy and to override federal law by shipping the weapons although they had not been paid for. Such arrangements obviously could not be resorted to on a routine basis, not least because of time and financial pressures.[12]

Finally, in 1949, a new policy was worked out. The catalyst was the North Atlantic Treaty; within a day of its ratification, Truman submitted to Congress proposed legislation that had been drafted and redrafted over the preceding several months. What eventually was enacted, in October, was the Mutual Defense Assistance Act of 1949, which explicitly recognized "the principle of continuous and effective self-help and mutual aid." The legislation provided for furnishing "equipment, materials, and services" to states with whom prior "agreements" had been worked out; this was the military counterpart to the surveillance arrangements laid out in the Marshall Plan. Arms sales were also envisioned, either from existing stocks or by new procurement. However, the Latin American countries were not included in the legislation: only signatories to the North Atlantic Treaty, Greece, Turkey, Iran, Korea, and the Philippines. An "emergency fund" was also appropriated for the "general area" of China, to be used by the President on an unvouchered basis when it was "inadvisable to specify the nature of such expenditures" (Truman used most of this money to support the French war in Indochina).[13]

The Mutual Defense Act essentially put on a continuing legislative footing the ad hoc arrangements the U.S. had worked out over the preceding several years. A total of $1.3 billion was provided, most of which went to the North Atlantic Treaty countries; the next spring, Congress prepared to appropriate a similar amount of money for fiscal year 1951. These sums were small by comparison with those of the Marshall Plan, indicating yet again that in those years, the principal concern of U.S. policy makers was (except for Greece and Turkey) reconstruction planning rather than protection of Western Europe from the Soviet Union. (A partial exception a year before the Act's passage was Italy, but there the concern was with internal danger, not invasion.) Latin America was seen as still more peripheral and less endangered, and the Truman Administration did not even bother requesting funds for the countries in that region.

All this changed with the outbreak of the Korean War. As U.S. defense spending soared, Congress passed a supplemental appropriation of an additional $4 billion for military assistance, of which $3.5 billion was for the North Atlantic Treaty countries, now suddenly seen as potential targets of a Soviet invasion. Asia, though, was the immediate panic zone: Truman not only interposed the Seventh Fleet to protect the Nationalist Chinese regime in its Taiwan refuge, but sharply increased military aid to the French in Indochina and, a few months later, worked out a military aid agreement with Thailand, a country that certainly was within the "general area" of China but which no one, in the summer of 1949, had considered as a potential recipient of military aid. Other regions were not seen as in any great danger but could stand to be strengthened by military and economic means; the latter, however, would have to be subordinated to the former. This led, as we saw above, to the Mutual Security Act of 1951, in which every region in the world had a title of the Act devoted to it, with separate sections in each title devoted to both military assistance and economic and/or technical assistance.[14]

Thus, by 1951, the basic framework of military assistance had been set up, not coincidentally in the same piece of legislation that also opened the door to worldwide concessional bilateral economic aid. Henceforth, the U.S. would give weapons and other equipment to states with whom it had signed agreements specifying everything from the nature of the materiel to what local production would occur and what reimbursement, if any, would take place; in addition, the U.S. would also send to each recipient country a large Military Assistance Advisory Group (MAAG) which would, at the very least, oversee the use of the weapons and equipment and, when needed, train the local armed forces in their use, as well as more generally. Later legislation added some new wrinkles – the explicit possibility of making loans; more detailed language about sales; overseas weapons manufacture; and the introduction (mentioned above) of budgetary support – but did not alter the basic structure.[15]

What did change over time was the number and variety of specific military training programs. For the first few decades of military assistance, training could be carried out both in the recipient country and in the United States (including, for a number of decades, the Panama Canal Zone, where the School of the Americas operated); it could cover both general topics and the use of specific weapons systems. Up until 1976, training took place either through the U.S. military assistance grant or loan to the country involved, or as part of an arms sale. But in that year, a new program, International Military Education and Training (IMET) was set up, whereby armed forces personnel could be trained without their country necessarily receiving military assistance or buying weapons. IMET served as the model for a host of subsequent and more specialized programs, including in narcotics control and interdiction, peacekeeping, demining, disaster response, counterterrorism, and special operations forces.[16]

With the proliferation of training programs and the growth in arms sales (see below), new administrative arrangements had to be worked out. As we saw in Chapter 2, most arms transfers and some training programs came to be supervised by security assistance officers (SAOs), who are the functional successors to the chiefs of the MAAGs of earlier decades. However, as we might expect from the history of these programs – an initial setting up of various functions, followed by multiple programmatic variations – SAOs are not the only players in the game. Some training programs take place through the unified combatant commands; others involve individual armed services or other executive branch agencies. Still other programs, particularly those involving training in, and maintenance of, advanced weapons systems, are administered by private military companies under contract to the U.S. government.[17]

Political assistance

Many of the regimes in the United States's poorer and middle-income client states are weak politically. This does not mean that they face armed opposition or are in imminent danger of falling; but for various reasons – recent independence, perhaps; or limited tax revenues and administrative capabilities; or the political impossibility of incorporating important groups in society into the regime – they find themselves in a state of chronic political fragility. (This was not the case for most Western European countries after World War II: although they lacked funds to pay for economic reconstruction and the reequipping of their militaries, their regimes were politically strong. We will discuss one of the exceptions, Italy, in the next chapter.) As a result, U.S. officials therefore found it useful to act on various fronts to build up their clients politically. This went beyond simply helping economically and militarily.

One form of political assistance was direct payments in cash or kind to state officials and their nongovernmental supporters. For many decades, dating back to the early days of the cold war, the U.S. paid regular subsidies to component parts of client regimes. In Ecuador, for example, the CIA had on its payroll in the early 1960s the chief of the intelligence and personnel departments of the national police, the vice president of the Senate, one of the leading political journalists, leaders of several political parties, a cabinet minister, the manager of one of the largest banks, labor leaders, and an important figure in the federation of university students. Part of the purpose of these payments, of course, was to obtain information and to push particular campaigns (e.g., in favor of breaking diplomatic relations with Cuba); but the payments also served to hold together a configuration of political and economic power holders against some of their principal enemies. In addition, both the CIA and various organizations connected with the U.S. trade union movement provided funds and advice to local unions. From everything we know, operations similar to those in Ecuador took place (and still do) in dozens of countries around the world.[18]

In some cases, heads of state or government themselves were recipients of regular payments from the CIA. By their nature, such payments are not confirmed by the U.S. government, but news leaks by executive branch and congressional officials, especially in the 1970s, at the height of revelations about the CIA, indicate that regular stipends went to the leaders of Jordan ($750,000 per year to the King), Cyprus, Kenya, Zaire, Guyana, South Vietnam, Taiwan, the Philippines, South Korea, Chile, Mexico, Venezuela, Thailand, and Panama. In addition, the U.S. has subsidized various political exiles in hopes that later, as in Iraq, they would come to power.[19]

A second type of political assistance to poor and middle-income countries has to do with the tracking down and elimination of political opponents. In part, this occurs by furnishing intelligence information that the bureaucracy has already collected. Even though regimes in most countries have an acute sense of who is opposing and supporting them, the U.S. devotes considerable resources to collecting lists of names; these are often shared with a country's leaders on a routine basis (for example, the CIA station chief in Mexico regularly met with the president and sent him daily intelligence summaries about revolutionary organizations). The significance of these lists is particularly evident after *coups d'état* and other irregular changes of government, when the names may be passed to the country's new leaders. Thus, the CIA provided the Shah of Iran's government (both the intelligence agency SAVAK and the Shah himself) with information on the left-leaning Tudeh party, not only in the immediate aftermath of the coup against the Mosaddeq regime but for a number of years thereafter (see Chapters 3 and 6). The same thing occurred in Ecuador after the coup in 1963, in the Dominican Republic after the U.S. invasion in 1965, in Indonesia after the military's countercoup in 1965, and in Iraq after the Ba'ath coup in 1963; in the latter two cases, both of which involved a regime change (see Chapter 6), many of the persons whose names were furnished were subsequently arrested and executed.[20]

Another way in which the U.S. helps regimes with their political opponents has to do with assistance to national police forces. Through the early 1950s, such aid was offered on an ad hoc basis to several countries as part of technical assistance programs. In 1954, in NSC Action 1290D, the Eisenhower Administration initiated a review of its "current program to develop constabulary forces to maintain internal security." What resulted was a multi-agency Overseas Internal Security Program, with particular emphasis given on training and equipping police. The Kennedy Administration, particularly concerned about the prospect of communist insurgencies, placed still further emphasis on police assistance, creating an International Police Academy and setting up an Office of Public Safety (OPS) within AID. By 1968, OPS had over 450 advisers in some 34 countries and enjoyed a budget of $55.1 million. Controversy over the teaching of torture techniques led to the elimination of OPS in the 1970s; however, police aid was soon resumed in more targeted form through narcotics control assistance and, more recently, anti-terror assistance.[21]

On the issue of torture, we would make three points. First, torture was used by police and other internal security forces in many countries long before the U.S. got into the business of police aid; nor was the U.S. the only outside source of torture techniques: one U.S. ally, France, also provided training in torture methods (refined in the Algerian war) to several South American countries. Second, even though many U.S. police advisers had nothing to do with torture techniques, there is no doubt that the development and refinement of these techniques formed an important activity for a significant number of OPS officers. In this respect, they were pursuing much the same path as the U.S. Army's infamous School of the Americas (now moved and renamed as the Western Hemisphere Institute for Security Cooperation) and the CIA, in its advising in South Vietnam and Central America: the controlled use of torture was seen as an indispensable tool for obtaining information and terrorizing regimes' political opponents. As a prominent OPS official, Dan Mitrione, is reported to have said,

> the precise pain, in the precise place, in the precise amount to achieve the effect ... When you get what you want, and I always get it, it might be good to keep the session going a little longer with more hitting and humiliation. Not to get information now but as a political instrument, to scare him away from any further rebel activity.

Third, and most depressingly, torture seems now to have become well embedded in U.S. policy as a routine method for fighting certain kinds of enemies. The hue and cry over abuse in Iraq's Abu Ghraib prison and the Guantánamo Bay interrogation facility resulted only in certain techniques being prohibited; other coercive methods remained in use, justified by a variety of arguments (including appeals to psychology and anthropology), as did the routine resort to "extraordinary rendition" techniques to transport certain prisoners to other countries well known for torture.[22]

Maintenance of wealthier clients

Client states enjoying high income levels tend to have regimes which are reasonably secure internally. As a result, most of the resource flows developed to maintain regimes in economically deprived countries are unnecessary and when they do continue, are considered at best as temporary expedients and at worst as improper or even "shameful."[23] Instead, the focus of U.S. policy instruments is on maintaining regimes in a particular relation to other international, rather than domestic, political and economic actors: that of junior partner of the United States. This focus applies across a broad range of short-term and long-term goals, for both former great powers and smaller countries. It arose, as we might expect from the history of routine client maintenance for economically deprived clients, from repeated attempts to adapt a set of policy instruments, developed for other reasons, to new problems, especially those which arose after postwar reconstruction had largely been completed.

Economic contributions

By the early 1950s, the Marshall Plan was in the process of being wound up. Most of the money had already been disbursed; the U.S. focus was now on military assistance; and the rearmament spending spurred by the Korean War was contributing strongly to the rebuilding of the Western European and Japanese economies. This rapid growth made it possible for the U.S. to reduce concessional economic aid to a number of the countries in Europe, as well as Japan.[24] To be sure, economic assistance continued to flow to these countries, with funding being provided by the Ex-Im Bank, by the World Bank, and by budgetary assistance as part of the military aid program. In addition, the U.S., by stationing troops in Europe and Japan, also contributed to the local economies: throughout the 1950s, the amount the U.S. spent on its bases in these areas greatly exceeded its bilateral economic aid to those same countries. Nonetheless, economic assistance was clearly in the process of being reoriented away from Europe and Japan.[25]

This shift in resource flows created an organizational difficulty. As we saw, the U.S. agency in charge of Marshall Plan funds, the ECA, shed its skin a number of times over the next dozen years, eventually becoming AID. But what of the receiving side? Originally, the Europeans and Americans had set up an Organisation for European Economic Co-operation (OEEC), with the U.S. and Canada as associate members, to coordinate Marshall Plan aid requests and help in overseeing the functioning of the agreed-on spending programs. Soon after, at U.S. urging, the OEEC established a European Payments Union so that, in the absence of convertible currencies, intra-European trade could become multilateral. (If currencies could not be bought and sold, then the only way for importers in one country to buy goods from another country was by selling to that country. The Payments Union made it possible to avoid this problem by letting importers use earnings from third countries.) The OEEC also created and administered a Trade Liberalisation Code for cutting down on tariffs and restrictive quotas.[26]

The problem for the OEEC is that by the end of the 1950s, these newer tasks in trade and payments had ceased to be its responsibility. Currencies became convertible, so that the Payments Union was no longer necessary (this also had effects on the IMF, as we will see below). The European Economic Community was also created, liberalizing trade between its six members far beyond what the OEEC could have hoped. In reaction, seven other members of the OEEC established the European Free Trade Area, which liberalized trade for them. This led to considerable tensions between the two groups of countries because trade between the Six and the Seven risked being affected; the U.S. also feared discrimination. In these circumstances, the OEEC could do little.

In the meantime, the U.S. found itself with another problem. By the late 1950s, Eisenhower and his colleagues had become convinced that it was vitally important to have significant economic assistance programs in place for developing countries. With independence approaching for many African colonies, the need for funds would be even greater. These latter countries might receive aid from the former colonial powers, but those sums were unlikely to be sufficient. Congress, however, refused to appropriate more money, and in any case, concerns were growing about U.S. spending overseas. One solution was to increase the number of multilateral lending institutions, and this led the administration to support the creation of the IADB and IDA. Another solution was to push the Europeans (and the Japanese) to start or expand their own bilateral assistance programs, if possible with U.S. input so that the funding would be compatible with American priorities.

Revitalizing the OEEC was another, more general solution to these various problems in the late 1950s. The organization could be reconstructed to focus on trade liberalization and development issues, with the U.S. becoming a full member, along with Canada and, if possible, Japan. The Europeans went along with this and the OEEC was soon reconstituted as the Organisation for Economic Co-operation and Development (OECD). Even before that happened, a Development Assistance Group was created, with the Japanese being invited to join; once the OECD came into existence, the Group was absorbed into it as the Development Assistance Committee (DAC). Within a short time, the DAC, and the OECD more generally, were beginning to serve as forums in which pressures to increase development aid and liberalize trade could be applied by members to each other. The OECD has expanded greatly since then, but still relies on this kind of peer pressure.[27]

What the transformation of the OEEC shows is how, without aiming at it as a specific goal, the U.S. succeeded in getting Western European countries and Japan to play the role of junior partner. This outcome resulted from the use of an instrument created for one purpose to solve other problems. The policy was not goal-driven: it arose, cybernetically, from the connecting of an existing organization to a particular, newer set of problems. Much the same story can be told about other instances of Europe and Japan becoming junior partners. One example concerns the IMF and the role of the dollar. By the end of the 1950s, what had been a shortage of dollars turned into a glut. To solve this problem without jettisoning the dollar's centrality, the U.S. pushed for a number of policy changes – new forms of liquidity (e.g., Special Drawing Rights; central bank swap arrangements) and an end to fixed exchange rates – that resulted in the IMF's being remade as an agency capable of bailouts far beyond anything envisaged in 1944. In this way, European and Japanese capital could now be mobilized to support packages designed in Washington.[28]

It might be thought that the world now is very different than it was when the OECD was created and when the IMF was given new tasks. Surely, with the continued economic growth of Western Europe and Japan, we should no longer expect that the U.S. will still be able to harness the resources of those areas in the same way as it could do 30 or 40 years ago. In fact, the economic role of Western Europe and Japan is still very much that of junior partner to the United States. We will discuss how this works with emergency measures, such as economic bailouts, in Chapter 5; but the pattern is even more striking when it comes to development assistance. If we look at the OECD's statistics on bilateral economic aid (so that U.S. voting power in multilateral agencies is beside the point) we can see that in the most recent year for which numbers were available, the DAC countries made commitments of around $20 per capita to U.S. client states, whereas their commitments to states that were not U.S. clients were just under $9. In our view, this disparity is not due to U.S. pressure within the DAC but to a genuine convergence of views on the kind of states and development projects that merit large amounts of aid. One can if one wishes call this hegemony; our point is that it is reinforced by the regular experience of working together in organizations such as the OECD.[29]

With this example in mind, we can now say a bit more precisely what we mean by "junior partner." Being a junior partner with respect to development issues means that the United States can rely on a wealthy state to aid in the routine economic maintenance of poorer U.S. clients. Similarly, being a junior partner with respect to monetary issues means, as we will see, that the U.S. can rely on a wealthy state to aid in the interventionary economic maintenance of clients, whether wealthy or poor. By extension, being a junior partner also signifies that the U.S. can rely on a wealthy state not to aid in the maintenance of states which the U.S. deems to be enemies. Examples of this are legion, from full or partial agreement to restrict trade, aid, and investment links with (at various times) China, Cuba, Afghanistan, or Iran to the institutions set up both during and after the cold war to oversee trade in strategic materials with various states.[30] Of course, the Western European countries and Japan cooperate with the U.S. in many other ways related to global governance; but the concept of junior partnership, as we are using it, refers to the use, by wealthy countries, of their resources in support of the U.S. client state empire, specifically to help maintain other U.S. client states and to refrain from such help to U.S. enemies.[31]

For the most part, this role is taken for granted by both the United States and its wealthy clients. Certainly disagreements occur and pressure is applied from time to time (not only by the U.S., it should be added). There is, however, a general consensus among wealthy clients that the specific policies we have characterized as junior partnership are correct and justified on their own terms. As for the U.S., it tends to assume that as its clients become wealthier, they will become junior partners. Thus, to return to an issue we raised in Chapter 2, clients do not "graduate" to the status of nonclient; they "mature" to the status of junior partner.

We have been referring to "Europe and Japan," but in fact the very coupling of the two is itself an example of how the role of junior partner arose cybernetically. From the start, the U.S. treated the Western European countries as a group. Even Britain, which had an important empire and currency, was folded into the Marshall Plan and the North Atlantic treaty. Japan, however, was to a great degree isolated. There were no other states in the region at comparable levels of industrial development, and U.S. hopes that Japan would be the economic linchpin of Northeast Asia, mostly relative to its former possessions of Manchuria and Korea, were dashed by the Chinese Revolution and the Korean War. (Japan's principal trading partner, at least for the first decade and a half after the war, was the U.S.) In Western Europe, the U.S., which had already been cooperating with Britain and France in the occupation of Germany, created regional institutions in which the different states participated; but Japan was occupied solely by the U.S. and the only regional institutions created by the U.S. conspicuously excluded Japan. U.S. economic aid to Japan was bilateral, as was the defense arrangement worked out in 1951.[32]

Why then link Japan and Western Europe? As we saw, the issue first arose in late 1959, when the U.S. began to push for harnessing European and Japanese capital for development purposes. The Japanese, because of their resources, were obvious candidates for the DAC; once this institution was then folded into the OECD, it became only a matter of time until Japan acceded to membership in the latter. (The anomaly of its being a member of the DAC but not the OECD was grasped immediately by both Eisenhower and Kennedy; their advisers, and the Europeans, took a bit longer to come around.) Once that happened, it became impossible for the OECD to restrict itself to purely European issues and the institution rapidly became a set of forums in which policies in various domains were coordinated. This led to other non-European members joining, so that by the early 1970s, all of the U.S.'s wealthy allies had joined.[33]

Seen more generally, it is striking just how many wealthy U.S. clients have become members of the OECD. Canada, which was a founding member of NATO, was an associate member of the OEEC at the same time as the U.S. and became one of the OECD's original members. Spain (which arguably was then still quite poor) became an OEEC associate member in 1958 and was in on the OECD's founding, decades before it joined NATO. Japan, as we saw, joined the OECD in 1964. Australia did so in 1971, New Zealand in 1973, and Poland and South Korea joined in 1996. In short, it seems as if there is a sort of trajectory by which clients whose acquisition revolves around military issues will tend to end up as OECD members; to be a wealthy client means that, however one starts, one will end up as an economic junior partner. This is powerful, if indirect, evidence for the general status of junior partner; it also illustrates, yet again, a strong U.S. interest in multilateral institutions.[34]

Military contributions

One of the striking facts about wealthy U.S. client states has been how, with almost no exceptions, they have reconstructed, maintained, and regularly modernized their militaries for over half a century. This buildup occurred in the absence of threats from either Germany or Japan, and, during the cold war, in the understanding that the contribution which might be made by most U.S. clients in the event of a Soviet or Chinese invasion would be trivial. The end of the cold war brought a decline in military spending for several years, but this tendency soon reversed and modernization continued apace. Thus, even if the militaries of every other country are dwarfed in spending terms by that of the United States, wealthy U.S. clients still devote more resources to their armed forces than do most other states: of the countries ranked second through twelfth of total military expenditures (the U.S. being number one), wealthy U.S. clients occupy all but three slots.[35]

The task of reconstructing the militaries of Western Europe began shortly after the North Atlantic Treaty was ratified, although planning took place more than a year before. Reconstruction involved several elements, the costliest and most visible being arms transfers. Initially, as we saw above, military aid was considered by U.S. policy makers for its "psychological effect, rather than the intrinsic military value." The Europeans agreed, although both the French and the Italians had specific military tasks in mind (respectively, the war in Indochina and protecting against a domestic Communist takeover). However, as agencies in Washington began to hammer out the details of what would be sent, they had to posit specific functions which the European armed forces would perform. This led them, and the Europeans in their formal request, to focus on land warfare in Europe itself: "artillery, small arms, trucks, and communications supplies."[36]

The next step occurred when the individual military assistance agreements were signed and the North Atlantic Council began creating NATO's organizational forms. A European-wide defense plan – inherited from the North Atlantic Treaty's predecessor, the Brussels Pact – was drafted and roles assigned to each state's military. This opened the door to heavier weapons, aircraft, and naval vessels, but the size of European armed forces and U.S. budget limitations made this seem only a long-term goal. But in June 1950, when the Korean War broke out, Congress quadrupled its spending on military aid and the Europeans began large-scale rearmament, complete with expansion of their own armed forces. By the end of the year, the NATO countries had agreed to establish an "effective integrated defense force," headed by a Supreme Allied Commander (always an American; Eisenhower was the first) and a Defense Production Board to coordinate weapons spending in the U.S. and Europe; they also created a Finance and Economic Board (which was placed in Paris and linked to the OEEC) to oversee issues of mobilization, conversion, and scarce materials.[37]

With these instruments in place, arms transfers to, and joint production with, Europe became a constant in U.S. policy. Military aid continued through the early to mid-1960s; at that point, arms transfers were financed through Ex-Im Bank loans for another few years. By the early 1970s, arms transfers to the wealthiest European clients took the form of either government-to-government or commercial sales. These programs continue, and the amounts are considerable, as we will discuss below. In addition, the U.S. set up weapons research and production programs with a number of wealthy countries. Some of these concerned advanced technology: with France, for example, the U.S. made agreements on research into titanium alloys, free electron laser technology, composite propellants, helicopter aeromechanics, image/information reformatting for reconnaissance system interoperability, and intercooled recuperated gas turbine engines. To a considerable degree, the armed forces of America's wealthiest European clients have for years operated with U.S. weapons, worked on weapons with the U.S., trained with the U.S., and have been developed in common with the U.S. To suspect junior partner status is not a major leap.[38]

The situation with Japan is quite similar. Numerous economic and political concerns led the U.S. to adopt a "reverse course" policy in Japan, encouraging conservatives and others active in the imperial government to come back into power while also supporting the large industrial conglomerates (*zaibatsu*) which it had earlier tried to suppress. Rearmament was part of this policy: first, for purposes of domestic security against labor unions and the left; next, as the Pentagon began to plan for a Communist China and a still-divided Korean peninsula, for assisting the U.S. in the defense of Japan. With the conclusion of the peace and defense treaties in 1951, this process continued, the Japanese understanding that their role was to supply "military goods and strategic materials by repairing and establishing defense industries with the technical and financial assistance from the United States." By the summer of 1952, Truman had formally adopted a policy summarized as having Japan engage in

(1) Production of goods and services important to the United States and the economic stability of non-Communist Asia; (2) Production of low cost military material in volume for use in Japan and non-Communist Asia; (3) Development of its own appropriate military forces as a defensive shield and to permit the redeployment of United States forces.

Not surprisingly, the U.S. supplied military aid to Japan for the next decade or so; subsequently, Japan became one of the largest buyers of U.S. arms (deliveries of weapons bought as "direct commercial sales" are estimated at $1.6 billion for fiscal year 2004, $1.7 billion for fiscal 2005, and $2.7 billion for fiscal 2006).[39]

Thus, in both Western Europe and Japan, the U.S. began a program of military assistance for one set of reasons (reassurance, internal security), then, when the program had been established, adjusted it to address new, more region-specific and war-fighting, goals. This classically means-driven, cybernetic process can also be seen in the case of wealthy clients who never received military aid. These states – Canada, Australia, New Zealand, and Sweden – were seen by U.S. planners as having neither the political nor the financial needs of Japan and most of the Western European countries. However, this did not rule out arms sales and joint production. In Australia, a Mutual Defense Act agreement – which resulted in sales, not grants or loans – was signed over half a year before the ANZUS Pact was concluded, to a great degree as a way of supplying arms during the Korean War. The Pact led to regional defense planning, which resulted in shifts in the kind of weapons sold and thence to a mutual weapons development program being set up in 1960. In Canada, the Permanent Joint Board on Defence, created in 1940, was deliberately maintained after the end of World War II (and to the present day), when it was complemented by a Military Cooperation Committee. Sales and production were to be hemispheric; but then, as the North Atlantic Treaty was being signed, a Joint Industrial Mobilization Committee was set up, with an agreement on economic cooperation for defense the following year. These opened the possibility of sales and production for European defense as well. In Sweden, which had a larger arms industry, an agreement on the procurement of military equipment, materials, and services was concluded in 1952. This permitted U.S. weapons technology to be transferred to Sweden, a regular occurrence over the next two decades, complete with numerous friendly visits of officers and other defense officials. As this institutional cooperation deepened, the Swedes sought missiles from the U.S., which had not originally been part of the Americans' plans but which Sweden's significant arms spending (much more in relative terms than the NATO members Denmark and Norway, so that Sweden was viewed as a reliable partner) made more palatable to Washington. Finally, in the early 1970s, the floodgates opened and Sweden started to buy significant quantities of arms from the U.S., a practice which continues to this day.[40]

Hence, time and again, whether immediately or after some decades, the U.S. set up arms sales and production agreements with its wealthy clients. These, as we have seen, resulted in the militaries of those clients being restructured along American lines, thereby facilitating other forms of cooperation (see below). Indeed, arms sales have now come to be the dominant way by which the United States transfers weapons to other states more generally. Originally, there was a separation between sales, which occurred through commercial channels, and military assistance, which involved grants or loans to pay for government to government transfers, whether from existing stocks or through new procurement. However, this began changing, in part because of an increase in the sheer volume of sales and in part because of a desire to restrict grant and loan assistance. Eventually, wealthy clients became the programmatic norm and the military assistance program was merged into what became known as Foreign Military Financing (FMF); since 1990, all arms are technically transferred in the form of sales, either by direct purchases from private companies (though subject to U.S. export licenses) or by government to government sales. The latter may be financed by grants or loans from the U.S. government, with the presumption being that as clients become wealthier, their FMF account will drop to zero. As it stands, and as we will discuss below, total U.S. arms sales in fiscal year 2004, both commercial and by the government, came to around $20 billion; only $4.6 billion of this was paid for by FMF.[41]

In addition to arms sales, the U.S. has extensive and ongoing cooperative arrangements with the militaries of wealthy clients. Some of these arrangements, such as joint exercises, also exist with poorer clients; others, though, go much farther. For example, the U.S. carries out extensive operational planning with its wealthier clients, in NATO above all but also in ANZUS and with Japan. More generally, the U.S. has a broad array of programs carried out jointly with its wealthy clients. These range from weapons research and production to telecommunications, early warning systems, and exchanges of personnel. A simple count of the number of treaties and executive agreements listed under "Defense" gives a sense of the density of these ties: the U.S. has 5 agreements with Indonesia, 10 apiece with Brazil and Pakistan, 26 with France, 55 with Japan, 58 with Germany, and 77 with the United Kingdom. Each of these agreements involves a number of persons working together, on often highly sensitive topics, for periods that can last up to 20 years. To the client militaries, these arrangements are matters for pride, providing them the opportunity of working with the world's leading armed force.[42]

To a considerable degree, these various resource transfers and cooperative agreements are in effect an end in themselves. U.S. officials want to have close ties with the militaries of other states and they consider it desirable that those armed forces be equipped with U.S. weapons and integrated into U.S. plans. However, it is also expected that problems with poorer clients and enemies will arise from time to time and that wealthy clients will be able to serve as junior partners relative to the U.S. military; these eventualities are how many of the arms transfers and cooperative arrangements are explicitly justified. The point is not that junior partnership is an explicit goal but that it is assumed by both the U.S. and its wealthy clients as a natural state of affairs.

For decades, the most important military form of junior partnership for wealthy U.S. client states was, as we saw above, for deployment in the eventuality of an attack by the Soviet Union or its allies. The fact that such an attack was judged to be highly unlikely during most of the Cold War had little effect on procurement, standardization, joint training, and other aspects of contingency planning. At times, the existence of war-fighting units was considered by both the Americans and their allies as an essential part of a general deterrence policy: being able to fight a conventional war was, the argument went, vital to demonstrate the credibility of the U.S. nuclear deterrent. Similarly, the fact that U.S. allies would in the event of war be subordinate to U.S. command did not discourage them from maintaining and modernizing their forces, even if the extent of their military spending was less than the U.S. wished. In the end, and in spite of the various crises that organizations like NATO underwent, neither the Americans nor their allies seriously envisioned that, in an emergency, the latter would not fight alongside the former.

This basic presumption, as well as the habits and routines of day-to-day cooperation, go a long way to explaining why the end of the cold war did not lead to the dissolution of the post-World War II alliances. NATO not only continued to exist but added new members in several waves of expansion. Even before NATO expanded, its forces had begun to be used for combat purposes, with the Europeans in a classic junior partner status. (We will discuss these examples in detail in Chapters 5 and 6.) The earliest instance of this was in the first Gulf War, when the units and many of the operational plans for the attack on Iraqi forces in Kuwait were taken wholesale from NATO's forces in Europe. Interestingly, at the start of the war, the French, who had withdrawn from NATO's integrated command in 1966, placed their forces under U.S. command.[43] Several years later, NATO itself went into action, first in Bosnia-Herzegovina, then against Serbia over Kosovo. The invasion of Afghanistan involved military forces from a number of wealthy U.S. clients, both NATO members (including Germany) and other countries (e.g., Australia, Japan); in 2003, NATO began to take over command of forces in parts of Afghanistan. A number of U.S. allies, again including several NATO members, contributed forces to the second Gulf War against Iraq; once again, a few years afterward, NATO itself began to train Iraqi government forces. Most recently, in May 2005, NATO decided to become involved in supporting the African Union in its peacekeeping efforts in Darfur (Sudan), providing strategic airlift and training. Given Sudan's status as a U.S. enemy and its ties to the militia the African Union mission was intended to control, NATO's action should be seen as a combination of routinely hostile and humanitarian activities.

The expansion of NATO and other allied operations against enemies other than the Soviet Union illustrates nicely the cybernetic quality of how junior partner status developed. Originally, each of the U.S. post-World War II alliances was connected with planning for a particular region. Once created, these alliances then interacted with military assistance programs to shape arms transfers, production, and training for decades. That in turn created a policy instrument – capable militaries accustomed to working with the U.S. – which was used after the end of the cold war for combat operations in regions where the founders of the alliances would never have imagined getting involved.

A similar cybernetic process has occurred in support of U.S. clients. It began at the very dawn of the post-World War II era, with U.S. reliance on the British and French to take charge of military problems in their colonies and, if possible, their former colonies. American backing was not only political: the U.S. heavily subsidized the French war in Indochina with money, weapons, and advice; and French political and military officials, including the theatre commander, went so far as to give briefings in Washington (see Chapter 5). As we saw in Chapters 2 and 3, the U.S. also worked closely with and gave military and political support to the British during their intervention on behalf of King Hussein in Jordan in 1958. In the 1980s, as we also saw in Chapter 2, the U.S. both pressured and helped France to launch anti-Libyan operations in Chad. More generally, the U.S. has favored the preservation of British and French influence in their former colonies, so much so that when the British moved toward withdrawing their military presence in the Persian Gulf and Southeast Asia ("East of Suez"), high-level officials in Washington were notably upset: the U.S. Secretary of State exhorting his British counterpart to "for God's sake act like Britain."[44]

Thus, from an early date, the U.S. was accustomed to helping at least some of its wealthy clients maintain their military forces for possible intervention. To be sure, those interventions were not on behalf of U.S. clients but once in place, the policy instrument could be applied to other types of circumstances. For example, over the last decade, the U.S. has begun to back its wealthy clients in their contributions to UN military operations. One example of this is the intervention led by Australia in East Timor in 1999, following violence occasioned by a UN-sponsored referendum on independence from Indonesia. The United States helped Australia militarily (airlift, intelligence, combat reserves, plus planning) and politically (pressure on the Indonesian government and support in the Security Council). Similarly, the U.S. gave political and budgetary support to the British military stiffening of the UN's operation in Sierra Leone and to similar French activity in Côte d'Ivoire.[45]

Given this pattern of cooperation, it was not much of a stretch for the U.S. to organize wealthy clients intervening on behalf of poorer U.S. clients. The reasons for this were varied, although most involved a combination of U.S. reluctance to commit its own troops and wealthy clients' eagerness, or at least willingness, to commit theirs. This is particularly true of interventions on behalf of poorer clients perceived by U.S. officials as disorganized and lacking strong indigenous forces which the U.S. could support directly (see the discussion of "basket cases" in Chapter 5). A classic arena for the U.S. use of European clients as junior partners is the Democratic Republic of the Congo, formerly known as Zaire. We mentioned in Chapter 3 that the U.S. carried out extensive CIA paramilitary operations in 1964 (see Chapter 5 for details) to support the central government in the face of an insurgency, but this was only because the U.S. had earlier tried and failed to get the Europeans to intervene, on the grounds that "the African continent was above all their responsibility." In the end, the Belgians agreed, and dropped paratroopers from U.S. planes into two cities. In 1977, insurgents again threatened, and so the French flew Moroccan troops to Zaire, where they were given logistical support by the U.S. The next year, the insurgents launched another invasion; this time, the French and Belgians both sent troops in U.S. C-141 heavy transport planes.[46]

More recent examples are Liberia and Haiti (see Chapter 5 for details). In Liberia, worsening violence in the summer of 2003 led to calls for the U.S. to intervene on the grounds that "a long tradition" linked the two countries and accordingly that it was "normal for the United States to play a special role" there. Instead, the U.S. put together a sort of package for Liberia: it applied pressure on the president of the country, a faction leader under indictment for war crimes, to go into exile; it assembled a West African peacekeeping force, obtaining UN approval for it, having a senior U.S. official named as the Secretary General's special representative, authorizing the UN force in Sierra Leone to assist, and persuading the British to contribute troops to a future UN peacekeeping force in Liberia; and finally it sent a small number of marines into Liberia as part of these operations, with a larger contingent remaining offshore in reserve. The next year, in Haiti, the U.S. pressured the country's elected president into resigning in the face of a rebellion, flying him to the Central African Republic to reduce his future influence; it then organized an interventionary force composed of troops from the U.S., France, Canada, and Chile, and obtained both a request for its deployment by the new Haitian government and a UN resolution approving of that deployment. In both Liberia and Haiti, the U.S. rapidly withdrew its troops, leaving other states to do the peacekeeping; it also organized donor conferences (for economic reconstruction and development funds) for both states in the months after the intervention. Note, once again, the deep and routine use of the United Nations and other multilateral institutions (in West Africa, Latin America, and the Caribbean).[47]

In addition to their interventionary activities on behalf of U.S. clients and against U.S. enemies, wealthy clients are junior partners in less spectacular ways. One is by helping provide training for developing countries to take over from them in future peacekeeping operations, just as they and the UN did, in effect, from the United States. The U.S. has been carrying out this training for some of its clients and other African states since 1996, using both U.S. soldiers and private contractors. This program was then expanded into a Global Peace Operations Initiative and, as such, endorsed by the G-8 group of wealthiest countries (the U.S. plus six client states, plus Russia). It involved both bilateral training programs by the U.S., France, and the United Kingdom; and a multilateral center in Ghana, subsidized by Germany, the U.K., Canada, Italy, France, the Netherlands, and the European Union. A similar center for training constabulary forces in peacekeeping missions was also established in Italy.[48]

An additional type of military support by wealthy clients comes in the form of arms sales. Although consistent data are hard to come by, the two leading data bases on the subject both show that wealthy U.S. clients are among the world's leading weapons suppliers, accounting for between one-third and two-thirds of total sales by countries other than the U.S., and around 40 percent of sales to developing nations. The buyers of these weapons are overwhelmingly U.S. clients: they comprise 33 of the world's top 38 recipients and 96 percent of the total sales by U.S. clients. Insofar as arms sales are a means of transferring resources to help maintain regimes in power, U.S. clients' sales, which range from 57 percent to 77 percent of U.S. sales, are an important adjunct to U.S. individual efforts, even if they cut into potential profits from U.S. firms.[49]

Political contributions

We have seen that the wealthy U.S. client states became junior partners in both economic and military relations, helping support poorer U.S. clients while opposing U.S. enemies. A similar role can be seen in the sphere of political relations, although with one important difference. Political assistance to poorer clients is often either low key or completely covert, since payoffs, furnishing of enemy names, and police support are not the kind of activities either the U.S. or recipient states wish to have widely discussed. In addition, certain forms of assistance, notably bribes and support payments, tend to be exclusive: if an official of a state is regularly given cash by a local CIA officer, the former can generally assume that the latter would not be happy if he were also to be paid off by someone from a third state. (There are of course exceptions to this.) Hence, we would not expect that wealthy clients would play much of a supporting role in providing political assistance to U.S. clients. One exception is, as we mentioned above, French assistance in counterinsurgency (including torture) techniques to Argentina and Chile – and, for that matter, to the U.S.[50]

On the other hand, wealthy clients were and are active in giving the U.S. political support against its (and their) enemies. This policy began early on, when the OPC (the CIA's original covert action branch; see Chapters 5 and 6) set up "stay-behind armies" in many Western European countries. The purpose of these was to serve as a nucleus for resistance if there were to be a takeover by communist forces, whether indigenous ones or by means of an invasion by the Soviet Union. When NATO was created, coordination (including furnishing supplies and technical advice on matters such as planting explosives) passed to a committee of the organization, run out of its headquarters in first Paris, then Brussels. The committee was dominated by U.S. officials from both the CIA and the military, although the U.S. formed an Executive Group, together with Britain and France, within the committee. Long after the fear of a communist takeover had passed, the stay-behind armies remained and, in several countries, began carrying out political actions against actual or suspected leftists, including assisting military *coups d'état* (in Greece and Turkey) and engaging in terrorist actions (in Italy, Spain, Turkey, Germany, and Belgium).[51]

For much of the cold war, the intelligence agencies of the United States cooperated with their counterparts in Western Europe and elsewhere. Many of the arrangements set up were bilateral: the CIA, for example, would receive information from the French or the Germans about certain Soviet activities either locally or in third countries. This was not simply a matter of handing tips to the Americans but of using U.S. expertise in signals intelligence and in turn receiving certain kinds of material. There were also multilateral arrangements set up. One was a signals intelligence sharing agreement in 1948 between the U.S., Britain, Canada, Australia, and New Zealand, with other countries, such as Japan and Norway, playing a more limited role. The targets of this program were Soviet and Warsaw Pact communications around the world. Another arrangement, concluded in the late 1960s with the same English-speaking countries, involved the sharing of counterintelligence information, again about the Soviet Union. Other groups, with broader membership among wealthy countries (most of them U.S. clients), were set up starting in the late 1970s to exchange information about different types of terrorism. In addition, as we will see in the next chapter, the U.S. also cooperated with the British and other states on covert interventions designed to overthrow enemy regimes.[52]

Since the end of the cold war, cooperation between intelligence agencies has if anything intensified. The "Global War on Terror," for all its controversial aspects, has involved routine coordination between the U.S. and all of its wealthy clients. Signals and human intelligence are being exchanged; counterintelligence agencies (e.g., the FBI in the U.S.; MI5 in the U.K.) are cooperating on tracking down and arresting suspects (and, in some cases, in "rendering" them to third countries for interrogation and torture); and financial records are being pored over and bank accounts frozen. These joint activities are being carried out both against groups accused of terrorism and states accused of sponsoring terrorism. Other U.S. enemies accused of possessing or of aiming to possess weapons of mass destruction are also targets of political cooperation, not only across intelligence and law-enforcement agencies but by coordinated diplomacy.[53]

Trends and transitions

As we have presented them, the two types of U.S. clients, economically deprived and wealthy, are both distinct and overlap. They differ from each other not only in terms of whether they contribute or receive grants and loans but, as we have seen, with regard to the presumed strength of their regimes and their status as junior partners. On the other hand, some of the programs – notably arms sales – first developed for one type of client have subsequently been used for the other type and even for nonclients. More significantly, there is in principle no barrier preventing economically deprived clients from becoming wealthy ones. At the end of World War II, many states which were then in dire need of grants and loans to reconstruct their economies and which also could not afford to reconstruct their militaries soon became wealthy enough no longer to require such resource flows. Other, poorer, states, such as South Korea, began to go through a similar process. For these reasons, it is useful to take a broader look at the post-world War II period when many of the client maintenance instruments were developed.

We can begin by looking at resource flows over time. Although, as we saw, there are and have been many different programs for transferring resources, those programs fall into four general budget categories: (1) economic assistance (mostly grants and concessional loans); (2) military assistance (again, grants and concessional loans; also training); (3) nonconcessional loans (mostly from the Export-Import Bank); and (4) arms sales (both government-to-government and direct commercial). It is possible, for any given country, to get an idea of total resource flows by adding up the numbers for each budget category across all the years that the programs have been in operation. We have done this in Figure 4.1 for four different types of client states: wealthy countries which received reconstruction aid after World War II; wealthy countries which did not receive such aid (e.g., countries like Australia); less wealthy countries; and poor countries.[54]

What Figure 4.1 shows is how, for the almost 60 years in which most of the resource flow programs have been in operation, the composition of those flows has varied

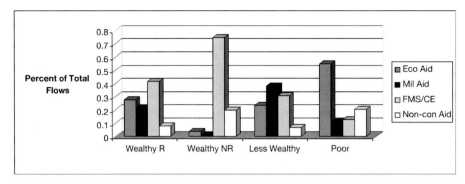

Figure 4.1   Distribution of resource flows by client type, 1946–73
Sources: U.S. Agency for International Development (2005) and U.S. Defense Security Cooperation
   Agency (2004 and predecessor volumes) as per note 54.

considerably from wealthy clients to poorer ones. For wealthy clients which received reconstruction aid, economic assistance and military assistance were of roughly the same magnitude, with arms sales (which, as we saw, took over from military aid for those states in the 1970s) accounting for close to half of total flows. The less wealthy clients, being unable to afford to purchase arms until more recently, received greater amounts of military aid than the value of the weapons they bought; their proportion of economic aid was around the same as for the reconstructing wealthy states. By contrast, the nonreconstruction wealthy clients received practically no aid of any sort, with arms sales serving as the only means of transferring resources. Finally, the poorest clients received a relatively low proportion of their resources in the form of arms, whether as aid or as purchases; most resource transfers were economic grants and loans, the latter being both concessional and nonconcessional. None of these results are surprising, although they do confirm the large differences between wealthy and poorer clients.

The story becomes more interesting if we split the post-World War II era into two parts and compare the 1946–71 period with the 1972–2003 one. Figure 4.2 shows a clear convergence between the two types of wealthy clients: although those receiving reconstruction assistance began, evidently, with greater percentages of economic and military grants and loans than those not reconstructing, this difference had vanished by the more recent time period, with neither type of client getting any significant concessional aid and the main resource flowing to both types of clients being purchased weapons. On the other hand, Figure 4.3 tells a different story. Less wealthy clients diminish sharply their reliance on economic assistance; they continue, though on a reduced basis, receiving military aid; but when they can afford to start buying arms, they do so in a very large way. Poor clients still have a high percentage (just over 40 percent) of their resource inflows in the form of economic assistance and a low (though increased) percentage in the form of military assistance. The real shift over time is that arms sales went up considerably. Thus, even poor clients, for whom economic aid represents a significant portion of total resource inflows, are buying many more weapons now than in the past. This points to both a major push in terms of arms sales as well as a diminution, in real terms, in concessional aid since its heyday in the first two decades after World War II.[55]

If we turn now to specific countries, we can see some interesting patterns. A central argument in Chapter 3 was that the acquisition of clients involved the U.S. making a

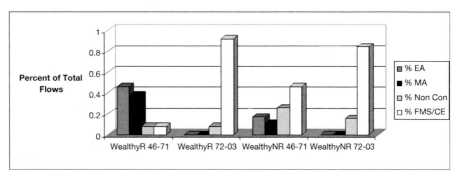

Figure 4.2 Changes in distribution of resource flows to wealthy clients, 1946–2003
Sources: U.S. Agency for International Development (2005) and U.S. Defense Security Cooperation
Agency (2004 and predecessor volumes) as per note 54.

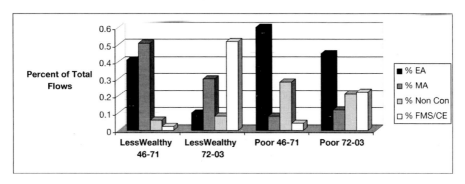

Figure 4.3 Changes in distribution of resource flows to less wealthy clients, 1946–2003
Sources: U.S. Agency for International Development (2005) and U.S. Defense Security Cooperation
Agency (2004 and predecessor volumes) as per note 54.

commitment; combining that with the discussion earlier in this chapter about the development of policy instruments for maintaining clients leads to the implication that when clients were acquired after those instruments had been developed, there should have been an increase in resource flows (this also happened, as we saw, in the pre-World War II period, but there were far fewer instruments and the flow of resources was much lower). An example of this can be seen in Figure 4.4, which shows that as Egypt was moving toward client status, the flow of economic aid sharply increased from a level of zero to almost $3 billion in constant 2003 dollars (this was also connected with the Sinai withdrawal agreements). When, in 1978, Egypt became a client, it was rewarded for its switch with over $3 billion in military aid (we discussed this in Chapter 3) and practically $5 billion in arms sales.

The reverse of this process can be seen in Figure 4.5. This depicts flows to Iran, which had been a client from 1953 to 1979, when the Islamic Revolution ended that status. For close to two decades, the U.S. sent economic assistance programs, military aid, and nonconcessional loans to the country. The amounts transferred in these programs were not trivial, running between $100 million and $800 million per program, in constant dollars, depending on the year (the length of the y-axis, necessary to capture arms sales, tends to obscure these transfers). This ended in the early 1970s, when the

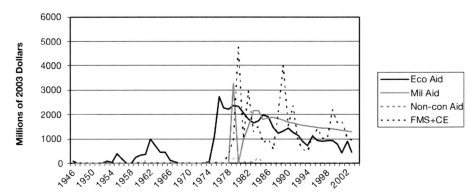

Figure 4.4   Resource flows to Egypt, 1946–2003
Sources: U.S. Agency for International Development (2005) and U.S. Defense Security Cooperation
Agency (2004 and predecessor volumes) as per note 54.

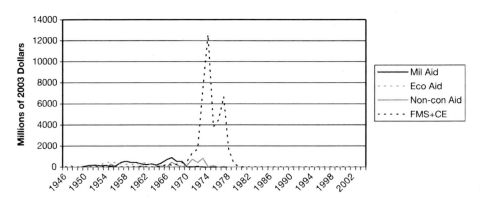

Figure 4.5   Resource flows to Iran, 1946–2003
Sources: U.S. Agency for International Development (2005) and U.S. Defense Security Cooperation
Agency (2004 and predecessor volumes) as per note 54.

run-up in oil prices left the Shah with greatly increased revenues, thereby obviating his
need for aid and making it possible for him to go on an arms-buying spree (over $12
billion worth, in constant 2003 dollars, in 1974 alone). This coincided perfectly with U.
S. policy which, under the Nixon Doctrine, encouraged several countries to act as
regional policemen for the United States. When demonstrations in 1978 forced the
Shah out of power, the Islamic regime that replaced him quickly became considered by
the U.S. as an enemy and arms sales crashed to zero.[56]

The case of El Salvador reveals a different pattern (see Figure 4.6). For decades after
the abortive peasant uprising, the country was for the U.S. a backwater, ruled by a
succession of military dictators and military-backed oligarchs. Then, in 1979 and 1980,
when it looked as if a coalition of leftist groups might take power (first by political, then
by military, means), the U.S. sharply increased all three kinds of aid: economic, military,
and nonconcessional (see Chapter 5). Throughout the 1980s, as a war raged between

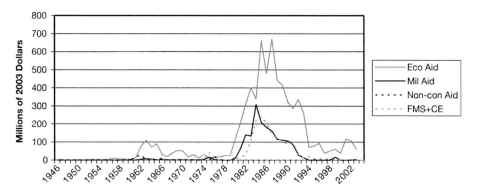

Figure 4.6 Resource flows to El Salvador, 1946–2003
Sources: U.S. Agency for International Development (2005) and U.S. Defense Security Cooperation
Agency (2004 and predecessor volumes) as per note 54.

insurgents and the state, the latter was strongly backed by the U.S. with advisers, equipment, and massive resource flows. Once a peace agreement led to the insurgency's end, each kind of aid, including economic, declined. This "spike" – a sudden increase in aid, followed by a precipitous fall-off – in assistance illustrates not only the essentially political nature of even economic aid but also the extent to which routine maintenance of clients is a relatively low-cost affair. For most of El Salvador's history as a U.S. client, resource flows to it were tiny; only when the regime needed the U.S. to intervene on its behalf did aid rise to appreciable levels.

In short, resource flows over the past 60 years illustrate much about the routine maintenance of both wealthy and poorer clients. The former, though originally receiving more military (and for that matter, economic) aid than the latter, have for several decades now had their U.S.-supplied resources restricted only to purchased weapons. Poorer clients, though, while receiving higher percentages of economic aid, have had their flows pumped up or down depending on their political situation; but they, too, have ended up more and more as purchasers of U.S. arms. Indeed, for all clients of whatever type and indeed, for all countries, the two principal trends after World War II are, first, the decline in all forms of assistance – economic, military, and nonconcessional – in both absolute and relative terms (see Figures 4.7 and 4.8) and second, the significant rise in arms sales (Figure 4.7).[57]

Client maintenance today

We indicated above that there has been a considerable proliferation of policy instruments by which U.S. clients are maintained. Programs were not only replaced by other programs but subdivided into new and ever more specialized forms, diffusing as well from the states for which they were originally intended to other states in completely different regions. At times, existing programs were used in pursuit of entirely new goals. In all these ways, particular client states have been the arena for ever greater numbers of U.S. government organizations even if the state in question is not experiencing a crisis. This general pattern can be seen clearly by taking a programmatic view of current resource flows as a whole.

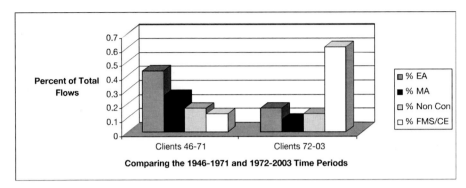

Figure 4.7 Changes in distribution of resource flows to all clients, 1946–2003
Sources: U.S. Agency for International Development (2005) and U.S. Defense Security Cooperation
Agency (2004 and predecessor volumes) as per note 54

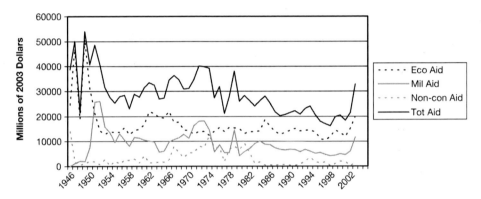

Figure 4.8 Aid Flows to All Countries, 1946–2003
Source: U.S. Agency for International Development (2005) as per note 57.

To see this, we can look at the latest data available on resource flows to all countries, rather than at individual countries or a sample of recipients, as we did above. Although, as we saw, some types of maintenance activities do not involve significant financial outlays, many do, including arms sales. (Whether weapons are paid for by the U.S. or the recipient state, they are a real transfer of resources from the former to build up the capabilities of the latter.) This will give us an idea of the U.S. resources involved in routine client maintenance, as well as how those resources are divided up by type of client, geographical region, and, more generally, how many resources go to clients as opposed to nonclients. In this way, we can begin to answer the broader question of just how expensive the U.S. client state empire is on a day-to-day basis, and hence what, if any, resource constraints there are on that empire's longevity.[58]

In 2004, the U.S. transferred some $35.8 billion in resources to other states, either through direct bilateral arrangements or through its contributions to multilateral lending agencies (see Table 4.1). Of this sum, around a quarter was in the form of economic aid, with another seventh being military aid. By far the largest resource component was weapons sold through the U.S. government or by private firms; some of those sales

Table 4.1 Resource flows to clients and non-clients by region in 2004

Region	Clients/ Non-clients	Economic Aid	Military Aid	Military Sales	Total Aid
Western Hemisphere	Clients	3286.2*	913.1	555.2	4754.6
	Non-Clients	21.6	0	0	21.6
Europe	Clients	537.1	104.3	4751.6	5393.1
	Non-Clients	1260	89.1	644.4	1993.5
Middle East and	Clients	1502.8	3711.6	2647.9	7862.4
Littoral North Africa	Non-Clients	318.3	29.2	106.8	454.2
Africa	Clients	631.8	4.7	0.7	637.2
	Non-Clients	2843.7	29.8	36.1	2909.7
Caucasus, Central and	Clients	2110.6	741.8	70.3	2922.8
South Asia	Non-Clients	2241.8	43.1	36.5	2321.5
East Asia and Pacific	Clients	382.9	31.6	5089.0	5503.6
	Non-Clients	1047.7	7.7	19.0	1074.4
World Total	Clients	8451.4	5507.1	13114.7	27073.7
	Non-Clients	7733.1	198.9	842.8	8774.9

Sources: U.S. Department of State (2005b), World Bank (2004c), Inter-American Development Bank (2005a), Asian Development Bank (2005), European Bank for Reconstruction and Development (2005), African Development Bank (2005), U.S. Central Intelligence Agency (2005), as per note 58.
Note: * In millions of 2004 dollars.

Table 4.2 Largest recipients of resources, 2004

Rank	Country	Total resource flows
1	Egypt	2886.3*
2	Afghanistan	1771.7
3	Japan	1645.0
4	Israel	1530.5
5	Saudi Arabia	1489.2
6	Brazil	1110.2
7	United Kingdom	1067.3
8	Pakistan	1050.2
9	South Korea	1008.6
10	India	964.4
11	Colombia	942.2
12	Jordan	912.3
13	Australia	756.9
14	Thailand	636.0
15	Turkey	603.1
16	Democratic Rep. of Congo	561.4
17	Netherlands	506.0
18	United Arab Emirates	505.2
19	Italy	495.5
20	Vietnam	481.2

Sources: U.S. Department of State (2005b), World Bank (2004c), Inter-American Development Bank (2005a), Asian Development Bank (2005), European Bank for Reconstruction and Development (2005), African Development Bank (2005), U.S. Central Intelligence Agency (2005), as per note 58.
Note: * In millions of 2004 dollars.

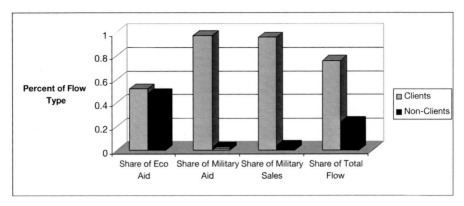

Figure 4.9   Distribution of resource flows between clients and non-clients, 2004
Sources: U.S. Department of State (2005b), World Bank (2004c), Inter-American Development
    Bank (2005a), Asian Development Bank (2005), European Bank for Reconstruction and
    Development (2005), African Development Bank (2005), U.S. Central Intelligence Agency
    (2005), as per note 58.

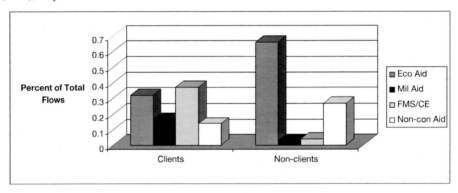

Figure 4.10   Distribution of types of resource flows to clients and non-clients, 1946–2003
Sources: U.S. Agency for International Development (2005) and U.S. Defense Security Coopera-
    tion Agency (2004 and predecessor volumes) as per note 54.

were paid for by military aid but most were not. These resources went disproportionately
to client states (who comprise the top 10 resource recipients and 18 of the top 20; see
Table 4.2): they received slightly over half (52 percent) of all economic aid (including
from multilateral agencies), in spite of having many more people, and almost all the
military aid (97 percent) and arms sales (95 percent). Combining all resources, U.S.
clients received over three times as much as nonclients (see Figure 4.9).

As we might expect, the difference between clients and nonclients is not simply that
the former receive greater resources than the latter but that the type of resources they
receive is different as well. Figure 4.10 shows that over the past half century or so as a
whole, the resources clients received were divided into proportions that were not grossly
different: arms sales, followed by appreciable amounts of economic aid, and with military aid and nonconcessional loans being of roughly equal amounts. By contrast,
nonclients received the vast majority of their resources in the form of economic aid,
with nonconcessional loans being less than half that amount and the other two categories
close to zero. This indicates just how significant military resources (aid and sales) are to
client status. To be a client, as we defined it in Chapter 2, means that the U.S. is committed

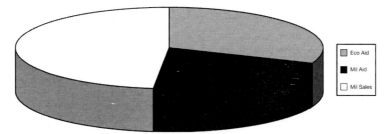

Figure 4.11 Distribution of resource flows to clients, 2004
Sources: U.S. Department of State (2005b), World Bank (2004c), Inter-American Development Bank (2005a), Asian Development Bank (2005), European Bank for Reconstruction and Development (2005), African Development Bank (2005), U.S. Central Intelligence Agency (2005), as per notes 58, 59.

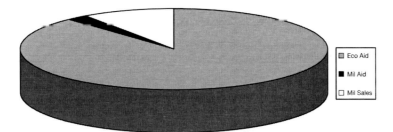

Figure 4.12 Distribution of resource flows to non-clients, 2004
Sources: U.S. Department of State (2005b), World Bank (2004c), Inter-American Development Bank (2005a), Asian Development Bank (2005), European Bank for Reconstruction and Development (2005), African Development Bank (2005), U.S. Central Intelligence Agency (2005), as per notes 58, 59.

to the maintenance of the state's regime; although there are a number of ways of keeping that commitment, one set of ways – the transfer of military resources – is directed overwhelmingly toward client states. Nonclients may be helped out economically but viewed over the long run, the U.S. has done very little on behalf of their militaries.

This may now be starting to change. Figure 4.11 summarizes the distribution of resource transfers in 2004 across all clients, showing once again the dominating role of arms sales. When those sales are added to military aid, the percentages are even higher: U.S. clients receive something like 69 percent of their total resource transfers from the U.S. in the form of weapons, training, and other forms of military assistance. The corresponding figures for nonclients, of course, are much lower (Figure 4.12). Most of what nonclients receive from the U.S. is economic assistance; when resource transfers from junior partners are included, this disproportion can grow still further. However, something like 10 percent of resource transfers to nonclients are arms sales, all the more significant because most of those sales are not subsidized by U.S. foreign military financing. If we add in the arms sales made by wealthy U.S. clients, many nonclients turn out to be receiving (mostly buying) important portions of their foreign resources in the form of weapons. Recent efforts by the Pentagon to carry out "counterterrorist" military training in Africa (mostly among nonclients), although relatively inexpensive in budgetary terms, may open the door to further arms transfers.[59]

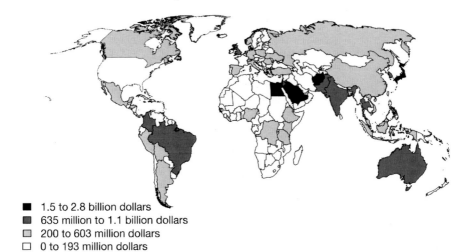

■   1.5 to 2.8 billion dollars

■   635 million to 1.1 billion dollars

☐   200 to 603 million dollars

☐   0 to 193 million dollars

Figure 4.13 Total resource flows for 2004
Sources: U.S. Department of State (2005b), World Bank (2004c), Inter-American Development
Bank (2005a), Asian Development Bank (2005), European Bank for Reconstruction and
Development (2005), African Development Bank (2005), U.S. Central Intelligence Agency
(2005), as per note 58.

U.S. resource transfers are geographically highly concentrated. The region receiving
the most resources in fiscal year 2004 was the Middle East and North Africa, which in
total transfers (Figure 4.13) is easily in first place. East Asia and the Pacific comes
second, followed by Europe and then the Western Hemisphere. Africa comes dead last,
indicative of just how few clients the U.S. has there. More generally, we can say that
there are three types of regions from the standpoint of U.S. resource transfers to clients:
the areas of long-standing clients (Europe, the Western Hemisphere, and East Asia and
the Pacific), which receive roughly similar amounts; the Middle East and North Africa,
which, beset by conflicts and possessing many U.S. clients, is the region in which the U.S.
sees the most urgent need to maintain clients; and Africa, which by all accounts is in
U.S. eyes a backwater best left to the French and British.[60]

How expensive is the U.S. client state empire from the standpoint of routine maintenance? Total U.S. resource transfers to its clients in 2004 cost $27 billion. Of course
there are other costs of maintaining the empire, notably those connected with intervention, but by itself, the figure of $27 billion is almost ludicrously small. (In fact,
considering that close to half of U.S. transfers to its clients take the form of unsubsi-
dized arms sales, the real budgetary incidence is even tinier.) The fiscal year 2004
budget outlay for the U.S. government was $1.9 trillion; routine maintenance of 81
client states cost slightly over one percent of that figure.[61] This is low-cost empire with
a vengeance: the vast majority of U.S. clients are stable and indeed, when wealthy
enough, contribute to helping out the U.S. At least for most clients, most of the time,
maintenance is really routine. This was not always the case in the past: for example, in
the early days of the cold war, U.S. resource transfers ran to over 20 percent of the
federal budget (see Figure 4.14). However, as the situation normalized, the cost of
routine maintenance declined significantly, stabilizing in the early 1980s (ironically, the
years when Reagan was president and the cold war is supposed to have worsened) to

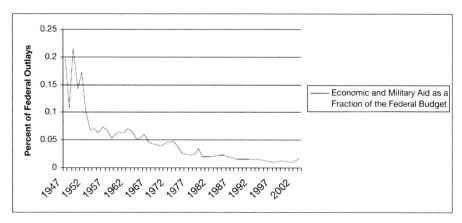

Figure 4.14 Budgetary cost of economic and military assistance, 1946–2003
Sources: U.S. Agency for International Development (2005), U.S. Office of Management and Budget (2005), as per note 61.

just around 2 percent of total federal spending. The end of the cold war led to a further decline, and so far the evidence is that the new war on terror has not appreciably increased routine maintenance costs. We will return to this issue in the concluding chapter of this book; but for now, note that if in the future a problem arises of "imperial overstretch" or some other resource difficulty in maintaining the U.S. empire, it cannot come from the day-to-day costs of its maintenance. The costs of interventions on behalf of clients or against enemies, however, are potentially another story.

5   Client maintenance by interventions

Most of the time, policy makers in Washington consider the problems faced by U.S. client states to be routine. This does not mean that those problems are trivial from a human or moral point of view (for example, the spread of AIDS, or the effects of global warming); what it does mean is that the problems are not considered to have any appreciable chance of resulting in the clients' regimes losing power. For routine problems, as we saw in Chapter 4, there are multiple programs that can be administered to transfer resources to clients and otherwise help them, at least as seen through U.S. eyes.

Other kinds of problems raise more dire prospects. There may be an economic crisis, or an impending election, or an insurgency, any of which presents the possibility that the regime might fall from power or, that if it continues in power, might give rise to an enemy or even become one itself. In these situations, the U.S. risks the loss of the client, a prospect which, in Dr. Johnson's well-known phrase, "concentrates [the] mind wonderfully." Suddenly, special task forces are created, high-level policy makers get involved, ambassadors are recalled, and crisis meetings are scheduled; even if the chances of actually losing the client are slight, the situation calls for special measures. But which ones? Here we have to consider, yet again, the cybernetic quality of U.S. policy making.

If the country in question is already a U.S. client, then, prior to the moment when loss becomes seen as a possibility, there will be a set of programs revolving around routine maintenance. Hence, unless those programs come under sudden and massive pressure, the newest problem is likely to be seen as involving some incapacity on the part of the client itself: something that the regime is either unable to do adequately or perhaps making worse. If, on the other hand, the country in question is not yet a client, then the newest problem is by definition due to the incapacity of the state or its patron, if there is a patron. In either case, the emerging problem has to do with tasks which others are performing inadequately. This means that policy making in Washington will of necessity involve considering how to assume some degree of responsibility for tasks which had been carried out by local authorities (who had perhaps been aided by some other state). We define this taking over as *intervention in the affairs of the client*.

Our aim in this chapter is to discuss the principal types of intervention on behalf of clients, as they have been developed over the last century. We begin with a general overview of the concept of intervention, distinguishing it from other phenomena, including routine maintenance of clients. We introduce the concept of families of intervention situations, then, in the rest of the chapter, turn to concentrate on three different "subfamilies" of client maintenance intervention: those which involve taking over economic or political tasks from the client; those which involve taking over military tasks; and those which involve replacing the personnel of the regime. As we will see, these three subfamilies are distinguished from each other less by the policy instrument employed (since instruments can be used in more than one situation) than by the nature of the situations common to each subfamily.

The concept of intervention

As we have defined it, intervention goes well beyond the sending of troops or other members of the armed forces. It involves any policy in which an activity by a regime, essential to its survival, is taken over by an outside actor. As we will see, those activities range from assuring creditors or soliciting votes to stay in power to accompanying troops into combat or carrying out bombing raids. If the leaders of the regime are themselves considered the problem, then, in effect, the U.S., or those it is supporting, will take over their activities, i.e., overthrow the leaders. (See Chapter 6 for an extension to the case of intervention against enemies.) Whatever the type of taking over, policy making in such dire situations involves the substitution of a U.S. policy instrument for that of an existing or new client. This permits officials in Washington to focus their attention rather than to disperse their resources; it also gives, yet again, a strong programmatic and organizational cast to policy making even under circumstances of grave worry.[1]

Of course, it could be argued that it is misleading to distinguish between intervention and routine maintenance. After all, to be a client state is to accept surveillance and problem solving by a patron, who thus has a permanent presence in the client's internal affairs. There is, however, an important difference between a normal presence and a takeover of local responsibilities on an urgent basis. Under normal circumstances, the regimes of U.S. clients are competent enough to maintain themselves in formal and informal positions of political and economic power. They may need resources to do so over and above those available internally – although, as we saw in Chapter 4, they may have enough cash on hand actually to pay for certain of those resources (e.g., weapons) by themselves – but those resources are transferred on behalf of the regime's own personnel. The archetypal example of this relationship is the military assistance provided by the U.S. to the armed forces of its less wealthy clients: the U.S. trains the clients' troops and furnishes them with weapons. Similarly, economic assistance involves building hospitals or schools or courthouses, activities that the clients would normally undertake themselves and which, following the act of construction, they will use in providing health care or teaching children or holding trials. As states become wealthier, their need for externally-supplied resources to carry out these activities decreases.

In situations where a regime's maintenance of power is threatened, however, the issue, at least in Washington's eyes, is no longer whether the regime needs more resources to do the job but whether, even if such resources were provided, it would be capable of doing the job. That is why the issue is whether to take over some of the regime's activities, not simply furnish resources to it. To both the U.S. and its client, this is a significant step: it means that the relationship has passed, if only for a limited time, from being one of tutelage and advice-giving to one in which the client is, in essence, an onlooker. Issues of national pride are accentuated; and it is difficult for the U.S., even if technically its takeover of activities is at the invitation of the host government, to avoid responsibility for failure in carrying out the activities. It is for this reason that U.S. policy makers consider the stakes high enough for senior officials to get involved: not that the cost of the takeover is so high, at least in budgetary or manpower terms, but that the costs of losing are high and therefore that there will be a built-in motive to escalate. Even when the activities in question are supposedly covert, the assumption is that other states, at least, are aware of what the U.S. is doing (although the secrecy permits "plausible deniability" of the U.S. role), thereby again engaging U.S. prestige. In this way, intervention in a client's affairs is, as takeover, a matter of great political significance both to the U.S. and to the client.

To be a client is to acquiesce in U.S. surveillance and concern with regime performance, whether domestic or foreign. All clients, whether rich or poor, routinely maintained or undergoing intervention, are accustomed to U.S. officials checking up on their performance and offering advice. In all clients, the U.S. plays a high-profile role, even if this may be done with tact and delicacy. None of this is unusual, so much so that it is taken for granted by both clients and the U.S. But when regimes risk no longer holding onto power, the U.S. responsibility is suddenly brought to the foreground and made hyper-visible. Intervention, even if cheap, is considered exceptional and hence is of great political significance. When we speak of intervening "in the affairs" of a client state, the emphasis should not be on particular affairs as opposed to others but on the sense that the affairs are those of the client, so that a U.S. takeover is a deviation from whatever the norm has been for that state up until that time.

Almost by definition, intervention is expected to be uncommon. The regimes of most client states, even if not performing at a high level of competence, are nonetheless assumed by U.S. officials to be capable of maintaining themselves in power. And when a regime is seen as incompetent, it is not necessarily considered to be in a condition of free fall, such that it might be considered as a "failed state," one "utterly incapable of sustaining itself as a member of the international community," and "in which public authorities are either unable or unwilling to carry out their end of what Hobbes long ago called the social contract, but which now includes more than maintaining the peace among society's many factions and interests." In such states, as the State Department's director of policy planning put it while still an academic, "national authority structures" are "failed, weak, incompetent, or abusive ... The best that people living in such countries can hope for is marginal improvement in their material well-being; limited access to social services, including health care and education; and a moderate degree of individual physical security."[2]

Regimes on behalf of whom the U.S. intervenes are not, indeed cannot be, perceived as across-the-board incompetent, since, as we shall see, the U.S. would otherwise not bother trying to keep them afloat. Rather, such regimes are viewed as confronting much the same type of situation as in South Vietnam in 1961: "critical but not hopeless." Most of the time, the U.S. steps in long before some Hobbesian state of anarchy is reached; on the rare occasions when a U.S. client finds itself in that situation, the odds are that the U.S. has helped bring about that state of affairs (see examples later in this chapter) as a way of destabilizing an unacceptable regime and replacing it by one more to American tastes. Otherwise, even if a regime is incompetent at providing certain basic services to the population, such as physical security or basic education, it may still be capable of maintaining its hold on power, provided, perhaps, that the U.S. takes over certain tasks. Clients need not be well governed for their regimes to survive, regardless of whether or not the U.S. intervenes in their affairs.[3]

This mixed picture gives U.S. policy making a particular characteristic. Since, in cases of intervention, regimes are not failing across the board, deliberations in Washington become a matter of characterizing the task at which the client regime is deficient and then finding a U.S. policy instrument capable of being applied to that task. The first of these activities – characterizing the deficiency – is potentially highly complicated. In fact, because clients (and, for that matter, some potential clients) are closely surveilled, field officials in any given client are constantly sending back a stream of situation descriptions, focusing on the regime's performance across a range of activities (see the discussion in Chapter 2 about links with Washington). When the performance in a particular activity is deemed as potentially failing, a report along those lines is sent to Washington and that in turn sets the agenda for subsequent discussion. The accuracy of those reports is, of course, another matter.

The second activity in Washington which engages the attention of top officials involves finding a policy instrument with which to take over the task at which a regime is said to be failing. Here, the cybernetic mechanisms we discussed in Chapter 1 are relevant. When a report of a regime's failure at a task is received, officials engage in a search of existing U.S. policy instruments similar to whichever instrument the regime is using; the first one found is usually argued for as appropriate. For example, if an insurgency has broken out and the regime's troops are unable to put it down, then some type of troop-related policy instrument will be seized on by U.S. officials. (This means that some of the same policy instruments used for routine maintenance can also be used for intervention.) If there is no U.S. instrument corresponding to the regime's, one is put together by giving an organization a new task, something which happened in the early years of the CIA.[4]

Of course, taking over a task does not guarantee that it will be accomplished sufficiently to solve the problem. Other inadequacies may arise or be discovered, thereby placing policy makers in a new situation, triggering new attempts at instrument matching, and so forth. Even a resource insufficiency in U.S. policy instruments, such as a short-fall in the number of troops, is in effect understood as an additional inadequacy on the part of the client regime (the competence of U.S. soldiers and officials is almost never questioned, as we will discuss in Chapter 7) which puts additional stress on the U.S. program. For this reason, intervention policy for a given client may need to be remade with some frequency, with each instance of policy making being tantamount to a new situation. Since, in a given country, a particular policy instrument was identified as appropriate to the situation for which it was employed, a change in that situation will normally be thought of as indicating a need to change instruments.

It follows, then, that intervention policy making is above all a matter of specifying the situation in which the client finds itself. A given situation is seen as indicating the need for a particular instrument; although several instruments are in principle possible for a given situation (recalling, again, that the same instrument can be applicable to multiple situations), if the situation is specified with enough precision, only one instrument seems to fit. This is why much of high-level policy making revolves around attempts to characterize the situation in a given place and time; it is why high-level officials who just returned from a visit that lasted perhaps forty-eight hours are considered to have valuable firsthand knowledge; and it is why rejected recommendations (e.g., to send troops, or to offer negotiations) are typically castigated as inappropriate to the particularities of the situation. To understand which policy instrument is used under what conditions, we therefore need to specify, as parsimoniously as possible, the range of situations identified by policy makers. We do this in Figure 5.1, which represents the top of what we call a "pseudo-decision tree."

What Figure 5.1 represents are the principal factors that distinguish situations, and hence appropriate interventions (and noninterventions), in the eyes of U.S. policy makers. Although couched as a series of questions, this is a presentational device and

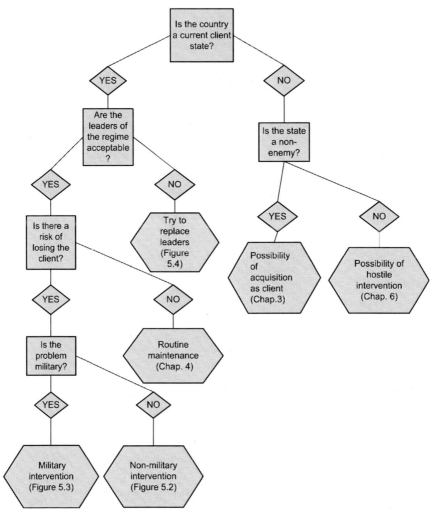

Figure 5.1 Client intervention situations, 1: Overview

the questions should be thought of as simultaneous; hence the adjective "pseudo." Our claim is that each decisional node (see below) corresponds to one particular intervention situation; although there are only a small number of criteria which we think high level policy makers take into account, those criteria combine to generate a large number of nodes, and thus types of interventions. The nodes fall into two basic families, each being divided into several subfamilies. To see how this works, look at the very top of the tree where the question is asked "Is the country a current client state?" If the country in question is not, then we proceed to the right-hand side of the tree, asking the follow-up question "Is the state a non-enemy?" Here there are two possibilities. The first is that the state is a non-enemy, which then raises the possibility of its being acquired as a client through one of the five different contexts of acquisition discussed in Chapter 3. The other possibility is that the state is in fact identified as an enemy of the U.S., in which case we enter the logic of hostile intervention, the topic of Chapter 6.

There, the fundamental question is, as we can see, "Is the regime strong militarily?" which gives two subfamilies of intervention types to be discussed.

If, on the other hand, the answer to the question at the top of the tree is yes, then the next question to distinguish situations is "Are the top political leaders of the regime acceptable?" The answer to this question may be no, in which case U.S. officials will want to replace the regime's leaders by those deemed more competent or less repulsive. This gives us one subfamily for interventions aiming at maintaining clients. We will discuss this subfamily at the end of this chapter; as we will see, the first question to ask about it is "Does the military back the regime's top political leaders?" Alternatively, if the regime is acceptable, the next question is "Is there a risk of losing the client?" The answer here, of course, may be no, in which case intervention is not indicated and U.S. efforts are directed at routine maintenance. However, if there is a risk of losing the client, then policy makers will consider intervention. One of their principal considerations in such cases will be "Is the problem military?" If the answer to this is yes, then some type of intervention employing military policy instruments will be on the table; this is an entire subfamily which we will discuss later in this chapter. Instead, the problem may be nonmilitary, in which case a third sub-family of other types of policy instruments may be indicated. We now turn to this set of situations.

Non-military intervention situations

As policy makers in Washington understand it, situations in which nonmilitary intervention is perhaps appropriate fall into four categories: those which call for emergency economic aid (node 1), those which call for emergency covert political operations (node 2), those which call for emergency action to separate the military from the top political leader (node 3), and those for which it is too late for intervention to have any appreciable chance of success (node 4). Figure 5.2 depicts these four situations as they are related to each other and to the more general tree. The basic question is whether, in the face of a nonmilitary problem which risks losing the client, the problem is due to a massive loss of political support. If not, then some type of emergency assistance is indicated: economic, if overt aid to the regime is politically possible; and covert political, if overt aid is out of the question.

Our procedure here and for the rest of this and the next chapter will be to present each node, explain its logic, and give one or more detailed historical examples of that kind of intervention situation. Other detailed examples will be mentioned in the text and can be found on the book's website. Still other examples are mentioned briefly in the endnotes to this and the next chapter. A list of all the examples for each node is presented at the start of the node.

Emergency economic assistance: Node 1

> Dominican Republic (1908: text); Nicaragua (1911: text); El Salvador (1921: text); Cuba (1922: text); Dominican Republic (1922 and after: text); Italy (1946–48: text); France (1946–48: text); Mexico (1994–95: text); Turkey (2001: website); Brazil (2002: website)

We saw in Chapter 4 that routine client maintenance for less wealthy clients usually includes a transfer of financial resources in the form of different types of grants and

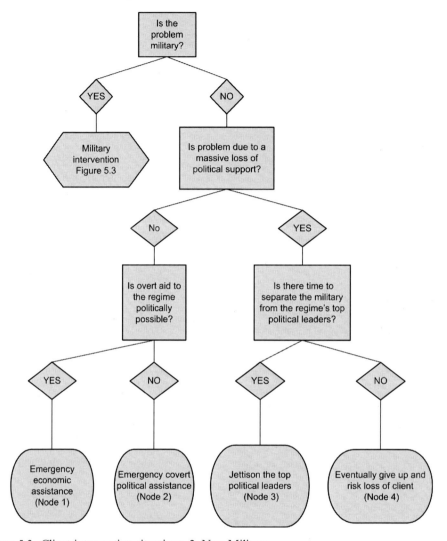

Figure 5.2   Client intervention situations, 2: Non-Military

loans. These transfers are typically programmed with a long lead time: for example, bilateral development assistance funds for a given fiscal year are requested by the president in January in the budget he submits to Congress; if approved on time, the funds will be disbursed starting in October and stretching to the following September. The prospect of a regime falling from power, however, requires a considerably more expedited procedure: if the problem is financial, such as a possible default that might result in the regime's being unable to pay the armed forces or supply them with weapons, then the U.S. will quickly have to take over the regime's debt payments or other obligations.

In the early days of the client state empire, this takeover involved emergency loans or other financial arrangements, more often than not made by Wall Street banks, whether individually or in consortia. We have already discussed in Chapter 3 how the acquisition of the Dominican Republic and El Salvador revolved around a customs arrangement in the first case and a loan in the second, with the regimes in both countries facing imminent threats (from European creditors and from domestic opponents, respectively). Emergency loans were also made after states in the region had become clients. For example, in Cuba, less-than-clean elections in the early 1920s left the new president facing a depleted treasury and an inability to pay the basic wages needed to keep the government functioning and him in power. A loan of $50 million was arranged by J.P. Morgan and Company, with the explicit approval of the State Department and promises by the Cubans to carry out various reforms. Around the same time, in the Dominican Republic, as U.S. military withdrawal approached, American diplomats were concerned that a new Dominican government would need emergency funds if it were to have a chance to survive. Five New York banks bid on, and provided, a loan of $10 million.[5]

On occasion, emergency loans could be made by the U.S. government itself. An example of this concerns Nicaragua, with whom the Taft Administration had negotiated the Chamorro-Weitzel treaty providing for an exclusive U.S. option on a Nicaraguan canal route as well as basing and leasing rights, all these in ostensible exchange for providing the Nicaraguan government with an emergency $3 million loan. Interestingly, even after Taft left office and the populist William Jennings Bryan had succeeded the corporate lawyer Philander Knox as Secretary of State, the Wilson administration, at Bryan's urging, opted to support the treaty for fear that the Díaz government would fall and instability ensue.[6]

By the later 1930s, the U.S. had begun to rely more and more heavily on government funds rather than private capital as a source of emergency loans. One instrument for this was the Exchange Stabilization Fund (ESF), controlled by the Treasury Department and created in 1934. The initial idea behind the Fund was to stabilize the exchange value of the dollar; however, within a few years, it had begun to be used for lending dollars to poorer countries (most of them U.S. clients, many in Latin America) on a short-term basis, although most of those loans were not prompted by fears of client regime collapse. Mexico was the first country for which emergency ESF arrangements were made, and for many years thereafter, it, and to a lesser degree other Latin American countries, were the principal objects of ESF solicitude (in 1976, the UK also received a large loan). However, the first use of the ESF for interventionary purposes – occasioned precisely by concerns over the political survival of the regime – did not take place until the Mexican financial rescue of 1995 (see below).[7]

The 1940s saw two other mechanisms created for providing emergency loans. One of these mechanisms, the Marshall Plan, was time-and-place specific; the other, the IMF, is still very much with us today. In Chapter 3, we discussed the importance of the Marshall Plan as a means of client acquisition in the context of postwar planning and as a means of providing surveillance and control through the use of counterpart funds. However, it is worth recalling that the Plan was put forward in a situation perceived as one of "crisis" in several European countries, notably France and Italy, where the economic distress was considered so grave as to raise the spectre of communist government, whether by elections or as a result of a general strike. Both France and Italy were major recipients of Marshall Plan aid; in the nearly 12 months between Marshall's speech and when Congress finally passed the necessary legislation, both countries also received emergency aid from Washington.[8]

The mechanism still around today is the International Monetary Fund (IMF). This institution, one of whose creators was the same official (Harry Dexter White) who first used the ESF for emergency loans, had from the beginning as one of its central missions the provision of foreign exchange in financial crises. There have of course been many such crises over the past half-century and the IMF, in which the U.S. plays a preponderant role (the number two official is American and a high percentage of the staff are either U.S. citizens or trained in the U.S.; the U.S. also exercises enormous influence on policy decisions), has regularly helped U.S. clients and kept funds out of the hands of U.S. enemies. In the same way as the multilateral development institutions discussed in Chapter 4, the IMF permits the U.S. to mobilize the resources of other countries, with a multiplier of around six times the current U.S. contribution. The IMF also carries out what it calls "surveillance" of the economic situation in member countries, thereby permitting performance to be assessed and problems anticipated (in theory) in a way which may be politically more palatable than if done by the U.S.

The Mexican financial rescue of 1995 exemplifies nicely the policy instruments invented in the 1930s and 1940s. By 1994, Mexico had liberalized its investment and trade policies; this led to an increase in exports but an even greater increase in imports. Private capital inflows had gone up, but most of this took the form of portfolio investments which could easily be sold off if investors got frightened. They did, due to a series of political shocks: armed attacks by a guerrilla movement in the state of Chiapas; the kidnappings of two prominent businessmen; and the assassinations of the ruling party's presidential candidate and secretary general. Money began to flow out of the country and the U.S., which had been closely monitoring the situation, gave increasingly urgent advice to Mexican officials while also putting together a series of short-term swap arrangements to support the peso. The situation only got worse and, on the advice of the secretary of the treasury, President Clinton proposed a $40 billion loan guarantee package for Mexico (with another $8 billion from the IMF), modeled after a similar package (a quarter the size) approved by Congress for Israel in 1992. In spite of backing by the Republican leadership in Congress, legislators balked and, with Mexico facing imminent bankruptcy, something that the national security adviser saw as "terribly threatening to the Zedillo government" and that the secretary of state saw as unleashing "a very serious government crisis in Mexico" with potential repercussions in the U.S. and elsewhere, Clinton finally ordered the ESF to provide a total of $20 billion in short-term swaps, medium-term loans, and long-term securities guarantees; in addition, the IMF agreed to increase the size of its standby credit arrangement for Mexico by another $10 billion, the Bank for International Settlements (an organization of central banks) by another $5 billion, and the Bank of Canada to deliver on its earlier pledge of $1 billion. The total amount of money thus mobilized by the U.S. on Mexico's behalf was $48.8 billion.[9]

The Mexican bailout, as it came to be called, illustrated the extent to which the U.S. was willing to intervene on behalf of a client regime. Not only were the amounts of U.S. funds considerable and agreed on in a matter of hours, but massive pressure was applied to mobilize far larger contributions from multilateral lending institutions than was common, thereby leading to some grumbling by states such as Germany and the U.K. Hence, when the next round of financial crises hit, starting in 1997, the U.S. reverted to a more orthodox role, especially since none of the American client states being rescued were perceived to run serious risks of the regime losing power. However, in 2001 and 2002, the U.S. was alarmed enough about Brazil and Turkey to intervene financially in both countries (these cases, and the lower-key reaction to other financial crises, are discussed on the book's website).

Emergency covert political assistance: Node 2

Italy (1946–48: text); Bolivia (1963–64: text); Chile (1964: text); Guyana (1964: text); El Salvador (1982–84: text); Afghanistan (2004: text)

However embarrassing or intrusive financial rescues may be, they usually are considered as responses to a complex set of events for which responsibility is widely diffused. Thus, there is no compelling reason for a regime to keep secret the fact that a rescue took place, even if it might not want to disclose the specific details of the agreement. Other types of regime threats, though, are more sensitive, and the mere fact that those threats were combated by outside aid is by tacit agreement a secret on both the client and the U.S. side. Indeed, as we shall see, the client's regime may not even be told of some of the U.S. programs put in place to help it survive. This typically was the case when client regimes faced elections which the U.S. feared they would lose: one way of helping them was to pass out money on their behalf, something too delicate to reveal to the beneficiaries of this largesse.

We saw in Chapter 4 how, as a matter of routine, the CIA transfers financial resources to various organizations and individuals in regimes it supports. The capacity to carry out these kinds of operations was in fact built up in a situation of real panic in which U.S. officials feared the imminent loss of a newly-acquired client, Italy. From mid-1946, Italy had a coalition which included the Communists; as the economy declined, popular unrest grew and the principal noncommunist party, the Christian Democrats, suffered a major loss in local elections. U.S. officials became concerned about the prospects of a political takeover by the Communists and, over the next few months moved to give economic aid to the regime and to encourage the prime minister, Alcide De Gasperi, to evict the Communists from the coalition. When he did so, the U.S. backed him in the face of Communist outrage and increasing economic and political turmoil, with Truman going so far as to call Congress back into session to pass emergency funding for Italy (and France) a good six months before it enacted the Marshall Plan legislation. The National Security Council proclaimed that the U.S. had "security interests of primary importance in Italy" and called for action "without delay" to prevent or at the least plan for the possibility of the Communists coming to power in the scheduled 1948 elections, something that Truman did by delaying to the last possible second the withdrawal of U.S. troops from Italy and by circumventing the law to transfer weapons from the U.S. Army to the Italians.[10]

In the meantime, the U.S. was in the middle of a set of major changes in the areas of intelligence gathering and covert operations. At the end of World War II, Truman had dissolved the Office of Strategic Services (OSS), the agency responsible for coordinating and carrying out those activities, which had been created shortly before the U.S. entered the war. The branch of the OSS responsible for "secret intelligence and counterespionage" was transferred to the War Department, but, some months later, after Truman had decided to constitute a Central Intelligence Group, it was transferred again to that organization and renamed as the Office of Special Operations (OSO). There matters remained through the rest of 1947, during which time Congress passed the landmark National Security Act, which established an independent Air Force and a coordinating group of military leaders, the Joint Chiefs of Staff; merged the War and Navy Departments into the Department of Defense; set up the National Security Council; and transformed the Central Intelligence Group into the Central Intelligence Agency. During this time, the idea of what was then called "psychological warfare" – essentially, propaganda, both overt and covert – began to develop. There was concern that the Soviet Union was "conducting an intensive propaganda campaign" against the U.S. "designed to undermine non-Communist elements in all countries." The U.S., it was argued, should come up with counterpropaganda, with this task devolved upon the State Department. This proposal was resisted by the Secretary of State on the ground that the commingling of covert and overt activities would serve to discredit the latter. Instead, a compromise was put forward in which covert activities would be placed under the CIA but subject to guidance from the State Department and other agencies. In turn, the CIA assigned responsibility for covert propaganda to the only administrative unit in the agency having both experience in and capabilities for carrying out such activities: the OSO. Within a few days, the OSO had set up a Special Procedures Branch (later known as Special Procedures Group: SPG) to execute this order.[11]

The flurry of activity leading to the SPG's establishment climaxed as U.S. concern over the impending Italian elections was growing. Accordingly, of the $20 million in unvouchered funds (i.e., money which would not be accounted for to Congress) given to SPG, half went for operations in Italy. Since there was no time to lose, it was out of the question to ask that a special budget supplement be passed by Congress; nor were there as yet any Marshall Plan counterpart funds. Hence the SPG was given "bags of money" for its Italian operations from the Treasury's ESF. The money was used for a wide array of activities: assistance to non-Communist political parties, trade unions linked to them, local political leaders, the Roman Catholic Church (including payments to the cardinal who later would become Pope Paul VI), journalists, and other writers. In the end, the Communists lost the elections, although just what the effect of the SPG's activities were is difficult to determine. As we saw in Chapter 4, even after the emergency passed, payments continued for almost two decades.[12]

The CIA's intervention in the Italian elections of 1948 set the pattern for a series of such operations in many countries and for many years. Most of these cases were what we earlier characterized as routine maintenance: the covert supply of funds to support individuals or groups in client regimes. In some cases, however, U.S. officials were concerned that elections and demonstrations might lead to a radical shift in power and thus to the loss of those clients. These circumstances led to the same kind of large-scale action program as in Italy in 1948, with both overt and covert components. One example of this is Bolivia, where the U.S. gave covert subsidies to the incumbent president "to overcome the emergency situation" in 1963–64, and to the junta which succeeded him in 1965–66 "as the only apparent feasible alternative for the time being to chaos and the eventual dominance of extremist groups." Another example is Chile, in which the U.S., concerned that the "extreme leftist" Salvador Allende might win the presidential election of 1964, supplied considerable covert political funding to Allende's opponents, both its preferred candidate and a spoiler who was seen as drawing votes from Allende (see below for the U.S. reaction to the following election). Still another example is Guyana, where, as we saw in Chapter 3 and will further discuss below, the U.S. carried out covert action that destabilized the government of Cheddi Jagan and when the British had been persuaded to change the electoral rules, led to his defeat in the 1964 elections. Several years later, the Jagan forces were still strong and U.S. officials remained concerned that if they were to win the next election, it "would be disastrous for Guyana, would prove a dangerous stimulus to Castro, and would introduce an unacceptable degree of instability into the Caribbean area." As a result, the CIA provided the incumbent prime minister with covert political funding.[13]

By definition, covert political support, whether routine or emergency, is difficult to verify. We know about the three Western Hemisphere examples above because of recently published volumes in the *Foreign Relations of the United States* series, for which the State Department's historians obtained CIA documents. At the time of this writing, that series had just begun to cover the early years of the 1970s, and so any knowledge of more recent covert political actions has had to come from press leaks or scandal investigations. An example of the former is the U.S. support of the Christian Democrats in the El Salvador elections of 1982 and 1984. In that case, the concern was not that leftists might come to power but that extreme rightists would, an eventuality that threatened to endanger political backing for the U.S.-led counterinsurgency war. Accordingly, the CIA spent several million dollars, some of it passed circuitously through foundations in West Germany and Venezuela. A post-cold war example is Afghanistan, where evidence is that the U.S. passed money to local warlords to support its preferred candidate, Hamid Karzai, during the 2004 presidential elections. Apparently plans were also made, though not implemented, to support anti-Iran candidates in Iraq's 2005 elections. In short, emergency covert political assistance appears to be one of the policy instruments most frequently resorted to for maintaining clients by intervention.[14]

Jettisoning the president: Node 3

South Korea (1960: text); Philippines (1986: text); Haiti (1986: text); Indonesia (1998: text)

For most client states in which regimes might fall from power, the U.S. has policy instruments permitting a takeover of one or more of the regimes' essential activities. In the case of nonmilitary problems, money can be found for both emergency loans and covert political support. However, when the problem is a massive loss of political support in which the public takes to the streets to demand the regime's overthrow, it becomes far more difficult for the U.S. to respond. The essential activity for the regime is then a matter of maintaining the military or other security forces until such time as the crowd can be appeased (for example, by jettisoning the president or other hated members of the regime). This is exactly what happened when the U.S. pushed Syngman Rhee to resign as president of South Korea in 1960, after rigged elections and years of autocratic rule had led to large-scale and repeated popular demonstrations.[15]

A more recent example, with an even longer-serving president, is that of the Philippines. By the 1980s, the country had been a valued U.S. client for decades. It harbored several massive American military bases that served to project U.S. power throughout Southeast Asia. Politically, the Philippines had helped provide a multilateral fig leaf for U.S. military intervention in Vietnam, sending (for a handsome fee) 2,000 soldiers to fight alongside the U.S. More generally, the Philippines, as a former U.S. colony, was a client for whom officials in Washington felt particularly responsible. It was against this backdrop that the long-time dictator, Ferdinand Marcos, found himself confronted by mass political protest.

In the early 1980s, about a year and a half after then-Vice President George H.W. Bush proclaimed to Marcos that "we love your adherence to democratic principles," the principal Philippine opposition figure, Benigno Aquino, was assassinated by a mechanic working for the country's military. This triggered a massive outpouring of public opposition to Marcos: a million people participated in Aquino's funeral and at regular intervals thereafter, huge numbers poured into the streets for demonstrations and other mass gatherings. In the meantime, the communist New People's Army, which for years had been carrying out an insurgency, grew in strength. U.S. officials began to worry that Marcos was "the problem, not the solution," and pushed, in vain, for him to reform, going so far as to send a close political ally of Reagan's, Senator Paul Laxalt, to convey this message in person. Instead, Marcos called a snap election for 7 February 1986, expecting to confront Washington with evidence of his legitimacy. The plan backfired, as Aquino's widow, Corazon (Cory), was persuaded to present herself as the principal opposition candidate. Cory was overwhelmingly popular, mobilizing enormous crowds and gaining support as well from segments of the Philippines economic elite, the U.S. mass media, and even some U.S. officials. To win, Marcos had to stuff the ballot boxes, but he did so in such a clumsy and blatant fashion that no one – with the exception of Reagan – was fooled.

At this point, high-level State Department officials decided that Marcos had to go. Their problem was to convince Reagan, since Marcos knew well that otherwise he could hang on to power. A special envoy was sent; but then events took a sudden turn: on 16 February Cory Aquino declared victory and launched a nationwide nonviolent protest ("people power") to bring down the regime; on 19 February the U.S. Senate voted 85 to 9 to declare the election fraudulent; and on 20 February the Philippines defense minister and one of the top generals resigned and established themselves at a military base on the outskirts of Manila where they told their forces to disobey any orders from Marcos. Troops loyal to Marcos tried to assault the rebel forces but were turned back by crowds of Aquino supporters protecting them. Finally, on 23 February, Shultz and his allies succeeded in convincing Reagan to tell Marcos not to use force against the rebels and to establish a transition government. The next day, the White House stated that "attempts to prolong the present regime by violence are futile." Marcos, desperate, telephoned Laxalt, who told him that he should "cut and cut cleanly." That evening, a U.S. Air Force plane transported him to the U.S. territory of Guam.[16]

The policy the U.S. adopted in the Philippines did not appear out of thin air. Just two weeks before, an even older U.S. client, Haiti, found itself in a similar situation. In the late 1950s, François "Papa Doc" Duvalier had seized power; after some disgruntlement, the U.S. accommodated itself to his rule, which lasted until his death in 1971. His son, Jean-Claude ("Baby Doc") then took over and the U.S. continued its support. But in late 1985, riots broke out in the town of Gonaives and spread to other cities; after only two months, the U.S. decided to cut off budgetary support to the government and began sending signals that Duvalier's days were numbered. By 7 February 1986, Baby Doc was on a U.S. Air Force plane on his way to Paris and a military council was in charge. A similar situation arose some dozen years later in Indonesia, where the U.S., after staunchly backing long-time dictator Suharto (although extracting concessions in exchange for IMF loans), finally disengaged from him in the face of continuing student protests. Suharto's own allies, worried that the military might split and the regime collapse, pressured him into ceding power to his vice president.[17]

Losing the client: Node 4

Iran (1978–79: text)

In both Haiti and the Philippines, the Reagan administration's policy makers acted in painful awareness that if they were to wait too long, the risk was that the armed forces would disintegrate, with the U.S. then being faced with the choice of either large-scale armed intervention or else giving up and risking the loss of the client. This is exactly what happened in the case of Iran in 1978.

As we saw in Chapters 3 and 4, the CIA-assisted coup against Mossadeq in 1953 led to Iran's becoming a U.S. client state, with considerable resources being invested by the U.S. in building up the shah's regime. By the early 1970s, the U.S had come to rely on Iran as a regional policeman, the shah providing overt and covert military support for U.S. objectives in the area, selling – albeit at a high price – oil to the U.S. and Israel in the face of short-term or long-term Arab boycotts, and purchasing over $40 billion worth of sophisticated U.S. armaments. Both Republican and Democratic U.S. presidents staunchly supported the shah, appointing high-level, trusted officials as ambassador to Iran and brushing aside accusations of human rights abuses from the U.S.-trained security services. Thus, when protests against the regime broke out in early 1978, the first U.S. reaction was to urge the shah to crack down on the opposition.

Repression, however, failed, and as time went by, street demonstrations became larger and more far reaching in their aims. By the autumn of 1978, the U.S. ambassador, William Sullivan, was writing that the time had come to start contingency planning for a post-shah Iran, with the focus being on preserving a strong, pro-American military. To this end, he argued, the U.S. should explore having the younger officers in the military make contacts with the religious opposition and noncommunist political figures so that, "should this unthinkable contingency [i.e., the shah abdicating] occur," the military would have a chance of prevailing. Other, mid-level State officials went farther, advocating that the U.S. should simply force the shah out of power. These views, though, were not accepted, in part because Carter and his top advisers did not believe that the shah could not hold on and in part because they thought that his departure might open the door to communist influence in Iran, would dishearten other U.S. allies, and could result in chaos in the petroleum markets. But as one high-level envoy after another visited Iran, their reports made it harder for Carter to maintain his position. Finally, Sullivan was ordered to meet with the shah and counsel him strongly to establish a government capable of maintaining order, if need be a military government. The shah, though, rejected this as unfeasible, instead holding to his earlier decision to set up a civilian coalition to run the country.

For Carter's advisers, the shah's refusal to go along with the U.S. recommendations was a sign that he no longer could be relied on and the decision was made to urge him to leave Iran. The U.S. would back the civilian government but would also send a top general to urge his Iranian counterparts to stick together and make contingency plans for a takeover if need be. Carter's national security adviser, in fact, wanted him to urge the military to stage a coup. However, by this time the Iranian military was falling apart, with the U.S. general quoting desertion rates of 500 to 1000 per day and the army leadership demoralized and without plans. The Ayatollah Khomeini was able to return from exile and set up a provisional government without the military doing anything to stop him; under these circumstances, the U.S. was reduced to issuing statements in support of the other, shah-appointed coalition government and encouraging vaguely the military to support it. Several days later, the last act took place: an air force unit rebelled against the coalition government, receiving support from other parts of the military as well as from revolutionary militia backing Khomeini. Whatever thoughts Carter's hardliners had about a military government now evaporated, as it became clear that the only slight chance of this happening would for the U.S. to send troops to the middle of

Teheran. At this point Washington bowed to the inevitable, announcing it would work with the Khomeini-appointed government; a U.S. defense attaché in Teheran cabled, "Army surrenders; Khomeini wins. Destroying all classified."[18]

Military intervention situations

Although the vast majority of the problems faced by U.S. client regimes are non-military, the story is different when it comes to problems that threaten the loss of those regimes. Since the early days of the U.S. empire, a number of its clients have faced armed insurgencies. Although many of those rebellions were easily repressed or contained, Washington could not be so sanguine as the fighting was occurring and thus considered intervening in one way or another. In some cases, the threatened regimes were not clients at the time of the crisis and, as we saw in Chapter 3, the U.S. adopted those states as clients precisely in order to protect the regimes. In other circumstances, insurgencies arose in existing clients and the U.S. was led to intervene on their behalf.

By our count, just over half of all U.S. clients experienced, at least once, either a military rebellion or a prolonged terrorist campaign directed against the regime (see Table 5.1).[19] The countries in this category can be found on every continent and range in time from 1906 (Cuba) to 2008 (Iraq, Afghanistan, Israel, Colombia, Ethiopia, the Philippines, and Indonesia). In slightly more than half of these countries, at least one of the uprisings was responded to by U.S. military interventions in our use of the term (the taking over of military tasks essential to a regime's survival, anywhere from the emergency furnishing of arms and training to large-scale bombing and ground combat). Not surprisingly, such interventions were most common in poorer countries or those with relatively weak militaries; we will come back to this point below. For the most part, the interventions were also successful in preserving the regimes, though often at a terribly high price in money and lives on all sides and, as we will see, with some flagrant exceptions.

Situations of military intervention can be divided into several categories, again using the pseudo-decision tree approach (see Figure 5.3). The first question that needs to be asked about military problems is whether or not the client regime can hold on long enough to make a difference. If not, then nothing can be done; otherwise, the issue becomes whether the client has sufficient manpower to counter the insurgency on its own. A yes answer indicates the need for emergency military aid and advisers (node 5); a no answer, presuming that there are no troops already committed (see below) raises the possibility of sending troops, whether from the U.S. or a proxy. To determine where those troops will have to be from and what their mission will be, two other questions need to be asked: whether the client's military is competent, and, for either possible answer, whether the enemy forces are formidable as well.

Emergency military aid and advisers: Node 5

> China (1943–49: text); Greece (1947–48; website); Philippines (1950: website); France-Indochina (1950–54: text); South Vietnam (1961–74: text); El Salvador (1980–92: text); Colombia (2000–present: text); Pakistan (2001–present: text)

One of the most common and low-cost types of military intervention involves the emergency use of military advisers and equipment. We saw in Chapter 4 that

Table 5.1 U.S. Clients having experienced at least one rebellion*

Clients	US military intervention
Cuba	Yes
Haiti	Yes
Dominican Republic	Yes
Trinidad and Tobago	No
Mexico	No
Guatemala	No
Nicaragua	Yes
El Salvador	Yes
Costa Rica	No
Honduras	Yes
Panama	Yes
Canada	No
Bolivia	No
Peru	No
Ecuador	No
Colombia	Yes
Argentina	No
Uruguay	No
Paraguay	No
Guyana	No
Greece	Yes
Turkey	No
Bosnia-Herzegovina	No
Macedonia	No
Spain	No
UK (Northern Ireland)	No
Italy	No
Germany	No
France	No
Lebanon	Yes
Tunisia	No
Jordan	No
Israel	No
Iraq	Yes
Ethiopia	No
Liberia	Yes
Congo/Zaire	Yes
Ghana (inter-ethnic)	No
China	Yes
Philippines	Yes
South Vietnam	Yes
Laos	Yes
Thailand	No
Cambodia	Yes
Pakistan	Yes
Indonesia	No
Afghanistan	Yes
South Korea	Yes

Sources: Sarkees (2000); Eriksson and Wallensteen (2004); Wars of the World (2003), as per note 19.
Note: * One or more rebellions against the regime either when the state was already a U.S. client or which, as a result of the U.S. response to the rebellion, became a client; rebellions do not include *coups d'état* but do include sustained campaigns of terror.

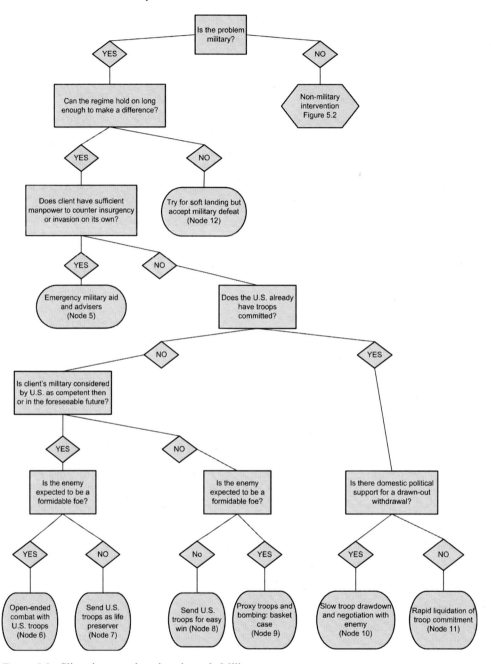

Figure 5.3 Client intervention situations, 3: Military

nonemergency military assistance is an important form of routine client maintenance; what distinguishes emergency aid is the fact that the U.S. is not only providing resources but in fact taking over essential tasks that the client had until then been performing. One such task is the preparation of specific units for combat, with the units ranging in size from battalions up to corps. Routine training, of the sort covered by the

IMET program discussed in Chapter 4, focuses on individual soldiers; by contrast, emergency training aims, minimally, at preparing units for imminent combat. Emergency training may also involve advice, if not de facto command, during field and combat operations. Clearly, for regimes facing insurgencies, these are essential tasks, and it is usually only a U.S. assessment that the client's armed forces are badly led or grossly incompetent that triggers emergency training.

The other main component of emergency aid is the furnishing of large quantities of combat equipment on an emergency basis. Most types of routine arms transfers may take years to be negotiated, financed, and delivered; at times, as we saw, the weapons are only produced once the order is confirmed. In effect, the arms are understood as a kind of insurance policy, to be drawn upon in case some type of crisis should break out. Insurgencies are such crises, and endangered regimes, in spite of whatever plans they may have, typically find themselves desperately short of certain kinds of weapons, ammunition, or other supplies (e.g., fuel). Under these circumstances, the U.S. response will be to ship quickly a broad array of weapons and other arms-related resources, always from existing U.S. stocks, with payment either being waived entirely or postponed until conditions improve. Note that when the client's military is deemed competent, only weapons will be shipped on an emergency basis; no advisers will be sent at all (this was the case, for example, during the 1973 October War, when the U.S. shipped "everything that will fly" to Israel).[20]

A classic example of emergency aid and advisers is the program set up by the U.S. in South Vietnam in the early 1960s. Several years earlier, following the U.S.-induced cancellation of Vietnam-wide elections and the increasingly exploitative and despotic rule of the South Vietnamese regime of Ngo Dinh Diem, the remnants of the Vietminh (the forces that had fought against the French in the 1940s and 1950s) pulled themselves together and began an insurgency against the regime. Soon, they had created a new military organization, the People's Liberation Armed Forces (PLAF) and were the object of a government-run counterinsurgency campaign. The United States, having essentially set up the state of South Vietnam from scratch with massive political and economic aid, was not about to let its client be lost, and the head of its military advisory group (MAAG) switched his planning focus from a North Vietnamese invasion to the PLAF insurgency. The MAAG's mean's were limited, however, and the plan it produced, centered on paying for additional South Vietnamese soldiers in exchange for administrative reforms, rapidly was overtaken by events. One was the perception that U.S. reverses in the spring of 1961 (the failure of the Bay of Pigs invasion, discussed in Chapter 6; and a decision to settle for a neutral, rather than pro-Western, Laos, discussed below) meant that a line had to be drawn somewhere; the other was an increase in PLAF attacks in September of 1961, with the result being a request by Diem for a defense treaty with the U.S. and the possible sending of U.S. troops.

Kennedy responded by sending two of his top aides to Saigon. They made two recommendations. The first, which was not accepted, was to send combat troops to the central plateau, partly for symbolic reasons and partly as a way of taking pressure off the South Vietnamese forces. The second recommendation, which was accepted and immediately implemented, was to provide a wide array of combat equipment to South Vietnam's various military units as well as

> such new terms of reference, reorganization and additional personnel for United
> States military forces as are required for increased United States military assistance

in the operational collaboration with the GVN [government of South Vietnam] and operational direction of U.S. forces and to carry out the other increased responsibilities which accrue to the U.S. military authorities under these recommendations.

What this meant was not only a large build-up in numbers of advisers (from 685 in April 1961 to 3,400 a year later; by the start of 1967, there were almost 7,000 advisers) but a lower-level focus on training: advisory teams for the South Vietnamese army at both the battalion and province level, as well as for the Civil Guard and the Self Defense Corps, which in fact was suffering the highest number of casualties. The MAAG was folded into a Military Advisory Command, Vietnam (MACV), which would be headed by a four-star general and, by October 1963, would comprise almost 17,000 U.S. troops. Soon, U.S. soldiers were advising their South Vietnamese counterparts on any number of tactical issues; in many cases, the advisers accompanied battalion commanders into the field and gave advice (by no means always heeded) during combat.

A sense of the intensity of the advisory relationship can be obtained in this account of the battle of Ap Bac on 2 January 1963. The principal U.S. adviser to the South Vietnamese battalion commander, Bui Dinh Dam, was John Paul Vann, who followed the battle from a spotter plane; his planner was Richard Ziegler, and James Scanlon was the adviser to the armored regiment, with Ly Tong Ba in command of a company of M-113 armored personnel carriers:

> While they were regaining altitude after the last pass, Scanlon came back on the air with bad news. "I've got a problem, Topper Six," he said. "My counterpart won't move." "Goddammit, doesn't he understand this is an emergency?" Vann asked. "I described the situation to him exactly as you told me, Topper Six, but he says, 'I don't take orders from Americans,'" Scanlon answered. "I'll get right back to you, Walrus," Vann said. He switched frequencies and raised Ziegler at the command-post tent beside the airstrip. He gave Ziegler a capsule account of what had occurred and told him to ask Dam to order Captain Ba to head for Bac immediately with his M-113s.

In addition to infantry advisers, MACV included air combat forces, the use of which could be triggered by the advisers. The U.S. Air Force provided both logistical services for the South Vietnamese military and unpublicized tactical air support (including the use of napalm) for combat operations in its Farmgate operations. Additional air support was provided by U.S. Army helicopter crews: during the battle of Ap Bac, for instance, U.S. helicopters strafed and rocketed PLAF positions, with no fewer than five of them being shot down. As the account of the battle suggests, although the policy of emergency aid and advisers enjoyed initial success, the combination of falsified U.S. intelligence, South Vietnamese military timidity (imposed by Diem for political reasons), and, above all, PLAF advantages (learning from mistakes and sufficient popularity to keep a constant flow of recruits) limited its effectiveness. Nonetheless, even after the U.S. began committing large numbers of its own troops for combat and, as we will see, during the period when those troops were being withdrawn (i.e., for at least another decade), it continued the emergency aid and advisory policy, which came to be seen as indispensable as long as the South Vietnamese armed forces were being counted on to fight.[21]

Vietnam was by no means the first case of emergency aid and advisers. The U.S. had been furnishing routine military assistance since early in the twentieth century, with at least one case (Cuba in 1924) of emergency weapons shipments.[22] But for these kinds of operations to be transformed into Vietnam-style actions capable of being carried out in distant countries simultaneously, it was necessary for the U.S. military to grow in size, along with its weapons stocks and logistical capacities. World War II spurred this growth, with Lend-Lease in particular serving as a means of building up arms transfer capacities. Thus, it is not surprising that the first cases of emergency aid and advisers, including the development of the MAAG machinery, date to the later part of the war and the immediate post-World War II period, when the U.S. was acquiring clients, including endangered ones, on a wholesale basis. One of these cases, discussed in Chapter 3 and also on the book's website, is Greece.

Another, less successful, effort, took place in China. As we saw in Chapter 3, the U.S. began military assistance to China during World War II, with U.S. officers "assigned to ground units to give operational advice on all levels and under all conditions, including active combat." When the war ended and it was clear that there would be a race between the forces of the Nationalist government and the Communists to receive the surrender of the Japanese in Manchuria and North China, the U.S. transported half a million Nationalist soldiers by air and sea to key sectors, while also sending U.S. marines to Beijing and other key areas until the Nationalist forces could arrive. In early 1946, Truman created a Military Advisory Group, which provided both training and advice (usually unheeded) to the military and the supreme leader, Chiang Kai-shek (Jiang Jieshi). (Toward the end, Chiang went so far as to request U.S. officers to assume operational command of Nationalist army units.) The U.S. also furnished vast quantities of weapons (including aircraft) and supplies to the Nationalists, equipping scores of divisions; although, due to the combination of Nationalist ineptitude and Communist competence, "much" of this equipment fell into Communist hands.[23]

It is worth noting that most of the cases of emergency military aid and advisers involved far more aid than advisers. Even the U.S. effort in South Vietnam did not, as we saw, exceed 7,000 advisers all told. This meant that it was possible to mount an emergency effort which would expose relatively few U.S. soldiers to hostile fire, thereby lessening political controversies raised by the possibility of the advisers being followed by U.S. combat troops. An early, but quite effective, demonstration of this is the emergency aid and advisory operation mounted by the U.S. in the Philippines (discussed on the book's website). Another example involving small numbers of advisers is that of the Reagan administration in El Salvador. The policy was in fact initiated under Reagan's predecessor, Jimmy Carter, who found himself confronted at the end of his term with a sudden offensive by the rebel Farabundo Martí Front for National Liberation (FMLN). Carter sent around $6 million in weapons and military supplies, an amount further increased by Reagan; by the next year, military aid had gone to $82 million and, by 1984, to $197 million, all this in a small country with a military of under 50,000 men. Aid included not only weapons for the infantry but an entire air capacity, including fighter planes, fixed-wing gunships, and attack helicopters. Meanwhile, a self-imposed restriction of 55 on the number of military advisers in El Salvador itself (because of fears of "another Vietnam") was circumvented in part by accounting tricks (adding numerous advisers on "temporary duty") and in part by forming and then training entire battalions (and half the country's officer corps) in the U.S., Panama, and a special training center built for this purpose in Honduras. As elsewhere, advisers in El Salvador were inserted from headquarters down to brigade levels, occasionally accompanying Salvadoran forces on combat missions.[24]

A more recent – indeed, ongoing – example of an emergency military aid and advisory effort involving relatively few advisers is the set of operations known as Plan Colombia. Since the mid-1970s, the U.S. had provided funds to Colombian police and security forces for narcotics control; but as cocaine production rose in Colombia and its neighbors, the U.S. began to increase its efforts. In the 1990s, Congress passed legislation giving the Defense Department authority to provide transportation, intelligence, and various kinds of equipment to foreign law enforcement agencies engaged in counter-narcotics efforts. But when violence continued to increase, with both narcotics traffickers and long-time insurgent forces facing off against Colombian government forces and paramilitary groups, the newly elected Colombia president proposed a comprehensive spending plan aimed at establishing peace through both development and counter-narcotics efforts. The U.S. enthusiastically signed onto the plan, while shifting its emphasis primarily in the counternarcotics direction. This was in July 2000, when Congress voted $1.3 billion for a region-wide Plan Colombia, with over $860 million set aside for Colombia itself and half of that amount in turn directed to be spent on setting up and organizing Colombian Army Counternarcotics Battalions, tasked with fumigating narcotics crops and dismantling cocaine laboratories.

This, however, was only the opening shot in an ever-intensifying campaign. Within a year, the Bush administration had folded Plan Colombia into a broader, Andean-wide policy; the following year, an additional justification – action against "terrorists" – was added; and the result was that between fiscal years 2000 and 2006, the U.S. spent $5.8 billion on Colombia alone, with around 80 percent of that funding being used for military and police assistance programs. In the meantime, the plan was transforming into a straightforward counterinsurgency effort: in August 2002, Congress permitted U.S. aid to be used for "counter-terrorist" activities, which in light of the designation of the two main leftist guerrilla groups as "narcoterrorists rather than romantic guerrillas crusading for the downtrodden," meant that the U.S. military was now back in the business of aiding and advising a war against domestic insurgents. By 2003, the U.S. embassy in Bogotá had 2,000 employees from 32 U.S. agencies and was the largest U.S. embassy in the world (the one in Baghdad recently surpassed it). In 2004, Congress raised the ceilings on U.S. defense-related personnel in Colombia, permitting up to 800 military advisers and 600 U.S. civilian government contractors (there is no limit on non-U.S. citizens employed by those contractors). Numerous battalions, comprising thousands of Colombian troops, were trained, while dozens of helicopters, attack aircraft, patrol boats, and other military equipment were shipped. U.S. civilian pilots, while fumigating crops, at times engaged in combat.[25]

It will be recalled that many types of political assistance, both routine and emergency, are too sensitive to be provided openly. Similarly, certain situations indicating emergency military aid and advisers are of equal sensitivity. In these cases, the U.S. operates through proxies or other third parties, a practice which, as we shall see, is also true of other military intervention situations, both on behalf of clients and against enemies. One example of aid to intermediaries is the policy the United States followed from 1950 to 1954 with respect to France's colonial war in Indochina. The U.S. shipped large quantities of weapons to the French, with aid running as high as $6 billion a year in 2008 dollars (for a detailed discussion, see the book's website).

In Indochina, the U.S. was constrained to operate through intermediaries. In recent years, however, new types of third parties have arisen in such a way that the U.S. can now use them as proxies when the politics of emergency aid and advisers are too delicate for overt bilateral action. Starting as early as the 1940s, but with faster growth in the 1980s and 1990s, a number of private military companies (PMCs) were formed, often comprising or even run by former professional soldiers. The companies garnered various sorts of contracts from defense ministries, covering any number of activities from construction and logistics to actual combat. A particularly important PMC activity is combat training, which, even if not terribly secret, affords sufficient deniability for states to avoid explicit condemnation. An example of this – ironically, much publicized after the fact – is the role of Military Professional Resources Incorporated (MPRI) in Croatia and Bosnia in 1994–95 (see Chapter 3 and, for a detailed discussion, the book's website).

Private military companies are also used in conjunction with overt programs of (emergency) aid and advisers. We saw this above in the case of Colombia; it also is true of Iraq where, in the autumn of 2007, over 160,000 PMC employees, working for hundreds of companies, were active. Among their ranks were a number of former soldiers whose job was to train the Iraqi army and security forces. One of the companies providing training services was the Vinnell Corporation, a subsidiary of the defense contractor Grumman; one of Vinnell's subcontractors, responsible for training Kurdish forces, was MPRI. A third company, DynCorp, whose employees flew helicopters in Colombia, was in charge of training the police.[26]

In addition to the proliferation of PMCs, recent years have also seen the development of another policy instrument as a way of providing emergency military aid and advisers. After the attacks of 11 September 2001, the U.S. stepped up its efforts to go after groups associated with Al-Qaeda. A major geographical focus of these efforts was the region of Pakistan bordering on Afghanistan and soon large quantities of weapons and cash began flooding into this area. All told, between September 2001 and August 2007, some $10.5 billion in total overt assistance was given to Pakistan, with the bulk of those funds going to support military operations and arms transfers. In addition, U.S. forces provided various forms of military training. Much of the funding for these activities was shoehorned into existing programs, a situation that both State and Defense found sufficiently unsatisfactory that they proposed setting up a specialized, permanent "Train and Equip" program to "act in months rather than years." In effect, the U.S. would give itself the standing ability to fly in and rapidly establish a MAAG for whatever new client was endangered.[27]

We have spent some time on the policy of emergency military aid and advisers. One reason for this is that the policy is often used. It is easy for a wealthy and populous country like the U.S. to supply large quantities of weapons and provide, directly or indirectly, the few hundred or, at most, few thousand advisers needed to train the client's military. At best, this policy enables the U.S. to support clients faced with military insurgencies without committing U.S. troops; but, as we saw with the Vietnam and Iraq examples, even when the U.S. does send troops, their number can be kept down by building up the client's military. However, there is also a theoretical reason for concentrating on this phenomenon. When providing aid and, even more, when furnishing training, the U.S. often works with clients whom it considers inept, corrupt, often dictatorial, and overly concerned with matters of sovereignty and national pride. The clients, in turn, find the U.S. insistence on efficiency and modern war-fighting techniques to be clumsy and politically tone-deaf. What results is a bureaucratized power relationship built around surveillance and fraught with all the resentments inherent in patron–client interactions. The policy of providing emergency aid and advisers thus illuminates some of the essential characteristics of a client-state empire.

Combat troops

Although U.S. officials have a strong preference for responding to insurgencies by sending emergency aid and advisers, there are circumstances in which the client simply does not have sufficient manpower to put down a rebellion or an invasion without outside troops. In these situations (and when the U.S. does not already have troops committed: see below), even though aid and advisers might be of great value, the U.S. will have to find some way of sending combat troops, whether its own or those of a proxy. The key question for determining the identity of those troops and their number is whether the client's military is considered by U.S. officials to be competent then or in the foreseeable future, i.e., capable of fighting a series of battles if well supplied, trained, and officered. If so, then one set of alternatives opens up, depending on whether the enemy is expected to be a formidable foe for U.S. troops (node 6) or, conversely, is not expected to be formidable (node 7). If, on the other hand, the client's military is considered incompetent, then other courses of action will be indicated, depending, again, on whether the enemy is assessed as formidable (node 8) or not (node 9). This gives us two pairs of alternatives.

Before discussing each of those combat nodes, it should be noted that the choice of a particular type of combat is fairly definitive. That is, once U.S. officials decide that it is necessary for U.S. forces or proxies to engage in ground combat, they do not "switch" to another type of combat. We will discuss the reasons for this below, after we have gone over each of the different nodes; but note for now that this feature of policy making places important constraints on the types of escalation considered if and when things go badly.

Competent clients: open-ended combat: Node 6

South Vietnam (1965–68: text)

For many years, the image that many people had of U.S. combat activities on behalf of client states was the ground war fought by American forces in South Vietnam between 1965 and 1973. That war had a profound effect on U.S. policy for years to come; as we shall see in Chapter 7, the "Vietnam syndrome" served for some years as a source of cautionary lessons on how and how not to conduct future wars. An impact of this sort is striking, not least because the ground war in which U.S. soldiers fought was practically unique among the century or so of combat operations against anti-client insurgents. This is because the situation in South Vietnam – a combination of a competent client and a formidable enemy – was responded to by a troop commitment seen in Washington as open-ended; and in no other client was there that type of situation and hence the need for that type of response.[28]

We saw above that in late 1961, the U.S. initiated a program of emergency aid and advisers for the regime in South Vietnam and that, for some time, this program succeeded in keeping the PLAF insurgency to a controllable level. However, as time went on, it became clear that the military situation in Vietnam was deteriorating and that time was "running out swiftly": the South Vietnamese military (ARVN) was "stretched to the limit" and needed an infusion of outside combat troops; North Vietnamese military units had entered South Vietnam; and the bombing campaign against North Vietnam (see Chapter 6) was having little effect. Accordingly, Johnson approved plans to place some 82,000 U.S. troops in "enclaves" (for example, at U.S. air bases) and have them go on combat patrols dozens of kilometers from the edge of the enclaves; they would be aided by the beginning of B-52 saturation bombing over South Vietnam. It was expected that these actions, aimed above all at "avoiding – for psychological and morale reasons – a spectacular defeat of GVN [Government of South Vietnam] or US forces," would take several years to "demonstrate VC [Viet Cong, the derogatory term used for the PLAF] failure in the South." In approving this policy, Johnson was aware that both one of his top advisers and a joint CIA-State-Defense assessment of the 82,000 troop plan had concluded that the insurgency would respond by simply "stepping up" its efforts.[29]

Within a month, the enclave troop commitments had been overtaken by events. The PLAF began attacking the South Vietnamese government forces (ARVN) in regimental-size units; by "early summer they were annihilating ARVN battalions as a blast furnace consumes coke." In response, the head of MACV and the secretary of defense put forward various plans for large, new troop deployments – 100,000 more in 1965 (in addition to the 82,000 already decided on), plus another 100,000 in 1966 – to take over, in essence, from the ARVN in two of the country's four provinces. Johnson had considerable trepidation about these proposals, fearing, along with his national security adviser and the number two official in the State Department, that U.S. troops, as "a white ground force of whatever size," would be incapable of fighting against guerrillas, that they risked ending up, after ever-greater troop commitments, like the French, and thus that the proposed deployments were "rash to the point of folly." However, there was general agreement that a failure to escalate would call into question the "integrity of the U.S. commitment"; if it became

> unreliable, the communist world would draw conclusions that would lead to our ruin and almost certainly to a catastrophic war. So long as the South Vietnamese are prepared to fight for themselves, we cannot abandon them without disaster to peace and to our interests throughout the world.

Thus, the proposals were accepted and the U.S. embarked on a policy that its leaders well knew could lead to huge numbers of U.S. troops in South Vietnam (at the peak, there were to be over half a million) and years of combat by those troops (they were to fight for seven years), not to mention considerable casualties (the final total would be some 50,000 U.S. deaths, a figure dwarfed by the two million or so Vietnamese who died).[30]

It may seem extraordinary that policy makers would knowingly enter into a war they considered open-ended and in which winning was very much an open question. In fact, though, this pessimism was a characteristic of U.S. officials' decisions about Vietnam practically from the start: again and again, presidents adopted courses of action that either they, or their leading advisers, or both, thought would fail to succeed in the long term. The short term, however, was another question. From the perspective of the White House, there were two disasters to avoid: all-out escalation, such as invading North Vietnam or using nuclear weapons, which could well lead to a Korean-style Chinese intervention (see below) or to a war with the Soviet Union; and a policy of staying put or pulling out, which would assuredly lead to the fall of the Saigon regime in short order and, it was feared, to another right-wing, McCarthy-style backlash such as befell the Democrats after the "loss" of China. Hence, even though the middle ground finally chosen (middle, of course, relative only to the alternatives, not in terms of the numbers of soldiers or deaths) was forecast as likely only to postpone defeat, that was good enough.[31]

Of course, as we saw above and will discuss in some detail later, the U.S. has at times opted to let a client be lost rather than to escalate. But to anticipate, the reason for this is that no organizationally feasible alternatives were seen as available in those situations. In South Vietnam, by contrast, U.S. officials saw themselves as capable of taking over some of the ARVN's tasks, at least against the PLAF; and the logic of commitment to a client meant that a failure to act on that capability would, as the quotation about "integrity" indicated, signify U.S. weakness. In the words of the assistant secretary of defense, U.S. aims in South Vietnam (SVN) were:

1 70% – To avoid a humiliating US defeat (to our reputation as a guarantor).
2 20% – To keep SVN (and then adjacent) territory from Chinese hands.
3 10% – To permit the people of SVN to enjoy a better, freer way of life.
4 ALSO – To emerge from crisis without unacceptable taint from methods used.
5 NOT – To "help a friend," although it would be hard to stay if asked out.

McNaughton continued:

> It is essential – however badly SEA [Southeast Asia] may go over the next 2–4 years – that US emerge as a "good doctor." We must have kept promises, been tough, taken risks, gotten bloodied, and hurt the enemy very badly.

This notion of the doctor whose responsibility is to get bloodied, presumably from his patient, goes a long way to accounting for the terrible interaction between patron–client relations and U.S. capabilities.[32]

Competent clients: life preserver: Node 7

> Panama (1904: note 37); Cuba (1912–13: note 37); Cuba (1917: note 37); Panama (1918: note 37); Panama (1925: note 37); Nicaragua (1927–33: text); South Korea (1950–51: text); Afghanistan (2003–present: text)

Another type of combat troop situation, more common than that which occurred in South Vietnam, is the combination of a competent (or soon to be competent) client and an enemy not anticipated to pose a problem for U.S troops. When policy makers in Washington see a given country as in this situation – whether or not that perception turns out to be accurate (see below) – they respond by sending enough troops to help out the client in its hour of need. Logically, that commitment is anything but open-ended: it does not involve an open spigot for U.S. troops nor does it presume that fighting will go on for more than a limited time (usually, between several months and a year at the most). An optimistic, perhaps a cocksure, attitude is typical; and this means, as we will see later, that if and when assumptions turn out to be incorrect, panic ensues.

A case in point is the initial U.S. decision to send troops for ground combat in South Korea. We saw in Chapter 3 that U.S. troops were put into the southern part of Korea originally to receive the Japanese surrender there; this led rapidly to the establishment of a regime which, because of its ties to large landlords and former collaborators of the Japanese, was highly unpopular with major segments of the population and hence had to rely heavily on U.S. support. For the next few years, uprisings and guerrilla insurgencies broke out in various parts of the south and were duly repressed by the new regime's forces, armed, trained, and advised (far more intrusively than later in South Vietnam) by the U.S. However, the U.S. presence in South Korea was both broader and deeper than this. In 1948, following elections held only in the south and acquiescence by the United Nations, South Korea became formally sovereign. Although the Pentagon, believing that the country was a geopolitical cul de sac, insisted on withdrawing U.S. troops, this was compensated for by a significant program of both military and economic aid, the latter administered through the Marshall Plan agency (ECA). By 1950, before the war broke out, South Korea contained the largest U.S. MAAG, the largest ECA aid mission, and the largest U.S. embassy. The U.S. ran major parts of the economy, provided around 2/3 of the government budget, and participated in decisions both major and mundane. At the same time, the U.S. kept a leash on the regime, controlling military aid to prevent it from invading the north and setting off a potentially major war.[33]

War, though, did come. Fighting broke out on 25 June 1950 (Korean time; the U.S. was a day behind), with the U.S. ambassador characterizing it as an "all-out offensive" by the North Koreans, a phrase repeated by Secretary of State Acheson in both a telegram and a phone call to Truman. Immediately, the situation was seen as a "clear-cut Soviet challenge which … US should answer firmly and swiftly as it constitutes direct threat our leadership of free world against Soviet Communist imperialism." The next evening, after the Security Council had condemned the fighting and called for North Korean withdrawal, Truman began a series of meetings that, by the end of the month, would eventuate in a decision to send ground troops to fight against the North Korean forces. (As we saw above, Truman also stepped up U.S. military aid in the Philippines and Indochina; in addition, he interposed the Seventh Fleet between Taiwan and mainland China, thereby saving Nationalist forces in the former and preventing them from offensive operations against the latter.) Initially, it was thought that the South Korean (ROK) army would be able to hold on with only added ammunition and supplies, but by the end of the week, even after U.S. air power had begun to be used, ROK effectives were so disorganized and demoralized that, in order to be sure of holding the air-head through which they were being resupplied, General MacArthur advocated sending a regimental combat team (around 3,000 men) and, to build up "for an early counter-offensive," two divisions (20,000 men) as well.[34]

At this point, the crisis atmosphere suddenly lifted. The day after the troop commitment was announced, the U.S. ambassador reported that ROK forces "held their ground well," with "steadying effects" being attributed to U.S. air attacks and the announcement that U.S. ground forces were on their way. Although the South Koreans continued retreating and only a small number of U.S. troops had yet been deployed, the National Security Council cut down sharply on the number and extent of its meetings about Korea. On 7 July, at a time when he had less than 800 troops in combat, MacArthur was already planning a counteroffensive. Within ten days, at a time when U.S. forces were still arriving in Korea (by the start of August there would be 47,000), Truman had set the bureaucracy to work on what policy "should be pursued by the United States after the North Korean forces have been driven back to the 38th parallel." By 7 September, before MacArthur had even launched his counteroffensive at Inchon, it had been decided that the parallel would be crossed, North Korea occupied, and the peninsula reunified. All of these decisions clearly show that U.S. political and military leaders had no doubt that North Korean forces would easily be overcome and that the principal stakes were geopolitical: to rescue a U.S. client and thereby preserve U.S. credibility. As for Chinese forces, which soon would wreak havoc on U.S. troops, leaders were almost as confident. Truman's decision to cross the 38th parallel made it clear that if the Soviet Union committed forces, MacArthur should act defensively; but if the Chinese were to come in (an eventuality seen as unlikely), he should continue fighting unless it appeared that a general war would break out. MacArthur in fact was not only supremely confident, predicting that "formal resistance" would be ended by late November and that he might be able to withdraw over half his forces by Christmas, but also contemptuous of Chinese power, stating that if China were to intervene "there would be the greatest slaughter" and planning a post-combat ten-division Korean army that, by itself, would be "a tremendous deterrent to the Chinese Communists moving south." In short, up until the moment of Chinese intervention in November, U.S. officials (with rare exceptions) saw the war as much more a test of U.S. will than of serious military challenge.[35]

Although MacArthur may have been extreme in his rhetoric, the discussion above shows clearly that he was part of a broad consensus that the war would not be open-ended in terms of either time or force deployments. (Indeed, as the counteroffensive was proceeding, Acheson was closeted for weeks with his European counterparts, working out plans to send additional troops to NATO rather than to Korea.) That consensus, which extended to a number of U.S. allies, did not downplay the massive commitment that would be required if the Soviet Union or China were to enter the war on a large scale – MacArthur's orders were to stay south of the 38th parallel if either state occupied North Korea beforehand – but estimated that the chances of such intervention were fairly low. The reason for this confidence, as best we can ascertain, is that the U.S. and its allies assumed that both the Soviets and the Chinese would understand that there were no U.S. designs on either country and that war aims did not extend beyond eliminating North Korea as an independent state. That is why, in the several weeks that passed between the initial deployment of Chinese forces and the large-scale assault in late November, there were repeated discussions in Washington and elsewhere about how to convey to the Chinese that the Yalu would not be crossed and China not attacked. Such reassurances missed the point, which was that China, in whose army 100,000 North Koreans had fought, could not let North Korea disappear without suffering a serious blow to its credibility, especially at a time when it was not even allowed to be seated in the UN. To most Americans and Europeans, the idea that China, a figure of ridicule under Chiang Kai-shek, could have Great Power concerns over credibility and prestige, was ludicrous; only the handful of China experts in Washington (who were later fired for their pains) and officials in countries such as India and Burma, as befitting newly independent and ferociously anticolonialist states, grasped this.[36]

U.S. actions in Korea are the classic example of the use of combat troops as a life preserver until the client can be built up. Another example, of far more limited scope, was the war carried out by the U.S. marines in Nicaragua in the early 1930s (this is certainly the most widely known of numerous other life preserver interventions in the region[37]). As we saw in Chapter 3, Nicaragua became a U.S. client in 1910, when marines intervened on behalf of a revolt against the government, then, two years later, put down a rebellion against the U.S.-backed president. The limits of political action having been made clear, the marine detachment was reduced to around one hundred men, who were stationed at the U.S. Legation in Managua for the next thirteen years. This, however, was too thin a reed for long-term stability and so, after several abortive efforts, the

State Department and banks in New York finally managed to work out a series of financial arrangements in which customs receipts and government spending would be subject to U.S. control. The next problem dealt with was the electoral system, the U.S. dispatching a political science professor to write a bill (duly enshrined in law by the Nicaraguan Congress) which made elections slightly less corrupt, thereby supposedly reducing the chances that the losing side would take up arms against the government. Finally, the U.S. proposed setting up a constabulary, the National Guard, which would have as its principal task the maintenance of domestic order. Rapidly, the Nicaraguan Congress ratified this decision and in June 1925 the government arranged with a retired U.S. Army major to train the new force. Two months later, the marines sailed for home.

Almost immediately, chaos broke out. After numerous twists and turns, it became a full-fledged civil war, with the U.S. recognizing one side as the legitimate government while claiming to have "the most conclusive evidence" that the other side was being armed by the U.S. bête noire, Mexico. The day after the U.S. accorded recognition, a consortium of U.S. banks made an emergency loan to the government; this was followed by arms sales, bombing of insurgent positions by former U.S. Army pilots in Nicaraguan planes, and the deployment of U.S. marines, over 5,000 of them by February. This policy, which was in effect a scaled-up version of what the U.S. had been doing in Nicaragua over the preceding decade, led to an almost-immediate freezing of the situation. Coolidge's actions, though, were criticized strongly in the U.S. and Latin America as one-sided and so, in April, the White House sent a special envoy with a peace plan that included additional measures from the past: disarmament by both sides (this would benefit chiefly the government forces); the creation of a National Guard, this time to be commanded (not simply trained) by an active-duty (not retired) U.S. officer; and elections to be supervised by the large contingent of marines then in the country.

Although most of the belligerents agreed to this plan, one of them, Augusto Sandino, did not. What followed was a nasty little war in which the marines, now with little else to do, pursued Sandino's forces around the sparsely populated northern and eastern parts of the country. Although the marines had far greater firepower at their disposal, including the use of dive-bombing aircraft, they were unable to put an end to the insurgency. Indeed, even though Sandino had little effect on "the normal political and economic life of Nicaragua," his resistance, along with the marines' tactics, led to increased criticism of the war in the U.S. Congress. In response, the U.S. increased the size of the National Guard, stepped up the pace of its training, and had it take over most combat operations. The Guard's performance was more than adequate, permitting the marines to withdraw the bulk of their forces by 1929; the rest left at the start of 1933 (the day before the departure, the U.S. installed an English-speaking officer, Anastasio Somoza, to take over command of the Guard). Almost immediately, Sandino agreed to stop fighting and the next year was assassinated on Somoza's orders.[38]

A contemporary, example of using combat troops as a life preserver for a client is that of Afghanistan after 2001. As we will see in Chapter 6, the U.S. overthrew the Taliban regime using a combination of its own air power, ground troops from the Northern Alliance, a small number of special forces troops to act as target spotters, and CIA operatives to serve as recruiting agents and go-betweens. Only after the principal cities had been conquered were regular units of U.S. combat forces sent to Afghanistan, their mission being to "pressure the Taliban" and "prevent Taliban and Al Qaeda terrorists from moving freely about the country." The first to arrive was a Marine detachment, toward the end of November 2001; by early January 2002, there were almost 4,000 troops, and the number continued to climb: 7,000 by June 2002, 9,800 by September 2003, and then a jump to 18,000 by August 2004. At that point, deployments leveled off, so that a year later, there were still the same number of U.S. troops, with an additional 2,000 "coalition forces" counted as part of the same Operation Enduring Freedom (OEF). In addition, as we saw in Chapter 4, an International Security Assistance Force (ISAF) of foreign troops (some 8,500 in August 2005) was created to play a peacekeeping role, with NATO becoming the leader. All this was over and above Afghan government troops (gradually replacing the warlords' militias), who were paid for, equipped, trained, and accompanied on combat operations, mostly by the United States: 25,000 in the army and around 50,000 in the police, both as of August 2005. To round out the picture, the U.S. was also running Bolivian- and Colombian-style antidrug operations with the Afghans and the United Kingdom.

The original mission of U.S. ground forces was to pursue the remnants of the Taliban regime and to hunt down whichever Al Qaeda forces still remained in Afghanistan. Thus, for the next few years, there was a series of operations in which U.S. troops, joined by a smattering of coalition units and, increasingly, Afghan detachments, searched for both enemy forces and information about them. Typically, these operations would result in a certain number of casualties and prisoners, along with caches of weapons and documents. By late 2003, the Taliban had reverted to guerrilla warfare and begun targeting the Afghan government, the United Nations (which was providing various forms of economic and political aid), and some nongovernmental organizations. To respond to these new attacks and to lay the ground for the 2004 presidential elections, the Pentagon doubled the number of its troops and moved into what the general in charge of U.S. troops called "a counterinsurgency operation." This involved a revival of Vietnam-era efforts at joint security and development programs, now called "provincial reconstruction teams" of soldiers and aid-givers, as well as sweeps by ever-larger numbers of OEF troops (often, all 18,000 were said to be engaged). The Taliban, however, was not beaten and as parliamentary elections approached in 2005 began to target OEF and, to a lesser degree, ISAF forces directly. Although the U.S. intelligence estimate was that the Taliban did "not pose a strategic threat" to the regime, they were, very much like Sandino 70 years earlier, "a determined enemy." By April of 2008, ISAF was up to 47,000 troops, including 15,000 U.S. forces; in addition, the U.S. had some 12,000 troops fighting separately from ISAF, with 3200 more marines on the way. Clearly, the Taliban had not yet been defeated and it was an open question if Afghanistan would end up more like Korea or like Nicaragua.[39]

Incompetent clients: easy wins: Node 8

Cuba (1906: text); Nicaragua (1912: text); Haiti (1915: text); Dominican Republic (1916: text); Lebanon (1958: text); Dominican Republic (1965: website); Zaire (1978: text); Lebanon (1982–83: website); Saudi Arabia (1990–91: text); Iraq (2004–present: text)

Up to this point, we have been concerned with combat troop commitments on behalf of clients who were either perceived as competent at the time of the commitment or seen as becoming competent in a politically reasonable interval. The expected power of the client's enemy against U.S. soldiers, in turn, served as a kind of pointer to the magnitude, in time and troops, of the U.S. commitment. However, when the client's military is viewed as incompetent both at the moment of crisis and for the foreseeable future, the enemy's assessed strength in combat against the U.S. plays a different role. It affects, not the magnitude of the troops which U.S. leaders commit but the nature of that commitment, i.e., just who the troops are. To see this, we will reverse the order of presentation and begin with situations in which the client is deemed incompetent and the enemy not formidable.

In these circumstances of dual weakness, policy makers estimate that almost any deployment of combat troops will result in a rapid and low-cost victory, what we here call an "easy win." Hence, even more than with other troop commitments, there is no reason to worry about the specifics of the political and tactical situation at that moment; instead, deployments are simple adaptations of existing contingency plans or precedents, based on whatever forces are ready-to-hand. Those forces may be large or small, not because of the terrain or the estimated size of enemy forces but because the forces are, in classic cybernetic fashion, pulled off the shelf. By the same token, although it is not expected that troops will have to remain for years, there is no great concern among policy makers at the thought of a 12- or 18-month commitment. Furthermore, since the client is deemed to be as incompetent as the enemy is weak against the U.S., whatever training occurs is more a reflex and a symbol of commitment rather than a serious effort at turning over combat operations to the client; this is the principal difference with the life preserver situations discussed above.

A good example of an easy win troop deployment is the action undertaken in Lebanon in 1958. For several years, the U.S. had had good relations with the pro-Western regime – an arrangement combining Christian and Muslim office-holders with the avid pursuit of local and foreign business – in power since the mid-1940s. As we saw in Chapter 3, Lebanon was the only Arab state openly to endorse Eisenhower's offer of 1957 to send U.S. armed forces to any Middle Eastern country faced with "overt armed aggression from any nation controlled by International Communism." This alignment, although rewarded by Washington, was challenged by foes of the country's president, Camille Chamoun: they were upset both on foreign policy grounds and because Chamoun had shut them out of the spoils they expected. Not surprisingly, Chamoun labeled his opponents as communists and persuaded Washington to help him rig parliamentary elections to keep them out of power, a task vigorously undertaken by the CIA with the aid of large sums of money (one officer regularly visited Chamoun late at night and handed him briefcases full of cash for his preferred candidates). This operation was almost too successful, as so many pro-Chamoun legislators were elected that Chamoun began to contemplate having parliament amend the constitution so that he could serve a second term as president.

Chamoun's ambitions triggered a strong reaction from his opponents. In May, the assassination of an anti-Chamoun journalist sparked riots, street fighting, and, rapidly, an armed uprising in the north and east of the country. Predictably, Chamoun raised the possibility of U.S. troops; Washington, by now disenchanted with Chamoun, understood that under the Eisenhower Doctrine it would have no choice if there were to be a direct appeal for troops but was still not convinced that the Lebanese government really needed troops, at least not enough for the U.S. to suffer the inevitable criticisms of imperialism such a deployment would bring unless really necessary. For this reason, Dulles wrote to the U.S. ambassador, telling him that troops could only be sent for purposes of protecting Lebanon's independence, that Lebanon's "Western orientation" had to take precedence over Chamoun's possible reelection, and that if troops were to be sent, their mission would be to "release Lebanese forces" and, except in self-defense, not to attack rebel forces. U.S. officials simply did not think that the rebels posed a significant military threat – not only for U.S. troops but even for the small Lebanese armed forces. Hence, as the crisis continued, the U.S. contented itself with shipping first tanks, then fighter jets, to Lebanon. When the Lebanese armed forces saw fit to use this equipment (most of the time, they were extremely cautious so as not to ignite a sectarian war and risk their own disintegration), they were able to defeat the rebels in relatively short order.

For the next two months, the situation remained more or less the same. From time to time, fighting would flare up enough to prompt panicked messages from Beirut or intervention discussions in Washington, but with UN involvement, matters looked as if they would come under control. Indeed, as time went by, Eisenhower and his top advisers began to realize just how isolated Chamoun was and how little a threat to the regime's maintenance it would be for him to step down from power. This led the U.S. to attach new conditions to a possible troop deployment, such as participation by other Arab states; it also led to a joint démarche by the U.S., British, and French ambassadors advising Chamoun to start the process of finding a successor to him as president when his term ended. Suddenly, on 14 July, the pro-Western regime in Iraq was overthrown in a *coup d'état*, with both the prime minister and the king being executed. Both Chamoun and King Hussein of Jordan (cousin to the Iraqi monarch) immediately requested U.S. military intervention, a request seconded by the governments of Turkey, Iran, Pakistan, Israel, Saudi Arabia, Britain, and France – all U.S. clients and one of them an Arab country. Although this agreement on what the U.S. should do could not remove the imperialist taint of an intervention, it certainly reinforced the arguments that a decision not to intervene would "lose influence" for the U.S. and bring "into question throughout the world" the "dependability of United States commitments for assistance in the event of need." The one bright lining was that no one expected the marines actually to have to fight the anti-Chamoun forces: the U.S. troops were to be deployed mostly in Beirut and the surrounding areas, their objective being "a show of force with psychological overtones." In fact, to the extent that the troop landings were directed against an enemy, rather than simply being a theatrical demonstration that the U.S. would stand by its clients, the enemy was not the anti-Chamoun rebels but Nasserite and leftist forces who, in the future, might be tempted to overthrow an entire regime, as in Iraq.

Eisenhower thus sent troops to Lebanon but used their presence as a means to work out a political compromise. The troops were held in Beirut and not sent into rebel-controlled areas; neither the Lebanese army nor the rebels engaged in serious combat against each other (one observer described the action as "noisy shooting" instead of "heavy fighting"); and the entire ambience, with heavily-armed marines wading ashore among bikini-clad sunbathers while the U.S. ambassador persuaded the government forces not to fire on them, was more Kabuki than combat. Almost immediately, Eisenhower dispatched a top State Department official to Beirut and within a few weeks, he had worked out a deal with the rebels and Chamoun's erstwhile supporters for electing the country's top general as Chamoun's successor. In the meantime, the U.S. and Britain agreed not to intervene in Iraq and, against the wishes of Jordan's king, soon recognized the new regime. By the fall, when the marines finally departed, they could claim never to have gone into combat.[40] Several decades later, the U.S. sent troops to Lebanon again, this time with a different outcome (see the book's website for a detailed discussion of the intervention in 1982 and its subsequent escalation).

One of the regions in which marines have often been sent in anticipation of an easy win is Central America and the Caribbean. The first intervention of this sort was in Cuba in 1906, with the U.S. going so far as to set up a provisional government. We saw above that there was a similar intervention in Nicaragua in 1912; there was another, in Haiti, in 1915 (the marines remained until 1934, putting down rebellions along the way in 1918 and 1929), followed by one in 1916 in the Dominican Republic (there, the marines remained for eight years). One of the lessons that U.S. policy makers learned from these interventions was the desirability of organizing a constabulary, typically a National Guard, for the client so that, in the future, there would be a competent force to put down insurgencies. This is why the intervention in Nicaragua in 1927–33 was more in the nature of a rescue: the U.S. expected, correctly, that the National Guard would be able to take over from the marines in relatively short order. By the early 1930s, a number of the formerly chaotic U.S. clients in the region had powerful Guard-like militaries, thereby providing an armed forces backup for Franklin Roosevelt's Good Neighbor policy of not sending the marines. That policy held for over 30 years, although, as we will see below and in Chapter 6, it did not stop the U.S. from various covert military or paramilitary operations. What finally was the *coup de grâce* for the policy was the intervention, in 1965, in the Dominican Republic (see the book's website for a detailed discussion).

Thus far, we have been discussing easy win interventions of between 2,000 and 20,000 troops. A more recent instance involved a considerably greater deployment and is interesting because it illustrates the means-driven way in which situations are assessed as likely to be easy wins. On 2 August 1990, Iraq invaded Kuwait, easily overrunning the country. To officials in Washington, this immediately raised the prospect that a long-time U.S. client and neighbor of Kuwait, Saudi Arabia, could also be attacked and its oil fields seized. Within 12 hours, a meeting of the National Security Council was taking place, with participants from the president to the CIA director worrying about Saudi Arabia and the commander-in-chief of Central Command, General Schwarzkopf, presenting a reworked contingency plan for defending the Arabian peninsula. Two days later, Bush decided to push the Saudi king to accept the large numbers of American troops it was anticipated would be necessary to defend his regime. Schwarzkopf and the secretary of defense were duly dispatched to Jiddah and, following a briefing about the number of Iraqi troops and the danger they posed to the kingdom, permission was granted. Rapidly, tens of thousands of U.S. troops began arriving in Saudi Arabia, leading U.S. officials to begin to breathe more easily.

Practically from the beginning of the crisis, even before Bush stated that "this aggression" against Kuwait "will not stand," it was assumed by almost all U.S. policy makers that Iraqi forces could not be permitted to stay in Kuwait. There were several reasons for this, ranging from concern over Iraqi control of petroleum reserves to the longstanding U.S. antipathy to the Ba'athist regime in Iraq (notwithstanding the tactical alliance of the two countries against Iran in the 1980s); but one important motivation was the understanding that the Saudis could not be safe with the Iraqis "only forty kilometers from the Saudi oil fields." Moreover, the U.S. could not maintain 200,000 troops in Saudi Arabia indefinitely: quite apart from logistical and financial considerations, a permanent or even long-term troop deployment was politically impossible for the Saudis. Hence, almost immediately, policy makers began to discuss "warfighting" that would go beyond simply "deterring" an Iraqi invasion of Saudi Arabia. Schwarzkopf began planning for a massive air war to force the Iraqis out of Kuwait, even before

Bush had told the chairman of the Joint Chiefs of Staff that UN economic sanctions were unlikely to work (this six days after they were voted at U.S. urging) and long before the "Y in the road" meeting at the end of October in which it was decided formally that if Iraq did not withdraw from Kuwait, the U.S. would use force to do so.

Schwarzkopf initially focused on an air campaign because the troop deployments planned to defend Saudi Arabia were, he thought, inadequate for a short and low U.S.-casualty ground war in Kuwait; he also saw Iraq as "target rich" for air strikes. After some bureaucratic maneuvering, Schwarzkopf produced a ground war plan relying lavishly on U.S. troops and equipment in Europe, now available for use in the Middle East because of the end of the cold war. This new plan, which involved over half a million troops and the latest planes, tanks, and "smart" bombs, was projected to result in a rapid ground victory in Kuwait with low U.S. casualties, especially in conjunction with the punishing air strikes which would both precede and accompany it. The expected ease of the U.S. victory was increased still further when, shortly before Christmas, it was decided not to aim at removing the Ba'athist regime from power in Iraq; this meant that U.S. forces would not be required to invade Iraq and face guerrilla warfare. In fact, although policy makers had expected an easy win, the actual war went even faster and resulted in fewer U.S. casualties (137 killed) than had been anticipated; ground combat was ended in under 100 hours (leaving the regime in Baghdad free to repress domestic uprisings) because the wholesale slaughter of Iraqi forces was so great that Bush and his advisers feared damage to the image of the United States.[41]

Not all easy win interventions involve U.S. troops. If, for various reasons, the U.S. lacks forces in the vicinity of a client and, in the recent past, an alternative policy instrument was used on behalf of that client, then attention will focus on reviving that alternative instrument. A good example of this is Zaire in 1978. The year before, the country had been invaded by long-time foes of the Mobutu regime. Washington, skeptical about both the seriousness of the threat and its supposedly communist character, contented itself with sending "nonlethal" military aid; and neither the former colonial power, Belgium, nor the Organization of African Unity were much more forthcoming. However, as Zaire's army, never very competent, began to disintegrate, Morocco stepped into the breach, sending a 1,500-man paratroop brigade, assisted by Egyptian pilots and mechanics, paid for by Saudi Arabia, and flown in by France, which added additional weapons and paramilitary advisers. This tipped the balance and the invasion was quickly repulsed. It is impossible to know just what the U.S. role was in the operation: although Carter was criticized by Mobutu and former U.S. officials, such as Kissinger, for not helping, Paris apparently "informed" Washington beforehand and coordinated with it, including on intelligence matters; the Saudis were a long-time U.S. client; the Egyptians had lengthy discussions about Zaire with the U.S.; by law, the Moroccans could only use their U.S. weapons abroad if they had prior U.S. support; and the U.S. made it clear that it hoped the operation could "stabilize the military situation." There were also unconfirmed reports that the CIA was trying to find mercenaries to send to Zaire, as it had in fact done during an earlier proxy war (see below).[42]

The next year, in precisely the same province (Shaba), precisely the same group of invaders repeated their feat. This time, Mobutu's forces were even less competent than before, and the rebels managed to take the major mining center of the province, where Americans, French, and, in larger numbers, Belgians, lived and worked. Quickly, policy makers in the three countries worked on plans to evacuate their citizens; but when the relatively small number of U.S. nationals were ferried out by their own employer, Washington changed tack, instead reworking the 1977 troop lift by itself supplying large aircraft to ferry 700 French (mostly Foreign Legion) and 1,700 Belgian paratroopers for rescue missions. By the time they landed, the invaders had already begun to retreat and brief skirmishes led to the remaining ones being killed, captured, or expelled within two days. At this point, the Belgians began to withdraw, but the French stayed on, hunting for insurgents until such time as an international force could replace them (in the words of the French commander, "Zaire does not have the means to secure the region. There is no other way"). Within a week, such a force had been put together, composed of Moroccan troops and soldiers from several of France's former colonies. The U.S., which had coordinated closely with Paris on all these decisions, then ferried out the French troops and ferried in the international force. In the meantime, drawing on both its standard repertoire of policy instruments and those countries which had participated in the previous year's rescue, the U.S. arranged for Zaire to receive IMF-supervised loans, Saudi-supplied U.S. weapons, and Egyptian (and other) military advisers.[43]

A final, and at the time of this book's writing, ongoing, example of an intervention intended as an easy win is that which began in Iraq after the regime of Saddam Hussein was deposed (see Chapter 6 for a discussion of the 2003 war). Soon after, it became apparent that various fighters, whether former soldiers or new volunteers, were carrying out a guerrilla war against the U.S. occupation. Bush's instantly famous response was, "There are some who feel like that, you know, the conditions are such that they can attack us there. My answer is bring them on. We've got the force necessary to deal with the security situation." This view was hardly unique: the secretary of defense referred to the insurgents as "dead-enders" and said that they would be defeated; the next spring, by which time the insurgency had spread widely, U.S. generals still said (at least publicly) that there was no need "for more [U.S.] troops in the region, nor in the country" and that U.S. "combat power" was so "overwhelming" that the insurgents would surely be defeated, even before economic development projects would demonstrate to the population that the U.S. was not an enemy. Ideally, counterinsurgency operations would be carried out by the forces of the newly sovereign Iraqi state, but, at that point, there were so few of them and they were so poorly trained and equipped that they were for all practical purposes absent from Pentagon strategic plans. Ironically, this did not worry the U.S. military, which, as late as July 2004, "still seemed to live in a fantasyland. ... Its spokesmen were still talking about a core insurgent force of only 5,000" when "experts on the ground in Iraq saw the core as at least 12,000 to 16,000." The expectations of an easy win persisted, with the vice president claiming in 2005 that the insurgency was in its "last throes," a claim which he repeated a year later. By the end of 2006, with the fighting into Iraq having metastasized into intra- and inter-communal war as well as continued anti-U.S. attacks, Bush decided to "surge" U.S. forces by some 33,000 troops in order to tamp down on violence and provide breathing room for political reconciliation. Since the total number of troops even at the height (no more than a few months long) of the surge was less than during the 2003 invasion, and far less than U.S. military doctrine held necessary to fight an insurgency, it appears that, even several years into the conflict, U.S. leaders still anticipated no difficulties in snuffing out military threats to the Maliki regime. Their presumption continued to be that, faced with the practical impossibility of defeating the U.S. in battle, insurgents of various stripes would eventually make their peace with the regime.[44]

Incompetent clients: basket cases: Node 9

Laos (1962–73: text); Congo (1964–65: website); Cambodia (1970–73: website); Liberia (1991–92: text)

One of the striking features of a number of the life preserver and easy win interventions is how badly mistaken U.S. policy makers turned out to be. We will discuss some of the reasons for this in Chapter 7; here, we would simply indicate that in a number of those cases, situation estimates derived, in classic cybernetic fashion, from the policy means adopted in the preceding phase of decision making. Thus, in Korea, Iraq, and Lebanon, the fact that U.S. forces had earlier been committed to deal with a particular problem meant that those forces, and the Washington agencies that keyed off of their activities, looked and planned for additional manifestations of that specific problem, even though it was no longer the most important threat to the regime. It would, however, be incorrect to think that only in the case of the 1965 decisions in South Vietnam did a more pessimistic view prevail. There is a fourth category of combat commitments in which American officials had a considerably more lucid view, namely, those in which the client was deemed incompetent and the enemy formidable.

In these situations, the U.S. could count on neither a sure nor a rapid victory. Since there were no local forces on which to build, any troop commitment was likely not only to be open-ended but to necessitate the assumption of a colonial-style role by the United States. A role of this sort would pose a political problem, both for public opinion in the U.S. and elsewhere, and, interestingly, for U.S. policy makers themselves. For whom would they be fighting? In effect, on behalf of a basket case, incapable of being healed. However, since the U.S. was committed to defending its clients, doing nothing was not acceptable. The solution was to use proxy forces, operating at the behest of the U.S. and perhaps under direct U.S. control. This was a centuries-old imperial technique, but one which required organizational innovations if it was to be carried out by the U.S.

Throughout history, empires have used foreign troops, both to make up for manpower shortages and because the foreigners were deemed particularly appropriate for certain kinds of imperial policing tasks. In ancient Rome, for example, the army had for many years relied on foreign auxiliaries who would receive citizenship upon discharge, but as time went on, they were considered too civilized to be of value in the most hostile terrain. Instead, emperors began to recruit *numeri* from the provinces considered especially barbarous and these, because of their supposedly tougher qualities, were stationed in frontier areas of other provinces and, logically, did not become citizens after their discharge. In more recent times, the Russians used the Cossacks for similar purposes, as did the French with Moroccans and *tirailleurs sénégalais* (in fact, soldiers from various colonial possessions in Africa). The Cossacks were used systematically along the southern and eastern borders of the expanding empire; the Moroccans and "Senegalese" throughout the colonies, including during the Indochina campaign after World War II. The French also had an additional unit of proxies, the Foreign Legion, which served in a number of colonial campaigns; it still is in existence and, as we saw above, is used from time to time in operations, especially in Africa.

In the era of formal colonies, proxies were considered an effective instrument of imperial rule. However, in a sovereign state, a garrison of foreign troops who are commanded and paid for by a third party is anomalous (for both the country in which they are stationed and the one providing them) and seen as a kind of return to colonial rule. If there is an emergency and if the third party is the United Nations, this may be acceptable for a limited period of time. Otherwise, the situation is simply too awkward to maintain, and this is one reason that standing proxy forces have tended to dwindle or simply disappear, replaced by special forces or other, shorter-term, arrangements. A case in point is the fate of the famous Gurkhas. These troops, from Nepal, have been used by the British since 1815. They were sent throughout the Empire for various counter-insurgency operations, including Iraq in the 1920s, Malaya, and Borneo. Since the advent of independence for most British possessions, the Gurkhas have continued to be used, including in the reconquest of the Falklands and in the UN-sponsored mission in Sierra Leone. However, as the Empire shrank, then disappeared, the need for standing regiments of Gurkhas diminished and other forces were seen as substitutable for them (a similar story can be told of the French Foreign Legion); hence they have dwindled in size from some 16,000 at their non-World War peak to 3,300 today.[45]

For the United States, the fact that its empire was comprised of independent client states meant that, even if it had been politically possible to station garrisons from colonial possessions, there were practically no such places from which troops could regularly be drawn. From time to time, in emergency situations where the U.S. had already committed its own troops, other U.S. clients did offer soldiers either from a sense of solidarity or in hopes of a political or financial payoff, but the number of troops in these offers was small by comparison with those already furnished by the U.S. and there was no evidence that the other clients could in fact substitute their forces for those of the U.S. Hence, in basket case situations where the use of U.S. troops was ruled out, it was necessary to come up with ad hoc, situation-specific proxies for U.S. ground troops. Such proxies, though, were only worth sending if they could be effective, something which the for-midable nature of their enemy and the case-by-case nature of their recruitment called into question. The U.S. would therefore have to help them by providing equipment, advisers, and, above all, tactical support during their battles. This latter implied the use of air power, a policy instrument developed for use against insurgencies back in the 1920s. (The marines, as we saw, used bombing against Sandino's forces; they were preceded by the British in Iraq, who also used poison gas.)[46]

The dilemma for U.S. officials is that the only means by which they could have some confidence that ad hoc proxy forces might succeed is if they were to accompany those forces with American advisers and support them with bombing from planes flown by American pilots. A policy along these lines would be sure to raise political hackles, as it would raise the specter of an eventual U.S. ground troop commitment. The solu-tion to the dilemma was to keep the U.S. role secret, if not from the client or its ene-mies, then from the American public; only in this way could the circle be squared. This meant that the U.S. would have to develop policy instruments for covertly recruiting, training, equipping, transporting, advising, and supporting with bombing not one, but a series of, proxies.

In fact, the U.S. developed two policy instruments for these purposes. The first was what became the paramilitary branch of the CIA. As we saw above, in 1947, the Office of Special Operations (OSO) was given the responsibility for carrying out covert psycholo-gical warfare. However, by the following spring, U.S. officials began broadening their sights to what was then called "organized political warfare," which would include agitation, sabotage, and other activities. Within a short time, a new agency was born, the blandly named Office of Policy Coordination (OPC), responsible for "covert operations":

> [A]ll activities ... conducted or sponsored by this Government against hostile for-
> eign states or groups or in support of friendly foreign states or groups but which
> are so planned and executed that any US Government responsibility for them is
> not evident to unauthorized persons and that if uncovered the US Government can
> plausibly disclaim any responsibility for them. Specifically, such operations shall
> include any covert activities related to: propaganda, economic warfare; preventive
> direct action, including sabotage, anti-sabotage, demolition and evacuation measures;
> subversion against hostile states, including assistance to underground resistance
> movements, guerrillas and refugee liberation groups, and support of indigenous
> anti-communist elements in threatened countries of the free world.

OPC was placed within the CIA, although it would be several years before the CIA director
would acquire power over it. In the meantime, it grew quickly: from 300 employees in
1949 to almost 6,000 in 1952, and from a budget of $4.7 million to one of $82 million
over the same period. Finally, it was merged with OSO and became the CIA's Directorate
of Plans (later, the Directorate of Operations [DDO]; still later, the National Clandestine Service).[47]

Within a short time, the OPC and its successors had developed a significant paramilitary capacity. Arrangements were worked out with the military to provide personnel and training facilities as well as equipment when needed for specific operations.
(This cooperation was subsequently mandated by the National Security Council.) The
CIA also ended up buying an airline in Asia, Civil Air Transport (later renamed Air
America), thereby permitting OPC to transport equipment and troops without having
to rely on the air force or, as in Europe, on the British RAF. Over time, the CIA acquired
other airlines, notably Southern Air Transport and Intermountain Aviation, although
in the 1970s most of these were sold. At present, the CIA's paramilitary capacities are
concentrated in what had been DDO's Special Activities Division and in spite of budgetary and political ups and downs over the last half-century, those capacities still
follow along more or less the same lines as set up by the OPC.[48]

Initially, covert paramilitary operations were focused in Eastern Europe and China
(see Chapter 6). The military had slowly been moving to create its own covert units for
use in time of war, with the intention of complementing the OPC (which would be used
in nonwar situations). With the outbreak of the Korean War, these units, the core of
the second policy instrument for working with proxies, were greatly expanded, in
keeping with policy makers' desire to mount large numbers of operations in North
Korea. Even though the military enjoyed obvious logistical and budgetary advantages
over the OPC, the urgency of the situation meant that the latter, too, was called on to
participate in these missions. Conversely, the military's units were not dissolved at the
end of the Korean War and by the late 1950s, all three services had "special forces"
capabilities, thereby creating institutionalized resources upon which the CIA could
draw and against which it could compete. When Kennedy became president, his concern to find a way of combating what he saw as communist insurgencies gave additional impetus to this development: special forces units were beefed up and assigned
responsibility for what had been CIA operations in Vietnam. In 1987, Congress created
a Special Operations Command, bringing most of the military's units under a single
umbrella and facilitating Defense-run covert operations.[49]

Both the CIA's paramilitary capacity and the Pentagon's special forces have been
used in basket case situations. Typically, one or more proxy forces have been developed

or shipped in and then supported with weapons, advisers, and, not least, with bombing. A good case in point, involving mercenaries and other proxies, is the Republic of the Congo (later renamed Zaire; later still, the Democratic Republic of the Congo) in 1964–65 (see Chapter 4 and, for a detailed account; the book's website). Around the time of the Congo intervention, the U.S. was also confronting another basket case situation. This was in Laos, where since the late 1950s, the U.S. had been backing the rightist part of a collapsed coalition in a war against their former partners, namely neutralist forces and communist insurgents. Although Washington tried to build up its allies, sending them both overt and covert aid (the latter with special forces advisers), U.S. officials, who saw the rightists as "mush," without strength, and unwilling to fight (the British agreed, the prime minister describing them as "incompetent"), were dubious about their chances of success. Under these circumstances, it was hopeless to send U.S. troops and every time the prospect was brought up, it was either rejected or watered down into a contingent warning across the border in Thailand. Instead, U.S. leaders pursued a two-track strategy: one was to neutralize Laos, the other to construct a proxy which could do the fighting for the rightists. A neutralization agreement was signed in July 1962; prior to that date and subsequent to the agreement's slow-motion collapse in 1963–64, the U.S. avidly pursued the proxy option.

The most important proxy efforts revolved around a non-Lao ethnic group living in the highlands around the area most fiercely contested by the insurgents. This group, the Hmong (or Meo, as they were then widely called), was seen by U.S. officials as considerably more willing and able to fight; they were supplied by the CIA through Air America and trained and advised by a combination of CIA officers, special forces, and units of Thai soldiers who had themselves been organized by the CIA to put down an insurgency in their own country. By the mid-1960s, the CIA had built a Hmong army of some 30,000 soldiers. They were assisted by tactical air power, with U.S. T-28s operating from Thailand (where the CIA officer in charge of the Hmong program had his office) and flown by Thai, Lao, or U.S. pilots. Later, the T-28s would be assisted by U.S. jet fighters based in Thailand, South Vietnam, or the South China Sea. Similar, though smaller, programs were run with other non-Lao ethnic groups elsewhere in the country, as well as in the highland areas of South Vietnam.

The Hmong's principal task was to fight against the Laotian communist forces, not with the aim of eliminating them from the entire country but simply "of preserving [the] integrity and stability" of the zone between the country's royal and administrative capitals. Insofar as the Laotian communists were assisted by the North Vietnamese, the Hmong would need greater fire power, but it was assumed by U.S. officials that any North Vietnamese aid would be limited so as not to provoke a stronger U.S. reaction. This was in the northern part of the country; starting in late 1964, the U.S. also began a pair of systematic bombing campaigns in the southern "panhandle" of Laos, the region used by the North Vietnamese to transport men and equipment into South Vietnam. These campaigns, although controlled as to pace and targets by the U.S. ambassador to Laos, were distinct from the CIA's counterinsurgency efforts with the Hmong. Gradually, however, as the U.S. infiltration war intensified, the North Vietnamese began to get more heavily involved against the Hmong, which in turn led to higher casualties and a greater reliance on air power. This reached its apogee in the early 1970s, when the U.S. began using B-52s to bomb entire map grids in the northern part of the country. Almost all of these operations, in both northern and southern Laos, were kept secret for years, partly to preserve the fiction of a neutral Laos (the North

Vietnamese had the same incentive to keep their troop activities secret) and partly out of concern that if U.S. activities were to be acknowledged, a Congress fearful of escalation would begin to interfere.[50]

The operations by and in support of both the Hmong in Laos and the mercenaries in the Congo involved the full array of features characteristic of basket case interventions: the organization, equipping, training, and deployment of proxy infantry; the use of tactical air power in support of those forces; and the covert direction of both of the first two elements by CIA and special forces personnel. In Cambodia, the U.S. began its intervention with all three elements but then, within a short time, found that the proxy troops had disappeared so that the war became a massive bombing campaign by the U.S. against communist troops (for a detailed account, see the book's website).

The three basket case interventions we have mentioned all occurred during the heyday of U.S. counterinsurgency operations. However, the logic behind proxy wars is just as valid now as decades ago, even if the enemy is different. To see this, consider the case of Liberia from 1990–92. As we saw in Chapter 3, the country had been a U.S. client since 1942. Up through 1980, the situation was calm, with the descendants of American slaves monopolizing power and the U.S. using the extensive air and communications facilities it had constructed. Nothing much changed when an army sergeant from outside the elite, Samuel Doe, seized power, disemboweling the then-president and staging a public execution of cabinet ministers on the beach. The wealth was shared a bit more broadly but there was more of it, since Doe let the Reagan administration use Liberia as a staging ground for its anti-Libyan crusade (see Chapter 6) and was rewarded with large amounts of aid. Doe, however, was both thuggish and inept, and in late 1989, insurgents led by a former government official, Charles Taylor, entered the country and began advancing toward the capital.

Once the Bush administration realized that the rebels were likely to overwhelm Doe's forces, it was faced with a decision. The State Department advocated dropping Doe and arranging for Taylor to take power, with assurances that an election would then be organized. However, concern that Taylor was backed by Libya and that his coming to power would endanger U.S. facilities in Liberia led to a rejection of that policy: the U.S. would not do anything that might lead to Taylor's victory. Logically, this meant that some military force had to be found to block, or if possible, push back Taylor's forces; but the thought of U.S. forces being involved beyond a standard evacuation operation in such a chaotic situation was anathema. Instead, U.S. officials encouraged proxy forces to act. The first of these was one of Taylor's commanders, who broke with him on the grounds that he was too close to Libya and interposed his own forces between those of Taylor and Doe. The second proxy was a West African multilateral force (ECOMOG) led by Nigeria and the other U.S. client in the region, Ghana. This force was bitterly opposed by Taylor, all the more so when it began advancing into his territory. The U.S., claiming to be neutral, supported ECOMOG politically and financially, while closing the door on a ceasefire as the multilateral force was on the offensive.

Over the next year, political and military maneuvers took place. The U.S. paid for Senegal to contribute experienced troops to ECOMOG as a way of strengthening the force and weakening Taylor's francophone African support; it also put pressure on another francophone source of weapons to Taylor, Burkina Faso. When Taylor launched a new offensive in the fall of 1992, the U.S. strongly supported ECOMOG's aggressive response: it provided target spotters for a bombing campaign by Nigerian aircraft and tactical advice for a shelling campaign by the Nigerian navy; it called for "full support" to ECOMOG as the only way to avoid "direct United States or United Nations intervention"; and it engineered a Security Council resolution imposing "a general and complete embargo on all deliveries of weapons and military equipment to Liberia" except those destined for ECOMOG. All this led to alternate rounds of fighting and political agreements until, in 1995, a coalition executive was formed with Taylor as its key member; two years later, elections were held and an intimidated population voted Taylor into the presidency (his supporters' slogan was, "he killed my ma, he killed my pa, but I'll vote for him"). It is estimated that some 200,000 civilians (out of a total population of 2.5 million) died between the start of Taylor's insurgency and the day he took office. Taylor's rule, it should be noted, lasted six years, until another U.S.-brokered intervention occurred (discussed in Chapter 4 and in node 15 below).[51]

Liquidating a troop deployment

As we have seen, there are no fewer than four situations in which U.S. policy makers opt to send combat troops, whether their own or proxies, to take over some of the clients' military tasks. Since prior to the U.S. decision the state in question had been either a client maintained by routine means or by noncombat forms of intervention, or else a nonclient, the U.S. troop commitment represents an escalatory step from existing policy (even if that policy continues). Furthermore, given the U.S. commitment implied in the very fact of a state's being a client and the ease with which existing policy instruments can be scaled up, there tends to be a built-in bias toward expanding the scope and magnitude of combat operations if it turns out that the U.S. or its proxies are not making progress. In Vietnam, for example, Johnson sent in several hundred thousand more troops than those he had originally decided to deploy in July 1965. In Laos, the U.S. greatly increased the size of the Hmong, while intensifying air support bombing; this latter also occurred in Cambodia and, albeit to a much small degree, in Lebanon in 1983–84 (see below). In Nicaragua in the 1920s and in Afghanistan more recently, the U.S. stepped up the pace of patrols and began larger-scale military operations, something which was also the case in Iraq.

However, when there is a radical change in circumstances, it has the effect of placing U.S. policy makers before a quandary. They now find themselves faced with a situation quite different from that for which the combat commitment was intended and therefore must choose between an entirely new kind of intervention and scaling down or liquidating combat operations by U.S. or proxy forces. The first of these two possibilities is the one which initially tempts policy makers, not least because it represents one more move in a policy of saving the client. To escalate in this sense, though, is both difficult and dangerous. Difficult, because the necessary policy tools – for example, significant numbers of new troops, whether U.S. or proxy – may not be available quickly or even for several years. Dangerous, because some of the necessary tools, such as transforming a small or proxy force into a major troop commitment, or calling up the reserves, or increasing taxes, would be massively unpopular at home; other tools, such as an invasion of another country or the use of nuclear weapons, would run risks of a world war, something far beyond what policy makers had committed to in even open-ended intervention situations. Hence, although it is possible for the U.S. to move from a noncombat form of intervention to a combat one as well as to escalate within a given combat situation, escalation across combat nodes (say, from a life-preserver intervention to an open-ended one, or from an easy win intervention to a proxy one) is out of the question. (The same also applies, as we shall see, to escalation from an open-ended combat situation to a world war-type situation.)

If escalation of this sort is ruled out, then the only alternative to current policy is to reduce the number of U.S. troops. Ideally, this would not be done until the client's capabilities had been built up; to gain time for that to happen, negotiations would have to be undertaken with the enemy. In principle, the client should also be a party to these talks but as it is likely to see them as an American betrayal, the U.S. will probably to take over entirely the task of negotiations. (A consequence is that, when an agreement is reached, the U.S. has to apply great pressure to the client for it to be accepted, going so far as to contemplate a *coup d'état* against the country's president.) If, however, there is no domestic political support for a slow withdrawal, then the above strategy is untenable and the U.S. might have to pull out without having been able to arrange a backup.

It is important not to interpret these situations of liquidating troop commitments as indicative of some kind of constraint on the bloodiness or duration of combat interventions. The Korean and Vietnam Wars, for example, show clearly that U.S. officials are able to initiate and maintain high levels of fighting, often for years on end. (We will see below that even the liquidation of these commitments in the face of growing public disaffection involved from two to four years of additional war. The same can also be said of hostile interventions, as will be discussed in Chapter 6.) Rather, the point is that if things worsen enough so that the basic situation – the combination of a geographically contained conflict, a client either competent or incompetent, and an enemy either formidable or not – changes, then, and only then, U.S. policy makers will be led to scale down, perhaps very rapidly, their activities.

In terms of the pseudo-decision tree, these nodes are branched onto from the question asked higher up the tree about whether or not the client has sufficient manpower to put down a rebellion or invasion without foreign troops. If the answer is yes, then, as we saw, the situation indicates sending emergency aid and advisers. But if the answer is no, then the question that arises is whether the U.S. has already sent combat troops, whether its own or those of one or more proxies. If the answer to this question is no, then we end up with one of the four combat intervention nodes discussed above. If, though, the answer is yes, then, depending on whether or not there is political support for a drawn-out troop reduction policy, there are two ways in which the troop deployment can be liquidated: slowly, accompanied by a policy of building up the client and (over the client's objection) negotiating with the enemy (node 10); and rapidly, by a precipitate end to the combat intervention (node 11).

Political support: drawdown and negotiation: Node 10

> South Korea (1951–53: text); South Vietnam (1968–73: text and website); Laos (1973: text)

Even when a disaster occurs, presidents often retain political support for a gradual liquidation of a troop deployment. This may be due to the well-known "rally round the flag" effect; but it also occurs because much of the public is susceptible to arguments about sunk costs and preserving national honor. Both of these factors were at work in the first of the really major combat interventions to be liquidated, that of Korea. In late November 1950, the Chinese attacked U.S. and allied forces "in great and ever increasing strength." MacArthur, shaken, reported that, "We face an entirely new war" and declared that he did not have enough force at his disposal to repel the attack. This led to a somber meeting at the White House in which it was reported that there were "no more ground troops which we could now send" and that escalation risked general war with China and/or the Soviet Union. Although there was some discussion of withdrawing from Korea, both Truman and his secretary of state, Acheson, expressed a determination to fight in Korea as long as was possible. A series of talks with the British prime minister several days later (occasioned by panic over a remark by Truman on the possible use of nuclear weapons) reaffirmed this policy, effectively ruling out some of the ideas MacArthur – and, it should be added, leaders in the U.S. – had begun putting forward about extending the war into China. By 11 December, Truman had accepted the idea of a cease-fire in Korea, adding publicly several days later that he was willing to negotiate. (This meant negotiations with the Chinese communists, whom the U.S. had boycotted for several years.) That same day, Acheson specified that a cease-fire should establish a demilitarized zone "following generally the line of the 38th parallel," which is precisely what was finally agreed to some two and a half years later.

First, however, the negotiations had to start. This itself took six months of heavy fighting until both the U.S. and Chinese were satisfied that no major military gains or losses were likely. Although there was resistance from both MacArthur – who persisted in his calls for attacking China and was finally fired by Truman – and the South Korean president, Rhee – who still wanted to reconquer North Korea and was violently opposed to any talks with communists – most of the bureaucracy, much of Congress, and almost all the U.S. allies were in favor of negotiations. Such support was crucial for the U.S., because the negotiations rapidly became stalemated. Some of the stumbling blocks were predictable: disputes over the location of the demilitarized zone between the two Koreas; the ability of the U.S. to maintain troops after an armistice was signed (to protect its client, viewed as too weak to withstand another invasion); and other issues pertaining to U.S.-Chinese relations. In order to force agreement, the U.S. escalated the air (and also sea) war, bombing cities, power complexes, and dams (which resulted in catastrophic floods and the destruction of the rice crop); the Chinese responded by launching huge infantry offensives. Since Rhee opposed any concessions to China, U.S. officials gave serious thought to overthrowing him as well.

The most important stumbling block, however, had to do with prisoners of war. Early in the talks, the U.S. decided to insist on voluntary repatriation of prisoners, something which the Chinese and some of the U.S. commanders strongly opposed and which may have violated the Geneva conventions. This contributed in no small way to the stalemate, since on most other issues, progress was being made when talks resumed later in 1951 at Panmunjom. Truman, though, would not budge, and on this he was supported by most of his advisers and, critically, by Congress. The talks thus dragged on for over another year, during which the U.S. was able to start rebuilding the South Korean military in preparation for the armistice. Finally, with a flurry of last-minute moves – a new U.S. bombing campaign, a new Chinese offensive, a promise to Rhee that the U.S. would expand his army and offer him a mutual defense pact, and a decision to ride roughshod over South Korean objections and to agree to keep Rhee from sabotaging the armistice – an agreement was reached between China, North Korea, and the United States (South Korea did not sign). The war had been liquidated, South Korea preserved as a U.S. client with the same boundaries as before the war, and millions of soldiers and civilians had been killed.[52]

The ending of U.S. ground combat in Vietnam followed a logic similar to that in Korea, although, given the nature of the war, both the liquidation of the U.S. role in fighting and the eventual outcome diverged in important respects from the Panmunjom policy. By the end of 1967, U.S. ground troops had been fighting in South Vietnam for almost two and a half years. Their numbers had grown to over 500,000, although only a portion of those forces were "maneuver battalions," i.e., infantry units engaged in routine ground combat operations. In addition, the U.S. was engaging in extensive bombing operations over both South Vietnam and North Vietnam (and, as we saw, in Laos). "Progress" in the war was very much a matter of dispute: to the Johnson administration and its senior advisers (the "Wise Men") who had served presidents as far back as Franklin Roosevelt, the numbers showed that the U.S. was turning the corner; to the critics, now including the secretary of defense and growing numbers of citizens, the situation was as bad as ever, since communist recruitment, infiltration, and logistical support continued. This debate was recast when, at the end of January 1968, the communists launched a major offensive during the Tet lunar new year. Although they were beaten back, the scale of the offensive and its tactical successes (holding the former imperial capital for several days; attacking the U.S. embassy in Saigon) set off shock waves in Washington and among the general public. The military, worried about the prospect of being stretched thin if attacks were to resume, pushed for more troops, with General Wheeler, the chairman of the Joint Chiefs of Staff going so far as to press the commander in South Vietnam, General Westmoreland, to indicate that new deployments were urgent. At first, Johnson was told that 25,000 additional combat troops were needed, then 10,500 (a deployment he approved); and then, after Wheeler had visited South Vietnam, the president was presented with a request for no fewer than 206,000 new forces as a reserve for Westmoreland, whose "margin" had become "paper thin." Indeed, Wheeler told Johnson that "without the reserve, we should be prepared to give up the two northern provinces of South Vietnam. This ... would, I believe, cause the collapse of the ARVN [the South Vietnamese army]."

The enormous numbers of troops requested and the highly pessimistic way in which the situation was now being described provoked sharp debate in the administration. Within a week, a task force led by the new secretary of defense, Clark Clifford, had posed the question of why the communists (by now, principally the North Vietnamese) would not simply match a U.S. troop increase with one of their own; it pointed out that even with "200,000 additional troops ... we will not be in a position to drive the enemy from SVN or to destroy his forces" and that the result would instead be "the total Americanization of the war." In the end, the task force recommended to Johnson that he send only 22,000 additional troops and defer a decision on the bulk of the Wheeler request. During the meeting in which this recommendation was presented, Clifford made clear that the U.S. was now at a fork in the road: if the full request was approved, the U.S. would either have to deplete its forces around the world or else call up the reserves; U.S. casualties could be expected to increase; and, within a year, Westmoreland would probably be asking for yet another 200,000 troops. In effect, granting the request would be tantamount from transforming the intervention into something resembling the scale of the U.S. commitment in a world war.

Over the next few weeks, pressures grew for a change of course. One important factor was domestic politics: Johnson was challenged in his own party by two presidential candidates, one of whom was his predecessor's brother; public opinion polls showed that almost half the country thought that Johnson had made a mistake by sending troops to fight in Vietnam; and Johnson's top political adviser told him that many of his staunchest supporters desperately wanted him to start peace negotiations. In addition, senior advisers began to turn against the troop request. The secretary of defense and his principal civilian officials were opposed; so too was the State Department ("all of us in this building are against a troop increase," one newspaper story reported); and perhaps most significantly, many of the Wise Men, hitherto staunch defenders of escalation, now felt that "we can no longer do the job we set out to do in the time we have left and we must begin to take steps to disengage." Stunned and drained, Johnson buried the troop request, announced that he wanted peace negotiations and as an incentive was suspending bombing operations over most of North Vietnam, and indicated that he would not stand for reelection.[53]

The U.S. reaction to the Tet offensive is a classic example of how a changed situation, in the context of a combat intervention, can lead to the liquidation of that intervention. Johnson's reaction, though, was only the start of the reaction to Tet. Although, by the end of 1968, negotiations had begun and the bombing suspension had been extended to all of North Vietnam, the U.S. still had over half a million soldiers in South Vietnam. Nixon, who succeeded Johnson as president, was determined to eliminate U.S. ground combat operations but without losing South Vietnam as a client (for a detailed discussion of Nixon's prolonged withdrawal of U.S. combat forces, see the book's website.)

The end of the U.S. ground war in Vietnam drastically changed the situation of the U.S. proxy war in Laos. As the negotiations between the U.S. and North Vietnam reached their conclusion, both sides agreed that there should be a cease-fire in Laos shortly after the one in Vietnam. Although this was not part of the formal peace accord signed between the United States and the Vietnamese parties (Article 20 merely referred piously to recognition of Laotian and Cambodian rights and an end to foreign military activities there), both the U.S. and North Vietnam were able to pressure their respective clients to conclude a cease-fire before the end of February 1973. Some months later, a coalition government was formed. In the meantime, the U.S. began to withdraw its advisers and support personnel, and to send the Thai forces it had used back to their homes. The Hmong, who by the terms of the ceasefire were to have been demobilized, were incorporated into the Royal Lao Army, although in smaller numbers and at reduced pay from their days as a CIA-sponsored force. Military aid was also reduced and bombing eliminated, even before Congress wrote this latter into law. The proxy war had been liquidated, and for the next two years, Laos slumbered.[54]

At the time of writing (spring 2008), there was mixed evidence pointing to Iraq as another country in which a combat intervention was being transformed into a drawdown. By almost any objective standard, the insurgency in Iraq had increased enormously since its early days, with violent communal conflicts accompanying it; and certainly this was reflected in the lengthening time lines being put forward in the Pentagon for how long U.S. ground combat forces would have to remain. On the other hand, the insurgents had not as of yet been recognized – at least publicly – by the Bush administration, or, for that matter, many of the Democratic critics in Congress, as having become sufficiently formidable that the choice had become one of escalation or a combination of drawdown and negotiated settlement with the U.S.'s principal adversaries. The range of alternatives seemed to extend from holding the line to slowly withdrawing some number of combat troops if the situation permitted. If the Korean and Vietnam cases are any guide, it would take some high-profile event, like the Chinese or Tet offensives, to change policy makers' positions.

Lack of political support: rapid liquidation: Node 11

Cambodia (1973: website); Lebanon (1983–84: text)

Political support for a gradual liquidation of a troop commitment is most likely to exist when there is a large contingent of U.S. troops, especially if fighting has been going on for a while. This is not to say that the war is popular but simply that the public is susceptible to arguments against a rapid and nonnegotiated end to the deployment. If, however, relatively few troops are involved or if the intervention is being carried out by proxy means, then there is less of a political cushion to liquidate a combat commitment in a drastically worsened situation. An example of this is Cambodia in 1973 (see discussion on the book's website). Another combat intervention which was terminated rapidly due to a collapse in political support is that in Lebanon in the 1980s. In September and October of 1983 (see the discussion on the book's website), the U.S. began escalating its combat forces and operations on behalf of the Lebanese government. In late October, massive truck bombs hit the barracks of the U.S. marines and the French paratroops in the multinational force, killing over 200 soldiers. The French response was to carry out reprisal air strikes against the Iranian-backed forces thought to have been responsible for the truck bombing. Washington, however, was focused above all on strengthening the Lebanese government against what it saw as Syrian threats. A few days after the barracks bombing, Reagan loosened the rules of engagement to permit fire support to the Lebanese Armed Forces in additional situations. On 1 December, the rules were broadened further to order "a policy of *vigorous* self-defense against all attacks from any hostile quarter" (emphasis in the original); if it was unclear where those attacks stemmed from or if there were too many civilians around, "destructive fire" would be "directed against discrete military targets in unpopulated areas which are organizationally associated with the firing units," in other words, against forces deemed solely to be allied with those doing the shooting. This new policy had an almost immediate effect: three days later, after U.S. jets flying reconnaissance over central Lebanon were fired on by Syrian antiaircraft batteries, the Navy carried out an air strike on those positions, with two of the planes being shot down. On background, U.S. officials described the bombing as "a political signal to Syria" to withdraw its forces from Lebanon; Reagan, speaking with reporters, said that the U.S. would continue reprisals against Syria "until all the foreign forces can be withdrawn and until the Government of Lebanon can take over the authority of its own territory." Ten days later, the battleship *New Jersey* began using its 16-inch guns to shell other Syrian anti-aircraft positions.

The reaction to the U.S. escalation was anything but supportive. None of the other members of the multinational force in Lebanon had planned for a war against Syria and calls began to be heard for reducing their contingents or withdrawing them completely. At home, the military, shocked by the shooting down of two U.S. planes, began reevaluating just how formidable a foe Syria was; within a few days, leaks (subsequently disavowed) from the Pentagon began criticizing the reliance on air and naval power and describing plans for withdrawing the marines. Congress also became alarmed, fearing that the U.S. was moving toward a larger war. By January, Republicans as well as Democrats were criticizing U.S. policy as both pointless and dangerous, with one representative, asked if he agreed with the administration's optimistic depiction of events, responding, "It all depends on whether you believe in fairy tales."

Faced with this barrage of criticism, Reagan stood firm rhetorically while shifting his policy behind the scenes. He tried to negotiate an agreement with Syria; he also (secretly) began to encourage planning to shift the marines back onto ships, coupling this with a further broadening of the rules of engagement to permit "naval gunfire and air support against any units in Syrian-controlled territory in Lebanon firing into greater Beirut" and an increase in the number of advisers and equipment for the Lebanese army. This policy of what might be called "Lebanonization" was not yet put into effect, since the secretary of state, by then in a distinct minority among Reagan's advisers, was concerned that it would send a signal of U.S. weakness.

In early February, the anti-government forces launched fierce attacks. Rapidly, the army lost ground, hemorrhaging its Muslim soldiers along the way. Although after several days the U.S. carried out shelling and air strikes, they were of little consequence: the Lebanese cabinet resigned and the government's control was soon limited to the presidential palace and parts of East Beirut. At this point, with the secretary of state out of the country, Reagan implemented the late-January plans, ordering the marines to leave Beirut for their own safety, the new rules of engagement to be followed, and training and equipment deliveries stepped up. Congress rejoiced; but then, after several days of fierce bombardment, voices began to be raised (again, similar to what happened in Indochina) that with the marines leaving, there was no longer any legal basis for the shelling and air attacks. In response, the administration began to describe the shelling as only for protection of U.S. forces and the U.S. embassy, and the number of salvos fired declined markedly. Meanwhile, newspaper stories began quoting unnamed officials to the effect that the Lebanese army was not in any shape to take over from the marines (in fact, when they left, it was the rebels who occupied their former positions). By late February, with the army having collapsed completely, it was clear that unless the U.S. wanted to widen the air and naval war extensively, as the Lebanese government was desperately urging, the only possible way for that government to survive was for it to work out a deal with Syria. That deal would have to have as its centerpiece the abrogation of Lebanon's 1983 U.S.-brokered agreement with Israel. This soon came to pass and with State Department officials bitterly comparing the situation to the collapses of South Vietnam in 1975 and the Shah's regime in Iran in 1978–79, the Sixth Fleet sailed away.[55]

There are two ways to view the cases of rapid liquidation in this section. One is to see them as examples of democracy at work: illustrations of how public opinion, at least as expressed through Congress, constrains the executive on matters of war making. However, what is striking is how rarely combat interventions are liquidated rapidly – or, for that matter, at all. Only when a situation changes drastically do policy makers begin to try cutting down on fighting by U.S. forces; and only when the number of those forces is relatively small do policy makers succumb to political pressure and liquidate rapidly. This points, yet again, to the strongly inertial quality of U.S. foreign policy making we first discussed in Chapter 1 and suggests that unless repeated disasters occur, the U.S. is more than likely to continue resorting to combat interventions when its clients face military problems and have manpower shortages. We will return to this point in Chapter 7 when we discuss whether, and if so, how, U.S. officials learn from intervention disasters.

Military defeat: Node 12

China (1949: text); France-Indochina (1954: website); Cuba (1958: text); Laos (1975: website); Cambodia (1975: text); South Vietnam (1975: text); Zaire (1997: website)

As we have seen, most of the situations in which U.S. clients are facing military problems are responded to by military intervention. That intervention may take the form of emergency aid and advisers or, under some circumstances, of committing U.S. or proxy combat troops. In all these situations, however, the presumption by U.S. officials is that the client can hold on long enough for some type of American intervention to make a difference. Clearly, this is not always the case, and there are situations in which policy makers rule out either new or further intervention as pointless, deciding that there is nothing to be done that might stave off the client's military defeat. In these circumstances, escalation of any sort makes no sense: the policy that had been in place – whether one of routine maintenance or of some type of intervention – continues and the focus is on arranging what is usually termed a "soft landing," either in hopes of keeping a foothold for future action or as a means of rescuing key members of the soon-to-be defeated regime. The problem is not to liquidate an intervention (nodes 10 and 11) but to salvage bits and pieces from an imminent defeat.

A classic example of the U.S. watching a client go down to defeat without even sending emergency aid and advisers occurred in Cuba in 1958. For several years, the country's dictator, Fulgencio Batista, had been facing an insurgency in the island's eastern mountains. Batista was widely unpopular in the United States and the State Department from time to time restricted deliveries of certain types of weapons he had bought in the U.S. However, most U.S. policy makers were also "deeply worried" over the "orientation" of the leader of the rebellion, Fidel Castro and of the 26th of July movement (named after the date of an assault on Batista's forces) he headed. This was not because Castro was then considered a communist but because his movement had "given no indication of political or moral responsibility." Nonetheless, at least into November, U.S. officials did not see Batista as in any military danger from the insurgents. Although there was dissent within the U.S. government on whether or not arms shipments should continue to be suspended (the Joint Chiefs of Staff wanted to keep ties with the Cuban military; the embassy to encourage Batista to hold elections), the policy held: the U.S. would simply wait for Batista to end his term as president in February and try to assemble a wider and more democratic government to replace him.

Suddenly, the Washington bureaucracy began to perceive that Batista was in trouble. A new rebel offensive had begun and it now seemed unlikely that the army could hold out until February. In response, the State Department and the CIA sent a business executive who had been active in the overthrow of Guatemala's Arbenz regime (see below) to meet with Batista and try to persuade him to step down and go into exile in Florida; Batista refused. By mid-December, a special intelligence estimate was describing the regime's position as having "deteriorated even more rapidly," with there being "mounting apprehension that Castro may soon come to power." The estimate went on to say that "a military junta would be the most effective means of breaking the existing political impasse," but that such a junta "would require, on a large scale, military equipment and supplies such as have been denied to Batista, and the issue would remain [for] some time in doubt." This pessimistic outlook did not provide much of a basis for putting together a junta plan and when the idea was broached to Eisenhower two days later, discussion still revolved around persuading Batista to resign rather than encouraging a coup against him. In the meantime an alternative plan was being hatched, in which the CIA's paramilitary division would make air drops, starting on 2 January, to a third force which would be "both anti-Castro and anti-Batista." This idea was brought up before Eisenhower at the next meeting of the NSC, during which the director of the

CIA stated unequivocally that if "Castro takes over in Cuba" – an eventuality which now seemed likely, given that the Army did "not appear to have the stomach" for a coup – "Communist elements can be expected to participate in the government." Eisenhower approved the third force solution, receiving a special briefing on it the day after Christmas.

By then, however, the Batista regime was in its final hours. A major interdepartmental meeting on 31 December was held, with the participants returning repeatedly to where a third force might exist and how it could be helped. Although Pentagon representatives complained about the suspension of weapons to the army, the State Department retorted that even when the army had received weapons, they "had put on a disgraceful performance with the arms given them, and in fact the rebels actually had gotten arms by buying them from the Cuban Army." In any case, aid at this point would lead to major political damage to the United States. When, at the end of the meeting, news arrived that Batista would step down in favor of a junta (in fact, he seems to have been forced to this by pressure from the army and business leaders), there was general agreement that "because of his power," Castro "must be a member" of whatever junta would take over. As it turned out, the next day, while the CIA was still getting ready to support its third force, Batista fled and the 26th of July movement was immediately handed power.[56]

Twenty years later, a remarkably similar sequence played out in Nicaragua (a detailed description is on the book's website). In both that country and Cuba, the U.S. had to acquiesce in the loss of its client because of a rapid military collapse. This left no time for a proxy intervention by an internal "third force" and the regime was so unpopular that no other state, including the U.S., wanted to commit troops to save the client. Nonetheless, even if the collapse were slower, it is doubtful that the outcome would have been much different. The reason is that years of dictatorship had eliminated what Washington considered a moderate opposition, while also making outside military intervention politically taboo. To see this, consider a slower collapse during which the U.S. had time to consider alternatives: that of Mobutu in Zaire (see the book's website for a detailed description).

Thus far we have been discussing situations in which clients were defeated without military intervention by the United States. In all three cases, dictatorial behavior by the client had eliminated any possible third force which could be given military support before the rebels took power; this meant that the only other way to save the regime militarily was to organize an emergency combat intervention on behalf of the very dictator whom the U.S. had until then been denouncing. By this logic, what was "too late" about the cases of Cuba, Nicaragua, and Zaire was not the fact that the rebels' final offensive lasted only a few weeks but that alternative possibilities had long before been stamped out. By extension, this same situation could exist in a country with an even lengthier military collapse and prior, or existing, U.S. military intervention. This was the case with China in the late 1940s. As we saw above, the United States had been supporting the Nationalist regime of Chiang Kai-shek against the communists. U.S. policy had been to work out a political settlement and thereby avoid a new civil war since, it was thought, the economy was too weak and Chiang's forces too extended to hope to prevail in direct combat. Chiang rejected this advice, grabbing cities in Manchuria and reigniting the civil war. Although the U.S. lavished aid on Chiang's armies, they were so poorly led that when the communists passed to the offensive in 1947, they rapidly lost enormous chunks of territory and abandoned or surrendered large numbers of weapons. By March 1948, the "political and military disintegration" was sufficiently advanced to make it clear that if the war continued, the Nationalists' only hope was to withdraw their troops from Manchuria and other exposed regions. This advice, strongly pressed on Chiang by the senior U.S. military officer in China, was of course disregarded, leading to communist control over most of the north by the end of the year. The next month, Beijing fell; three months later, the capital, Nanjing, and the principal commercial city, Shanghai; and on 1 October, while Chiang's forces were still retreating, Mao Zedong proclaimed the People's Republic of China.

During this time, the U.S. continued to send economic and military aid to Chiang Kai-shek. The legislative vehicle for this was the China Aid Act of 1948, requested by Truman in February and approved by Congress in April as part of the Marshall Plan legislation. At that time, although it was evident that Chiang could not win, the U.S. still hoped for a third-force solution (Truman spoke of widening the government to include "liberals") for which, it was thought, aid might buy time; in addition, no one wanted to be accused of acquiescing in a communist military victory. However, it was well understood by everyone that the U.S. would not go beyond aid and advisers: for Marshall, who had passed a hellish year as Truman's envoy in China, a deeper involvement would be "an unending drain upon our resources." The Senate had the same point of view, the chairman of the Foreign Relations Committee arguing that

> China is too big. ... this process must be completely clear of any implication that we are underwriting the military campaign of the Nationalist Government. No matter what our heart's desire might be, any such implication would be impossible over so vast an area.

The debacle that then ensued did nothing to change this estimate. In November, the embassy's senior military personnel agreed that "short of actual employment of United States troops no amount of military assistance could save the present situation in view of its advanced stage of deterioration." As the end drew near, the U.S. position remained unchanged, one diplomat reporting he had responded to a "desperately" expressed plea for additional aid by "our axiom 'God helps him who helps himself.'" Chiang never did, and, after he had withdrawn the remnants of his forces to Taiwan, it was only the outbreak of the Korean War that saved him from the alternatives of a third-force coup or a communist invasion of Taiwan.[57]

What the example of China shows is that, in a situation of rapid collapse, combat intervention is not seriously considered. In the case of China, this was due both to the enormous size of the country and to Chiang's notorious venality, incompetence, and autocratic nature. The size argument – that China was just too big – was in fact a political concern: had there been a World War II-type situation, perhaps the U.S. would have considered committing a million troops; but since the U.S. itself was not militarily endangered and its ally was so grotesque, sending even a small number of combat troops was politically out of the question. This is precisely the situation that arose in Cuba, Nicaragua, and Zaire. Interestingly, the fact that the U.S. was already intervening militarily in China by providing emergency aid and advisers counted for nothing in the U.S. acceptance of Chiang's defeat.

A similarly dispassionate attitude toward sunk costs is also evident in U.S. policy toward Indochina in 1954 as well as toward Laos in 1975, on behalf of whom the U.S. had earlier run a proxy war (see discussion of both cases on the book's website). Much the same occurred next door in Cambodia, where the U.S. also accepted a client's military defeat on the basis that it was too late to make a difference, with just as much bitterness as in Laos but considerably more bloodshed. On the book's website, we discuss how U.S. combat operations in Cambodia ended in 1973; after that, the Lon Nol government's principal source of U.S. support was military and economic assistance. In December 1974, Congress cut the administration's aid request by about a third, leading the Pentagon to forecast that ammunition supplies would run out by April. In the meantime, the Khmer Rouge insurgents had begun another offensive. Within days, supplies carried on the government's principal lifeline, the Mekong River, were severely restricted and soon the U.S. launched an emergency airlift from Thailand and South Vietnam. At this point, the Ford Administration asked Congress for supplemental funds for Cambodia (and South Vietnam; see below), arguing that with "adequate assistance" Lon Nol's forces "could hold their own" and thereby force negotiations on the enemy. As Congress debated the issue, the administration increased the pressure: the secretary of defense said that without new aid, the Lon Nol government would "absolutely" collapse and the U.S. would acquire a reputation for being "perfidious," comments echoed two days later by Kissinger and Ford.

To a remarkable degree, Congress stood up against the pressure. Although senators and representatives were unhappy about the prospect of a communist victory, particularly in light of the horrifying stories that were already surfacing about the Khmer Rouge, they thought that the Lon Nol government was hopeless and that aid could at best buy a few months' time while at the same time prolonging the bloodshed. Even staunch Republican conservatives like Senator Barry Goldwater shared this view, remarking that "Cambodia will fall about anyday now and probably should." Legislators also suspected strongly that Ford and Kissinger had already written off Cambodia and were looking to put the best face on a loss: if Lon Nol fell even as the U.S. voted new aid, then the U.S. would be seen by other states "as a loyal ally and the fault would clearly be put on the Cambodians." If, however, Congress refused to vote more aid, then it could be blamed for the loss (this finger-pointing was already well underway) and thereby shamed into approving aid for South Vietnam. This, and not simply the complete lack of a third force, is why the administration seemed uninterested in pushing Lon Nol out of power, or pressing negotiations with the exiled Prince Sihanouk (Kissinger sarcastically referred to the U.S. ambassador who pushed this idea as "that genius in Phnom Penh"), or pursuing a compromise aid bill with Congress. In the end, the aid request was not approved; the next month, the regime collapsed; and 24 years later, Kissinger still blamed the Khmer Rouge victory on the actions of Congress.[58]

What we have seen thus far is that when it is too late to stave off military defeat, the U.S. contents itself with continuing existing policy while trying to arrange a political settlement that might weaken the eventual enemy takeover. When even this latter is not possible, then all that is left is to put a good face on things domestically, whether by keeping the issue low-key (Laos), defending itself publicly (China), or blaming Congress (Cambodia). In Vietnam, not surprisingly, it was the third option that was chosen. On the book's website, we discuss how Nixon's liquidation of U.S. ground combat operations was followed in short order by the collapse of his plans for bombing North Vietnamese troops and targets. Hence, U.S. policy toward South Vietnam became one of providing emergency military aid (the peace agreement had drastically reduced the number and activities of U.S. advisers), although Congress had gradually been reducing the amount of this assistance. Nonetheless, by late 1974, the situation still seemed relatively stable: although the communist forces were "more powerful than ever before" and would likely be "in a position of significant advantage" in anticipated fighting, it was not thought that they would launch "an all-out offensive" during the coming dry season. There was thus no sense of urgency and when the predicted communist attacks took place, Ford coupled his supplemental budget request for Cambodia (see above) with a similar request for South Vietnam, asking for the amount that Congress had cut the month before. Refusal, it was reported, would mean that the North Vietnamese would "take over little by little."

Over the next month and a half, the question of aid for South Vietnam receded from view. The principal political battle was over the Cambodian aid request and the administration did not make much of Congress's equal reluctance to grant more money for the Thieu regime. When a congressional delegation returned from Indochina, its members, who largely favored the Vietnam request, saw the money as a way of spurring negotiations; they expected that the fighting would continue for several years, with some disagreements among them as to the regime's long-term prospects. Ford and his advisers largely agreed: although they were deeply troubled by what Kissinger called "the most serious consequences" that they saw would arise from "losing South Vietnam," they did not see such a loss as either imminent or inevitable and for this reason were open to fallback solutions, such as an agreement to eliminate aid after three years, or to forget the supplemental request and concentrate on longer-term financing, or simply to give up on Congress and obtain funding from other countries, such as Saudi Arabia.

Suddenly, in mid-March, the situation changed drastically. The North Vietnamese conquered a provincial capital in South Vietnam's central highlands; as the city was falling, President Thieu decided to withdraw troops from other capitals in the region in the hopes of massing them for a counterattack. This order, which may have been warranted on purely tactical grounds, provoked a disaster: armies streamed to the coast, disintegrating as they went and leaving vast quantities of U.S.-supplied military equipment. Civilians, panicked, began fleeing along with the soldiers. Several days later, as the scale of the disaster was becoming apparent, Thieu ordered another withdrawal, this time from the country's northern provinces. Again, chaos resulted. In Washington, officials were stunned, expecting a South Vietnamese counterattack that never materialized. However, with Thieu's forces facing a "catastrophic" situation, little could now be done. Ford duly sent the Army Chief of Staff to Saigon, who returned with a report in which he duly advocated increased aid, not because it would make much of a military difference but on the off-chance that it might raise South Vietnamese morale and thus encourage them to keep fighting. The report also wistfully raised the prospect of U.S. air strikes, an action which was expressly forbidden by a 1973 law.

General Weyand wrote his report on 4 April. It took almost a week to be debated in the National Security Council, suggesting that everyone thought the situation was now hopeless and that the only decision was how to react to the approaching defeat of the Thieu regime. In the end, although furious with the South Vietnamese for not having fought harder (Kissinger wanted Thieu to have made the North Vietnamese "bleed"), Ford decided to shift the blame to Congress: over the objections of his secretary of defense and his principal political advisers, he asked for almost a billion dollars in military and economic aid which, he added, should be approved within nine days. Predictably, Congress massively opposed the request which, again predictably, led to a number of finger-pointing speeches by both Ford and Kissinger. At last, Thieu resigned (with bitter complaints at U.S. betrayal); Ford declared the war "finished – as far as

America is concerned" (when he uttered the word "finished," his audience burst into applause); and on 29 April 1975, Saigon fell to the communists, thereby putting an end to a quarter-century of U.S. military intervention.[59]

Interventions against unacceptable leaders

Up to this point, we have been focusing on two "subfamilies" of intervention situations: those in which the client is facing a nonmilitary problem and those in which the problem is military. Early in the chapter, we indicated that there is a third subfamily of situations: those in which the top political leaders of the client's regime are unacceptable. There are a number of reasons why this might be the case – the leaders could be insufficiently repressive, or conversely, gratuitously violent; they could also be too corrupt, or even too strange, to keep the rest of the regime in hand – but what matters is that the leaders are considered by U.S. policy makers as incompetent at basic tasks. The logical U.S. response in these circumstances is not to take over those tasks themselves but to find others in the client who can do so and to transfer executive power to that new set of leaders.

Notice that we are focusing here on political leaders, not regimes. If the regime, i.e., the configuration of political and economic arrangements that give formal and informal power in the country to certain types of actors, is seen by the U.S. as not worth maintaining, then the state is not a U.S. client; moreover, depending on whether or not that regime is seen as choosing systematically to differ with the U.S. on key issues of foreign and domestic economic and political policy, then the state may even be considered in Washington as an enemy. In such situations, as we will discuss in Chapter 6, the United States will try to intervene and overthrow the regime. However, in this section, we are concerned with U.S. client states in which the regime's leaders are unacceptable but in which the configuration of political and economic power is, at least for the time being, satisfactory. In fact, it is precisely when leaders are seen as endangering the maintenance of the regime (e.g., by threatening the military or major private investors) that U.S. officials become alarmed and decide to act. Note that in light of the numerous reasons why leaders may be seen as bad for a regime (similarly as to why states may be seen as enemies), there is no ideological litmus test used by the U.S. for determining whether leaders of client states are unacceptable.[60]

For U.S. policy makers, the difficulty with unacceptable political leaders is that they risk remaining in power for a long enough time to pose serious problems for the maintenance of the client. The issue is thus not simply one of waiting until they leave office on a voluntary or forced basis but of intervening to force their exit. Here there are, broadly speaking, four possibilities, with the critical question being whether or not the regime's leaders are backed by important segments of the country's military (see Figure 5.4). If the answer is no, then the course of action is obvious: the U.S. will try to persuade the military to carry out a *coup d'état*, either by simply deposing the leaders or by triggering the imposition of martial law (node 16). If, however, the military is neutral toward or weakly supportive of the regime's leaders, then a coup is either impossible or at least considerably more difficult to engineer and the U.S. will have to act by other means, ranging from psychological warfare to sponsoring invasions. These means may be harnessed to induce a sufficient state of fear (of chaos; of punishment) in key officers that they break with the regime's leaders (node 15). Conversely, if it is clear – after having tried to foment a coup or otherwise eliminate the leaders – that an

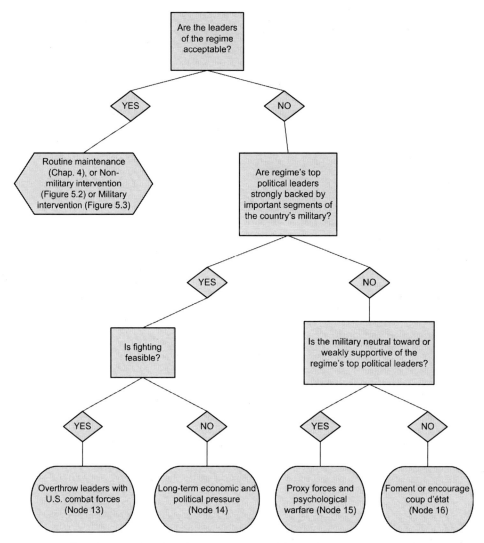

Figure 5.4 Client intervention situations, 4: Unacceptable Leaders

important segment of the military strongly supports the leaders, then neither of the above policies will work. In these circumstances, U.S. officials will, if they think it militarily feasible, opt for intervention by U.S. combat forces aimed at decapitating the client's military (node 13). If, however, U.S. troops would face a militarily difficult task, then longer-term pressures will instead be applied (node 14). We will discuss these possibilities beginning with the third and fourth situations.

It should be noted that all four situations of clients with unacceptable leaders will be responded to, at least initially, by policies that are necessarily covert in nature. Most of the time, U.S. officials cannot publicly admit to encouraging *coups d'état*, or facilitating assassinations, or carrying out psychological warfare, or sponsoring paramilitary operations aimed at replacing the leaders of sovereign states. This means that the documentary record on such operations will, of necessity, be far more limited than for the various overt interventions we have been discussing throughout this chapter. We will signal these limitations and discuss in detail only those cases for which we have independent and concordant information; but, so as not to leave the misleading impression that these kinds of interventions are rare or unusual, we will also list other cases for which there is convincing evidence, even if the details are still obscure.

Military supportive, fighting feasible: overthrow by U.S. combat forces: Node 13

Honduras (1911: text); Dominican Republic (1912: text); Dominican Republic (1961: text); Panama (1989: text); Haiti (1994: website)

Long before the CIA or most other instruments of intervention were created, presidents had at their disposal the U.S. Marines. It stands to reason, then, that some of the earliest cases of overthrowing unacceptable leaders in client states involve landings and combat operations by the marines. Early examples of this occurred in Honduras in 1911 (see Chapter 3), as well as in the Dominican Republic in 1912, when U.S. commissioners, accompanied by marines, weighed in on behalf of a revolt against a particularly nepotistic set of leaders (the president had been installed by his nephews, one of whom was Minister of War; the other was commander of the army) and deposed the lot. However, with the development of National Guards and constabularies in the region, the U.S. was able to rely on military-led regimes in which it had confidence, and so for some decades, Honduran- and Dominican-style interventions became uncommon.[61]

During those years, the U.S. was able to use contacts with its clients' militaries to foment or at least encourage *coups d'état* in cases where particular leaders were unacceptable. There were a number of such cases (we will discuss a few of them below) and attempts at fostering a coup seem to have become the default procedure for U.S. officials in other situations, notably those in which the military backed the leaders. In fact, it was only when coup attempts failed that policy makers in Washington began to understand that leaders were supported by the military and that other policy instruments would have to be used. This was all the more true in situations where top military officers enjoyed a revenue stream outside the control of the U.S. government (e.g., because of narcotics trafficking), thereby rendering them even less susceptible to pressure for a coup. A good case in point is Panama, in which a military leader associated for decades with the U.S. was overthrown by U.S. troops. Manuel Noriega was the head of military intelligence and later the head of the Panamian Defense Forces (PDF), from which post he essentially ran the country. Noriega had worked closely with various U.S. agencies, including the CIA (which paid him from time to time), the DEA, and the Defense Department; he provided intelligence information and helped in the U.S. proxy war against Nicaragua (see Chapter 6). Although it was known that Noriega himself was involved in trafficking and arms smuggling, the U.S. was willing to look the other way because of the services Noriega provided. Thus, in 1979, the Carter administration stopped federal prosecutors from indicting Noriega; in 1984, the U.S. acquiesced in vote fraud that resulted in Noriega's hand-picked candidate being "elected" as the country's new president.

The next year, the relationship began to sour. Opponents of Noriega within the regime began to speak out against him but they were forced out of office or tortured and murdered. The U.S. began to distance itself from Noriega, a process accelerated in 1987 when Noriega's own deputy denounced him, triggering massive protests and a crackdown in response by the PDF. The U.S. Senate then called on Noriega and his top officers to resign, which led to a mob attack on the U.S. embassy in Panama City, a suspension of U.S. military aid to the PDF and contacts with it, and a public call by the State Department for the PDF to remove Noriega from power. In addition, over the next six months, the U.S. tried and failed at least three times to negotiate Noriega's resignation. The situation then intensified when U.S. prosecutors, supposedly acting without "adequate consultation," indicted Noriega on criminal charges. This led to a U.S.-backed, but unsuccessful, coup against Noriega, the first of at least four that Washington either supported or tried to foment over the next 20 months. Negotiations aimed at trading Noriega's exile for dropping the indictments failed when junior officers in the PDF balked, fearing that without Noriega they would no longer be safe. The U.S. also imposed economic sanctions on Panama and mounted a covert operation to aid the opposition candidate in the May 1989 presidential elections; the former had too many loopholes to affect the PDF's revenues and the latter failed when Noriega, once again, stole the elections and put down protests by force.

By the end of 1989, it was clear that the only way of removing Noriega from power was to go after the PDF itself. The U.S. military was already preparing plans to use its armed forces in the Canal Zone to seize Noriega, but those plans looked unlikely to succeed and raised the prospect of subsequent PDF retaliation against U.S. forces and their dependents. Accordingly, the plans were reworked, principally by adding an 11,000-man force and removing most U.S. dependents. When in early December clashes broke out between PDF and U.S. soldiers and the Panamanian legislature appointed Noriega to head the government, declared him "maximum leader of national liberation," and declared that Panama was in a state of war with the United States, Bush finally acted. Operation Just Cause was launched on 19 December: 27,000 U.S. troops fought for six days against the 3,500 combat troops of the PDF. Noriega was eventually captured and shipped off to Florida to stand trial; and the PDF, shorn of its top officers, was transformed into a new Fuerza Publica de Panama.[62]

In Panama, the U.S. was targeting a former ally whom it had come to see as unacceptable. A similar situation, though from the other end of the ideological spectrum, occurred in Haiti several years later (see the discussion on the book's website). In both countries, the U.S. tried unsuccessfully to provoke a coup before deciding to send its own troops. By contrast, in the Dominican Republic in 1961 it was able to use other means to overthrow the country's leader and his family, though sending U.S. troops was under active consideration at several key moments. The leader in question was the country's long-time military dictator, General Rafael Trujillo. For years, the U.S. had accommodated itself to Trujillo, but by the end of the 1950s his repressiveness was coming to be seen as both embarrassing and contributing to leftist revolutions, such as had occurred nearby in Cuba with the fall of Batista. In February 1960, U.S. officials began discussing covert political assistance to some of Trujillo's opponents; two months later, Eisenhower approved the first steps in the direction of "political action to remove Trujillo from the Dominican Republic as soon as a suitable successor regime can be induced to take over with the assurance of U.S. political, economic, and – if necessary – military support." Soon afterward, the deputy chief of mission, Henry Dearborn, was designated as the principal communications link between the CIA and anti-Trujillo dissidents. Within several months (during which time the U.S. suspended diplomatic relations with the Dominican Republic), Dearborn and his superiors had come around to the dissidents' view that Trujillo's control of the armed forces made a coup unlikely unless and until Trujillo was killed. Nor was there any hope that Trujillo might step down on his own or that, if he was induced to do so, the situation would improve: "he will devote his life from exile to preventing stable government in the D.R., to over-turning democratic governments and establishing dictatorships in the Caribbean, and to assassinating his enemies." Instead, Dearborn continued:

> If I were a Dominican, which thank heaven I am not, I would favor destroying Trujillo as being the first necessary step in the salvation of my country and I would regard this, in fact, as my Christian duty. If you recall Dracula, you will remember it was necessary to drive a stake through his heart to prevent a continuation of his crimes. I believe sudden death would be more humane than the solution of the Nuncio who once told me he thought he should pray that Trujillo would have a long and lingering illness.

Thus, when the dissidents with whom Dearborn was meeting asked for weapons with which to assassinate Trujillo, the U.S. agreed and duly arranged for shipments. Although later Kennedy and his aides got cold feet (both because of fear that an assassination could be pinned on the U.S. and because of uncertainty over Trujillo's successor), the Dominicans' plans went ahead and Trujillo was ambushed and shot to death on 30 May 1961.

It quickly became clear that the military's backing of Trujillo was such that his death by itself would not end the policies which the U.S. found so repugnant. Trujillo's son Ramfis had taken over the armed forces, who immediately began to carry out retaliatory killings and, in anger against the United States, were rumored to be flirting with Castro's Cuba. Two days after the assassination, a high-level meeting was convened in which leading officials discussed the prospect of sending U.S. troops into the Dominican Republic. In preparation, a naval flotilla was ordered to the coast with 12,000 marines abroad and consideration was given to creating an incident (blowing up the U.S. consulate) that would serve as an excuse for landing the troops. The recommendation was not agreed to, partly because information was still limited and partly because of strong State Department reluctance to pay the international political costs of sending marines to the Caribbean for the first time in over 30 years. Within a few days, Ramfis had given assurances of democratic and pro-U.S. tendencies, and the immediate crisis subsided. However, as months went by and Ramfis not only failed to relinquish power but was joined by other Trujillo family members, U.S. officials once again grew agitated at the thought that this situation could lead to a shift leftward in Dominican policies. The U.S. responded by making extremely strong statements in public and private, and by moving ships into sight of land in order to support the civilian government. This led the chief of the air force to back that government and the Trujillo family members to leave the country. Although Washington's intention was not to send troops, refusal by the armed forces to break with Ramfis might well have embarrassed the U.S. into following through on its implicit threats, in much the same way that embarrassment led Bush and Clinton to send troops to Panama and Haiti.[63]

Military supportive, fighting not feasible: long-term pressures: Node 14

Chile (1971–73: text); Venezuela (2002–present: text)

The interventions carried out in both Panama and Haiti, as well as the intervention discussed for the Dominican Republic, aimed at removing the top layer of the military as a way of toppling each country's leaders. In Panama, we know that the U.S. tried other ways of removing Noriega before settling on an invasion; in Haiti, it was only the leaders' obduracy which led the U.S. to the brink of an invasion; in the Dominican Republic, sending troops was clearly a last resort. Once troops did land and the leaders in Panama and Haiti were deposed, each country's military was, at least initially, reconstituted, very much along the lines of the creation of constabularies in the 1920s and 1930s. In the meantime, both before and after the actual and recommended invasions, the U.S. maintained close ties with the economic elite of each country. All these points suggest that policy makers in Washington saw at least a portion of the military in the three countries as a potential ally and did not believe that the remaining portion would pose much of a combat challenge to U.S. troops. The expectation was for a rapid and quick victory akin to the easy win situation discussed above.

All of the combat overthrow cases, from the early 1900s until the present, have involved countries in the Caribbean and Central America. Although the interventions prior to World War II may have been due in part to the relatively few policy instruments then available, what both the older and the more recent examples have in common is not so much the proximity to the U.S. as the small size of the countries involved. This means that the U.S. would not face a difficult military problem if and when it sent its own combat troops; but it also means that if a much larger U.S. client, especially one with a large surface area and difficult topography, were to have a leader considered to be like Noriega, Cédras, or Trujillo, the U.S. would be much less likely to send its own combat forces. (The situation is different, of course, when it is a question of intervening on behalf of a client's military: in those cases, as we saw above, the U.S. is willing to send combat troops into much larger countries.) For example, although it seems evident that U.S. officials were eager to depose the president of Venezuela, Hugo Chávez, their first inclination was to back a *coup d'état*. Only when that failed, due to support for Chávez among key segments of the military, was a longer-term policy adopted of applying economic and political pressure. As we will see below in the case of Chile, this is similar to the policy the U.S. resorted to for several years after the failed efforts of 1970, when the military proved itself unwilling at that point to break with the country's elected president.[64]

Military neutral: proxy forces and psychological warfare: Node 15

Costa Rica (1919: text); Guatemala (1954: text); British Guiana (1963: website); Liberia (2003: text); Haiti (2004: text)

In operations Just Cause and Restore Freedom (Haiti), the leaders were backed by the top levels of the military and so the point of sending U.S. forces was to neutralize or destroy those levels. By contrast, when the military had a more neutral stance toward the regime's leaders, then U.S. policy could be less direct and more economical, with the aim being to turn the military against the leaders. An early example of this occurred in Costa Rica in 1919, as we saw in Chapter 3. But a more recent, and now canonical, example of this type of intervention is Operation PBSUCCESS, through which the U.S. induced the Guatemalan military to turn against the country's elected president (and former military officer), Jacobo Arbenz. The story began in 1944, when Guatemala's long-time dictator was toppled by popular unrest. Eventually, elections were held and an exiled opposition figure was elected president; he soon implemented democratic and labor reforms, thereby incurring the hostility of the country's upper classes, the Catholic Church, and the U.S.-headquartered United Fruit Company, which had vast Guatemalan holdings. On the other hand, the army was hostile to the government and was moving in the direction of a coup when its leading officer was murdered. This mixed picture led the United States to place its hopes in Arbenz, whom it predicted correctly would win the next presidential elections, in late 1950, and whom it also predicted, incorrectly, would, once he took office, be "an opportunist," not "an honest leftist," and would "rid Guatemala of its leftist penetration."

Arbenz was inaugurated in March 1951. Within a few months, U.S. diplomats and journalists were voicing worries about communism and continuing the policies that they had already begun of restricting Guatemala's access to European armaments and World Bank loans. In April 1952, Arbenz introduced an agrarian reform bill which infuriated his opponents and provoked a lobbyist for United Fruit to approach the CIA; around this same time, the Nicaraguan dictator Somoza visited Washington and began lobbying for the U.S. to back an invasion of Guatemala by a former military officer, Carlos Castillo Armas. The CIA, which for some months had been keeping tabs on Castillo Armas and compiling lists of communists to be executed if and when Arbenz was overthrown, apparently was told to ship weapons to Castillo Armas, an order countermanded several months later by the top officials in the State Department. This revocation, however, was only temporary, and once the Eisenhower administration was installed, pressure once more began building to get rid of Arbenz. Formal authorization was given on 12 August 1953 and planning began immediately. Soon, a CIA special project office near Miami was running a multi-pronged operation: training and equipping a new force under Castillo Armas; creating and disseminating anti-Arbenz propaganda both inside Guatemala and elsewhere, including the U.S. news media; attempting to suborn officers of the Guatemalan army; and, the one public aspect of the plan (and the only one known to most U.S. diplomats), isolating Guatemala from other states in Latin America. Each of these activities represented a policy instrument which the U.S. had already developed and employed elsewhere; during its early stages, PBSUCCESS was simply a collection of efforts by the CIA to do what it could against Arbenz.

Gradually, it began to dawn on senior officials that Castillo Armas would never have enough troops at his disposal to win pitched battles against the Guatemalan military. It also became clear that few if any officers could be recruited for fifth column operations. On the other hand, the propaganda and diplomatic campaigns were making it clear that the U.S. was unremittingly hostile to Arbenz and that no other state, both in Latin America and elsewhere, was willing to confront the U.S. over Guatemala. These facts were stapled together into a new policy logic when, realizing that it could no longer hold off Castillo Armas, the CIA gave him permission to "invade" Guatemala. Almost immediately, the rebels bogged down, leading both the officer in charge of the operation and the U.S. ambassador to plead frantically ("Bomb repeat Bomb") for permission to launch bombing raids (by ex-U.S. pilots, in cast-off planes furnished to Castillo Armas) on the capital and elsewhere. The reply by the CIA director's special assistant was instructive: bombing would "consolidate army's loyalty to regime and we still believe defection of army is best chance." This rationale was expanded on later the same day in a memo which was sent to Eisenhower, specifying that the "controlling factor in the situation is still considered to be the position of the Guatemalan armed forces" which, if they "should move within the next few days against the Arbenz regime," had "the capacity to overthrow it." The memorandum continued:

> The action of Colonel Castillo Armas is not in any sense a conventional military operation ... The entire effort is thus more dependent upon psychological impact rather than actual military strength, although it is upon the ability of the Castillo Armas effort to create and maintain for a short time the impression of very substantial military strength that the success of this particular effort primarily depends. The use of a small number of airplanes and the massive use of radio broadcasting are designed to build up and give main support to the impression of Castillo Armas' strength as well as to spread the impression of the regime's weakness.

This analysis was to prove prescient, although the "impression of very substantial military strength" pertained not to Castillo Armas but the United States: apparently Guatemalan officers thought that if they defeated the rebels, as they could easily have done, then the U.S. would be angered and would use its own armed forces to crush the Guatemalan army. The military thus refused to fight and Arbenz, abandoned, resigned, thereby triggering celebrations in Washington and decades of massacres in Guatemala.[65]

Half a century later, a similar operation seems to have been carried out in Haiti. As we mentioned above, the U.S. had overthrown the country's military leaders in 1994 and reinstalled the elected president, Jean-Bertrand Aristide. However, some of Aristide's policies (on economic matters and on the army, which he dissolved) irritated the Clinton administration, thereby adding to the hostility already evident in the CIA and segments of the military. Fast forward to the elections of 2000, in which Aristide's party gained control of the legislature and Aristide, after having sat out the preceding term of office, was returned to the presidency. At this point, several factors came together: a boycott of the election by anti-Aristide forces, a friendly policy toward Venezuela and Cuba by Aristide's government, and the inauguration of a new U.S administration, which quickly named virulently anti-Aristide figures to run policy making toward the Western hemisphere. Soon, bilateral and multilateral development loans to Haiti were being blocked and a "Haiti Democracy Project" was funneling resources to Aristide's internal opponents (who were for the most part the same "small economic elite" that had dominated the country for decades). Behind the scenes, the U.S. appears to have begun equipping and training former Haitian army soldiers, by now in exile next door in the Dominican Republic.

In February 2004, the exiles invaded Haiti. Their numbers, their weapons, and their training made it easy for them to overwhelm the National Police forces, which had replaced the army in 1995; in some cases, the police or local militias (e.g., the "Cannibal Army" in the city of Gonaives) joined the rebels. Various intermediaries attempted to work out a compromise between Aristide and his political opponents, but the latter repeatedly refused any solution short of Aristide's leaving office. Ostensibly, the U.S. supported a compromise but its arm-twisting efforts were noticeably half-hearted (the principal State Department negotiator spent only four hours with the opposition), not least because it repeatedly ruled out the use of force to back Aristide against the "criminal gangs," as it called the armed exiles. Within days, the U.S. formally switched position, calling on Aristide to "examine his position carefully." Two days later, Aristide was induced by the U.S. ambassador and his deputy to go to the airport; there, he was made to understand that his life was in danger from the rebels and that he could no longer be protected by the private U.S. security service he employed. He resigned and was flown in a U.S. military jet to a French client state, the Central African Republic. Several hours later, Bush sent U.S. troops to Haiti to restore order (they were soon joined by French and Canadian soldiers) and the police miraculously reappeared, patrolling pro-Aristide neighborhoods together with the armed exiles. As U.S. congressional representatives bitterly denounced what they referred to as a *coup d'état*, the U.S. vice president announced, "I'm happy he is gone. He'd worn out his welcome with the Haitian people."[66]

In both Guatemala and Haiti, the outside invading force had only limited military strength. Its success was due to a more general campaign of psychological warfare and political destabilization in which the regime's security forces – the army, in the case of Guatemala; the national police, in Haiti – were frightened into passivity or, indeed, deserted to the side of the exiles. Much the same process took place in British Guiana, although in this case, the United States did not even need to sponsor or wink at an invasion (see the discussion on the book's website). A similar intervention, relying on proxy forces for varous countries, was used to expel the leader of Liberia in 2003 (see Chapter 4 for a discussion); in this case, too, the point of the operation was not to fight the leader's faction but to intimidate it into acquiescence.

The array of policy instruments used to induce a regime's military to drop its neutrality and turn against the country's leaders is in fact a standard set of tools which can also be used when the military is already hostile to the leaders (see the next section) or, indeed, when the state in question is an enemy which the U.S. wishes to overthrow (see Chapter 6). This "off the shelf" quality to the policy instruments is why, yet again, it makes more sense to talk about policy as means-driven rather than crafted in pursuit of a goal. In Guatemala, the techniques employed by the U.S. had been developed in other circumstances (e.g., operations in Italy and Iran, and against Albania; as well as diplomatic isolation techniques employed as far back as the early 1930s), and it was only when the officers in charge of the operation realized that there would not be either a military coup or a domestic uprising that they focused on using those instruments to frighten the army into believing that the U.S. would soon send its own troops. In British Guiana, the CIA's efforts were again standard and succeeded only indirectly. In Liberia, well-established instruments (UN, British, and regional troops) as well as a small number of marines, were used. Finally, in Haiti, the denial of economic aid was both an attempt at pressuring Aristide and, along with the funneling of resources to the opposition, an instrument that had been used in many other places to weaken the government for the upcoming elections; but when the exiles invaded (which the U.S. seems to have abetted), the police had been so weakened by the government's budgetary problems (a direct result of the U.S. aid cutoff) that they were unable to resist. This is not to deny that in all four cases, the U.S. set out to get rid of the country's leader; but it is to point out that in practice, the policy instruments adopted triggered this consequence via sequences quite different than had been planned in Washington. It is also possible that the U.S. could have failed and thus been forced to coexist, at least for a while longer, with the leaders.

One implication of policy being means-driven is that there may have been other cases of attempts to topple leaders in a context of military neutrality. If policy instruments are standard tools easily employable if leaders are disliked, and if their effects are often different, in practice, than intended, then there may well be other client states in which the U.S. tried but failed to end the military's neutrality. Since in those cases there would be no deposed leaders to cry scandal, documents or other inside information would be less likely to surface. For example, there are bits of evidence to suggest that in 1976 the U.S. tried unsuccessfully to depose the prime minister of Jamaica, Michael Manley, but the documentary record on this is almost nonexistent and is likely to remain so even when the *FRUS* volumes for 1976 are published.[67]

Military opposed: coups d'état: *Node 16*

Guatemala (1920: text); Cuba (1934: text); South Korea (1961: text); South Vietnam (1963: website); Brazil (1964: text); Chile (1970: text)

From the discussion above, it is clear that if a client's military is either supportive of the country's leaders or neutral toward them, the process of deposing those leaders involves the U.S. acting to counter or sway the military. If, however, the military, or at least a segment of it, is opposed to the leaders, then paradoxically, the U.S. task becomes more complicated. At least since World War II, overthrowing leaders of American clients by sending in U.S. troops only occurs or is contemplated in circumstances where the leaders can be accused of gross malfeasance; similarly, the methods used to depose leaders such as Arbenz or Aristide lend themselves to claims that the overthrow was effected by ordinary citizens or neutral administrators who were unhappy with the situation. By contrast, if the military carries out a coup d'état which results in the exile, or perhaps even the death, of the leaders, then either of the above arguments are harder to put forward. Harder, but not impossible: the deposed leaders must be presented as having been corrupt, or subversive, or woesomely incompetent; and the military must be seen as responding to broad civilian demands. Early examples of coups justified by the U.S. along these lines are the removal of the Guatemalan dictator in 1920 (see Chapter 3) on grounds of his "insanity" and the overthrow of the Cuban president in 1934 (pressured diplomatically, and with U.S. ships anchored in Havana harbor) on grounds that he did not enjoy the "confidence" of "the Cuban people."[68]

Several decades later, the president of Brazil, João Goulart, was deposed by the military. This was not the first time that the country's military had meddled in presidential politics – it had overthrown Goulart's mentor on two occasions and had intervened unsuccessfully to prevent two other presidents from taking office – but on this occasion the United States played a particularly significant role. Although initially suspicious of Goulart's "past associations with Communists and his anti-US positions," the U.S. finally decided to back Goulart and offer both long-term development aid and limited short-term financial assistance to Brazil. Over the next twenty months or so, relations oscillated. Goulart alternated between moves to the left and reassurances to U.S. officials (including Kennedy's brother, sent as a special envoy for talks at the end of 1962); the U.S., now seeing Goulart as a "clever opportunist" with enough military support to make a coup "highly unlikely" and covert action in pursuit of that as not "feasible," opted to "seek to change the political and economic orientation of Goulart and his government." A new financial agreement was thus reached in the spring of 1963, leading officials in Washington first to describe themselves as "encouraged" by Goulart's actions and then, as his anti-inflation program "began to sag," as "gravely concerned about the deterioration." This in turn triggered new cycles of warmth and coolness.

By January of 1964, the U.S. had begun to consider the prospect of an "interim military takeover" in Brazil. There was "in the military a very considerable reservoir of good will toward the United States and sympathy toward U.S. objectives and policy"; to protect against further "political erosion" in the armed forces, it was of "high political importance" to cultivate them, including by lending money to buy U.S. planes and other material. This attitude sharpened after Goulart expropriated land and oil refineries and, the same day, held a rally in which he called for constitutional amendments, among them the legalization of the communist party. The U.S. mission characterized these actions as "rapid deterioration of situation," with the prospect that "substantial amounts of ground may be lost irrevocably." Within a week, the ambassador, Lincoln Gordon, was reporting that the Brazilian military was discussing conditions under which a coup could be triggered and appealing for U.S. assistance. Two days later, Gordon sent an emergency telegram through the CIA, requesting that it be passed to the top policy makers in Washington. "My considered conclusion," he wrote, "is that Goulart is now definitely engaged on campaign to seize dictatorial power, accepting the active colla- boration of the Brazilian Communist Party, and of other radical left revolutionaries to this end." Gordon went on to argue that unless the U.S. was willing to have Brazil end up like China, it should support the main group of coup plotters in the military by clan- destinely furnishing them weapons of non-U.S. origin and by providing them fuel and lubricants, again without U.S. markings. In the meantime, he continued, the U.S. mis- sion was providing "covert support" for street rallies, discreetly making it clear that the U.S. was "deeply concerned at events," and encouraging anti-Goulart sentiment "in Congress, armed forces, friendly labor and student groups, church, and business."

Gordon's message set off a flurry of high-level meetings. It was agreed that day (28 March) to send fuel and lubricants and, two days later, to ship arms, although, in the absence of an airlift, none of these supplies could arrive for another week. In Rio de Janeiro, the mission maintained its contacts with leading generals. On 31 March, the coup began. Gordon contacted state governors, encouraging them through intermediaries to join the coup to give it the "color of legitimacy" and if possible to engineer a cov- ering vote by the Brazilian Congress. The pro-coup forces quickly gained ground and, on 2 April, Goulart fled the country. That same day, Johnson sent his "warmest good wishes" to Goulart's successor, stating that the "American people ... have admired the resolute will of the Brazilian community to resolve [its] difficulties within a framework of constitutional democracy." The military, as it turned out, would remain in power for a quarter of a century.[69]

We have discussed this case in some detail because it illustrates the combination of reaction and approval that is evident when the U.S. supports *coups d'état*. Brazil, as Rusk pointed out to Gordon, was a country "of over 75 million people, larger than con- tinental United States" and to depose its president was "not a job for a handful of United States Marines." U.S. intervention would therefore have to take the form of sup- porting "those elements" of the military who would themselves "move." This, however, does not only mean that if Brazil had been smaller, the U.S. would have contemplated intervening with its own troops. Rather, the point is that the military's hostility to Goulart provided a lever to get rid of him and that until that hostility was manifest, the U.S. had little choice but to accept him. Only when the military turned against Goulart and voiced its alarm to the CIA station and the military attachés could U.S. officials, with impeccable cybernetic logic, characterize the situation as rapidly deteriorating. Had the military maintained a neutral posture, then the only basis on which Gordon could have drafted a "sky is falling" cable would have been reports from the right-wing forces from whom the U.S. was already distancing itself or from the major industrialists or landowners whom the U.S. had already been willing to sell out. Similarly, had seg- ments of the military supported Goulart after his 13 March rally, then the U.S. would have had to claim malfeasance by the top officers to have even imagined sending troops, something that would have been difficult in light of Goulart's constitutional legitimacy. In short, the U.S. did not have multiple alternatives for dealing with Goulart: its ties with the military meant that the situation was defined, and U.S. policy set, in terms of the military's reactions. A coup was in effect the only possibility at that point, and this is what we mean by the U.S. as reacting.[70]

On the other hand, the Brazilian military definitely sought U.S. approval, and indeed assistance, for the coup. Does this mean that if Washington had not given its blessing, the coup would not have taken place? There is no way of knowing; but certainly U.S. opposition, accompanied by a threat of an even more stringent aid cutoff, would have given pause to the generals. Of course, a policy of this sort is rarely carried out, not least because most coups seem to offer the prospect of strengthening client regimes, at least by comparison with the predecessor leaders now overthrown. Undoubtedly, U.S. officials feel "repugnance" for certain military takeovers, as in Argentina in 1966; but just as clearly, "cool analysis" militates in favor of uninterrupted collaboration after a "decent interval." In effect, the U.S. has the power to stop, or at least hinder, coups, but rarely bothers to do so.[71]

Why this policy? To answer this question, it is important to keep in mind two facts. One is that, for a variety of reasons, the military in many states already played an important role in government before those states were acquired as U.S. clients. The second fact is that routine U.S. surveillance and maintenance of clients involves close contact with their militaries. Hence, since situation reports from the field will tend to stress threats to stability (see Chapter 2), those threats will often be defined through the military's perspective. This does not mean that U.S. officials agree with everything their military informants say or that they have a preference for military rule; but it does lead to a sense that a coup may be (or may have been) useful, even if regrettable. This, we think, is why the U.S. so rarely takes active steps to prevent coups from taking place and why so many U.S. clients have at some point during their status as client either continued as a client after experiencing a military coup that overthrew the countries' leaders or became a client by a coup. By our count, all but one Spanish-speaking country in Latin America (plus Brazil and Haiti) fall into this category, as do most U.S. clients in Asia and Africa. Only in Europe and the Middle East have U.S. clients generally escaped this fate.[72]

These considerations help to decipher the U.S. role in a particularly notorious *coup d'état*, that carried out in Chile against the country's elected president, Salvador Allende, on 11 September 1973. The story, as we saw earlier in this chapter, began with the 1964 elections, in which the U.S. used the CIA to give emergency political assistance to the Christian Democrats so that their presidential candidate, Eduardo Frei, would defeat Allende. By 1970, though, the left had become stronger and in the election of 4 September, Allende received a plurality, though not a majority, of the popular vote. Under the constitution, this result threw the election into the hands of the Chilean congress, and the U.S. decided on a covert operation with political, economic, and propaganda components aimed at inducing the congress to elect someone other than Allende or, failing that, to create a sufficient degree of panic that the military would feel compelled to stage a coup. Neither goal was achieved.

However, even as the covert operation was being launched by an interagency group, Nixon ordered a second, deeply secret intervention. The director of the CIA, Richard Helms, was summoned to the White House the next day and told that Allende was "unacceptable" and that the CIA should do whatever it needed to prevent him from taking office. Nixon made clear that no other agencies of government were to be informed, including the State Department, the Defense Department, and the interagency group that was in charge of the other operation. Helms thus cabled his station chief in Santiago that "Purpose of exercise is to prevent Allende assumption of power. Parliamentary legerdemain has been discarded. Military solution is objective." In pursuit of this "Track Two" strategy, the CIA contacted Chilean officers and let them know the U.S. would support a coup. When the officers asked for weapons without serial numbers, the CIA obliged, sending them by diplomatic pouch. Nonetheless, the staunch constitutionalism of the army's top officer, Rene Schneider, made a coup unlikely at that time and Kissinger decided that although it was still "firm and continuing policy that Allende be overthrown by a coup," the plotters be advised to suspend their activities for the time being. They refused (perhaps being encouraged by the delivery two days later of U.S. machine guns) and tried on two occasions to kidnap General Schneider. During a third attempt, Schneider was killed while trying to defend himself. Although this triggered martial law and the appointment of the chief plotter to a key position, the army refused to budge and Allende was elected by the congress.

At this point, the U.S. embarked on a longer-term effort at pushing Allende out of office (node 14 above). Economic aid from the U.S. and, as we saw in Chapter 4, from multilateral development banks, was cut, even as military sales and training increased sharply. Money was passed to opposition parties, to supposedly independent groups opposed to Allende, and to anti-Allende communications media, notably the newspaper *El Mercurio*. In the meantime, close intelligence ties were maintained with the Chilean military, and even though the CIA station was told that the U.S. would not support instigating a coup, it was clear to the military that the U.S. would take a benevolent attitude in such an event. Thus, on 10 September 1973, a Chilean officer reported to his CIA contact that a coup was being planned and asked for U.S. assistance. Although he was duly told that none would be provided, "because this was strictly an internal Chilean matter," he was also told that the request "would be forwarded to Washington." The next day, the coup took place and Allende, defending himself in the presidential palace, seems to have committed suicide.[73]

As these examples show, the degree of U.S. involvement in a coup can vary considerably. At the high end of the scale (Chile Track Two), the CIA and other agencies can initiate contact with military officers, offering them political, financial, and weapons support. Not far below this comes U.S. receptivity to coup requests (Brazil 1964), in which the military first raises the prospect of a coup, asking for and receiving U.S. support. A somewhat lower-key posture is also possible (Chile 1973), with U.S. hostility to the leader being clear, covert support being given to opposition movements, and friendly contacts being maintained with the military.[74] A further limitation in the U.S. role comes in situations where, although the leader may be minimally acceptable to Washington, other segments of the regime – with whom the U.S. has good relations – are extremely worried, and, after indicating their intentions to the embassy, launch a coup. This occurred in Thailand in 1957, in Pakistan in 1958 (afterward, the U.S. ambassador congratulated the leader of the coup, saying that it was a "most pleasant task" to do so), in Turkey in 1960, and, it appears, in Ecuador in 1963. It is noteworthy that in these, as in all the other cases, of *coups d'état*, the new leaders quickly call in the U.S. ambassador to explain why a coup was necessary and how friendly they are to the U.S. (in Thailand, the ambassador was told that the new prime minister "would be pleasing to U.S. and to me personally"). Finally, the least active way in which the U.S. supports coups is what we might call the "lesser of two evils" strategy, in which the military acts, against U.S. advice, to head off a situation where a truly unacceptable leader risks coming to power. In these circumstances, Washington's preference is for some action short of a coup (e.g., significant changes in policy, or coalition rule); it therefore condemns the seizure of power but without going any farther and, within a few weeks, works out a *modus vivendi* so that relations continue. One example of this is in Argentina in 1962, where the U.S., alarmed at the prospect of elections which might bring supporters of Juan Peron back to power, decided to "let events take their course" and not interfere with the military-induced resignation of the country's president. Another example is in Greece in 1967, where the U.S., deeply worried that elections in May would result in the eventual rule of Andreas Papandreou, did not use its extensive contacts with the military coup plotters to warn them off and contented itself with a "fairly starchy posture" toward the new government.[75]

We do not mean by this discussion to suggest that all *coups d'état* in U.S. client states result either in getting rid of leaders disliked by American policy makers or in imposing new leaders preferred by those policy makers. Clearly, some coups are considered by U.S. officials as resulting in governments with leaders worse than those who were overthrown. Nor do we mean to suggest that every coup that occurs is known about in advance by the U.S. or that the U.S. can simply let its wishes be known for a coup to take place. Nonetheless, given that the patron–client relation involves active surveillance of the regime (the government, the military, prominent business leaders, and so forth) by U.S. officials, it should be expected that when coups are planned, the U.S. is more often than not aware of plots well beforehand. Recently declassified communications to and from military attachés and CIA station officers bear out this expectation. Such foreknowledge is asymmetrical in its power: the U.S. can encourage fearful coup plotters by making it clear that they will receive support both before and after the event; but, as we saw in the case of Chile in 1970, the U.S. has less power to prevent the coup, since both sides are aware that there is no enthusiasm for confronting its own client's military or other influential sectors of the regime. The same logic applies even more strongly after the coup and helps explain why the U.S. almost always reconciles itself even to those coups it opposes (e.g., that in Pakistan in 1999).[76]

One additional observation. As the above discussion makes clear, the United States has nearly a century of experience in dealing with client states having undergone coups and also has close ties with the military of most of its clients. This means that the possibility of encouraging a coup is always a policy instrument available to U.S. officials whenever they are confronted with unacceptable leaders in a country. From a cybernetic point of view, it becomes easy to push the coup button in such circumstances, regardless of whether the military is indeed opposed to the leaders. If it is, the chances of a coup are increased; if not, then the U.S. will (perhaps after several more efforts) be led to recategorize the situation and opt for one of the other overthrow strategies discussed above. In this sense, the resort to coup encouragement as a default policy instrument serves in itself as a surveillance and information-gathering mechanism.

These aspects of coup plotting are particularly noteworthy in cases where there is an active military enemy. In such circumstances, U.S. ties with the client are likely to be even more concentrated on the military parts of the regime. One classic example, discussed at length on the book's website, is the coup which resulted in the deposition and murder of South Vietnam's president Ngo Dinh Diem. Another, less well-known case, is South Korea, where the U.S. had kept a significant number of troops; there, the 1961 coup by Park Chung Hee was reported on by the CIA a month in advance, with no message of discouragement being passed on to the plotters. On the day of the coup, the Korean chief of staff was constantly in touch with the commander of U.S. forces, General Magruder, pleading with him to use American soldiers to block Park's troops. Magruder refused, although both he and the U.S. chargé d'affaires, Marshall Green, issued statements condemning the coup and reiterated this position during a three-hour meeting with the country's president. This activism alarmed Washington, which was distinctly cool to the South Korean prime minister (who, with his cabinet, was the real target of the coup, being disavowed by his own president) and which issued a wait-and-see statement of its own, adding conspicuously that Magruder's and Green's comments were made solely "within the scope of their authority in their posts." Magruder, who in fact commanded one of the South Korean armies and could have ordered it to suppress the coup, realized which way the wind was blowing and refrained from further action.[77]

Maintenance interventions in perspective

Over the past century, the United States has often resorted to one or another type of intervention in order to address problems which might threaten the loss of a client state. Of course, there are far fewer of these interventions than there are routine maintenance operations, since the former take place only in dire situations, whereas the latter occur year-in year-out, in clients around the world. Interventions, however, can easily end up leading to many deaths and costing considerable sums of money, and since the very possibility of their occurrence is part of the definition of a client state, we have spent considerable time discussing them. What, apart from their situation-specificity, have we learned about them?

It is useful to begin with a few totals. Over the course of this chapter, we have either mentioned or presented narrative accounts of some 68 interventions in 35 different countries (out of 89 current or former clients), spread across 16 different nodes (three of emergency assistance [nodes 1–2, 5], four of combat forces [nodes 6–9], five of overthrowing or jettisoning leaders [nodes 3, 13–16]). That is, not counting situations where the client was being lost and the U.S. finally decided that intervention was not feasible (nodes 4, 12), or in which the U.S. liquidated an ongoing troop deployment (nodes 10, 11), in at least 68 times over the past century, the U.S. has taken over a vital task, whether economic, political, or military, from one of its clients in order to maintain that client in power. These numbers, it should be pointed out, are conservative: they do not cover every instance of emergency financial, political, or military assistance; they exclude cases in which the U.S. role was merely one of encouraging others to act (e.g., Shaba I in Zaire); they only refer to *coups d'état* which the U.S. explicitly aided or attempted to trigger, and even then not to more than two instances or so per country;[78] and, as we indicated above, they likely omit some lower-profile covert operations. Nonetheless, even with this undercounting, a general pattern to U.S. maintenance interventions still emerges.

Of the 68 interventions, 33 were nonmilitary, while another 8 involved emergency military aid and advisers. That leaves 28 cases in which U.S. or proxy combat forces were the principal policy instrument; and of those, 24 in which the U.S. overtly employed its own ground combat forces on behalf of the regime. Thus, although the chances are slim that the United States is engaging in an intervention on behalf of a given client at a given moment in time, when that eventuality does occur, it is more likely to be military than nonmilitary, almost as likely to involve combat forces as other means, and reasonably likely to involve U.S. ground troops. This is quite emphatically not the kind of inverted pyramid we would expect from simple notions of escalation ladders in which force is a last resort and therefore quite rare. Certainly in some cases, Vietnam being the most prominent example (also Panama and Haiti), American policy makers were reluctant to commit ground troops (air power was less of a concern) on behalf of a client; but in most of the instances where U.S. ground troops were sent, that policy instrument was decided on quickly and with few or no lower-level means being tried first. What mattered was the situation: when the problem was military, the regime seen as able to hold on but as lacking sufficient manpower, and the enemy not judged as formidable, the U.S. moved rapidly to committing troops. In a purely formal sense, these decisions can be seen as escalation, if we take as our baseline the status quo ante (in some cases, a policy of emergency military aid and advisers); but the point is that once the situation was identified as being of a particular sort, a troop commitment was seen as the appropriate policy, rather than as the last resort, to be tried only after every other measure had failed.

How to explain this relatively high percentage of client maintenance interventions involving U.S. ground combat forces? In part, it has to do with the reporting bias discussed above: there were certainly additional instances of emergency economic assistance, and most likely of emergency covert political assistance as well. However, even if there were more nonmilitary interventions than we discussed, it remains true that military problems were both common and more likely to be dealt with by U.S. combat forces than by other means. A second explanation has to do with perceived or expected U.S. dominance. Officials in Washington, and usually in the field as well, expected that most of their clients' enemies would prove relatively easy to defeat (nodes 7, 8); the same also applied if it was the client's own military that stood in the way of removing an unacceptable leader (node 13). Of course, this expectation was flagrantly wrong in several cases, but as we will discuss in Chapter 7, such disasters did not significantly hinder subsequent life preserver and easy win U.S. troop commitments. The problem with U.S. dominance as an explanation is that it is applicable only to the particular situations listed above. When the client's military was deemed incompetent and the enemy formidable (node 9), policy makers opted for proxies, not U.S. ground troops; when there was not a manpower shortage, they instead turned to emergency military aid and advisers (node 5); and when the regime's military collapse was either rapid or massive, they tried simply to arrange a third force solution (node 12). In other words, the relatively high number of U.S. ground troop interventions on behalf of clients has relatively little to do with either a general condition of U.S dominance or a simple comparison between the U.S. and the forces it opposes.

A better explanation has to do with the cybernetic quality of U.S. policy making. In essence, there are five types of policy instruments available to the U.S. for interventionary client maintenance: (1) emergency economic aid, mostly in the form of emergency loans and advice; (2) emergency covert political aid, mostly in the form of propaganda, material assistance to political parties, and encouragement of coups and insurrections; (3) emergency military aid; (4) U.S. ground troops; and (5) proxy military forces (perhaps aided by U.S. air power). Two of these instruments – U.S. ground troops and emergency economic aid – date back to the early years of the twentieth century and have long had a particular organizational form: military units, on the one hand, and the ESF and IMF, on the other. Two other instruments – emergency covert political aid and emergency military aid – were developed and given organizational form after World War II, with further development still occurring in the 2000s. By contrast, the final instrument, proxy military forces, needed not only an organizational form (which it received with the OPC and its successors) but the proxy forces themselves. As we will see in the next chapter, the U.S. actively searched for proxies in its various hostile interventions, but they were considerably more scarce when it came to intervening on behalf of clients. The closest the U.S. ever came to acquiring a standing proxy force like the Gurkhas was the Cuban exiles it relied on in the Congo, hardly an all-purpose tool.

Thus, when all was said and done, the United States had only a handful of policy instruments available for intervention. These tools could certainly be adapted to the specifics of the situation and they were often cumulated (for example, continuing with emergency military aid even after combat forces were sent) but they were what economists call "lumpy": there were no hybrid tools available and very little possibility of crafting something novel, especially in light of the pressing nature of many of the problems faced by U.S. clients. As we have emphasized throughout this chapter, policy making involved matching situation descriptions to the tools in the U.S. repertoire. Since there were relatively few tools available overall, and for military problems even fewer, it is not surprising that quite often, Washington's solution was to send U.S. combat forces.

How often does U.S. intervention succeed in maintaining the client? By our count, as of early 2008, ten states were lost to the U.S. as clients, eight of them without being regained. Of the ten, one was lost in an uprising (Iran), another in a coup (Ethiopia), and eight more by military defeat. (Another U.S. client was defeated – France in Indochina – but was not lost as a client.) Of those eight, four losses occurred without the U.S. sending any military forces (China, Cuba, Zaire, Nicaragua), two more after the U.S. had sent proxy forces (Cambodia, Laos), and the last two after the U.S. had sent ground troops (South Vietnam, Lebanon). Thus, from Washington's perspective, if most interventions succeed, nonmilitary instruments tend to work out considerably better than military ones, and among the latter, emergency aid is more likely to succeed than combat forces. There is of course a selection bias here, since insurgencies tend to be more immediately dire than other problems and the odds may still be in favor of winning (almost three-quarters of all insurgencies in U.S. clients are crushed), but what is striking is (1) that U.S. military power is unable to prevent a significant number of client regimes from being defeated by rebellions and (2) that nonetheless the U.S. continues to intervene militarily on behalf of clients.

One final note. In the preceding section, we have mentioned or discussed 18 cases (in 13 countries) where the U.S. set out to get rid of the top political leaders of its clients, and four more cases in which the U.S. jettisoned the leaders in the face of popular discontent. In almost all of these cases, the U.S. succeeded, though it is pointless to come up with exact percentages in light of the numerous other coups we have not mentioned. What is striking is just how often the U.S. made the attempt. In other words, with some regularity, American officials decided that the top political leaders of a client themselves posed a problem to the continued maintenance of the regime and intervened to depose those leaders. We would therefore expect that when it comes to enemies, the U.S. would act with at least equal energy to overthrow their regimes. This was in fact the case, as we will now see.

6 Hostile interventions against enemy states

The U.S. client state empire is large, expanding, and long-lived. As we saw in Chapter 2, it stretches around the globe, accounting for over 40 percent of the world's countries, over a third of its population, and over 80 percent of its economic output. As we saw in Chapter 3, the empire began over a century ago and is still growing, with the latest acquisition as recent as 2004. And as we saw in Chapters 4 and 5, the empire is remarkably robust, with most clients being routinely maintained in that status and those with problems being maintained through U.S. intervention. At first blush, this track record would seem to be one of great success, leading U.S. policy makers to no small measure of satisfaction. However, to be a client is to have the U.S. continually concerned with the regime's maintenance and hence highly attentive to any problems which it deems potentially or actually threatening to that condition. A significant number of these problems involve real or imagined activities by those identified as opponents of the clients' regimes. Some problems, though, are attributed to other states, with the majority of such problems coming from states considered to be enemies of the United States.

In Chapter 3, we briefly discussed enemy states, which we defined as nonclients whose regimes are seen as choosing systematically to differ with the U.S. on key issues of foreign and domestic economic and political policy. These enemies, we pointed out, come in various ideological hues and have nothing in common except the U.S. perception that they have opted deliberately for across-the-board disagreements with Washington. Those disagreements are seen as extending to U.S. clients: enemy states are pictured as at the very least attempting to impede or disrupt U.S. policy regarding certain client states, and quite possibly as attempting to subvert the regimes of those clients. Enemies may also be perceived as posing a physical or ideological threat to the United States itself, but this danger is usually seen as accompanying threats to clients instead of substituting for those threats. Indeed, few of the enemies listed in Figure 3.1 were viewed by U.S. officials as a military danger to the U.S. itself; and the level of those officials' concern with specific enemies was unrelated to that danger.

In using words such as "perceive," "see," "view," "picture," and "imagine," we do not mean to imply that states categorized as enemies by U.S. policy makers in fact do nothing to undermine U.S. policy or aid domestic opponents of U.S. client regimes. Certainly such acts do occur, as they have in the past against both imperial powers and other states. Our point, rather, is to suggest that there is an important ideological and, as we will see, cybernetic connection between the categorization of a state as having chosen to differ systematically with the U.S., on the one hand, and its categorization as a danger to the U.S., on the other. In a world of theoretically separate and independent political units, a state that is seen as rejecting the norms proclaimed by existing or rising imperial powers will tend to be seen by the latter as endangering other units, so much so that there can be no genuine peace with that state unless and until it has changed not only its foreign policy but above all its internal power arrangements. Which of these – the nature of a regime or its foreign policy – comes first is a chicken-and-egg question; but imperial powers assuredly perceive some sort of connection. Thus, Philip II of Spain saw Elizabeth's England as impelled to its anti-Spanish naval raids and its support of Dutch rebels by the Protestantism it espoused, a faith that had already led to Elizabeth's condemnation by the Pope. Two centuries later, the British prime minister, William Pitt the Younger, proclaimed revolutionary France "a system which was in itself a declaration of war against all nations," with security impossible until "either the principle [of the system] has extinguished or its strength is exhausted." This rhetoric was repeated yet again after World War II, when one of the leading thinkers of the State Department informed Truman that:

> our free society finds itself morally challenged by the Soviet system. No other value system is so wholly irreconcilable with ours, so implacable in its purpose to destroy ours ... and no other has the support of a great and growing center of military power.[1]

A corollary of this point is that there is no necessary relation between enemy status and war. Imperial states can oppose enemies by various means short of war and may even decide that such attempts have so little chance of success and so many disadvantages that some sort of truce is the only reasonable solution. This, however, does not mean that genuine peace can be envisaged with the enemy: suspicions are dormant and can at any time be rekindled into active hostility. The U.S. attitude toward the Soviet Union is a good case in point, with periods of fierce animosity punctuating more relaxed inter-vals. Conversely, it is possible to go to war against a particular state without that state being seen as an enemy: there may be a specific dispute justifying war but not a per-ception of the adversary as systematically choosing to differ. Examples of this are Spain in the Spanish-American War, condemned only for its actions in Cuba and not as a Pitt-style "system"; Austria-Hungary in World War I, whom Wilson qualified as "not her own mistress but simply the vassal of the German Government" (Germany's other allies were described as "mere tools" not worth fighting unless they were to take up arms against the U.S.); and Italy in World War II, which U.S. policy makers mostly ignored before and during the war (even as they invaded it) and whose internal political and economic system was mostly left alone once the leading Fascists were deposed.[2]

These considerations point to a fundamental distinction between U.S. policy toward those whom it considers enemies and toward other states with whom it may be hostile. Since, as per our definition, enemies are seen as having chosen to differ systematically with the United States, only temporary agreements are possible with them and routine relations (see below) involve a considerable measure of mistrust and perhaps of obses-siveness (the Cuban case, which we will discuss later, is only the most prominent example of this). On the other hand, U.S. policy toward nonenemy states is con-siderably more limited in its scope, its duration, and, significantly, its emotional charge. This can be seen for three sets of nonenemy states. The first set pertains to the period prior to the establishment of the client state empire, when the U.S. fought wars against foes such as Britain, Mexico, and Spain, even though none of those states were seen as being ruled by regimes which had opted to oppose everything that the U.S. favored.

Wars could end with territorial adjustments and without a sense that the only long-term solution was for the foe to be destroyed. The second set covers states considered by U.S. policy makers to be "tools," as Wilson put it, or "satellites," as certain clients of the Soviet Union were described. The U.S. may have found it expedient to undertake some type of hostile action against these states but only as part of its policy against their patrons; if, as often happened, the hostile action failed, then the U.S. would move on, no longer aiming at overthrowing the enemy's clients. A good example of this is the way in which, after a brief flirtation with "para-military operations against the Soviet orbit, particularly those operations designed to weaken Kremlin control over the satellites," it was recognized that "Soviet domination of the Eastern European satellites remains firm," that "sustained resistance activities" had no chance of succeeding, and that the best policy was to "encourage such national Communist movements where we believe the effect will be to disrupt the tie between the satellite state and the USSR" (see below). Finally, there have been other states which, although perceived as being opposed to elements of U.S. policy, were also seen as dependent on Western aid and therefore as incapable of differing systematically with the United States. These "steady nuisances," as one official described them, were not viewed as particularly worrisome and, even when local U.S. officials were criticized or expelled, bilateral economic aid continued.[3]

The differences between U.S. policy toward enemies and toward other types of adversaries suggest that Washington surveils far more closely nonclients who are already enemies than those with whom it has limited disagreements. Clients, of course, are surveilled more closely still via the field apparatus discussed in Chapter 2. These differing levels of observation point to basic cybernetic mechanisms by which U.S. policy makers categorize states as entering or exiting enemy status. First, as we saw in Chapter 5, when clients are "lost" through military defeat or the disintegration of the military chain of command, the state is quickly perceived as an enemy. For nonclients, who are observed less closely, the bar to being seen as an enemy is higher: a policy perceived as anti-U.S. combined with a significant change in the reported internal or external base of the regime (e.g., Japan, Syria, Ghana). The same mechanisms apply when it comes to leaving enemy status. If an enemy switches sides (Chapter 3) and/or throws its lot in with the United States, it automatically becomes a U.S. client. However, if the regime does not agree to align itself with the U.S., then the only other ways of losing its enemy status are, as we will discuss below, to make an explicit agreement with Washington to change a broad array of policies and/or its internal or external political base (e.g., Angola, Libya); to change regimes for reasons other than U.S. pressure (e.g., the fall of the Communist Party in the Soviet Union); or, ironically, to become the client of another U.S. enemy (e.g., Cambodia). Note once more that we are focusing on policy tools and reporting mechanisms, not ideological or strategic criteria. Enemies are every bit as diverse as are clients.

It might be asked whether nonstate actors can be enemies as we are using the term. Certainly some of those actors, such as narcotics trafficking organizations, national liberation movements, and networks specializing in acts of terror against particular states, are often seen as rejecting systematically many or all U.S. policies. However, what distinguishes enemies from other adversaries is not only the choice they are supposed to have made to differ systematically with the U.S., but the sense that this choice is that of a regime, i.e., of an arrangement of political and economic power in a particular society. This is what makes it possible for policy makers to think of deposing an enemy or having it switch to the U.S. side: namely, that the citizens of the country can, in principle, be governed by a very different regime, perhaps even a U.S. client. Indeed, U.S. policy makers routinely consider enemies to be in the grip of regimes which oppress their populations and which the latter ought to be encouraged to overthrow. Here, for example, is an appeal by one secretary of state in words which, changing the proper nouns, could have used by his predecessors going back to the early 1900s and by his successors up to the present day:

> The needless prolongation of your suffering and moral slavery rests in your hands. The United Nations demand your honorable surrender, your unconditional military surrender. Overthrow Hitler and his corrupt colleagues, turn your arms against their Gestapo and their SS. Thus you will speed the day of Germany's restoration to a position of respectability in the family of nations.

Rhetoric of this sort is common and corresponds to the operational logic of many forms of hostile intervention which, as we will see, are premised on an attempt at cutting the ties between the enemy regime and the population of its country. Enemies, hence, are imagined capable of being transformed into nonenemies. By contrast, the various nonstate adversaries listed above cannot, it is thought, be so transformed: they either can be destroyed completely or else are seen as representing a danger that will last forever. Hence, the objects of U.S. enemy policy, as of its client policy, are states.[4]

Whatever their ideological complexion or even the resources they command, enemies are seen as dangerous to U.S. clients (and, in rare instances, to the U.S. itself). This danger is both specific and general. Particular enemies may be perceived as threatening individual clients by subversion or, less commonly, invasion. These threats, as we saw in Chapters 4 and 5, are addressed by various policy instruments ranging from routine forms of resource transfers and other assistance to different types of intervention on behalf of the clients. The general danger is structural in character: even if enemies are certified as being on good behavior and not trying to subvert U.S. clients, the systematic nature of the policy choices they are supposed to have made means that they represent – if only by their continued existence – an ongoing potential threat to various clients. To counter this, U.S. policy makers have been led over the years not only to act on behalf of clients but against enemies. There are two sorts of anti-enemy actions, analogous to those used for client maintenance: routinely hostile activities and hostile interventions.

What *routinely hostile activities* have in common is the displeasure they express. The point is not to overthrow an enemy's regime (although this would be welcome) but to act on the basis that the enemy is in some sense abnormal and unfit for regular state-to-state relations. Hence, the U.S. may withhold diplomatic recognition, block UN membership, decree or intensify a trade embargo, vote against multilateral loans, forbid normal travel by citizens of either country, offer asylum to immigrants from the enemy, attempt to restrict weapons and technology transfers, verbally support exiled opposition leaders, electronically broadcast propaganda, and, of course, denounce the enemy as illegitimate and a violator of basic norms (e.g., human rights). Most of these policy instruments can be carried out in tandem and are, from a symbolic perspective, mutually substitutable; this makes it possible for some of them to be repealed as part of a limited agreement with the enemy, even as others are maintained or perhaps imposed. Note further that there is nothing special or even, for the most part, contrary to international law, about these instruments: several of them presume the backing of other states, or indeed of international organizations such as the United Nations or the Organization of American States (OAS), indicating that much of the time, the U.S. is leading multilateral opinion even when it comes to expressing anger at enemies. For example, when Japan was condemned by the League of Nations for its actions in Manchuria, the League's action was instigated by the United States, which was only an observer in Geneva. Similarly, as we saw in Chapter 4, the U.S. has for decades administered export controls aimed at the Soviet Union and other enemies through a multilateral agency, COCOM, and its successor. This international backing for hostile activities extended even against enemies on whom it was acknowledged that the U.S. had a particular fixation: China, whose seat in the UN the General Assembly voted to deny to Beijing for 20 years; Cuba, against whom the OAS decreed a trade embargo and banned diplomatic relations (this policy stood for over a decade), and, as of 2008, was still excluded from participation in the organization; and Iran, target of a U.S.-led investment boycott and anti-nuclear campaign.

For the most part, policies of routine hostility are maintained toward enemies regardless of what the enemies do. If an enemy persists in acting contrary to U.S. wishes, American policy makers take this as indicative of virulent opposition and therefore as a license both to continue routinely hostile activities and, if the situation warrants it, to engage in hostile intervention (see below). If the enemy negotiates an agreement with the U.S. on a specific matter of disagreement, that is usually seen in Washington as a sign that its policy is paying off and hence as grounds for continuing or even escalating most forms of pressure except for the points on which accord was reached (see below, on negotiations). As mentioned above, it takes really major changes by the enemy (typically the subject of a lengthily negotiated package deal) or else a significant change in the international environment for U.S. officials to end routinely hostile activities; even then, bureaucratic resistance goes hand in glove with those activities and makes it difficult for them to be scrapped. A classic case in point is the Roosevelt–Litvinov agreement extending diplomatic recognition to the U.S.S.R. in 1933 and negotiating a solution to a host of outstanding disputes. This agreement necessitated a new U.S. president, the exclusion of the State Department from policy making, significant policy changes on the part of the Soviet Union, and a common recognition by both states that Japan's actions in Manchuria and elsewhere in China signalled a threat to the area. There are a handful of other cases in which the U.S. negotiated an end to enemy status; we will discuss them at the end of the chapter.[5]

Routinely hostile activities are the background, the standard way in which the United States deals with enemies. However, from time to time, these activities are supplemented by specific operations directed against an enemy regime's military support at home or the maintenance of its forces in one or more geographical areas. These operations are what we mean by the term *hostile intervention*, and several aspects of this definition should be noted. First, hostile interventions are directed against one or more of several related types of targets: the armed forces of an enemy in one of its client states as well as the armed forces of the client state itself; an enemy's occupation of a particular province which it claims as part of its own territory; and the military basis of the enemy regime itself. To policy makers in Washington, these various targets are closely linked as alternative ways in which a given enemy might manifest itself, even though the distinction between them may be seen as opening up space for diplomacy (for example, as we will see below, the U.S. wanted to have North Vietnam cease its military activities in South Vietnam, while at the same time reassuring it that, unlike in the Korean War, there was no intention of invading the north or overthrowing the regime in Hanoi).

Second, hostile interventions are directed against the military of an enemy regime: either its status as the key component of the regime at home or its presence in a province or client. This does not mean that the authors of these interventions expect the enemy's military immediately to launch a coup, or to be destroyed in battle, or to withdraw quickly from a province or client in the near future, but it does mean that the operations are expected to impinge on the military at some point and thus to present the possibility of the regime's overthrow or of its retreat from some location. In this sense, hostile interventions are the mirror image of interventions on behalf of clients. If policy makers think that a given operation has no chance of affecting the regime's military anywhere or at any time, then the operation is purely expressive or symbolic and hence falls into the category of routinely hostile activities. It should also be noted that even though initial authorizing orders may refer to more limited goals, those goals typically expand, with both high level policy makers and their subordinates soon proclaiming far more grandiose ambitions.

Third, there is a strong connection between hostile intervention, as we have defined it, and acts of war against a state. If an act of war is carried out against an enemy, then, unless it is purely punitive or symbolic, it is at the same time an intervention. (The definition of hostile intervention in terms of enemies means that, as we discussed above, acts of war against nonenemies are not interventions.) However, this link is not just a matter of overlapping situations: even when the intervening state does not use its own armed forces, its proximate target is the armed forces of the enemy, so as to make it impossible for them to maintain themselves in a given territory or to support a given regime. In this sense, hostile intervention shares some of the same aims as traditional war, though in its frequent targeting of the enemy regime, it is considerably more far-reaching. Put differently, just as client intervention is a means of maintaining clients, so hostile intervention is a means of undermining, if not outright overthrowing, enemies.[6]

Although routinely hostile activities differ significantly from hostile interventions, the policy that the U.S. follows toward any given enemy may be a combination of both. We pointed out above that routinely hostile activities are a sort of baseline carried out against enemies year after year. On top of that baseline, the U.S. may also engage in hostile interventions, depending, as with client interventions, on the type of situation it perceives. Although, as we will see, a failed hostile intervention will lead to a change in the situation and thus indicate an end to that particular operation, if another promising situation should later arise, the U.S. would in that case initiate a new hostile intervention appropriate to the changed circumstances. Just as various types of intervention are always possible as means of maintaining clients, so too are various types of intervention possible against enemies. The only limitations on such repetitions are practical: for example, if exile raids fail, it is unlikely that an internal guerrilla movement will arise any time soon or that the enemy will engage in some action which turns it into a pariah, thereby justifying U.S. overt intervention of some sort (see below). In this sense, as we will discuss later, there are similarities between escalation constraints on interventions against enemies and those on behalf of clients.

Consider now the different types of hostile intervention situations (see Figure 6.1). Using the pseudo-decision tree approach introduced in Chapter 5, we can start with the top-level questions: is the country a current client state and if not, is it a nonenemy? If

Figure 6.1 Hostile intervention situations, 1: Overview

the answer to this latter question is also no, then hostile intervention is a possibility providing that actions against the enemy's military are assessed as having some chance of success, i.e., of leading to the overthrow of the enemy regime or its withdrawal from a province or client. (This assessment, it should be noted, is made cybernetically, i.e., by determining whether proxy or multilateral policy instruments exist; see below.) Should success be seen as out of the question, then policy reverts to the default position, i.e., routinely hostile actions. (Such actions may, on rare occasions, be interrupted by attempts at negotiation, a possibility we will discuss at the end of the chapter.) If, on the other hand, hostile intervention is indicated, the issue is then the form of that intervention. Here, the basic question is whether or not the enemy is perceived by U.S. policy makers as having some degree of international legitimacy (see below): if the answer is yes, then hostile intervention must be covert in nature; if not, then intervention will be overt.

Covert intervention situations

Since the 1990s, the United States has widely come to be perceived as violating international law. The examples most frequently cited of these violations are the bombing of Serbia in 1999 and the invasion of Iraq in 2003, both of which we will discuss below. However, it must be recognized that actions of this sort are fairly rare, and that the U.S. has, in the vast majority of cases, refrained from the overt use or support of force in

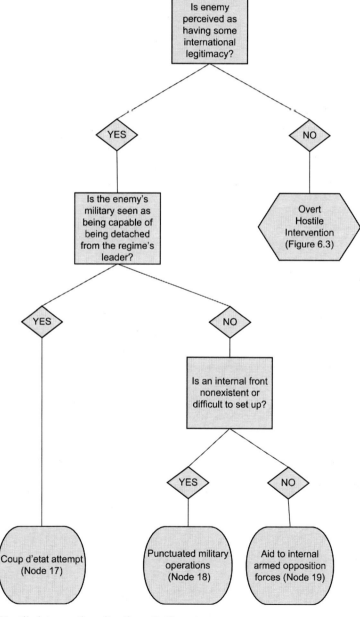

Figure 6.2 Hostile intervention situations, 2: Covert

cases where the enemy is a sovereign state or where the legal status of U.S. combat units or trainers is in question (e.g., because they are not present at the invitation of a sovereign state). If these conditions do not apply, then only if the enemy in question is seen internationally as committing barbaric or uncivilized acts and hence as politically illegitimate will the U.S. feel free explicitly to violate international law. Otherwise, the U.S. will intervene against the enemy covertly, i.e., without acknowledging its actions.[7]

Of course covert interventions are hypocritical, in the famous definition of François de la Rochefoucauld ("hypocrisy is the homage which vice pays to virtue"). Nonetheless, constraints on overt military action revolve around the maintenance of the U.S. self-image as a state which does not lightly (or at all) infringe on the sovereignty of other states and which does not bully weaker states. Policy makers take this self-image for granted, only bothering even to mention it when a subordinate puts forward a plan which violates it. For example, when, during the deliberations over the collapse of the French in Indochina (see the book's website), the official in charge of foreign aid proposed that the U.S. send combat troops even if the French, as the colonial power, refused to act, Eisenhower reacted sharply, saying that action of this sort would lead to a loss of "all our significant support in the free world. We should be everywhere accused of imperialistic ambitions. ... Without allies and associates the leader is just an adventurer like Genghis Khan." Some years later, when the CIA's initial plan for using U.S. forces to land an exile army in Cuba was being presented (see below), the secretary of state warned that "such an operation could have grave effects upon the U.S. position in Latin America and at the U.N." Covert operations offer the possibility of avoiding these kind of difficulties because they are "plausibly deniable," to use the standard paraphrase of the original order authorizing such operations (see Chapter 5).[8]

Covert intervention situations are distinguished from each other by two criteria (see Figure 6.2). First, it matters considerably whether or not the enemy's military is seen as capable of being detached from the regime's leaders. If so, then *coups d'état* or other violent action can be plotted against those leaders, similar (though, as we will see, more difficult) to the actions undertaken against unacceptable leaders of U.S. clients (node 17). However, if U.S. policy makers assess the military as unlikely to be separated from the regime's leaders, then the military itself will be combated by some kind of larger-scale action. The question in this case is whether an internal front is either nonexistent or difficult to establish. If so, then the U.S. will opt for punctuated military operations: landings, airdrops, and brief raids (node 18). On the other hand, should an internal front be judged possible, then American policy will aim at supporting continuing armed opposition operations within the enemy's territory (node 19). In both these cases of larger-scale action, the ones doing the actual fighting will of necessity be proxies which are organized, paid, equipped, and trained by the United States.

Coups d'état: *Node 17*

> Syria (1949: website); Iran (1953: website); Egypt (1956–57: text); Syria (1956–57: website); Iraq (1963: text); Indonesia (1965: text); Ghana (1966: website); Iraq (1996: text)

For U.S. policy makers to have a chance of fomenting a *coup d'état* against the regime of an enemy state, they need at the minimum to have some contacts with the enemy's military. However, the U.S. has relatively limited connections of this sort, whether in the form of training, arms transfers, or even military observers. This contrasts sharply with the extensive links (see Chapters 2 and 4) between Washington and the militaries of its client states. Of course, on purely prudential grounds, it might be rational for the U.S. to cultivate such ties with the military of each enemy, but in the vast majority of cases, it is unlikely that this would occur. U.S. officials would not want to take the risk of strengthening an enemy and the latter would be loath to provide an opening for fifth column activities. Hence in general, the odds are slim that the U.S. would even try to set off a coup against an enemy.

There are, however, two situations in which a coup is likely to be pursued. First, if the regime has only recently come to power, there may still be ties from the period before it was a U.S. enemy. One example of this is Egypt, where it appears, first, that the U.S. helped Nasser and his military colleagues come to power and fend off internal foes; and then, that the U.S. tried to induce the military to overthrow Nasser after he had turned to the Soviet Union for arms.[9] Another example, for which considerably more internal documents are available, is Syria, where the United States moved from having splendid relations with the regime to full-fledged enemy status in just a few years (for a discussion, see the book's web site).

Another enemy state in which the U.S. attempted to foment *coups d'état* shortly after the regime had come to power is Iraq. Up until the summer of 1958, Iraq was a British client state, ruled by a staunchly pro-Western regime. A coup in July led to considerable turmoil, including U.S. intervention in Lebanon (see Chapter 5) and British intervention in Jordan. Soon, disaffected military officers were asking the U.S. to fund a coup and passing on information about plans for an uprising and an assassination attempt on the regime's strongman, Abdel Karim Qassim. Although the U.S. did not apparently participate in these efforts, it moved toward "preliminary contingency planning" for covert action of its own. Soon after, the CIA was privy to information on another assassination attempt (carried out by the young Saddam Hussein), meanwhile developing its own plan for sending Qassim "a monogrammed handkerchief containing an incapacitating agent." Although this plan did not work out, Qassim's days were numbered: the CIA worked with Ba'ath party militants in the army and in February 1963, Ba'ath soldiers overthrew and executed Qassim. (In the words of the party's secretary general: "we came to power on a CIA train.") As we saw in Chapter 4, the CIA also transmitted names of those it considered leftist sympathizers and the new regime killed at least hundreds, and perhaps thousands, of them over the next weeks. While this was happening, the U.S. secretly supplied the Ba'ath regime with military equipment. Nonetheless, the regime did not survive and before the year was out, it was overthrown in another coup, this time by officers then sympathetic with Nasser. It would take five years for the Ba'athists to rebuild their networks among the military and stage a pair of coups in 1968 that would bring them back to power; once back in, they shifted to the left and, with the help of Soviet and East German advisers, purged the military and put it under tight party control, thereby reducing drastically the possibility of future coup attempts against them (see below).[10]

A second type of situation in which the U.S. is likely to pursue a coup against an enemy state is when the regime of that state is judged to be a rickety coalition of elements at odds with each other. In these circumstances, it makes sense for the U.S. to try and peel away the military from other components of the regime. The classic example of a coup attempted under these conditions is Operation TPAJAX, the CIA-sponsored overthrow of Prime Minister Mohammad Mossadeq in Iran (see Chapter 3 for the coup's consequences, and the book's website for a detailed account of the coup).

The coup against Mossadeq could only be envisaged, much less carried out success-fully, because of his loss of support among the military. Much the same situation was perceived as holding, and as justifying a coup, in two other U.S. enemies, Indonesia and Ghana (on this latter case, see the description on the book's website). In Indonesia, the U.S. had for a number of years been hostile to the regime of Achmed Sukarno. When a CIA-supported rebellion fizzled out in 1958 (see the book website), the U.S. began focusing its efforts on establishing ties with "the strongest anti-communist force in Indonesia," the country's army. These were above all personal, with top army officers being trained in the United States at military institutions and younger officers, as part of "civic action" programs, at leading U.S. universities. Small arms were also provided for internal security purposes. Although at this point the odds of a coup taking place were still "less than even," the expectation was that when Sukarno died or retired (his health was supposed to be bad), there would be a struggle for power among the regime's other main components – the Communist Party (PKI) and the military – and if the U.S. main-tained close ties with the military, it might turn out to have bet on a winning horse.

The pro-army policy was inherently unstable. If, as most in Washington thought, the PKI was continuing to gain in power, then unless Sukarno were to fall from power quickly (his assassination was "contemplated"), the army risked being sidelined. How-ever, broadening U.S. support beyond the army would only help to "consolidate an essentially unacceptable regime." This was the hardliners' view; but in fact Kennedy, who flirted with the idea of extending aid, found it impossible to break with the policy of routinely hostile activities. The reason was the regime's foreign policy. In the summer of 1963, Indonesia launched a bitter attack on Britain's plans to create a Malaysian federation that would include territories in the north of Borneo, the rest of which belonged to Indonesia. Relations with both Britain and the newly formed state of Malaysia rapidly worsened and, very much as had been the case with Iran in 1953, the U.S. found itself compelled to choose. In this case, there was no hesitation and Kennedy suspended his plans for economic aid. Relations rapidly went downhill, the U.S. gra-dually reducing its nonmilitary assistance and Indonesia taking foreign policy positions increasingly at odds with those of the United States (e.g., defending North Vietnam and recognizing North Korea). Nonetheless, lacking any alternative, the U.S. main-tained its ties with the Indonesian military, continuing its civic action program, having detailed talks about delicate subjects (e.g., "Indonesian paramilitary" efforts against Malaysia), and giving "obvious hints of U.S. support in time of crisis." This policy was noticeably supported by the Indonesian military as an "investment" in the "future." In addition, the U.S. expanded its existing covert programs of "assistance to individuals and organizations prepared to take obstructive action against the PKI" and of "black and grey propaganda" against the PKI. Around this time, the U.S. ambassador was also contacted by an Indonesian about the prospects of a *coup d'état* and "conveyed clearly [his] own sympathy." Nothing materialized at that point, and U.S. policy remained one of "playing for the breaks."

At the end of September 1965, the situation changed drastically. Several anticommunist generals were kidnapped and killed by forces sympathetic to the PKI, although whe-ther this was a coup attempt or a feint by the army was unclear. In any case, the army reacted ferociously, launching a campaign of repression against the PKI involving legal actions, propaganda, arrests, and killings, both by the military and by civilians allied with it. The U.S. response was to keep a low profile so as not to provide a target for Sukarno; at the same time, the embassy would "indicate clearly to key people in the army ... our desire to be of assistance where we can" and would "spread the story of PKI's guilt, treachery and brutality" through the Voice of America and various covert channels. Shortly after the propaganda campaign was launched, various figures connected with the military contacted the U.S. army attaché and the deputy chief of the CIA station and asked for communications equipment so that top officers could stay in touch with each other and, presumably, so that anti-PKI militias could communicate with the army. The U.S. supplied this equipment; it was also agreed to furnish small arms, again presumably for the militias. In addition, it appears that subsidies were given to an important militia which was carrying the "burden of current repressive efforts targeted against PKI." Finally, at the height of the hunt for the PKI, the U.S. embassy passed to the military a list containing the names of PKI leaders and senior cadres (see Chapter 4); this list, the ambassador indicated, was "used by Indonesian security authorities who seem to lack even the simplest overt information on PKI leadership." The net effect of these contributions was to facilitate not only the removal of the PKI from power but its physical destruction as well: the ambassador reported afterward that between 300,000 and 400,000 persons suspected of being PKI members had been killed, with other estimates ranging far higher (travelers reported roads strewn with headless bodies and rivers clogged with corpses). Several months later, the army stripped Sukarno of his powers, thereby clearing the way for the U.S. to send aid overtly to the new regime and establish a patron–client relationship (see Chapter 3).[11]

In all of the above examples, the U.S. became involved in coup attempts when officials thought that the enemy regime was shaky. This perception may have stemmed, as in the first set of cases, from the fact that the regime had not been in power for long and thus had not yet had a chance to establish itself; or, as in the second set of cases, from the fact that the regime was seen as made up of disparate components very much at odds with each other. In both sets of cases, U.S. links to the regime's military made it possible to encourage or at least aid a coup if and when the opportunity presented itself – something which might not occur for several years, even with economic and diplomatic pressure being applied. However, if U.S. officials neither saw the regime as shaky nor had close ties to its military, they would be much more reluctant to involve themselves in any kind of coup attempt. A classic example of this reluctance is the U.S. campaign against Iraq's Saddam Hussein in the 1990s. As we saw above, after the 1968 coups, the country's military was purged and put under tight party control, thereby ruling out other coup attempts for the foreseeable future. For the next 20 years, U.S. intervention efforts were confined to aiding a guerrilla war by the Kurds in the early 1970s (see below); outside of that, U.S. policy was one of routinely hostile activities, interspersed with tactical collaboration during the Iran-Iraq war. Even when Iraq invaded and annexed Kuwait, U.S. combat forces were sent to defend Saudi Arabia (see Chapter 5) and not overthrow the Ba'athist regime:

LOWELL BERGMAN: I thought we had two interests. One was to evict the Iraqi army from Kuwait. But the other really was to get Saddam out of power.
BRENT SCOWCROFT: No. No, it wasn't.
LOWELL BERGMAN: Well, either covertly or overtly.
BRENT SCOWCROFT: No. No, it wasn't. That was never – you can't find that anywhere as an objective, either in the U.N. mandate for what we did or in our declarations, that our goal was to get rid of Saddam Hussein.

This did not mean that the U.S. had become friendly toward Iraq, but simply that the use of U.S. combat forces was not a policy tool which then corresponded to the situation. As Bush and Scowcroft presciently put it in their joint memoir, although "we hoped that popular revolt or coup would topple Saddam," to have converted the Gulf War into a hostile intervention would have led to the U.S. to "be an occupying power in a bitterly hostile land."

Bush's decision was strongly criticized, all the more so as the U.S. stood by and let the regime crush uprisings in both the north and south of the country. To relieve the political pressure on himself, Bush ordered the CIA to try and get rid of Saddam by giving money to anyone (including family members or close aides) who could pull off a *coup d'état*, whether triggered by a Kurdish uprising or by economic sanctions. This was an extremely limited program, presupposing that the regime would most likely continue in power; Bush also refused to support a larger-scale guerrilla campaign such as the U.S. had done in Afghanistan (see the book's website). Even with these restrictions in mind, U.S. actions were desultory. In 1995, for example, officials in Washington distanced themselves from a plan combining a Kurdish offensive and actions by military units near Baghdad. In 1998, Congress passed legislation proclaiming the overthrow of Saddam to be explicit U.S. policy, but little more was done. Only for a brief moment, when disaffected military officers and Ba'ath members contacted British intelligence and when the CIA had direct access to Baghdad through the UN's weapons inspectors, did the U.S. decide, rather half-heartedly at that, to try for a coup. The attempt (in 1996) did not get off the ground and was not renewed. Thus, in spite of the fact that Saddam had become an American obsession, the fundamentals of the situation – lack of dissent among most components of the regime and few U.S. contacts with the military – led to a policy during the 1990s almost identical to that followed for the preceding two decades. Only when the situation changed in 2001 did intervention move back onto the agenda (see below).[12]

Punctuated military operations: Node 18

> Soviet Union (targets: Baltic Republics, Ukraine, Poland, Albania; 1948–54: text); China (targets: Yunnan and Fujian provinces; 1951–54: text); China (target: Tibet; 1958–74: web); North Vietnam (1961–68: website); Cuba (1961–65: text); South Yemen (1980–82: website); Libya (1985–?: website); Nicaragua (1982–88: website); Iran (2005–present: text)

Until 2003, Iraq was a rather typical American enemy, at least as regards its perceived lack of suitability for a Washington-backed *coup d'état*. Most enemies are seen by U.S. policy makers as enjoying considerable backing by their military, which means that any hostile intervention against them must involve an assault on that military. For enemies deemed to enjoy some degree of international legitimacy, this in turn implies that the U.S. must participate in some kind of covert military operations, i.e., operations in which the U.S. role is plausibly deniable. Hence the importance of proxy forces: Americans can train, fund, equip, and even accompany them into combat, but a significant number of U.S. combat troops would make it impossible to keep up the fiction of noninvolvement. There are two types of covert operations with proxy forces: situations where the proxies are implanted within the country, carrying out a protracted campaign of armed resistance (see below) and those in which, lacking any such implantation, proxy forces are restricted to raids by sea, land, or air, what we have called punctuated operations.

The difference between the two types of proxy force interventions is not simply a question of whether or not indigenous armed opposition forces are already in place. On the one hand, U.S. control over raiding forces is considerably greater than with an indigenous armed opposition: the latter is usually only supplied with weapons and money, whereas the former are also recruited, trained, and advised by U.S. operatives. This has important implications for the U.S. response to failure and the "disposal problem" raised by an unsuccessful proxy force. In addition, the situations that tend to trigger one versus the other type of U.S. intervention also differ. As we will see in the next section, where there are indigenous armed opposition forces present inside an enemy's country or the territory it occupies, the U.S. will support them, provided their level of activity triggers their being assessed as having some chance of success. Punctuated operations, however, require considerably less manpower: what matters is simply that there be some exiles who can be trained and transported to enemy territory with at least a slight possibility of succeeding. Such assessments are necessarily speculative and there are two kinds of situations in which organizational mechanisms tend to induce them. The first are those in which a U.S. client is carrying out operations against one of its enemies; the second, similar to the "recent enemy" cases of coup attempts, are those in which the enemy had been lost as a client not long before. In both these types of cases, the paramilitary instruments available to U.S. policy makers will be focused on indications that exiles can be or are being transformed into raiding parties capable of triggering an enemy withdrawal or defeat. To see this, let us take a look backward at the CIA's early history.

In Chapter 5, we discussed the development of U.S. proxy force activity, starting with the Office of Policy Coordination (OPC) of the CIA. As we saw, the OPC's initial efforts were very much along the lines of its World War II predecessor organization, the Office of Strategic Services (OSS), and involved various types of punctuated operations in areas of enemy control. The earliest of these overlapped extensively with OSS activities and in many ways look as if they could have taken place during the Second World War. We refer here to the raiding programs carried out against the Soviet Union in its recently acquired provinces and in countries deemed to be its puppets. As Soviet armies swept toward Berlin, they reconquered territories, such as Ukraine and the Baltic states, which had been occupied by the Germans during the war; they also installed regimes centered around the Communist Party in most of the East European states. In several of these places, insurgencies broke out against Soviet control, with fighting usually lasting from a year to 18 months before the inevitable happened and the uprisings were crushed. What then occurred was a westward flow of exiles, a number of whom contacted the British Secret Intelligence Service (MI6), with whose agents they had collaborated in wartime resistance efforts against Germany and, prior to 1941, the Soviet Union. Unlike the OSS, MI6 had never been dismantled and was marked by strong anti-Soviet sentiments. The result, in Ukraine, Poland, and the Baltic republics, was the launching of raiding programs designed to train, equip, and most importantly, transport small groups of exiles back home in order to run sabotage campaigns and if possible to serve as a nucleus for a new uprising.

During this time, the U.S. played almost no role. In part, this was because, as the CIA's first Soviet Division chief put it, "In 1946 Washington knew virtually nothing about the U.S.S.R." and it was natural for the British to take the lead. In addition, the OPC had not yet come into existence and the U.S. had no organization capable of carrying out paramilitary activities. It was only in 1948, after OPC had been created, that the British turned to the U.S. for help in running their anti-Soviet raiding operations, much as they had done the year before regarding their activities in Greece (see the book's website). In each case, an important motive was financial: to get the U.S. to defray the cost of the exiles (Ukraine and Poland) and of amphibious operations (the Baltic states). The U.S., which by this time had begun to develop ties of its own with different groups of exiles and which was in the process of working with a pre-existing German intelligence net-work, was ready to agree. Soon, the U.S. had adopted as a goal "the gradual retraction of undue Russian power and influence from the present perimeter areas around traditional Russian boundaries and the emergence of the satellite countries as entities independent of the USSR" and the OPC was participating actively in training exiles and organizing raids. These operations almost always failed, being not only several years too late to make any difference but also betrayed by double agents. Nonetheless, they continued for many months, ending only when the supply of cannon fodder ran out or when show trials made it clear that the operations were fatally compromised. In the words of Kim Philby, the MI6 officer (and Soviet double agent) who served as the liaison with the CIA,

> [The] operation now takes on an independent existence ... Money that was allocated for it has already been partially spent, people have been recruited and continue to be recruited, equipment is being supplied ... You can't turn back the clock – it would mean a colossal scandal.[13]

This triggering by MI6 of U.S. support for anti-Soviet exile raiding operations reached its high water mark regarding Albania. During World War II, the British had worked closely with various anti-German resistance groups in the country but were unable to prevent the communists from taking over after the Germans withdrew. Over the next few years, as the regime cracked down and as state-to-state relations with Britain worsened, MI6 maintained contact with various of its wartime allies, now mostly in exile. By late 1948, senior civil servants were considering an operation against Albania, the hope being that it would lead to removing the country from Soviet control. Given a paucity of resources ("church mice do not start wars"), it was expected that the U.S. would have to be brought in. Once approval had come from the top, the British immediately flew to Washington, where they presented their plans to the State Department and the OPC. The response was positive, an Albanian operation offering the chance of "slicing off" a satellite of the Soviet Union, and the OPC began both working with the British on paramilitary matters and with Albanian exiles on setting up a government in exile. By the autumn, operations were ready to proceed, even though there were no clear ideas about what would happen if raids should indeed trigger the regime's fall (for example, the British foreign secretary asked if there were "any kings around that could be put in"). The first raid – a British-planned landing by nine men – took place several weeks later. It was followed by other landings, then by U.S.-sponsored parachute drops (using Polish pilots), each at intervals of several months. None of these succeeded, the reasons including Philby's treason, security lapses among the exiles, lack of secrecy (e.g., articles in the *New York Times*), and general incompetence as compared with the Alba-nian regime; and in spite of high levels of funding and energy, Operation BGFIEND was finally terminated in 1954, when show trials, torture and executions of agents, and a wave of repression made it impossible to continue (the British side of the program,

Operation Valuable, had in effect ended several years earlier). Nonetheless, even as the operation was sinking, the CIA's director defended it: "At least we're getting the kind of experience we need for the next war." Forty years later, the officer in charge of BGFIEND had not changed his mind: Albania was where the OPC "cut its teeth."[14]

The OPC's early anti-Soviet interventions illustrate clearly the cybernetic aspects of punctuated operations programs. Although the U.S. had displayed some interest in the internal situation in Poland toward the end of World War II and shortly afterward, this had markedly faded by the time the OPC began its raids. U.S. interest in the Baltic states and Ukraine was considerably more limited, and until the British brought up the possibility of collaborating, there is no evidence that anyone in Washington gave any attention to the Soviet role in Albania. Nor were the interventions an instrumentally rational response: they occurred months or years after whatever uprisings had taken place had been crushed, and the CIA persisted, for years, in running World War II-type operations that patently failed to succeed on even the narrowest tactical grounds. Instead, the interventions were means-driven: they took place only when the U.S. had (re)developed a particular policy instrument, when that instrument had been triggered, and when that instrument was still able to function on its own terms, e.g., training raiders, transporting them, and so forth. The particular locales – Poland, the Baltic area, Albania – were distinctly secondary compared with their being categorized as places which the Soviets were occupying and from which there were exiles who were willing to be trained. Note that there are other examples of exile raids being means-driven and triggered by clients: North Vietnam, Libya, and South Yemen (descriptions of all three cases can be found on the book's website).

In addition to punctuated military operations triggered by U.S. clients, there is a second set of enemies against whom the U.S. carries out such operations without any encouragement by third parties. These are former U.S. clients which were "lost" and, as we saw in Chapter 3, became enemies. In such cases, the U.S. policy making apparatus will be particularly focused on remnants of the former regime who, if they have gone into exile, will be natural candidates for some type of paramilitary operations against their homeland. The earliest, and to a great degree paradigmatic, example of this is China. We saw in Chapter 5 how the U.S. intervened with emergency military aid and advisers in hopes of maintaining in power Chiang Kai-Shek's Kuomintang (KMT). As defeat loomed, the remnants of the KMT forces and of the U.S. supply effort tried to preserve themselves. Most of the KMT army fled to Taiwan, though a few columns headed southwest to Burma, where some 1000 of them established a strategic foothold, and to Laos, where a larger number were captured and interned by the French colonial forces. During the civil war, the KMT had been supplied by airplanes belonging to Civil Air Transport (CAT), a company set up by a former U.S. military officer who was linked to Chiang and had good connections in Washington. With the KMT collapsing and CAT's revenue sources drying up, the staunchly anticommunist owners of the airline managed to obtain cash advances from the CIA to keep operating, an arrangement that, in the summer of 1950, was transformed into an actual purchase of CAT by the CIA (see Chapter 5).

The stage was thus set to use CAT to supply the remnants of the KMT. Already in April 1950, the Joint Chiefs of Staff were noting "evidences of renewed vitality and apparent increased effectiveness of the Chinese Nationalist forces"; they called for a "program of special covert operations designed to interfere with Communist activities in Southeast Asia." CAT accordingly began to supply arms to the KMT forces in

Burma and to reinforce them with troops flown in from Taiwan; by 1951, their numbers had grown to over 4,000. This ongoing reinforcement operation was then folded into a larger set of covert OPC missions approved by Truman after the Chinese entered the Korean War: in June 1951, and then again in August, the KMT forces in Burma launched an invasion of China, assisted by CAT resupply flights and with the support of CIA embedded advisers. Both attacks failed. Undeterred, the U.S. launched a new resupply effort and by early 1952, KMT forces in northeast Burma numbered nearly 13,000 well-equipped troops, whose weapons were paid for partly by CIA largesse and partly by large-scale opium smuggling through Thailand to the international market. In August 1952, another invasion took place, again without success. At this point, the KMT forces gave up any idea of a major invasion, contenting themselves with minor raids, gradually becoming enmeshed with local Burmese secessionist forces and ensconcing themselves ever more deeply into the international opium trade. Evidence suggests that throughout this time, they continued to be supplied with U.S. arms and munitions. Finally, after repeated Burmese protests and a combined Burmese-Chinese military operation, the KMT remnants left, some being shipped to Taiwan by CAT and the others making their way to Thailand and Laos (where they were recruited by the Lao government in its fight against the Pathet Lao).

At the same time as the Burmese operations were going on, the OPC also was using other Taiwanese forces to carry out paramilitary raids on the China coast. Initially, the idea was to train a group of raiders (200 men) to land and then head toward mountainous regions, where they were supposed to form bases, be supplied by airdrops, and link up with the numerous guerrillas who were thought to exist in the area. There were, of course, no guerrillas, and the team was wiped out within a few days of its landing. This led to a change of tactics in which units, now baptized as part of the Anti-Communist National Salvation Army (NSA), would carry out hit-and-run raids up and down the coast. All told, 55 of those raids took place over the next twelve months, with several of them considered to be successes (though by what criteria is unclear). However, with time, China began to build up its capabilities along the coast and even go on the offensive: by 1954, it had recaptured several islands from the NSA and the following year, the U.S. Navy had to evacuate the remaining islands on which the raiders were located.[15] This, however, did not signal a final end to raiding operations against Beijing, for three years after the NSA operations were wound down, a new, long-running, though ultimately unsuccessful operation was launched at the other end of the country, in Tibet (see the book's website for details).

It might seem as if the combination of long-term operations and meager results in the Albanian and Tibetan operations was due to the relative isolation of those two locations. In fact, exactly the same pattern arose much closer to home: in the CIA's various efforts to overthrow the Castro regime in Cuba. One of these operations, the landing at the Bay of Pigs in 1961, is well known. However, Operation ZAPATA, as it was called, was only one in a long sequence of punctuated military operations carried out against the Castro regime. As we saw in Chapters 3 and 5, Cuba was one of the earliest U.S. client states and the United States regularly intervened to try and maintain the regime in power. With the fall of the Batista regime, a new era began. By October of 1959, the State Department had concluded that by the end of the next year, there should be a government in Cuba with drastically different "domestic and foreign policies" and that, to this end, the U.S. should in a non-overt fashion "encourage and coalesce opposition" to the regime, above all by helping "suitable elements presently outside of the Castro regime." Within a month, the CIA had developed a plan involving propaganda, paramilitary training, and the possible "elimination" of Castro; and it was this plan, revised slightly (the explicit reference to Castro's elimination was deleted), which was put forward by a new branch of the CIA's Western Hemisphere Division (WH/4) and accepted by Eisenhower himself. The plan (JMATE) aimed at overthrowing the Castro regime while avoiding "any appearance of U.S. intervention." Specifically, WH/4 would build up exile groups, broadcast propaganda, establish covert networks inside Cuba, and train "an adequate paramilitary force outside of Cuba," the idea being to infiltrate it to the island as the nucleus of future resistance groups. Those groups would presumably engage in guerrilla warfare and perhaps sabotage (which exiles had been doing for some months) along the lines of other punctuated military operations. Over the next six months, WH/4 vigorously pursued JMATE activities; in the meantime, leading CIA officials began to contact U.S. organized crime figures about assassinating Castro.

By the autumn of 1960, it was becoming clear that the underground opposition in Cuba was either "virtually non-existent" or else "so amorphous as to be useless." In addition, the regime's internal security was much better than had been anticipated, so that half of all the agents infiltrated to that point "were picked up within 12 or 24 hours." As a result, JMATE was refocused away from guerrilla warfare organized by infiltrated exiles and toward a large-scale raid in the form of an "amphibious and airborne assault" which could serve as a "base for further ops." The hope was that the invaders would hold on, capture several nearby towns, and thus "help create the catalyst necessary to trigger uprisings throughout Cuba." This new concept, with some of its tactical elements reworked, would eventually become the Zapata plan for the landings in April 1961 at the Bay of Pigs.

As was the case with almost all the other OPC and CIA raids we have discussed in this section, Zapata was a failure, though given its size and the long-standing U.S. role in Cuba, the operation led to considerably greater policy making turmoil. Predictably, the focus of the attention was tactical, for example on whether intelligence was accurate, whether the landing site was flawed, and whether Kennedy was right to have called off a second air strike. Just as predictably, plans immediately began to be laid for additional raids: these began within two weeks of Zapata and by the summer were approved by Kennedy to include consideration of "sabotage, terrorist and guerrilla activities"; in November, Kennedy authorized a new and large-scale effort called Operation Mongoose. At the heart of this new plan was an entire CIA station, JMWAVE, employing some 400 Americans and 2000 Cubans and with a fleet of speedboats at its disposal. The boats would be used for running various types of missions both outside and inside Cuba, with the aim being to train dissidents and eventually encourage them sufficiently that "the people themselves" would "overthrow the Castro regime." In the meantime, assassination efforts continued, with the CIA officer in charge of JMWAVE reestablishing contact with Mafia figures and with Kennedy himself being told about other "opportunities ... worth vigorous development."

By the spring of 1962, the inherent limitations of jump-starting a guerrilla war by infiltrating exiles were once more coming to the fore. Although the CIA was duly infiltrating agents into the island and recruiting potential guerrillas, progress was slow and limited. At first the head of JMWAVE, then the head of Mongoose itself, made clear that even if, against all odds, a "spontaneous uprising" were to occur, it would be "ruthlessly and rapidly crushed" in the absence of overt U.S. military intervention and/

or turmoil (perhaps from assassination?) at the top of the regime. Since at this point, a U.S. invasion would likely lead to a lengthy war and intense condemnation of the United States throughout the hemisphere, the only remaining option was to turn away from internal guerrilla activities, give up on an uprising, and use the exiles in a campaign of sabotage against domestic Cuban targets and foreign Cuban assets, activities in which they had been engaged for several years, though without tight U.S. control. This policy was already on the cards by the early autumn of 1962 and it was reinforced by the Cuban Missile Crisis, which committed the U.S. not to invade Cuba, at least without apparent cause. During the next year, CIA-supervised exiles carried out an extensive raiding campaign against Cuban economic targets, a subject in which Kennedy showed "a particular interest"; the CIA also gave support to autonomous exile groups. In addition, the head of the CIA's sabotage activities pursued assassination attempts against Castro, this time using a high-level Cuban official. Although the exile raids did considerable economic damage, they also caused political and potential military problems for the U.S. and were eventually shut down in 1964 and 1965.[16]

For five years, in three successive operations, the United States intervened against the Castro regime. At various times, it tried to manufacture an internal guerrilla force or to spark an uprising by a World War II-style landing; but in each case, it ended up falling back on the small-scale infiltration and sabotage operations which the exiles had begun on their own soon after Castro first came to power. This is one of the reasons why assassination kept being plotted: if the U.S. was not going to follow up raids, even major ones, by overtly sending its own combat troops, then the only other chance the officials saw of raids triggering an overthrow is if they were to be accompanied by the death of the regime's top leaders. Conversely, and very much along the lines of the other raiding examples against China or the Soviet Union, this also meant that the repeated failures of the raids – the capture of many raiders and their inability to generate an internal uprising – were in and of themselves insufficient to stop the U.S. program: only when the raids were seen as making the situation worse were they finally ended. Even then, and for the decades of routinely hostile actions which subsequently ensued, U.S. leaders displayed obsessive animosity toward the Castro regime.

As we have seen, the U.S. resort to punctuated military operations is triggered either by the existence of such operations being carried out by U.S. clients against their own enemies or else by the availability of exile groups capable of being used for operations against recently "lost" U.S. clients. In neither case is it necessary for the raiders to succeed in order for the U.S. to continue backing them: all that counts is a continued supply of cannon fodder and an absence of obvious negative consequences. A good example of this is U.S. support for the Nicaraguan "contras" under the Reagan Administration (see the book's website for a detailed description). Another, more recent example pertains to Iran, which, as we saw in Chapter 5, was lost to the U.S. as a client state in 1979. Almost immediately after the Islamic regime came to power, U.S. officials began to look around for exile groups with whom they could work, an effort repeated when Reagan became president. The one exile group that was carrying out military operations (mostly assassination efforts and attacks on government buildings), the Mujahedin-e-Khalq (MEK) was in effect unavailable: prior to the Shah's overthrow, it had opposed the U.S. and, since the mid-1980s, was headquartered in and supported by another U.S. enemy, Iraq. However, after the U.S. invasion of Iraq in 2003 (see below), the MEK fell under U.S. military control and apparently began to be used by it in 2005 for operations against Iran, the hope being to spark an insurgency by Iran's Sunnis with which a possible U.S. invasion could be coordinated (see Chapter 7). Complaints that the MEK was a terrorist organization were finessed by having its members formally resign from the organization before they were trained by U.S. forces. There were also reports that separatist groups on the fringes of the country (notably the PEJAK organization of Kurds and the Jundollah one of Baluchis) were being supported by the U.S.[17]

One final note. Although for half a century the U.S. has had the institutional capacity for conducting punctuated military operations using exile groups, the mere existence of the latter is, as we have seen, insufficient to trigger those operations. The exiles must already be running some kind of raids, whether by themselves or with the help of a U.S. client. In the absence of such activities, standard organizational reporting mechanisms will generate negative assessments of the exiles and block a raiding program from getting off the ground. This, as we saw, is what happened in Iraq throughout the 1990s and regarding Iran until after 2003; it also occurred regarding Suriname in the 1980s.[18]

Aid to internal armed opposition forces: Node 19

Indonesia (1957–58: website); Iraq (1972–75: text); Soviet Union (target: Angola; 1975: text); Vietnam (target: Cambodia; 1979–91: website); Cuba (target: Angola; 1985–91; text); Soviet Union (target: Afghanistan; 1979–91: website); Somalia (2006: text)

Punctuated military operations are not the only type of covert military intervention using proxy forces. In situations where an enemy is confronted with an internal armed opposition movement, the United States will channel aid to those forces. The aid, for the most part, will take the form of weapons or cash to pay fighters, since except when the weapons in question are technologically complex, there is no need for the U.S. to engage in the kind of training programs typical of exile raids. Although this makes for a simpler operation, it also reduces the possibilities of U.S. control, which in turn means that the armed opposition cannot simply be turned off if Washington decides that supporting it has become a political liability. On the other hand, if a particular opposition aid program is aimed at evicting an enemy from the territory of a state considered as a tool or satellite (see above), then to have an arm's-length relationship with the opposition permits the U.S. to reach an agreement for enemy withdrawal, opening up the possibility of a disengagement or, as it is usually seen by the opposition, a sellout.

In fact, although aid to armed opposition forces usually involves roughly the same mixture of tactical instruments, U.S. policy after the termination of aid differs considerably depending on how officials in Washington perceive the local regime. If the regime is itself a U.S. enemy, then ending aid to the armed opposition only means that that particular policy instrument has been abandoned at that moment. The regime will still be very much in the cross-hairs of U.S. planners, even if for the moment, they judge the situation more propitious for routinely hostile activities than for some sort of intervention. A classic example of this is U.S. policy toward Indonesia in 1957–58 (see the book's website for a detailed discussion of this case).

A second example of U.S. covert assistance to internal armed opposition movements, showing a similar willingness to cut off aid and return to routinely hostile activities, pertains to the Kurds in Iraq in the early 1970s. For some time, U.S. clients in the region had been aiding the Kurds in their struggle against the Ba'ath regime and knowing that the U.S. was also hostile to the regime, asked it to join in. Washington rebuffed these requests, concerned that the Kurds already had "enough money" from other states and that an expanded insurgency would "provoke a further influx of Soviet arms and influence" in Iraq and might alarm the Turks, whose territory contained large numbers of Kurds. However, in April 1972, Iraq signed a friendship treaty with the Soviet Union, and when the Shah of Iran again pressed for U.S. aid, Nixon acquiesced. His decision, to pay the Kurds and also supply them with ammunition and small arms, was a closely held secret, with even the government's own interagency committee being bypassed. By 1973, Kissinger was supporting a CIA request for additional resources, on the grounds that Iraq "had become the principal Soviet client in the Middle East"; a year later, when the Iraqis showed signs of stepping up an offensive, Ford approved compensating the Israelis for some $28 million of Soviet equipment they had captured and which was sent to the Kurds; and at the end of 1974, the Kurds evidently had received U.S.-made surface to air missiles from Iran (which presumably also was compensated by Washington), which they used to shoot down Iraqi fighter jets. At this point, the Iranians and Iraqis plunged into secret talks, emerging in March 1975 with an agreement. Immediately, the Iraqis launched an offensive and Iran closed its border to the Kurds and cut off all weapons and logistical support. Stunned, the Kurds pleaded with the CIA and Kissinger to supply them with arms or pressure the Iranians to rescind their closure of the frontier, a plea seconded by the CIA Chief of Station in Tehran on the grounds that otherwise, the Kurds "are likely to go public. Iran's action has not only shattered their political hopes; it endangers lives of thousands … [to help] would be the decent thing to do." All this was to no avail: Kissinger remained silent, Ford did not intercede with the Shah or even let Kurds into the U.S. as refugees; and when, later that year, the congressional committee investigating the CIA asked Kissinger about his actions, it received this response: "covert action should not be confused with missionary work."[19]

Indonesia in 1958 and Iraq in 1975 were both states viewed by U.S. policy makers as enemies. Thus, even after the U.S. cut off aid to the guerrillas it had been backing, it continued to oppose the two regimes and work to set up the conditions in which, at some point in the future, it could once more intervene to overthrow them. By contrast, there are other guerrilla groups the U.S. has aided which, at least as seen from Washington, were struggling against a puppet regime kept in place only by the troops of a different, enemy state. In these situations, once the enemy had withdrawn its forces, the U.S. could and did envisage normal relations with the indigenous regime. From the standpoint of the guerrillas, this was also a sellout, but from the U.S. perspective, it was a victory. A simple and clear example of this concerns Cambodia and the Khmer Rouge from the late 1970s until the early 1990s; another, far more acclaimed, example during much the same time period, is the CIA's support of anti-Soviet guerrillas in Afghanistan (both cases are discussed in detail on the book's website).

Around the same time that the U.S. was ending its support for the guerrillas in Cambodia, it was doing the same, thousands of miles away, in Angola. The story there began in the 1970s, when, with the country nearing independence from Portugal, three movements vied for power. One of them, the MPLA, was backed by the Soviet Union; a second group, the FNLA, had for years received some support from the U.S. A third movement, UNITA, was smaller and had in the past flirted with various outside forces, ranging from China to Portugal itself. In January 1975, the CIA and the State Department proposed giving aid to both the FNLA and UNITA. The reasoning, as the director of the CIA later testified, was simplicity itself:

MR. COLBY: They are all independents. They are all for black Africa. They are all for some fuzzy kind of social system, you know, without really much articulation, but some sort of let's not be exploited by the capitalist nations ...

MR. ASPIN: And why are the Chinese backing the moderate group?

MR. COLBY: Because the Soviets are backing the MPLA is the simplest answer.

MR. ASPIN: It sounds like that is why we are doing it.

MR. COLBY: It is.

Only the FNLA was funded this time around, but soon the policy changed. The president of Zambia visited Washington and pushed strongly for the U.S. to aid UNITA; soon after, Zaire's leader, Mobutu Sese Seko, whose regime the U.S. had helped maintain for over a decade (see Chapters 3 and 5), insisted that his protégé, the head of the FNLA, be armed. This led to an interagency task force and to the predictable options paper, in which a paramilitary operation, seen as risky, was contrasted with the alternatives of neutrality and (the first choice) of a diplomatic initiative to halt the fighting. Ford's response to the three recommendations was simple: "doing nothing is unacceptable. As for diplomatic efforts, it is naive to think that's going to happen." The CIA was thus told to plan aid to the FNLA and UNITA, and although the State Department's assistant secretary of state for African affairs vigorously protested (since by then it was clear that UNITA was also being backed by South Africa, the one pariah state in the region), Kissinger overrode him, arguing that a failure to intervene would boost the Soviet Union in Africa and adding, for good measure, that "coupled with Indochina [where the U.S. had just lost in South Vietnam, Laos, and Cambodia], it is not a trivial thing which is happening in Southern Africa." Even before there was an independent Angolan state, the prospect that it would be backed by the Soviet Union was enough to trigger an American intervention.

Thus the U.S. launched Operation IAFEATURE, immediately shipping weapons, doling out cash, and providing advisers. As with most of the other interventions we have discussed in this chapter, a number of countries participated along with the U.S. or ran parallel and coordinated operations; in this case, Zaire, Zambia, Britain, and France. By far the most important U.S. partner and for obvious reasons, the most secret one, was South Africa. The two countries collaborated "at all CIA levels," as the officer in charge of IAFEATURE put it, with the South Africans supplying not only weapons and advisers but, in mid-October 1975, a column of troops. This helped hold off the MPLA, which by then was pummeling UNITA; and the column rapidly swept north, toward the Angolan capital, Luanda. Suddenly the tide turned. The Cubans, who had been advising the MPLA and supplying it with arms, grew alarmed at the South African advance and in early November sent their own infantry. Within three weeks, the FNLA was a broken rabble and the South Africans had been stopped. Washington responded with panic, considering plans for more advisers, more powerful weapons, and above all, more funds. By then, news of both IAFEATURE and of the South African "regular troops" had leaked into the press. Congress, nervous at the prospect of greater U.S. involvement and links to South Africa and shocked (as was the Vichy captain in "Casablanca") at having been lied to, moved to cut off funds for the program. Before the bill was signed into law, the CIA desperately searched Europe for mercenaries, but their numbers were few and their competence limited. The MPLA took over the Angolan state; South Africa, "ruthlessly left in the lurch" to face the Cubans on their own, retreated; UNITA fled and took up low-level guerrilla warfare.

Act II of the Angolan war now began. At first, UNITA carried out desultory combat operations in the most deserted and isolated corner of the country. By the early 1980s, it had expanded the war, aided significantly by South Africa and, covertly, by Saudi Arabia at what seems to have been the behest of the United States. In 1985, Reagan persuaded Congress to lift restrictions on military assistance in Angola and the next year began supplying UNITA with sophisticated weapons, including Stinger anti-aircraft missiles. This aid arrived in the midst of seesawing and escalating offensives by the Angolan government forces (still with considerable Cuban assistance), on the one hand, and by UNITA and South Africa, on the other. By 1988, the Cubans were at the doorstep of South African-occupied Namibia, which finally led to serious negotiations among Angola, Cuba, South Africa, and the United States. The result was a series of agreements in which the Cubans and South Africans agreed to withdraw their forces from Angola and, for good measure, for South Africa to pull its troops out of Namibia as well. UNITA's initial reaction was to denounce the accords as a sellout; it was mollified by continued U.S. military aid but with the withdrawal of Cuban troops, reports of UNITA atrocities, and the end of the cold war, it became difficult to maintain congressional support for a military solution. Aid began to decline and in 1991, the U.S. helped to broker an agreement between the Angolan government and the MPLA which provided for an end to all foreign military support. Elections were held in 1992; UNITA lost and once again took up arms, an act which pushed the U.S. to recognize the MPLA government and to support a U.N. arms embargo against UNITA. One more round of peace accords and fighting then occurred before the death of UNITA's leader led to the movement's disintegration.[20]

As we have seen, in situations where internal guerrillas are carrying out an ongoing struggle against the forces of an enemy regime, the United States has consistently had a policy of aiding the guerrillas as a way of overthrowing the enemy regime or removing its forces from a province or other country. However, if the only guerrillas actually doing any fighting are secessionists, it raises a potential problem. In cases where the enemy is not a successor to a U.S. client state (e.g., Indonesia in 1958; Iraq in 1972), U.S. officials are willing to play the secessionist card in order to facilitate the regime's overthrow. If, though, the enemy overthrew a U.S. client, then American policy makers are likely to want to make good their loss and therefore will shy away from identification with secessionist guerrillas. An example of this latter case is Ethiopia from 1977 to 1991. We saw in Chapter 3 how, from the late 1950s, Ethiopia had been a U.S. client state. In 1974, the country's long-time ruler was deposed in a *coup d'état* and executed not long afterward. The regime that took power, the Derg, moved to the left and in 1977 ended military ties with the U.S. Soon after, Ethiopia was invaded by Somalia, with the Derg finally being rescued by weapons and advisers from the Soviet Union and combat troops from Cuba. Throughout the war, the U.S. walked a narrow line, supplying defensive weapons to Somalia but refusing to support its invasion.

By 1981, when Reagan took office, the Somali threat had been repulsed. The remaining military danger was a secessionist movement in the northern province of Eritrea, attached for several decades to Ethiopia. Guerrilla movements, which had for some time been fighting for independence, took advantage of the Somali invasion to occupy most of Eritrea. They were aided by Saudi Arabia, an arrangement about which the U.S., having "no current interest in an Eritrean settlement ... consult[ed] closely" with Riyadh, while at the same time being careful to "avoid identification with the Eritrean insurgents." As a temporizing measure, the U.S. set up a small covert propaganda operation against the Derg, using local members of a royalist group. Predictably, the operation was discovered and the plotters arrested (including their CIA case officer); pleas for training other exiles in paramilitary techniques were turned down as hopeless. Over the next few years, the situation did not change, and although conservatives mounted a campaign for military aid to nonsecessionist forces, those latter were not engaged in any guerrilla activities which could be supported. Hence the U.S. waited, denouncing the Derg while sending humanitarian assistance to respond to repeated famines and droughts.

By the end of the 1980s, the situation had begun to change. A government offensive against the Eritrean guerrillas failed; the guerrillas counterattacked in strength and gained territory. A secessionist movement in Tigre, the province bordering Eritrea, strengthened and put additional pressure on the Derg. The Cubans, who had in any case never fought in Eritrea or Tigre, withdrew their troops and the Soviets reduced their subsidy. Meanwhile, the leader of the Derg was almost overthrown by his fellow officers in a coup. All of this led the Derg to moderate its domestic policies and try to improve relations with the United States. These moves were reciprocated and talks between the regime and the guerrillas began under American auspices; they were resumed after Ethiopia had sided with the U.S. in the Gulf War. Then, in the spring of 1991, the regime crumbled, leaving the U.S. in what one official called "a de facto advisory role for the three opposition groups about to inherit all military and political power." The head of the Tigrean guerrillas, a former Marxist whom the U.S. had been grooming for a year, arrived in Addis Ababa within a few days; he soon received, as a "personal guest" for three weeks, a former U.S. official (CIA and NSC staff), who pronounced him "pragmatic." Ethiopia was now back in the fold, and without the U.S. ever having thrown its lot in with the internal guerrillas.[21]

Two recent examples of aid to internal armed opposition forces concern Somalia and Palestinian territories. For a number of years, Somalia essentially lacked a regime, as no groups were able to constitute themselves in positions of clear political and economic control over most of the population. By the early 2000s, several Islamic movements had set up a court system in the capital and were moving toward greater power. At this point, the United States, alarmed at the prospect of an Al Qaeda-backed alliance coming to power, quietly began funneling financial and other support to a new coalition ("Alliance for the Restoration of Peace and Counter-terrorism") of warlords and splinter government militias. Using these resources, the coalition purchased arms and, in the spring of 2006, fought several pitched battles with the Islamists. By early June, however, they had lost and the U.S. had joined with other states (and, it appears, private military companies) in finding an alternate way of countering the Islamists. A similar pattern occurred in the Palestinian territories, where the United States, after watching the Hamas movement win elections in January 2006, began trying to undermine it by working with the security forces controlled by the territories' other principal political movement, Fatah. As months went by and U.S. allies, emboldened by arms transfers, training, and increased financial resources, launched one attack after another on Hamas, the latter finally reacted by driving Fatah out of the Gaza portion of the territories entirely.[22]

The Somalia case illustrates a more general reluctance on the part of the U.S. to escalate qualitatively in situations of military defeat. In Chapter 5, we saw that escalation will occur only within combat intervention nodes and not across nodes. Much the same is true of hostile intervention, although the reasons are not always the same.

Consider the three types of covert intervention. If a coup fails, it of course can be tried again later on. However, the chances of a coup being attempted against the backdrop of a group of exiles who until then have not been used for raids, or an internal armed group which up to that point was not supplied by the U.S., are relatively slim. The same logic applies to exile raids: there is no reason that if an internal armed force existed while the exiles were trying and failing that the U.S. would not have already been aiding it. Indeed, as we saw above, the most common response to failure of exile raids is to continue them until there are no more raiders available to be launched (and captured). Finally, if a covert operation built around an internal armed force fails, the only way for there to be an escalation into some sort of overt intervention is, as we will see below, for there to be a major shift in the status of the enemy, a condition unlikely to be triggered simply by the defeat of internal armed forces (thus, for example, the U.S. never seriously entertained the prospect of sending American forces to help out the mujahedin in Afghanistan or UNITA in Angola). For these reasons, the chances are slim of cross-node escalation from one situation of covert intervention either to another such situation or to one of overt intervention. As to qualitative escalation from one type of overt intervention to another type, this too is unlikely and for reasons similar to those discussed in Chapter 5: organizational difficulty and political/military danger; we will discuss this issue below.

Overt intervention situations

As we have seen, the United States has engaged in a number of covert interventions against enemy states. Those operations, if not exactly secret, were nonetheless plausibly deniable, thereby sparing the U.S. the onus of admitting publicly that it was trying to overthrow the regime of a sovereign state or to evict forces whose presence was at the formal invitation of another state. From time to time, however, a particular enemy is viewed by U.S. officials as engaging in policies so outrageous that they assume it will be seen by other U.S. citizens and by diplomats and the mass public in many other states as a pariah; in these cases, hostile intervention is viewed as self-evidently justified and need not be concealed. Here, there are four types of situations (see Figure 6.3). First, the enemy in question may be seen as warring against another state (whether or not that state is a U.S. client) or illegitimately occupying territory that is not its own. In such situations, the question is whether the enemy's forces are judged to be sufficiently well-anchored (because of their number, their prowess, or the enemy's fanaticism) that the only way of dislodging them is via ground combat. If so, then the enemy is for-midable enough that U.S. policy makers see no option other than large-scale combat, with the risks of escalation (including of war aims; see below) that that entails (node 20). If, however, the enemy's forces are seen as capable of being dislodged from the territory they occupy without resorting to ground combat, then the U.S. response is to carry out sustained and asymmetrical attacks on the enemy in the hopes of compelling it to cease its aggression and/or withdraw its troops (node 21). As we will see below, these attacks have tended to take the form of bombing campaigns. On the other hand, the enemy in question may not be seen as warring against another state (at least at that moment) but rather as generally egregious (including against its own population), a perception that, if a particularly outrageous event occurs, serves as grounds for an overt attempt at overthrowing the enemy regime by the use of combat forces. Should local insurgent forces be present in significant numbers, then the U.S. will use them to do

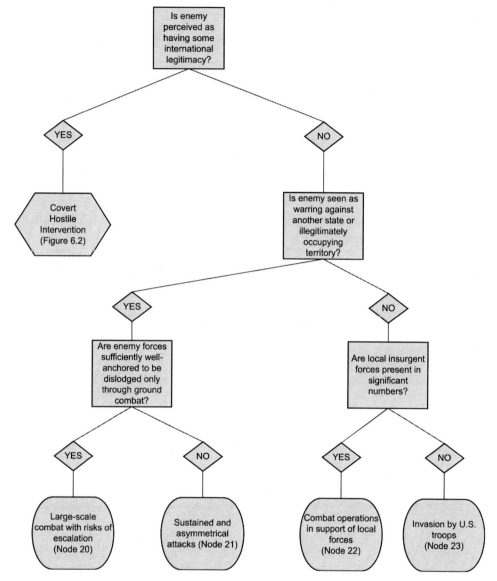

Figure 6.3 Hostile interventions situations, 3: Overt

most of the fighting (node 22); otherwise, the U.S. will invade the enemy with its own troops providing the bulk of the infantry (node 23).

Large-scale combat: Node 20

Germany (1917–18: website); Germany (1941–45: website); Japan (1941–45: text); Soviet Union (target: North Korea; 1950–51: text)

Earlier in this chapter, we distinguished between interstate wars and hostile interventions, arguing that although there was certainly some overlap on specific cases, many wars were not against enemies, in our use of the term. Certainly the adversaries in many of the best-known great power wars, for example, did not see each other as having chosen to differ systematically on issues of foreign policy and even less so on domestic issues. Thus one state could try to snatch territory from its neighbor without being perceived by that neighbor as differing systematically with it; and even expansionist states, such as the France of Louis XIV, could be combated by broad coalitions without the latter being alarmed at the Sun King's internal power arrangements. As we saw, several U.S. wars fit this broad category: the War of 1812, the Mexican War, the Spanish-American War, and the operations against Italy in World War II.

However, we also indicated that participants in some interstate wars characterize their foes as enemies, making the war a type of hostile intervention. In modern Europe, wars of this sort, if less common than the first type, have been noteworthy because of the strong ideological overtones. If the adversary is seen as choosing to differ systematically on both foreign and domestic issues, then the war becomes a kind of crusade. Not surprisingly, in light of the long list of U.S. enemies (see Figure 3.1), the U.S. historical record includes a number of such wars, including three against enemies which were seen as difficult to dislodge from the territories they occupied without the use of American troops. These three interventions, in the context of World Wars I and II, are particularly striking because of the way in which the U.S., as an intervening state, was allied with nonintervening ones.

The first two large-scale combat interventions were against Germany in the two world wars (for detailed descriptions, see the book's website). In both of those situations, the U.S. intervened in an ongoing conflict. This meant that it was constrained in its operations, though the degree of constraint was noticeably less in World War II than in World War I. (Partly as a result of this constraint, U.S. leaders used some of their aid-based leverage to obtain concessions on postwar international arrangements rather than focus entirely on Germany.) By contrast, in the war against Japan (as in the postwar occupation), the U.S. had an almost entirely free hand. It planned and executed practically by itself all the air and naval, and the vast majority of the ground combat, operations outside of China. This, however, was only the tip of the iceberg, for, unlike the case of Germany, the U.S. largely pushed Japan into war. For ten years, key Washington policy makers had seen Japan as an enemy, a perception which took root at the time of the so-called Manchurian Incident. The use of force to take over a Chinese province and block a diplomatic settlement was immediately seen as evidence that "the Japanese military" had begun "a widely extended movement of aggression," was willing to "destroy [Japan's] most important link with other countries," and hence could no longer be regarded "as a normal Government." This view, at first restricted to the secretary of state and a smattering of diplomats and other elites, soon broadened after Japan sent troops to Shanghai. Suspicions continued after Roosevelt became president (this contributed, as we saw above, to recognizing the Soviet Union), heightened still further by Japan's withdrawal from a naval limitation treaty and, most significantly, the large-scale war it began with China in 1937.

The initial U.S. response to the war was not to interfere with the shipment of arms to China and Japan, a measure which disproportionately favored the arms-importing Chinese. Next year, the U.S. initiated naval talks with the British about how to respond to Japanese threats and, some months later, announced that it was "strongly opposed to the sale of airplanes" that could be used for "bombing civilian populations from the air" and that any export licenses for this purpose would be issued "with great regret."

This "moral embargo," as it came to be known, could not affect Japan very much and so, in mid-1939, the U.S. began using its considerable economic weight by announcing that it would abrogate the commercial treaty then in effect between the two countries. Even then, it was not until the summer of 1940 when the U.S. finally began to go after Japan's war-making capacity, a step advocated for several years by Roosevelt's new secretary of war (who had been the secretary of state at the time of the Manchurian Incident). The policy instrument chosen was the National Defense Act, a law that had just been passed and that permitted the president to suspend export of strategic materials. At first, the U.S. ended exports of aviation fuel and scrap iron and steel, materials on which Japan was heavily dependent. Over the course of the next six months, new items were added to the list, each time triggering outraged complaints of discrimination by Japan and bland denials by the U.S. In the meantime, loans were made to China, vague words of encouragement were passed on to Britain and the Netherlands (whose East Indies colonies contained many raw materials coveted by Japan), and new condemnations made of Japan's latest "predatory" actions of allying with Germany and forcing its troops into northern Indochina. This was as far as Roosevelt could go, given the priority he attached to Europe, the still-limited buildup of U.S. forces in the Pacific, and the general reluctance of Congress to get into a shooting war.

What moved the U.S. away from harassment and toward intervention was the Japanese decision, in July 1941, to move its troops into southern Indochina. Roosevelt, still reluctant to start a war at this point but recognizing that a stronger signal was needed if there was to be any hope of deterring a further Japanese advance, agreed to yet another policy instrument advocated by the hardliners for six months and only recently imposed on Germany and Italy: the freezing of all Japanese assets in the U.S. Over the next month, as the Japanese searched for unfrozen funds with which to purchase oil and other products, zealous bureaucrats raised administrative obstacles which, one after another, had the effect of transforming the financial freeze into a total embargo on all exports to Japan, a policy then joined in by the British and the Dutch. At this point, Roosevelt made the conscious decision not to restore trade. Japan was now condemned to economic strangulation unless a diplomatic settlement could be reached with the Americans. There was none, the U.S. contenting itself with what Stimson called "diplomatic fencing to be done so as to be sure that Japan was put into the wrong and made the first bad move – overt move." A month later, Roosevelt echoed his ambassador's warning that war "may come with dangerous and dramatic suddenness":

> [he] brought up the event that we were likely to be attacked perhaps next Monday, for the Japanese are notorious for making an attack without warning, and the question was what we should do. The question was how we should maneuver them into the position of firing the first shot without allowing too much danger to ourselves.

The answer, unsettling both to top U.S. army and navy officials, who wanted the war to be postponed until U.S. forces were ready, and to the British, who "certainly [did] not want an additional war," was to reiterate its diplomatic demands on the Japanese and to encourage the British in the event of an attack by Japan. Soon after, the Japanese attacked and the U.S. was finally, and formally, at war.

Over the next several years, the war was essentially under the control of the United States. None of Japan's other foes had the resources or the maneuver room to strike back in more than a local fashion, and so the offensive against Japan was planned and executed by the U.S. Since Washington's priority was Germany, this meant that the U.S. was restricted to an island-hopping strategy, accompanied, once U.S. forces drew closer, with a strategic bombing campaign (see below). Both of these policy instruments left practically no space for forces other than those of the U.S. The one exception, a planned Soviet invasion of Manchuria, was seen as an adjunct to U.S. strategy, one about which U.S. leaders had second thoughts as the date approached and the atomic bomb was tested. For these reasons, the decision to continue insisting on Japanese unconditional surrender was almost entirely an American one. There was a broad consensus among country specialists and military leaders that if the surrender terms could be softened to permit the continuation of the emperor – though now as a constitutional monarch – the Japanese could be persuaded to give up without an invasion of the home islands. This view, which was shared by the British, was rejected by Truman and his secretary of state; the British gave in; the Soviets were "not ... informed until after" the fact; and at the end of the Potsdam conference, the U.S. (and, technically, Britain and China) issued a declaration maintaining harsh terms for Japan. Two weeks later, the U.S. changed position, deciding on its own to respond to the Japanese surrender offer by language which made it possible to envision the emperor continuing. Again, this change was swallowed by U.S. allies (including the Soviet Union, which "did not consider it unconditional surrender") who, for good measure, also acquiesced in the appointment of a U.S. general (MacArthur, who later headed U.S. and UN forces in Korea) to oversee the surrender and the subsequent occupation.[23]

In both the Japanese and the two German cases, U.S. policy makers responded to the combination of an enemy seen as entrenched in its occupation of others' territory and a *casus belli* by that enemy with the instrument of U.S. ground combat forces. In turn, the commitment of those forces and the perceived radicalism of the enemy regime led the U.S. to expand its war aims beyond the liberation of occupied territories and to the overthrow of the regime itself. An accelerated variant of this same process can be seen in the Korean War. There, the enemy in question was the Soviet Union, which was assumed to be operating through a puppet, North Korea. (In fact, North Korea's very status as a state with a "lawful government" was called into question at the United Nations even before the war began.) As we saw in Chapter 5, when fighting broke out on 25 June 1950 and North Korean forces rapidly advanced southward, the U.S., with strong UN support, reacted by defending its South Korean client, even as it also made sure to guard against the possibility of Soviet feints elsewhere. When, over the next few weeks, it became clear that the Soviet Union was not about to send its own military forces to the Korean peninsula, Truman decided that the planned U.S. offensive would extend beyond the 38th parallel and, in effect, aim at expelling the Soviets from their position in North Korea, a decision which, given the recent division of the peninsula, was tantamount to eliminating North Korea as a state. (Once again, the UN backed the U.S. decision on the familiar grounds that South Korea was the only "lawful government" in Korea and that "the unification of Korea [had] not yet been achieved.") This decision meant that the maintenance intervention would be transformed into a hostile intervention aimed at expelling an enemy from a puppet. Nonetheless, the latter differed from the other, covert, expulsion interventions discussed earlier in this chapter. In the Korean case, an overt policy instrument was already in the process of being used; moreover, since the puppet's legitimacy had been denied by the UN, an extension of the original mission was seen as justified. In both of these ways, the invasion of

North Korea resembles the World War II interventions, even if its organizational development was grafted onto puppet expulsion aims.

MacArthur's orders, as we saw, were to proceed carefully and not to advance should it appear that the Soviets were intervening. Such caution was eminently reasonable in light of the invasion's origins as an easy-win maintenance intervention. Soon after the Chinese intervened and the extent of the debacle became known in Washington, the U.S. tossed overboard the goal of puppet expulsion, Acheson making it clear that a ceasefire would roughly follow the 38th parallel (see Chapter 5). From this point on, the hostile intervention had ended, even if it took several years of bloodshed before a formal armistice was signed. Ironically, the decision to give up on eliminating North Korea meant that the country now became a target for massive bombing raids intended not only to hit military targets but to influence the negotiations which were beginning. These began in the summer of 1951 and were then renewed (interdiction and tactical bombing went on without stop) in the spring of 1952, when the military began looking for "ways and means of exerting maximum pressure" as a way of breaking the stalemate then prevailing on the battlefield and at the negotiating table. Within a few months, the U.S. had attacked hydroelectric plants, major cities, and dams and reservoirs; as this happened, policy makers in Washington gradually began to focus on how it might affect not only the communists in general but North Korean "continued recalcitrance" in particular. "If we keep on, tearing the place apart, we can make it a most unpopular affair for the North Koreans." In short, not only was the hostile intervention only a few months in duration, but the continuing client intervention paved the way for North Korea to be transformed from a puppet into an enemy, a change similar to the less-harsh transformations (into nonenemies) of Cambodia, Angola, and Afghanistan we saw above.[24]

In all three of the world war interventions, U.S. policy makers resorted to armed ground combat because they saw no other way of dislodging the enemy from the territories it occupied and, for that matter, of even trying to bring about the fall of the regime. Because the enemy was both militarily powerful and, by definition, seen as having deliberately chosen to differ with the U.S. across the board, the view in Washington is that it would therefore have been unsafe only to aim at evicting the enemy from its occupied lands: the goal of regime change grew out of the means chosen. A similar cybernetic process also occurred in the North Korean intervention, although in that case it led from the projected ease with which U.S. forces would triumph in saving the client to a brief and abortive attempt to expel and destroy the supposed puppet in Pyongyang. By extension, then, if the initial occupation situation is one in which the use of U.S. ground forces is not indicated because the enemy is not seen as well entrenched in occupied territory, then U.S. war aims will be more limited. Those war aims may still change considerably over time, but they will always be fitted to the more limited, if no less violent, means employed. To see how this works, we now turn to a second set of intervention situations.

Sustained and asymmetrical attacks: Node 21

North Vietnam (1965–72: text and website); Serbia (in Kosovo; 1999: text)

For centuries, imperial powers have used military force not only to annex certain territories but to control the actions of other, nominally independent, political units. Up until the sixteenth century, this was primarily a matter of close-range fighting by infantry and cavalry, sometimes with the aid of proxy forces. However, with the development of artillery powered by explosives, it became possible to equip ships with long-range guns, thereby enabling shelling operations to be carried out against enemy sites. If, as was usually the case outside of Europe, the target of the bombardment lacked the same firepower, then the attacker could pound away for days, weeks, or even months at a time without running much of a risk. Such asymmetrical and sustained campaigns lent themselves to what would later be called coercive diplomacy, in which the aim was to force policy changes from a still-capable defender rather than the annexation of part or all of its territory. This was the technique employed by the British during the First Opium War, when they sent 15 warships to bombard forts and cities in China; and it served as the archetype for other, briefer, exercises in naval intimidation elsewhere, such as in South America. Operations of this sort, though, were spatially limited, since even the most powerful guns could not carry more than 20 miles or so (recall the U.S. naval bombardments in Lebanon in 1983–84; see Chapter 5). The technical fix for this problem would be airpower.[25]

In the 1920s and 1930s, defense intellectuals developed ideas about how cities could be bombed from the air in order to break the enemy's morale. Although even then there was considerable controversy about targeting civilians directly, air forces soon began teaching a variant of the policy, in which bombing would be directed at factories, transportation lines, and above all the electrical grid. During World War II, the U.S. carried out this sort of strategic bombing against both Japan and Germany; and although the accuracy of the bombing was low and its morale effects limited, it remained a basic tool in the American policy repertoire, one which the U.S. continued to build up. By the end of the 1950s, scholars in various fields had begun writing about how "steady weekly damage" could be inflicted as a "compellent threat" intended "to make an adversary do something." Strategic bombing seemed tailor-made for such a policy: the U.S. could send its planes over new targets each week, perhaps also calibrating the number of aircraft in each sortie and the types of explosives they were dropping. Of course, the bombing could still fail, either because the targets were not hit or because their destruction turned out not to have much effect on the enemy's morale; but with enough material asymmetry between the United States and its foe, a bombing campaign could be carried on for a long enough period of time to make it likely that some type of morale-sensitive targets (if they existed) would eventually be hit. Over the next several decades, as technological improvements made it possible for bombing to be considerably more precise than in the past, additional scenarios were developed for the use of airpower as an instrument of coercive diplomacy.[26]

It should be noted that strategic bombing is a tool that can be used for more than one purpose. If combined with ground combat operations, as it has been for most of its history, it is part of a general war-fighting policy. However, the use of ground troops is seen by policy makers not only as costly in lives and treasure but as potentially triggering a much wider, and harder to control, war. If officials estimate that an adversary, even an enemy, can be expelled without ground combat, then they are much less likely to escalate their war aims. For these reasons, when the enemy is seen as having a weak-enough hold on neighboring territory that there is little risk of it reentering once evicted, U.S. policy will accordingly be aimed only at expelling it. Under these circumstances, officials in Washington will gravitate toward strategic bombing on its own, at least initially or at key diplomatic turning points. A classic example of this is the U.S.

air war against North Vietnam from 1965, on and off, through 1972. This war began to be planned in 1964, when it had become clear that the covert raids then being carried out (see the book website) were not affecting Hanoi's support of the insurgency against the Saigon regime. In response, mid-level policy makers began preparing an "integrated political-military plan for graduated action against North Vietnam," the "theory" of the plan being that the U.S. "should strike to hurt but not to destroy, and strike for the purpose of changing the North Vietnamese decision on intervention in the south." This plan, prepared by a former colleague of the scholar whose writings on "compellence" we quoted above, was rejected by Johnson on several grounds, ranging from concern over possible Chinese intervention to lack of domestic and international support for what would be viewed by "many members" of the UN as "aggression." However, over the course of the next months, the situation changed significantly. The insurgent forces did better against Saigon's troops, inflicting "disastrous" losses on the latter. As U.S. officials saw it, the explanation for this trend was due both to "sharply increased" infiltration from North Vietnam and to governmental chaos in Saigon, with coups and demonstrations making it impossible to motivate troops. This latter problem raised the alarming possibility of a neutralist regime coming to power, asking the U.S. to leave, and reaching an accommodation with Hanoi. Such a result, with the U.S. being "thrown out in a matter of months," would be "as just as humiliating a defeat as any other" scenario. A related nightmare, as Washington saw it, was the rising chorus of calls in the UN and by other states for an international conference in which North Vietnam would of necessity play a central role. Thus by early 1965, the U.S. perception was that Hanoi had moved from being simply a supporter of insurgency in South Vietnam to a hovering threat to Saigon's continued existence as an independent and pro-U.S. state. The U.S. would have to act directly against "the very heavy role and responsibility of Hanoi."[27]

In late February 1965, the United States began a sustained and overt policy of bombing North Vietnam. The campaign was known as Rolling Thunder; it consisted of strikes carried out by navy and air force jets, under the command of the admiral in charge of U.S. forces in the Pacific, with the targets being reviewed directly by the Defense Department and the White House. As this level of control indicates, Rolling Thunder was conceived above all in political terms, both as pressure designed to lead to Hanoi's disengagement from South Vietnam and to foster a shifting set of other goals, such as rallying morale in Saigon, demonstrating U.S. firmness, and, at least initially, heading off a U.S. troop commitment. How exactly the strikes were to accomplish the first of these objectives, i.e., North Vietnamese withdrawal, was very much an open question and a quintessentially cybernetic one at that. The U.S. could engage in sustained massive bombings of a wide variety of strategic targets in North Vietnam, but, as the U.S. ambassador put it, "if you lay the whole country waste, it is quite likely that you will induce a mood of fatalism in the Viet Cong. Also, there will be nobody left in North Viet Nam on whom to put pressure." (His successor was more succinct: "It is important not to 'kill the hostage' by destroying the North Vietnamese assets inside the 'Hanoi do-nut.'") Instead, bombing would in principle be escalated over time, gradually moving north "in a slow but steadily ascending movement" and striking ever more significant targets until the U.S. could "persuade Hanoi" to engage in "meaningful negotiations." However, as the U.S. escalated, its air strikes resembled ever more closely those envisaged for the first strategy, until, by 1967, almost every target that had been on the military's original wish list had been struck, including those in the city of

Hanoi and the port of Haiphong. Major escalation beyond this (e.g., a ground invasion of North Vietnam, or bombing China), though, was never seriously considered. Not only was there concern that such actions would lead to another Korean-style war against Chinese forces, but the assumption was that U.S. air power was sufficiently punitive to force North Vietnam into a deal of some sort.

From the beginning, Rolling Thunder was very much a distinct hostile intervention, linked far less tightly to the maintenance intervention in South Vietnam than might be expected. The bombing was conceived a good year before U.S. troops entered into combat operations in the South; it continued even after the U.S. ground war began; and its command and control arrangements were completely separate from those for South Vietnam. Instead, Rolling Thunder was intertwined with diplomatic efforts directed at the North, not with counterinsurgency in the South. Repeatedly, Washington used third parties to try to induce Hanoi into negotiations, attempting to trade an end to bombing for a North Vietnamese withdrawal. In addition, the U.S. paused the bombing on five occasions and restricted it geographically on several others. As we saw in Chapter 5, when Johnson finally decided in 1968 to turn down a large troop increase and to invite serious talks, he suspended most Rolling Thunder strikes in hopes of inducing serious talks with the North. This was followed some months later by an agreement with Hanoi on the modalities of negotiations, in exchange for ending all bombing and other acts of force against North Vietnamese territory. (It should be noted that throughout the more than three years of the Rolling Thunder program, the air strikes, though condemned by a number of states, were nonetheless viewed, in the reported words of one leader, as "careful" responses to "North Vietnamese aggression.") In effect, as Rolling Thunder's targets became increasingly indistinguishable from the standard ones developed before World War II, policy makers in Washington found that the only way they had of using bombing as a bargaining tool was to turn it on and off. And since, logically, it was impossible to know whether negotiation would be enhanced by resuming or further escalating the bombing, or instead by pausing it for short or longer periods of time, Rolling Thunder's apparent lack of success was never seen as a good enough reason to stop it.[28] Indeed, when Nixon resumed strategic bombing of North Vietnam, with the operation being renamed "Linebacker," it soon came to be used for various purposes, with North Vietnamese concessions being only one among them (see the book website for a detailed discussion).

A later, and supposedly more successful, case of overt bombing being used to bring about an enemy's withdrawal is Operation Allied Force, directed against Serbia's presence in Kosovo in 1999. Up through the late 1980s, most U.S. efforts relative to Serbia had revolved around the eventual U.S. clients of Bosnia-Herzegovina and Macedonia (see Chapter 3); policy toward Serbia itself was primarily a matter of routinely hostile actions, numerous tense negotiations, and a warning that the U.S. would be prepared to use military force against Serbia should the latter cause conflict in its province of Kosovo. By 1998, it looked as if this promise would have to be fulfilled. The regime in Belgrade had begun to use increasingly repressive means against the majority population, leading U.S. and NATO (with whom the U.S. had worked on Bosnia) officials to begin making contingency plans for a bombing campaign against Serb forces in Kosovo and against targets in Serbia proper. Although precise details of these plans were not divulged, both their existence and their general outlines were openly discussed, thereby permitting U.S. and NATO diplomats to brandish the threat of air operations in their negotiations with the Serb leader, Slobodan Milošević. On the other hand, both in

Washington and among the NATO allies, there was considerable unease at the thought of actually carrying out a bombing campaign: Serbia had significant enough air defenses that a large-scale campaign would have to be carried out, a policy that "might amount to overkill against Milošević and could incite powerful popular resentment against NATO." Serbia at this point was not a pariah and thus through the rest of 1998, the U.S. and NATO contented themselves with toothless negotiations.

In January, the situation began to change. A particularly horrible massacre was promulgated by Serb forces, giving advocates of force the upper hand. The Serbs were given an ultimatum and, upon their refusal, NATO began to bomb, at first in a limited way, then after Milošević expelled hundreds of thousands of Kosovars and was blamed for a World War II-type refugee catastrophe, in an escalating and considerably more systematic fashion. Rapidly, Operation Allied Force took on the trappings of a classic "coercive pressure" campaign, with bombing continuing until "President Milošević complies with the demands of the international community." Not surprisingly, the U.S. military, which had bitter memories of the White House approving targets in the Rolling Thunder campaign, once more found itself transmitting lists of targets to politicians. The problem, as with Rolling Thunder, was that although there were numerous strategic targets, the relation between their destruction and a Serb agreement to withdraw from Kosovo was loose; and even when the military was able to convince the politicians to approve particular targets, still others would continue to be vetoed. Nor could these deficiencies be made up by tactical strikes on Serb forces in Kosovo, who were not easily spotted by aircraft flying at the high altitudes insisted on by the Pentagon. Thus by late May, the U.S. general in charge of NATO's forces had concluded that "we had gone as far as possible with the air strikes" and "were reaching the end of the strategic campaign": further escalation of Allied Force would lead to many more civilian casualties and split the alliance. For this reason, major escalatory possibilities began to be considered, among them arming the Kosovars and launching a ground invasion with U.S. forces; but the Defense Department had "strong reservations" about a ground war (particularly one that involved an invasion of Serbia), one house of Congress had voted to prohibit funds for ground troops, many U.S. allies had "strong opposition" to any action other than a continued air campaign, and nothing in the contemporary record shows that the U.S. was likely to escalate to a different kind of intervention. Luckily for Clinton, a combination of other factors, notably Russian diplomatic pressure, led Milošević to concede in early June and withdraw his forces.[29]

It should be noted that, even more so than in Korea, the U.S. intervention in Kosovo relied heavily on multilateral institutions. Operation Allied Force was carried out through NATO, even though the U.S., as the dominant member, was able to shape the policy in most details. NATO operated on a unit veto principle, so both the initial decision to bomb and each subsequent escalation in the bombing were acquiesced in by every member of the organization. This provided the United States important political support and served as a model for future NATO operations in Asia and Africa. In addition, even though the bombing campaign did not receive UN approval (the Russians would have vetoed a resolution and so no attempt was made), the Security Council passed a resolution, one day after NATO's military agreement with Yugoslavia, giving its blessing both to that agreement and to the role of NATO in Kosovo. This points to just how widely shared was the perception of the Serbs as egregious and of the U.S. and its allies as justified in their overt use of force.[30]

Combat operations alongside local insurgent forces: Node 22

Nicaragua (1909–10: text); Mexico (1913–14: text); Libya (1986: text); Afghanistan (2001: text); Somalia (2006–07: text)

The kind of sustained and asymmetrical attacks that are carried out to force an enemy to withdraw from a province or other state are not seen by U.S. policy makers as the appropriate way of reducing or eliminating an enemy regime's military support in its own territory. This task, even when there are no occupied countries or provinces, is usually thought as requiring ground troops, and thus whatever bombing may be employed will have to be in the service of infantry. If the enemy regime has some kind of internal armed force opposing it, then in situations where that regime is considered to have crossed the line into pariah status, the U.S. will overtly use its own military power to support the insurgents. Operations of this sort are among the oldest types of U.S. hostile interventions, mostly because the policy instrument they involve – the use of elite ground troops backed by mobile fire power – predates almost all the other instruments discussed above and in Chapter 5. Long before its client state empire was established, the U.S. was using warships and marines, both by themselves and in support of indigenous insurgent groups. Among the earliest examples is the expedition against Tripoli in 1804; at the end of the century, U.S. forces were used in support of a coup against the monarch in Hawaii. In neither these nor other nineteenth-century cases was the target an enemy, as we are using the term in this book, but when such enemies did arise, the policy instrument was ready at hand (for more details, see Chapter 7).[31]

The first state really to be considered an enemy was Nicaragua in the early 1900s. Its ruler, José Santos Zelaya, was seen, starting around 1907 (almost 15 years after having taken office) as having chosen to differ systematically with the United States on issues ranging from Zelaya's policy toward other Central American countries to the way he treated U.S. investors. This led Washington to express hostility through diplomatic maneuvers, economic pressure, and propaganda disseminated through compliant journalists (e.g., "a tyrant, a mischiefmaker … he has ruled Nicaragua from his palace in the dirty little town of Managua on the hot shores of Lake Managua … Sucking his country's strength in sensual enjoyment, Zelaya promotes the gangrene of degeneracy"). The problem was that although "this ruffian," a "harsh and unscrupulous ruler … fond of engineering wars and revolutions in neighboring states" deserved, in U.S. eyes, to be overthrown, any direct U.S. action along those lines would be massively unpopular throughout Latin America. Instead, the U.S. seems to have encouraged Zelaya's domestic opponents to prepare an uprising. When it broke out, Zelaya's forces captured and executed two U.S. citizens who were fighting with the rebels. This was seen as contrary to "the modern enlightened practice of civilized nations" and the U.S. immediately dropped its pretense of neutrality, sending naval vessels to help the insurgents. Soon after, Taft broke diplomatic relations, having his secretary of state announce that the Zelaya regime was "a blot upon the history of Nicaragua." Several weeks later, Zelaya went into exile. His replacement, however, was seen by the U.S. as too close to the departed president and as not "capable of directing a responsible government." The anti-Zelaya rebels clearly received the message that Washington was "steadily against anything like a revival of the Zelaya régime" and continued their insurgency, protected by the U.S. Navy from the government's offensive against them. Although the

Nicaraguan president protested at this violation of "the principles of neutrality proclaimed by the law of nations," the handwriting was on the wall and the rebels soon took over, thereby opening the way for Nicaragua to become a U.S. client (see Chapter 3).[32]

Soon after Zelaya's overthrow, the U.S. acquired a far more significant enemy. Mexico had for several years been in the throes of a revolution when, with the encouragement of the U.S. ambassador, the country's elected president was overthrown by his leading general and the next day shot to death. This murder led to "unconcealed indignation" on the part of officials in the outgoing Taft administration and to similar, if even stronger, views by its successor: Wilson called the new Huerta regime in Mexico a "government of butchers," refused to recognize it, and ended its occasional arms imports from the U.S. By the autumn of 1913, Huerta still clung to power and so Wilson escalated his rhetoric:

> Usurpations like that of General Huerta menace the peace and development of America as nothing else could. They not only render the development of ordered self-government impossible; they also ... impair both the national credit and all the foundations of business, domestic or foreign. It is the purpose of the United States, therefore, to discredit and defeat such usurpations whenever they occur. The present policy of the Government of the United States is to isolate General Huerta entirely; to cut him off from foreign sympathy and aid and from domestic credit, whether moral or material, and so to force him out. It hopes and believes that isolation will accomplish this end, and shall await the results without irritation or impatience. If General Huerta does not retire by force of circumstances, it will become the duty of the United States to use less peaceful means to put him out.

Accordingly, Wilson began to make plans "for the invasion and occupation of Mexico," but as the Huerta government was recognized by a number of Latin American and European states, this course of action was seen as unwarranted and was "strongly opposed" by the U.S. Army's chief of staff.

Wilson thus had to find another way to move militarily. The insurgency was the obvious choice, since it had made considerable progress over the last year. On 27 January, the U.S opened discussions with the rebels; a week later, it lifted the arms embargo, a step which disproportionately favored the rebels and "elated" them. In April, an incident occurred, much as in Nicaragua in 1909: a small number of U.S. sailors were detained briefly by Huerta's army, enraging the U.S. admiral on the spot. He considered it a "hostile act," a view shared by Wilson, who saw it as the "culminating insult of a series of insults to our country and our flag." The upshot was that the navy seized Mexico's principal port of Veracruz and made it possible for the rebels to take Tampico, center of the country's oil trade. Thus deprived of customs and export revenues, Huerta was unable to resist much longer and he resigned in mid-July. Nonetheless, the rebels were staunch nationalists and Wilson was not able to obtain assurances as to the policies they would follow; eventually, U.S. forces had to withdraw from Veracruz without any sort of quid pro quo. Although relations waxed and waned, Mexico remained a U.S. enemy for another 25 years (see Chapter 3).[33]

Almost a century after Wilson's Veracruz adventure, another U.S. president committed American military power to the overt support of internal insurgents halfway around the world, in Afghanistan. As we mentioned earlier in this chapter (a discussion is on the book's website), after the Soviet Union withdrew its troops, the United States began to terminate its support to the mujahedin. By 1992, when they finally took over, the U.S.

was in a neutral posture. This stance continued for almost ten years, throughout an intra-mujahedin conflict, throughout the triumph of the Islamic fundamentalist Taliban in 1996, and practically up until the Al Qaeda attacks on the U.S. of 11 September 2001. Although the U.S. was not enamored of the Taliban, it was also less than happy with the Taliban's principal opponents, the Northern Alliance (and former mujahedin) forces under Ahmed Shah Massoud, whom it accused (correctly) of trafficking in heroin and of military weakness. Although the CIA maintained low-level relations with Massoud, these were mostly on a contingency basis; as regards arms aid, the U.S. restricted itself to lukewarm encouragement to Iran's and Russia's covert transfers of weapons to the Northern Alliance.

Although the Taliban were off the agenda as an enemy, policy makers in Washington were willing to consider action against Al Qaeda, whose leaders by then had relocated to Afghanistan. Up until September 2001, Al Qaeda's attacks on the U.S. were considered too small to warrant some kind of U.S. ground response – "our closest allies would not support us," Clinton said in 1998 – and so the U.S. response when two of its embassies in Africa were bombed was a series of cruise missile strikes, criticized widely as disproportionate and ineffective. This reaction led the CIA to come up with a plan for a significant covertly financed war by Massoud's forces against Al Qaeda, but that, too, was disapproved in Washington on the grounds, among other reasons, that it would elevate the standing of Al Qaeda's leader, Osama bin Laden, and make him "a hero." Several months later, as U.S. intelligence began to be flooded by reports of planned Al Qaeda strikes, the CIA resuscitated its previous plan. This time, policy makers were more responsive and a presidential finding authorizing covert arms aid to the Northern Alliance began wending its way to Bush's desk. The finding set out as a goal "eliminating" Al Qaeda, though it was clearly understood that this would involve action against the Taliban itself. What would have happened had there been no attacks on 11 September cannot be ascertained: the day before, Massoud was assassinated and no one in Washington knew whether the Northern Alliance could hold together sufficiently to justify a covert war.

Within 36 hours, everything had changed. The Taliban, seen as harboring Al Qaeda, was now a prime U.S. enemy, indeed "really the same" as Al Qaeda. However, attacking "Afghanistan would be uncertain. … 100,000 American troops [could be] bogged down in mountain fighting … six months from then"; and since the country "had few roads and little infrastructure," it "would be hard" to find "anything to hit" with air power by itself. If the U.S. was to act on its own, perhaps it would have to launch "military action elsewhere as an insurance policy in case things in Afghanistan went bad." Instead, the CIA's existing plan of aid to the Northern Alliance was bulked up in size and extended to potential rebels in the south of the country; and to this was added a Defense Department plan for air strikes combined with commando operations. What this meant in practice, a few weeks hence, was that the CIA dispensed funds to Northern Alliance and other warlords to pay for their troops and subsidize defections among the Taliban, while the air force engaged in battlefield bombing against Taliban units, with targets being spotted by special forces teams. This combination was powerful: after an initial scare, when the Northern Alliance stalled and Powell had to fend off contingency plans for "Americanizing the war," the Taliban collapsed by mid-November. The U.S. then turned to Al Qaeda, trying at first for a similar marriage of its own airpower and Afghan forces and then, several months later, using larger numbers of American ground troops to carry out what would become a regular series of operations against suspected Al Qaeda fighters and, later, resurgent Taliban guerrillas (see Chapter 5).[34]

The anti-Zelaya operation of 1909, the Veracruz occupation of 1914, and the Afghanistan war of 2001 involved U.S. forces operating overtly and in tandem with indigenous troops against an enemy regime. This combination is relatively rare because, as we pointed out earlier, most states which the U.S. considers to be enemies are not also considered by it to be international pariahs, as was the case with both the Huerta and Taliban regimes. Hence, where there are indigenous forces fighting against a U.S. enemy, Washington's aid is usually covert. (As we saw in Chapter 5, this is also the case when the U.S. uses proxies to aid client states.) If, though, the enemy's international standing is perceived to have changed, then the situation is different. An example of this, in which the enemy was seen to have made itself a pariah and therefore to be a fitting target of U.S. overt force in support of proxies (military dissidents in this case, not insurgents) is Libya in 1986. We mentioned above (a discussion is on the book's website) that the U.S. had been trying covertly to organize punctuated military operations by exiles. As those operations failed, Washington grew increasingly frustrated and began to contemplate the use of the U.S. military to attack Qaddafi directly, with the hopes of either assassinating him or triggering a *coup d'etat*. Reagan, however, was unwilling to order such an attack in the absence of strong evidence that the Libyan regime was behind some particularly egregious act of terrorism. Thus, although U.S. forces were sent off the coast of Libya in hopes of baiting Qaddafi into striking first, the Defense Department authorized only a tit-for-tat response.

A few days after the U.S. task force was withdrawn, an incident occurred which changed the situation. A discotheque in Berlin was blown up, with numerous Americans being wounded. U.S. officials immediately claimed that their intelligence showed this was a Libyan terrorist operation and Reagan authorized an air strike against Libya. Two of the targets were Qaddafi's tent and his family house; bombs hit them, killing one of the leader's daughters and injuring other members of his family. Qaddafi himself escaped. Two days after the bombing attempt, Shultz, whose State Department lawyers had laid the groundwork for the strike by claiming that "in the context of military action what normally would be considered murder is not," consoled himself with the thought that there was "considerable dissidence" within the Libyan armed forces and that the bombing raid had at least sent "messages" to those forces.[35]

A more recent variant of the Libyan raid occurred in Somalia from late 2006 to early 2007. We saw above that the CIA's efforts at aiding internal armed forces had badly backfired in the middle of 2006; this led, some months later, to an alignment with the Ethiopian-supported (and toothless) "Transitional Federal Government" (TFG). However, as the TFG's foes began to advance on the little territory it had left, the Ethiopians grew alarmed and in December invaded Somalia. By this time, the U.S. had been training Ethiopian troops for several years; during the invasion, it supplied them with intelligence. The following month, with the TFG's enemies on the run, a U.S. naval task force patrolled off shore, looking for "terrorists" who might try to flee the country or resupply those chased from power. In addition, two U.S. airstrikes took place, aiming at killing individuals said to be connected to Al Qaeda.[36]

A note on assassination

The 1986 raid against Libya was among other things a barely disguised assassination attempt; those of 2007 in Somalia were not even disguised. As we have seen, these were not the first such attempts. The U.S. tried on numerous occasions to assassinate Castro, planned to kill Qassim in Iraq, contemplated assassinating Sukarno in Indonesia, bombed the dwelling and headquarters of Milošević in Serbia, and trained guerrillas and raiders in several other states in techniques which could certainly be used to assassinate leaders. We also saw in Chapter 5 that the U.S. initially approved, and in fact sent weapons for, the assassination of Trujillo in the Dominican Republic; and that it gave the green light to the kidnapping of Schneider in Chile and to the coup against Diem in South Vietnam (this coup, and the resulting assassination, is discussed on the book's website). Although these three cases did not involve any kind of order to kill the individuals in charge, such actions were understood by various U.S. officials to be a clear possibility. (At one point, assassination was also considered, though not carried out, against various leaders in the Arbenz regime in Guatemala; see Chapter 5.) In addition to these well-documented cases (plus another plot against the already-deposed Congolese leader Lumumba, and the air strikes in Somalia and, as we will see, Saddam Hussein in Iraq), there have been recurring rumors for many years about U.S. attempts at assassinating other leaders.[37]

This range of situations in which assassination is pursued, considered, or tacitly permitted indicates that it is not a particular type of intervention but more an action which can be incorporated into one or more policy instruments. From time to time, there have been discussions about institutionalizing an assassination capacity in the CIA (the Senate uncovered references to a "Health Alteration Committee" and a subsequent "Executive Action" capability known as ZR/RIFLE), but even when some type of bureaucratic mechanism is set up, it tends to be thought of only in a specific context of other hostile activities. At the very minimum, killing a particular foreign leader has various potential consequences for the nature of the regime which would presumably succeed his death. This is one significant difference between enemy states and other sorts of enemies, such as terrorists or narcotics traffickers: the former will certainly continue to exist, while the latter can be imagined to disintegrate after a leader's death. Perhaps this explains why, after the attacks of 11 September 2001, consideration was given to assassinating the leaders of Al Qaeda, but not (so far as we know) of enemy states.[38]

A further difference has to do with moral compunctions. Assassination has traditionally been distinguished from killings that occur as part of a broader attack on cities or enemy fortifications during wartime. However tenuous this distinction may be in practice (or however one-sided, in light of the large numbers of nonleaders who have died in certain interventions), it underlies the controversies when particular assassination attempts come to light, the various orders outlawing it issued by a series of presidents, and the elaborate avoidance behavior by bureaucrats aimed at making sure that presidents and top-level policy makers are never presented with written or explicit oral proposals for a particular enemy leader to be killed. This may also help explain why, when assassination was considered or resorted to, it often was done on an ad hoc basis, with the involvement of actors outside of the U.S. government, such as the Mafia. By contrast, when the targeted leader is not in charge of a state but of some other type of organization, whatever arguments are made against assassination tend to be far more pragmatic than moral.

In the end, assassination can be expected to come up from time to time as a possible component in various types of client and hostile interventions. Because of the stigma attached to it and because by definition it aims at only one or a small number of leaders, it will rarely, if ever, be the centerpiece of a particular intervention. Whatever the fantasies or obsessions of U.S. officials about particular leaders, "executive action" with regard to those leaders can never be more than one part of a broader policy.[39]

Invasion by U.S. troops: Node 23

Grenada (1983: text); Iraq (2003: text)

As we have seen, apart from situations combining entrenched occupation and a *casus belli*, most hostile interventions have not involved an invasion whose principal ground forces are American. Either the enemy in question is not a pariah, thereby ruling out any kind of overt operation; or the situation is seen as one demanding coercive bombing or fighting in which local forces take the lead. Up until the 1980s, in fact, there were no hostile intervention situations of either pure attacks on a regime's military support or pure territorial expulsion which did not fall into the covert, bombing, or proxy war categories. In other words, through the first 80 or so years of its client state empire, with the important exception of the two world wars, the U.S. acted against its enemies by means short of invasion; when hostile interventions did take place, they were relatively cheap, a point we will return to below and in Chapter 7. However, when the enemy in question is considered a pariah; when the issue is not to force its withdrawal from a province or territory but only its overthrow pure and simple; and when there are few or no indigenous forces capable of playing the role of a proxy, then U.S. policy makers see themselves as facing no option but that of invading the enemy, preferably at the head of a multinational coalition but in any case with their own troops.

The first case of hostile invasion occurred in 1983, against Grenada. Since 1979, the island had been governed by a leftist party with ties to Cuba; almost as soon as this governance began, Carter reacted with concern and ordered the CIA to carry out covert activity to undermine the regime. Congress, however, bristled at this decision and pressured the CIA into calling off the operation. Instead, a policy of routine hostility was put into effect and over the next few years, the U.S. tried to isolate Grenada diplomatically and financially, to intimidate it militarily, and to raise the rhetorical temperature (e.g., Grenada "now bears the Soviet and Cuban trademark, which means that it will attempt to spread the virus amongst its neighbors"). The U.S. also encouraged Grenada's island neighbors to set up a regional security organization; and there is some evidence that new covert operations were being planned as part of a "coordinated" effort in early October 1983.

Some days later, an internal dispute broke out within the ruling party. This spurred mid-level meetings in Washington, with one official on the NSC staff advocating an armed intervention that would involve nominal participation by Caribbean states alongside the U.S. Ostensibly, the purpose of this would be to prevent U.S. medical students on Grenada from being taken hostage, and the next day, contingency evacuation planning began. As this was occurring, the political struggle on the island intensified, with the prime minister, Maurice Bishop, being arrested; and over the next few days, intense discussions began to take place in the region, with heads of government in several Caribbean states urging the U.S. at the least to rescue Bishop and perhaps to intervene and overthrow the Grenadan regime. This the U.S. resisted, since "overt military action without" actual signs of danger to U.S. citizens "would have been impossible." On 19 October, Bishop was killed; this raised the spectre of hostages and radical leftist control, sparked a formal request for intervention by Caribbean states, and led those in Washington who had until then been reluctant to change their minds and back an invasion. On 25 October, Operation Urgent Fury took place and the U.S. military stormed into the small island, deposed its government, and evacuated the medical students.[40]

Almost 20 years later, the U.S. mounted another invasion. This one was considerably larger and, as we saw in Chapter 5, was soon transformed into a counterinsurgency war. The target in 2003 was a 40-year old enemy: Iraq. To summarize the various hostile interventions discussed above: the U.S. helped foment a coup in 1963 and may have done so again in 1968; it supported the Kurds' armed struggle between 1972 and 1975; and following the Gulf War in 1991, it hoped for the overthrow of the regime but gave only half-hearted support to a coup attempt in 1996. In addition, U.S. forces fought against Iraqi ones in the 1991 Gulf War, but this did not go much beyond a maintenance intervention on behalf of Saudi Arabia. Thus, by the end of the 1990s, U.S. leaders found themselves in a situation where an enemy against whom they had gone to war as well as intervened against on several occasions was still around. None of the covert policy instruments had worked or was feasible to try and an overt invasion did not seem justified, particularly as the regime was forbidden to use aircraft in the north and south of the country and as the UN had succeeded in forcing the destruction of weapons of mass destruction (i.e., chemical and biological weapons, as well as a program aimed at developing nuclear weapons). What was left at this point was symbolism – Congress passed the Iraq Liberation Act of 1998, stating that it "should be the policy of the United States to support efforts to remove the regime headed by Saddam Hussein from power" and authorizing $97 million in military aid to "Iraqi democratic opposition organizations" – and pinprick bombing operations designed to goad the Ba'athist regime into war.

The attacks of 11 September 2001 changed everything. Immediately, high-level policy makers understood that whether or not Iraq had anything to do with the attacks, doubts could be raised, thereby serving as a *casus belli* for an invasion of the country. Thus, that very afternoon, in preparation for policy meetings, the secretary of defense ordered his subordinates to get "[b]est info fast ... judge whether good enough. Hit S.H. [Saddam Hussein] @ same time. Not only UBL [Usama bin Laden]. ... Hard to get a good case. Need to move swiftly. ... go massive – sweep it all up, things related and not." The next day, after Bush had spent several hours with his advisers discussing Al Qaeda and Afghanistan, he told the senior counterterrorism official on the National Security Council staff to "go back over everything, everything. See if Saddam did this." The official responded that Al Qaeda was behind the 11 September attacks, at which point Bush reiterated his order to "see if Saddam was involved. ... I want to know any shred." This interest persisted throughout the planning for the war in Afghanistan, with a classically cybernetic policy recommendation by one official serving as a model for other anti-Iraq arguments:

> Another risk they faced was getting bogged down in Afghanistan ... which led to a different discussion: Should they think about launching military action elsewhere as an insurance policy in case things in Afghanistan went bad? They would need successes early in any war to maintain domestic and international support ... Wolfowitz seized the opportunity. Attacking Afghanistan would be uncertain. He worried about 100,000 American troops bogged down in mountain fighting in Afghanistan six months from then. In contrast, Iraq was a brittle, oppressive regime that might break easily. It was doable. He estimated that there was a 10 to 50 percent chance Saddam was involved in the September 11 terrorist attacks. The U.S. would have to go after Saddam at some time if the war on terrorism was to be taken seriously.

Soon afterward, the Bush administration began planning for a war against Iraq. As fighting was still raging in Afghanistan, the general in charge of Central Command, whose area of responsibility encompassed both countries, was ordered to "look at options" and revise the now-outdated contingency plans for Iraq. This took months to do, but even as the Pentagon was developing and refining its options, Bush ordered troops to be moved to the Gulf region, where they would be housed in the various bases the U.S. had established following the Gulf War of 1991 (see Chapter 3). The harder problem was a political one: to establish that if Iraq were not invaded, other 11 September-style attacks were more likely. This task gave rise to a multipronged effort, aimed at amassing whatever scraps of evidence could be found to demonstrate that the Ba'ath regime still had weapons of mass destruction (WMD) and that it was likely to give some of those weapons to terrorists. As the head of the British foreign intelligence service put it, following a trip to Washington: "Military action was now seen as inevitable. Bush wanted to remove Saddam, through military action, justified by the conjunction of terrorism and WMD. But the intelligence and facts were being fixed around the policy." Since at this point the CIA was reporting that there was no good evidence that Iraq had either weapons of mass destruction or links with Al Qaeda, the Defense Department set up an Office of Special Plans whose job it was to bypass the CIA, taking unconfirmed rumors and invented or exaggerated claims by defectors and making sure that those types of materials made it to high-level policy makers. This operation, plus intense pressure on the CIA to soften its views, led to a flood of alarmist stories about Iraq, which were in turn disseminated to the mass media, the Congress, and foreign governments. By the autumn of 2002, the view of Iraq as still possessing WMD, even if not necessarily having links to terrorists, was widely held.

Nonetheless, to many elites both at home and abroad, there remained a gap between an Iraq armed with WMD and an Iraq sufficiently dangerous to justify an invasion there and then. In part, this skepticism was due to the well-known history of mutual hostility between the Ba'ath and Al Qaeda; the extensive air patrols by the U.S. and the U.K. also made it difficult to imagine Iraq posing a major and imminent threat to its neighbors, much less to the U.S. Hence, Bush shifted ground, arguing that the UN should insist on Iraq being disarmed and that if Iraq refused, the UN should then authorize its member states to do the job militarily. This tactic, designed to back Iraq into a choice between verified disarmament of its supposed WMD and the role of an internationally condemned pariah, was successful: Congress authorized Bush to use force "(1) to defend the national security of the United States against the continuing threat posed by Iraq; and (2) enforce all relevant United Nations Security Council resolutions regarding Iraq." The next month, the Security Council passed a resolution requiring Iraq to readmit weapons inspectors and verifiably disarm; failure to do so would be a "further material breach" of its obligations and would be brought before the Council "in order to consider the situation and the need for full compliance." By now, the U.S. was assembling a coalition to support it in the war everyone considered as inevitable, once the Iraqis defied the UN.

Instead, Iraq readmitted the weapons inspectors and submitted a declaration of almost 12,000 pages in which it denied possessing WMD ever since their destruction some years earlier. Although this was true, the declaration was incomplete in certain respects and the interpretation in Washington and elsewhere was that it was still concealing its activities. Nonetheless, since with each passing day, the UN's inspectors failed to find WMD and since the very U.S. troop buildup in the area made Iraq that much less of an imminent threat, cracks began to appear at the UN. Several important U.S. allies, of which France was the most significant, made it clear that there was not yet enough evidence for them to join in a war and urged that the inspectors be given more time. In the meantime, the harshness of Bush's rhetoric and his apparent willingness to go to war led to massive peace demonstrations around the world. The U.S., faced with a deterioration in its political position, therefore gave up on a second Security Council resolution and, with UK backing, launched its war. (Operations began earlier than planned with an anti-Qaddafi-style airstrike on a compound where the Iraqi president supposedly was at the moment.) Interestingly, military operations were assisted by several U.S. clients who had either been silent on the war or publicly opposed to it. Moreover, once the Iraqi regime's armies had ceased fighting and before the insurgency began in earnest (Chapter 5), the UN recognized the U.S. and British occupation; called on member states to support Iraqi reconstruction, in particular by financial contributions; and for good measure reaffirmed the "importance" of WMD destruction and of pursuing "members of the previous Iraqi regime who are alleged to be responsible for crimes and atrocities." The U.S., it seemed at the time, had won its bet, converting international outrage at the 11 September attacks into broad, if at times grudging, support for an invasion of a long-term U.S. enemy.[41]

The invasion of Iraq illustrates one of the principal differences between hostile interventions which are covert and those which are overt. When we first introduced the distinction, we emphasized the importance of being seen to respect sovereignty and of the necessity that the enemy in question be considered by U.S. policy makers as a pariah. That status is emphatically not a matter of polling the mass public in the U.S. or elsewhere, or of acting against only those regimes which have been condemned by the UN Security Council. Indeed, the invasions of both Iraq and Grenada were widely unpopular, as were the bombing/assassination raid on Libya, the occupation of Veracruz, and the bombing of North Vietnam. Rather, the point is that U.S. officials conceived of themselves as being unable to act overtly unless and until the enemy had done something which in their minds, in those of opinion leaders at home, and perhaps also in the view of leaders of other states (e.g., NATO regarding Kosovo, the Eastern Caribbean states regarding Grenada), was egregious and beyond the pale. Such actions – the massacre in Racak (Kosovo), say, or the attacks on 11 September – were thus indicators that the situation was now different, whether or not that view was widely held outside of Washington. Of course, U.S. policy makers, often eager to act, waited for such egregious acts to occur or even, as in the case of Japan, pushed the enemy to them.

Hostile interventions in perspective

Hostile interventions, like maintenance interventions, are a recurring feature of United States foreign policy. Just as the U.S. has frequently intervened on behalf of clients which it was unable to maintain by routine means, so too the U.S. has tried regularly to overthrow various of its enemies rather than simply manifest its hostility to them in routine ways. As we have seen, these hostile interventions display the same cybernetic logic as the maintenance interventions, a point to which we will return in Chapter 7 when we discuss the origins and likely future of U.S. client state and enemy policy. For now, though, one of the obvious questions to ask about hostile interventions is how often they succeed in overthrowing or expelling the enemy regime in question.

To answer this question, we can begin by adding up the successes and failures of operations for each situation of hostile intervention discussed in this chapter. From 1909 to the middle of 2008, the U.S. fomented eight separate *coups d'état* (that we know of) against enemy regimes; five succeeded and three failed. Among exile raid operations, the figures are one success and eight failures; among internal armed movements, one success and six failures.[42] Over all, covert interventions have succeeded seven times and failed 17 times. The picture is quite different for overt interventions: one case of bombing success and one of bombing failure; three of proxy assistance success and two of failure, and five of invasion success (at least in the short term) and one failure, for a total of nine overt successes and four failures. Thus, overt interventions are more likely to overthrow or expel an enemy regime than are covert interventions; though if we add together all interventions, there are more failures (21) than successes (16). Finally, if we redivide all hostile interventions into nonmilitary (i.e., coups) and military (i.e., everything else), we see that nonmilitary interventions succeed most of the time (five successes, three failures), whereas military interventions fail most of the time (11 successes, 18 failures). This gives a slightly different picture: coups and overt military interventions are most likely to succeed; covert military interventions are highly likely to fail.

These mixed results can be both contrasted and compared with client interventions. As we saw in Chapter 5, most clients can be maintained by routine means. For those who require intervention, nonmilitary responses work out better than military ones and among the latter, emergency aid is more likely to succeed than combat forces. On the other hand, hostile interventions involving either the enemy's own military deposing the regime's leaders or else American military forces operating overtly, are more successful than those involving the use of proxy forces. Intermediate situations of intervention, where the U.S. relies on local forces, are about as unsuccessful in dealing with enemies as combat interventions (which, it should be recalled, usually rely on local forces) are in dealing with clients. Most generally, though, the U.S. is simply much more effective at maintaining its clients – above all, by nonmilitary (routine and interventionary) means – than at overthrowing its enemies.

In the face of this mixed track record, the obvious question is whether U.S. officials see alternative ways of eliminating enemies. In fact, there are two such paths: as a result of negotiations with the United States and as a result of internal collapse or overthrow by states other than the U.S. The paradox, as we will see, is that both of these paths are surer ways of eliminating enemies than are the various interventions discussed above.

Most frequently than one might imagine, the U.S. negotiates with its enemies. These negotiations are opened from time to time while the U.S. is carrying out a policy of routinely hostile activities; and they bear on a particular, limited subject (e.g., the withdrawal of the enemy's troops from another state; the modalities for refugees to travel from the enemy's territory to that of the United States). Most of the time, as we discussed above, negotiations do not change the basic thrust of U.S. policy. If the talks fail, routinely hostile activities continue and, as always, may escalate into hostile intervention if the situation permits. On the other hand, if the talks arrive at an agreement, that usually is the end of it, with some chance of U.S. officials even interpreting that accord as a sign of the enemy's weakness and doubling their efforts at looking for opportunities to overthrow the enemy regime or evict it from a territory. However, there is a slight chance for negotiations to widen into more general talks about relations with the U.S. and thus to offer the chance of ending the state's status as an enemy; although if an external shock occurs, such as the enemy engaging in new policies the U.S. considers unacceptable, then the negotiations will remain circumscribed and the chances for subsequent broadening will be reduced. Viewed in this way, negotiating an end to enemy status is a possibility but not a very probable one. That is one reason why successful negotiations over status usually conclude only after the state in question has been an enemy for a number of years: from 9 years in the case of Sudan (in 1976) to 16 years for the Soviet Union (in 1933), 24 for Libya, 29 for China, 36 for Mexico, and 41 for Vietnam (former North Vietnam).

To get a better idea of the essentially random way in which negotiations either succeed in ending enemy status or are aborted due to some kind of external shock, it is useful to list the immediate reasons for success or failure in particular cases. One example, which we briefly discussed above, is of the U.S. normalization of relations with the Soviet Union in 1933: what permitted negotiations to broaden was a confluence of events, including Roosevelt's election and the looming threat of Japan. Another example, discussed in Chapter 3, is that of Mexico, with whom the U.S. had repeatedly entered into limited negotiations. Some of those efforts had succeeded, others failed and even led the U.S. to contemplate the possibility of renewed intervention; what expanded the talks which began after Mexico's oil expropriations in 1938, thereby permitting an end to enemy status and subsequent acquisition as a client, was a variety of factors, chief among them Roosevelt's Good Neighbor policy and the War Department's attempts to organize hemispheric defense in anticipation of a war against the Axis powers.

Thus far, it may appear that the key issue accounting for a negotiated end to enemy status is the presence of another enemy. In both the Soviet and Mexican cases, the U.S. was willing to make significant concessions because of concern over a recently aggressive Japan and newly threatening Axis powers. However, this particular factor is either less significant or absent in other cases of negotiation. For example, the U.S. reached an agreement with China in part because of shared concern over the Soviet Union but that concern was hardly recent, even if it was enhanced by a chill in the cold war during the Carter administration. By all accounts, Nixon and Kissinger began their trilateral diplomacy with multiple and partly conflicting goals in mind, ranging from spurring detente with the Soviet Union to serving "as a counterweight to Russia"; the significant point was that "we want normalization and we want friendship," and this led almost immediately to ending hostile activities and reorienting covert efforts in the direction of "improv[ing] relations with us." Normalization moved forward under Ford and was concluded under Carter, mostly out of concern that if diplomatic relations were not established, the situation would become untenable, with potentially high foreign and domestic costs. This latter motivation was similar to that underlying the normalization of relations between the U.S. and Vietnam. Washington launched talks following Vietnam's withdrawal from Cambodia, arguing that Vietnam's behavior was now acceptable to the U.S.; but only when American business interests grew alarmed at the prospect of losing out on future trade and investment opportunities did the Clinton Administration finally summon the courage to defuse the issue of soldiers missing in action from the earlier war. In another case, U.S. alarm over terrorists led it to expand negotiations with Libya, specifically by responding to offers of information about terrorists. A final accord was then reached when the Libyans agreed to cease work on nuclear weapons and the U.S., pleased at the possibility of its 2003 invasion of Iraq intimidating other so-called rogue states, agreed to let the Qaddafi regime stay in power. One last example is Sudan, with whom good U.S. relations were temporarily reestablished in the mid-1970s, following the former's cooling of its links with the Soviet Union.[43]

This same heterogeneity of motives and simultaneity of external shocks is what derailed several otherwise promising negotiation efforts. For example, in the 1970s the U.S. opened fairly broad talks with Cuba on normalizing relations; these were killed off by domestic U.S. changes and by Cuba's intervention in Angola. The talks were then resumed under Carter, only to be aborted because of a flood of Cuban refugees and another Cuban intervention, this time in Ethiopia. The window then closed and U.S. policy reverted to its customary one of seething anti-Castroism. Similarly, on several occasions starting around 2000, it looked as if the United States was going to broaden discussions with Sudan on specific issues (e.g., terrorism, the rebellion in the south), but the rise of a new conflict in the region of Darfur, with the regime being accused of mass killings, torpedoed this possibility (see Chapter 7). U.S. relations with Syria display the same pattern, with specific agreements on numerous occasions (the 1974 Golan Heights accord, the 1978 arrangements for Lebanon, the 1991 Gulf War, and the post-11 September 2001 anti-terror hunt) being sidetracked or undercut by new hostile actions when other issues – relations with Israel, Iraq, or Iran, for example – flared up. Another rapprochement, this one with Iran, never occurred, in spite of several promising openings (one in fact involved an apology by the U.S. for the coup against Mossadeq). The obstacles came above all from hardliners in both countries who, through legislative and other means, torpedoed both implicit cooperative arrangements and broad proposals for settling outstanding issues. Finally, the same pattern holds with North Korea: on various occasions from the 1970s to the present, the U.S. and the Koreans have talked, with the agenda ranging from specific issues (e.g., troops, nuclear activities) to general relations; but each such effort was short-circuited or limited by untoward events or insistence on more far-reaching concessions.[44]

An alternate pathway by which enemy regimes disappear is if they collapse internally or are overthrown in war for reasons having little or nothing to do with U.S. actions. In fact, there are a number of such cases, ranging from coups or other political upheavals with which the U.S. is not associated to wars in which the U.S. role was fairly minor. The most prominent example of the former is the collapse of the Soviet Union, an event related only tangentially to any U.S. efforts directed against the communist regime. Other examples include the overthrow of the Derg in Ethiopia in 1991, something carried out by a coalition of insurgents mostly unsupported by the U.S. (see above); the democratic ending of the Bouterse regime in Suriname from 1988–91, an event in which the U.S. played no direct role (see above and also Chapter 3); and the collapse of the Milošević regime in Yugoslavia, an action triggered by domestic discontent largely unrelated to any explicit U.S. policy. Still other instances of enemy removal occasioned by non-U.S.-related internal changes include Egypt (Sadat's reversal of Nasser's policies) and South Yemen (disappearance of the state via merger with North Yemen). In both these cases, the U.S. was carrying out a policy of routinely hostile actions at the time the enemy regime disappeared and had not engaged in a hostile intervention for a number of years, if ever.

Other enemy regimes have been overthrown as a result of foreign war or invasion in which the U.S. role was nonexistent or minor. For example, the Khmer Rouge regime was, as mentioned above, deposed by Vietnam, which invaded the country in 1978. In Afghanistan, the Khalq-PDPA regime, which the U.S. was already combating via aid to rural insurgents (see discussion on the book's website), was eliminated by the Soviet invasion of 1979 in which KGB agents actually went into the palace and shot dead the regime's leader. Even when the U.S. did intervene, the enemy may have collapsed for other reasons, as for example with the Hohenzollern regime at the end of World War I (see discussion on the book's website): although this was a war aim of the United States, it did not come either at the hand of the U.S. or of its allies. Nor was it an indirect effect, because although U.S. entry into the war may have provided the *coup de grâce*, the bulk of the fighting did not involve the U.S.; even the collapse of the Ludendorff offensive in 1918, which led the German high command to sue for peace, was due mainly to efforts by the British and the French. In short, several cases of war-induced enemy regime elimination cannot with any real justice be described as a consequence of U.S. intervention: either the U.S. did not intervene or its actions had little or no effect.

If we now compare the different pathways to enemy disappearance, the result is striking. Applying the World War I correction to our above totals, 15 enemy regimes have been overthrown or forced to withdraw from territory as a clear effect of U.S. interventions (with another 21 interventions failing). On the other hand, no fewer than 15 enemy regimes left that status as a result of either negotiation with the United States or of actions (internal overthrow; wartime defeat) not primarily attributable to U.S. intervention. Hostile intervention is thus no more successful as a means of eliminating enemies than are negotiation, noninterventionary war, or simply waiting for domestic actors to force regime change. This contrast is even more apparent when we add in the failure rate of interventions, already discussed above. The U.S. can and does eliminate enemies but hostile interventions are much less likely to achieve this outcome than are other policies. Since most U.S. enemies eventually leave that status (in 2008, only five states were still enemies), this calls into question the utility of hostile intervention. When to these considerations are added the enormous potential human costs of those interventions for both target states (combat deaths, civilian casualties, deliberate massacres) and the U.S., not to mention the budgetary implications, such operations appear even more means-driven than their client counterparts. Are they really likely to continue? Can the U.S. empire be envisioned without them or, for that matter, without a constant supply of enemies? It is to these questions that we now turn.

7 The persistence of client-state imperialism

The United States has pursued essentially the same foreign policy for over a century. It has acquired client states, maintained them routinely through a limited number of policy instruments, and when necessary, intervened on their behalf with another, equally small, set of instruments. Throughout most of this same time span, the U.S. has also, and in ways often connected with its support of clients, opposed various states deemed as enemies both through routinely hostile activities and, again with a small set of policy instruments, through hostile interventions. These various pro-client and anti-enemy activities are the dominant feature of U.S. foreign policy both through the mundane operations of the various programs the U.S. carries out in scores of countries around the world and in terms of the major issues of war and peace debated on significant occasions by the highest-level policy makers in Washington.

Up to this point, we have discussed two kinds of continuity in U.S. foreign policy. The first of these is micro-continuity, the recurring resort by the U.S. to the same type of policy instruments in a given context. This is certainly the case for routine policies of maintenance and hostility but it is also true of the interventionary policies carried out from time to time on behalf of clients and against enemies. Indeed, as we saw in numerous cases of intervention, particular policy instruments continue to be carried out even when they are patently failing (we will return to this point below). The second kind of continuity is meso-continuity, the recurring deployment of particular policy instruments in contexts where they had not previously been used. Time and again, when U.S. officials found themselves confronted in a given country by a situation which had never before been the case there, they used exactly the same type of policy instruments to deal with that situation as they or their predecessors used in similar situations in other countries. This kind of continuity can give apparently aberrant results, as when policy makers, perfectly aware that a given instrument led to disastrous consequences the last time it was deployed, nonetheless resort to it again (this, too, will be discussed below). Although the cybernetic approach used in this book is compatible with a picture of policy makers consciously and deliberately choosing specific courses of action, both types of policy continuity indicate just how limited the range of choice actually is. There may be multiple variants of a given type of policy instrument but there are only so many types in the first place. Policy making in this sense is indeed mechanistic.

Machines, of course, can be scrapped and new ones built. Is this a likely prospect? Should we expect that for decades to come, the United States will continue acquiring and maintaining clients, often by interventionary means? Similarly, will the U.S. continue to intervene from time to time against states it considers as enemies? For obvious policy reasons, these are important questions; but just as obviously, any answers put forward here can only have their truth or falsity determined years in the future. What we can do, first, is to go over the various arguments against what, in Chapter 1, we called macro-continuity and see if, in terms of both their logic and the evidence usually cited on their behalf, they are at least plausible. What we will see is that they are not and that, as a result, there are no good reasons to predict that the U.S. will adopt a significantly different foreign policy any time in the foreseeable future. Instead, we will argue in the second half of the chapter, the cybernetic approach points strongly to a continuation of U.S. clientilism and anti-enemy policy.

Standard arguments for policy discontinuity

From time to time, often when a war is begun or liquidated, intellectuals in the U.S. engage in debates about how long the U.S. will be able to maintain its position in the world. For the most part, these debates presume that U.S. dominance is beneficial and/ or necessary, with writers arguing about what can and ought to be done to extend that dominance. Although the question we pose in this chapter – whether the U.S. will continue to engage in the same kinds of client-state and anti-enemy policies as in the past – is only tangentially addressed in these debates, it is nonetheless possible to construct an answer from among the various exchanges. In fact, there are four answers, all arriving at the same conclusion but doing so by different paths.

Imperial overstretch

In 1987, the historian Paul Kennedy published a monograph which quickly became a bestseller. In it, he argued that great powers need both wealth to "underpin military power" and military power "to acquire and protect wealth." However, if a state invests too much in military power, it thereby robs itself of future wealth production and hence, in the long run, of the wherewithal to retain its military position abroad, at least relative to other states. By the same token, if a great power tries to conquer too many territories or fight too many wars, it will again deplete the resources it could use to maintain its position in the future. These two dangers, which soon acquired the label of "imperial overstretch," applied to all great powers and Kennedy gained considerable notoriety for arguing that they applied to the United States as well. The U.S., he claimed was in "relative decline" and would be unable to "preserve its existing position" indefinitely in the face of other, rising, states.[1]

There are two general ways in which imperial overstretch can affect the foreign policy a state pursues. First, it may be that a decline in resources reduces the amount of money available for the state to maintain its empire, leading to a decision to retrench. For example, a state may no longer have enough money to maintain a large army, or to keep a significant number of ships afloat, or to undertake what might be long and costly campaigns. In these cases, the leaders of the state may opt to scale down their ambitions, at the very least by ceasing to acquire new clients; perhaps by leaving existing clients to their fate or turning over the role of patron to another state (e.g., as Britain did with Greece); or by opting to live and let live with enemies in situations which previously would have evoked an interventionary response. Those types of decisions may be approached gradually rather than all at once: for example, an ongoing war may require so many resources that too few soldiers are left available for carrying out a counterinsurgency in another country, thereby triggering compromise policies or, perhaps, acceptance of the "loss" of the client.

The second way in which overstretch might affect foreign policy is via some type of serious loss. If an imperial power is led to expand into areas beyond its capabilities, then the effect of a defeat might lead to an end to the practice of acquiring new clients or engaging in large-scale combat against new enemies. Again, there may not be a once-and-for-all deliberate decision to make those changes, but if it takes time for a state to reconstitute its armed forces (or for its allies to do likewise), it may find itself unable to respond with the full array of military instruments the next time a situation might otherwise indicate such a response. If several incidents like this occur, then a new precedent for nonaction can begin to be created, even as the earlier loss begins to take on larger proportions in policy makers' deliberations.

At first blush, both of the overstretch arguments would seem to apply to the United States as a result of the 2003 Iraq war and the resulting counterinsurgency. Certainly the cost of the war was staggering, with over $800 billion appropriated by Congress through fiscal year 2008 and one well researched estimate putting the total bill (including operational expenses of a withdrawal that would begin in 2009, long-term care for the wounded, replacement of lost or damaged equipment, and interest on borrowed money) at some $3 trillion.[2] In addition, the war absorbed so many of the army's combat troops that few were left for other wars, notably the counterinsurgency effort being prosecuted in Afghanistan (see Chapter 5). To be sure, some advocates of the war described it as a success but by the time of the 2008 elections, there was a broad consensus that the U.S. had become bogged down in a ruinously expensive war from which it would take years to recover. When added to the general cost of the U.S. military, the Iraq war would, on this view, represent the high water mark of U.S. client maintenance and anti-enemy foreign policy.[3]

On closer examination, though, this argument does not hold up. To begin with, we need to separate costs into several categories, then to determine just how much of a constraint they are on foreign policy decisions. We saw in Chapter 4 that direct U.S. resource transfers to U.S. clients are fairly small, amounting to some $35 billion in 2004. This figure, which as we pointed out does not include resource transfers in Iraq or the costs of the military, can be taken as part of the baseline cost of U.S. foreign policy. To that should be added some portion of the general budget for the Department of Defense, as well as client- or enemy-related expenditures incurred by other agencies, such as the Veterans Affairs Department (health care), the Justice Department (narcotics control), the State Department (diplomacy), and the Treasury Department (exchange stabilization).[4] It is impossible to determine just what percentage of these various costs are attributable to the acquisition and maintenance of client states and to policies of hostility toward enemies. Arguably, some expenditures, such as for nuclear missiles, should not be counted since they are not intended for purposes of either intervention or routinely hostile activities carried out against enemy states. However, it is the nature of policy instruments that they are available for use and so even the most devastating weapons can, on occasion, at least be considered for use in the context of an intervention (e.g., Truman's allusions to the atomic bomb at the time of the Chinese offensive in the Korean War; Nixon's nuclear alert during the 1973 Arab-Israeli War); thus the safest procedure is simply to treat the entire Defense Department budget as relevant to maintaining clients and intervening against enemies. This surely overestimates the non-major war costs of U.S. foreign policy but even so, the numbers are revealing in terms of their relative importance.

In 2008, the United States was projected to spend some $600 billion in the Department of Defense, not counting the cost of the Iraq War. This represents a bit over 4 percent of the total economic output of the entire country, a figure which was approximately 1 percentage point less of economic output than in 1975, when the U.S. had just wound down the Vietnam War, and 2 percent less than in 1985, when Carter and Reagan had been increasing the military budget for several years (see Figure 7.1). That percentage was roughly half of the corresponding figure for the years between the end of the Korean War and the height of the Vietnam War, and less than an eighth of that in World War II.[5] Certainly, as Figure 7.1 shows, the U.S. spends considerably more on its military now than in the early decades of the twentieth century when the number of clients and enemies was far lower; but in relative terms, it is hard to make the case that the U.S. empire is, in terms of resources, overstretched as compared with earlier decades.

Of course, the spanner in the works is the 2003 Iraq War. Once the war had been transformed into a client maintenance intervention, it ended up costing around $200 billion a year; and as we pointed out above, some significant fraction of that sum will continue to be incurred for decades to come. Nonetheless, even $200 billion adds only 1.4 percent to the total impact of military spending on the U.S. gross domestic output. For the fact remains that the U.S. is an enormously large and wealthy country, and although many of its citizens might understandably wish for the military budget to be cut in favor of schools, hospitals, and transportation lines, the cost of even a major budgetary black hole like the Iraq War is relatively minor. Only if the war were to drag on for decades would it begin to have the kind of impact on the country's resource base that might conceivably lead to changes in foreign policy. As evidence of this, the 2008 presidential campaign was marked by agreement on the major party candidates that the U.S. military needed to be rebuilt as soon as possible: no one called for budgetary retrenchment.[6]

The second overstretch argument fares no better. In order for an imperial defeat to affect future foreign policy, there either has to be a significant hobbling of the military long enough for new responses to become habitual or else some kind of lesson-learning such that overstretch-type policies are consciously avoided. The first of these possibilities, we have seen, is more hypothetical than real as regards the United States. Although the Iraq counterinsurgency war reduced the number of U.S. troops available for a similar

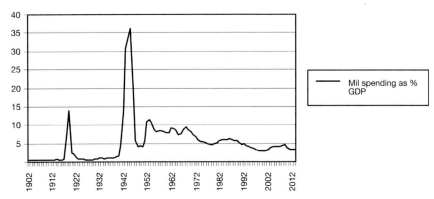

Figure 7.1 U.S. Military spending as a percentage of Gross Domestic Product
Source: USGovernmentSpending.com (2008) as per note 5.

mission in Afghanistan, this consequence was limited in time, with policy makers resolving to shift troops from Iraq to Afghanistan as soon as the situation permitted and to expand the size of the U.S. military more generally. In the meantime, the U.S. attempted to plug the gaps in other ways, by pressuring its allies to send more forces to Afghanistan, by carrying out air strikes on Afghan insurgents who retreated across the border in Pakistan, and by stepping up aid transfers and training programs in Afghanistan. At no point was any serious consideration given to liquidating the U.S. intervention in Afghanistan; nor, conversely, was there much evidence that other possible combat troop intervention situations were being taken off the agenda, or indeed were even on the agenda in the first place.[7]

As to lesson-learning, this, too, is far more limited than one might imagine. Even assuming that a particular intervention is seen in Washington as a U.S. defeat, the lessons usually learned from such experiences tend, in cybernetic fashion, to revolve around errors of execution rather than of broader policy choices. This tactical learning, as we call it, is a classically cybernetic response to mission failure, one discussed in Chapter 1 and in certain of the cases in Chapter 6. When the mission of a deployed policy instrument is not satisfied, it is incumbent on those reporting the failure to isolate its proximate causes (e.g., inadequate training, money supplied to the wrong proxies, etc.), very much in the way that daily operations are critiqued and then adjusted the next time they are tried. These cybernetic mechanisms for reporting and recommending of course do not preclude broader types of lesson learning, but here, too, individuals are focused on improvements, not on fundamental shifts in the very thrust of U.S. policy. Anyone advocating such shifts either is not a member of the policy making community to begin with or else, through advocacy of that sort, excludes himself or herself from it. This accounts for the tendency to keep carrying out unsuccessful operations such as BGFIEND (Albania), or, if the political and military problems connected with such operations are such as to lead to their termination (for example, the exile raids against Cuba), the tendency to continue carrying out such operations in other countries.[8]

Tactical learning can be seen very clearly in the aftermath of three combat troop interventions by the United States. The Korean War, as we saw in Chapter 5, dragged on for another 30 months after the Chinese intervention led the U.S. to a 38th parallel solution. After the war, which became massively unpopular and ended Truman's political career, the U.S. political elite absorbed the lesson that it should avoid a future land war in Asia. There is considerable evidence that this lesson was one of the reasons the U.S. did not commit ground troops to help the French hold onto Indochina the year after the Korean armistice, Eisenhower commenting that such a war "would absorb our troops by divisions" and one senator warning against pouring "money, materiel, and men into the jungles of Indochina without at least a remote prospect of victory." Nonetheless, a number of Eisenhower's advisers, including his own secretary of state, seriously considered deploying U.S. forces, something which in fact occurred the next decade in Vietnam. This intervention, too, provoked a greater caution about various types of military intervention, so that the policy of furnishing emergency military aid and advisers to El Salvador had a self-imposed ceiling of 55 advisers.[9] However, even though U.S. officials were wary of "foot in the door" pathways to another Vietnam-style war, they were undeterred from a significant aid and advisory effort in El Salvador and, since this effort proved sufficient to defeat the insurgency, the so-called "Vietnam syndrome" cannot really be said to have headed off a U.S. troop commitment.

Moreover, by the time of the 1991 Gulf War, the U.S. once again committed large numbers of troops in a war on behalf of a client. To be sure (see Chapters 5 and 6), that war was understood as an easy win, as was the U.S. counterinsurgency effort in Iraq when it first began; but this again points to the principally tactical nature of the primary lesson learned from Vietnam: if policy makers are fairly sure that, by sending limited numbers of troops, they are likely to get involved in an endless counterinsurgency war, then they should try to come up with some other solution. That kind of lesson excludes neither mistakes in calculation nor deployments of large numbers of troops in one fell swoop; it hardly is evidence of the kind of inhibiting effect that the overstretch argument might suggest.[10]

As to the Iraq counterinsurgency war, the lessons learned were resolutely tactical in nature. At the end of 2006, with the war having already dragged on for over three years, one high-level panel argued in favor of a diplomatic solution and against both an increase in troop levels (a recommendation rejected by Bush) and a rapid withdrawal. Two years later, the army issued its own report in which it concentrated on weaknesses in pre-invasion planning. Even politicians who wanted to liquidate the Iraq war, while arguing that it should never have been fought, advocated increased emphasis on the counterinsurgency war in Afghanistan, including sending additional troops. In short, important U.S. military setbacks tend not to be attributed to imperial overstretch in any way that could lead to a fundamental shift in U.S. foreign policy.[11]

War weariness

A second standard argument for policy discontinuity has to do with general war weariness. This argument, which in certain ways resembles the "loss" version of the overstretch position, focuses on a growing discontent with prolonged wars (such as the U.S. fought in both Iraq and Afghanistan), whether or not they are considered to have been lost. In part, the discontent is a response to the casualties suffered by U.S. forces (certainly not those of the civilian population where the war is being fought), particularly in conflicts which the mass public does not see as being marked by high stakes. Wars that go on for a long time result in higher casualties; even allowing for some desensitization over time, the public eventually turns against a prolonged war. If presidents do not respond to this discontent by moving toward withdrawal, they will face opposition from other politicians. More relevant for our purposes here, policy makers will also face pressure to avoid future interventions with U.S. combat forces: "No matter how the war in Iraq turns out ... the likelihood of any coherent application of military power or even of a focused military threat ... has substantially diminished." Much the same could be said of the Vietnam War, although the casualties there were significantly higher.[12]

In addition to their casualty-driven effects on mass opinion, prolonged wars also lead to disaffection among current and former policy makers and opinion leaders more generally. We saw in Chapter 5 how, following the Tet offensive in Vietnam, the so-called Wise Men turned against the war. Their words were revealing: "Time is limited by reactions in this country"; "Unless we do something quick, the mood in this country may lead us to withdrawal"; "A bombing halt would quieten the situation here at home." The concern was not with casualties but with the fact that the public was no longer following their leaders. As one journalist put it, things had "all gotten out of hand, and it was time to bring it back to proportion. It was hurting the economy, dividing the country, turning the youth against the country's best traditions." In addition, the army had begun to fall apart, with drug use rampant and officers starting to come under attack by their own troops. Much the same occurred several decades later as the Iraq counterinsurgency dragged on: commentators began to worry about the army being "broken," with recruitment down, officers resigning their commissions, and, once again, widespread drug use.[13]

We discussed above the tactical learning spurred by the wars fought in Korea, Vietnam, and Iraq. Another kind of lesson, with potentially greater inhibiting effect on future interventions, is that learned by the military after the second of those wars. Within a decade after the final U.S. helicopter had departed the embassy in Saigon, the Reagan Administration's secretary of defense, Caspar Weinberger, had formulated what came to be known as the Weinberger Doctrine about how and under what conditions U.S. troops should be committed to a future war (see Chapter 2). For example, the U.S. had to have vital interests at stake; troops should be committed with the clear intention of winning, and so forth. By some accounts, the Weinberger Doctrine as reformulated by the chairman of the joint chiefs of staff, Colin Powell, was used to inhibit both the older Bush and Clinton from intervening in the wars of the former Yugoslavia, leading the UN ambassador to complain, "What's the use of having this superb military you're always talking about if we can't use it?" Although this may not seem like much, particularly in light of subsequent troop interventions, it does represent a certain constraint on U.S. foreign policy.[14]

However, war weariness is unlikely to prove much of a constraint. For one, mass public opinion is uninformed about the vast majority of foreign decisions (not only the secret ones) and thus is unable to play any role except in high-profile issues. Even when the mass public is aware of a potential policy and expresses an opinion on it, the public is considered malleable enough by policy makers that they feel free to embark on interventions. A good case in point is the Iraq War of 2003, which the U.S. fought in spite of large-scale protests throughout the U.S. (and the world). Once the war began, the so-called "rally 'round the flag" effect kicked in, with public support for the war rising rapidly to high levels before, many months later, it declined. Moreover, mass opinion can easily be manipulated by the very politicians who then vaunt its support. This has been known since the 1920s and the pioneering work of Walter Lippmann; and it was consciously played on by the Bush Administration in the run-up to the Iraq War. A constant stream of speeches and background briefings poured out of the White House and the Defense Department, all hammering away at the message that Saddam Hussein was a threat to the United States because of his interest in nuclear weapons (destroyed some years earlier), in chemical and biological weapons (ditto), and because of the links he supposedly had to Al Qaeda (nonexistent). By the time of the war, over half of the public was convinced that Iraq had something to do with the attacks of 11 September 2001; even though this figure dwindled as no weapons of mass destruction were found and as the truth about Al Qaeda began to circulate, by September 2007, four and a half years after the war began, some 33 percent of the public still believed that Saddam Hussein was personally involved in the 9/11 attacks. If a given foe (whether an enemy state or a client regime's own enemies) can be sold to the American public as dangerous and having committed some outrageous act, then an overt war can be begun and supported by the general public for a number of years.[15]

One might imagine that elites are much less capable of being manipulated, but if anything, they serve as even less of a check on client and enemy policy than does the mass public. We will discuss below the shared ideology that, crystallized in the form of policy instruments, underlies this policy, but for now, note that there is a second aspect of elite opinion that also attenuates any constraining effect that war weariness may have. For decades, there has been a curious paradox about coverage of foreign policy issues in the United States: there is far more written about such issues than ever before but the range of opinion on those issues is far narrower than during an earlier era. Thus in the 1930s, it was possible to find correspondents in even such establishment newspapers as the *New York Times* praising the Soviet Union under Stalin, as well as other influential figures in the press advocating isolationism and deep hostility to France and Great Britain; no equivalent is even imaginable today. Much the same can be said about research institutes, with the dominant range of opinion on issues such as "humanitarian intervention" being restricted to matters of tactics; with skeptics on key issues such as the 2002 push for war in Iraq holding their tongues; and with particular critical views such as those calling into question U.S. support for Israel being policed. In short, if elite opinion is reflected in, if not shaped by, the writings of specialists on foreign affairs, then the chances are slim for war weariness to translate into a real break with U.S. foreign policy regarding clients and enemies.[16]

Changed international structure

Up to this point, we have been concentrating on the way in which ground combat by U.S. forces might (but in fact does not) lead to a break in the macro-continuity of United States foreign policy. However, only a few of the different modalities of inter-vention on behalf of clients or against enemies involve ground combat by the army or marines. There are many other ways in which intervention occurs, with policy instru-ments ranging from military aid and training to emergency economic and political aid or to a *coup d'état* against a regime's leader. On top of that, routine maintenance does not involve the use of U.S. ground combat forces, nor for that matter do most of the contexts of client acquisition. Thus, it is somewhat narrow to focus on threats to macro-continuity only from problems with U.S. troops fighting a ground war. In fact, there are two further ways in which the U.S. might switch to a different kind of foreign policy. One of them has to do with changes in the structure of the international system; the other with changes in the policies of U.S. clients.

When political scientists talk about the structure of the international system, two of the principal features they have in mind are polarity and polarization. Polarity has to do with how power (usually military) is distributed across states: there may be multiple powerful states, or two of them, or only a single one. Polarization, on the other hand, has to do with how tightly less powerful states align themselves with one or another pole. Thus, in Europe, the nineteenth century was supposed to have been a multipolar era with more than two great powers; as time wore on, the system became increasingly polarized into two antagonistic alliances, one involving Germany and Austria-Hungary, the other Britain, France, and Russia. By contrast, the cold war is said to have been characterized by a highly polarized bipolar system in which each of the two poles, the U.S. and the U.S.S.R., had allies closely bound to it. If we recall that those allies were, without exception, client states of one side or the other, then we can begin to see how changes in the structure of the international system might usher in changes in the general thrust of U.S. foreign policy.[17]

During the cold war, an important context in which states became U.S. clients was the perception of certain states as endangered, with the Soviet Union or its allies sometimes being seen as the source of that danger. Occasionally, the U.S. engaged in hostile interventions against states considered as either clients or puppets of the Soviet Union. In many more cases, the U.S. intervened on behalf of its own clients when they were seen as either at risk of overthrow by insurgents perceived to be ideologically aligned with the U.S.S.R., or else out of fear that to let a client be toppled would discourage other actual or potential clients and open the door to them to them keeping their distance from the U.S., perhaps even aligning with the Soviet Union. Presumably, the end of the cold war would drastically reduce all these occasions for client acquisition, client intervention, or hostile intervention. There would be less need to acquire clients and less need to protect them; there would also be fewer enemies to worry about. At the same time, not only would polarization diminish but the number of poles would increase, so that the U.S. might face competitors for acquiring new clients.[18]

These types of arguments are weak. To begin with, as we pointed out repeatedly in Chapter 3, the context of acquisition for at least half of all client states, including many taken on during the cold war, had little or nothing to do with the Soviet Union or a fear of communism. We know, in fact, that many U.S. enemies were never considered as aligned with the Soviet Union; and the persistence of clients, the acquisition of new clients, and the attempt to act against enemies have all continued even twenty years after the end of the cold war. Moreover, during the cold war, although the U.S. avidly pressed certain states to become U.S. clients, such alignment almost never occurred in the context of a competing offer from the Soviet Union. Certainly, the two superpowers tried to attract neutral or nonaligned states, but those moves were taken with respect to regimes which were considered fickle and hence not as real candidates for client status. For example, the U.S. tried on various occasions to overthrow Nasser and to attract him away from the Soviet Union (see Chapter 6); in carrying out the latter policy, there were no illusions about the Egyptian regime and thus how far the U.S. could ever be able to go: "They will use the Soviets as a source of arms or investment whenever it suits their purpose (precisely as they will use us)." Similarly, in the post-9/11 era, the U.S. from time to time wooed other states, such as certain Central Asian republics, in order to establish military bases or gas pipelines, but there is no evidence that in doing so, the intention was to take them, perhaps from Russia, as clients. In some cases, at least in the planning for the intervention against the Taliban, the U.S. went through the Russians; in other cases, the U.S., engaged in "real rug-merchant work," was careful not to commit itself to the regime, and shied away from a "bilateral treaty of mutual defense, love, cooperation, and economic support" that would be "permanent."[19]

Thus, neither the disappearance of the Soviet Union nor the supposed growth of potential rivals seems to have ushered in any kind of an era in which fewer clients are being acquired (whether because there was no longer a need to do so, or, conversely, because there were rivals for acquiring clients). There were many contexts of acquisition that had nothing to do with enemy status; even when danger from an enemy led to client acquisition, the enemy in question need not have been linked to the U.S.S.R.; and, as we have seen, at no point before, during, or after the cold war did the United States really compete with other states such as the Soviet Union for new clients. Quite the contrary: the U.S. and the Soviet Union displayed considerable deference to each other's sphere of influence, neither trying to poach an existing client nor competing against each other for the favors of potential new clients. Such competition as existed had to do with temporary alignments, not with client status. Although, of course, it was possible for a state to undergo a major shift and cease to be a client (see below), behavior of this sort was not encouraged by either superpower. Moreover, as we saw in Chapter 3, the U.S. was happy during the cold war for its various European clients to hold on to their own clients.

As for intervention, the end of the cold war is unlikely to lead to any changes. The thrust of this book, as articulated in Chapter 1 as well as in the chapters on intervention, is that U.S. policy is means-oriented, with long-term goals being multiple, changeable, secondary, and often stapled on after the fact. Thus, the U.S. commitment to defend regimes has nothing to do either with their ideological complexion or that of their enemies. Similarly with enemy states: what matters is that a state be seen as systematically choosing to differ with the U.S. on key issues of foreign and domestic political and economic policy. Over the years, U.S. enemies have come in various ideological flavors, from Zelaya's regime in Nicaragua to the Taliban in Afghanistan. On the other hand, a state can have a communist-dominated regime and not be considered by the U.S. as an enemy (e.g., China and Vietnam today; Yugoslavia under Tito). If, as some in the Pentagon are predicting (see below), China once more becomes an enemy, it will have very little to do with the cold war having revived.

Changes in clients' policies

In point of fact, U.S. client and enemy policy has relatively little to do with the external affairs of states. Many of the states which come to be categorized as enemies are classified in this way because of their domestic and not their foreign policy. More importantly, the vast majority of threats to client regimes are within rather than without. Thus to a great degree, it is misleading to focus on changes in the international system as a possible source of interruption in U.S. foreign policy. A stronger claim, at least in theory, has to do with the possibility of clients changing in such a way that a core feature of client status – the fact that dominant political forces in the state consider that U.S. concern over the maintenance of its regime is legitimate and worth considerable U.S. effort (see Chapter 2) – is no longer the case. What, in other words, are the prospects for clients to exit that status?

It is possible to glean two arguments about this prospect from recent literature in international relations. First, there may be increasing turmoil in many states, sufficient to depose the regimes of existing or potential clients and of a nature to which the U.S. is unable to respond. One often-cited cause of such turmoil is the phenomenon of global warming, which, it is argued, will lead to resource crises and mass population shifts that will overwhelm the capacities of many of the poorer states, particularly those in Africa and in low-lying areas of Asia. As one study put it,

> Climate change acts as a threat multiplier for instability in some of the most volatile regions of the world. … Unlike most conventional security threats that involve a single entity acting in specific ways and points in time, climate change has the potential to result in multiple chronic conditions occurring globally within the same time frame.

These same kinds of problems, however, are also said to present the United States with considerable difficulties, as there are few policy instruments in place for many of the most dire scenarios (e.g., the combination of crop failures, large trans-border refugee movements, and limited supplies of fuel) in even one country, much less a dozen or so countries simultaneously. Thus, it is to be expected that the U.S. will be faced with a triage situation in which the scope of clientilistic policies ends up being reduced geographically.[20]

An oft-cited example of the difficulty of U.S. military intervention to address the kind of humanitarian crises seen as likely in a world of global warming is the situation in the Darfur region of Sudan. A combination of persistent drought, conflicts over land, and violence deliberately provoked by the central government in reaction to an insurgency led to the deaths of perhaps a quarter of a million persons and the transformation of some two million others into refugees. In the face of these conditions, there were loud calls among some in the Washington foreign policy community for the U.S. to intervene militarily against the Sudanese regime – an enemy of almost 40 years – if and when the United Nations failed to act. The Bush administration resisted, one of its members arguing that military intervention would "endanger" rather than assist the humanitarian operations being carried out by the UN and other organizations. Moreover, even if U.S. actions were to be concentrated on attacking the Sudanese regime and its proxies, high-level officials pointed out that the size of the region and the country meant that "there would never be enough troops to impose order."[21]

Darfur could be argued to represent a break in the continuity of United States policy as regards enemies. As regards clients, the broader point about turmoil is that, irrespective of the cause, if the U.S. finds itself confronted by a situation to which its existing policy instruments do not easily correspond then it may be unable to act successfully, if at all. We saw in Chapter 5 how massive protests against the Shah led to a rapid loss of Iran as a client, with the U.S. unable to intervene to save the regime. In that case, although the U.S. had numerous policy instruments at its disposal, most had to do with phenomena such as armed insurgency or conventional party organizing; the rapid growth of mass street protests was something for which available U.S. responses (government shuffles; a possible military coup) were totally inadequate. By extension, analogous phenomena, whether induced by global climate change or by other factors (e.g., a sudden rise in religiously-based militance), can also lead to a break in the macro-continuity of U.S. client policy. That, at least, is an argument that can be constructed, although as we will see below, it is not strong.

A second and somewhat more convincing scenario about how clients might exit that status has to do with the unpopularity of U.S. foreign policy. During its eight years, the administration of George W. Bush engaged in numerous policies which enraged both elites and the mass public in countries around the world, including the United States. Actions such as the "unsigning" of the Rome statute for an international criminal court; refusal to agree to restrictions on greenhouse gas emissions; the use of torture and the denial of legal rights to persons accused of terrorism; denigration of the United Nations and of long-standing U.S. allies; and, above all, the U.S. invasion and continued occupation of Iraq all contributed to a widespread hatred of Bush, most of his top advisers, and more generally, the United States. Public opinion surveys showed that favorable views of the U.S. declined precipitously following Bush's accession to the presidency, particularly after the run-up to and invasion of Iraq in 2003. This fall-off was especially strong in long-time clients such as Britain (decline in favorable views from 83 percent in 2000 to 53 percent in 2008), Germany (78 percent to 31 percent), Turkey (52 percent to 12 percent), Japan (77 percent to 50 percent), Argentina (50 percent to 22 percent), and, for a client of slightly shorter duration, Indonesia (75 percent to 37 percent). These declines correlated strongly with negative views of Bush himself, who received staggeringly high negative ratings practically around the world.[22]

The unfavorable opinions of the United States are not simply a matter of distaste. Largely as a result of the U.S. invasion of Iraq, public opinion came to see the U.S. as dangerous and threatening to many other countries, not necessarily because the latter were considered as enemies but because American policies were seen as likely to boost terrorism. In addition, public opinion in many clients also identified extensive U.S. influence on those countries as a bad thing. Under these circumstances, accepting U.S. oversight and willingness to maintain a regime might be considered by key personnel of that regime as more a liability than an asset and the regime might move to diminish the U.S. role. If those moves continued, then at some point the state would cease to be a U.S. client. Arguably, several countries in South America began this process in the 2000s, though without, as of yet, going so far as to lose their client status. An example is Ecuador, whose government, angered by U.S. counterinsurgency policy in Colombia and fearing that the long-standing military to military relations between the U.S. and Ecuador threatened the government, concluded that the country had been "relying too much on military relations with the United States, with President Bush showing little regard for national borders or sovereignty." Accordingly, the government decided not to renew the U.S. lease of a military base and dismissed the country's top military officials for having close ties to the U.S. in general and the CIA in particular.[23]

As with the other arguments for a break in the continuity of U.S. foreign policy, neither of the claims about changes in clients' policies holds up to close analysis. Consider first the argument about the increasing irrelevance of U.S. policy instruments in the face of turmoil provoked by climate change, religious zealotry, or other factors. The general problem with this argument is that as we have seen, policy making is means-driven: instruments are used without some sort of prior assessment that they pass some sort of test for their relevance to the situation. This implies that if a reasonably novel or unforeseen situation arises, it is not necessarily the case that no action will be undertaken. Quite the contrary: policy makers can deploy a policy instrument, even though that instrument ends up failing to succeed in its mission and even though such failure may have been anticipated. Thus, to return to the Iran example mentioned above, the U.S. repeatedly and unsuccessfully used the instruments it had on hand, notably political advice and contacts with the military. It is true that in 1978, the U.S. had no instruments specifically designed to deal with repeated large-scale protests, but we can also imagine that if the protests had been somewhat smaller or less frequent, or the regime had survived longer, some type of hybrid military-police aid program might have been cobbled together. Note that one of the lessons the U.S. learned from Iran was to pressure the regime's leader to step down before the military fell apart, a policy put into place just a few years later in the Philippines (see Chapter 5). In other words, looked at more closely, the U.S. did not fail to carry out clientilistic policies in Iran in the face of mass turmoil; rather, it intervened as it normally did in support of clients, though without success. The fact that no U.S. troops were sent hardly means that the U.S. was bereft of ideas or found itself unable to support the client.

It might be argued that with all the surveillance mechanisms in place, some type of maintenance response to mass turmoil in a client is more likely than is a hostile intervention in response to similar turmoil in an enemy. In fact, though, that is the case only if the reference is to intervention with a particular policy instrument, namely the deployment of U.S. ground combat forces. The reason for this, as we saw in Chapter 6, is that hostile interventions are violations of state sovereignty and thus require some sort of outrageous or triggering act if they are to be carried out openly by the United States. (Maintenance interventions occur formally with the permission of the client and so the sovereignty issue does not arise.) This asymmetry between hostile and maintenance interventions, however, applies only to the overt use or support of military force by the United States. Covert hostile intervention remains possible, provided that there are levers (e.g., rebel forces) available and that the U.S. is upset with the regime; and overt hostile intervention is also possible if some sort of triggering condition occurs. The apparent novelty of the situation is of little importance; if the means and, if necessary, a trigger are present, then intervention will occur, even if the chances of success were in retrospect relatively slim. A good case in point is the U.S. in Somalia in 1993.

When Clinton took office, some 25,000 U.S. troops were present in Somalia. They had been sent the preceding December by Bush, already a lame duck, to respond to the widespread famine caused by the combination of drought and civil war, specifically to insure that UN relief supplies reached the large numbers of starving Somalis. This operation was neither one of taking over an essential activity from a client nor one directed against an enemy regime's military support at home or the maintenance of its forces in one or more geographical area; for that reason, Operation Restore Hope was not, by our definitions, an intervention. However, although some 80 percent of the U.S. troops were soon withdrawn from Somalia, several thousand remained as part of a UN operation (led in fact by the U.S.) designed to set up a new government. This operation, predictably, faced armed opposition from various Somali political factions and soon morphed into a counterinsurgency campaign, albeit one fought more against the militia of a particular faction in the capital city and on behalf of the UN operation itself than against an enemy regime or in support of a Somali state.[24] Thus, a humanitarian crisis was responded to by a moderate troop deployment; a fraction of those troops, in turn, were used for a UN "nation-building" operation; and when it became clear that the latter would be resisted by force in a large and chaotic city, the remaining troops were reinforced by a few hundred more soldiers and used for counterinsurgency. This is not an example of shying away from hostile actions in a situation of great turmoil but of using policy instruments ready at hand, even though their appropriateness was very much in question at the time. The failure of the counterinsurgency operations did not end the troop deployment; if anything, it acted as a magnet, pulling more forces into Somalia. Only when the U.S. troops started to incur casualties (the famous "Black Hawk down" incident) were they withdrawn.[25] This suggests that whatever situations of mass turmoil may occur in the future will not occasion a break in the macro-continuity of U.S. enemy policy.

Of course, that policy does not always involve sending troops or indeed intervening at all. We saw in Chapter 6 that the key element in the pseudo-decision tree for whether or not the U.S. moves from a policy of routine hostility toward an enemy to an actual intervention against that enemy is whether actions against the enemy's military have some chance of success; that assessment, we also saw, is made cybernetically, by determining whether particular policy instruments exist and are ready at hand. Moreover, as we also saw, if the only available policy instruments are U.S. military forces which would be used overtly, then there must be some kind of triggering event which in the eyes of U.S. policy makers destroys the legitimacy of the enemy regime. The result of these conditions is that most of the time, the United States does not intervene against most of the states it considers enemies. Thus, the fact that, in a given situation, such as one of mass turmoil in an actual or potential enemy, the U.S. fails to intervene either overtly or covertly has no particular bearing on the issue of a possible break in the continuity of U.S. foreign policy. To see this, it is worth returning to the Darfur situation discussed above.

Sudan first became an enemy of the United States in 1967, when it broke relations with the U.S.; it left that status in 1976 after its president helped the U.S. in a hostage crisis and was rewarded with a restoration of economic assistance. During this time, the regime's principal opponent was the Sudanese Communist Party which, because of its links to the Soviet Union, was unavailable as an insurgent force to back for either punctuated military operations or internal armed attacks. Given the absence of relations, U.S. ties to the military were not good enough to back a coup; and no outrageous event occurred which, to U.S. officials, sufficiently discredited the Sudanese regime to justify an overt intervention. Most of these conditions had not appreciably changed the second time that Sudan was classified as an enemy, when U.S. attacks on Libya (see Chapter 6) led to a dramatic reduction in diplomatic personnel. Within several years, the U.S. had again eliminated development assistance, suspended embassy operations, labeled Sudan as a state sponsor of terrorism, and, following bombing attacks on U.S. embassies in other African countries, launched cruise missile strikes against a pharmaceutical factory in Khartoum suspected of housing chemical weapons. None of these hostile actions were directed against the regime's military support.

However, one policy instrument had become available: support for a somewhat more acceptable insurgency. This was the Sudanese People's Liberation Army (SPLA), an autonomist movement in the southern part of the country. Its leader, educated and militarily trained in the United States, reportedly received some military aid indirectly from the U.S. and may also have been given some operational support by several U.S. army detachments;[26] this was followed by a pledge of direct humanitarian aid, with expressions of support from the U.S. Congress. The military aid, which took over a year to wend its way through the bureaucracy, was unaccompanied by a "finding" and appears to have been resisted by the CIA, in part because the prospects for the SPLA were limited and in part because the SPLA was an unsavory organization with obscure goals. In effect, the U.S. moved up to the edge of a hostile intervention but, somewhat as in Ethiopia (see Chapter 6) never opted for such a policy. Instead, when the countries the U.S. had used to transfer aid themselves became involved in other wars, the U.S. decided to pursue a diplomatic track with the Sudanese government and the SPLA, a decision confirmed by Sudanese intelligence cooperation on terror issues after the attacks of 11 September 2001. A preliminary agreement was finally reached in May 2004 and a final one in January 2005.[27]

All this meant that when the Darfur situation was at its worst, the U.S. was actively cooperating with Sudan on some issues, negotiating with it on other ones, and although weighing the possibility of a hostile intervention in a context that was certainly qualified as a humanitarian catastrophe, finally decided not to do so for exactly the same kind of cybernetic reasons that applied in other enemy state situations for many decades. It simply is not true that U.S. officials were unable to respond to the turmoil in Darfur because it was a novel humanitarian situation for which its array of policy instruments were unsuited; instead, they reacted as they did to any other potential opportunities vis-à-vis enemy states. Initially, the U.S., focused on working out an arrangement between the SPLA and the Sudanese government, was not terribly concerned by the large number of deaths and of refugees in the Darfur region.[28] As the tenor of Western opinion changed and the regime in Khartoum came more and more to be seen as actively complicit in the Darfur situation, the U.S. once more opted for a series of hostile actions short of intervention. Even more than their SPLA counterparts, the Darfur insurgents were seen as disorganized and violent, so that there were no possibilities of a proxy intervention; on the other hand, there were no high profile events which served as a justification for overt intervention. However, this did not stop the U.S. from acting on the humanitarian front, first by existing policy instruments (e.g., significant bilateral programs and contributions to international relief agencies) and second by stapling other instruments (e.g., airlift capacity through NATO; training) to multilateral peacekeeping operations by the African Union and the UN. In other words, U.S. failure to intervene in Darfur was not due to being overwhelmed by the novelty of the turmoil there but to the same factors that account for nonintervention most of the time against other enemies. There was no break in the continuity of U.S. enemy policy; and given the asymmetries between clients and enemies, there is all the less reason to expect that massive turmoil will result in clients exiting that status.[29]

Let us now turn to the other argument about client exit, this one pertaining to the growing unpopularity of U.S. foreign policy. Here, several points need to be made. The first is that there is nothing new about American actions being unpopular. During the 1980s, U.S. interventions in El Salvador and Nicaragua were denounced around the world; the same thing happened in the 1960s and 1970s with respect to the U.S. interventions in Indochina. Various coups and proxy operations (e.g., the Bay of Pigs invasion of Cuba) also were quite unpopular. Going even further back, there is evidence from public opinion polling of unpopularity in Europe in the first decade of the cold war, with more respondents disapproving than approving of the role the U.S. was playing in world affairs. These episodes, however, were always followed by a recovery of positive views about the United States; more importantly, they were decoupled from any consequences for the client status of the countries concerned. Alliances were not broken; cooperation was not ended; U.S. personnel were not expelled; bases were not really closed. A recent example of this concerns precisely the unpopularity of the U.S. in the post-Iraq invasion period. As we pointed out in Chapter 6, U.S. allies took great care not to take their opposition to the invasion very far: they permitted the U.S. overflight rights during the war and supported the Iraqi government the U.S. set up after the invasion. More significantly, public opinion distinguished, whether rightly or wrongly, Bush administration policy from the general position of the U.S. in the world. Thus, in 2008, the presidential candidate from the opposition Democratic Party, who had opposed the invasion, found himself adulated by elites and mass publics alike in countries around the world, with newspapers remarking on the thirst for a return to support for U.S. leadership.[30]

Second, it is important to emphasize that there is a vital distinction between the U.S. role as patron for a given client state, on the one hand, and approval of U.S. policy toward other countries, on the other. The status of a state as a client involves an acquiescence in U.S. surveillance and potential intervention to maintain the regime of that state; the state in question need not cooperate with the U.S. or even refrain from criticizing it. Quite the contrary: it is common to see clients who regularly exasperate the United States or blackmail the U.S. into supporting its positions. The former was the case, notoriously, for France when DeGaulle was president; the latter has frequently been true of Israel. For this reason, public disapproval of the U.S. in a particular state can be quite strong and still have no bearing on the state's continuation as a client.

The third and final point about public opinion, and indeed client exit more generally, has to do with a remarkable statistic. At least through 2008, there never was a U.S. client state which, though not undergoing a change in regime, nonetheless decided to end its status as a client. We saw in Chapter 4 that states do not graduate from client status when they become wealthy and more stable; combining this with the cyclical nature of public opinion, the implication is that there is a deep sense among both critics and supporters of specific U.S. policies that it is normal and natural for their states to exist in a clientilistic relation to the United States. This suggests that instead of U.S. foreign policy facing a break in macro-continuity, it is quite likely to go on as it has for years to come. However, the fact that none of the standard arguments about a break in policy macro-continuity holds up takes us only part of the way to understanding that continuity. To explain why U.S. policy continues in the face of major, perhaps historical, changes, we need to abstract from the arguments we have been discussing.

Ideology and policy instruments

The relation between the United States and its clients is both a matter of power and of consent. On the one hand, there is an enormous asymmetry in control, with the U.S. overseeing internal developments in clients while the latter play no comparable role toward the U.S. On the other hand, as we have repeatedly emphasized, there is an acceptance by clients, in practice if not in so many words, of that very asymmetry. Client state regimes acquiesce on a continuing basis in U.S. surveillance, support, and possible intervention on their behalf. Moreover, U.S. elites also accept this way of dealing with other countries. What the discussion above points to is that the acquisition and maintenance of clients, if need be by intervention, is considered perfectly normal and legitimate by government officials and other influential citizens. Indeed, when situations arise in which one might expect a break in clientilism, the reaction of U.S. elites is to continue acquiring and maintaining clients. This double acceptance, in which both client regimes and U.S. elites (and, for that matter, large segments of the mass public) consider as normal U.S. client state policy, we would label as *ideological hegemony*.[31]

All four of the standard arguments presented and critiqued above presume that ideological hegemony can be interrupted or broken by people changing their minds. For example, imperial overstretch might lead to retrenchment decisions; war weariness to disaffection; changes in international structure to a lack of concern about enemies; or humanitarian crises to a sense of discomfiture. These sorts of thoughts, or beliefs, or emotions are further presumed to lead to the suspension, or even the disappearance, of the deployment of certain policy instruments, particularly those connected with the overt use of U.S. ground or air combat forces. Neither one of these presumptions is correct and seeing just why this is so sheds light on how ideological hegemony operates and why clientilism is likely to continue for many years to come.

Ideology

When we use the term "ideological" as a way of describing the acceptance by U.S. and client elites of the relationship between the two states as normal, we are doing so in a shorthand fashion. *Ideologies* are connected sets of ideas about how the world does and should work; they are used to understand, evaluate, and predict existing and future situations.[32] Thus, various liberal ideologies, such as those mentioned in Chapter 1, link together representative democracy and open markets, characterize countries with these types of institutions as admirable and advanced, castigate political forces opposed to such systems as retrograde and dangerous, and conclude that it is a moral duty for open market democrats to distance themselves from such forces and perhaps to work against them. By the same token, to say that clientilism is ideological is to say that U.S. surveillance and maintenance activities are seen as complementary, that client status (with its attendant surveillance and maintenance activities) is considered as a normal and unexceptional relationship for states to occupy relative to the U.S., that those who object to client status for their country are benighted or dangerous opponents of the U.S., and that no matter how unsavory a client regime may be, the U.S. must be willing to make significant efforts to maintain it.

The various interconnections and inferences in clientilist ideology go a long way to explaining the weakness of arguments about a break in the macro-continuity of U.S. foreign policy. Those arguments, as we saw, are premised on some sort of new situation having arisen – imperial overstretch, war weariness, change in international structure, or internal turmoil – which will occasion a nonclientilist response from the U.S. However, if U.S. policy making is permeated by clientilist ideology, then historically new situations will be evaluated as relevant to one or more typical client problems, which in turn will be responded to by the corresponding client maintenance policy instruments. Ideology in this sense is like a factory which discards some deliveries, transforms others into standard inputs, and produces the same kind of products no matter how the suppliers or the market may have changed. Ideologies can do this because they connect "is" to "ought": if a given type of situation is seen as normal then one should be on the lookout to protect it and act accordingly.

The question then is how ideology performs these tasks. Most analyses of ideology and foreign policy depict ideologies as residing in people's heads and playing a double mapping function: events in the world are mapped onto specific ideas in the ideology; those ideas, by dint of their connections to other ideas, are then mapped from the latter back onto the world.[33] For example, a leftist politician denouncing a U.S. client regime as corrupt may be perceived by officials with a clientilist ideology as a threat to the regime, the inference drawn that this threat should be opposed by the United States, and a recommended U.S. policy response (e.g., blackmailing him) put forward. Here, however, we run up against the same translation problems which, as we saw in Chapter 1, apply to structural arguments for the continuity of U.S. foreign policy: in the absence of numerous other, unspecified mechanisms, there is no way to map ideologies onto concrete situations in client states or actions by the U.S. regarding those states. Consider again the case of the leftist politician. Why do U.S. officials perceive him as a threat to the regime rather than as a reformer who might in fact strengthen it? Are there ideas in clientilism which distinguish between some types of denunciations and others? Or instead, are there ideas which distinguish between political parties? What then to do if the ideas conflict in a particular instance?

Even if somehow clientilist ideology were to contain the hundreds, if not thousands, of ideas required for mapping situations, the second half of the depiction fares no better. Assume now that somehow the politician has been categorized as a threat to the client regime and that the inference has been drawn that he should be opposed by the U.S.[34] How exactly should U.S. officials map this stance onto a concrete policy? In Chapter 5, we went over the criteria by which particular policy instruments are deployed in specific situations. Should we assume that each of those criteria is represented in the ideology by an idea? But that would not be enough: each such idea would also have to be accompanied by other ideas about each of those policy instruments: their nature, their recent history, and so forth. Since as we know, policy instruments are often copied or reconfigured, this would mean that the ideology would also have to contain components about budgets, Congress, the United Nations, and various other aspects of the world. In addition, the ideology would have to change to take account of changes in policy instruments. These are stringent requirements.

The problem with the mapping depiction of clientilist ideology is that it requires the heads of most policy makers to be filled with massive numbers of the same highly specific ideas, most of which will never enter into consciousness. Not only is this exceedingly unlikely but if it were true, so that each policy maker had the same myriad of ideas about what to do in all sorts of highly specific circumstances, there would never be debate among officials as to what should be done in a given situation.

A far more realistic approach is to return to the notion of policy instruments. As we have pointed out, they are used to accomplish particular time-and-place-specific missions and thus, when deployed, are of necessity crafted to the situation – even if they fail to succeed. Moreover, the reporting that goes on about their success or failure is used both to adjust them – for example, to send more troops to a given region – and to signal that they need to be complemented by other instruments. (Similar reporting occurs for the client's performance of certain tasks.) In this sense, the cycle by which policy instruments are deployed, reported on, and adjusted or complemented is itself exactly what the mapping approach to ideology is about, but without the mentalism and the thousands of ideas all held at the same time and in the same order. Moreover, since policy instruments are only budgeted for on the expectation that there is some chance, however remote, of their being used to solve certain problems, then the instruments can be seen as the organizational embodiment of expectations that such problems are somewhat likely to occur. For example, an institutionalized military training capability (these days, through programs such as IMET and JCET; see Chapter 4), presupposes an institutional expectation that the militaries of various countries will need training, whether against domestic insurgencies, terrorist threats, or future disasters in which rapid mobilization may be needed.

The connection to ideology should now be clear. We said above that ideologies are connected sets of ideas about how the world does and should work. If ideas are not simply thoughts that individuals happen to have, then policy instruments are precisely such institutionalized connections: between the situation in a given country and how it should be dealt with, and between expectations about the kinds of problems likely to arise in certain places and the ways in which those problems should be responded to. *Policy instruments, in effect, are crystallized ideologies.* Whatever may be going on inside people's heads, in the domain of foreign policy making, ideology takes an organizational form.

With this in mind, we can now start to answer the question of how clientilist ideology can help explain the macro-continuity of U.S. foreign policy. Imagine a situation which, to U.S. policy makers, is new. Standard surveillance mechanisms will report problems in U.S. clients (as well as opportunities in U.S. enemies), including problems caused or exacerbated by the new situation. Such reports, as we saw, are accompanied or shortly followed by recommendations for how particular policy instruments ready at hand can be deployed so as to address the problems. Those instruments may not be ideal and they may fail to address key issues, but such concerns are secondary. Thus, in the first instance, clientilist policy would continue. In order for there to be a break in macro-continuity, the new situation would eventually have to lead (1) to the construction of policy instruments that have little or nothing in common with the existing stock of clientilist instruments and/or (2) to the wholesale discarding of instruments from that stock. How likely is this?

The persistence of policy instruments

We saw in Chapter 1 that policy instruments are capabilities for generating specific sequences of purposeful activities, housed bureaucratically in a particular organization. Concretely, these capabilities involve professional personnel, many of whom have considerable experience in carrying out certain sequences; they in turn may be given money to spend and perhaps various types of tools, such as weapons, to use. This implies that in order to distinguish one policy instrument from another, we look first at the degree to which the skills, training, and experience of the personnel differ across instruments (this includes not only which sequences they are capable of performing but also where and in what language); second, at the number of personnel, their budget, and the tools allocated to them; and third, at the personnel's bureaucratic autonomy, to whom they report, and whether or not they are expected to perform other sequences. Using these criteria, we can identify three ways in which a given policy instrument is different than the instruments which previously existed.

First, an instrument can be assigned far greater resources and given greater bureaucratic autonomy. A bureau or command consisting of a few dozen personnel can be bulked up to several hundred or even thousand employees, with the latter given regular training and specialized equipment, perhaps a building of their own, a program with its own line item in the budget, and maybe an administrator of high rank. This, in effect, is what happened to the military's training and arms transfer programs, as we saw in Chapter 4. Training, in particular, went from an ad hoc series of tasks carried out by marines in places they were occupying to congressionally mandated programs with soldiers and civilian administrators who devoted a number of years of their careers to these tasks.

Second, an instrument can, in effect, be cloned. An organization can be set up whose personnel and typical programs are modeled after counterparts in another organization. In some cases, the former's early months are eased by temporary or permanent transfers of personnel from the latter, whether at the operational or command level. This is what happened to military training. The original IMET program expanded in several ways: across branches of the armed services (JCET); into regions that had previously been a low priority (ACRI); and into new issue areas, such as narcotics, under the authority of other executive branch agencies (ILEA).[35]

It may be thought that neither resource expansion nor cloning really involve creating a new policy instrument since the tasks in question are already being carried out in some form. However, this is not a strong objection, partly because some resource changes are significant enough – for example, increasing the number of employees from single digits to the thousands – to constitute major changes, as are some differences in hierarchy (e.g., reporting directly to the president as opposed to an intermediate-level bureaucrat). More significantly, though, the idea of a new policy instrument that starts afresh and does not borrow from existing instruments is a fantasy. To see this, consider a third type of different instrument, one that is not constructed by augmenting the resources of an existing instrument or copying one or more such instruments. In theory, those who are designing this third type of instrument are free to choose as employees anyone they want. In practice, that would make no sense. Policy instruments are designed to solve certain kinds of actual or expected problems and the idea that, in the face of such problems, one would construct an organization whose personnel would be neophytes or those without any relevant background is farfetched indeed. What makes more sense is to grab specialists from other agencies or perhaps from outside the government or even the country. Thus, when Roosevelt approved the creation of the United States's first coordinating intelligence agency (which eventually became known as the OSS; see Chapter 5), its personnel, although coming from different backgrounds, were already specialists: military intelligence officers (the War and Navy Departments); commandos (from the armed services, as well as the British Special Operations Executive); international lawyers, business executives, and former diplomats; and research analysts from academia.[36] As we will see below, even the most important change in U.S. foreign policy, over a century ago, involved building on existing instruments; such building is one of the two important mechanisms by which policy has been macro-continuous at major historical turning points.

The other mechanism is in a sense the converse of the first: the fact that older policy instruments are simply not discarded wholesale. Of course some specialties become obsolete because of changes in technology: the disappearance of the horse cavalry or of telegraph operators. Other organizations are eliminated because their principal mission has become overtaken by events (e.g., the CIA proxy intervention in Laos: see Chapter 5); even if the personnel are reassigned to other jobs, they may have spent so many years on an operation that they are unable to adjust to new responsibilities. Nonetheless, when policy instruments are eliminated in these types of circumstances, they tend to be terminated on an individual rather than general basis. There are several reasons for this, which we will label inheritance, innocuousness, inertia, and in-case-ness.

- *Inheritance.* Even if it has been years since the last occurrence of a particular problem with a client, a policy instrument may still be deployed to deal with that or earlier occurrences. For example, as we saw in Chapter 5, the U.S. engaged in emergency military aid and assistance in South Vietnam for over a dozen years; similar policy in Colombia had, at the time of writing, lasted almost as long. Other instruments may originally have been deployed in a situation of intervention and then, because of expectations, maintained for years after the situation became one of routine maintenance. This is the case, as we saw in Chapters 4 and 5, for the cash payments given to Italian politicians, trade unionists, and others. Although specific operations can be and have been terminated, the fact that other operations are inherited from previous years means that it is difficult simply to eliminate a policy instrument, much less a whole set of instruments.
- *Innocuousness.* The personnel connected with a given policy instrument are not constantly engaged in emergency operations. There are often months, if not years, between crises and during this time specialists nonetheless keep reporting to work. Partly, this is a matter of recovery from earlier operations as well as of maintaining readiness for future ones, but there are also other tasks that employees perform during these periods. Often, specialists are rotated between the field and headquarters, where they may carry out supervisory or training activities. Work of this sort may not be glamorous but its very innocuousness makes it harder to eliminate the employees. Of course, certain programs may still be ended, but it takes a formal and often

contested decision to do that: the fact that employees are currently doing something else will not, by itself, result in either single or wholesale instrument elimination.

- *Inertia.* U.S. foreign policy making is, as we have seen, means-driven. If a policy instrument has recently been in use, or is at least seen as ready at hand, then it is more likely to be employed for a given situation than otherwise. Obviously, this does not mean that there is some kind of a queue such that the next instrument in line, as it were, is deployed regardless of the situation; but it does mean that in complicated situations, where more than one problem can be diagnosed, an instrument's availability will facilitate its deployment to address the appropriate problem. Even if the last operation for that instrument failed to accomplish the mission, it can still be argued that this situation is different, that greater resources should be allocated, and so forth. Thus, paradoxically, a recent failure may protect an instrument (though spurring reforms) more than it may expose it to elimination.
- *In-case-ness.* By this made-up word, we mean the kinds of arguments that are used to defend policy instruments which are on the chopping block. Such claims are common, particularly as regards certain types of military and intelligence capabilities. For example, even though the U.S. had no enemies with significant naval capacities since the fall of the Soviet Union, the navy nonetheless argued for maintaining and indeed expanding its surface warfare abilities, claiming that at some point in the future, China, North Korea, or Iran might constitute a threat.[37] Although these sorts of arguments are sometimes rejected, they make it difficult simply to eliminate entire groups of policy instruments.

Thus, policy instruments tend to persist, both because new instruments are built on existing ones and because old instruments are simply not eliminated on a wholesale basis. This in turn means that clientilist ideology, in its crystallized, policy instrument form, will mandate macro-continuity at historical turning points: the United States will diagnose the same kinds of problems and respond in the same kind of ways in the presumably new environment as it did in earlier years. (Although there is macro-continuity regarding client acquisition (see the next section), there is no equivalent macro-continuity regarding the U.S. perception that certain states have become enemies. This, as we implied in Chapter 3, is essentially a random process; to see this graphically, consider Figure 7.2, which shows a sharp distinction between the continued increase in the number of clients (with certain big jumps) and the long-term stability in the relatively small number of enemies.) To see this clearly, let us travel back in time to key historical turning points.[38]

The clientilist time machine

On three occasions in the past 11 decades, officials and commentators on U.S. foreign policy have found themselves confronted with a situation which they considered as qualitatively different from the past, so much so that a fundamental debate broke out on how to respond to that situation. In each case, policy makers opted for a particular solution that, as it turns out, either continued clientilism as the basic thrust of United States foreign policy or installed clientilism in the first place. In each case, as well, that choice was controversial and resisted, though unsuccessfully, by a significant segment of opinion makers. Eventually the debate ended, with external events hastening that

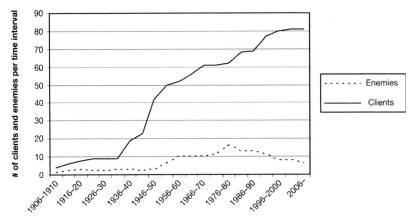

Figure 7.2 U.S. clients and enemies over time
Sources: Tables 3.1–3.5 and Figure 3.1.

end in some instances. As we will see, the debates became less acrimonious with each new turning point: an indication that clientilism had, in effect, become not only the dominant ideology of U.S. foreign policy but the only one.

In the process of navigating these turning points, policy instruments developed much along the lines discussed above. First, some existing instruments were adapted to construct new ones, with the latter exhibiting many of the same qualities, whether activity sequences or personnel, of the former. Second, other existing instruments were maintained and deployed, in spite of the apparent novelty of the situation. Thus, clientilism was not discarded but continued; and when, during the first of the turning points, clientilism was first turned to, it was very much a constrained innovation with respect to existing policy, which itself continued for several decades. This pattern has clear implications for the future, an issue we will return to below.

End of the cold war

The fall of the Berlin Wall and the dissolution of the Soviet Union were understood to have ushered in an end to the cold war. This was supposed to lead to various changes, from diminished use of the veto in the UN Security Council and hence a greater number of UN operations to a decline in military spending.[39] One might also have expected, as we mentioned above, that the U.S. would have turned away from those of its policy instruments linked most closely to the cold war in general and to its conflict with the Soviet Union in particular. In fact, nothing of the sort occurred, and one of the principal means by which Western European clients played the role of junior partners – NATO – not only continued in existence but was expanded (see Chapter 4). By the mid-1990s, the Clinton administration had decided, and had convinced the other NATO members, to extend membership invitations to three former clients and military allies of the Soviet Union: Poland, Hungary, and the Czech Republic.

The decision to expand NATO led to an acrimonious debate among the U.S. foreign policy elite. Several dozen former high-ranking officials strongly opposed expansion and published articles, op-ed pieces, and open letters in major newspapers and periodicals. The grand old man of containment policy, George Kennan, characterized expansion as a "fatal error," given the adverse consequences it was likely to have on Russian foreign and domestic policy. Nonetheless, within a year or so, the tempest had come to an end and expansion went through. Indeed, as we pointed out in Chapter 5, NATO was formally expanded precisely during the Kosovo air war, which was fought by NATO under American command. Three years later, a second round of expansion took place, this time with former component republics of the Soviet Union becoming members; again, formal accession occurred when NATO was once more at war, this time in Afghanistan (see Chapter 5). A third round followed, with two additional states receiving invitations and two others having their invitations postponed. Although the postponement did involve some controversy among other NATO members, the other states accepted in the second and third rounds occasioned very little debate in the United States. Opposition to NATO's wars underwent a similar shift, with several of the American opponents of expansion also criticizing the Kosovo war, but little controversy in the U.S. over NATO's role in Afghanistan.[40]

NATO's expansion was contested among the U.S. foreign policy elite. Other, equally clientilistic decisions also were made – for example, the acquisition of several Persian Gulf states as clients; the raft of free trade agreements that were concluded during the Clinton and second Bush administrations[41] – but these were far more consensual among current and former policy makers, with client acquisitions being practically unnoticed and trade agreements being combated (unsuccessfully) primarily by labor unions and other groups with relatively little influence in foreign policy. Interestingly, even though, as we saw above, the Bush administration was widely unpopular almost from its inception, its policies regarding NATO expansion, free trade, and a host of other programs aimed at maintaining clients were for the most part continuations of what the Clinton administration had done; they occasioned no more debate, either at home or abroad, than had been the case in the 1990s. In this regard, the principal consequence of the end of the cold war was to increase the number of clientilistic policy instruments. From time to time, certain of those instruments were restructured, but for the most part, existing instruments were either given greater resources or cloned to cover new domains. NATO's war fighting is probably the newest of the instruments, though if one looks back at other maintenance interventions (e.g., in support of South Korea, South Vietnam, Lebanon, and Saudi Arabia), U.S. allies have already fought alongside American troops. In short, clientilistic ideology led to the macro-continuity of U.S. foreign policy after the end of the cold war.

World War II

By the late 1930s, the Roosevelt administration and many members of the U.S. foreign policy elite had decided that what later became known as the Axis powers posed a significant threat to various countries and that if, as seemed likely, war were to break out, the U.S. would have to back the latter. Up to that point, U.S. support for other states fell into two categories: short-term wartime alliances, of the sort concluded with Britain and France as part of the anti-German hostile intervention in World War I; and clientilism (primarily against domestic opponents) with countries in Central America and the Caribbean. What Roosevelt and his advisers opted to do was to extend both types of support. Thus, as we saw in Chapter 3, the U.S. began to establish various types of military links with South American countries, beginning with attachés and staff discussions, then going on to officer training, arms transfers, and, in the case of Brazil, the coordinated dispatch of troops. Some of these programs simply involved the deployment of existing policy instruments; others, as we saw, regularized what had been ad hoc arrangements. In addition, and using much the same methods of deploying existing instruments and regularizing others, the U.S. also set up financial and other economic arrangements. In effect, the South American states, along with Mexico and Canada, became U.S. clients, with the Rio Treaty and other postwar accords simply adding multilateral machinery to the arrangements.[42]

U.S. policy toward the Western Hemisphere was little noticed and mostly uncontroversial in Washington. By contrast, policy toward European countries was bitterly combated. In Chapter 6, we saw that prior to the U.S. formal entry into the war, it instituted programmatic arms transfer arrangements to the United Kingdom, then to the Soviet Union. Several of these programs required legislative approval and it was around those votes that ferocious debates broke out. In each case, Roosevelt prevailed, but there was strong opposition from various political forces, many of them being somewhat misleadingly labelled as isolationist. Only after Pearl Harbor was attacked did the debates subside.[43]

However, opposition was renewed after the war's end when, as we discussed in Chapter 3, the Truman administration responded to what it saw as the dangerous combination of old and new problems in Western Europe, first by ad hoc arrangements and then by transforming and expanding those into new policy instruments (the most important being the Marshall Plan) through which most of the countries in that area would be supported. In other words, the U.S. responded to the problem of an economically weakened and politically fragile Western Europe by acquiring many of the states there as clients. That decision was unpopular among many of those who had earlier fought against Roosevelt's interventionary tendencies but their numbers had diminished during the war and none of the various policy instruments requiring legislative approval were in any serious danger. Thus, World War II was very much a hinge in the macro-continuity of United States foreign policy. What had been a localized policy of clientilism, involving a small number of policy instruments and restricted to less than a dozen countries in the Caribbean and Central America became generalized into an overall policy: numerous new or expanded policy instruments, with far greater resources devoted to them, and applied to states throughout the hemisphere and then, after the war's end, to states in Europe and a smattering of countries elsewhere. Whether anticipating a war or tidying up after it, U.S. officials opted for clientilism: a reflex that, with time, became less and less controversial.[44]

The Spanish-American War

In 1898, the United States went to war against Spain. The campaign was brief and unproblematic; the result, driven by available means, was, within a few years, the establishment of a client state empire. That empire required new means, which were pieced together from the array of policy instruments available at century's end. The latter, in turn, crystallized an older ideology which underlay much of the opposition to the war and its immediate aftermath. However, that older ideology did not simply disappear and for several decades was evident from time to time in other U.S. foreign policy actions.

Clientilism and its predecessors

The war that broke out in 1898 was ostensibly about Cuba; various reasons were put forward, but all involved the situation on the island. However, the day that war began,

McKinley ordered the U.S. fleet then in Hong Kong to proceed immediately to the Philippines, a Spanish possession for nearly four centuries. Some weeks later, still before U.S. forces had landed in Cuba, another order went out for an invasion of Puerto Rico, which also belonged to Spain. Soon afterward, as an American army expedition was heading to Manila, it detoured to capture another Spanish possession, the island of Guam. Not surprisingly, when peace negotiations got under way, the U.S. demanded, and soon received, all four territories. In the meantime, while the war was still going on, Hawaii, which had no relation whatever to Spain, was annexed (see Chapter 3). The next year, it was Samoa's turn, with the U.S. reaching an agreement with Germany to divvy up the islands. Although there was opposition to the annexation of the Philippines (as, afterward, to the counterinsurgency war there and as, earlier, to the annexation of Hawaii), it was unable to stop this initial thrust. The U.S. now had an overseas empire.[45]

Of course, there was nothing new about the United States expanding or going to war with other countries. From the moment it gained its independence, the U.S. had annexed territory, buying or taking it from Spain, France, Russia, Mexico, and a large number of native American political groupings. Although most of this expansion had been on lands contiguous to existing U.S. territory, the Alaskan purchase was separated from the rest of the United States by almost a thousand miles. Nonetheless, several of the places annexed or occupied in 1898 and 1899 differed from all of the preceding land grabs in one vital respect: they were intended to be colonies, not states. Until then, whenever the U.S. added new lands, Congress enacted legislation that organized them as territories which would, eventually, become states, i.e., the population would have full citizenship rights; they would elect representatives and, indirectly, senators; they would be able to vote for president; and the goods they produced could be sold to residents of other states without tariffs or restrictions. By contrast, the laws that set up Puerto Rico and the Philippines as U.S. territories defined the local inhabitants not as U.S. citizens but as citizens of those places "entitled to the protection of the United States." Guam and Samoa were not even the objects of legislation about citizenship for decades afterward. The first two territories were administered within the War Department instead of the Interior Department, as was the case for territories on the North American mainland (this eventually became true as well for Puerto Rico); the latter two were run by the navy. In addition, Congress imposed a tariff on goods imported into the U.S. mainland from Puerto Rico.[46]

The legal term for what was being created in these four places (Cuba and Hawaii were treated differently; see below) was "unincorporated territories." In effect, these lands would be part of the United States but with a status that was distinct from, and clearly inferior to, that of other past and present territories, since they had not been "incorporated" into the U.S. as the latter had been. What this implied, legally, was worked out in a set of Supreme Court decisions, known collectively as the Insular Cases and which, although decided a century ago, still apply in important respects today. Accompanying this jurisprudence was a set of policy instruments, all adapted from existing instruments in order to administer these colonies. The standard territorial government machinery was revised somewhat to be put under the War Department's newly created Bureau of Insular Affairs, with correspondingly greater involvement by officials appointed from Washington than in incorporated territories to take account of the supposedly childlike and unsophisticated character of the bulk of the local population. In setting up this system, U.S. policy makers studied European colonial practices, although it is unclear just how much they borrowed from them.[47]

What we do know is that standard U.S. territorial administrative techniques, somewhat adapted for the presumed racial mixtures overseas, were combined with decades-old U.S. techniques used in administering peoples who were considered incapable of rule: native Americans. Up to the mid-nineteenth century, this had been the responsibility of the War Department; even after the relevant bureau was transferred to the newly-created Interior Department, the army was in charge of military order and punitive expeditions. Early in the Spanish-American War, the army was involved in the Philippines and Puerto Rico, and while hostilities ended quickly in the latter, a vicious counterinsurgency war went on for three years in the former. Similar, if less well-developed, machinery was created in the Navy Department for the territories it administered. Thus, the new U.S. colonial empire was to a great degree a transplantation of well-established policy instruments for setting up territories with large numbers of non-English-speaking peoples considered as savage or uncivilized.[48]

That empire, however, never grew. Instead, it had certain built-in limitations which quickly led to a second type of empire being invented, namely the client state one that subsists today.[49] One of the limitations was precisely the racial concerns mentioned above. Until 1898, newly annexed territories were either granted statehood immediately (Texas, California) or else set up in a way that anticipated this status later on. That day duly arrived, although in several cases when Congress deemed that there were too many non-English speakers and/or non-whites it postponed statehood until the population was "thoroughly Americanized." As a result, Oklahoma, Arizona, and New Mexico remained as territories until the early years of the twentieth century, the latter because of the Hispanic population and the former because it had been "Indian Territory" reserved originally for native Americans.[50] However, it was obviously more difficult for English-speaking whites to migrate to overseas territories and so the statehood path appeared rockier. Hawaii, for example, was refused annexation until non-whites were deprived of citizenship, non-English speakers disenfranchised, and a centralized government set up by those who carried out the coup against the Queen, changes which presumably would make it more attractive for future migration from the mainland. This could not be said of the Philippines, which was seen as populated by a minority of "semicivilized" people and a majority that was "as ignorant and savage as the aboriginal Indians" whom the U.S. needed "to educate ... and uplift and Christianize them." (Most Filipinos had been Catholic since the early days of Spanish rule.) These views, which were widely shared by both proponents and opponents of Philippine annexation, also underlay the army's counterinsurgency tactics in the Philippines. The result was that overseas annexations were deemed to be incompatible with statehood, which in turn meant that the U.S. would have to maintain, indefinitely, controls over the subject populations of its new territories lest they do something (revolt? migrate to the U.S. mainland?) unacceptable. Small wonder, then, that the next time the possibility of taking over another population arose, Roosevelt, who once had been the advocate *par excellence* of Philippine annexation, retorted that he had no more desire to do so "than a gorged boa constrictor would be to swallow a porcupine wrong-end-to."[51]

Roosevelt's concern was not only with the idea of having to administer a large number of people who, for him, were childlike, savage, or both. He and his colleagues were also concerned with practical questions of military order. The Philippines, far from the United States, were vulnerable to attack from nearby powers such as Japan; and since the islands' population was considered incapable of defending itself anytime soon, this would have to be a U.S. responsibility. On the other hand, places in the Western

Hemisphere were in less danger of outside attack and, by dint of being closer to the U.S. mainland, were easier to defend. The peoples of these countries were also considered more advanced, which meant that they would either be accustomed to self-adminis-tration or, as in Cuba, expect to govern themselves; if instead they were annexed or placed under indefinite occupation, there would be a risk of another Philippine-style insurgency. For this reason, the somewhat accidental congressional promise to "leave the government and control of [Cuba] to its people" was honored, at least formally. As we saw in Chapter 3, the U.S. eventually set up an independent government for the island, being sure to restrict the franchise to "the decent element" and, for good mea-sure, to destroy the ballots cast for opposition candidates. These techniques, borrowed from multiple U.S. experiences (e.g., southern U.S. states after Reconstruction, Tam-many Hall and other urban political machines, and of course the recent case of Hawaii), permitted the U.S. to turn over power to an indigenous Cuban regime. This, along with other policy instruments (see below) provided an alternative to colonial empire. The U.S. would no longer annex overseas territories; and, some 15 years later, Congress even voted to grant independence to the most prominent such territory, the Philippines, "as soon as a stable government can be established."[52]

Racial and military considerations thus truncated the U.S. colonial empire. What replaced it was clientilism, constructed haltingly and in piecemeal fashion. In earlier chapters we discussed the development of the various policy instruments used in the early years of the twentieth century to acquire and maintain client states; however, those new and adapted instruments were preceded by two intermediary mechanisms stemming from colonialism but ultimately serving as dead ends. The first was a legal mechanism giving the U.S. the right to intervene. This was the Platt Amendment (see Chapter 3) which was explicitly designed by the secretary of war to provide a right which would "never be terminated" to "protect" Cuba. Such a right was necessary because

> if we should simply turn the government over to the Cuban administration, retire from the island, and then turn around to make a treaty with the new government, just as we would make treaties with Venezuela, and Brazil, and England, and France, no foreign state would recognize any longer a right on our part.

None of the countries in this list were then client states and what Root was attempting to do was to imagine a way of institutionalizing regime maintenance. However, what he failed to recognize was that an explicit legal provision for intervention would galvanize opposition in Cuba, weakening the regime and necessitating more frequent and pro-longed interventions. If the U.S. did need to intervene, it could simply engineer a request by the Cuban government. Eventually, the Platt Amendment would be repealed.[53]

The second intermediary mechanism was the creation of extraterritorial zones. There was nothing new about this practice, which dated back centuries; the U.S. itself had been granted extraterritorial rights in a number of countries during the 1800s. The U.S. thus set up such a zone in Cuba on which it established a naval base in perpetuity. (As we saw in Chapter 2, this base, Guantánamo, would a century later become infamous as a site for detention and torture of individuals captured in Afghanistan and elsewhere.)[54] A few years later, after the U.S. detached Panama from Colombia (see Chapter 3), it set up the Panama Canal Zone, an area subject to U.S. law. Much as with the Platt Amendment, the Canal Zone was sufficiently unpopular that the U.S. finally decided to abolish it. In this way, too, the colonial empire served as a way station between pre-1898

U.S. policy and the client state empire that briefly began with Hawaii and then, after the war, began in earnest with Cuba, Panama, and the Dominican Republic.

The continuation of older policy instruments

Many of the policy instruments created for routine and interventionary maintenance of clients had their origins in ad hoc governmental or private activities. One set of instruments, though, involved adaptation of much older capabilities residing in the U.S. military. Up until the early years of the twentieth century, neither the army nor the navy had been used in support of clients for the simple reason that until Hawaiian annexation was refused in 1893, there were none. Nor, in the strong sense of the term (see Chapter 6) were they used for hostile interventions since at that point, the U.S. did not really have enemies, at least in terms of the definition used earlier in this book. As John Quincy Adams characterized what was the U.S. doctrine, America "goes not abroad in search of monsters to destroy." Instead, both the army and the navy were deployed on other kinds of missions: land grabs (as in the war against Mexico); rescue operations for U.S. citizens; punitive and raiding expeditions; and gunboat diplomacy aimed at forcing commercial treaties on "barbaric" states.[55]

These various operations added up: all told, the United States used military force abroad more than 100 times during the nineteenth century, even though many of these operations were highly limited in terms of the number of troops and the period of time during which they were deployed (see Figure 7.3). Interestingly, those troop deployments occurred in some 33 locations spread across every region of the globe. In short, there never has been a time when the U.S. did not use its military forces around the world. This relativizes considerably the idea that somehow the U.S. had pursued a policy of isolation or that its dealings with other countries were restricted to commercial exchanges. It also shows clearly that when the U.S. began using its armed forces to establish or prop up client states, or later to strike at enemy states, it was using a well-established set of policy instruments.[56]

Toward the end of the nineteenth century, those instruments were modernized and given greater resources. This started with the navy even before the war with Spain, though

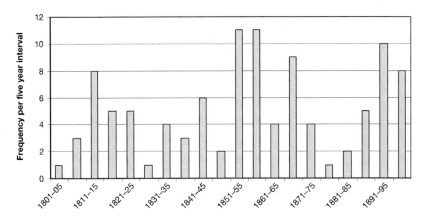

Figure 7.3   Use of military force in the nineteenth century
Source: Grimmett (2008) as per note 56.

Roosevelt accelerated the process. The army, whose performance during the war left much to be desired, was overhauled by the energetic new secretary, Elihu Root. These changes were aimed at giving both services, especially the navy, the ability to hold their own against the militaries of other great powers, even though, ironically, the deployments up until World War I were directed only at small or weak opponents. There would now be more troops available, equipped with more modern weapons, to be deployed for longer periods of time in support of a regime or its opponents.[57]

Nonetheless, older types of military operations continued. A case in point is the suppression of the Boxer Rebellion in China, where the United States, in collaboration with all the European powers and Japan, contributed armed forces to rescue their citizens besieged in Beijing in 1900. The U.S. sent two kinds of troops (so too did the British, French, and Italians): marines and armed sailors (both accustomed to raids and rescue operations) from barracks in China, ships near its waters, or bases in nearby colonial possessions; and when larger, more heavily armed forces turned out to be necessary, army units with experience in fighting colonial or counterinsurgency wars (the U.S. contributed troops from the Indian wars as well as from the Philippine anti-guerrilla war). This kind of deployment was nothing new: it could have occurred at any point in the preceding decades.[58] Other, similar deployments would take place up through the 1930s: Pershing's raid into Mexico against Pancho Villa (1916) and the marines' operations in China to protect U.S. citizens (1927–41).

U.S. foreign policy in perspective

We now can take a longer view. The Spanish-American War ushered in a new foreign policy for the United States, one of clientilism. That change did not take place immediately: there was a notable false start (colonial annexation), with clientilist policy instruments only being developed on a piecemeal basis over the following two decades. Even so, the new instruments did not involve wholesale replacement of existing ones. Rather, the former were built from the latter, combining, adapting, and augmenting them; at the same time, the old policy instruments continued to be used for decades to come. There was a break in the continuity of U.S. foreign policy, but it did not mean that the existing policy was disavowed or forgotten.

If we look at all three turning points over the past eleven decades, what jumps to the eye is the uniqueness of the post-1898 policy shift. Up to the war with Spain, U.S. foreign policy had been fairly stable. Not long after the war, that foreign policy changed, with a whole array of policy instruments starting to be developed. Those instruments then drove policy cybernetically; they also were the crystallized form of the U.S. foreign policy elite's ideology, providing built-in mechanisms for linking expectations about foreign policy problems to the responses put forward to those problems. (That ideology was palatable even to opponents of U.S. colonialism in 1899.) When new historical turning points were reached, the ideology, through the mechanism of the existing policy instruments, operated to channel policy further in a clientilist direction. The result in each case was a multiplication of clientilist policy instruments and the acquisition of additional client states.

From this perspective, what is distinct about 1898 is the relative paucity of policy instruments used at that time for maintaining order outside of the United States. Policy makers had few ready-to-hand responses for dealing those problems and as a result, were ready to adapt domestic instruments and think about the instruments of other states. By the 1940s, and even more so, by the 1990s, the situation was radically different. The U.S. then had a set of developed policy instruments which had become the standard way of interacting with, first, nearby countries, then with scores of countries. Under those circumstances, for the U.S. to have broken with clientilism would have been astonishing and have required a revolution, not in other countries, but at home.

The situation is no more fluid today. There are more well-established clientilistic policy instruments than ever before and they are better funded than in the past, even if certain agencies are favored at the expense of others. Although U.S. foreign policy elites disagreed about what to do in Iraq, they agreed that more troops should be sent to Afghanistan; that the U.S. should continue to support the full range of its client states, including those with contested or corrupt regimes; and that the U.S. military, in spite of its enormous budget, should be expanded. An 1898-like situation is not likely to come about any time soon; the United States will continue to maintain clients and oppose enemies for many years to come.

Notes

1 Explaining the continuity of U.S. foreign policy

1 NATO press briefing, Informal Session of the Ministers of Defence in Portorož, 28 September 2006; "U.S. Increases Support for Labor and Environmental Protection Improvements in Central America-Dominican Republic Free Trade Agreement Countries," U.S. Department of State Press Statement 2006/879, 28 September 2006; "RP-US Relations Stronger Than Ever, Says PGMA," press release, Malacañang Palace, Philippines, 17 September 2006; "U.S. Government Refuses Entry Visa to Cuban Minister of Public Health," *Granma* (Havana), 26 September 2006; U.S. Department of State daily press briefing, 28 September 2006.
2 Buell (1931a); Munro (1934: 21–33, 106–112; 199–201); Minger (1961). These cases are discussed at greater length in Chapter 3.
3 Kirkpatrick (1979); Smith (1994); Layne (2006); Dueck (2006); and many of the works referenced in both Layne and Dueck.
4 Quotations from Dueck (2004: 208); Hartz (1991: 285); Cumings (1990: 31). In our view, the claim that U.S. foreign policy is continuous back as far as George Washington incorrectly conflates policy instruments with supposed long-term goals. See Chapter 7 for a discussion of policy instruments in the pre-1898 period.
5 See Leffler (1992); Mearsheimer (2001); Ikenberry (2002); Krasner (1978).
6 Sylvan and Majeski (2006). To be clear: the point is to show why long-term goals of any sort are of little use in explaining the continuity of U.S. policy, not whether particular goals are in fact pursued by U.S. officials. Both issues, though, are linked, since as we point out above, if an objective such as democracy-promotion is usually subordinated to other concerns, then there is some doubt that it is a goal at all.
7 Tocqueville (1969: vol. 2, pt. 1, Ch. 8; pt. 3, Ch. 16); Winthrop (1630), Kennedy's inaugural address, 20 January 1961; Weinberg (1935); Tuveson (1968); Drinnon (1980); Williams (1980); Horsman (1981); Hunt (1987); Stephanson (1995); Lipset (1996); McDougall (1997); Nau (2002).
8 Klingberg (1952, 1996); Holmes (1985); Hoff (1999); Pollins and Schweller (1999). As with long-term goal explanations, even the existence of clear "moods" is debatable: for example, John Quincy Adams's famous speech against slaying monsters abroad (see Chapter 7) was made during a phase Klingberg qualifies as "extrovert."
9 Eisenstadt (1963); Fieldhouse (1966); Choucri and North (1975); Liska (1978); Doyle (1986); Ferguson (2004); Meinig (2004); Maier (2006).
10 Wiener (1942: 6); Rosenblueth *et al.* (1943: 19); Rosenblueth and Wiener (1950: 326); Galison (1994).
11 Ashby (1952, 1956); Shannon and Weaver (1949); Wiener (1948); Masani (1990: Chs. 14–18); Richardson (1991: Chs. 3, 4); Pickering (2002); Mirowski (2002: Ch. 2). Technically, negative feedback loops involve taking information about the difference between the performance of a system and the condition which it was set to satisfy, and using that information to change the behavior of a system in such a way as to reduce that difference. The standard example is that of a thermostat, which, if the preset temperature is greater than the actual temperature, turns on (or keeps on) the furnace, turning it off once the actual temperature is the same as, or greater than, the preset temperature. By contrast, positive feedback would take information and use it to increase the difference between the system's performance and its preset condition.

12 Beer (1959); Simon (1947); March and Simon (1958); Sent (2000); Pickering (2004); Mirowski (2002: Ch. 7). It is worth noting that the most frequent use of cybernetic approaches to explain the design and operation of organizations was in the study of business and, to a lesser degree, public administration (see Simon 1952: 248, for an explicit connection). Applications to foreign policy were far less common and, except for work on military spending (Davis *et al.* 1966; Ostrom 1977; Marra 1985; Majeski 1989) and several celebrated monographs on more general issues (Deutsch 1963; Allison 1971; Steinbruner 1974), interest waned (all three general works went into second editions, but those broke no new ground). We have opted for a cybernetic approach in this book because it seemed to us best suited to capture many of the salient features of U.S. foreign policy.

13 Wiener (1950: Ch. 10); Cyert and March (1963: Chs. 5, 8); March and Simon (1958: Chs. 6, 7); Simon (1964). The word "sequence" or the reference to purposeful machines should not be taken as implying that the activities in a purposeful sequence are purely mechanical, habitual, or unconscious, even if many of them may be. Often the activities that comprise the pursuit of a particular task are themselves deliberately and thoughtfully pursued, so that purposeful activities are made up of sequences of other purposeful activities, and so forth. This is one of the reasons that the references in this note are, on the whole, to work in the field of organization theory, i.e., particular arrangements of people, with the latter carrying out sequences of purposeful activities. (In large formal bureaucracies, these sequences are sometimes referred to as standard operating procedures.)

14 Lindblom (1959; 1965: Ch. 9); Levinthal and March (1981).

15 Certain components of capabilities, such as personnel, budget, and hardware, may be deployed to generate more than one sequence of purposeful activities. A given individual, for instance, may at some times work at bribing politicians and at other times at writing copy for a radio broadcast. However, the particular set of capabilities deployed to generate one sequence of purposeful activities will differ, at least to some degree, from the set of capabilities deployed to generate another sequence; for this reason, each capability, understood as a specific package of skilled personnel, with certain amounts of money and specialized hardware at their disposal, is a separate policy instrument. From this point of view, there are thus two ways of characterizing organizations: as sets of employees, budgets, hardware, and so forth; and as collections of policy instruments. The latter we find of greater interest in the analysis of foreign policy than the former.

16 We have borrowed the term "policy instrument" from the public policy literature (Bemelmans-Videc *et al.* 1998; Eliadis *et al.* 2005), although have given it a cybernetic twist. Note that although all policy instruments are authorized by legislative enactment or executive order, some are in the nature of standing, regularly funded programs whereas others (notably those in the CIA) are capabilities which are expected only episodically to be deployed.

17 U.S. Government Accountability Office (2008); U.S. Department of State (2008: 40); U.S. Congress, House (2008a); Berrigan (2008). There are in fact dozens of policy instruments involving bilateral cash transfers.

18 Skowronek (1982: Part 3); DiMaggio and Powell (1983); Sparrow (1996: Ch. 1); Sahlin-Andersson (1996); Aldrich (1999); Carpenter (2001: Chs. 5, 7, 8). Claims about long-term trends in the professionalization of state bureaucracies date back to 1922, when Weber's *Economy and Society* was first published.

19 Hudson (2005: a good overview of the foreign policy analysis literature, with particular emphasis on various psychological processes); Simon (1955); Newell *et al.* (1958); Newell and Simon (1972).

20 See Hudson (2005) for references on groupthink and bureaucratic politics; on argumentation and competing recommendations, Majeski and Sylvan (1999). Note that the bureaucratic/editorial processes of writing by committee and of cutting and pasting parts of one policy position into another are themselves means-oriented, sequential, and purposeful.

21 In practice, most studies of foreign policy making using psychological categories deal with the issue of translation between those categories and the specifics of a policy making situation through the act of data coding. The problem is that many coding decisions are neither explicit nor systematic.

22 These possibilities illustrate nicely the limitations of explanations that require translation into concrete terms. Arguments that failure is not yet clear, or that with enough time, competence,

and resources the situation can improve may exemplify concern about sunk costs or optimistic cognitive biases. Just as logically, however, they could represent a preemptive move in some kind of bureaucratic politics struggle, or an incremental search strategy, or for that matter, a sober judgment that policies often take many years to succeed. The point is that these types of motives add no explanatory power over and above the policy making convention that reports of failure are about missions and that they be accompanied by concrete suggestions for how the mission can be made to succeed. (Note incidentally that this logic applies also to the failure of instruments in nonclient states. What matters from a cybernetic point of view is not the existence of a commitment but of a surveillance and reporting apparatus, something which coincides only partly with client status.)

23 U.S. Department of State (2008: 245, 246, 247); our emphasis.

24 In the case of an enemy regime, a similar process occurs: policy recommenders diagnose insufficiencies in the efforts of the enemy's domestic or foreign adversaries and propose substituting U.S. policy instruments for those of the adversaries.

25 Guided search is a classically cybernetic process, as Levinthal and March point out in their discussion of "discoveries in the near neighborhood of the present activities" (1981: 309).

26 At-hand availability is similar to so-called "garbage can" models of decision, in which organizations are

> viewed for some purposes as collections of choices looking for problems, issues and feelings looking for decision situations in which they might be aired, solutions looking for issues to which they might be an answer, and decision-makers looking for work.
> (Cohen *et al.* 1972: 1)

See also Padgett (1980); Olsen (2001); Peters (2002).

27 Many states in Africa and, to a lesser extent, in Asia, which are neither enemies nor clients, have some of the same policy instruments deployed on their territory as do clients. There are nonetheless significant differences (see Chapter 4) between the two categories of states, particularly as regards the scale of resource transfers and certain types of political and military missions.

28 Roosevelt, press conference, 17 December 1940.

2 An empire of client states

1 Wallace-Hadrill (1989); see also Gellner and Waterbury (1977); Schmidt *et al.* (1976); Scott (1972); Folsom (1968); Eisenstadt (1963); and Eisenstadt and Lemarchand (1981). The study by Eisenstadt and Roniger (1980) contains extensive citations in political science, sociology, and anthropology; the monographs by Lugard (1922) and Barth (1959) are still worth consulting.

2 Plutarch, *Life of Cato the Elder*, 3.

3 Besides the United States, we would list, minimally, Britain, France, Russia, and India as having client states. Some 30 years ago, during the cold war, Knorr (1975: 25–26) enumerated at least a half-dozen patrons, each with a network of clients; a view of how the cold war played out, in terms of patron-client relations, in one particular region, can be found in Efrat and Bercovitch (1991: Chs. 1, 2). The classic ancient example is that of the Roman empire and its clients; see Badian (1958). To Knorr's theoretical discussion can be added that of Gasiorowski (1991: Ch. 1, esp. 2n), who also has applied the term to Latin America (1986) and to East Asia (Gasiorowski and Baek 1987); see also Murphy (1961).

4 Johnson telephone call to McGeorge Bundy, 27 May 1964, 11:24 a.m, in Beschloss (1998: 370).

5 Most states in the world have been independent for a far shorter period of time than has the U.S. Many of the states extant when the U.S. Constitution was adopted have since disappeared or have changed radically their political system. Thus only a handful of states have political systems older than that of the United States.

6 Schuman (1933: 187).

7 Figures are as of 1 January 2005, derived from U.S. Department of State (2005c: 16); FY 2009 budget request figures are slightly higher. Other figures on employment obtained from the U.S. Office of Management and Budget (2004) and U.S. Department of State (2004a) give slightly different results. The quotation is from ibid.

8 *FRUS 1964–1968*, vol. 31. Clearly, the 521 cables reproduced in the volume are only a tiny fraction of those in fact sent from State to the embassies and vice versa; however, discussions we have had with the department historians show that their criterion for selecting particular cables for *FRUS* series is precisely the degree to which the telegrams in question track the most pressing problems dealt with by higher-level policy makers in Washington.

9 U.S. Congress, Senate (1976: 33); U.S. Central Intelligence Agency (2004); Johnson (1991: 44–47). Until 2005, the clandestine service was called the Directorate of Operations.

10 Daalder and Destler (2000, 2001). In mid-2004, there were six regional directorates and six functional ones (Miller Center of Public Affairs 2004). See also Rothkopf (2004).

11 U.S. Department of the Treasury (2004); U.S. Agency for International Development (2004a).

12 Daft and Noe (2001: Ch. 15).

13 Some 23,000 persons work at the Pentagon, over 1500 in the Office of the Secretary of Defense (U.S. Department of Defense 2004a; more recent figures are similar). This does not count employees in various "defense agencies," such as those in charge of security assistance.

14 U.S. Department of Defense (2004b). The formal responsibilities of the under-secretary of defense for policy, under whose authority International Security Affairs falls, include the development of "policy on the conduct of alliances and defense relationships with foreign governments [and] their military establishments" and "political-military policy on issues of DoD interest that relate to foreign governments and their defense establishments" (U.S. Department of Defense 1999).

15 The Defense Security Cooperation Agency (DSCA); two of its directorates are regional, divided in turn into subregional divisions. DSCA's *raison d'être* is to arrange for arms transfers and military training, which it does on a country-by-country basis, an orientation reflected in the country-level data entries of its annual fact book (U.S. Defense Security Cooperation Agency 2004).

16 For a brief overview of the current unified command arrangements, see the Defense Department's website and the links it contains to the five (six as of 2007) geographical and four functional commands (U.S. Department of Defense 2004c). In fact, as we will see below, unified commands exercise a policy role well beyond that of war-planning and fighting; the officers in charge of these commands have, in terms of their role in foreign policy making, been referred to as "proconsuls" and "viceroys" (Priest 2003; Reveron and Gavin 2004).

17 A classic statement of the military's reluctance is the speech given by Secretary of Defense Caspar Weinberger in 1984, listing six criteria to be met for military intervention to be justified. This "Weinberger Doctrine" was opposed by Secretary of State George Shultz. Some years later, a similar episode pitted Colin Powell, then chairman of the Joint Chiefs of Staff, against Madeleine Albright, at the time UN ambassador (Garofano 2002).

18 For example, Nixon's opening to China was largely negotiated in secret by the national security adviser, with the State Department and other agencies kept in the dark. The sale of arms to Iran during the Reagan administration was also a secret, executed by NSC staffers.

19 This coordination is considered as essential. Thus, George W. Bush's first National Security Presidential Directive established no fewer than 17 National Security Council policy coordination committees (National Security Presidential Directive 1).

20 *FRUS 1964–1968*, vol. 24: docs. 99–109.

21 Gleijeses (2002: 280–330).

22 U.S.C. 3927.

23 The discussion of country teams in the State Department's website (U.S. Department of State 2004a) omits as members the CIA's head of station and, where present, the Drug Enforcement Administration's attaché. For a more complete membership list, see U.S. Department of the Army (1994: Ch. 2). It is interesting to note that the country team concept is used by other governments and political actors, including the United Nations.

24 For example, see the routine described by the U.S. ambassador to Greece in the mid-1970s: a daily briefing for the ambassador, the deputy chief of mission, and a few others by the CIA station chief; meetings three times a week of the "immediate country team" (the above group, plus the embassy's counselors and the defense attaché); and once a week, the "enlarged country team," (including all the attachés), a group of around 25 persons (Mak and Kennedy 1992: 52). In other embassies, especially during crisis situations, the country team would meet every day.

25 U.S. Department of Defense (2003: figure 22–2).

26 U.S. Defense Intelligence Agency (2002); U.S. Defense Institute of Security Assistance Management (2005: Ch. 5); on the (often charged) relations between defense attachés and security assistance officers, see Marisa (2003).

27 Listings drawn from U.S. Department of State (2004b: Bolivia) and U.S. Embassy La Paz (2004).

28 Washington Office on Latin America (2003, 2004). All told, there were 27 U.S. military personnel present in Bolivia in 2003.

29 In La Paz, Cochabamba, Santa Cruz, and Trinidad (US Drug Enforcement Administration 2004a). We have not been able to track down the number of U.S. personnel connected with anti-narcotics efforts; however, in fiscal year 2004, the budget for this single line item (i.e., the salaries and personal expenses of the U.S. citizens carrying out the 26 separate counter-narcotics programs in Bolivia) was $830,000 (U.S. Department of State 2003). The programs continued even after Morales was elected president: "Bolivia is an Uneasy Ally as U.S. Presses Drug War," *New York Times*, 28 August 2008.

30 U.S. Agency for International Development (2004b: Program Summary). The budget request submitted by George Bush for fiscal year 2006 included $80 million destined in anti-drug funds for Bolivia (U.S. Department of State 2005a: 77).

31 Our argument here is similar to the one popularized by Gould and Lewontin (1979) in evolutionary theory.

32 Lodge to State, 23 October 1963, quoted in *FRUS 1961–1963*, vol. 4: doc. 209. Harkins eventually found out he had been bypassed and was able to get the Joint Chiefs of Staff to intercede but, in addition to their move being too late, they were only able to force a minor change in Lodge's instructions (i.e., to discourage a coup if he thought it would fail). Earlier in October, Lodge had succeeded in getting Kennedy to transfer back to Washington another official close to Diem: the CIA head of station in Saigon. For discussion of these episodes, see *Pentagon Papers* (1971: 2: 252–263). This case is treated at greater length in the book's website.

33 One example among many: Uruguay in the mid-1960s (Agee 1975: entry for 11 August 1964).

34 Rusk to Bruce [ambassador to UK], 19 February 1962 (*FRUS 1961–1963*, vol. 12: doc. 264).

35 See the matter of fact tone that characterizes Johnson's 16 October 1964 meeting with his top national security officials (*FRUS 1964–1968*, vol. 14: docs. 53–54). In fairness, it should be noted that the Chinese exploded their first nuclear bomb the day after Khrushchev's fall, and so the meeting in the White House had both items on the agenda.

36 Nicolson, writing in the 1930s, gives a view of the embassy's information sources as comprising the military, the top officials in the Foreign Ministry, and "men of business"; the ambassador in "major embassies" is able to avail himself of the services of a press attaché in understanding local newspapers (1939: Chs. 8, 9).

37 Almost three-fourths of the total civilian employees were U.S. citizens (Federal Jobs Net 2005).

38 U.K. Foreign and Commonwealth Office (2004). It is difficult to make strict comparisons between employment figures across countries because of differences in budget and accounting systems. We tried to come up with comparable numbers by distributing a survey to the embassies of some seven states in around two dozen countries; but the response was too spotty to provide more than informal confirmation of our sense of the relative size of the U.S. overseas presence.

39 The classic anecdote about fair elections is about Richard Nixon's visit to South Vietnam in 1967, when he was out of office. Nixon's old acquaintance Edward Lansdale, then back in Saigon,

> seized on the idea of using Nixon to build support for the elections, really honest elections this time. "Oh sure, honest, yes, honest, that's right," Nixon said, "*so long as you win!*" With that he winked, drove his elbow into Lansdale's arm and slapped his own knee.
>
> (Halberstam 1972: 207, emphasis in original)

40 Conversation between Johnson and Mann, 11 June 1964, *FRUS 1964–1968*, vol. 31: doc. 16.

41 State to Montevideo, 12 June 1964; letter from Mann to Coerr, 23 June 1964; Montevideo to State, 8 July 1964; Mann to Rusk, 1 December 1964; Oliver to Rusk, 18 August 1967, ibid., docs. 459–461, 463, 467. Eventually the constitution was amended and, amid rumors of an impending coup, the U.S. arranged for two economic aid packages.

42 For example, neither the prison surveillance regimes invented by Jeremy Bentham and his successors nor contemporary urban video monitoring operate with the explicit cooperation of those surveilled. On the financial side, bond-rating companies and international institutions such as the IMF do receive cooperation (if grudging) from the states whose performance they assess, but this voluntarism is restricted in both scope and frequency.

43 Of course, Germany and Japan were viewed as economically vital to the world economy which U.S. policy makers wanted to construct (Cumings 1984, 1990: 49; Kolko and Kolko 1972: Ch. 1). But they were also seen as important barriers to Soviet expansion, as former enemies who needed to be controlled, as vehicles for the projection of U.S. power, and as laboratories for developing new political arrangements. As we pointed out in Chapter 1, there are multiple motives at play in most policies; there is no one-to-one mapping of ends (whether economic or otherwise) and means. The empire of client states the U.S. constructed was (and is) multifaceted in nature.

44 A brief introduction, with a good bibliography, can be found in Kaminsky (1986); see also Dewey (1993: Ch. 1). Ferguson (2003: 184n) points out that other British colonies were similarly thinly staffed: Africa, for example, with over a dozen colonies and 43 million people, was administered by some 1200 British civil servants.

45 The "princely states" in India have been characterized by one author as a "patron-client system" (Ramusack 2004: 92). On indirect rule, see Fieldhouse (1966: Chs. 12, 14).

46 One of the problems with both sides of the famous "imperialism of free trade" debate about British policy before the scramble for Africa (Louis 1976) is that the innovativeness of the administrative arrangements in the later nineteenth century is underplayed.

47 There is some evidence that U.S. officials were from time to time nervous about this. For example, during the height of the crisis with Diem, the Americans began to be concerned that Diem's brother Nhu would cut a separate deal with North Vietnam and call for the U.S. to leave. *FRUS 1961–1963*, vol. 4: docs. 110, 113–114; Kahin (1986: 153–156, 168–169). We will discuss in Chapter 5 certain cases in which the U.S. used military force to depose presidents or other leaders of clients whose continued tenure in office was seen as a problem for the regime's maintenance.

48 The literature on empires is enormous. For starters, see the references in Doyle (1986: Ch. 1), although we disagree somewhat with his discussions of some of that literature and, indeed, with his definition of empires; also see Eisenstadt (1963, 1968), who explicitly draws the link with patron–client relations and whose definition is closer to ours. Much of our thinking about U.S. foreign policy was influenced by the work of Franz Schurmann (1974) and the formal definition we have put forward can be seen as an unpacking of his recent characterization: "a political entity that rules over diverse peoples and territories" (Schurmann 2002). See also Nexon and Wright (2007).

49 Significantly, the process sketched out by Lenin in his pamphlet on imperialism culminates with territorial annexations and clashes between European states. Similarly, the British East India Company, which administered major portions of India, was replaced by direct state rule after the Uprising of 1857.

50 Or, alternatively, to confine "the scope of decision-making to relatively 'safe' issues" (Bachrach and Baratz 1962: 948).

51 On the Peloponnesian League, de Ste. Croix (1972: ch. 4) is still an excellent overview; note that the Spartans not only limited the policies of their allies vis-à-vis each other, but required them to have oligarchical political systems. (The Athenians went further in the Delian League, exacting tribute and judging certain local lawsuits in Athenian courts.) On Rome, see Badian (1958).

52 Zorzi (2004); although eventually, the cities were absorbed into a Florentine territorial state.

53 Wauthier (1995); Rouvez (1994); Hack (2001).

54 Arguably, Cuba was a Soviet client (although, as with many U.S. clients, it was hardly submissive to its patron) and, for a time in the 1970s, it had Guinea-Bissau as a client (Gleijeses 2002: 393).

55 In fact, the missiles airlifted by France in U.S. C-5As were Hawk air defense batteries, themselves made in the U.S. (Rouvez 1994: 160). In 2008, the president of the UN Security Council – in which, of course, the U.S. had veto power – called on the regime in Chad to be defended, which the French then used as permission to use military force.

56 We used several criteria for determining which states are currently U.S. clients. (The rationale
for these criteria is discussed at various points in the next three chapters.) First, we assumed,
unless there was strong evidence to the contrary (e.g., the case of Cuba), that all states with
whom the U.S. concluded a bilateral or multilateral mutual defence treaty before the end of
the cold war are U.S. clients. Second, we added to that list those countries with whom the U.S.
has close military-to-military ties, principally via treaty arrangements permitting extensive
arms transfers and military training; as well as those states over whom the U.S. at some point
established detailed budgetary monitoring and control. (Information on both the first and
second points was obtained from the State Department's *Treaties in Force* publication: U.S.
Department of State 2004c.) Other countries, notably those in which there are U.S. military
bases, or with whom the U.S. recently concluded a mutual defense treaty, or for which there is
evidence of CIA budgetary support or emergency military assistance, or which are in the
same region as other U.S. clients, we added to the list if: (1) there was verbal evidence (e.g.,
from the State Department budget "justification" to Congress – U.S. Department of State
2005b) that the state in question is considered as an ally or otherwise important to U.S.
security or (2) there is no countervailing evidence of U.S. deferral to other states (e.g., France,
Russia). Finally, states that at some point had been U.S. colonies, territories, or trusteeships,
or were occupied militarily by the U.S., were also included if they did not fall into any of the
above categories. As of February 2008, the list of U.S. clients was unchanged.

3 Acquiring client states

1 Certain military basing agreements in the past few years have not been communicated publicly. For example, agreements governing U.S. facilities in Qatar and Saudi Arabia were not
listed in the State Department (U.S. Department of State 2004c) compendium of treaties in
force, nor were the facilities themselves included in the Defense Department's (U.S. Department of Defense 2004d) report on military bases. Defense (U.S. Department of Defense
2004e) does list a certain number of troops as being present in both countries and State
(2004d) mentions Central Command's headquarters (though not its military bases) in Qatar.
In these cases, it is necessary to get information from non-Executive Branch agencies (e.g.,
Sharp 2004: 8–9) and nongovernmental sources, both organizations (e.g., GlobalSecurity.org
2004b) and individual journalists (e.g., Arkin 2005).
2 The principal source in which these agreements can be found is the State Department's (U.S.
Department of State 2004c) *Treaties in Force* publication; although, since, as per the discussion above, certain recent agreements are secret, it is also necessary to consult other sources.
The most important categories of agreements are defense arrangements providing for military
assistance and training, plus of course formal defense treaties; and economic and financial
treaties providing for aid or, in earlier times, customs monitoring. However, key features of
certain arrangements can only be seen in the operational details, which means that for some
countries, it is necessary to supplement treaty information with reports of diplomatic or
military cables.
3 Marcus (1983: 104); Lefebvre (1991, 1998); Schraeder (1994: Ch. 4, esp. pp. 120–123).
4 Leffler (1992: 150).
5 Kaplan (1975); Ovendale (1994); Little (1995). The 1960 reference to "collapse" is from an
internal U.S. policy paper, NSC-6011, "U.S. Policy Toward the Near East," cited in Little
(1995: 528); the Nixon comments are reported by Haldeman (1994: 195), although Garfinkle
(1985) reports that U.S. overt intervention was in fact unlikely.
6 The reference to consultations on Somalia comes from Schraeder (1994: 170); the reference to
Syria is from Little (1990: 55–58).
7 Even when U.S. leaders are piqued at a client's actions, they are loathe to renounce their
patronage. Thus, although the U.S. was miffed when New Zealand barred nuclear-armed
and–powered ships from its ports, leading the former to "suspend its ANZUS security obligations" to the latter, both countries continue to maintain close ties, including in the security
field, and there is little doubt that the U.S. would still come to New Zealand's aid in case of
threat. Hence, "the United States would welcome New Zealand's reassessment of its legislation to permit the country's return to full ANZUS cooperation" (U.S. Department of State
2004f). For the U.S. really to end its role as patron of a given state, there must have been a

major regime change in the client; even then, officials are reluctant simply to accept that the state is "lost."

8 For example, see comments about the Atlantic Alliance by De Gaulle in his press conference of 29 July 1963, and by Mitterrand in his speech before ambassadors of 31 August 1994. Even at the height of the U.S.-French disagreement over the 2003 war against Iraq, Chirac emphasized France's friendship and alliance with the United States (e.g., in his 16 February 2003 interview with *Time*).

9 Lundestad (1986; also 1998, 1999).

10 In technical terms, we employ a "grounded theory" approach (Glaser and Straus 1967), refining theoretical categories by deliberately looking for apparent coding anomalies in the "predicted" features of particular cases.

11 Kolko and Kolko (1972: 528–533).

12 The full text of the Platt Amendment can be found in Munro (1934: 11–12); see also Collin (1990: Ch. 17) and Schoultz (1998: Ch. 8).

13 Schirmer and Shalom (1987: Chs. 4–6); Brands (1992: 227–233); Cullather (1994: 36–43, 51–59).

14 See, for example, the statements by the president of Afghanistan and the U.S. secretary of defense, reported in the *New York Times*, 14 April 2005. In the spring of 2008, the U.S. entered into negotiations with the government of Iraq for a status of forces agreement that would regularize the presence of American troops after counterinsurgency operations would, it was hoped, have ended.

15 Figures as of 30 September 2004 (U.S. Department of Defense 2004e); the "civilian" numbers pertain to U.S. citizens directly hired by the Department of Defense in connection with the U.S. troop presence (so-called "foreign nationals" are also hired). More recent data show a slight decline in military personnel in most of these places; civilian data are no longer readily available.

16 The list was constructed on the basis of speeches and writings by U.S. officials, both for public consumption and behind the scenes. We began with a set of countries drawn from our general sense of U.S. diplomatic history, then checked each one for evidence that it was perceived by U.S. policy makers along the lines of the definition. This led us to take certain countries off the list; we then added to the list by looking for evidence of other enemies whose existence seemed compatible with the "danger" context of acquisition of particular clients (see below) and with various types of hostile intervention (see Chapter 6). In the meantime, note that certain states considered by U.S. officials as satellites (and hence as not having chosen to differ with the U.S.) of enemies are not themselves included as enemies. Dates are our best guess, within a year, as to when the state in question came to be seen as an enemy, although often this perception crystallized only gradually. In some cases, states entered enemy status, left it, and then reentered it.

17 The discussion in the following paragraphs is on rewards following regime change. U.S. efforts to foment such change are described in Chapter 6.

18 Gasiorowski (1991: Ch. 4).

19 Little (1990: 56–58, 60–62).

20 Nwaubani (2001); Noer (1984); U.S. Agency for International Development (2005); *FRUS 1964–1968*, vol. 24: docs. 262–274.

21 Hersh (1983: Chs. 15–16); Bundy (1998: 148–153, 220–223, 373–375, 391–393); Clymer (1999). The U.S. was already engaging in "secret" bombing of Cambodia from 1969.

22 Shultz (1993: 292–297); Woodward (1987: 240–241); U.S. Department of State (2004g); Cairo (2005); Payne (1996).

23 *FRUS 1964–1968*, vol. 26: docs. 206–262; Simpson (2004: docs. 10–11); U.S. Agency for International Development (2005); Roesad (2001: tables 3, 4).

24 U.S. Agency for International Development (2005); U.S. Department of State (2005b); Hersh (1983: 405); Bundy (1998: 337); Quandt (1993). The one billion dollar figure is in current dollars; see Chapter 4 for a discussion in terms of constant dollars.

25 Buell (1931a); Munro (1934: Chs. 5–6); LaFeber (1984: Ch. 1); Collin (1990: Ch. 16); Schoultz (1998: Ch. 11).

26 Aid data from 1946–2003 generated from U.S. Agency for International Development (2005); narrative account of post-1991 period from U.S. Department of State (2005d);

characterization as "key" from U.S. Department of Defense and U.S. Department of State (2004: sect. III.A.15).

27 Kolko and Kolko (1972: Chs. 8, 12); Yergin (1978: Ch. 11); Pach (1991: 104–116, 134–136).
28 See, for example, Henderson to Acheson, Dunn, and Hickerson, n.d. [probably late Dec. 1945], *FRUS 1946*, vol. 7: 1–6.
29 Little (2003: 127–137; 2004: 678–684). The text of the Eisenhower Doctrine is widely available online, for example, at www.eisenhower.archives.gov/midleast.htm. The Suez crisis of 1956 was another impetus to the Doctrine's promulgation.
30 Gendzier (1997: 217–224); *FRUS 1955–1957*, vol. 13: doc. 140.
31 Dulles, 12 July 1957, quoted in Little (1995: 525); Macmillan, in conversation with Eisenhower, 14 July 1958, quoted in Ovendale (1994: 291); Little (1996: 45–49).
32 *FRUS 1964–1968*, vol. 24: docs. 145–180, esp. 163. 166, 168–169, 175. Later on, when Egypt had ceased to be considered as a threat, Tunisia was seen as being endangered by Libya (Hechiche 1989).
33 Kissinger (1999: Chs. 25–26); Brzezinski (1983: 178–190); Carter (1982: 254); LeoGrande (1998a: Chs. 2–3).
34 Fienberg (1992); Zunes (2003); Williams (1997: 133–134); Knight and Persaud (2001: 38); Arkin (2005).
35 Kolko (1968: Chs. 10, 21); Tuchman (1971).
36 This also applies to the Democratic Republic of the Congo (ex-Zaire). The pivotal moment was 1964, when concern over leftist rebels led the Johnson Administration to set up a CIA-run paramilitary war, with weapons from the Defense Department, planes piloted by Cuban exiles who had participated in the Bay of Pigs invasion, and Belgian paratroopers and white mercenaries brought in (see Chapter 5). After this, the U.S. strongly backed the armed forces chief, Mobutu, in his overthrow of the civilian government; for years to come, he enjoyed close ties with the CIA. Schatzberg (1989: 324–329); Schraeder (1994: 68–80); Gleijeses (2002: Ch. 3); Devlin (2007). On a different region, Southeast Asia, see McMahon (1999).
37 Smith (1972: Chs. 2–4, 9); Munro (1934: Ch. 4); Schoultz (1998: Ch. 12).
38 The quotation from Baker is reported by many authors (e.g., Halberstam 2001: 46); the Bush warning is reported in the *New York Times*, 28 December 1992.
39 Holbrooke (1998); Daalder (2000); Halberstam (2001); Hamilton (1996).
40 The troop commitment in 1993 is reported in the *New York Times*, 11 June 1993; and Clinton's letter to Congress, 9 July 1993. On relations with Macedonia, see U.S. Agency for International Development (2005) and U.S. Department of State (2004c; 2004h).
41 Rouvez (1994: 155–162).
42 The State Department's Treaties in Force publication (U.S. Department of State 2004c) says that the Southeast Asia Collective Defense Treaty remains operative in spite of the fact that the organization created along with it, SEATO, ceased to exist in 1977. Both Thailand and Pakistan signed the treaty, although Pakistan withdrew in 1972. Pakistan had been asking for tighter relations with the United States as far back as 1950, but the request was only granted in 1954, when the two states signed the first of a series of military aid and training agreements and when, with strong U.S. encouragement, Pakistan and Turkey signed a pact of mutual cooperation (*FRUS 1952–1954*, vol. 9: docs. 136–241).
43 Kaplan (1980; 1984); Pach (1991: Ch. 7).
44 Yergin (1978: 351); Kolko and Kolko (1972: 498–502).
45 See, for example, the various statements by Secretary of State Warren Christopher; they are conveniently collected in Federation of American Scientists NATO expansion website (2001).
46 U.S. Agency for International Development (2005); U.S. Department of State (2004c; 2005e); Grafton (2003: 100).
47 South Vietnam became a client as soon as Washington installed Ngo Dinh Diem as president, helped him defeat his enemies, lavished money on him, supplied and trained his army, and turned what had been conceived of as a temporary holding ground for French-backed forces into a bona fide, if externally dependent, state (Karnow 1983: Ch. 6; see Chapter 5 below). Laos, like South Vietnam an associated state under the SEATO treaty, became a client some years later when its prime minister, who until then had had an arm's-length relation with the United States, asked for help against communist rebels. The U.S. rebuilt the Laotian air force, began "armed reconnaissance" and bombing missions against the rebels,

and then asked for, and received, permission to engage in bombing against North Vietnamese infiltrating into South Vietnam via Laos (see Chapter 5). U.S. Library of Congress (1994); South East Asia Community Resource Center (2002).

48 As regards the Philippines, note the U.S. ambassador's explanation to the Philippines president that "our public statements regarding the defense and security of the Phils do in fact constitute a closer alliance than is the case with Australia and New Zealand," and Washington's exasperated reference to "unique Phil-Amer relations which totally unlike anything US has ever had with any other country and that therefore Phils wld consider its relations with US something far more intimate." Cowen to State 17 July 1951; State to Cowen 18 July 1951, both in *FRUS 1951*, vol. 6: 223, 225.

49 Mecham (1961: Ch. 7); Lieuwen (1961: 188–195).

50 Mecham (1961: 217–218); Smith (1972: Chs. 4, 7, 9); Gellman (1979: 136).

51 Canada Department of Foreign Affairs and International Trade (2002); U.S. Department of State (2004c).

52 Rosenberg (1985); GlobalSecurity.org (2003).

53 Mecham (1961: 211–216); Schoultz (1998: 316–325).

54 Details on planning from Woodward (2004); the 21 November date is discussed on pp. 1–8. The eight countries in which the U.S. built up forces were Bahrain, Jordan, Kuwait, Oman, Qatar, Saudi Arabia, Turkey, and the United Arab Emirates. In the handful of weeks between the attacks on 11 September 2001 and the launching of the war in Afghanistan, the U.S. also established facilities or arranged for overflight privileges in Pakistan and five Central Asian countries; but there were no new clients acquired: Pakistan had for decades been a client, and, as we discussed above, the U.S. refrained from establishing clientilistic relations with the other states, one of the reasons presumably being a concern not to irritate the Russians (Arkin 2005: 4–5).

55 In fact, the U.S. did not intend initially to liquidate its war investment in 1918. Wilson, of course, participated actively in negotiations in Paris, and for a while, it appeared as if the U.S. would accept a mandate over Armenia, and possibly over the Dardanelles and Anatolia as well (MacMillan 2001: 386, 447).

56 Clayton quote from his memorandum to Acheson, 27 May 1947, in *FRUS 1947*, vol. 3: 221–223. The story of the genesis of the Marshall Plan is well known and the literature on it is immense. We would cite two recent articles discussing that literature, one a review article by Burk (2001) and the other an extended argument about the nature of the Plan (Cox and Kennedy-Pipe 2005).

57 George C. Marshall Foundation (2004); Pisani (1991: Ch. 4); U.S. Congress, Senate (1976: 25–41). The official who in fact disbursed counterpart funds to the OPC, Richard Bissell, later became the CIA's deputy director for plans, taking over as head of the successor to the OPC. As implied in the text, Plan recipients whose economies the U.S. was not able to control via counterpart funds did not become U.S. clients: Switzerland (which never received grant money from the ECA) and Ireland, whose continued membership in the Sterling Area meant that its economy remained under the control of the United Kingdom (Geiger 1999). By contrast, another neutral state, Sweden, was subject to the same control mechanisms as most Marshall Plan countries and so we have coded it as a client. As partial confirmation, we would note that Sweden, though refusing NATO membership the next year, nonetheless developed close military ties with the U.S.

58 See Acheson's letter to Marshall, 24 November 1950, emphasizing that Australia's concern was "not for security reasons, but as a vehicle to achieve a closer participation for Australia in all stages of high level Washington planning" and reassuring him that Canberra no longer expected a power of decision. *FRUS 1950*, vol. 6: 226–227; U.S. Department of State (2004c). Although neither the Australians nor the New Zealanders were happy about Japanese rearmament, there is no evidence that the U.S. saw them as endangered by Japan: U.S. reassurances to them were a distinctly secondary concern in Washington.

59 Kolko and Kolko (1972: 636, 661–662); Leffler (1992: 417); U.S. Department of State (2004c). Truman was quite unhappy with the opening to Franco, referring laconically to his decision as being "the result of the advice from the Department of Defense" and, months after negotiations were underway, saying bluntly that he had "never been very fond of" the Franco regime. Press conferences of 19 July 1951 and 7 February 1952.

60 Balfour-Paul (1991); Rugh (1996: 68–69); Katzman (2004: 19–21); U.S. Department of State (2004c, 2004e); Arkin (2005).

61 Schoultz (1998: Chs. 8–9; "splendid little war" is by Secretary of State Hay, on p. 140; other quotations are from pp. 170 and 168); Collin (1990: Chs. 9–11).

62 Roosevelt to Theodore Roosevelt, Jr., 10 February 1904, quoted in Schoultz (1998: 183).

63 Roosevelt to Root, 20 May 1904, quoted in Schoultz (1998: 184); Platt (1968); Mitchener and Weidenmier (2004).

64 The most detailed histories of the Dominican affair are by Collin (1990: pt. 3) and Veeser (2003). The Roosevelt "corollary" to the Monroe Doctrine was worded almost identically to his 20 May 1904 letter to Root (see above); it was in his annual message to Congress, 5 December 1904. Interestingly, in his 15 February 1905 message to the Senate about the Dominican treaty, Roosevelt made it clear that the value of the treaty was less to protect U.S. investors than to maintain order in the region.

65 Rosenberg and Rosenberg (1987); Rosenberg (1998, 1999: Chs. 3–4, 6).

66 Buell (1931a: 175–176); LaFeber (1984: 42–46); Lindvall-Larson (2002: Honduras).

67 Munro (1934: Ch. 4); Schmidt (1971); Healy (1976); Schoultz (1998: 231–233).

68 Buell (1931a: 177–184); Jones (1934: 157); LaFeber (1984: 54–58); Lindvall-Larson (2002: Costa Rica).

69 Buell (1931a: 185–186; 1932b: 188–189, 200); Munro (1974: 152–156), LaFeber (1984: 75–76); Rosenberg and Rosenberg (1987: 68–70).

70 Jones (1934: 154–156); Munro (1974: 145–152, 283–290); LaFeber (1984: 69–74); Rosenberg and Rosenberg (1987: 71–72); Lindvall-Larson (2002: El Salvador). For an example of the U.S. role in presidential politics, see Corrigan to State, 29 July 1937, *FRUS 1937*, vol. 5: 522–525.

71 Little (2003: Ch. 3); *FRUS 1948*, vol. 5: 1208, 1233, 1299, 1306, 1313, 1391, 1432, 1468, 1476, 1507, 1514, 1633. A typical passage is this:

> On all of fundamentals, two parties were in agreement. Examples of such agreement are: Existence of Israel as independent state, early and full recognition of new government of Israel, admission of Israel to UN, economic assistance, and peaceful settlement Jewish-Arab difficulties through UN.
>
> (Rusk to Lovett, 2 October 1948, in *FRUS 1948*, vol. 5: 1448)

The loan agreement in question was from the Export-Import Bank, for $100 million, and was made on 19 January 1949. Starting in 1949, the Israelis regularly asked for U.S. officers to train their army. Intelligence cooperation seems to have begun very early on, in 1951 (Cockburn and Cockburn 1991).

72 One example of the presumption of U.S. backing for Israel, even prior to independence, comes through in the meeting of 26 March 1948 between the top two State Department officials (both of whom were opposed to recognition) and two representatives of the Jewish Agency for Palestine. With some concern, the Secretary of State questioned his visitors "on the ability of the Palestine settlement to defend itself, and ... whether they were counting on foreign assistance if the Arabs began to get the upper hand." This conversation took place two days after a White House meeting in which there was a "general understanding" that if a truce could not be obtained, "steps would be taken to release the [arms] embargo." *FRUS 1948*, vol. 5: 762, 755. To get a sense of the political consensus underlying the U.S. commitment to Israel, see the figures and discussion in Mark (2004): from 1949 to 2006, the U.S. provided total military and economic aid to Israel of $105.01 billion, with particularly generous financial arrangements for much of this aid; in addition, around $3 billion a year is transferred through tax deductible philanthropic contributions, commercial loans, and Israel Bond sales. However, the fact that relations are now much more extensive than they were in 1948 (Bar-Siman-Tov 1998) should not obscure the real U.S. commitment to Israel from the very beginning.

73 The quotations are from Kissinger (1979: 1266, 1267). On support for Solidarity, see Brzezinski (1983: 463–468) and Bernstein (1992). The State Department description is from a recent budget justification (U.S. Department of State 2005b: 409).

74 U.S. Department of State (2004c, 2004i, 2005b: 500).

75 *FRUS 1961–1963*, vol. 12: docs. 241–299; Rabe (1999: 79–95); Waters and Daniels (2005); *FRUS 1964–1968*, vol. 32: docs. 370–440.
76 Tate (1965: 115–299); Kuykendall (1967: 648).
77 Little (2002: 45–58); Vitalis (2002; 2006).
78 The Truman letter is 31 October 1950; it was reaffirmed by Eisenhower's Under Secretary of State in a meeting with the Saudi ambassador on 16 March 1953. The letter from Eisenhower to the king (containing the "true friend" phrase) was written on 15 June 1953, several months after he authorized grant military assistance (this never was worked out, the Saudis opting for arms purchases as less politically risky) and just a few days before the agreement for military training was signed. *FRUS 1952–1954*, vol. 9: docs. 1451, 1452, 1461, 1465, 1506; U.S. Department of State (2004c). The linkage between U.S. military contacts (including arms sales) and Saudi internal security was occasioned by labor unrest in the kingdom's Eastern Province and by U.S. domestic controversy over the sale of tanks in early 1956, following on the sale of B-26 aircraft the year before (Citino 2002: 80, 93–94, 100–101).
79 The maps in Figures 3.3 through 3.6 are derived by aggregating the client acquisition data across all five contexts of acquisition and then periodizing them.
80 Ambrose (1970).

4 The routine maintenance of client states

1 To be precise: the median number of years that client states (as of February 2008) have been in that status is 57.33.
2 Ex-Im Bank history from Becker and McClenahan (2003); recent figures are authorizations for fiscal years 2004 and 2007, from U.S. Export-Import Bank (2004: 22–26; 2007: 18–21). The other agencies referred to are the Overseas Private Investment Corporation and the U.S. Trade and Development Agency; both support private investment and trade activities in very much the way that Ex-Im was originally designed to do (and in part still does) for exports.
3 World Bank figures derived from chronological listing of "first funding" for the period 1947–57 (World Bank 2004a). Interestingly, the Bank's very first loan, to France in 1947, was, in inflation-adjusted dollars, the largest it ever made ($250 million, accounting for more than a third of its loanable funds at the time), although, as we saw in Chapter 3, it was dwarfed by U.S. direct and Ex-Im Bank loans of $1.5 billion during the same fiscal year (World Bank 2004b; U.S. Agency for International Development 2005).
4 These are not the only multilateral sources of development assistance to which the U.S. contributes. The IMF has a Poverty Reduction and Growth Facility, and the UN Development Programme Group also has funding programs. For the most part, though, the loans available through these institutions tend to be considerably smaller and less regular than those made by the World Bank's agencies and the regional development banks.
5 Nixon in meeting with Helms (CIA director), 15 September 1970; National Security Decision Memorandum No. 93, "Policy Toward Chile"; Crimmins to Kissinger, 4 December 1970 (Kornbluh 1998). Loan information pertains to World Bank (IBRD/IDA) "commitments" with "approval date" (World Bank 2005) and to IADB "approved loans by country and fund" (Inter-American Development Bank 2005b); for a narrative account of the pre-coup loan situation, see Sigmund (1974: 326–29); note that the Ex-Im Bank, too, suspended loans during the Allende years.
6 "The China Aid Act of 1948": Title 4 of the Foreign Assistance Act of 1948 (the Marshall Plan was Title 1), 62 Stat. 137; George C. Marshall Foundation (2004). Mutual Security Act of 1951, Title 5, Sec. 511, 65 Stat. 381; Mutual Security Act of 1954, 68 Stat. 859; Mutual Security Act of 1957, 71 Stat. 355. Note the statement by the chairman of a Senate subcommittee that "in the future economic aid is to be primarily for the purpose of assisting friendly countries to strengthen their individual and collective defenses" (Theodore Green, quoted in Kaplan 1980: 157).
7 Foreign Assistance Act of 1961, 4 September 1961, 75 Stat. 424. There are other economic assistance programs – for example, food aid under P.L. 480 – but these tend to be mostly for emergency purposes, even if they have in the past been used as rewards for clients acquired through switching.

8 Treaty of Tipitata, 11 May 1927: *FRUS 1927*, vol. 3: 434–39; Nalty (1961); Schoultz (1998: Chs. 13, 15). A similar situation took place in Panama, with the replacement of the army by a National Police force in 1904; although since it was the U.S. that had created the country just the year before, this was more a matter of switching policy instruments.

9 69 Stat. 334. Aside from Sandino's rebellion in Nicaragua, which was handled by the marines prior to their withdrawal, the only significant use of armed force by domestic opponents against the regime of a client state prior to World War II was the communist-inspired peasant uprising in El Salvador in 1932. On the insurgents' side, this was a minor affair, with perhaps five towns taken over. The army, shocked more by the fact of the uprising than by its extent (the U.S. ambassador was quite unconcerned, unlike his European colleagues), bought large quantities of weapons in the U.S. and, even before they arrived, summarily executed over 10,000 people, most of them Nahuatl-speaking peasants, within a few weeks (Anderson 1971).

10 Schoultz (1998: 310); Pach (1991: Chs. 1, 3–4). There were two training missions sent to Iran in 1942, one for the army and the other for the gendarmerie; the latter was headed by Col. H. Norman Schwarzkopf, whose son, decades later, would be the general in charge of the first U.S. war against Iraq.

11 An Act to Promote the Defense of the United States (Lend-Lease Act), 11 March 1941, 55 Stat. 31; Pach (1991: Chs. 1–2).

12 Republic of the Philippines Military Assistance Act, 26 June 1946, 60 Stat. 315; Greek-Turkish Aid, 22 May 1947, 61 Stat. 103; Surplus Property Act of 1944, 3 October 1944, 58 Stat. 765; Pach (1991: 26, 137–44). By 1948, the Truman Administration had decided that the Nationalist regime in China was a lost cause; but although it resisted arms transfers, Congress insisted on supplying weapons up to (and beyond) the bitter end (Pach 1991: Ch. 6).

13 Mutual Defense Assistance Act of 1949, 6 October 1949, 63 Stat. 714.

14 Chap. 11, Supplemental Appropriation Act of 1951, 27 September 1950, 64 Stat. 1063; Agreement with Thailand Respecting Military Assistance, 17 October 1950, 3 UST 2675. Title IV of the Mutual Security Act of 1951, which dealt with the American republics, only listed military and technical assistance; there was no provision for economic assistance (cf. Schoultz 1998: 332–333). It was not until the Mutual Security Act of 1954 that economic assistance for Latin America was authorized, and even then the amount was derisory: $9 million, as contrasted with $115 million for the Near East and Africa, and $75 million for South Asia.

15 Kaplan (1980: Ch. 4); the principal modifications were made in the Mutual Security Act of 1954. The MAAGs were preceded by survey teams, which often led to numerous clashes with European countries over which types of materiel were and were not needed, as well as over the possible retransfer of lend-lease goods. Although the size of the MAAGs was reduced somewhat from what was originally planned (for example, the initial idea for Norway was that the MAAG should consist of 66 persons, which would have made it larger than the staff of the country's foreign ministry), their surveillance tasks made it impossible to cut down the numbers by more than a third.

16 Title I, Sect. 106, International Security Assistance and Arms Export Control Act of 1976, 30 June 1976, 90 Stat. 729. For a recent partial listing (training connected with arms transfers is classified; and there is no clear indication of the range of arrangements offered through unified combatant commands in their "deployments for training"), see U.S. Department of Defense and Department of State (2004: Ch. 3). Training by special operations forces through the Joint Combined Exchange Training (JCET) program has for a number of years served as a means of circumventing congressionally imposed restrictions (for example, forbidding IMET to the Indonesian military from 1992 to 2005 because of its human rights abuses) on contact with certain armed forces (Priest 2003: Chs. 8–10). A study of the School of the Americas is Gill (2004).

17 U.S. Defense Institute of Security Assistance Management (2005: Chs. 4, 21, 23); U.S. Department of Defense and Department of State (2004: Ch. 3); Singer (2003); Vitalis (2002).

18 Agee (1975: 117–130, 243–256). The operations in Ecuador helped contribute eventually to the overthrow of the elected president, and then, some months later, of his successor. On the more general issue of CIA payments and other forms of routine support of state officials, journalists, union leaders, and so forth, the best sources are memoirs and biographies of former CIA officers (e.g., Copeland 1989; Prados 2003; Holm 2003; Paseman 2004), although

these, understandably, omit many of the types of day-to-day details laid out in Agee's diary-based text. Official collections, such as *FRUS*, have only recently begun to include CIA operational documents, and then only the ones bearing on major covert actions. One exception is the online collection of 5120 documents (U.S. Central Intelligence Agency 2003) on the overthrow of Guatemala's president in 1954 (we will discuss this case in the next chapter): many of the documents point to the kind of routine payments detailed by Agee. On the role of U.S. labor unions, see Rathbun (1996); Morgan (1999); and, on more recent activities, Sims (1992).

19 "CIA Paid Millions to Jordan's King Hussein," *Washington Post*, 18 February 1977, "White House Reviewing Intelligence Operations," 19 February 1977; "More Heads of State are Reported to Have Received C.I.A. Payments," *New York Times*, 19 February 1977; Kempe (1990: 83); *Counterpunch*, 26–27 June 2004. See note 23 for references to payments to politicians in wealthy countries.

20 Gasiorowski (1991: 91–92, 116–121); Agee (1975: 295, 525–526); Santo Domingo to State, 3 August 1965, *FRUS 1964–1968*, vol. 32: doc. 119; Green to State, Airgram A-74, 10 August 1966, *FRUS 1964–1968*, vol. 26: doc. 386; King Hussein interview with Hasanein Heikal, *al-Ahram*, 27 September 1963, quoted in Ali (2003: 88). The U.S. Federal Bureau of Investigation provided the Chilean regime with information about an opponent of the regime who was arrested in Paraguay; he was transferred to Chilean custody and disappeared there: "F.B.I. Watched an American Who was Killed in Chile Coup," *New York Times*, 1 July 2000. On Mexico, an account of the former CIA head of station is revealing (Morley 2008: esp. Ch. 7).

21 Rempe (1999); McClintock (1992: Ch. 7); NSAM 114, 22 November 1961, and NSAM 132, 19 February 1962, both *FRUS 1961–1963*, vol. 8: docs. 59, 72; NSAM 177, 7 August 1962, *FRUS 1961–1963*, vol. 9: doc. 150. On current police aid via narcotics control and anti-terrorism assistance, see U.S. Department of State (2005b: 75–102, 142–153); we count at least six programs with funding going to 32 countries, most of them U.S. clients, although in some of these cases, the local partners are the armed forces rather than the police.

22 Armony (1997: 9–12; 2005); Haugaard (1997); Prados (2003: Chs. 11–12); Langguth (1978: 312–313); Hersh (2004); Suskind (2006); McCoy (2006); Sands (2008); Mayer (2008); "Bush Vetoes Bill That Would Limit Interrogations," *New York Times*, 8 March 2008. Mitrione spent a number of years advising Latin American internal security forces; he was kidnapped and executed by Uruguay's Tupamaro guerrillas in 1970.

23 McGeorge Bundy, referring to the continuation of the covert subsidies to Italian political parties as late as 1965: Memorandum for the Record, 28 June 1965, *FRUS 1964–1968*, vol. 12: doc. 113 (the actual phrase Bundy used was that the subsidies were an "annual shame"). There were apparently CIA payments to the Liberal Democrats in Japan up through the early 1970s, as well as a so-called "M-Fund" that had been used by U.S. military intelligence and was then turned over to the Japanese: "C.I.A. Spent Millions to Support Japanese Right in 50's and 60's," *New York Times*, 8 October 1994; Johnson *et al.* (1995).

24 For example, economic assistance and grants to Belgium went from almost $230 million in fiscal year 1950 to $59.8 million the following year, to $9.2 million the year after that, and to $1.1 million one year later. Economic aid to France tailed off abruptly in fiscal year 1954 and practically ended the next year. For the Netherlands, economic aid crashed to $3.1 million in fiscal year 1953; for Norway, in fiscal year 1954; and for the United Kingdom, in fiscal year 1956 (with a sharply reduced amount the year before). Portugal and Japan showed a similar pattern, with economic aid going to zero in fiscal years 1952 and 1953, recovering to modest amounts for a few years, then going down to tiny amounts in fiscal year 1958. For Germany and Japan, economic aid declined in fiscal year 1954 to a fraction of what it had been, though modest sums then continued to be provided. Only in Greece did economic aid continue at significant levels (though still lower than through the early 1950s). All data from U.S. Agency for International Development (2005).

25 Block (1977: 141–143, 247 n4). In the early 1960s, the U.S. began to receive "offsets" of its overseas military expenditures from some host countries but these did not cover all the costs.

26 Milward (1984); Eichengreen (1993).

27 Griffiths (1997); Herter to Eisenhower, 24 November 1959, *FRUS 1958–1960*, vol. 4: doc. 26; *FRUS 1958–1960*, vol. 7, pt. 1: docs. 81, 83, 85, 87, 89, 93, 95–98, 100, 103, 105–108, 117; Führer (1996: 14); Pagani (2002).

28 Block (1977: Ch. 7); Eichengreen (1996: Chs. 4, 5).

29 The numbers are calculated by adding together "ODA/OA Commitments from DAC Countries Combined to Individual Recipients" (Organisation for Economic Co-operation and Development 2005a: 86–87) for 2003, for all U.S. client states and for all other recipients, and dividing those totals by total populations for those states (see Table 2.1 for the data source). The DAC figures include U.S. bilateral aid, but in fact, the U.S. only accounts for a quarter of all DAC commitments (Organisation for Economic Co-operation and Development 2005b: Table 1) and subtracting the U.S. amounts from the totals does not appreciably change the per capita figures.

30 The original institution created to apply export controls was the Co-ordinating Committee for Multilateral Export Controls (COCOM), set up in 1950 and headquartered in an annex to the U.S. embassy in Paris. Japan, a non-NATO state, became a member two years later. Other non-NATO members adopted policies compatible with COCOM controls. In 1994, COCOM disbanded but its members continued applying controls; the following year, a new institution, the Wassenaar Arrangement on Export Controls for Conventional Arms and Dual-Use Goods and Technologies, was set up and pursues similar policies (Cupitt and Grillot 1997; Wassenaar Arrangement 2004).

31 When we use the phrase "refrain from such help to U.S. enemies," we do not mean that wealthy clients fall into lockstep with the U.S. on matters such as trade embargoes. Rather, the point is that, at the very least, wealthy clients do not even try to make up most of the resource flows cut off by the U.S.; and quite often, they agree with the U.S. assessment of the state in question and differ, if at all, only on tactics. An example of the former situation is the reaction by Western European nations to the U.S. embargo on Nicaragua in the 1980s: the aid and trade credits they provided were only a fraction of what was lost and not even as much as the Soviet Union provided (LeoGrande 1998a: 428–431, 689–690). An example of the latter, particularly striking in light of subsequent disagreements, is the general Western European agreement in 1964 that only minimal trade should occur with Cuba and that there should be no credits granted (*FRUS 1964–1968*, vol. 32: docs. 241, 255). In recent years, the same situation has arisen with regard to Iran, with Europe and Japan vacillating between active diplomatic pressure alongside the U.S. and tacit, though grudging, acquiescence in U.S. Treasury-led financial sanctions. "The March 20, 2008 US Declaration of War on Iran," *Japan Focus*, 22 March 2008.

32 Barnhart (1997); Gallicchio (1997).

33 Dillon to Eisenhower, 15 January 1960, *FRUS 1958–1960*, vol. 7: doc. 99 (and ftn. 1); Memorandum of Conversation, 21 June 1961, *FRUS 1961–1963*, vol. 22: doc. 336 (and footnote. 1).

34 Other U.S. clients being considered for possible membership (as of 2008) are Chile and Israel.

35 International Institute for Strategic Studies (2008: 443–450). The data are for 2006; the second through twelfth countries are (in order) China, Russia, the U.K., France, Japan, Germany, Italy, Saudi Arabia, South Korea, India, and Australia.

36 Lovett to Harriman, 3 December 1948, *FRUS 1948*, vol. 3: 306; Kaplan (1980: 27).

37 Final Communiqué, North Atlantic Council, 18–19 December 1950, North Atlantic Treaty Organization (2005); Kaplan (1980: Chs. 6–8).

38 Becker and McClenahan (2003: 127–128); U.S. Department of State (2004c: France/Defense).

39 Suto to Marquat, 12 February 1952; Dodge, "Japan: Post-Treaty Relationship," 17 January 1952, both quoted in Kolko and Kolko (1972: 533); the language is similar, though more prolix, in NSC 125/2, "United States Objectives and Courses of Action with Respect to Japan," 7 August 1952, *FRUS 1952–1954*, vol. 14, pt. 2: 1300–1308. Good general histories of Japanese rearmament are Dower (1972) and Brands (1986). Direct sales data from U.S. Department of State (2005b: 588).

40 U.S. Department of State (2004c); Canada Department of National Defence (1994: Ch. 5); Australia Department of Defence (2004: pars. 69–86); Moores (2002); Stenlås and Nilsson (2004). Data on military assistance and arms sales are from the sources discussed in note 58. New Zealand, which signed its Mutual Defense Assistance agreement with the U.S. two months after the ANZUS Pact went into effect, is the only one of the wealthy clients with whom the U.S. does not appear to have a production agreement.

41 U.S. Defense Institute of Security Assistance Management (2005: Ch. 2); figures derived from U.S. Department of State (2005b: 555, 592, 624). The numbers we report are for deliveries; authorizations for direct commercial sales are considerably higher but may fall through or be

stretched out over several years. It is worth noting, though, that the State Department's projections (U.S. Department of State 2005b: 592) for fiscal year 2006 commercial deliveries are almost $21 billion, as contrasted with $7.6 billion in 2004. Government sales are also likely to increase: the Defense Department's notifications of possible sales for Australia alone, from May 2004 to May 2005, come to $1.7 billion (U.S. Defense Security Cooperation Agency (2005)).

42 Data on defense arrangements from U.S. Department of State (2004c). For an example of pride, see Canada Department of National Defence (2005).

43 Japan, of course not a member of NATO, helped out financially, contributing some $10 billion to the U.S.-led effort (U.S. Department of Defense 1992: 725).

44 Gibbons (1986: Chs. 2, 3); Hack (2001: 286).

45 Schwartz (2001); "Fourth Report of the Secretary General on the United Nations Mission in Sierra Leone," 19 May 2000, S/2000/455, par. 69; UN Security Council Resolution 1299 (2000), 19 May 2000; "Third Progress Report of the Secretary-General on the United Nations Operation in Côte d'Ivoire," 9 December 2004, S/2004/962, paras. 17–18; Statement by the President of the Security Council, 6 November 2004, S/PRST/2004/42. In recent years, the U.S. has paid around a quarter of the costs of each of the above UN peacekeeping operations, while also providing logistical support (in many cases, channeling the funds through private contractors) to West African peacekeepers active in these missions (Whelan 2003). This is in addition to direct funding of training for potential peacekeeping forces through bilateral and multilateral means (see below).

46 Statement by Rusk to the Belgian ambassador (Scheyven), 21 August 1964, quoted in Gleijeses (2002: 68); on the different episodes, see also Lemarchand (1976); Weissman (1979); Mangold (1979); Odom (1988); Schatzberg (1989); and Schraeder (1994: Ch. 3).

47 Interview by de Villepin (French foreign minister), *Le Figaro*, 10 July 2003; UN Security Council Resolution 1497 (2003); "Report of the Secretary-General to the Security Council on Liberia," 11 September 2003, S/2003/875, pt. 3; UN Press Release 11 July 2003, SG/A/848/Rev.1; GlobalSecurity.org (2004a); UN Security Council Resolution 1529 (2004); "Report of the Secretary-General on Haiti," 16 April 2004, S/2004/300. Interestingly, when the UN peacekeeping force for Liberia, UNMIL, was first created, it had 151 troops from the U.K. and only three from the U.S. (UN Department of Peacekeeping Operations 2003). Once the initial Multinational Interim Force in Haiti was replaced by the longer-term UN peacekeeping operation MINUSTAH, France and Canada also withdrew most of their troops.

48 Jones (2005); Serafino (2005).

49 Figures calculated from Grimmett (2004: 3–4, 60, 84) and Stockholm International Peace Research Institute (2005: Table 10.1). The first of these sources covers arms transfer deliveries for calendar year 2003, expressed in constant 2003 U.S. dollars, including "weapons and ammunition, military spare parts, military construction, military assistance and training programs, and all associated service" (ibid., p. 2). The second source covers major conventional weapons – but not "small arms/light weapons, trucks, artillery under 100-mm calibre, ammunition, support equipment and components, [or] services or technology transfers" (ibid., p. 523) – for calendar years 2000–2004, expressed in constant 1990 U.S. dollars.

50 Armony (1997, 2005).

51 Ganser (2005).

52 Lefebvre (2003); Rudner (2004); and, for a general bibliographical listing, Clark (2005: Intelligence Liaison).

53 Segell (2004); e-Journal USA (2004); Archick (2005); Mayer (2005); "CIA Expanding Terror Battle Under Guise of Charter Flights," *New York Times*, 31 May 2005; Council of Europe (2007).

54 Economic assistance, military assistance, and nonconcessional loan figures from U.S. Agency for International Development (2005); arms sales figures from U.S. Defense Security Cooperation Agency (2004) and predecessor volumes (some available online at http://www.dsca.osd.mil/data_stats.htm). For details of which volumes were used to construct the arms sales series and how they were pieced together, see the website for this book. All figures in current dollars were converted into constant 2003 dollars using a Gross Domestic Product deflator, available online at http://www1.jsc.nasa.gov/bu2/inflateGDP.html. These sources apply to Figures 4.1 through 4.7, and to 4.10. The bar charts for each of the four different "client types" shown in Figure 4.1 (and also Figures 4.2, 4.3, 4.7, and 4.10) are constructed from a

sample of countries which have been clients since the early post-World War II era; for each country, we calculated what percentage of the total resource flows from 1946 to 2003 fell into each of the four budget categories, then averaged those percentages across the countries in the sample for that client type. Here are the countries for each sample: wealthy clients receiving reconstruction aid after World War II: Belgium, Denmark, France, Germany (earlier, West Germany), Italy, Japan, Netherlands, Norway, and United Kingdom; wealthy clients not receiving reconstruction aid: Australia, Canada, New Zealand, Saudi Arabia, and Sweden; less wealthy clients: Greece, Portugal, South Korea, Spain, and Turkey; and poor clients: Chile, Colombia, El Salvador, Guatemala, Indonesia, Jordan, Liberia, Mexico, and Pakistan (neither Indonesia nor Jordan became clients until the 1960s, but we included them to give greater geographical balance).

55 The amount of economic assistance sent to the poor countries in our sample actually dropped from the first to the second period, in 2003 constant dollars, from $39.2 billion to $33.4 billion; this in spite of the fact that two of the states did not even become clients until the 1960s and that all the states underwent significant population increases.

56 There was a secret attempt under Reagan to sell arms to Iran in exchange for the release of hostages in Lebanon, which, when knowledge of it leaked out, was considered so scandalous that to this day, the U.S. refuses to sell arms (and tries to discourage others from doing the same) to Iran.

57 Figure 4.7 covers all 28 countries listed in endnote 54. Figure 4.8 is drawn from U.S. Agency for International Development (2005) for all states in the world, converted to constant 2003 dollars. It does not include arms sales, as our figures on those sales do not cover every country.

58 The data used for the tables and figures in this section (except for Figure 4.10, which involved the sources and sample used earlier in the chapter, and Figure 4.14, for which see below) come from U.S. Department of State (2005b: 553–555, 566–567, 587–592, 617–622) and from project approval figures in World Bank (2004c [both the IBRD and the IDA]); Inter-American Development Bank (2005a); Asian Development Bank (2005); European Bank for Reconstruction and Development (2005); African Development Bank (2005); and (for population) U.S. Central Intelligence Agency (2005). Depending on the source, data cover either calendar or fiscal year 2004. Economic assistance category includes funding under the following bilateral programs: Child Survival and Health, Development Assistance, Economic Support, Assistance for Eastern Europe and the Baltic States, Assistance for the Independent States of the Former Soviet Union, as well as multilateral funding from the international or regional institutions listed above as sources. Aid from multilateral agencies is multiplied by the percentage of votes in each agency controlled by the U.S. Military assistance includes funding under the following programs: Foreign Military Financing, International Military Education and Training, the Andean Counterdrug Initiative, and International Narcotics Control and Law Enforcement. (It is impossible to get country breakdowns for other Defense Department forms of military assistance.) Arms sales include transfers under the following programs: Foreign Military Sales, Direct Commercial Sales, and Excess Defense Articles Grants. For exchange rate conversions, as well as details and justifications of data sources, see the book website. In order not to double count military aid, foreign military financing is not counted when calculating total resource transfers; this is why the three categories of resource transfers do not add up to the total. In fiscal year 2004, the U.S. disbursed some $18 billion in Iraq as part of a special fund; this figure was not included in our totals, nor was the cost of U.S. military operations there.

59 Figures for arms sales in Figures 4.11 and 4.12 are net of foreign military financing. On wealthy clients' arms sales to Africa see, for example, "U.K. Arms Sales to Africa Reach £1 Billion Mark," *Observer* (London), 12 June 2005. On U.S. counterterrorist training (the Pan-Sahel Initiative, its successor, the Trans-Sahara Counterterrorism Initiative, and other programs), see Hartung and Berrigan (2005) and LeMelle (2008).

60 The map in Figure 4.13 is derived from the data sources listed in note 58 above and pertains to 2004. Since then, the U.S. has become increasingly concerned about Pakistan and has poured nearly $10 billion into various security-related programs for that country (see Chapter 5).

61 Combined military and economic aid figures from U.S. Agency for International Development (2005); federal budget outlays ("on-budget") from U.S. Office of Management and Budget (2005: Table 1.1).

5 Client maintenance by interventions

1 Our definition of intervention is closest to that used by international lawyers (e.g., Brownlie 1963: 44–45; Jennings and Watts 1996: 428–434; Cassese 2004: 98–100), even if our emphasis on taking over tasks is more programmatic than theirs. Note that intervention, on this account, need not be counter to the will of the intervened-in state (cf. Hoffmann 1984). The important point is that intervention need not be military in nature, something implicitly recognized in other authors' work on clients (Gasiorowski 1991: 18–19; Morley 1994: Ch. 1).

2 Helman and Ratner (1993: 3); Gros (1996: 456); Krasner (2004: 85). Failed states were the subject of a major CIA-funded study by prominent academics in the 1990s: see Goldstone *et al.* (2000). Most of the failed states typically cited are essentially patronless, hence the concern in the literature for interventions sponsored by multilateral institutions.

3 Southeast Asia Task Force to Kennedy, "A Program of Action to Prevent Communist Domination of South Vietnam: Appraisal of the Situation," 26 April 1961 (*Pentagon Papers* 1971: vol. 2, 36). The quip at the time was that Laos, in which the U.S. was also considering introducing combat troops, was the reverse of Vietnam: hopeless but not critical.

4 Majeski and Sylvan (1999).

5 Munro (1974: Chs. 2–3).

6 Healy (1988: 182–186).

7 Schwartz (1997); Henning (1999: Ch. 3); Bordo and Schwartz (2001). From the time of the ESF's creation in 1934 up to, but not including, the financial rescue of February 1995, Mexico had been offered ESF loans (usually in the form of six-month "swap" arrangements between dollars and pesos) totalling $27.3 billion in current dollars, although not all of those loans ended up being drawn on; after the 1995 rescue, another $18 billion was offered through 2002 (U.S. Department of the Treasury 2005).

8 The word "crisis" comes from Acheson (1969: Ch. 26); for the sense of panic about France and Italy, see Kolko and Kolko (1972: Ch. 13) and Leffler (1992: 157–164, 188–198).

9 U.S. General Accounting Office (1996); Henning (1999: Ch. 6); Rubin and Weisberg (2003: Ch. 1); Clinton (2004: 641–645); Jim Hoagland, "More to It Than the Peso," *Washington Post*, 15 February 1995. On earlier Mexican financial rescue operations and the role of the IMF, see Gold (1988) and Lustig (1977).

10 NSC 1/1, "The Position of the United States with Respect to Italy," 14 November 1947, *FRUS 1948*, vol. 3: 724–726; Barnes (1981: 412); Miller (1983).

11 National Security Act; U.S. Congress, Senate (1976); *FRUS, 1945–1950*: docs. 241–268; Daugherty (2004: Ch. 7).

12 "F. Mark Wyatt, 86, C.I.A. Officer, is Dead," *New York Times*, 6 July 2006; NSC 1/3, "Position of the United States with Respect to Italy in the Light of the Possibility of Communist Participation in the Government by Legal Means," 8 March 1948, *FRUS 1948*, vol. 3: 775–779; Barnes (1981); Daugherty (2004: Ch. 7). At one point, the State Department's director of policy planning lost his cool and advocated outlawing the Communist Party and reoccupying the country militarily: Kennan to Marshall, 15 March 1948, *FRUS 1948*, vol. 3: 848–849.

13 *FRUS 1964–1968*, vol. 31: docs. 147–148, 158, 161, 245–269; *FRUS 1964–1968*, vol. 32: docs. 423, 431, 433, 439;

14 LeoGrande (1998a: 160, 249–250, 627, 646); Sulehria (2004); "The Bush Administration Takes Heat for a CIA Plan to Influence Iraq's Elections," *Time*, 4 October 2004; Hersh (2005b).

15 The key moment came when, after demonstrations broke out after some days of relative quiet, the U.S. ambassador telephoned the Korean Defense Minister and told him to pass on to Rhee the message that he should "consider his future political role." Within hours, Rhee announced that he was willing to resign (which he did, and in a few days flew to Hawaii). Seoul to State, 26 April 1960, *FRUS 1958–1960*, vol. 18: doc. 308; also docs. 299–319. It was reported at a White House meeting on 27 April (doc. 313) that the ambassador and the U.S. commanding general were spontaneously cheered the next time they appeared in public, something which worried Eisenhower.

16 Bonner (1987: 362–376); Shultz (1993: 610–628); "Marcos Reported to Lose Support in Administration"; "U.S. Sees Marcos Losing High Aides"; "Challenge to Marcos: How It Looks From Washington; Days of Decision: As Options Narrow, U.S. Moves Against an

'Old Friend'"; "Washington's Harder Line on Despots," all *New York Times*, 26 January, 17, 25 February, 2 March 1986.

17 *FRUS 1961–1963*, vol. 12: docs. 373–374, 384; *FRUS 1964–1968*, vol. 32: doc. 329; Shultz (1993: 620–623); "Haitian Conflict Imperils U.S. Aid; Protests Against Duvalier Escalate," *Washington Post*, 22 December 1985; "U.S. Acts to Reduce Aid to Haiti, Charging Human Rights Abuses," *New York Times*, 31 January 1986; "U.S. Laid Groundwork for Duvalier's Departure, Officials Say," *Washington Post*, 8 February 1986; "Duvalier Flees Haiti to End Family's 38 Years in Power; General Leads New Regime; Jamaica Said to Play a Key Role in Persuading Duvalier to Leave," *New York Times*, 8 February 1986; "Shultz's Words Heeded; Duvalier Saw Omen in Televised Remark," *Washington Post*, 10 February 1986; Priest (2003: Ch. 10); "U.S. Urges Suharto to Show Restraint," *Washington Post*, 2 May 1998; "U.S. Backs Indonesian Loans but Cancels Military Exercise"; "U.S. Urges Indonesia to Reform"; both *New York Times*, 9, 13 May 1998; "Clinton Administration Fears Suharto Impedes Stability," *Washington Post*, 14 May 1998; "U.S. to Appeal to Indonesian Military to Stop Crackdown"; "Unrest in Indonesia: The Policy; Halting Loans Isn't Enough, Both Parties Tell Clinton"; both *New York Times*, 14, 19 May 1998; "Washington Cool to Suharto Pledge; Suspension of IMF Bailout Likely"; "Albright Encourages Suharto to Leave Office; Suharto Should Arrange Transition of Power, Albright Says"; both *Washington Post*, 20, 21 May 1998; "Fall of Suharto: The Policy; Clinton Welcomes Suharto's Exit but Says Indonesia Still Needs 'a Real Democratic Change,'" *New York Times*, 21 May 1998; "Seven Days in May that Toppled a Titan; Back-Room Intrigue Led to Suharto's Fall," *Washington Post*, 23 May 1998.

18 Sullivan to State, "Thinking the Unthinkable," 9 November 1978, ProQuest (2005); "Carter Held Hope Even After Shah Had Lost His"; "Failing to Heed the Warning Signs of Iran's Revolution"; "As Turmoil Turns to Crisis, the U.S. Urges a 'Crackdown'"; "Vance, Predicting Disaster, Deflects Call for Toughness"; "Vance, for a Moment, Turns the President Around on Iran," all *Washington Post*, 25–29 October 1980; Sullivan (1981); Brzezinski (1983: Ch. 10); Vance (1983: Chs. 14–15); Sick (1985: 114–156 [attaché quote on 156]); Kennedy (2004); U.S. Agency for International Development (2005).

19 Sources for the list of insurgencies and extended terrorist campaigns against the regime: Correlates of War Intra-State War Data Set, V 3.0 (Sarkees 2000); PRIO/Uppsala Armed Conflict Dataset, V 3.0 (Eriksson and Wallensteen 2004); and Armed Conflicts Events Data, V Beta 1.2 (Wars of the World 2003). Interventions are coded using the measurement rules listed in the nodes in this section of the chapter, on the basis of primary and secondary sources. The coding is conservative, as there are several cases of insurgencies for which we have not been able to obtain enough information to ascertain if interventions in fact occurred; we have therefore coded those cases as nonintervention. Specific numbers and percentages are as follows: out of 92 states that at one time or another have been clients, 48 (52 percent) of these have had one or more rebellions. Of those 48 states, 21 (44 percent) experienced U.S. military interventions aimed at putting down those rebellions.

20 Little (2003: 106). Some 11,000 tons of equipment, including tanks, were sent in one month.

21 National Security Action Memorandum No. 111, 22 November 1961, *FRUS 1961–1963*, vol. 1: doc. 272; *Pentagon Papers* (1971: vol. 2, Chs. 1, 6); Sheehan (1988: bks. 1, 3, 4); Newman (1992: Chs. 8–13, 19); Clarke (1988: 59, Chs. 10, 18, 20, 24). The account of the battle of Ap Bac is from Sheehan (1988: 228).

22 Munro (1934: 51). The other example in this period is the Salvadoran government's emergency purchase of weapons from the U.S. to put down a rebellion in 1932, but this is a peculiar case in several ways (see chapter four, note 9). For the most part, the U.S. did not resort to emergency military aid and advisers in Central America and the Caribbean, in part because the marines were ready to hand, in part because the client militaries were rarely short of arms, and in part because the U.S. did not in that era have large stocks of weapons readily available for sale to foreign armies.

23 U.S. Department of State (1949: 346, 357, and more generally, Ch. 7; see also doc. 135, app. D; and docs. 170–174). This is the so-called "China White Paper" issued after the fall of the Nationalist regime and its flight to Taiwan.

24 Bacevich *et al.* (1988); Corum (1998); Valenzuela and Rosello (2004); Coutsoukis (2005).

25 Sec. 1004, National Defense Authorization Act of 1991, 104 Stat. 1485; Sec. 1033, National Defense Authorization Act of 1998, 111 Stat. 1629; "U.S. Military Contractors Involved in

Colombian Gun Battle," *Scotsman*, 23 February 2001; Serafino (2003: 1–2); Vaicius and Isacson (2003: 3); Veillette (2005: 1); Bouvier (2005: 2); Center for International Policy (2005: 1); U.S. Agency for International Development (2005 [most recent version contains 2006 data]). The statement about narcoterrorists comes from the testimony of the head of Southern Command (U.S. Congress, House 2004a: 2). The same legislation which authorized spending on "counter-terrorist" activities also provided $99 million to "train, equip, and assist" two Colombian battalions to protect 75 miles of an oil pipeline – jointly owned by the state oil company and the U.S.-based Occidental Petroleum – from guerrilla attacks (Washington Office on Latin America 2005).

26 "Specialists in Suits Train New Iraqi Army," *Scotsman*, 30 September 2003; Singer (2003: Ch. 13; 2005; 2007). In addition to the training, other PMCs directly provide protection services and participate in interrogations (Scahill 2007; Shorrock 2008).

27 Gates in testimony before the House of Representatives Armed Services Committee, 15 April, 9:30 A.M.; Cohen (2007); U.S. Government Accountability Office (2008); "U.S. Hopes to Use Pakistani Tribes Against Al Qaeda," "U.S. Plan Widens Role in Training Pakistani Forces in Qaeda Battle," "U.S. Lacks a Pakistan Plan, Report Finds," all *New York Times*, 19 November 2007, 2 March 2008; 18 April 2008; "Going Native: The Pentagon's New Pakistan Plan," MotherJones.com, 6 March 2008.

28 This point should not be exaggerated: the fact that, for over a century, there was no other combination of a competent client and a formidable foe does not imply that such a combination could not have occurred anywhere else. If in fact the provision of emergency military aid and advisers had succeeded in building up a client's army and suddenly the foe became much tougher, we can imagine that U.S. officials would have decided that they had no option except to send ground troops for open-ended combat.

29 H.K. Johnson [the Army Chief of Staff] to McNamara and Chiefs of Staff, "Report on Survey of the Military Situation in Vietnam," 14 March 1965: 15, 1, 10, Lyndon B. Johnson Library, National Security Files (NSF), Country File Vietnam; *Pentagon Papers* (1971: vol. 3: 433–62); Gibbons (1989: 148–181, 194–205, 225–237); McNamara to Johnson, 21 April 1965, *FRUS 1964–1968*, vol. 2: doc. 266; "Memorandum on Reactions to a US Course of Action in Vietnam," 21 April 1965: 6, Lyndon B. Johnson Library, NSF, Country File Vietnam.

30 Sheehan (1988: 536); Ball to M. Bundy, "A Compromise Solution in South Viet-Nam," 1 July 1965; M. Bundy to McNamara, 30 June 1965; Rusk to Johnson, "Viet-Nam," 1 July 1965, all *FRUS 1964–1968*, vol. 3: docs. 40, 35, 39; Gibbons (1989: Chs. 5–6); *Pentagon Papers* (1971: vol. 3: Ch. 4).

31 This argument is taken from Ellsberg (1972) who, as a marine in Vietnam, an adviser to high officials in the Defense Department, and a co-author (and later, leaker) of the *Pentagon Papers*, was in a position to know.

32 McNaughton to Bundy, Unger, McNamara, and Vance, "Action for South Vietnam," 10 March 1965, *FRUS 1964–1968*, vol. 2: doc. 193.

33 Cumings (1990: Ch. 15).

34 Muccio to State, 25 June 1950, *FRUS 1950*, vol. 7: 126; State to Truman, 24 June 1950, Truman Presidential Museum and Library (2003); Truman to Elsey, 27 June 1950, Truman Presidential Museum and Library (2003); Kirk to State, 25 June 1950; MacArthur to JCS and State, 30 June 1950; both *FRUS 1950*, vol. 7: 139, 249.

35 Muccio to State, 1 July 1950, *FRUS 1950*, vol. 7: 273; Paige (1968: 261); Truman (1956: 347); Halliday and Cumings (1988: 82); Lay to NSC, "Future United States Policy with Respect to North Korea," 17 July 1950; NSC 81/1, "United States Courses of Action with Respect to Korea," 9 September 1950 [approved by Truman 11 September 1950]; "Substance of Statements Made at Wake Island Conference on 15 October 1950," all *FRUS 1950*, vol. 7: 410, 712–721, 953, 949; Stueck (1983).

36 Cumings (1990: Ch. 11); for accurate assessments of China see, for example, Clubb to Rusk, 1 November 1950; India, as reported in Rusk, Memorandum of Conversation, 6 October 1950, Annex 4; and Burma, as reported in Key to State, 14 November 1950; all *FRUS 1950*, vol. 7: 1023–1025, 896–897, 1147.

37 By our reckoning, the U.S. carried out life preserver interventions in Cuba in 1912–13, and 1917; and in Panama in 1904, 1918, and 1925 (Munro 1934: 33–35, 38–42, 91, 94–95, 98–99).

38 "Agreement Between the United States and Nicaragua Establishing the 'Guardia Nactional de Nicaragua,' Signed December 22, 1927, *FRUS 1927*, vol. 3: 434–39; Cox (1927: Ch. 5, apps. 3–4); Stimson (1927); Munro (1934: Ch. 6); Nalty (1961); Jennings (1986); Schoultz (1988: 260–271); Lindvall-Larson (2002). The quote on Mexico is by Coolidge in his message to Congress of 10 January 1927; the claim about Sandino is by the then-chargé d'affaires of the U.S. who, incidentally, negotiated the details of the 1927 agreement on the National Guard (Munro 1934: 259). For a sense of the opposition, both foreign and domestic, to the decision to send the Marines back to Nicaragua, see the articles in the *New York Times* of 29, 30 December 1926; 9, 12, 14 January, 24 February, 10 March ("Coolidge Policy Under Hot Fire of Senate Critics"), and 25 March 1927.

39 Barno (2004: 9); O'Hanlon and de Albuquerque (2005: Foreign Military Troop Levels); Powell (2005); GlobalSecurity.org (2005a); "Coalition Steps Up Raids as Afghan Elections Approach"; "G.I. Death Toll in Afghanistan Worse Since '01'"; both *New York Times*, 20, 22 August 2005; Katzman (2008: 59); "U.S. To Deploy 3,200 Marines to Afghanistan," American Forces Press Service, 15 January 2008. The phrases about the initial combat troop deployment are from the U.S. secretary of defense, quoted in GlobalSecurity.org (2005a: Operations). OEF operations in fact aimed at three enemies: the Taliban, al Qaeda (these mostly involved small Special Forces units), and the Hezb-e-Islami Gulbuddin group.

40 Eisenhower Doctrine speech, 5 January 1957; Little (1996: 27, 35–36, 43), Dulles to McClintock, 13 May 1958, *FRUS 1958–1960*, vol. 11: docs. 31, 75, 84, 106, 112, 123 [quotes on failure to intervene], 127, 141–143, 146, 209–210; J-3 to Joint Chiefs of Staff, "Lessons Learned from the Lebanon and Quemoy Operations," 31 December 1958: 20, quoted in Gendzier (1997: 312 n51); "A U.S. Ship Lands 18 Tanks in Beirut"; "U.S. and Britain to Send 50 Jets to 3 Arab Lands"; "Dulles Sees Gain by U.N. in Lebanon"; "Back of Rebel Drive Broken, Beirut Says"; "Chamoun Backers Shift to Opposition After U.S. Landing"; "U.S. and Britain Will Limit Intervention"; "Presence of U.S. Forces in Lebanon Fails to Step Up Fighting"; "Iraq is Recognized by U.S. After Giving U.N. Pledges"; all *New York Times*, 29 May, 11 June, 2, 3, 18, 18, 22 July, 3 August 1958; Ovendale (1994: 292); Yaqub (2002: 572–575); Gendzier (1997: 20, 241–321); U.S. Agency for International Development (2005a).

41 Bush exchange with reporters, 5 August 1990; Woodward (1991: pt 2); Schwarzkopf (1992: 313–362); Powell (1995: 463–497); Bush and Scowcroft (1998: 2328–2478).

42 Mangold (1979); Odom (1993: Ch. 3); "Washington Seems to Favor Assistance Given Zaire Regime"; "C.I.A. Denies Aiding Recruitment of Mercenaries to Fight in Zaire," both *New York Times*, 9, 17 April 1977; "The Proxy War in Zaire," *Newsweek*, 25 April 1977.

43 Mangold (1979); Odom (1993: Chs. 4–7); Van Nederveen (2001: 47–52); "French Commander in Zaire Says Troops Will Stay Until an International Unit Arrives"; "Saudis Said to Offer Their U.S.-Made Arms for Zaire's Defense"; "U.S. Planes to Ferry French Out of Zaire and Fly in Africans"; all *New York Times*, 24 May, 2, 3 June 1978. In addition to the cybernetic features of the intervention – taking the planes it had intended for an evacuation and using them to transport foreign troops, much as the French had done the year before – the U.S. role in the 1978 operation was limited because of concern that neither Congress nor the public would stand for any direct commitment of U.S. troops so soon after the Vietnam War, no matter how easy the win was projected to be. The administration also claimed (unconvincingly, including to its own congressional allies) that Cuba was involved in the invasion, although not in a militarily threatening fashion.

44 Bush answer to reporters' questions, White House, 2 July 2003; Rumsfeld speech to Veterans of Foreign Wars, San Antonio, TX, 25 August 2003; Kimmitt news briefing, Baghdad, 1 April 2004; all widely available online; Cordesman (2005: 16; on training, 28–37). Cordesman sarcastically titled one section of his report (15), "Denial as a Method of Counter-Insurgency Warfare." Cheney's "last throes" remarks were made in an interview with CNN on 20 June 2005 and he reaffirmed them in a speech at the National Press Club on 19 June 2006. On the U.S. military response to the insurgency, including the "surge," see Packer (2005: Chs. 9, 16); Cockburn (2006: Ch. 16); Ricks (2006: Chs. 9, 11, 13–15, 18); Woodward (2006); Allawi (2007: Ch. 9); Dale (2008: 30, 51–59); Sanchez (2008: pt. 3).

45 Information about the Gurkhas and the other proxies discussed in these paragraphs is widely available, including on the Web. The reference to "the non-World War peak" is because several of these groups fought in both world wars.

46 Sluglett (1976: 262–270); Omissi (1990: 19–23); "A Report on Mesopotamia by T.E. Lawrence," *Sunday Times*, 22 August 1920. Winston Churchill, first as secretary of state for war, then as colonial secretary, was a particular enthusiast for the use of bombing and gas, arguing that the combination was both particularly fitting against "uncivilised tribes" and permitted cutting down the number of ground troops by tens of thousands.

47 Policy Planning Staff Memorandum, 4 May 1948; NSC 10/2; both *FRUS 1945–1950*, docs. 269, 292; U.S. Congress, Senate (1976: Bk. 4, 31–38).

48 Prados (1996: 35–36, 62–64); NSC 10/5, "Scope and Pace of Covert Operations," 23 October 1951, ProQuest (2005); U.S. Congress, Senate (1976: Bk. 1, Ch. 11); Woodward (2002: 139–143). Although the CIA sold off its proprietary airlines, it still works closely with other airlines (e.g., Aero Contractors) who do most or all of their business with the agency and whose executives had earlier worked for one of the proprietaries: "C.I.A. Expanding Terror Battle Under Guise of Charter Flights," *New York Times*, 31 May 2005.

49 Prados (1996: Chs. 5, 13); U.S. Special Operations Command (2002); Best and Feickert (2005). From time to time, turf wars have erupted between the Pentagon and the CIA (Hersh 2005a).

50 Quotations by Rusk before Senate Foreign Relations Committee, 11 April 1961; and Macmillan (1972: 347–348); Bowles to Rusk, 27 April 1961, *FRUS 1961–1963*, vol. 24: doc. 65; Gibbons (1986: Ch. 1); Lansdale to Taylor, "Resources for Unconventional Warfare," July 1961 (*Pentagon Papers* 1971: vol. 2, doc. 100); Warner (1996); Prados (1996: Ch. 14); Unger to State, 1 March 1964, *FRUS 1964–1968*, vol. 28: doc. 11; U.S. Congress, Senate (1971); Vongsavanh (1978); Castle (1993: Chs. 3–6); Leary (1999); Finlayson (2002); Troung *et al.* (2003).

51 Cohen (2000: Ch. 5); Kramer (1995); Adeleke (1995: 575–76); "West African States May Send Troops into Liberia," *Times* (London), 6 July 1990; Mortimer (1996); "The Perils of Peacekeeping," *Newsweek*, 16 November 1992; "US Agents 'Directed Air Raids in Liberia'"; "Confusion Marks US Policy on Liberia"; both *Independent*, 7, 13 November 1992; "Liberia's Crisis Tests U.S.-French Cooperation," *International Herald Tribune*, 19 November 1992; Statement by U.S. Ambassador Edward Perkins, UN Security Council, 19 November 1992; UN Security Council Resolution 788, 19 November 1992; both in Weller (1994: docs. 197–198); Gberie (2005: 61). It should be noted that contemporary accounts of the Liberian intervention presented it as an example of U.S. non-involvement, an interpretation fostered by the then-Assistant Secretary of State for African Affairs. Whether this was sour grapes at his losing the policy argument (there is considerable evidence of this), or ignorance of some of the U.S. operations (for example, the U.S. ambassador to Nigeria apparently was unaware of the naval deployment), or an aspect of the policy itself is impossible to determine.

52 MacArthur to Joint Chiefs of Staff, 28 November 1950; "Notes on NSC Meeting, November 28th, 3:00 pm, The White House"; "Note on Meeting of the National Security Council, 11 December 1950"; Acheson to United States Mission at the United Nations, 15 December 1950"; all *FRUS 1950*, vol. 7: 1237, 1244, 1520, 1550; Truman radio and television address, 15 December 1950; Joint Chiefs of Staff to Ridgway, 13 October 1951, *FRUS 1951*, vol. 7, pt. 2: 1034–1035; Murphy to State, 19 May 1953, *FRUS 1952–1954*, vol. 15, pt.1: 1057; Truman statement on General Ridgway's Korean Armistice Proposal, 7 May 1952; Bernstein (1983); Halliday and Cumings (1988: 172, 187–189, 194–201); Stueck (1995: 133, 142, 202, 306, 310, 332–333, 337); Stueck (2002: 119–123); Kimball (2003: 107–113).

53 Wheeler to Westmoreland, 7 February and 9 February 1968; McNamara in meeting of Johnson with Joint Chiefs of Staff, 9 February 1968; Wheeler to Johnson, 27 February 1968; Wheeler at White House meeting, 28 February 1968; all *FRUS 1964–1968*, vol. 6: docs. 63n1–2, 64, 68–70, 90, 91; Clifford Task Force draft report, 1 March 1968 (*Pentagon Papers* 1971: vol. 4, 563–564); Draft Memorandum for Johnson, 4 March 1968; Notes of Meeting, 4 March 1968; both *FRUS 1964–1968*, vol. 6: docs. 103–104; "Gallup Poll Reports 49% Believe Involvement in Vietnam an Error," *New York Times*, 10 March 1968; O'Brien to Johnson, 27 March 1968, *FRUS 1964–1968*, vol. 6: doc. 161; State Department official quoted in "Westmoreland Requests 206,000 More Men, Stirring Debate in Administration," *New York Times*, 10 March 1968; M. Bundy, quoting Acheson, in Notes of Meeting, 26 March 1968, *FRUS 1964–1968*, vol. 6: doc. 158; Johnson television speech of 31 March 1968; Berman (1989: 85–116, 166–90).

54 Kissinger (1979: 1372, 1383, 1465); "Agreement on Ending the War and Restoring Peace in Vietnam," Paris, 27 January 1973, Ch. 7, art. 20; Warner (1996: 343–344, 352–355); U.S. Congress, Senate (1973: 11–21); U.S. Congress, House (1974: 26–27); Brown and Zasloff (1974); Castle (1993: Ch. 8).

55 National Security Decision Directives #111, "Next Steps Toward Progress in Lebanon and the Middle East," 28 October 1983; #117, "Lebanon," 5 December 1983; #123, "Next Steps in Lebanon," 1 February 1984; all Federation of American Scientists (2003); "A Message for Damascus"; "Vow by President;" "U.S. Analysts Upgrade Opinion of Syrian Units"; "Air Power in Lebanon: Limits to Effectiveness"; "U.S. Said to Draw Plan for Shifting Marines in Beirut"; "Marine Chief Optimistic on Beirut Withdrawal"; all *New York Times*, 5 [3 articles], 7, 8, 9 December 1983; other *New York Times* articles on congressional opposition, 6, 30 December 1983, 3, 4 [containing "fairy tale" quote], 12 January 1984; on talks with Syria and Shultz's opposition, 12 January, 9 February 1984; on problems with the Lebanese army, 9, 16, 29 February; on the Lebanese government's eleventh-hour request for U.S. help, 29 February; on comparison with South Vietnam and Iran, 17 February; Pézard (2008: Ch. 8).

56 Quotations: Arneson in meeting of Intelligence Advisory Committee, 2 April 1958; "Preliminary Memorandum on Considerations for Policy Recommendations for Cuba," 25 July 1958; Special National Intelligence Estimate, "Developments in Cuba Since Mid-November," 16 December 1958; all *FRUS 1958–1960*, vol. 6. docs. 47n2, 112, 182; Pfelffer (n.d.: 1.14); A. Dulles in meeting of National Security Council, 23 December 1958; Rubottom in conference, 31 December 1958; both *FRUS 1958–1960*, vol. 6: docs. 188, 201, also docs. 158, 161, 164, 173, 186, 191, 203; "U.S. Aides Wary on Cuba's Future"; "Batista Asserts Army Ousted Him"; both *New York Times*, 2, 10 January 1959.

57 Stuart to State, 17 March 1948; report by General Barr, 1949; Truman in press conference, 11 March 1948; all U.S. Department of State (1949: 844, 325–38, 273); Marshall in meeting of National Security Council, 12 February 1948, quoted in Kolko and Kolko (1972: 540); Vandenberg in Senate, 29 March 1948; Stuart to Marshall, 6 November 1948; Minister-Counselor in Canton to State, 21 April 1948; all U.S. Department of State (1949: 352–353, 894, 306). The hope that a third force might be found died hard: in April 1949, when the communists were crossing into the south, Congress voted to let the president use whatever funds had not yet been spent from the preceding year for aid to areas not subject to communist control. This led smoothly to the $75 million in Mutual Defense funds several months later for "the general area of China" (see discussion of emergency military aid and advisers for Indochina on the book's website).

58 Ford message to Congress, 28 January 1975; Schlesinger on television, 23 February 1975; Goldwater in speech, 3 March 1975; attributed words of Kissinger and Schlesinger; all *New York Times*, 29 January, 24 February, 4 March, 27 February 1975; also articles of 31 January 1974; 8, 17 January, 26 February, 6, 7, 10, 11, 14, 19 March 1975; Kissinger in meeting, 3 March 1975 (Jespersen 2002: 451; also 447, 452); Dean to State, 6 February 1975 (Gerald R. Ford Library 2000); U.S. Congress, Senate (1975a: 2, 4–6, 21); Shawcross (1979: Chs. 22–23); Kissinger (1999: 514); Clymer (2004: Ch. 3).

59 NIE 53/14.3-2-74, "Short-Term Prospects for Vietnam," 23 December 1974 (U.S. National Intelligence Council 2005); quotations by Byrd, 28 January 1975; Kissinger, 26 February 1975; "senior Western official," 28 March 1975; attributed to Kissinger, 8 April 1975; Ford, 23 April 1975; all *New York Times*, 24 December 1974; 29 January, 27 February, 29 March, 9, 24 April 1975; also articles 19, 20, 24 March; 3, 4, 6, 11, 22 April 1975; Memorandum of Conversation: Ford, Kissinger, congressional delegation, 5 March 1975; Weyand, "Report to the President of the United States on the Situation in South Vietnam" 4 April 1975; both Gerald R. Ford Library (2000); Snepp (1977: 142–149, 279–291); Isaacs (1983: Chs. 10–11); Jespersen (2002: 450–451); Berman (2002: 267–268) reports that the CIA station chief and the U.S. ambassador in Saigon wanted to stage a coup to overthrow Thieu and replace him with a third force, but that this was not agreed to by Washington, more evidence that the situation was seen as too hopeless to do anything.

60 For example, when Bolivia had a revolution in 1952, the U.S. was favorable to it, granting emergency aid to a regime which it defended as "Marxist rather than Communist" (quoted in Lehman 1997: 193). In this particular case, there were a number of reasons, ranging from the nature of the predecessor regime to the reporting mechanisms of U.S. bureaucracies, why

Bolivia's new leaders were considered acceptable; the point is that, in a means-oriented policy making apparatus, ideological orientation is more a rule of thumb for figuring out what to do in particular circumstances (e.g., whether to insist on a purge of suspected communists) than a fundamental motive in determining the client or enemy status of a given state.

61 Munro (1934: 112–115).

62 Shultz (1993: 1052; also Ch. 48); Gilboa (1995: 588); Scranton (1991); Woodward (1991: Chs. 7–15); Cole (1995: 51–68).

63 Herter to Eisenhower, 14 April 1960; Dearborn to Mann, 27 October 1960; both U.S. Congress, Senate (1975b: 192, 195); *FRUS 1961–1963*, vol. 12: docs. 302, 307, 310–314, 323, 326–331; "Trujillo Enemies See Long Unrest," *New York Times*, 3 June 1961; Schlesinger (1965: 769–771).

64 "Venezuela Coup Linked to Bush Team," *The Observer*, 21 April 2002; Bevin and Mitchell (2005); Golinger (2007).

65 Siracusa to Wise, 29 July 1949, quoted in Gleijeses (1991: 125); Peurifoy to A. Dulles, 19 June 1954; CIA to PBSUCCESS Headquarters, 20 June 1954; both *FRUS 1952–1954, Guatemala*: docs. 208, 211, also docs. 5, 20, 40, 51, 113, 151, 165 (the "manifest threat" of U.S. troops as "the sole lever" to induce the military to desert Arbenz), 173, 185, 197, 199, 210, 214; A. Dulles to Eisenhower, 20 June 1954, *FRUS 1952–1954*, vol. 4, *Guatemala Compilation*: doc. 69; Eisenhower (1963: 421–27); Schlesinger and Kinzer (1983); Cullather (1999); Kirkland (2003: 73–75); Holland (2005).

66 Quote on elite from World Bank (2002: 3); quote on gangs from Noriega in testimony, 3 March 2004 (U.S. Congress, House 2004b: 46); Powell quote, 26 February 2004, "Powell Puts Pressure on Haitian Leader to Resign," *Washington Post*, 27 February 2004; Cheney quote in Valenzuela (2004); Stromsem and Trincellito (2003); Maguire (2003); Farmer (2004); Mitchell (2005); Hallward (2007).

67 Payne (1995: Ch. 3); "Arms Cache Found, Jamaica Declares State of Emergency"; "Jamaica's Emergency Rule Reduces Political Violence"; both *New York Times*, 20 June, 16 July 1976. The former director of the CIA indicated that Carter authorized some type of covert intervention in the summer of 1979, i.e., prior to the elections which turned Manley out of power (Gates 1996: 151, 175, 178).

68 "The President on Cuba," *New York Times*, 25 November 1933; Schoultz (1998: 299–303). Ironically, the Cuban intervention is usually cited as the first example of the Good Neighbor policy, presumably because the overthrow of Grau San Martín was carried out without U.S. troops.

69 Quotations: Bond to State, 8 September 1961; Inter-Departmental Survey Team to Kennedy, 3 November 1962; Memorandum Prepared for the National Security Council Executive Committee Meeting, 11 December 1962; all *FRUS 1961–1963*, vol. 12: docs. 214, 228, 230; also 218 (Goulart as creating an "inimical regime"); "Brazilian Policy Encourages U.S."; "Brazil Economy is Worrying U.S.", both *New York Times*, 28 April, 21 June 1963; Burton to Mann, 8 January 1964; Embassy in Brazil to State (for Gordon), 18 March 1964; Gordon to State, 28 March 1964; Gordon to State (for Rusk), 31 March 1964; all *FRUS 1964–1968*, vol. 31: docs. 181 (on the military's request for U.S. assistance), 184, 187, 197; also 186, 188, 190, 192–193; "Washington Sends 'Warmest' Wishes to Brazil's Leader," *New York Times*, 3 April 1964; Stepan (1971: pt. 3); Gribbin (1979); Green (2003).

70 Rusk to Gordon, 30 March 1964, *FRUS 1964–1968*, vol. 31: doc. 194.

71 Saccio to State, 30 June 1966, *FRUS 1964–1968*, vol. 31: doc. 137.

72 A list of clients in this category is available on the website; we count 34 former or current clients out of 89 total, with a number of those states having experienced more than one coup. We constructed the list from histories and chronologies contained in standard secondary sources (none of the widely available political science data sets have a comparable "*coup d'état*" variable extending back as far as the late nineteenth century).

73 Helms, Memorandum/Genesis of the Project, 16 September 1970; CIA to Santiago, 21 September 1970; CIA to Santiago, 16 October 1970; all U.S. Congress, Senate (1975b: 228, 243); U.S. Central Intelligence Agency (2000: 13); U.S. Congress, Senate (1975c: pt. 3); Hersh (1983: Chs. 21–22).

74 The 1973 Chilean case is just below the threshold for inclusion in the list of coups at the start of this section; the Korean case, in which the U.S. had the power easily to stop the coup but did not (see below) is just above the threshold.

75 Thailand, quote: Bangkok to State, 20 September 1957, *FRUS, 1955–57*, vol. 22: doc. 524; also docs. 475, 486; Pakistan, quote: Karachi to State, 31 October 1958, *FRUS, 1958–60*, vol. 15: doc. 334; also docs. 321–22, 324; Turkey: *FRUS, 1958–60*, vol. 10, pt. 2: docs. 354, 356, 365; Ecuador: "Washington Sees Gain for Ecuador," *New York Times*, 14 July 1963; Agee (1975: pt. 2); Fitch (2005: 50); Argentina, quote: State to Buenos Aires, 26 March 1962, *FRUS 1961–1963*, vol. 12: doc. 178n6; Greece, quote: Athens to State, 22 April 1967, *FRUS 1964–1968*, vol. 16: doc. 277; also docs. 225, 245, 251, 255, 259–261, 264–265, 267–273, 275–276, 278–284, 286, 289–292. The examples discussed in this paragraph are all drawn from the later 1950s and 1960s, not because there have been no U.S.-supported coups since then, but because documents released before that date usually do not include cable traffic involving military attachés and the CIA; and because at the time of writing, there have been no systematic document releases for U.S. policy toward many countries since 1969.

76 The U.S. had supported Prime Minister Sharif and warned publicly that it would "strongly oppose any attempt to change the government through extra-constitutional means." But after Sharif was overthrown just a few weeks later by the head of the armed forces, General Musharraf, diplomatic condemnation went hand-in-hand with pragmatic cooperation and, notably, complimentary statements about Musharraf himself. (It did not hurt that Musharraf was viewed as a "good guy" by the commander-in-chief of the U.S. Central Command, whom he telephoned immediately after the coup to explain his actions.) "In Pakistan, Hold on Power Grows Tenuous"; "Army Gets a Foothold in Pakistan"; "Pakistan's Coup Leader: Strongman or Statesman?" ("I don't believe he is an extremist; quite the opposite," according to the U.S. ambassador); "Commonwealth Group Penalizes Pakistan" (the U.S. "will have to do business" with Musharraf); "Coup Puts U.S. Ideals and Interests to a Test" ("we crafted a process in the middle"); all *Washington Post*, 10, 16, 19, 19, 20 October 1999; "The Uses of a Coup" (by a former national security adviser: "in the short term, military control is inevitable and in Pakistan's interest"), *New York Times*, 14 October 1999; "good guy": quoted in Priest (2003: 112, also 109–114).

77 Dulles to Kennedy, 16 May 1961; State Department statement, 16 May 1961, quoted in State to Seoul, same date; both *FRUS 1961–1963*, vol. 22: docs. 217, 216; also docs. 213–215, 218–223 (doc. 218, in which Magruder – who had the previous year released South Korean troops to help Rhee during the first demonstrations – makes clear to Lemnitzer on 17 May how easily he could stop the coup, is poignant; doc. 221, Johnson to Rostow, 23 May, detailing U.S. options, none of which involves acting against the coup leaders, is briskly cynical).

78 For example, barely three months after Diem was overthrown in South Vietnam, his successor, General Minh, was toppled with clear U.S. complicity. A year later, the general who led the coup against Minh was himself deposed after a long campaign against him by the U.S. ambassador and a coup actively shaped by the top U.S. general in the country (Kahin 1986: 182–202, 294–305).

6 Hostile interventions against enemy states

1 Pitt, speech in the House of Commons, 3 February 1800; Paul Nitze, NSC 68, "United States Objectives and Programs for National Security," 14 April 1950 (ProQuest 2005).

2 Wilson, annual message to Congress, 4 December 1917. McKinley's message to Congress on Cuba, 11 April 1898, said practically nothing about Spain. As regards Italy, even Roosevelt's famous "hand that held the dagger" speech (10 June 1940) said nothing about the Mussolini regime but only its foreign policy; over the next few years of fighting, the only time the U.S. showed any serious interest in the nature of the Italian regime was in the summer of 1943, when following the invasion of Sicily, Mussolini was forced from power. At that point, the issue became how to work with the successor Badoglio government, even though this implied the continuation of the monarchy and of military dominance (*FRUS: The Conference at Washington and Quebec*: 516–609, 808–824). By the time the Yalta conference was being prepared, the provisional Italian government was already being referred to by the British and Americans as a normal interlocutor, even though fighting was still taking place (*FRUS: Malta and Yalta*: 276–283).

3 NSC 135/3, "Reappraisal of United States Objectives and Strategy for National Security," 25 September 1952, p. 9; NSC 5603/1, "U.S. Policy Toward the Soviet Satellites in Eastern

Europe," 18 July 1956, p. 2; both ProQuest (2005); Nixon in NSC meeting, 12 July 1956 (Byrne 2002: doc. 2); Haynes to Rostow, "Check List of African Problems," 8 June 1966, *FRUS 1964–1968*, vol. 24: doc. 212; U.S. Agency for International Development (2005).

4 Draft statement, Hull to Roosevelt, 11 August 1943, *FRUS: The Conference at Washington and Quebec*: 509. The U.S. has had many nonstate adversaries since the inception of its client state empire, including the Berber chief Raisuli in 1904 (who had kidnapped a former U.S. citizen), the Mexican revolutionary Villa in 1916, the former Congolese prime minister Lumumba in 1960, various Palestinian leaders beginning in the 1970s, the Colombian drug lord Escobar in the early 1990s, and since at least 1998, the Saudi Arabian jihad organizer Bin Laden.

5 Stimson to Borah, 8 September 1932, *FRUS 1933*, vol. 2: 778–779; Browder (1953: Chs. 3–6); Morris (1962).

6 The standard international law definitions of intervention (Chapter 5, note 1) much more typically presuppose what we are calling hostile interventions than they do interventions on behalf of clients. We will return below to the question of UN approval of hostile interventions.

7 The UN Charter prohibits member states from threatening or using force against each other, except for purposes of self-defense, without the approval of the Security Council. By most construals of the Charter, U.S. actions against Serbia and Iraq were therefore contrary to international law (Simma 1999; Sands 2005: Ch. 8), though as we shall see, the U.S. took care in both cases to construct a multilateral armed coalition and to obtain a Security Council resolution after hostilities had ended. The justification of overt intervention against states committing barbaric or uncivilized acts stretches back to the nineteenth century and more recently has been evoked in support of "humanitarian" intervention (Gong 1984; International Commission on Intervention and State Sovereignty 2001).

8 Eisenhower in meeting of the National Security Council, 29 April 1954, *FRUS 1952–1954*, vol. 13, pt. 2: 1440; Rusk in meeting with Kennedy, 8 February 1961, *FRUS 1961–1963*, vol. 10: doc. 40.

9 Little (2004: 678–683). There were separate coup plans in 1956 and 1957.

10 U.S. Congress, Senate (1975b: 181n); Sa'adi quoted in Little (2004: 696); Hashim (2003: 17–25). Some months after the first 1963 coup, the CIA's role in planning it and transmitting names for execution was revealed by another recipient of covert largesse, King Hussein of Jordan (Batatu 1978: 986; see also "A Tyrant 40 Years in the Making," *New York Times*, 14 March 2003). The U.S. role, if any, in the 1968 coup is murky: "Ex-U.S. Official Says CIA Aided Baathists," Reuters, 20 April 2003.

11 Joint Chiefs of Staff to McElroy, "Indonesia," 18 April 1958; Special National Intelligence Estimate 65–60, "The Short-Term Outlook in Indonesia," 3 May 1960; both *FRUS 1958–1960*, vol. 17: docs. 68, 252; also docs. 88, 107, 145–146, 238, 293; Bissell testimony, U.S. Congress, Senate (1975b: 4n1); CIA Far Eastern Division [probably FitzGerald], "Indonesian Perspectives," 22 March 1961, attachment in Bissell to Bundy *et al.*, 27 March 1961; Memoranda of Conversations, 26–29 November; both *FRUS 1961–1963*, vol. 23: docs. 155, 322; also docs. 152, 287, 291, 325; Djakarta to State, 6 March 1964; Djakarta to State, 19 March 1964; CIA, Political Action Paper, 19 November 1964; Memorandum for the 303 Committee, "Progress Report on … Covert Action in Indonesia," 23 February 1965; Jones to W. Bundy, 23 April 1965; M. Bundy to Johnson, 30 June 1965; Djakarta to State, 5 October, 2 December 1965, 10 August 1966; Green in briefing to Humphrey, 17 February 1967; all *FRUS 1964–1968*, vol. 26: docs. 33n4, 40, 86, 110, 120, 125, 147, 179, 185, 229; also docs. 64–65, 76, 89, 118, 124, 135–137, 148, 155, 160, 163–164,171–173, 177, 180, 189–190, 192, 195, 203, 205, 214, 232; Hilsman (1967: Chs. 25–27); Bunnell (1976; 1990 [esp. p. 59 n152]); Chomsky and Herman (1979: 208); Scott (1985); Brands (1989); Easter (2005); "Ex-Agents Say CIA Compiled Death Lists for Indonesians," *Spartanburg (SC) Herald-Journal*, 19 May 1990. During 1964 and 1965, Britain was also engaged in covert military operations against Indonesia, with the aim being to hamper Indonesia's similar operations against Malaysia; during the army's war against the PKI, Britain, Australia, and Malaysia disseminated propaganda.

12 Frontline (2001); Bush and Scowcroft (1998: 489); "Anti-Saddam Operation Cost CIA $100 Million," *Washington Post*, 15 September 1996; Cockburn and Cockburn (1999: Chs. 7, 9); Byman (2000–2001); Baer (2002: Chs. 14–18); Ritter (2005: 11–14, 17).

13 Rositzke (1975: 335); NSC 20/4, "U.S. Objectives with Respect to the USSR to Counter Soviet Threats to U.S. Security," 23 November 1948 (ProQuest 2005: 10); Philby quoted in Dorril (2000: 498); also NSC 58/2, "United States Policy Toward the Soviet Satellite States in Eastern Europe," 8 December 1949 (ProQuest 2005: par. 37); Prados (1996: Ch. 2); Dorril (2000: Chs. 14–16); Mitrovich (2000: Ch. 1). Rositzke was in the OSO (intelligence gathering and psychological operations) part of the CIA which, at the beginning of the Ukraine operation, was pressed into service as the organization most knowledgeable about the Soviet Union.

14 Foreign Office official, quoted in Dorril (2000: 366); Joyce in White House-State-Defense meeting, quoted in Powers (1979: 44–45); Bevin in Memorandum of Conversation, 14 September 1949, *FRUS 1949*, vol. 6: 415; also 438; Dulles, quoted in Prados (1996: 59); Macarger, quoted in Berger (1995: 14); also "West Held Easing Stand on Albania"; "Soviet Officials Restricted to Belgrade; Get Treatment Given Yugoslavs in Russia"; "Anti-Red Radio and Leaflets Spur Political War on Satellite Regimes"; "Axis Supporters Enlisted by U.S. in Postwar Role"; all *New York Times*, 27 March 1950, 31 March, 9 April 1951, 20 June 1982; CIA, "Current Situation in Albania," ORE 71–49, 15 December 1949 (U.S. Central Intelligence Agency 2006); Barnes (1982: 657–658); Heuser (1989: 75–80); Berger (1995: 12–15); Prados (1996: 45–52); Dorril (2000: Ch. 19). The Greeks, Italians, and Yugoslavs also began running operations in Albania, all with equally dismal results.

15 Joint Chiefs of Staff to Secretary of Defense, "Strategic Assessment of Southeast Asia," 10 April 1950 (*Pentagon Papers* 1971: vol. 1, doc. 3); also NSC 118/2, "United States Objectives and Courses of Action in Korea," 20 December 1951 (ProQuest 2005); "U.S. Arms 'Seen' on Burma Raiders"; "Chinese in Burma in Opium-Gun Deal"; both *New York Times*, 11 February, 9 March 1992; Lansdale to Taylor, "Resources for Unconventional Warfare, S.E. Asia," July 1961 (*Pentagon Papers* 1971: vol. 2, doc. 100); Office of Current Intelligence, CIA, "Chinese Nationalist Irregulars in Southeast Asia," 29 July 1961 (U.S. Central Intelligence Agency 2006); Schaller (1976); Robbins (1979); Leary (1984); Foot (1985); Belanger (1989); McCoy (2003); Lintner (1994); Holober (1999); Kaufman (2001); Callahan (2003); GlobalSecurity.org (2005b). The same organization created by the CIA to run the coastal raids also ran raids by ethnic Muslim horsemen in the far west of China.

16 "Current Basic United States Policy Towards Cuba," in Rubottom to Murphy, 23 October 1959, *FRUS 1958–1960*, vol. 6: doc. 376 (approved by Eisenhower 9 November: doc. 387n3); also docs. 423, 446, 454, 462, 486; King to Dulles, 11 December 1959, quoted in Pfeiffer (n. d.: 28–30, also 46–49); 5412 Committee to Eisenhower, "A Program for Covert Action Against the Castro Regime," 16 March 1960 (Ulbrich 2002); Bissell interview with Pfeiffer, 17 October 1975 (National Security Archive 2001: 27, 28); CIA Headquarters to senior agency officer in Guatemala, 31 October 1960, quoted in Gleijeses (1995: 10); statement by planner to Cuba Study Group, 26 April 1961; Johnson to Rusk, 22 July 1961; both *FRUS 1961–1963*, vol. 10: docs. 176, 251; also docs. 197, 202, 205, 214, 223, 227, 244, 250, 254, 258, 269–270, 272–278, 280–288, 291–297; Lansdale quoted in U.S. Congress, Senate (1975b: 140; also 171–180); Lansdale, "Meeting with the President, 16 March 1962," s.d. (Mary Ferrell Foundation 2006); Harvey to McCone, "Operation Mongoose – Appraisal of Effectiveness and Results which can be Expected from Implementing the Operational Plan Approved at the Meeting of the Special Group (Augmented) on 16 March 1962," *FRUS 1961–1963*, vol. 10: doc. 323; also docs. 359–360, 367, 371–380, 399, 413, 423; McCone, "Meeting at the White House concerning Proposed Covert Policy and Integrated Program of Action Towards Cuba," 19 June 1963, *FRUS 1961–1963*, vol. 11: doc. 348; also docs. 8, 10, 14, 19, 231, 261, 272–274, 302–307, 309, 311, 313, 318–320, 323, 346, 350–351, 354, 365, 368, 375–376, 388; *FRUS 1964–1968*, vol. 32: docs. 259, 296, 298; also "Inspector General's Survey of the Cuban Operation and Associated Documents," 16 February 1962 (U.S. Central Intelligence Agency 2006); Inspector General, "Report on Plots to Assassinate Fidel Castro," 23 May 1967 (Mary Ferrell Foundation 2006); Prados (1996: Chs. 10–11); Rabe (2000); Husain (2005).

17 Woodward (1987: 27, 111–112); Bruck (2006); Hersh (2006); "On Cheney, Rumsfeld Order, US Outsourcing Special Ops, Intelligence to Iraq Terror Group, Intelligence Officials Say," *Raw Story*, 13 April 2006; "In the Club: Iran, Iraq and America," *Economist* 15 April 2006: 47–48; "Iran Says U.S. Aids Rebels at Its Borders," *Los Angeles Times*, 15 April 2008.

18 Shultz (1993: 292–297); Woodward (1987: 240–241, 256). Shultz wanted to give naval support to a Dutch overt intervention (an option the Dutch flatly refused); proposals for covert raids

(including by Korean commandos) were knocked down in both Congress and the State Department.

19 Saunders to Haig, "Background for Your Talk with Kurdish Leaders," 23 June 1972 (*FRUS 1969–1976*, vol. E-4: doc. 318; also docs. 301, 313, 315, 319, 321–322, 325); Kissinger assessment, n.d.; Kissinger to Nixon, 29 March 1973; both Kissinger (1999: 581, 585); "2 Iraqi Fighters Downed in North," *New York Times*, 17 December 1974; Chief of Station to Colby, 10 March 1975; Kissinger, quoted; both in U.S. Congress, House (1976: 215, 198).

20 U.S. Congress, House (1976: 218 n481); Ford in NSC Meeting, "Angola," 27 June 1975 (National Security Archive 2002: doc. 6); Kissinger in conversation with Davis, 16 July 1975 (Kissinger 1999: 807; and generally Ch. 26); Stockwell (1978: 188); "S. African Regulars Fight Inside Angola," *Washington Post*, 23 November 1975; P.W. Botha, 17 April 1978, quoted in Gleijeses (2002: 299; and generally Chs. 13–16); "Yet Another Saudi Connection," *Time*, 29 June 1987; "What Congress Didn't Ask," *New York Times*, 23 November 1987; Bender (1988); McFaul (1989–90); Tvedten (1992); Shultz (1993: Ch. 50); Pereira (1994); Scott (1996: Ch. 5); Potgieter (2000); Hanhimäki (2004: 408–422); Gleijeses (2006). Note that even during Carter's presidency, the U.S. was still favorable to UNITA (Bender 1987: 128 n12). Ironically, in the fighting of 1992–94, the MPLA government had to rely on a South African private security company, Executive Outcomes, which accounts for the fact that the peace accords of 1994 required all mercenaries to be withdrawn (Howe 1998; Angolan Government and UNITA 1994: Annex 3.II.6). To support itself financially, UNITA had to rely on a diamond trade analogous to that of the narcotics sold by other U.S.-supported forces (Human Rights Watch 1999: Ch. 9).

21 National Security Decision Directive 57, "United States Policy Towards the Horn of Africa," 17 September 1982 (Federation of American Scientists 2003); Cohen, statement to House Subcommittee on African Affairs, "Political Crisis in Ethiopia," *Department of State Dispatch*, 24 June 1991; Henze, quoted in "Having Won the Civil War, Ethiopia's Present Regime Must Now Keep the Peace," *New York Times*, 22 September 1991; also 22 May, 16 August [on CIA covert funding], 24 August 1986, 21 June 1987 [on Saudi funding of the Eritrean rebels], 28 November 1988, 20 April, 7 August 1989, 14 February, 6, 22 March, 17 April, 22 September, 24 October 1990, 14 December 1990, 30 January, 28, 30 May 1991; also (on Saudi funding) 12 July 1986, 21 June 1987; "Ethiopian Security Police Seized, Tortured CIA Agent," *Washington Post*, 25 April 1986; Pascoe (1987: 10–11); Ottaway (1991); Schraeder (1992); Vollman (1993: 11–13); Tareke (2002); Gleijeses (2006: 13–16). For the last year or so of the Derg, it received military aid from Israel in exchange for its permission to let Ethiopian Jews emigrate. The U.S. strongly encouraged the latter and thus by implication the former.

22 Al-Nasser to president of the Security Council, "Report of the Monitoring Group on Somalia Pursuant to Security Council Resolution 1630 (2005)," S/S2006/229, 4 May 2006, p. 15; "Somalia Blames US for Backing Mogadishu Warlords," washingtonpost.com, 4 May 2006; "U.S. Denies Funding Warlords," *The Nation* (Nairobi), 11 May 2006; "Alliance of Somali Warlords Battles Islamists in Capital"; "Efforts by C.I.A. Fail in Somalia, Officials Charge"; both *New York Times*, 13 May, 8 June 2006; "US Accused of Covert Operations in Somalia," *Observer* (London), 10 September 2006; Stevenson (2007); "The CIA and Fatah; Spies, Quislings and the Palestinian Authority," *Global Research*, 21 June 2007; Rose (2008 [with documents]).

23 Stimson to Wilson, 22 September 1931, *FRUS 1931*, vol. 3: 26; Grew to Stimson, 23 February 1933; Stimson in conversation with Japanese ambassador, 5 January 1933; Green to airplane part manufacturers, 1 July 1938; all *FRUS Japan*, vol. 1: 110, 107, 201; Stimson, letters to *New York Times*, 7 October 1937, 11 January 1940; Grew to Hull, 12 September 1940, *FRUS 1940*, vol. 4: 602; Stimson, diary entry, 16 October 1941 (Stimson 1973); Grew to Hull, 3 November 1941, *FRUS Japan*, vol. 2: 704; Stimson, diary entry, 25 November 1941 (Stimson 1973); Churchill to Roosevelt, 26 November 1941, quoted in Feis (1950: 318); Molotov in Byrnes–Molotov meeting, 27 July 1945, Bohlen minutes, *FRUS: The Conference of Berlin (The Potsdam Conference)*, vol. 2: 450; Harriman to Byrnes, 11 August 1945, *FRUS 1945*, vol. 6: 629; also U.S. Congress, Joint Committee on the Investigation of the Pearl Harbor Attack (1946: app. D); Feis (1950); Langer and Gleason (1952: 577–606, 719–723; 1953: Chs. 2, 10, 20); Esthus (1963); Anderson (1975); Iokibe (1981); Reynolds (1981:

58–62, 182–185, 222–250); Heinrichs (1990); Alperovitz (1995: pts. 1, 5, 6); Hasegawa (2005: Chs. 4, 6).

24 UN General Assembly, GA/RES 195 (III), 12 December 1948, GA/RES 293 (IV), 21 October 1949; UN Security Council, S/RES 82, 25 June 1950, S/RES 83, 27 June 1950, S/RES 84, 7 July 1950; UN General Assembly, GA/RES 376 /V, 7 October 1950; Smart to Randolph and Mayo, n.d., quoted in Crane (1999: 911); Weyland to U.S. Air Force Headquarters, 29 April 1952; Lovett in Cabinet meeting, 12 September 1952; both quoted in Bernstein (1983: 292, 296).

25 References to the First Opium War can be found in any standard history; on the British and French bombardment of the Parana River from 1845–50, see Graham-Yooll (1983: 79–94; also 152–165 on French and German gunboat operations against Venezuela in 1902–03).

26 Schelling (1960: 196, 195; also 1966: Chs. 1, 4); George *et al.* (1971); Griffith (1994); Pape (1996); Lebow (1998); Lindqvist (2001); Hastings (2008: Ch. 12).

27 M. Bundy to Johnson, "Planning Actions on Southeast Asia," 22 May 1964, *FRUS 1964–1968*, vol. 1: doc. 167; Stevenson in conversation with Johnson, 27 May 1964 (Beschloss 1998: 373; also 362–378); "Six-Day Battle at Binh Gia Ends in Defeat for Saigon;" U.S. intelligence sources, quoted in "Infiltration From North Vietnam Now Held Bigger"; Nixon, quoted in "Nixon Asserts U.S. Risks Defeat Soon in Vietnam Conflict"; all *New York Times*, 3, 27 January (2 articles) 1965; W. Bundy to Rusk, "Notes on the South Vietnamese Situation and Alternatives," 6 January 1965; M. Bundy to Johnson, "Your Meeting with Couve de Murville at 11:30 This Morning," 19 February 1965; both *FRUS 1964–1968*, vol. 2: docs. 15, 143; also Kahin (1986: Chs. 10–11); Porter (2005: Chs. 6–7).

28 Lodge to Johnson, 15 May 1964, *FRUS 1964–1968*, vol. 1: doc. 157; Taylor in Honolulu meeting, 20 April 1965, quoted in McNamara to Johnson, 21 April 1965; Taylor to State, 8 March 1965; *FRUS 1964–1968*, vol. 2: docs. 265, 187n6; McNaughton, "Some Observations about Bombing North Vietnam," 18 January 1966 (*Pentagon Papers* 1971: vol. 4: 42); "'Two Wars' in Vietnam," *New York Times*, 4 March 1965; Pearson in meeting with Johnson, 28 May 1964, reported in Ball to Lodge, 30 May 1964, "Ellsberg Defense Accuses U.S. of Suppressing Documents," *Washington Post*, 30 January 1973; also Thies (1980: Chs. 1–4); Herring (1983: VI.C.I); Gibbons (1989: Chs. 1–2). The means-centered quality of Rolling Thunder can most luridly be seen in the few months before it began, when Johnson's advisers, desperate that he respond to the situation by bombing, advanced new and contradictory goals for air strikes and even claimed that a 75 percent chance of failure still justified bombing: Bundy to Johnson, "The Situation in Vietnam," 7 February 1965, *FRUS 1964–1968*, vol. 2: doc. 84.

29 Views of U.S. military officials, reported in "Military Doubtful on Kosovo Strikes," *Washington Post*, 17 June 1998; Clark: characterization; statement in press briefing, 24 March 1999; assessments in mid- and late May (Clark 2001: 205, 203, 305, 316); "U.S. Military Chiefs Firm: No Ground Force for Kosovo," *New York Times*, 3 June 1999; Cohen, interview (Frontline 2000); also Daalder and O'Hanlon (2000); Halberstam (2001: Chs. 38–43); Stigler (2002/3); Albright (2003: Chs. 23–25). As regards nonmilitary forms of hostile intervention, there is little evidence of such attempts until the Kosovo crisis worsened in late 1998, when apparently an operation was launched to undermine Milosevic via carrots and sticks directed at his supporters in Serb industry: "Ask Not for Whom the Phone Rings," washingtonpost.com, 11 October 1999.

30 UN Security Council Resolution S/RES/1244, 10 June 1999. Annex 2 to the resolution was the text of the political agreement on 2 June, in which Yugoslavia agreed to NATO's conditions; this served as the basis for the military agreement of 9 June. The idea of NATO's Kosovo intervention as a legitimate, if illegal, use of force was put forward by a number of scholars and policy makers in the years immediately afterward and reached its high water mark with the report on "the responsibility to protect" (International Commission on Intervention and State Sovereignty 2001).

31 The U.S. objection to Tripoli, as to other of the North African ("Barbary," in European parlance) states, was exclusively to their privateering and had nothing to do with their domestic policies; this is one reason that U.S. actions were for the most part limited to naval strikes rather than to attempts at overthrowing the regimes (Whipple 1991). As regards Hawaii, the Queen was not considered a U.S. enemy in any sense and the actions on behalf of the coup plotters were purely annexationist in motive (Tate 1965: 115–185; Kinzer 2006: Ch. 1).

32 "The Worst Governed Country," *New York Times*, 2 March 1909; Knox in conversation with Bryce, quoted in Salisbury (1997: 383); Taft, State of the Union Message, 7 December 1909; Knox to Rodriguez, 1 December 1909, *New York Times*, 2 December 1909; Knox's views, as reported in "Our Attitude Unchanged;" State Department's views, as reported in "Tired of Nicaragua War"; both *New York Times*, 21 December 1909, 7 July 1910; Madriz to Taft, 13 June 1910, *FRUS 1910*: 752; also Powell (1928); Munro (1958); Buchenau (1993).

33 Unnamed "high ranking officers of the Administration," quoted in "Taft Not to Relax Watch on Mexico," *New York Times*, 20 February 1913; Wilson, ca. 22 May 1913; Wilson, quoted in Bryan to all embassies and legations, 24 November 1913; both in Link (1956: 350, 386–387); Wood, reported in Rice to Grey, 23 January 1914; Wood, quoted in Hohler, Memorandum D, Rice to Grey, 14 February 1914; both (Link 1979: 168, 250 n1); "Carranza Elated"; also "Villa Waves His Hat in Joy"; both *New York Times*, 4 February 1914; Mayo to Morelos Zaragoza, quoted in Quirk (1962: 26); "A Conversation with President Wilson," *Saturday Evening Post*, 23 May 1914 (Baker and Dodd 1926: 117); also Smith (1972: 31–42).

34 Clinton quoted in Coll (2004: 408); senior U.S. official, quoted in "Killing for the Glory of God, In a Land Far from Home," *New York Times*, 16 January 2001; draft National Security Presidential Directive, quoted in "A Strategy's Cautious Evolution; Before Sept. 11, the Bush Anti-Terror Effort Was Mostly Ambition," *Washington Post*, 20 January 2002; Tenet, meeting of 11 September 2001; Wolfowitz, meeting of 15 September 2001; Cheney, meeting of 11 September 2001; discussion by Rice and others, meeting of 15 September 2001; Powell, meeting of 29 October; all Woodward (2002: 33, 83, 33, 83, 275); also Priest (2003: Ch. 7); U.S. National Commission on Terrorist Attacks Upon the United States (2004: Ch. 10); Schroen (2005); Berntsen and Pezzullo (2005); Crumpton (2005); Andres *et al.* (2005/06); and Feith (2008: Chs. 1, 3, 4).

35 State Department legal paper, quoted in "Target Qaddafi," *New York Times Magazine*, 22 February 1987, p. 71; Shultz in press conference, 17 April 1986, *New York Times*, 18 April 1986; also Shultz (1993: 677–687).

36 "U.S. Stages 2nd Airstrike in Somalia; Ethiopians Leaving Capital," *Washington Post*, 24 January 2007; "U.S. Used Base in Ethiopia to Hunt Al Qaeda," *New York Times*, 23 February 2007; Stevenson (2007).

37 Most of the cases listed in this paragraph are discussed in the text or on the book's website. For additional details, see the report of the Church committee on this subject (U.S. Congress, Senate 1975b) and, on Lumumba in particular, Devlin (2007: Ch. 8).

38 "Bush Gives Green Light to CIA for Assassination of Named Terrorists," *Guardian*, 29 October 2001.

39 U.S. Congress, Senate (1975b: 181–190); Cullather (1999: app. C); Hosmer (2001: Ch. 2); Richelson (2002).

40 Reagan, 8 April 1982, quoted in Williams (1997: 134); National Security Decision Directive 105, "Eastern Caribbean Regional Security Policy," 4 October 1983 (Federation of American Scientists 2003); U.S. official, quoted in "Reagan Sought to End Cuban 'Intervention,'" *Washington Post*, 6 November 1983; also Woodward (1987: 287–298); Menges (1988: Ch. 2); Shultz (1993: Ch. 20); Beck (1994); Gates (1996: 125–126, 143); Williams (1997).

41 An Act to Establish a Program to Support a Transition to Democracy in Iraq (Iraq Liberation Act of 1998), 31 October 1998, 112 Stat. 3178; Rumsfeld, in meeting of 2:40 PM, 11 September 2001 (Cambone 2001); Clarke (2004: 32); Woodward (2002: 82–83); Rumsfeld in meeting with Franks, 27 November 2001 (Franks 2004: 315); Rycroft to Manning, "Iraq: Prime Minister's Meeting, 23 July," 23 July 2002, "The Secret Downing Street Memo," *Sunday Times*, 1 May 2005; Authorization for Use of Military Force Against Iraq, 16 October 2002, 116 Stat. 1498; UN Security Council, S/RES 1441, 8 November 2002, S/RES 1483, 22 May 2003; also "How the US Set a Course for War in Iraq," *Financial Times*, 26 May 2003; Burrough *et al.* (2004); Hersh (2004: pts. 4–6); Woodward (2004); Mann (2004: Chs. 15, 19–21); (Meyer 2005: Ch. 22); Packer (2005: Chs. 1–4); Sands (2005: Ch. 8); Suskind (2006); Ricks (2006: Chs. 4–6); Gordon and Trainor (2006: Chs. 1–9); Risen (2006: Chs. 3–5); "German Intelligence Gave U.S. Iraqi Defense Plan, Report Says;" "Bush Was Set on Path to War, Memo by British Adviser Says"; both *New York Times*, 27 February, 27 March 2006; Feith (2008: Chs. 1, 6–12); Hoyle (2008).

42 The totals discussed above are derived from the lists of interventions at the start of each section of this chapter. When on occasion we have distinguished between interventions of the same type against the same enemy in the lists, we have done so because the interventions were widely separated in either time (e.g., 10 years difference), space (e.g., Tibet versus coastal China), or both. Ambiguous cases: we coded Nicaragua as a success, because even though the contras failed militarily, the war so drained Nicaragua that it provoked the electoral defeat of the Sandinistas. Afghanistan was also a success, in that it resulted in the expulsion of the Soviet-backed regime. However, the Cambodian operation is listed as a failure since the Vietnamese-backed regime stayed in power. We coded the intervention by aid to internal armed forces in Somalia and the intervention by punctuated military operations against Iran via the MEK and separatist groups as failures (at least at the time of writing).

43 Kissinger, in conversation with Nixon, 14 February 1972; Kissinger, in meeting with Zhou Enlai, 10 July 1971; "China Covert Action Program," 24 October 1972; all *FRUS 1969–1976*, vol. 17: docs. 192, 140, 257; also the Shanghai Communiqué, 27 February 1972; Brzezinski to Mondale, Vance, and Brown, "People's Republic of China," Presidential Review Memorandum/NSC 24, 5 April 1977 (ProQuest 2005); Tyler (1999); Goh (2005); U.S. Department of State (1991); Womack (1996); Manyin (2005); Zoubir (2002); Jentleson and Whytock (2005/06); *FRUS 1969–1976*, vol. E-4: docs. 224–235, 237–239 [the actions described in these steps are almost textbook examples of how to normalize relations]. In both the China and Vietnam cases, domestic politics played a permissive role. Nixon, as a leading anticommunist Republican, could open up to China in a way which the Democrats, accused of "losing" China and then having to fight against it in the Korean War, could not. Similarly, it was only when Clinton received protective backing from Vietnam War veterans of both political parties that he was able to clinch the deal with Hanoi.

44 Smith (1996); LeoGrande (1998b); Brenner *et al.* (2002); Ronen (2002); Dagne (2006); Syria Accountability and Lebanese Sovereignty Restoration Act of 2003, 17 Stat. 2482, 12 December 2003 (listing no fewer than 11 separate complaints about Syria); Hinnebusch (2005); Prados (2003); Iran and Libya Sanctions Act of 1996, 110 Stat. 1541, 5 August 1996; Chubin and Green (1998); Katzman (2006); Ansari (2006); "In 2003, U.S. Spurned Iran's Offer of Dialogue," *Washington Post*, 18 June 2006; North Korean Human Rights Act of 2004, 118 Stat. 1287, 18 October 2004 (again with a long list of complaints); Cumings (1997: 457–487; 2003: Ch. 2); Niksch (2006). In 2008, the U.S. reached an agreement with North Korea but whether it would be fully implemented was unclear at the time of writing.

7 The persistence of client-state imperialism

1 Kennedy (1987): xvi, 514, 533; also Gilpin (1981).
2 Stiglitz and Bilmes (2008); Belasco (2008). Note that if in fact the war's costs begin to affect future budgets, this may include a failure to replace equipment and rebuild the military to its state of readiness before the war began, thereby lowering the cost somewhat. On the other hand, the $3 trillion figure is for the federal budget only; other, very real costs, such as the loss of future output from combat deaths and family members taking care of the wounded, or the diversion of expenditures from output-producing investments such as schools and roads, or the rise in oil prices provoked by the war, add another $1.5 trillion to the bill.
3 "A Shortage of Troops in Afghanistan: Iraq War Limits U.S. Options, Says Chairman of Joint Chiefs," *Washington Post*, 3 July 2008; USA Today/Gallup Poll, 24 April 2008.
4 Appropriated funds for intelligence agencies such as the CIA and the NSA are hidden in accounts for other departments, notably that of the Defense Department.
5 Data for Figure 7.1 come from the entries for "Military defense" and for "GDP," both in USGovernmentSpending.com (2008); those data, in turn, are from the *Budget of the United States Government* and, for years prior to 1962, from the *Historical Statistics of the United States*.
6 Zakaria (2008), Ch. 6; speeches by McCain and Obama, 15 July 2008.
7 "Pentagon Plans to Send More than 12,000 Additional Troops to Afghanistan," USNews.com, 19 August 2008 ("Now that just means we have to figure out a way to get [the troops] there"); "Stronger U.S. Role Likely in Afghanistan," *Christian Science Monitor*, 12 August 2008. Although for several years, U.S. officials were actively contemplating the use of U.S. armed force against Iran, this was understood to be limited to specific, highly limited air

strikes. There was no particularly outrageous event, such as Bishop's murder in Grenada or the attacks of 9/11, that had occurred and was seen as justifying a U.S. ground campaign or even a sustained air war. Instead, U.S. policy makers were limited to accusations against Iran for its nuclear program and its supposed provision of roadside bombs to Iraqi insurgents: acts that were seen as sufficient to justify a one-time U.S. air strike against the relevant nuclear and/or bomb-production/insurgent-training facilities but certainly not enough to trigger an overt war.

8 There are numerous examples of claims (e.g., Summers 1982; Walton 2002) that the U.S. was not militarily defeated in the Vietnam War but instead squandered a victory or was prevented, by political pressures, from fully achieving a victory. As the dialogue from one Hollywood comedy ("A Fish Called Wanda") put it, "Shut up. We didn't lose Vietnam. It was a tie." A more detailed discussion of tactical learning is in Sylvan and Majeski (2007).

9 Concern over another Vietnam-style intervention also played a role, as we saw in chapter five, in Congress's prohibition of funds for a proxy war in Angola. However, there were other concerns at the time, including over links to South Africa; and as we also saw, within ten years, Congress repealed its earlier legislation and acquiesced in a new proxy war.

10 Quotations: Eisenhower in NSC meeting of 8 January 1954, *FRUS 1952–1954*, vol. 13: 949; Kennedy, colloquy in Senate, 6 April 1954, cited in Gibbons (1984): 204; unnamed official quoted in Woodward (1987: 174); Reagan, speech before the Veterans of Foreign Wars, 18 August 1980.

11 Iraq Study Group (2006); Wright and Reese (2008); Obama remarks on detainees and Afghanistan, 18 June 2008.

12 Mueller (2005: 53–54; 1973). Mueller's conclusions about Iraq were initially criticized by other political scientists on the grounds that the public will support casualties if a war is being "won" (Gelpi *et al.* 2005/06), but as he subsequently pointed out (Mueller 2006) in an exchange with one of those authors, most respondents interpret "success" as related to casualties and to the U.S. stakes in the war.

13 Acheson, Vance, Ball, all in Notes of Meeting, 26 March 1968, *FRUS 1964–1968*, vol. 6: doc. 158; Halberstam (1972: 653); Baritz (1986: Ch. 7); "Fatigue Cripples U.S. Army in Iraq," *Observer* (London), 12 August 2007; "America's Medicated Army," *Time*, 5 June 2008.

14 Weinberger, "The Use of Military Power," speech before National Press Club, 28 November 1984; Albright, reported by Powell (1995: 576); Halberstam (2001: Chs. 4, 25). It is unclear just how interested either Bush or Clinton were in sending combat troops to the Balkans.

15 Lippmann (1922); Lindsay and Smith (2003); Mueller (2005); "Poll: 70% Believe Saddam-9/11 Link," USAToday.com, 26 September 2003; "Polls, Truth Sometimes at Odds," CBSNews.com, 12 September 2007.

16 Crowl (1981); Carlisle (1974); Rieff (2005); Halper and Clarke (2005); Mearsheimer and Walt (2007: Chs. 4, 6).

17 Raymond and Kegley (1990), with numerous citations to other studies.

18 Although there is an extensive literature on the end of the cold war, most of it has nothing to do with client acquisition and very little with client intervention. A partial exception, with the principal concern being Eastern Europe, is Danner (1997). (The literature on the post-9/11 world, another candidate for an event symbolizing a structural shift, is focused on U.S. military action and the role or absence of the United Nations.) Similarly, the literature on the end of the cold war had little to say in general about the prospect of intervention against enemies other than the Soviet Union, the one exception being whether China would at some point become a military adversary of the United States (e.g., Layne 1997). Other literatures – for example, whether the world would become multipolar or unipolar, dominated by a "hyperpower" United States (Ikenberry 2001; Haass 2008) – are equally difficult to connect in a straightforward way to the macro-continuity of U.S. client and enemy policy.

19 Bowles to Kennedy, Rusk, and Hamilton, 21 February 1962, quoted in Little (1988: 509); Woodward (2002: 129, 172 [referring to Uzbekistan]).

20 CNA Corporation (2007: 6); see also Pumphrey (2008: Chs. 2, 6, 7); Podesta and Ogden (2007–08); and U.S. Congress, House (2008b).

21 Natsios (2008); Powell, quoted in "U.S. Promises on Darfur Don't Match Actions," *Washington Post*, 29 October 2007.

22 Pew Global Attitudes Project (2008: 21, 33–34).

23 Pew Global Attitude Project (2006; 2008); Ponce, quoted in "Ecuador's Leader Purges Military and Moves to Expel American Base," *New York Times*, 21 April 2008. Other countries whose governments began carrying out similar policies are Bolivia ("Evo Morales Supports Expulsion of Interventionist U.S. Agency From Bolivia," Digital *Granma* Internacional, 27 June 2008) and, to a much greater degree, Venezuela ("US-Venezuela Military Cooperation Indefinitely Suspended," venezuelanalysis.com, 25 April 2005; see also Chapter 5).

24 The mission of the U.S. troops was highly limited: against only certain militias, primarily in Mogadishu, and increasingly, against the individual who led the largest enemy faction. (The U.S. also set up a secret negotiating channel with him.) For these reasons, the counter-insurgency is difficult to describe as a full-fledged hostile intervention; it would be more accurate to see it as a kind of late twentieth-century version of the kind of punitive raids the U.S. practiced at various times in the nineteenth and early twentieth centuries (e.g., against the Barbary "pirates" and against Pancho Villa in Mexico; see below and Chapter 6).

25 de Waal (1998); Bowden (1999).

26 "Wielding Aid, U.S. Targets Sudan; $20 Million to Be Sent to Neighbors Who Are Backing Rebel Forces," *Washington Post*, 10 November 1996; "US Steps Up Support for South Sudanese Resistance," *Middle East Intelligence Bulletin*, November 1999; Hoile (2004); GlobalSecurity.org (2005c); de Waal (2005).

27 Dagne (2002) There were also pressures from evangelical Christians and from oil interests (Huliaris 2006).

28 This reaction is not unusual. Some ten years earlier, as genocide was being carried out in Rwanda, the U.S. carefully avoided action that might be construed as opening the doors to armed intervention. In the 1970s, the U.S. did nothing to stop the Khmer Rouge from massacring its own population. In all of these cases, U.S. allies were just as silent (Power 2002).

29 "Official Pariah Sudan Valuable to America's War on Terrorism," *Los Angeles Times*, 29 April 2005; Dagne (2008). As regards triggering conditions for overt military intervention, one former official described them in this way:

> The use of U.S. airpower against Sudan would be justified, ethically or politically, in only two instances: if the Sudanese armed forces launched an unprovoked attack against the south or if Khartoum tried to violently shut down the refugee camps in Darfur and massacre or forcibly return people to their homes.
>
> (Natsios 2008: 4)

30 Logevall (1993); Gallup (1976: 1.325); Isernia (2006, esp. figs. 7.1 and 7.2); Chicago Council on Global Affairs (2007); BBC World Service Poll (2008); "A Foreign Tour but a Home Crowd," *Guardian*, 26 July 2008.

31 We use the term "hegemony" to indicate the power relationship built into the relationship between the United States and its client states; the term "ideological" (see below for a discussion) here is shorthand for the acceptance of a particular social relationship as the normal order of things. Cf. Cox (1979).

32 The definition of ideology is drawn from standard definitions found in conceptual and literature review pieces: Mullins (1972: 510); Hamilton (1987: 38); and (aimed at U.S. foreign policy) Hunt (1987: xi).

33 Hunt (1987); Layne (2006); Mann (2004) A detailed discussion of the points raised in the rest of this section can be found in Sylvan and Majeski (2008).

34 In fact, this inference is also problematic, for much the same reasons as the first step of the mapping depiction. Not all threats to client regimes are necessarily opposed by the U.S. For example, if the leftist politician is deemed about to take power, then the U.S. may decide that the best course of action is to try to befriend him.

35 For a brief account of these and other programs, see Lumpe (2002: box 1). Since that report was issued, several programs have been combined and new ones created.

36 Warner (2000). The academics, grouped under a Harvard history professor in the Research and Analysis Branch, themselves had a predecessor in the so-called Inquiry of 150 academics who accompanied Wilson to the Paris peace negotiations in 1919 as his own research staff (Shotwell 1937).

37 Marfiak (2008); see also Klare (2008).

38 Note that the discussion above is focused on clientilism. This is not to deny that U.S. policy toward enemies is also macro-continuous, but that continuity primarily involves the way in which, during different historical periods, certain types of situations trigger a shift from routinely hostile activities to hostile interventions. That triggering is also means-driven, involving the availability of policy instruments, and since the instruments in question are used mostly for client maintenance, the way in which clientilism continues across historical turning points also helps explain why hostile interventions do as well.

39 How important these changes are to the thrust of U.S. foreign policy, and how much they are attributable to the end of the cold war, are debatable questions. Certainly the Security Council was able more easily to authorize military (usually peacekeeping) operations than in the past; however, many of the countries in which the operations occurred were either clients of the U.S. or of one of the U.S.'s own clients and it is difficult to believe that had the Security Council been blocked, those states would have been left to their own devices. As to military spending, although it declined in the United States and elsewhere, the decline began some years prior to the end of the cold war; was far smaller, proportionately, than after earlier, "hot" wars; and was nonetheless considered by policy makers to have sufficiently eroded U.S. readiness that, independently of the events of 11 September 2001, there were calls to reverse direction and raise military spending again. "Defense," *Time*, 7 September 1992; Davoodi *et al.* (1999); "Defense Spending Soars to Highest Levels Since World War II," McClatchy Newspapers, 20 March 2007.

40 "A Fateful Error," *New York Times*, 5 February 1997. A useful summary of the debate over NATO's 1999 expansion, with numerous references to the various writings by opponents and supporters alike, is MccGwire (1998); also Barany (2003: Ch. 1). The arguments of Kennan, Gaddis, and others against the Kosovo war were similar to their arguments against NATO expansion; see, for example, Mandelbaum (1999).

41 Export.gov (2008). The first free trade agreement – with Israel – was made under Reagan.

42 Conn and Fairchild (1960: Chs. 8–13).

43 Cole (1983); Steele (1984); Doenecke (2000). The most important of the policy instruments developed for arms transfers to European states, Lend-Lease, was in turn used for Latin America once the war broke out.

44 Grimmett (1973); Doenecke (1979); Rothbard (2007: Ch. 8). It should be noted that a leading conservative Republican, Robert Taft, both opposed the North Atlantic Treaty and supported the Marshall Plan. There were also opponents of the Truman Doctrine on the left of the Democratic Party.

45 Livermore (1943); Karp (1979: Ch. 5); Zimmermann (2002: Chs. 7–9). On opposition to annexation, see Beisner (1968). The Yale sociologist William Graham Sumner's (1899) requisitory against imperialism is still worth reading.

46 Secs. 7, 3, Organic Act of April 12, 1900, 31 Stat. 77; Sec. 4, Philippine Organic Act (1902), 32 Stat. 691; Leibowitz (1989: Chs. 8, 9); Sparrow (2006). The tariff on Puerto Rican goods was imposed primarily to protect sugar interests.

47 Pomeroy (1944); Kramer (2002); Schumacher (2002); Thompson (2002); Go (2003; 2007).

48 Williams (1980); Linn (1996; 1997); Hagan and McMaster (2008: Chs. 8–10).

49 Three of the four unincorporated territories still occupy that status; the Philippines became independent in 1946.

50 Utah was denied statehood until it outlawed polygamy.

51 *New Orleans Picayune*, writing about the territories ceded by Mexico, quoted in Sparrow (2006: 24; also 38–40); McEnery quoted in Williams (1980: 824–825); McKinley to Methodist clergymen, quoted in Zimmermann (2002: 320); Roosevelt, quoted in Love (2004: 197); Kramer (2006). It should be recalled that only two years before the Spanish-American War, the Supreme Court rendered its Plessy v. Ferguson decision, ruling that racial segregation was constitutional.

52 Teller Amendment, quoted in Schoultz (1998: 139; also Ch. 8); Philippine Autonomy Act of 1916, 39 Stat. 545; Zimmermann (2002: Ch. 11); also Abinales (2003). It should be noted that some of the strongest opponents of Philippine annexation were southern Democrats committed to racial segregation.

53 Root to Wood, 9 January 1901, quoted in Zimmermann (2002: 379). Many of the anti-imperialists who so vigorously opposed the annexation of the Philippines were in favor of the Platt Amendment.

54 Guantánamo was established pursuant to one of the clauses in the Platt Amendment, though it long outlived that legislation.
55 Adams speech, 4 July 1821; Robeson, quoted in Chang (2003: 1334). There was of course a division of labor between the army and the navy, with the latter active overseas (usually deploying the marines) and the former restricting its operations to North America.
56 The data in Figure 7.3 are derived from Grimmett (2008), arrayed by five-year intervals.
57 O'Connor (1974); Skowronek (1982: Ch. 7); Oyos (1996); Bönker (2001).
58 U.S. Department of War (1900); Levenson (1953); Bodin (1979); Plante (1999). A number of the forces deployed by the U.S., as well as by the British, French, and Russians, were non-whites and/or non-Europeans. For a more detailed discussion, see Sylvan and Majeski (2008).

Bibliography

Books, articles, and reports

Abinales, P.N. (2003) "Progressive-Machine Conflict in Early Twentieth-Century U.S. Politics and Colonial State-Building in the Philippines," in J. Go and Foster, A.L. (eds), *The American Colonial State in the Philippines: Global Perspectives*, Durham, NC: Duke University Press.

Acheson, D. (1969) *Present at the Creation: My Years in the State Department*, New York: W.W. Norton.

Adeleke, A. (1995) "The Politics and Diplomacy of Peacekeeping in West Africa: The ECOWAS Operation in Liberia," *Journal of Modern African Studies* 33(4): 569–593.

Agee, P. (1975) *Inside the Company: CIA Diary*, New York: Stonehill.

Albright, M. (2003) *Madam Secretary*, with B. Woodward, New York: Miramax Books.

Aldrich, H. (1999) *Institutions Evolving*, London: Sage.

Ali, T. (2003) *Bush in Babylon: The Recolonisation of Iraq*, London and New York: Verso.

Allawi, A.A. (2007) *The Occupation of Iraq: Winning the War, Losing the Peace*, New Haven, CT: Yale University Press.

Allison, G.T. (1971) *Essence of Decision: Explaining the Cuban Missile Crisis*, Boston, MA: Little, Brown.

Alperovitz, G. (1995) *The Decision to Use the Atomic Bomb and the Architecture of an American Myth*, New York: Alfred A. Knopf.

Ambrose, S.E. (1970) *Rise to Globalism: American Foreign Policy since 1938*, London: Penguin.

Anderson, I.H. (1975) "The 1941 *De Facto* Embargo on Oil to Japan: A Bureaucratic Reflex," *Pacific Historical Review* 44: 201–231.

Anderson, T.P. (1971) *Matanza: El Salvador's Communist Revolt of 1932*, Lincoln, NE: University of Nebraska Press.

Andres, R.B., Wills, C., and Griffith, T.E., Jr. (2005/06) "Winning with Allies: The Strategic Value of the Afghan Model," *International Security* 30(3): 124–160.

Ansari, A.M. (2006) "Iran and the US in the Shadow of 9/11: Persia and the Persian Question Revisited," *Iranian Studies* 39(2): 155–170.

Archick, K. (2005) "U.S.-EU Cooperation Against Terrorism," *CRS Report for Congress* RS22030, 13 April. Online. Available: http://www.mipt.org/pdf/CRS_RS22030.pdf (accessed 7 June 2005).

Arkin, W.M. (2005) *Code Names: Deciphering U.S. Military Plans, Programs, and Operations in the 9/11 World*, Hanover, NH: Steerforth Press.

Armony, A.C. (1997) *Argentina, the United States, and the Anti-Communist Crusade in Central America, 1977–1984*, Athens, OH: Ohio University Press.

—— (2005) Film Review: "Death Squadrons," *American Historical Review* 110(2): 450.

Ashby, W.R. (1952) *Design for a Brain*, London: Chapman and Hall.

—— (1956) *An Introduction to Cybernetics*, London: Chapman and Hall.

Bacevich, A.J. et al. (1988) *American Military Policy in Small Wars: The Case of El Salvador*, Washington, DC: Pergamon-Brassey's.

Bachrach, P. and Baratz, M.S. (1962) "Two Faces of Power," *American Political Science Review* 56: 947–952.

Badian, E. (1958) *Foreign Clientelae (264–70 BC)*, Oxford: Clarendon Press.

Baer, R. (2002) *See No Evil: The True Story of a Ground Soldier in the CIA's War on Terrorism*, New York: Crown Publishers.

Baker, J.A. (1995) *The Politics of Diplomacy: Revolution, War and Peace 1989–1992*, New York: G.P. Putnam's Sons.

Balfour-Paul, G. (1991) *The End of Empire in the Middle East: Britain's Relinquishment of Power in Her Last Three Arab Dependencies*, Cambridge: Cambridge University Press.

Barany, Z. (2003) *The Future of NATO Expansion: Four Case Studies*, Cambridge: Cambridge University Press.

Baritz, L. (1986) *Backfire: A History of How American Culture Led Us into Vietnam and Made Us Fight the Way We Did*, New York: Ballantine Books.

Barker, G. (2000) "The Survival of Saddam," *Frontline*, Program No. 1810, Public Broadcasting System, 25 January. Transcript online. Available: http://www.pbs.org/wgbh/pages/frontline/shows/saddam/etc/script.html (accessed 21 February 2006).

Barnes, T. (1981) "The Secret Cold War: The CIA and American Foreign Policy in Europe, 1946–56. Part I," *Historical Journal* 24(2): 399–415.

—— (1982) "The Secret Cold War: The C.I.A. and American Foreign Policy in Europe, 1946–56, Part II," *Historical Journal* 25(3): 649–670.

Barnhart, M.A. (1997) "A Secondary Affair: American Economic Foreign Policy and Japan, 1952–68," *Working Paper* No. 9, U.S.-Japan Project. Online. Available: http://www.gwu.edu/~nsarchiv/japan/barnharttp.html (accessed 28 May 2005).

Barno, D.W. (2004) "Afghanistan: The Security Outlook," Lecture, Center for Security and International Studies, Washington, DC, 14 May. Online. Available: http://www.csis.org/isp/pcr/040514_barno.pdf (accessed 23 August 2005).

Bar-Siman-Tov, Y. (1998) "The United States and Israel Since 1948: A 'Special Relationship'?" *Diplomatic History* 22(2): 231–262.

Barth, F. (1959) *Political Leadership among Swat Pathans*, London: University of London, Athlone Press.

Batatu, H. (1978) *The Old Social Classes and the Revolutionary Movements of Iraq*, Princeton, NJ: Princeton University Press.

BBC World Service Poll (2008) "Global Views of USA Improve," 1 April, WorldPublicOpinion. org, Program on International Policy Attitudes, University of Maryland.

Beck, R.J. (1994) *The Grenada Invasion: Politics, Law, and Foreign Policy Decisionmaking*, Boulder, CO: Westview Press.

Becker, W.H. and McClenahan, W.M., Jr. (2003) *The Market, the State, and the Export-Import Bank of the United States, 1934–2000*, Cambridge: Cambridge University Press.

Beer, S. (1959) *Cybernetics and Management*, London: English Universities Press.

Beisner, R.L. (1968) *Twelve Against Empire: The Anti-Imperialists, 1898–1900*, New York: McGraw-Hill.

Belanger, F.W. (1989) *Drugs, the U.S., and Khun Sa*, Bangkok: Siam Square.

Belasco, A. (2008) "The Cost of Iraq, Afghanistan, and Other Global War On Terror Operations Since 9/11," *CRS Report for Congress RL33110*, 14 July. Online. Available: http://www.fas.org/sgp/crs/natsec/RL33110.pdf (accessed 16 August 2008).

Bemelmans-Videc, M.-L., Rist, R.C., and Vedung, E. (eds) (1998) *Carrots, Sticks and Sermons: Policy Instruments and Their Evaluation*, New Brunswick, NJ: Transaction Publishers.

Bender, G.J. (1987) "The Eagle and the Bear in Angola," *Annals of the American Academy of Political and Social Science* 489, January: 123–132.

—— (1988) "Washington's Quest for Enemies in Angola," in R.J. Bloomfield (ed.) *Regional Conflict and U.S. Policy: Angola and Mozambique*, Algonac, MI: Reference Publications.

Berger, D.H. (1995) "The Use of Covert Paramilitary Activity as a Policy Tool: An Analysis of Operations Conducted by the United States Central Intelligence Agency, 1949–51," Marine Corps Command and Staff College, 22 May. Online. Available: http://www.fas.org/irp/eprint/berger.htm (accessed 23 February 2006).

Berman, L. (1989) *Lyndon Johnson's War: The Road to Stalemate in Vietnam*, New York: W.W. Norton.

—— (2002) *No Peace, No Honor: Nixon, Kissinger, and Betrayal in Vietnam*, New York: Touchstone).

Bernstein, B. (1983) "The Struggle over the Korean Armistice: Prisoners of Repatriation?" in B. Cumings (ed.) *Child of Conflict: The Korean-American Relationship, 1943–1953*, Seattle, WA: University of Washington Press.

Bernstein, C. (1992) "The Holy Alliance," *Time*, 24 February.

Berntsen, G., and Pezzullo, R. (2005) *Jawbreaker: The Attack on Bin Laden and Al-Qaeda: A Personal Account by the CIA's Key Field Commander*, New York: Crown Publishers.

Berrigan, F. (2008) "Indonesia's Arms Appetite," *Foreign Policy in Focus*, 27 February. Online. Available: http://www.fpif.org/fpiftxt/5018 (accessed 20 May 2008).

Beschloss, M.R. (ed.) (1998) *Taking Charge: The Johnson White House Tapes, 1963–1964*, New York: Touchstone.

Best, R.A., Jr. and Feickert, A. (2005) "Special Operations Forces (SOF) and CIA Paramilitary Operations: Issues for Congress," *CRS Report for Congress* RS22017, 4 January. Online. Available: http://www.fas.org/man/crs/RS22017.pdf (accessed 8 September 2005).

Bevin, M. and Mitchell, D. (2005) "US-Venezuela (1948–2005)," Center for Cooperative Research. Online. Available: http://www.cooperativeresearch.org/timeline.jsp?timeline = venezuela (accessed 26 November 2005).

Block, F.L. (1977) *The Origins of International Economic Disorder: A Study of United States International Monetary Policy from World War II to the Present*, Berkeley, CA: University of California Press.

Bodin, L.E. (1979) *The Boxer Rebellion*, London: Osprey.

Bönker, D. (2001) "Admiration, Enmity, and Cooperation: U.S. Navalism and the British and German Empires before the Great War," *Journal of Colonialism and Colonial History* 2(1): n.p.

Bonner, R. (1987) *Waltzing with a Dictator: The Marcoses and the Making of American Policy*, New York: Times Books.

Bordo, M. and Schwartz, A.J. (2001) "From the Exchange Stabilization Fund to the International Monetary Fund," *Working Paper* 8100, National Bureau of Economic Research, January. Online. Available: http://www.nber.org/papers/w8100.pdf (accessed 26 June 2005).

Bouvier, V.M. (2005) "Evaluating U.S. Policy in Colombia," Policy Report, IRC Americas Program, 11 May. Online. Available: http://americas.irc-online.org/pdf/reports/0505colombia.pdf (accessed 9 August 2005).

Bowden, M. (1999) *Black Hawk Down: A Story of Modern War*, New York: Grove/Atlantic.

Brands, H.W. (1986) "The United States and the Reemergence of Independent Japan," *Pacific Affairs* 59(3): 387–401.

—— (1989) "The Limits of Manipulation: How the United States Didn't Topple Sukarno," *Journal of American History* 76(3): 785–808.

—— (1992) *Bound to Empire: The United States and the Philippines*, New York: Oxford University Press.

Brenner, P., Haney, P.J., and Vanderbush, W. (2002) "The Confluence of Domestic and International Interests: U.S. Policy Toward Cuba, 1998–2001," *International Studies Perspectives* 3(2): 192–208.

Browder, R.P. (1953) *The Origins of Soviet-American Diplomacy*, Princeton, NJ: Princeton University Press.

Brown, M. and Zasloff, J.J. (1974) "Laos 1973: Wary Steps Toward Peace," *Asian Survey* 14(2): 166–174.

Brownlie, I. (1963) *International Law and the Use of Force by States*, Oxford: Clarendon Press.

Bruck, C. (2006) "Exiles," *New Yorker*, 6 March: 48–63.

Brzezinski, Z. (1983) *Power and Principle: Memoirs of the National Security Adviser 1977–1981*, London: Weidenfeld and Nicolson.

Buchenau, J. (1993) "Counter-Intervention against Uncle Sam: Mexico's Support for Nicaraguan Nationalism, 1903–10," *The Americas* 50(2): 207–232.

Buell, R.L. (1931a) "The United States and Central American Stability," *Foreign Policy Reports* 7(9): 161–186.

—— (1931b) "The United States and Central American Revolutions," *Foreign Policy Reports* 7 (10): 187–204.

Bundy, W. (1998) *A Tangled Web: The Making of Foreign Policy in the Nixon Presidency*, New York: Hill and Wang.

Bunnell, F.P. (1976) "The Central Intelligence Agency-Deputy Directorate for Plans 1961 Secret Memorandum on Indonesia: A Study in the Politics of Policy Formulation in the Kennedy Administration," *Indonesia* 22: 131–170.

—— (1990) "American 'Low Posture' Policy Toward Indonesia in the Months Leading Up to the 1965 'Coup'" *Indonesia* 50: 29–60.

Burk, K. (2001) "The Marshall Plan: Filling in Some of the Blanks," *Contemporary European History* 10(2): 267–294.

Burrough, B. *et al.* (2004) "The Path to War. Special Report: The Rush to Invade Iraq: The Ultimate Inside Account," *Vanity Fair*, May: 228–45, 281–294.

Bush, G. and Scowcroft, B. (1998) *A World Transformed*, New York: Alfred A. Knopf.

Byman, D. (2000–2001) "After the Storm: U.S. Policy Toward Iraq Since 1991," *Political Science Quarterly* 115(4): 493–516.

Cairo, I. (2005) "US to Sever Ties with Suriname if Former Dictator Becomes President," *Caribbean Net News*, 14 March. Online. Available: http://www.caribbeannetnews.com/2005/03/14/dictator.shtml (accessed 31 March 2005).

Callahan, M. (2003) *Making Enemies: War and State Building in Burma*, Ithaca, NY: Cornell University Press.

Carlisle, R. (1974) "The Foreign Policy Views of an Isolationist Press Lord: W.R. Hearst and the International Crisis, 1936–41," *Journal of Contemporary History* 9(3): 217–227.

Carpenter, D.P. (2001) *The Forging of Bureaucratic Autonomy: Reputations, Networks, and Policy Innovation in Executive Agencies, 1862–1928*, Princeton, NJ and Oxford: Princeton University Press.

Carter, J. (1982) *Keeping Faith: Memoirs of a President*, London: Collins.

Cassese, A. (2004) *International Law*, 2d edn, Oxford: Oxford University Press.

Castle, T.N. (1993) *At War in the Shadow of Vietnam: U.S. Military Aid to the Royal Lao Government, 1955–1975*, New York: Columbia University Press.

Center for International Policy (2005) "Rethinking Plan Colombia." Online. Available: http://www.lawg.org/docs/cip_rethinking.pdf (accessed 9 August 2005).

Chang, G.H. (2003) "Whose 'Barbarism'? Whose 'Treachery'? Race and Civilization in the Unknown United States-Korea War of 1871," *Journal of American History* 89(4): 1331–1365.

Chicago Council on Global Affairs (2007) "World Publics Reject US Role as the World Leader," 17 April, WorldPublicOpinion.org, Program on International Policy Attitudes, University of Maryland.

Chomsky, N. and Herman, E.S. (1979) *The Political Economy of Human Rights*, vol. 1, Boston, MA: South End Press.

Choucri, N. and North, R.C. (1975) *Nations in Conflict: National Growth and International Violence*, San Francisco, CA: W.H. Freeman.

Chubin, S. and Green, J.D. (1998) "Engaging Iran: A US Strategy," *Survival* 40(3): 153–169.

Citino, N.J. (2002) *From Arab Nationalism to OPEC: Eisenhower, King Saud, and the Making of U.S.-Saudi Relations*, Bloomington and Indianapolis, IN: Indiana University Press.

Clark, J.R. (2005) *The Literature of Intelligence: A Bibliography of Materials, with Essays, Review, and Comments*, New Concord, OH: Muskingum College. Online. Available: http://intellit.muskingum.edu/ (accessed 7 June 2005).

Clark, W.K. (2001) *Waging Modern War: Bosnia, Kosovo, and the Future of Combat*, New York: PublicAffairs.

Clarke, J.J. (1988) *Advice and Support: The Final Years*, The U.S. Army in Vietnam, Center of Military History, United States Army, Washington, DC: Government Printing Office.

Clarke, R.A. (2004) *Against All Enemies: Inside America's War on Terror*, New York: Free Press.

Clinton, B. (2004) *My Life*, London: Hutchinson.

Clymer, K.J. (1999) "The Perils of Neutrality: The Break in U.S.-Cambodian Relations, 1965," *Diplomatic History* 23(4): 609–631.

—— (2004) *The United States and Cambodia, 1969–2000: A Troubled Relationship*, London and New York: RoutledgeCurzon.

CNA Corporation (2007) *National Security and the Threat of Climate Change*, Alexandria, VA: CNA. Online. Available: http://securityandclimate.cna.org/report/National%20Security%20and%20the%20Threat%20of%20Climate%20Change.pdf (accessed 16 August 2008).

Cockburn, A. and Cockburn, L. (1991) *Dangerous Liaison: The Inside Story of the U.S.-Israeli Covert Relationship*, New York: HarperCollins.

Cockburn, A. and Cockburn, P. (1999) *Out of the Ashes: The Resurrection of Saddam Hussein*, New York: HarperCollins.

Cockburn, P. (2006) *The Occupation: War and Resistance in Iraq*, London and New York: Verso.

Cohen, C. (2007) "A Perilous Course: U.S. Strategy and Assistance to Pakistan," *CSIS Report*, August. Online. Available: http://www.csis.org/media/csis/pubs/071214_pakistan.pdf (accessed 18 April 2008).

Cohen, H.J. (2000) *Intervening in Africa: Superpower Peacemaking in a Troubled Continent*, Studies in Diplomacy, Houndmills, UK: Macmillan.

Cohen, M.D., March, J.G., and Olsen, J.P. (1972) "A Garbage Can Model of Organizational Choice," *Administrative Science Quarterly* 17(1): 1–25.

Cole, R.H. (1995) *Operation Just Cause: The Planning and Execution of Joint Operations in Panama, February 1988–January 1990*, Joint History Office, Office of the Chairman of the Joint Chiefs of Staff, Washington, DC, November. Online. Available: http://www.globalsecurity.org/military/library/report/1995/justcaus.pdf (accessed 20 November 2005).

Cole, W.S. (1983) *Roosevelt and the Isolationists, 1932–45*, Lincoln, NE and London: University of Nebraska Press.

Coll, S. (2004) *Ghost Wars: The Secret History of the CIA, Afghanistan, and bin Laden, From the Soviet Invasion to September 10, 2001*, New York: Penguin Press.

Collin, R.H (1990) *Theodore Roosevelt's Caribbean: The Panama Canal, the Monroe Doctrine, and the Latin American Context*, Baton Rouge, LA and London: Louisiana State University Press.

Conn, S. and Fairchild, B. (1960) *The Framework of Hemispheric Defense, United States Army in World War II: The Western Hemisphere*, Washington, DC: Office of the Chief of Military History, Department of the Army.

Copeland, M. (1989) *The Game Player: Confessions of the CIA's Original Political Operative*, London: Aurum Press.

Cordesman, A.H. (2005) "Strengthening Iraqi Military and Security Forces," with the assistance of P. Baetjer and S. Lanier, Update of 17 February 2005, Center for Strategic and International Studies. Online. Available: http://www.csis.org/features/iraq_strengtheningforces.pdf (accessed 27 August 2005).

Corum, J.S. (1998) "The Air War in El Salvador," *Airpower Journal* 12(2): 27–44.

Coutsoukis, P. (2005) "El Salvador: Foreign Military Influence and Assistance," photius.com, 27 March. Online. Available: http://www.photius.com/countries/el_salvador/national_security/el_salvador_national_security_foreign_military_inf~11422.html (accessed 8 August 2005).

Cox, I.J. (1927) *Nicaragua and the United States, 1909–1927*, Boston, MA: World Peace Foundation Pamphlets 10(7).

Cox, M. and Kennedy-Pipe, C. (2005) "The Tragedy of American Diplomacy? Rethinking the Marshall Plan," *Journal of Cold War Studies* 7(1): 97–134.

Cox, R.W. (1979) "Ideologies and the New International Order: Reflections on Some Recent Literature," *International Organization* 33(2): 257–302.

Crane, C.C. (1999) "Raiding the Beggar's Pantry: The Search for Airpower Strategy in the Korean War," *Journal of Military History* 63(4): 885–920.

Crowl, J.W. (1981) *Angels in Stalin's Paradise: Western Reporters in Soviet Russia, 1917–1937; A Case Study of Louis Fischer and Walter Duranty*, Washington, DC: University Press of America.

Crumpton, H.A. (2005) "Intelligence and War: Afghanistan, 2001–2," in J.E. Sims and B. Gerber (eds) *Transforming U.S. Intelligence*, Washington, DC: Georgetown University Press.

Cullather, N. (1994) *Illusions of Influence: The Political Economy of United States–Philippines Relations, 1942–1960*, Stanford, CA: Stanford University Press.

—— (1999) *Secret History: The CIA's Classified Account of Its Operations in Guatemala, 1952–1954*, Stanford, CA: Stanford University Press.

Cumings, B. (1984) "The Origins and Development of the Northeast Asian Political Economy. Industrial Sectors, Product Cycles, and Political Sequences," *International Organization* 38(1): 1–40.

—— (1990) *The Origins of the Korean War*, vol. 2: *The Roaring of the Cataract 1947–1950*, Princeton, NJ: Princeton University Press.

—— (1997) *Korea's Place in the Sun: A Modern History*, New York: Norton.

—— (2003) *North Korea: Another Country*, New York: New Press.

Cupitt, R.T. and Grillot, S.R. (1997) "COCOM is Dead, Long Live COCOM: Persistence and Change in Multilateral Security Institutions," *British Journal of Political Science* 27(3): 361–389.

Cyert, R.M. and March, J.G. (1963) *A Behavioral Theory of the Firm*, Englewood Cliffs, NJ: Prentice-Hall.

Daalder, I.H. (2000) *Getting to Dayton: The Making of America's Bosnia Policy*, Washington, DC: Brookings Institution Press.

Daalder, I.H. and Destler, I.M. (2000) "A New NSC for a New Administration," Brookings Institution Foreign Policy Studies, *Policy Brief* #68, November. Online. Available: http://www.brookings.edu/comm/policybriefs/pb68.htm (accessed 7 October 2004).

—— (2001) "How Operational and Visible an NSC?" Brookings Institution Foreign Policy Studies, 23 February. Online. Available: http://www.brookings.edu/views/op-ed/daalder/20010223.htm (accessed 7 October 2004).

Daalder, I.H. and O'Hanlon, M.E. (2000) *Winning Ugly: NATO's War to Save Kosovo*, Washington, DC: Brookings Institution Press.

Daft, R.L. and Noe, R.A. (2001) *Organizational Behavior*, Medford, MA: International Thomson Publishing.

Dagne, T. (2002) "Sudan: Humanitarian Crisis, Peace Talks, Terrorism, and U.S. Policy," *CRS Issue Brief for Congress* IB98043, 14 June. Online. Available: http://fpc.state.gov/documents/organization/11282.pdf (accessed 17 August 2008).

—— (2006) "Sudan: Humanitarian Crisis, Peace Talks, Terrorism, and U.S. Policy," *CRS Report for Congress* RL33574, 27 July. Online. Available: http://fpc.state.gov/documents/organization/70327.pdf (accessed 26 September 2006). [Authors' note: In spite of having the same title, this report differs markedly from the earlier version cited above.]

—— (2008) "Sudan: The Crisis in Darfur and Status of the North–South Peace Agreement," *CRS Report for Congress* RL 33574, 15 April. Online. Available: http://www.fas.org/sgp/crs/row/RL33574.pdf (accessed 17 August 2008).

Dale, C.M. (2008) "Operation Iraqi Freedom: Strategies, Approaches, Results, and Issues for Congress," *CRS Report for Congress* RL34387, 22 February. Online. Available: http://www.fas.org/sgp/crs/natsec/RL34387.pdf (accessed 19 April 2008).

Danner, M. (1997) "Marooned in the Cold War: America, the Alliance, and the Quest for a Vanished World," *World Policy Journal* 14(3): 1–23.

Daugherty, W.J. (2004) *Executive Secrets: Covert Action and the Presidency*, Lexington, KY: University Press of Kentucky.

Davis, N. (1978–79) "The Angola Decision of 1975: A Personal Memoir," *Foreign Affairs* 57, Fall: 109–124.

Davis, O.A., Dempster, M.A.H., and Wildavsky, A. (1966) "A Theory of the Budgetary Process," *American Political Science Review* 60(3): 529–547.

Davoodi, H. *et al.* (1999) "Military Spending, the Peace Dividend, and Fiscal Adjustment," IMF *Working Paper* WP/99/87, July.

de Ste. Croix, G.E.M. (1972) *The Origins of the Peloponnesian War*, Ithaca, NY: Cornell University Press.

Deutsch, K.W. (1963) *The Nerves of Government: Models of Political Communication and Control*, London: Free Press of Glencoe.

Devlin, L. (2007) *Chief of Station, Congo: Fighting the Cold War in a Hot Zone*, New York: PublicAffairs.

de Waal, A. (1998) "US War Crimes in Somalia," *New Left Review* 230: 131–144.

—— (2005) "Sudan's Chance," *Prospect Magazine*, web exclusive, Aug. 2005, no. 113. Online. Available: http://www.prospect-magazine.co.uk/article_details.php?id = 6996.

Dewey, C. (1993) *Anglo-Indian Attitudes: The Mind of the Indian Civil Service*, London and Rio Grande: Hambledon.

DiMaggio, P.J. and Powell, W.W. (1983) "The Iron Cage Revisited: Institutional Isomorphism and Collective Rationality in Organizational Fields," *American Sociological Review* 48(2): 147–160.

Doenecke, J. (1979) *Not to the Swift: The Old Isolationists in the Cold War Era*, Lewisburg, PA: Bucknell University Press.

—— (2000) *Storm on the Horizon: The Challenge to American Intervention, 1939–1941*, Lanham. MD: Rowman and Littlefield.

Dorril, S. (2000) *MI6: Inside the Covert World of Her Majesty's Secret Intelligence Service*, New York and London: Free Press.

Dower, J.W. (1972) "The Superdomino in Postwar Asia: Japan in and Out of the Pentagon Papers," in N. Chomsky and H. Zinn (eds), *The Pentagon Papers: The Senator Gravel Edition*, vol. 5: *Critical Essays*, Boston, MA: Beacon Press.

Doyle, M.W. (1986) *Empires*, Ithaca, NY: Cornell University Press.

Drinnon, R. (1980) *Facing West: The Metaphysics of Indian-Hating and Empire-Building*, Minneapolis, MN: University of Minnesota Press.

Dueck, C. (2004) "New Perspectives on American Grand Strategy," *International Security* 28(4): 197–216.

—— (2006) *Reluctant Crusaders: Power, Culture, and Change in American Grand Strategy*, Princeton, NJ: Princeton University Press.

Easter, D. (2005) "'Keep the Indonesian Pot Boiling': Western Covert Intervention in Indonesia, October 1965 – March 1966," *Cold War History* 5(1): 55–73.

Efrat, M. and Bercovitch, J. (1991) *Superpowers and Client States in the Middle East: The Imbalance of Influence*, London and New York: Routledge.

Eichengreen, B. (1993) *Reconstructing Europe's Trade and Payments: The European Payments Union*, Manchester and Ann Arbor, MI: Manchester University Press and University of Michigan Press.

—— (1996) *Globalizing Capital: A History of the International Monetary System*, Princeton, NJ: Princeton University Press.

Eisenhower, D.D. (1963) *The White House Years*, vol. 1: *Mandate for Change, 1953–1956*, Garden City, NY: Doubleday & Company.

Eisenstadt, S.N. (1963) *The Political System of Empires: The Rise and Fall of Historical Bureaucratic Societies*, New York: Free Press.

—— (1968) "Empires," in *International Encyclopedia of the Social Sciences*, New York: Macmillan.

Eisenstadt, S.N. and Lemarchand, R. (eds) (1981) *Political Clientilism, Patronage, and Development*, Beverly Hills, CA: Sage.

Eisenstadt, S.N. and Roniger, L. (1980) "Patron-Client Relations as a Model of Structuring Social Exchange," *Comparative Studies in Society and History*, 22: 42–77.

e-Journal USA (2004) "The Global War on Terrorist Finance," *e-Journal USA: Economic Perspectives* 9(3): entire issue. Online. Available: http://usinfo.state.gov/journals/ites/0904/ijee/ijee0904.htm (accessed 7 June 2005).

Eliadis, P., Hill, M.M., and Howlett, M. (eds) (2005) *Designing Government: From Instruments to Governance*, Montreal: McGill-Queen's University Press.

Ellsberg, D. (1972) "The Quagmire Myth and the Stalemate Machine," in *Papers on the War*, New York: Simon & Schuster.

Eriksson, M. and Wallensteen, P. (2004) "Armed Conflict 1989–2003," *Journal of Peace Research* 41(5): 625–636.

Esthus, R.A. (1963) "President Roosevelt's Commitment to Britain to Intervene in a Pacific War," *Mississippi Valley Historical Review* 50(1): 28–38.

Farmer, P. (2004) "Who Removed Aristide?" *London Review of Books* 26(8) (15 April).

Federal Jobs Net (2005) "Overseas Jobs with the Federal Government, All Occupations Hiring," 14 February. Online. Available: http://federaljobs.net/overseas.htm (accessed 19 February 2005).

Feis, H. (1950) *The Road to Pearl Harbor: The Coming of the War Between the United States and Japan*, Princeton, NJ: Princeton University Press.

Feith, D.J. (2008) *War and Decision: Inside the Pentagon at the Dawn of the War on Terrorism*, New York: Harper.

Ferguson, N. (2003) *Empire: How Britain Made the Modern World*, London: Allen Lane.

—— (2004) *Colossus: The Rise and Fall of the American Empire*, London: Allen Lane.

Fieldhouse, D.K. (1966) *The Colonial Empires: From the Eighteenth Century*, New York: Dell.

Fienberg, H. (1992) "The Revolution in Grenada," February. Online. Available: http://www.hfienberg.com/irtheory/grenada.html (accessed 6 April 2005).

Finlayson, K. (2002) "Operation White Star: Prelude to Vietnam," *Special Warfare* 15(2) (June). Online. Available: http://www.findarticles.com/p/articles/mi_m0HZY/is_2_15/ai_89859337 (accessed 10 September 2005).

Fitch, J.S. (2005) "Post-Transition Coups: Ecuador 2000. An Essay in Honor of Martin Needler," *Journal of Political and Military Sociology* 33(1): 39–58.

Folsom, K.E. (1968) *Friends, Guests and Colleagues: The Mu-fu System in the Late Ch'ing Period*, Berkeley, CA: University of California Press.

Foot, R. (1985) *The Wrong War: American Policy and the Dimensions of the Korean Conflict, 1950–1955*, Ithaca, NY: Cornell University Press.

Franks, T. (2004) *American Soldier*, with M. McConnell, New York: Regan Books.

Frontline (2000) "War in Europe: NATO's 1999 War Against Serbia Over Kosovo," February. Online. Available: http://www.pbs.org/wgbh/pages/frontline/shows/kosovo/ (accessed 15 June 2006).

—— (2001)"Gunning for Saddam," November, transcript. Online. Available: http://www.pbs.org/wgbh/pages/frontline/shows/gunning/etc/script.html (accessed 6 November 2008).

Führer, H. (1996) "The Story of Official Development Assistance: A History of the Development Assistance Committee and the Development Co-operation Directorate in Dates, Names and Figures," OCDE/GD(94)67, Organisation for Economic Co-Operation and Development, Paris. Online. Available: http://www.isc.niigata-u.ac.jp/~miyatah/nu/2004/N-S_relations/dac_story_of_oda.pdf (accessed 26 May 2005).

Galison, P. (1994) "The Ontology of the Enemy: Norbert Wiener and the Cybernetic Vision," *Critical Inquiry* 21(1): 228–266.

Gallicchio, M. (1997) "Japan in American Security Policy: A Problem in Perspective," *Working Paper* No. 10, U.S.-Japan Project. Online. Available: http://www.gwu.edu/~nsarchiv/japan/gallicchiotp.htm (accessed 28 May 2005).

Gallup, G.H. (ed.) (1976) *The Gallup International Public Opinion Polls: Great Britain, 1937–1975*, 2 vols., New York: Random House.

Ganser, D. (2005) *NATO's Secret Armies: Operation Gladio and Terrorism in Western Europe*, London and New York: Frank Cass.

Garfinkle, A.M. (1985) "U.S. Decision Making in the Jordan Crisis: Correcting the Record," *Political Science Quarterly* 100(1): 117–138.

Garofano, J. (2002) "The Intervention Debate: Towards a Posture of Principled Judgment," Strategic Studies Institute, U.S. Army War College, January. Online. Available: http://www.carlisle.army.mil/ssi/pdffiles/PUB293.pdf (accessed 30 November 2004).

Gasiorowski, M.J. (1986) "Dependency and Cliency in Latin America," *Journal of Inter-American Studies and World Affairs* 28: 47–65.

—— (1991) *U.S. Foreign Policy and the Shah: Building a Client State in Iran*, Ithaca, NY and London: Cornell University Press.

Gasiorowski, M.J. and Baek, S. (1987) "International Cliency Relationships and Client States in East Asia," *Pacific Focus* 2: 113–143.

Gasiorowski, M.J. and Byrne, M. (eds) (2004) *Mohammad Mosaddeq and the 1953 Coup in Iran*, Syracuse, NY: Syracuse University Press.

Gates, R.M. (1996) *From the Shadows: The Ultimate Insider's Story of Five Presidents and How They Won the Cold War*, New York: Simon & Schuster.

Gavin, F.J. (1999) "Politics, Power, and U.S. Policy in Iran, 1950–53," *Journal of Cold War Studies* 1(1): 56–89.

Gberie, L. (2005) "Liberia's War and Peace Process: A Historical Overview," in F. Aboagye and A.M.S. Bah (eds), *A Tortuous Road to Peace: The Dynamics of Regional, UN and International Humanitarian Interventions in Liberia*, Pretoria: Institute for Security Studies.

Geiger, T. (1999) "Why Ireland Needed the Marshall Plan but Did Not Want it: Ireland, the Sterling Area and the European Recovery Program, 1947–48," Queen's University of Belfast, August. Online. Available: http://www.art.man.ac.uk/HISTORY/research/workingpapers/wp_44.pdf (accessed 15 April 2005).

Gellman, I.F. (1979) *Good Neighbor Diplomacy: United States Policies in Latin America, 1933–1945*, Baltimore, MD: Johns Hopkins University Press.

Gellner, E. and Waterbury, J. (eds) (1977) *Patrons and Clients in Mediterranean Societies*, London: Duckworth.

Gelpi, C., Feaver, P.D., and Reifler, J. (2005/06) "Success Matters: Casualty Sensitivity and the War in Iraq," *International Security* 30(3): 7–46.

Gendzier, I. (1997) *Notes from the Minefield: United States Intervention in Lebanon and the Middle East, 1945–1958*, New York: Columbia University Press.

George, A.L., Hall, D.K., and Simons, W.E. (1971) *The Limits of Coercive Diplomacy: Laos, Cuba, Vietnam*, Boston, MA: Little, Brown.

George C. Marshall Foundation (2004) "Economic Cooperation Administration," *Marshall Plan*. Online. Available: http://www.marshallfoundation.org/marshall_plan_economic_cooperation_administration.html (accessed 15 April 2005).

Gibbons, W.C. (1984) *The U.S. Government and the Vietnam War: Executive and Legislative Roles and Relationships, Part 1: 1945–1961*, Congressional Research Service for the Committee on Foreign Relations, United States Senate, Washington, DC: U.S. Government Printing Office.

—— (1986) *The U.S. Government and the Vietnam War: Executive and Legislative Roles and Relationships, Part 2: 1961–1964*, Princeton, NJ: Princeton University Press.

—— (1989) *The U.S. Government and the Vietnam War: Executive and Legislative Roles and Relationships, Part 3: January–July 1965*, Princeton, NJ: Princeton University Press.

Gilboa, E. (1995) "The Panama Invasion Revisited: Lessons for the Use of Force in the Post Cold War Era," *Political Science Quarterly* 110(4): 539–562.

Gill, L. (2004) *The School of the Americas: Military Training and Political Violence in the Americas*, Durham, NC and London: Duke University Press.

Gilpin, R. (1981) *War and Change in World Politics*, New York: Cambridge University Press.

Glaser, B.G. and Straus, A.L. (1967) *The Discovery of Grounded Theory: Strategies for Qualitative Research*, New York: Aldine.

Gleijeses, P. (1991) *Shattered Hope: The Guatemalan Revolution and the United States, 1944–1954*, Princeton, NJ: Princeton University Press.

—— (1995) "Ships in the Night: The CIA, the White House and the Bay of Pigs," *Journal of Latin American Studies* 27(1): 1–42.

—— (2002) *Conflicting Missions: Havana, Washington, and Africa, 1959–1976*, Chapel Hill, NC and London: University of North Carolina Press.

—— (2006) "Moscow's Proxy? Cuba and Africa 1975–88," *Journal of Cold War Studies* 8(2): 3–51.

GlobalSecurity.org (2003) "History of Liberia," 15 August. Online. Available: http://www.global security.org/military/world/liberia/history.htm (accessed 14 April 2005).

—— (2004a) "Operation Secure Tomorrow," 11 June. Online. Available: http://www.globalsecuri ty.org/military/ops/haiti04.htm (accessed 23 August 2005).

—— (2004b) *U.S. Central Command Facilities*, 23 December. Online. Available: http://www.glob alsecurity.org/military/facility/centcom.htm (accessed 29 March 2005).

—— (2005a) "Operation Enduring Freedom – Afghanistan," 3 July. Online. Available: http://www.globalsecurity.org/military/ops/enduring-freedom.htm (accessed 23 August 2005).

—— (2005b) "Anti-Communist National Salvation Army," 27 April. Online. Available: http://www.globalsecurity.org/military/world/taiwan/nsa.htm (accessed 2 April 2006).

—— (2005c) "Sudan People's Liberation Army / Sudan People's Liberation Movement," 27 April. Online. Available: http://www.globalsecurity.org/military/world/para/spla.htm (accessed 16 August 2008).

Go, J. (2003) "Modes of Rule in America's Overseas Empire: The Philippines, Puerto Rico, Guam, and Samoa," paper prepared for the Louisiana Purchase Conference, 20–23 February 2003, Austin, TX.

—— (2007) "The Provinciality of American Empire: 'Liberal Exceptionalism' and U.S. Colonial Rule, 1898–1912," *Comparative Studies in Society and History* 49(1): 74–108.

Goh, E. (2005) "Nixon, Kissinger, and the 'Soviet Card' in the U.S. Opening to China, 1971–74," *Diplomatic History* 29(3): 475–502.

Gold, J. (1988) "Mexico and the Development of the Practice of the International Monetary Fund," *World Development* 16, 10: 1127–1142.

Goldstone, J.A. *et al.* (2000) *State Failure Task Force Report: Phase III Findings*, Center for International Development and Conflict Management, University of Maryland. Online. Available: http://www.cidcm.umd.edu/inscr/stfail/SFTF%20Phase%20III%20Report%20Final. pdf (accessed 22 June 2005).

Golinger, E. (2007) *Bush vs. Chávez: Washington's War on Venezuela*, New York: Monthly Review Press.

Gong, G.W. (1984) *The Standard of "Civilization" in International Society*, New York: Oxford University Press.

Gordon, M.R. and Trainor, B.E. (2006) *Cobra II: The Inside Story of the Invasion and Occupation of Iraq*, New York: Pantheon Books.

Gould, S.J. and Lewontin, R.C. (1979) "The Spandrels of San Marco and the Panglossian Paradigm: A Critique of the Adaptationist Programme," *Proceedings of the Royal Society of London*, ser. B, 205, 1161: 581–598.

Grafton, J.S. (2003) "Security Cooperation 2003 Conference: Strengthening Alliances for the Future," *DISAM Journal* 26(1): 99–107. Online. Available: http://www.disam.dsca.mil/pubs/ INDEXES/Journals/Journal_Index/v.26_1/Grafton.pdf (accessed 13 April 2005).

Graham-Yooll, A. (1983) *Small Wars You May Have Missed*, London: Junction Books.

Green, J.N. (2003) "Top Brass and State Power in Twentieth-Century Brazilian Politics, Economics, and Culture," *Latin American Research Review* 38(3):250–260.

Gribbin, P. (1979) "Brazil and CIA," *CounterSpy* 3(2) (April-May): 4–23. Online. Available: http://www.namebase.org/brazil.html (accessed 14 November 2005).

Griffith, T.E. Jr. (1994) "Strategic Attack of National Electrical Systems," Graduation Thesis, School of Advanced Airpower Studies, October, Maxwell Air Force Base, AL: Air University Press.

Griffiths, R.T. (1997) "'An Act of Creative Leadership': The End of the OEEC and the Birth of the OECD," in R.T. Griffiths (ed.) *Explorations in OEEC History*, Paris: Organisation for Economic Co-operation and Development.

Grimmett, R.F. (1973) "Who Were the Senate Isolationists?" *Pacific Historical Review* 42(4): 479–498.

—— (2004) "Conventional Arms Transfers to Developing Nations, 1996–2003," *CRS Report for Congress* RL32547, 26 August. Online. Available: http://www.fas.org/man/crs/RL32547.pdf (accessed 9 June 2005).

—— (2008) "Instances of Use of United States Armed Forces Abroad, 1798–2007," *CRS Report for Congress* RL32170, 14 January. Online. Available: http://www.fas.org/sgp/crs/natsec/RL32170.pdf (accessed 17 June 2008).

Gros, J.-G. (1996) "Towards a Taxonomy of Failed States in the New World Order: Decaying Somalia, Liberia, Rwanda and Haiti," *Third World Quarterly* 17(3): 455–471.

Haass, R.N. (2008) "The Age of Nonpolarity: What Will Follow U.S. Dominance," *Foreign Affairs* 87(3): 44.56.

Hack, K. (2001) *Defence and Decolonisation in Southeast Asia: Britain, Malaya and Singapore 1941–1968*, Richmond: Curzon.

Hagan, K.J. and McMaster, M.T. (eds) (2008) *In Peace and War: Interpretations of American Naval History*, 3d edn., Westport, CT: Praeger Security International.

Halberstam, D. (1972) *The Best and the Brightest*, London: Barrie & Jenkins.

—— (2001) *War in a Time of Peace: Bush, Clinton, and the Generals*, New York: Scribner.

Haldeman, H.R. (1994) *The Haldeman Diaries: Inside the Nixon White House*, New York: Putnam.

Halliday, J. and Cumings, B. (1988) *Korea: The Unknown War*, New York: Pantheon Books.

Hallward, P. (2007) *Damming the Flood: Haiti, Aristide, and the Politics of Containment*, London: Verso.

Halper, S. and Clarke, J. (2005) *The Silence of the Rational Center*, New York: Basic Books.

Hamilton, L.H. (1996) "Third-Country Arms Deliveries to Bosnia and Croatia," 11 June, 104th Cong., 2d sess., *Congressional Record* 142, Extensions of Remarks: E1054–1056.

Hamilton, M.B. (1987) "The Elements of the Concept of Ideology," *Political Studies* 35(1): 18–38.

Hanhimäki, J. (2004) *The Flawed Architect: Henry Kissinger and American Foreign Policy*, Oxford and New York: Oxford University Press.

Hartung, W.D. and Berrigan, F. (2005) "Militarization of U.S. Africa Policy, 2000–2005," *Fact Sheet*, Arms Trade Resource Center, World Policy Institute, March. Online. Available: http://www.worldpolicy.org/projects/arms/reports/AfricaMarch2005.html (accessed 16 June 2005).

Hartz, L. (1991) *The Liberal Tradition in America*, San Diego, New York, and London: Harvest/Harcourt Brace [orig. publ. 1955 Harcourt, Brace & World].

Hasegawa, T. (2005) *Racing the Enemy: Stalin, Truman, and the Surrender of Japan*, Cambridge, MA: Belknap Press of Harvard University Press.

Hashim, A. (2003) "Saddam Husayn and Civil-Military Relations in Iraq: The Quest for Legitimacy and Power," *Middle East Journal* 57(1): 9–41.

Hastings, M. (2008) *Retribution: The Battle for Japan, 1944–45*, New York: Alfred A. Knopf.

Haugaard, L. (1997) "Textbook Repression: US Training Manuals Declassified," *CovertAction Quarterly* 61. Online. Available: http://mediafilter.org/CAQ/caq61/CAQ61manual.html (accessed 17 May 2005).

Healy, D. (1976) *Gunboat Diplomacy in the Wilson Era: The U.S. Navy in Haiti, 1915–1916*, Madison, WI: University of Wisconsin Press.

—— (1988) *Drive to Hegemony: The United States in the Caribbean 1898–1917*, Madison, WI: University of Wisconsin Press.

Hechiche, A. (1989) "Conflict and Resolution in Libyan-Tunisian Relations," *Maghreb Review* 14(1)–2: 50–69.

Heinrichs, W. (1990) "Franklin D. Roosevelt and the Risks of War, 1939–41," in A. Iriye and W. Cohen (eds), *American, Chinese, and Japanese Perspectives on Wartime Asia 1931–1949*, Wilmington, DE: Scholarly Resources Books.

Helman, GB. and Ratner, S.R. (1993) "Saving Failed States," *Foreign Policy* 89: 3–21.

Henning, C.R. (1999) *The Exchange Stabilization Fund: Slush Money or War Chest?* Washington, DC: Institute for International Economics.

Henze, P.B. (1991) "Ethiopia in 1991 – Peace Through Struggle," *Ethiopian Review*, September. Online. Available: http://www.ethiopianreview.com/content/347 (accessed 6 November 2008).

Herring, G.C. (1983) *The Secret Diplomacy of the Vietnam War: The Negotiating Volumes of the Pentagon Papers*, Austin, TX: University of Texas Press.

Hersh, S.M. (1983) *The Price of Power: Kissinger in the Nixon White House*, New York: Summit Books.

—— (1997) *The Dark Side of Camelot*, Boston, MA: Little, Brown.

—— (2004) *Chain of Command: The Road from 9/11 to Abu Ghraib*, London: Allen Lanc.

—— (2005a) "The Coming Wars," *New Yorker*, 24/31 January: 40–47.

—— (2005b) "Get Out the Vote," *New Yorker*, 25 July: 52–57.

—— (2006) "The Iran Plans," *New Yorker*, 17 April: 30–37.

Heuser, B. (1989) *Western "Containment" Policies in the Cold War: The Yugoslav Case, 1948–53*, London and New York: Routledge.

Hilsman, R. (1967) *To Move a Nation: The Politics of Foreign Policy in the Administration of John F. Kennedy*, Garden City, NY: Doubleday.

Hinnebusch, R. (2005) "Defying the Hegemon," paper presented at the conference of the European Consortium on Political Research, Budapest, September. Online. Available: http://www.st-andrews.ac.uk/mecacs/R.%20Hinnebusch%20DefyingHegemonSyria_Iraqwa_copy.pdf (accessed 26 September 2006).

Hoff, J. (1999) "The American Century: From Sarajevo to Sarajevo," in M.J. Hogan (ed.), *The Ambiguous Legacy: U.S. Foreign Relations in the "American Century,"* Cambridge: Cambridge University Press.

Hoffmann, S. (1984) "The Problem of Intervention," in H. Bull (ed.), *Intervention in World Politics*, Oxford: Clarendon Press.

Hoile, D. (2004) "Promoting Democratic Governance," paper presented at conference on Sudan at the Crossroads, Fletcher School of Law and Diplomacy, Tufts University, Medford, MA, 12 March. Online. Available: http://fletcher.tufts.edu/sudanconference2004/outcomes/Hoile%20Fri.pdf (accessed 16 August 2008).

Holbrooke, R. (1998) *To End a War*, New York: Random House.

Holland, M. (2005) "Private Sources of U.S. Foreign Policy: William Pawley and the 1954 Coup d'Etat in Guatemala," *Journal of Cold War Studies* 7(4): 36–73.

Holm, R.L. (2003) *The American Agent: My Life in the CIA*, London: St. Ermin's.

Holmes, J.E. (1985) *The Mood/Interest Theory of American Foreign Policy*, Lexington, KY: University Press of Kentucky.

Holober, F. (1999) *Raiders of the China Coast: CIA Covert Operations during the Korean War*, Annapolis, MD: Naval Institute Press.

Horsman, R. (1981) *Race and Manifest Destiny: The Origins of American Racial Anglo-Saxonism*, Cambridge, MA: Harvard University Press.

Hosmer, S. (2001) *Operations against Enemy Leaders*, RAND Report MR-1385-AF, Santa Monica, CA: RAND Corporation.

Howe, H.M. (1998) "Private Security Forces and African Stability: The Case of Executive Outcomes," *Journal of Modern African Studies* 36(2): 307–331.

Hoyle, R. (2008) *Going to War: How Misinformation, Disinformation, and Arrogance Led America into Iraq*, New York: Thomas Dunne Books.

Hudson, V.M. (2005) "Foreign Policy Analysis: Actor-Specific Theory and the Ground of International Relations," *Foreign Policy Analysis* 1(1): 1–30.

Huliaris, A. (2006) "Evangelists, Oil Companies, and Terrorists: The Bush Administration's Policy towards Sudan," *Orbis* 50(4): 709–724.

Human Rights Watch (1999) *Angola Unravels: The Rise and Fall of the Lusaka Peace Process*, HRW Index No. 2335, 1 September. Online. Available: http://www.hrw.org/reports/1999/angola/ (accessed 25 April 2006).

Hunt, M. (1987) *Ideology and U.S. Foreign Policy*, New Haven, CT: Yale University Press.

Husain, A. (2005) "Covert Action and US Cold War Strategy in Cuba, 1961–62," *Cold War History* 5(1): 23–53.

Ikenberry, G.J. (2001) "Getting Hegemony Right," *The National Interest* 63: 17–24.

—— (2002) "Democracy, Institutions, and American Restraint," in G.J. Ikenberry (ed.) *America Unrivaled: The Future of the Balance of Power*, Ithaca, NY: Cornell University Press.

International Commission on Intervention and State Sovereignty (2001) *The Responsibility to Protect*, Ottawa, Canada: International Development Research Centre.

International Institute for Strategic Studies (2008) *The Military Balance 2008*, London: Routledge.

Iokibe, M. (1981) "American Policy Towards Japan's 'Unconditional Surrender,'" *Japanese Journal of American Studies* 1: 19–53.

Iraq Study Group (2006) *The Iraq Study Group Report*, United States Institute of Peace. Online. Available: http://www.usip.org/isg/iraq_study_group_report/report/1206/iraq_study_group_report.pdf (accessed 16 August 2008).

Isaacs, A.R. (1983) *Without Honor: Defeat in Vietnam and Cambodia*, Baltimore, MD and London: Johns Hopkins University Press.

Isernia, P. (2006) "Anti-Americanism and European Public Opinion during the Iraq War," in Sergio Fabbrini (ed.), *The United States Contested: American Unilateralism and European Discontent*, London and New York: Routledge.

Jennings, K.A. (1986) "Sandino against the Marines: The Development of Air Power for Conducting Counterinsurgency Operations in Central America," *Air University Review* 37(5): 85–95.

Jennings, R. and Watts, A. (eds) (1996) *Oppenheim's International Law*, London: Longmans.

Jentleson, B.W. and Whytock, C.A. (2005/06) "Who 'Won' Libya? The Force-Diplomacy Debate and Its Implications for Theory and Policy," *International Security* 30(3): 47–86.

Jespersen, T.C. (2002) "Kissinger, Ford, and Congress: The Very Bitter End in Vietnam," *Pacific Historical Review* 71(3): 439–473.

Johnson, C., Schlei, N.A., and Schaller, M. (1995) "Special Report: The CIA and Japanese Politics," *Working Paper* 11, Japan Policy Research Institute, July. Online. Available: http://www.jpri.org/publications/workingpapers/wp11.html (accessed 22 May 2005).

Johnson, L.K. (1991) *America's Secret Power: The CIA in a Democratic Society*, new edn, New York: Oxford University Press.

Jones, C.L. (1934) "Loan Controls in the Caribbean," *Hispanic American Historical Review* 14 (2): 141–162.

Jones, J.L. (2005) "Statement of General James L. Jones, USMC, Commander, United States European Command, Before the Senate Armed Service Committee on 1 March 2005." Online. Available: http://www.eucom.mil/english/Command/Posture/SASC_Posture_Statement_010305.asp (accessed 5 June 2005).

Kahin, G.M. (1986) *Intervention: How America Became Involved in Vietnam*, New York: Alfred A. Knopf.

Kaminsky, A.P. (1986) *The India Office, 1880–1910*, New York: Greenwood.

Kaplan, L.S. (1980) *A Community of Interests: NATO and the Military Assistance Program, 1948–1951*, Washington, DC: Office of the Secretary of Defense, Historical Office.

—— (1984) *The United States and NATO: The Formative Years*, Lexington, KY: University Press of Kentucky.

Kaplan, S.S. (1975) "United States Aid and Regime Maintenance in Jordan, 1957–73," *Public Policy* 23(2): 189–217.

Karnow, S. (1983) *Vietnam: A History*, New York: Viking.

Karp, W. (1979) *The Politics of War: The Story of Two Wars Which Altered Forever the Political Life of the American Republic (1890–1920)*, New York: Harper & Row.

Katzman, K. (2004) "The Persian Gulf States: Issues for U.S. Policy, 2004," *CRS Report for Congress* RL31533, Congressional Research Service, Library of Congress, 4 October. Online. Available: http://www.usembassy.it/pdf/other/RL31533.pdf (accessed 16 April 2005).

—— (2006) "Iran: U.S. Concerns and Policy Responses," *CRS Report for Congress* RL 32048, 11 September. Online. Available: http://fpc.state.gov/documents/organization/72448.pdf (accessed 26 September 2006).

—— (2008) "Afghanistan: Post-War Governance, Security, and U.S. Policy," *CRS Report for Congress* RL30588, Congressional Research Service, Library of Congress, 28 January. Online. Available: http://www.fas.org/sgp/crs/row/RL30588.pdf (accessed 19 April 2008).

Kaufman, V.S. (2001) "Trouble in the Golden Triangle: The United States, Taiwan and the 93rd Nationalist Division," *China Quarterly* 166: 440–456.

Kempe, F. (1990) *Divorcing the Dictator: America's Bungled Affair with Noriega*, New York: G.P. Putnam's.

Kennedy, C.S. (2004) "The Iranian Revolution: An Oral History with Henry Precht, Then State Department Desk Officer," *Middle East Journal* 58(1): 9–31.

Kennedy, P. (1987) *The Rise and Fall of the Great Powers: Economic Change and Military Conflict From 1500 to 2000*, New York: Random House.

Kimball, J. (2003) "The Panmunjom and Paris Armistices: Patterns of War Termination," in A.W. Daum, L.C. Gardner, and W. Mausback (eds), *America, the Vietnam War, and the World: Comparative and International Perspectives*, New York: Cambridge University Press.

Kinzer, S. (2006) *Overthrow: America's Century of Regime Change from Hawaii to Iraq*, New York: Times Books/Henry Holt and Company.

Kirk, M. (2001) "Gunning for Saddam," *Frontline*, Program No. 2005, Public Broadcasting System, 8 November. Transcript online. Available: http://www.pbs.org/wgbh/pages/frontline/shows/gunning/etc/script.html (accessed 21 February 2006).

Kirkland, R.O. (2003) *Observing Our Hermanos de Armas:U.S. Military Attachés in Guatemala, Cuba, and Bolivia, 1950–1964*, New York and London: Routledge.

Kirkpatrick, J. (1979) "Dictatorships and Double Standards," *Commentary* (Nov.): 34–45.

Kissinger, H. (1979) *White House Years*, New York: Little, Brown.

—— (1999) *Years of Renewal*, New York: Simon & Schuster.

Klare, M.T. (2008) "The China Syndrome," *Foreign Policy in Focus*, 5 March. Online. Available: http://www.fpif.org/fpiftxt/5041 (accessed 17 August 2008).

Klingberg, F.L. (1952) "The Historical Alternation of Moods in American Foreign Policy," *World Politics* 4(2): 239–273.

—— (1996) *Positive Expectations of America's World Role: Historical Cycles of Realistic Idealism*, Lanham, MD: University Press of America.

Knight, W.A. and Persaud, R.B. (2001) "Subsidiarity, Regional Governance, and Caribbean Security," *Latin American Politics and Society* 43(1): 29–56.

Knorr, K. (1975) *The Power of Nations: The Political Economy of International Relations*, New York: Basic Books.

Kolko, G. (1968) *The Politics of War: The World and United States Foreign Policy, 1943–1945*, New York: Random House.

Kolko, J. and Kolko, G. (1972) *The Limits of Power: The World and United States Foreign Policy, 1945–1954*, New York: Harper and Row.

Kramer, P.A. (2002) "Empires, Exceptions, and Anglo-Saxons: Race and Rule Between the British and United States Empires, 1880–1910," *Journal of American History* 88(4): 1315–1353.

—— (2006) "Race-Making and Colonial Violence in the U.S. Empire: The Philippine-American War as Race War," *Diplomatic History* 30(2): 169–210.

Kramer, R. (1995) "Liberia: A Casualty of the Cold War's End," *CSIS Africa Notes*, African Studies Program, Center for Strategic and International Studies, Washington, DC, 1 July. Online. Available: http://www.hartford-hwp.com/archives/34/042.html (accessed 12 September 2005).

Krasner, S.D. (1978) *Defending the National Interest: Raw Materials Investment and U.S. Foreign Policy*, Princeton, NJ: Princeton University Press.

—— (2004) "Sharing Sovereignty: New Institutions for Collapsed and Failing States," *International Security* 29(2): 85–120.

Kuykendall, R.S. (1967) *The Hawaiian Kingdom*, vol. 3: *1874–1893, The Kalakaua Dynasty*, Honolulu, HI: University of Hawaii Press.

LaFeber, W. (1984) *Inevitable Revolutions: The United States in Central America*, exp. edn, New York: W.W. Norton.

Langer, W.L. and Gleason, S.E. (1952) *The Challenge to Isolation 1937–1940*, New York: Harper & Brothers.

—— (1953) *The Undeclared War 1940–1941*, New York: Harper & Brothers.

Langguth, A.J. (1978) *Hidden Terrors: The Truth about U.S. Police Operations in Latin America*, New York: Pantheon.

Layne, C. (1997) "A House of Cards: American Strategy toward China," *World Policy Journal* 14(3): 77–95.

—— (2006) *The Peace of Illusions: American Grand Strategy from 1940 to the Present*, Cambridge, MA: Harvard University Press.

Leary, W.M. (1984) *Perilous Missions: Civil Air Transport and CIA Covert Operations in Asia*, Birmingham, AL: University of Alabama Press.

—— (1999) "CIA Air Operations in Laos, 1955–74," *Studies in Intelligence* 43(1): 71–86.

Lebow, R.N. (1998) "Beyond Parsimony: Rethinking Theories of Coercive Bargaining," *European Journal of International Relations* 4(1): 31–66.

Lefebvre, J.A. (1991) *Arms for the Horn: U.S. Security Policy in Ethiopia and Somalia, 1953–1991*, Pittsburgh, PA: University of Pittsburgh Press.

—— (1998) "The United States, Ethiopia and the 1963 Somali-Soviet Arms Deal: Containment and the Balance of Power Dilemma in the Horn of Africa," *Journal of Modern African Studies* 36(4): 611–643.

Lefebvre, S. (2003) "The Difficulties and Dilemmas of International Intelligence Cooperation," *International Journal of Intelligence and Counterintelligence*, 16(4): 527–542.

Leffler, M.P. (1992) *A Preponderance of Power: National Security, the Truman Administration, and the Cold War*, Stanford, CA: Stanford University Press.

Lehman, K. (1997) "Revolutions and Attributions: Making Sense of Eisenhower Administration Policies in Bolivia and Guatemala," *Diplomatic History* 21(2): 185–213.

Leibowitz, A. (1989) *Defining Status: A Comprehensive Analysis of United States-Territorial Relations*, Dordrecht, Netherlands: Martinus Nijhoff / Kluwer Law International.

Lemarchand, R. (1976) "The CIA in Africa: How Central? How Intelligent?" *Journal of Modern African Studies* 14(3): 401–426.

LeMelle, G. (2008) "Africa Policy Outlook 2008," *FPIF Policy Report*, 7 February. Online. Available: http://www.fpif.org/fpiftxt/4949 (accessed 28 March 2008).

LeoGrande, W.M. (1998a) *Our Own Backyard: The United States in Central America, 1977–1992*, Chapel Hill, NC and London: University of North Carolina Press.

—— (1998b) "From Havana to Miami: U.S. Cuba Policy as a Two-Level Game," *Journal of Interamerican Studies and World Affairs* 40(1): 67–86.

Levenson, J. (1953) "Western Powers and Chinese Revolutions: The Pattern of Intervention," *Pacific Affairs* 26(3): 230–236.

Levinthal, D. and March, J.G. (1981) "A Model of Adaptive Organizational Search," *Journal of Economic Behavior and Organization* 2(4): 307–333.

Lieuwen, E. (1961) *Arms and Politics in Latin America*, rev. edn., New York: Frederick A. Praeger for Council on Foreign Relations.

Lindblom, C.E. (1959) "The Science of 'Muddling Through'," *Public Administration Review* 19 (2): 79–88.

—— (1965) *The Intelligence of Democracy: Decision Making through Mutual Adjustment,* New York: Free Press.

Lindqvist, S. (2001) *A History of Bombing*, trans. L.H. Rugg, New York: New Press.

Lindsay, J.M. and Smith, C. (2003) "Rally 'Round the Flag': Opinion in the United States Before and After the Iraq War," *Brookings Review* 21(3): 20–23.

Lindvall-Larson, K. (2002) *Latin American Election Statistics: A Guide to Sources*, Social Sciences and Humanities Library, University of California at San Diego, June. Online. Available: http://sshl.ucsd.edu/collections/las/index.html (accessed 19 April 2005).

Link, A.S. (1956) *Wilson: The New Freedom*, Princeton, NJ: Princeton University Press.

Linn, B. (1996) "The Long Twilight of the Frontier Army," *Western Historical Quarterly* 27(2): 141–167.

—— (1997) *Guardians of the Empire: The U.S. Army and the Pacific, 1902–1940*, Chapel Hill, NC: University of North Carolina Press.

Lintner, B. (1994) *Burma in Revolt: Opium and Insurgency Since 1948*, Boulder, CO: Westview Press.

Lippmann, W. (1922) *Public Opinion*, New York: Macmillan.

Lipset, S.M. (1996) *American Exceptionalism: A Double-Edged Sword*, New York: W.W. Norton.

Liska, G. (1978) *Career of Empire: America and Imperial Expansion Over Land and Sea*, Baltimore, MD: Johns Hopkins University Press.

Little, D. (1988) "The New Frontier On the Nile: JFK, Nasser, and Arab Nationalism," *Journal of American History* 75(2): 501–527.

—— (1990) "Cold War and Covert Action: The United States and Syria, 1945–58," *Middle East Journal* 44(1): 51–75.

—— (1995) "A Puppet in Search of a Puppeteer? The United States, King Hussein, and Jordan, 1953–70," *International History Review* 17(3): 512–544.

—— (1996) "His Finest Hour? Eisenhower, Lebanon, and the 1958 Middle East Crisis," *Diplomatic History* 20(1): 27–54.

—— (2003) *American Orientalism: The United States and the Middle East Since 1945*, London and New York: I.B. Tauris.

—— (2004) "Mission Impossible: The CIA and the Cult of Covert Action in the Middle East," *Diplomatic History* 28(5): 663–701.

Livermore, S.W. (1943) "American Strategy Diplomacy in the South Pacific 1890–1914," *Pacific Historical Review* 12(1): 33–51.

Logevall, F. (1993) "The Swedish-American Conflict over Vietnam," *Diplomatic History* 17(3): 421–446.

Louis, W.R. (ed.) (1976) *Imperialism: The Robinson and Gallagher Controversy*, New York and London: New Viewpoints/Franklin Watts.

—— (2004) "Britain and the Overthrow of the Mosaddeq Government," in M.J. Gasiorowski and M. Byrne (eds) *Mohammad Mosaddeq and the 1953 Coup in Iran*, Syracues, NY: Syracuse University Press.

Love, E.T. (2004) *Race Over Empire: Racism and U.S. Imperialism, 1865–1900*, Chapel Hill, NC: University of North Carolina Press.

Lugard, F.J.D. (1922) *The Dual Mandate in British Tropical Africa*, London: Frank Cass.

Lumpe, L. (2002) "U.S. Foreign Military Training: Global Reach, Global Power, and Oversight Issues," *Foreign Policy in Focus Special Report*, May. Online. Available: http://www.fpif.org/papers/miltrain/index.html (accessed 17 August 2008).

Lundestad, G. (1986) "Empire by Invitation? The United States and Western Europe, 1945–52," *Journal of Peace Research* 23(3): 263–277.

—— (1998) *"Empire" by Integration: The United States and European Integration, 1945–1997*, Oxford: Oxford University Press.

—— (1999) "'Empire by Invitation' in the American Century," *Diplomatic History* 23(2): 189–217.

Lustig, N. (1977) "Mexico in Crisis, the U.S. to the Rescue: The Financial Assistance Packages of 1982 and 1995," *Brookings Discussion Paper*, Brookings Institution, January. Online. Available: http://www.brookings.edu/dybdocroot/views/articles/lustig/1997BI.pdf (accessed 26 June 2005).

Macmillan, H. (1972) *Pointing the Way 1959–1961*, New York: Harper & Row.

MacMillan, M. (2001) *Peacemakers: The Paris Conference of 1919 and its Attempt to End War*, London: John Murray.

Maguire, R. (2003) "US Policy Toward Haiti: Engagement or Estrangement?" *Haiti Papers* 8, November, The Haiti Program, Trinity College, Washington, DC.

Maier, C.S. (2006) *Among Empires: American Ascendancy and Its Predecessors*, Cambridge, MA: Harvard University Press.

Majeski, S.J. (1989) "A Rule Based Model of the United States Military Expenditure Decision-Making Process," *International Interactions* 15(2): 129–154.

Majeski, S. and Sylvan, D. (1999) "How Foreign Policy Recommendations Are Put Together: A Computational Model with Empirical Applications," *International Interactions* 25(4): 301–332.

Mak, D. and Kennedy, C.S. (1992) *American Ambassadors in a Troubled World: Interviews with Senior Diplomats*, Westport, CT: Greenwood.

Mandelbaum, M. (1999) "A Perfect Failure: NATO's War Against Yugoslavia," *Foreign Affairs* 78(5): 2–8.

Mangold, P. (1979) "Shaba I and Shaba II," *Survival* 21(3): 107–115.

Mann, J. (2004) *Rise of the Vulcans: The History of Bush's War Cabinet*, New York: Viking.

Manyin, M.E. (2005) "The Vietnam-U.S. Normalization Process," *CRS Issue Brief for Congress* IB98033, 17 June. Online. Available: http://www.fas.org/sgp/crs/row/IB98033.pdf#search = %22mark%20manyin%20vietnam%20normalization%22 (accessed 25 September 2005).

March, J.G. and Simon, H.A. (1958) *Organizations*, New York: Wiley.

Marcus, H. (1983) *Ethiopia, Great Britain, and the United States, 1941–1974: The Politics of Empire*, Berkeley, CA: University of California Press.

Marfiak, T. (2008) "Where Are the Ballistic Missile Defense Cruisers?" U.S. Naval Institute *Proceedings Magazine* 134(5). Online. Available: http://www.usni.org/magazines/proceedings/story.asp?STORY_ID = 1453 (accessed 17 August 2008).

Marisa, K.M. (2003) "Consolidated Military Attaché and Security Assistance Activities: A Case for Unity of Command," *FAO Journal* 7(2): 6–10, 21–24.

Mark, C.R. (2004) "Israel: U.S. Foreign Assistance", *CRS Issue Brief for Congress* IB85066, 12 July. Online. Available: http://www.fas.org/man/crs/IB85066.pdf (accessed 22 April 2005).

Marra, R.F. (1985) "A Cybernetic Model of the US Defense Expenditure Policymaking Process," *International Studies Quarterly* 29(4): 357–384.

Masani, P.R. (1990) *Norbert Wiener 1894–1964*, Basel, Boston, MA and Berlin: Birkhäuser Verlag.

Mayer, J. (2005) "Outsourcing Torture," *New Yorker*, 14 February.

—— (2008) *The Dark Side: The Inside Story of How the War On Terror Turned Into a War On American Ideals*, New York: Doubleday.

MccGwire, M. (1998) "NATO Expansion: A Policy Error of Historic Importance," *Review of International Studies* 24(1): 23–42.

McClintock, M. (1992) *Instruments of Statecraft: U.S. Guerrilla Warfare, Counterinsurgency, and Counterterrorism, 1940–1990*, New York: Pantheon.

McCoy, A.W. (2003) *The Politics of Heroin: CIA Complicity in the Global Drug Trade*, rev. edn, New York: Lawrence Hill Books.

—— (2006) *A Question of Torture: CIA Interrogation, from the Cold War to the War on Terror*, New York: Metropolitan/Owl.

McDougall, W.A. (1997) *Promised Land, Crusader State: The American Encounter with the World Since 1776*, New York: Houghton Mifflin.

McFaul, M. (1989–90) "Rethinking the 'Reagan Doctrine' in Angola," *International Security* 14 (3): 99–135.

McMahon, R.J. (1999) *The Limits of Empire: The United States and Southeast Asia Since World War II*, New York: Columbia University Press.

Mearsheimer, J.J. (2001) *The Tragedy of Great Power Politics*, New York: W.W. Norton.

Mearsheimer, J.J. and Walt, S.M. (2007) *The Israel Lobby and U.S. Foreign Policy*, London: Allen Lane.

Mecham, J.L. (1961) *The United States and Inter-American Security, 1889–1960*, Austin, TX: University of Texas Press.

Meinig, D.W. (2004) *The Shaping of America: A Geographical Perspective on 500 Years of History*, vol. 4: *Global America, 1915–2000*, New Haven, CT: Yale University Press.

Menges, C.C. (1988) *Inside the National Security Council: The True Story of the Making and Unmaking of Reagan's Foreign Policy*, New York: Simon & Schuster.

Meyer, C. (2005) *DC Confidential: The Controversial Memoirs of Britain's Ambassador to the U.S. at the Time of 9/11 and the Iraq War*, London: Weidenfeld & Nicolson.

Miller, J.E. (1983) "Taking Off the Gloves: The United States and the Italian Elections of 1948," *Diplomatic History* 7(1): 35–55.

Miller Center of Public Affairs (2004) "National Security Council Staff Organization Chart." Online. Available: http://www.americanpresident.org/action/orgchart/a_index.shtml?/action/orgchart /administration_units/nationalsecuritycouncil/orgchart.xxml (accessed 10 November 2004).

Milward, A.S. (1984) *The Reconstruction of Western Europe, 1945–1951*, London: Methuen.

Minger, R.E. (1961) "William H. Taft and the United States Intervention in Cuba in 1906," *Hispanic American Historical Review* 41(1): 75–89.

Mirowski, P. (2002) *Machine Dreams: Economics Becomes a Cyborg Science*, Cambridge: Cambridge University Press.

Mitchell, D. (2005) "The 2004 Removal of Jean-Bertrand Aristide," The Center for Cooperative Research. Online. Available: http://www.cooperativeresearch.org/timeline.jsp?timeline = the_2004_removal_of_jean-bertrand_aristide (accessed 4 November 2005).

Mitchener, K.J. and Weidenmier, M.D. (2004) "Empire, Public Goods, and the Roosevelt Corollary," *Working Paper* 10729, National Bureau of Economic Research, August. Online. Available: http://dsl.nber.org/papers/w10729.pdf (accessed 18 April 2005).

Mitrovich, G. (2000) *Undermining the Kremlin: America's Strategy to Subvert the Soviet Bloc, 1947–1956*, Ithaca, NY, and London: Cornell University Press.

Montague, L.L. (1992) *General Walter Bedell Smith as Director of Central Intelligence: October 1950–February 1953*, University Park, PA: Pennsylvania State University Press.

Moores, S. (2002) "Neutral on Our Side: US Policy towards Sweden during the Eisenhower Administration," *Cold War History* 2(3): 29–62.

Morgan, T. (1999) *A Covert Life: Jay Lovestone: Communist, Anti-Communist, and Spymaster*, New York: Random House.

Morley, J. (2008) *Our Man in Mexico: Winston Scott and the Hidden History of the CIA*, Lawrence, KS: University Press of Kansas.

Morley, M.H. (1994) *Washington, Somoza, and the Sandinistas: State and Regime in U.S. Policy toward Nicaragua, 1969–1981*, Cambridge: Cambridge University Press.

Morris, R.L. (1962) "A Reassessment of Russian Recognition," *The Historian* 24(4): 470–482.

Mortimer, R.A. (1996) "Senegal's Role in Ecomog: The Francophone Dimension in the Liberian Crisis," *Journal of Modern African Studies* 34(2): 293–306.

Mueller, J.E. (1973) *War, Presidents, and Public Opinion*, New York: Wiley.

—— (2005) "The Iraq Syndrome," *Foreign Affairs* 84(6): 44–54.

—— (2006) "Reply," *Foreign Affairs* 85(1).

Mullins, W.A. (1972) "On the Concept of Ideology in Political Science," *American Political Science Review* 66(2): 498–510.

Munro, D.G. (1934) *The United States and the Caribbean Area*, Boston: World Peace Foundation.

—— (1958) "Dollar Diplomacy in Nicaragua, 1909–13," *The Hispanic American Historical Review* 38(2): 209–234.

—— (1974) *The United States and the Caribbean Republics, 1921–1933*, Princeton, NJ: Princeton University Press.

Murphy, G.G.S. (1961) "On Satelliteship," *Journal of Economic History* 21(4): 641–651.

Nalty, B.C. (1961) *The United States Marines in Nicaragua*, rev. edn., Washington, DC: Historical Branch, G-3 Division, Headquarters, U.S. Marine Corps. Online. Available: http://www.1stbattalion3rdmarines.com/war-related/NICARAGUA.htm (accessed 13 May 2005).

Natsios, A.S. (2008) "Beyond Darfur," *Foreign Affairs* 87(3): 77–93.

Nau, H. (2002) *At Home Abroad: Identity and Power in American Foreign Policy*, Ithaca, NY: Cornell University Press.

Newell, A., Shaw, J.C., and Simon, H.A. (1958) "Elements of a Theory of Human Problem Solving," *Psychological Review* 65(3): 151–166.

Newell, A. and Simon, H.A. (1972) *Human Problem Solving*, Englewood Cliffs, NJ: Prentice-Hall.

Newman, J.M. (1992) *JFK and Vietnam: Deception, Intrigue, and the Struggle for Power*, New York: Warner Books.

Nexon, D.H. and Wright, T. (2007) "What's at Stake in the American Empire Debate," *American Political Science Review* 101(2): 253–271.

Nicolson, H. (1939) *Diplomacy*, London: Home University Library/Oxford University Press.

Niksch, L.A. (2006) "North Korea's Nuclear Weapons Program," *CRS Report for Congress* RL33590, 1 August. Online. Available: http://fpc.state.gov/documents/organization/71870.pdf (accessed 27 September 2006).

Noer, T.J. (1984) "The New Frontier and African Neutralism: Kennedy, Nkrumah, and the Volta River Project," *Diplomatic History* 8(1): 61–80.

Nwaubani, E. (2001) "Eisenhower, Nkrumah and the Congo Crisis," *Journal of Contemporary History* 36(4): 599–622.

O'Connor, R.G. (1974) "The U.S. Marines in the 20th Century: Amphibious Warfare and Doctrinal Debates," *Military Affairs* 38(3): 97–103.

Odom, T.P. (1988) *Dragon Operations: Hostage Rescues in the Congo, 1964–1965*, Leavenworth Papers No. 14, Fort Leavenworth, KS: Combat Studies Institute, U.S. Army Command and General Staff College, Fort Leavenworth. Online. Available: http://cgsc.leavenworth.army.mil/carl/resources/csi/odom/odom.asp (accessed 5 June 2005).

—— (1993) *Shaba II: The French and Belgian Intervention in Zaire in 1978*, Combat Studies Institute, Combined Studies Institute, U.S. Army Command and General Staff College, Fort Leavenworth, KS: Combined Arms Research Library. Online. Available: http://cgsc.leavenworth.army.mil/carl/resources/csi/odom2/odom2.asp (accessed 7 September 2005).

O'Hanlon, M.E. and de Albuquerque, A.L. (2005) "Afghanistan Index," Brookings Institution, 30 June. Online. Available: http://www.brookings.edu/fp/research/projects/southasia/afghanistanindex.pdf (accessed 23 August 2005).

Olsen, J.P. (2001) "Garbage Cans, New Institutionalism, and the Study of Politics," *American Political Science Review* 95(1): 191–198.

Omissi, D.E. (1990) *Air Power and Colonial Control: The Royal Air Force, 1919–1939*, Manchester: Manchester University Press.

Ostrom, C.W., Jr. (1977) "Evaluating Alternative Foreign Policy Decision-Making Models: An Empirical Test Between an Arms Race Model and an Organizational Politics Model," *Journal of Conflict Resolution* 21(2): 235–266.

Ottaway, M. (1991) "Mediation in a Transitional Conflict: Eritrea," *Annals of the American Academy of Political and Social Science*, 518, November: 69–81.

Ovendale, R. (1994) "Great Britain and the Anglo-American Invasion of Jordan and Lebanon in 1958," *International History Review* 16(2): 284–303.

Oyos, M.M. (1996) "Theodore Roosevelt and the Implements of War," *Journal of Military History* 60(4): 631–655.

Pach, C.J., Jr. (1991) *Arming the Free World: The Origins of the United States Military Assistance Program, 1945–1950*, Chapel Hill, NC and London: University of North Carolina Press.

Packer, G. (2005) *The Assassins' Gate: America in Iraq*, New York: Farrar, Straus and Giroux.

Padgett, J.F. (1980) "Managing Garbage Can Hierarchies," *Administrative Science Quarterly* 25 (4): 583–604.

Pagani, F. (2002) "Peer Review: A Tool for Co-operation and Change: An Analysis of an OECD Working Method," SG/LEG(2002)1, General Secretariat, Directorate for Legal Affairs, Organisation for Economic Co-operation and Development, 11 September. Online. Available: http://www.oecd.org/dataoecd/33/16/1955285.pdf (accessed 26 May 2005).

Paige, G.D. (1968) *The Korean Decision, June 24–30, 1950*, New York: Free Press.

Pape, R.A. (1996) *Bombing to Win: Air Power and Coercion in War*, Ithaca, NY: Cornell University Press.

Pascoe, W. (1987) "Time for Action against Mengistu's Ethiopia," Heritage Foundation *Backgrounder* #568, 11 March.

Paseman, F.L. (2004) *A Spy's Journey: A CIA Memoir*, St. Paul, MN: Zenith Press.

Payne, A.J. (1995) *Politics in Jamaica*, 2d rev. edn., New York: St. Martin's Press.

Payne, D.W. (1996) "The 1996 Suriname Elections: Post-Election Report," *Western Hemisphere Election Study Series* 14(4), 19 September. Online. Available: http://www.parbo.com/information/census.html (accessed 31 March 2005).

Pereira, A.W. (1994) "The Neglected Tragedy: The Return to War in Angola, 1992–93," *Journal of Modern African Studies* 32(1): 1–28.

Peters, B.G. (2001) "Governance: A Garbage Can Perspective," Institute for Advanced Studies, Vienna, *Political Science Series* 84, December. Online. Available: http://www.ihs.ac.at/publications/pol/wp_84.pdf (accessed 27 May 2008).

Pew Global Attitudes Project (2006) "America's Image Slips, But Allies Share U.S. Concerns over Iran, Hamas," 15-Nation Pew Global Attitudes Survey, 13 June. Online. Available: http://pewglobal.org/reports/pdf/252.pdf (accessed 16 August 2008).

—— (2008) "Global Economic Gloom – China and India Notable Exceptions," 24-Nation Pew Global Attitudes Survey, 12 June. Online. Available: http://pewglobal.org/reports/pdf/260.pdf (accessed 16 August 2008).

Pézard, S. (2008) "Beating a Retreat: Military Interventions, Surprising Setbacks, and the Decision to Disengage," Ph.D. diss., Graduate Institute of International and Development Studies.

Pfeiffer, J. (n.d. [1970s]) *Official History of the Bay of Pigs Operation*, vol. 3. Online. Available: http://www14.homepage.villanova.edu/david.barrett/bop.html (accessed 27 September 2005).

Pickering, A. (2002) "Cybernetics and the Mangle: Ashby, Beer and Pask," *Social Studies of Science* 32(3): 413–437.

—— (2004) "The Science of the Unknowable: Stafford Beer's Cybernetic Informatics," *Kybernetes* 33(3/4): 499–521.

Pisani, S. (1991) *The CIA and the Marshall Plan*, Lawrence, KS: University Press of Kansas.

Plante, T.K. (1999) "U.S. Marines in the Boxer Rebellion," *Prologue Magazine* 31(4).

Platt, D.C.M. (1968) *Finance, Trade, and Politics in British Foreign Policy 1815–1914*, Oxford: Clarendon Press.

Podesta, J. and Ogden, P. (2007–08) "The Security Implications of Climate Change," *Washington Quarterly* 31(1): 115–138.

Pollins, B.M. and Schweller, R.L. (1999) "Linking the Levels: The Long Wave and Shifts in U.S. Foreign Policy, 1790–1993," *American Journal of Political Science* 43(2): 431–464.

Pomeroy, E.S. (1944) "The American Colonial Office," *Mississippi Valley Historical Review* 30 (4): 521–532.

Porter, G. (2005) *Perils of Dominance: Imbalance of Power and the Road to War in Vietnam*, Berkeley, CA: University of California Press.

Potgieter, J. (2000) "'Taking Aid From the Devil Himself': UNITA's Support Structures," in J. Cilliers and C. Dietrich (eds) *Angola's War Economy: The Role of Oil and Diamonds*, Pretoria: Institute for Security Studies.

Powell, A.I. (1928) "Relations Between the United States and Nicaragua, 1898–1916," *Hispanic American Historical Review* 8(1): 43–64.

Powell, C. (1995) *My American Journey*, with J. Persico, New York: Random House.

Powell, N.J. (2005) "Situation in Afghanistan," Testimony Before the House of Representatives Armed Services Committee, 22 June (released 15 August). Online. Available: http://www.state.gov/p/inl/rls/rm/51067.htm (accessed 23 August 2005).

Power, S. (2002) *A Problem from Hell: America and the Age of Genocide*, New York: Basic Books.

Powers, T. (1979) *The Man Who Kept the Secrets: Richard Helms and the CIA*, New York: Knopf.

Prados, A.B. (2006) "Syria: U.S. Relations and Bilateral Issues," *CRS Report for Congress* RL33487, 18 August. Online. Available: http://fpc.state.gov/documents/organization/71843.pdf (accessed 26 September 2006).

Prados, J. (1996) *Presidents' Secret Wars: CIA and Pentagon Covert Operations from World War II Through the Persian Gulf*, rev. edn, Chicago, IL: Elephant Paperbacks/Ivan R. Dee.

—— (2003) *Lost Crusader: The Secret Wars of CIA Director William Colby*, New York: Oxford University Press.

Priest, D. (2003) *The Mission: Waging War and Keeping Peace with America's Military*, New York and London: W.W. Norton & Company.

Pumphrey, C. (ed.) (2008) *Global Climate Change: National Security Implications*, Carlisle, PA: Strategic Studies Institute, U.S. Army War College.

Quandt, W.B. (1993) *Peace Process: American Diplomacy and the Arab-Israeli Conflict since 1967*, Washington, DC: Brookings Institution.

Quirk, R.E. (1962) *An Affair of Honor: Woodrow Wilson and the Occupation of Veracruz*, Lexington, KY: University of Kentucky Press.

Rabe, S.G. (1999) *The Most Dangerous Area in the World: John F. Kennedy Confronts Communist Revolution in Latin America*, Chapel Hill, NC and London: University of North Carolina Press.

—— (2000) "After the Missiles of October: John F. Kennedy and Cuba, November 1962 to November 1963," *Presidential Studies Quarterly* 30(4): 714–726.

Ramusack, B.N. (2004) *The Indian Princes and Their States, The New Cambridge History of India*, vol. 3.6, Cambridge: Cambridge University Press.

Rathbun, B. (1996) *The Point Man: Irving Brown and the Deadly Post-1945 Struggle for Europe and Africa*, London: Minerva Press.

Raymond, G.A. and Kegley, C.W., Jr. (1990) "Polarity, Polarization, and the Transformation of Alliance Norms," *Political Research Quarterly* 43(1): 9–38.

Rempe, D.M. (1999) "An American Trojan Horse? Eisenhower, Latin America, and the Development of US Internal Security Policy," *Small Wars and Insurgencies* 10(1): 34–64.

Reveron, D.S. and Gavin, M.D. (2004) "America's Viceroys," in D.S. Reveron (ed.) *America's Viceroys: The Military and U.S. Foreign Policy*, New York and Houndmills: Palgrave Macmillan.

Reynolds, D. (1981) *The Creation of the Anglo-American Alliance 1937–1941: A Study in Competitive Co-operation*, London: Europa Publications.

Richardson, G.P. (1991) *Feedback Thought in Social Science and Systems Theory*, Philadelphia, PA: University of Pennsylvania Press.

Richelson, J.T. (2002) "When Kindness Fails: Assassination as a National Security Option," *International Journal of Intelligence and CounterIntelligence* 15(2): 243–274.

Ricks, T.E. (2006) *Fiasco: The American Military Adventure in Iraq*, London: Allen Lane.

Rieff, D. (2005) *At the Point of a Gun: Democratic Dreams and Armed Intervention*, New York: Simon & Schuster.

Risen, J. (2006) *State of War: The Secret History of the CIA and the Bush Administration*, New York: Free Press.

Ritter, S. (2005) *Iraq Confidential: The Untold Story of the Intelligence Conspiracy to Undermine the UN and Overthrow Saddam Hussein*, New York: Nation Books.

Robbins, C. (1979) *Air America*, New York: Avon Books.

Roesad, K. (2001) "ODA in Indonesia: A Preliminary Assessment," *Economics Working Paper Series*, Centre for Strategic and International Studies, Jakarta, March. Online. Available: http://www.csis.or.id/papers/wpe058 (accessed 31 March 2005).

Ronen, Y. (2002) "Sudan and the United States: Is a Decade of Tension Winding Down?" *Middle East Policy* 9(1): 94–108.

Rose, D. (2008) "The Gaza Bombshell," *Vanity Fair*, April: 192–197.

Rosenberg, E.S. (1985) "The Invisible Protectorate: The United States, Liberia, and the Evolution of Neocolonialism, 1909–40," *Diplomatic History* 9(3): 191–214.

—— (1998) "Presidential Address. Revisiting Dollar Diplomacy: Narratives of Money and Manliness," *Diplomatic History* 22(2): 155–176.

—— (1999) *Financial Missionaries to the World: The Politics and Culture of Dollar Diplomacy, 1900–1930*, Cambridge, MA: Harvard University Press.

Rosenberg, E.S. and Rosenberg, N.L. (1987) "From Colonialism to Professionalism: The Public-Private Dynamic in United States Foreign Financial Advising, 1898–1929," *Journal of American History* 74(1): 59–82.

Rosenblueth, A. and Wiener, N. (1950) "Purposeful and Non-purposeful Behavior," *Philosophy of Science* 17(4): 318–326.

Rosenblueth, A., Wiener, N., and Bigelow, J. (1943) "Behavior, Purpose and Teleology," *Philosophy of Science* 10(1): 18–24.

Rositzke, H. (1975) "America's Secret Operations: A Perspective," *Foreign Affairs* 53(1): 334–351.

Rothbard, M.N. (2007) *The Betrayal of the American Right*, Thomas E. Woods, Jr. (ed.), Auburn, AL: Ludwig von Mises Institute.

Rothkopf, D. (2004) *Running the World: The Inside Story of the National Security Council and the Architects of American Power*, New York: PublicAffairs.

Rouvez, A. (1994) *Disconsolate Empires: French, British and Belgian Military Involvement in Post-Colonial Sub-Saharan Africa*, Lanham, MD: University Press of America.

Rubin, R.E. and Weisberg, J. (2003) *In an Uncertain World: Tough Choices from Wall Street to Washington*, New York: Random House.

Rudner, M. (2004) "Hunters and Gatherers: The Intelligence Coalition against Islamic Terrorism," *International Journal of Intelligence and Counterintelligence* 17(2): 193–230.

Rugh, W.A. (1996) "The Foreign Policy of the United Arab Emirates," *Middle East Journal* 50 (1): 57–70.

Sahlin-Andersson, K. (1996) "Imitating by Editing Success: The Construction of Organization Fields," in B. Czarniawska and G. Sevón (eds) *Translating Organizational Change*, Berlin and New York: Walter de Gruyter.

Salisbury, R.V. (1997) "Great Britain, the United States, and the 1909–10 Nicaraguan Crisis," *The Americas* 53(3): 379–394.

Sanchez, R.S. (2008) *Wiser in Battle: A Soldier's Story*, New York: HarperCollins.

Sands, P. (2005) *Lawless World: America and the Making and Breaking of Global Rules from FDR's Atlantic Charter to George W. Bush's Illegal War*, New York: Viking.

—— (2008) *Torture Team: Rumsfeld's Memo and the Betrayal of American Values*, New York: Palgrave Macmillan.

Sarkees, M.R. (2000) "The Correlates of War Data on War," *Conflict Management and Peace Science* 18(1): 123–144.

Scahill, J. (2007) *Blackwater: The Rise of the World's Most Powerful Mercenary Army*, New York: Nation Books.

Schaller, M. (1976) "American Air Strategy in China, 1939–41: The Origins of Clandestine Air Warfare," *American Quarterly* 28(1): 3–19.

Schatzberg, M.G. (1989) "Military Intervention and the Myth of Collective Security: The Case of Zaire," *Journal of Modern African Studies* 27(2): 315–340.

Schelling, T.C. (1960) *The Strategy of Conflict*, New York: Oxford University Press.

—— (1966) *Arms and Influence*, New Haven, CT: Yale University Press.

Schirmer, D.B. and Shalom, S.R. (1987) *The Philippines Reader: A History of Colonialism, Neocolonialism, Dictatorship, and Resistance*, Boston, MA: South End Press.

Schlesinger, A.M., Jr. (1965) *A Thousand Days: John F. Kennedy in the White House*, Boston, MA and Cambridge: Houghton Mifflin/The Riverside Press.

Schlesinger, S. and Kinzer, S. (1983) *Bitter Fruit: The Untold Story of the American Coup in Guatemala*, 2d edn., Garden City, NY: Anchor Books.

Schmidt, H. (1971) *The U.S. Occupation of Haiti*, New Brunswick, NJ: Rutgers University Press.

Schmidt, S.W., Guasti, L., Landé, C.H., and Scott, J.C. (eds) (1976) *Friends, Followers, and Factions*, Berkeley, CA: University of California Press.

Schoultz, L. (1998) *Beneath the United States: A History of U.S. Policy toward Latin America*, Cambridge, MA: Harvard University Press.

Schraeder, P.J. (1992) "The Horn of Africa: US Foreign Policy in an Altered Cold War Environment," *Middle East Journal* 46(4): 571–593.

—— (1994) *United States Foreign Policy Toward Africa: Incrementalism, Crisis and Change*, Cambridge: Cambridge University Press.

Schroen, G.C. (2005) *First In: An Insider's Account of How the CIA Spearheaded the War on Terror in Afghanistan*, New York: Ballantine Books.

Schumacher, F. (2002) "The American Way of Empire: National Tradition and Transatlantic Adaptation in America's Search for Imperial Identity, 1898–1910," German Historical Institute (Washington) *Bulletin* No. 31.

Schuman, F. (1933) *International Politics: An Introduction to the Western State System*, New York and London: McGraw-Hill.

Schurmann, F. (1974) *The Logic of World Power: An Inquiry into the Origins, Currents, and Contradictions of World Politics*, New York: Pantheon.

—— (2002) "America: The World's Next Great Empire," Pacific News Service, 1 February. Online. Available: http://www.doublestandards.org/schurm1.html (accessed 31 October 2004).

Schwartz, A.J. (1997) "From Obscurity to Notoriety: A Biography of the Exchange Stabilization Fund," *Journal of Money, Credit, and Banking* 29(2): 135–153.

Schwartz, E. (2001) "The Intervention in East Timor," National Intelligence Council Project on Intervention and Internal Conflict, Center for International and Security Studies, University of Maryland School of Public Affairs, December. Online. Available: www.cissm.umd.edu/NIC/Schwartz.pdf (accessed 4 June 2005).

Schwarzkopf, N. (1992) *It Doesn't Take a Hero: The Autobiography*, with P. Petre, New York: Bantam Books.

Scott, J.C. (1972) *Comparative Political Corruption*, Englewood Cliffs, NJ: Prentice-Hall.

Scott, J.M. (1996) *Deciding to Intervene: The Reagan Doctrine and American Foreign Policy*, Durham, NC: Duke University Press.

Scott, P.D. (1985) "The United States and the Overthrow of Sukarno, 1965–67," *Pacific Affairs* 58(2): 239–264.

Scranton, M.E. (1991) *The Noriega Years: U.S.-Panamanian Relations, 1981–1990*, Boulder, CO: Lynne Rienner.

Segell, G.M. (2004) "Intelligence Agency Relations Between the European Union and the U.S.," *International Journal of Intelligence and Counterintelligence* 17(1): 81–96.

Sent, E.-M. (2000) "Herbert A. Simon as a Cyborg Scientist," *Perspectives on Science* 8(4): 380–406.

Serafino, N.M. (2003) "Colombia: Summary and Tables on U.S. Assistance, FY1989 – FY2004," *CRS Report for Congress* RS21213, Congressional Research Service, Library of Congress, 19 May. Online. Available: http://www.ndu.edu/library/docs/crs/crs_rs21213_19may03.pdf (accessed 9 August).

—— (2005) "The Global Peace Operations Initiative: Background and Issues for Congress," *CRS Report for Congress* RL32773, Congressional Research Service, Library of Congress, 16 February. Online. Available: www.fas.org/sgp/crs/misc/RL32773.pdf (accessed 5 June 2005).

Shannon, C.E. and Weaver, W. (1949) *A Mathematical Model of Communication*, Urbana, IL: University of Illinois Press.

Sharp, J.M. (2004) "Qatar: Background and U.S. Relations," *CRS Report for Congress* RL31718, Congressional Research Service, Library of Congress, 17 March. Online. Available: http://fpc.state.gov/documents/organization/33741.pdf (accessed 5 April 2005).

Shawcross, W. (1979) *Sideshow: Kissinger, Nixon and the Destruction of Cambodia*, New York: Pocket Books/Simon & Schuster.

Sheehan, N. (1988) *A Bright Shining Lie: John Paul Vann and America in Vietnam*, New York: Random House.

Shorrock, T. (2008) *Spies for Hire: The Secret World of Intelligence Outsourcing*, New York: Simon & Schuster.

Shotwell, J.T. (1937) *At the Paris Peace Conference*, New York: Macmillan.

Shultz, G.P. (1993) *Turmoil and Triumph: My Years as Secretary of State*, New York: Scribner's.

Sick, G. (1985) *All Fall Down: America's Tragic Encounter with Iran*, New York: Random House.

Sigmund, P.E. (1974) "The 'Invisible Blockade' and the Overthrow of Allende," *Foreign Affairs* 52(2): 322–340.

Simma, B. (1999) "NATO, the UN and the Use of Force: Legal Aspects," *European Journal of International Law* 10(1): 1–22.

Simon, H.A. (1947) *Administrative Behavior: A Study of Decision-Making Processes in Administrative Organizations*, New York: Macmillan.

—— (1952) "On the Application of Servomechanism Theory in the Study of Production Control," *Econometrica* 20(2): 247–268.

—— (1955) "A Behavioral Model of Rational Choice," *Quarterly Journal of Economics* 69(1): 99–118.

—— (1964) "On the Concept of Organizational Goal," *Administrative Science Quarterly* 9(1): 1–22.

Sims, B. (1992) *Workers of the World Undermined: American Labor's Role in U.S. Foreign Policy*, Boston: South End Press.

Singer, P.W. (2003) *Corporate Warriors: The Rise of the Privatized Military Industry*, Ithaca, NY: Cornell University Press.

—— (2005) "Outsourcing War," *Foreign Affairs* 84(2): 119–133.

—— (2007) "Can't Win with 'Em, Can't Go to War without 'Em: Private Military Contractors and Counterinsurgency," *Policy Paper* No. 4, Brookings Foreign Policy, September. Online. Available: http://www.brookings.edu/~/media/Files/rc/papers/2007/0927militarycontractors/0927militarycontractors.pdf (accessed 18 April 2008).

Skowronek, S. (1982) *Building a New American State: The Expansion of National Administrative Capacities, 1877–1920*, Cambridge: Cambridge University Press.

Sluglett, P. (1976) *Britain in Iraq: 1914–1932*, London: Ithaca Press.

Smith, R.F. (1972) *The United States and Revolutionary Nationalism in Mexico, 1916–1932*, Chicago, IL: University of Chicago Press.

Smith, T. (1994) *America's Mission: The United States and the Worldwide Struggle for Democracy in the Twentieth Century*, Princeton, NJ: Princeton University Press.

Smith, W.S. (1996) "Cuba's Long Reform," *Foreign Affairs* 75(2): 99–112.

Snepp, F. (1977) *Decent Interval: An Insider's Account of Saigon's Indecent End Told by the CIA's Chief Strategy Analyst in Vietnam*, New York: Random House.

South East Asia Community Resource Center (2002) "Chronology Lao – The War Years." Online. Available: http://www.seacrc.org/pages/ravenschrono.html (accessed 26 April 2005).

Sparrow, B.H. (1996) *From the Outside In: World War II and the American State*, Princeton, NJ: Princeton University Press.

—— (2006) *The Insular Cases and the Emergence of American Empire*, Lawrence, KS: University Press of Kansas.

Steele, R.W. (1984) "The Great Debate: Roosevelt, the Media, and the Coming of the War, 1940–41," *Journal of American History* 71(1): 69–92.

Steinbruner, J.D. (1974) *The Cybernetic Theory of Decision: New Dimensions of Political Analysis*, Princeton, NJ: Princeton University Press.

Stenlås, N. and Nilsson, M. (2004) "Cold War Neutrality and Technological Dependence: Sweden's Military Technology in the East-West Trade," Royal Institute of Technology. Online. Available: http://www.cc.jyu.fi/~pete/EWStenlas.pdf (accessed 3 June 2005).

Stepan, A. (1971) *The Military in Politics: Changing Patterns in Brazil*, Princeton, NJ: Princeton University Press.

Stephanson, A. (1995) *Manifest Destiny: American Expansion and the Empire of Right*, New York: Hill and Wang.

Stevenson, J. (2007) "Risks and Opportunities in Somalia," *Survival* 49(2): 5–20.

Stigler, A.L. (2002/3) "A Clear Victory for Air Power: NATO's Empty Threat to Invade Kosovo," *International Security* 27(3): 124–157.

Stiglitz, J.E. and Bilmes, L.J. (2008) *The Three Trillion Dollar War: The True Cost of the Iraq Conflict*, New York: W.W. Norton.

Stimson, H.L. (1927) *American Policy in Nicaragua*, New York: Charles Scribner's Sons.

—— (1973) *Diaries of Henry Lewis Stimson*, microfilm edn, H. Kahn, B. Collier, and P. Goldstein (eds), New Haven, CT: Yale University Library, Manuscripts and Archives.

Stockholm International Peace Research Institute (2005) *SIPRI Yearbook 2005: Armaments, Disarmament and International Security*, Oxford: Oxford University Press. Chapter Ten online. Available: http://www.sipri.org/contents/armstrad/ch10.MASTER.050513.pdf (accessed 9 June 2005).

Stockwell, J. (1978) *In Search of Enemies: A CIA Story*, New York: W.W. Norton & Company.

Stromsen, J.M. and Trincellito, J. (2003) "Building the Haitian National Police: A Retrospective and Prospective View," *Haiti Papers* 6, April, The Haitian Program, Trinity College, Washington, DC.

Stueck, W. (1983) "The March to the Yalu: The Perspective from Washington," in B. Cumings (ed.) *Child of Conflict: The Korean-American Relationship, 1943–1953*, Seattle, WA: University of Washington Press.

—— (1995) *The Korean War: An International History*, Princeton, NJ: Princeton University Press.

—— (2002) *Rethinking the Korean War: A New Diplomatic and Strategic History*, Princeton, NJ: Princeton University Press.

Sulehria, F. (2004) "Ballots in Battlefields: The Afghan Election," *ZNet*, 31 October. Online. Available: http://www.globalpolicy.org/security/issues/afghan/2004/1031ballots.htm (accessed 5 July 2005).

Sullivan, W.H. (1981) *Mission to Iran*, New York: Norton.

Summers, H.G. (1982) *On Strategy: A Critical Analysis of the Vietnam War*, Novato, CA: Presidio Press.

Sumner, W.G. (1899) "The Conquest of the United States by Spain," *Yale Law Journal* 8(4): 168–193.

Suskind, R. (2006) *The One Percent Doctrine: Deep Inside America's Pursuit of Its Enemies Since 9/11*, New York: Simon & Schuster.

Sylvan, D. and Majeski, S. (2006) "Reviving the Cybernetic Approach to Foreign Policy Analysis: Explaining the Continuity of U.S. Policy Instruments," paper presented at the Annual Convention of the International Studies Association, San Diego, CA, March.

—— (2007) "A Cybernetic Approach to Continuity in U.S. Foreign Policy," paper presented at the Annual Convention of the International Studies Association, Chicago, IL, February.

—— (2008) "Ideology and Intervention," paper presented at the Annual Convention of the International Studies Association, San Francisco, CA, March.

Tareke, G. (2002) "From Lash to Red Star: The Pitfalls of Counter-Insurgency in Ethiopia, 1980–82," *Journal of Modern African Studies* 40(3): 465–498.

Tate, M. (1965) *The United States and the Hawaiian Kingdom: A Political History*, New Haven, CT: Yale University Press.

Thies, W.J. (1980) *When Governments Collide: Coercion and Diplomacy in the Vietnam Conflict, 1964–1968*, Berkeley, CA: University of California Press.

Thompson, L. (2002) "The Imperial Republic: A Comparison of the Insular Territories under U.S. Domination after 1898," *Pacific Historical Review* 71(4): 535–574.

Tocqueville, A. (1969) *Democracy in America*, trans. G. Lawrence, ed. J. P. Mayer, Garden City, NY: Anchor Books [from edn. of 1850].

Troung, Grandolini, A., and Cooper, T. (2003) "Laos, 1948–89," pts. 1–3, Indochina Database, Air Combat Information Group, 13 November. Online. Available: http://www.acig.org/artman/publish/cat_index_17.shtml (accessed 10 September 2005).

Truman, H.S. (1956) *Memoirs*, vol. 2: *Years of Trial and Hope*, Garden City, NY: Doubleday & Company.

Tuchman, B.W. (1971) *Stilwell and the American Experience in China, 1911–45*, New York: Macmillan.

Tuveson, E.L. (1968) *Redeemer Nation: The Idea of America's Millennial Role*, Chicago, IL: University of Chicago Press.

Tvedten, I. (1992) "U.S. Policy Towards Angola Since 1975," *Journal of Modern African Studies* 30(1): 31–52.

Tyler, P. (1999) "The (Ab)normalization of U.S.-Chinese Relations," *Foreign Affairs* 78(5): 93–122.

Ulbrich, D.J. (2002) "Research Note: 'A Program for Covert Action Against the Castro Regime, 16 March 1960,'" *SHAFR Newsletter*, September.

USGovernmentSpending.com (2008) "United States Federal, State, and Local Government Spending," 23 August. Online. Available: http://www.usgovernmentspending.com/defense_spending_30.html#usgs302 (accessed 23 August 2008).

Vaicius, I. and Isacson, A. (2003) "The 'War on Drugs' Meets the 'War on Terror'," *International Policy Report*, February, Center for International Policy.

Valenzuela, A. (2004) "A Betrayal of Democracy," *Salon.com*, 10 March. Online. Available: http://www.salon.com/opinion/feature/2004/03/10/haiti/ (accessed 4 November 2005).

Valenzuela, A.A. and Rosello, V.M. (2004) "Expanding Roles and Missions in the War on Drugs and Terrorism: El Salvador and Colombia," *Military Review* 84: 28–35.

Vance, C. (1983) *Hard Choices: Critical Years in America's Foreign Policy*, New York: Simon & Schuster.

Van Nederveen, G.K. (2001) "USAF Airlife into the Heart of Darkness, the Congo 1960–78: Implications for Modern Air Mobility Planners," *Research Paper 2001–04*, Airpower Research Institute, College of Aerospace Doctrine, Research, and Education, Air University, September. Online. Available: http://www2.hickam.af.mil/ho/Past/Airlift_History/USAF_Airlift_Congo_AirUniv_Sep01.pdf (accessed 7 September 2005).

Veeser, C. (2003) "Inventing Dollar Diplomacy: The Gilded-Age Origins of the Roosevelt Corollary to the Monroe Doctrine," *Diplomatic History* 27(3): 301–326.

Veillette, C. (2005)"Plan Colombia: A Progress Report," *CRS Report for Congress* RL32774, Congressional Research Service, Library of Congress, 22 June. Online. Available: http://fpc.state.gov/documents/organization/50264.pdf (accessed 9 August 2005).

Vitalis, R. (2002) "Black Gold, White Crude: An Essay on American Exceptionalism, Hierarchy, and Hegemony in the Gulf," *Diplomatic History* 26(2): 185–213.

—— (2006) *America's Kingdom: Mythmaking on the Saudi Oil Frontier*, Stanford. CA: Stanford University Press.

Vollman, D. (1993) "Africa and the New World Order," *Journal of Modern African Studies* 31(1): 1–30.

Vongsavanh, S. (1978) *RLG Military Operations and Activities in the Laotian Panhandle*, Indochina Monographs, Fort McNair, Washington, DC: U.S. Army Center of Military History.

Wallace-Hadrill, A. (ed.) (1989) *Patronage in Ancient Society*, London: Routledge.

Walton, C.D. (2002) *The Myth of Inevitable U.S. Defeat in Vietnam*, London and Portland, OR: Frank Cass.

Warner, M. (2000) "The Office of Strategic Services: America's First Intelligence Agency," Central Intelligence Agency, May. Online. Available: http://webroots.org/library/usamisc/oss-cia0.html (accessed 17 August 2008).

Warner, R. (1996) *Shooting at the Moon: The Story of America's Clandestine War in Laos*, South Royalton, VT: Steerforth Press. [Rev. edn of *Back Fire: The CIA's Secret War in Laos and Its Link to the War in Vietnam*, New York: Simon & Schuster, 1995.]

Wars of the World (2003) "A Timeline of Events 1800–1999," 2 October. Online. Available: http://www.onwar.com/aced/chrono/index.htm (accessed 5 August 2005).

Washington Office on Latin America (2003) *Security Assistance Organizations (Overseas Military Program Management)*. Online. Available: http://www.ciponline.org/facts/sao.htm (accessed 11 October 2004).

—— (2004) *Training Data: Bolivia*. Online. Available: www.ciponline.org/facts/fmtrbo.htm (accessed 11 October 2004).

—— (2005) "Protecting the Pipeline: The U.S. Military Mission Expands," *Colombia Monitor*, May.

Waters, R. and Daniels, G. (2005) "The World's Longest General Strike: The AFL-CIO, the CIA, and British Guiana," *Diplomatic History* 29(2): 279–307.

Wauthier, C. (1995) *Quatre présidents et l'Afrique: De Gaulle, Pompidou, Giscard d'Estaing, Mitterrand*, Paris: Seuil.

Weinberg, A.K. (1935) *Manifest Destiny: A Study of Nationalist Expansionism in American History*, Baltimore, MD: Johns Hopkins Press.

Weissman, S.R. (1979) "CIA Covert Action in Zaire and Angola: Patterns and Consequences," *Political Science Quarterly* 94(2): 263–286.

Weller, M. (ed.) (1994) *Regional Peace-keeping and International Enforcement: The Liberian Crisis*, Cambridge International Documents Series, vol. 6, Research Centre for International Law, University of Cambridge, Cambridge: Grotius Publications/Cambridge University Press.

Whelan, T. (2003) "Remarks to IPOA Dinner," 19 November. Online. Available: http://www.defenselink.mil/policy/isa/africa/IPOA.htm (accessed 4 June 2005).

Whipple, A.B.C. (1991) *To the Shores of Tripoli: The Birth of the U.S. Navy and Marines*, New York: William Morrow and Company.

Wiener, N. (1942) "Summary Report for Demonstration," Report to D.I.C. 5980 A.A. Directors, 10 June. Cited in Galison (1994: 236).

—— (1948) *Cybernetics: or Control and Communication in the Animal and the Machine*, Cambridge, MA: MIT Press.

——(1950) *The Human Use of Human Beings: Cybernetics and Society*, Boston, MA: Houghton Mifflin

Williams, G. (1997) "Prelude to an Intervention: Grenada 1983," *Journal of Latin American Studies* 29(1): 131–169.

Williams, W.A. (1980) *Empire as a Way of Life: An Essay on the Causes and Character of America's Present Predicament along with a Few Thoughts about an Alternative*, New York and Oxford: Oxford University Press.

Williams, W.L. (1980) "United States Indian Policy and the Debate Over Philippine Annexation: Implications for the Origins of American Imperialism," *Journal of American History* 66(4): 810–831.

Winthrop, J. (1630) "A Modell of Christian Charity," repr. *Collections of the Massachusetts Historical Society*, Boston (1838), 3d ser., 7: 31–48. Online. Available: http://history.hanover. edu/texts/winthmod.html (accessed 22 January 2008).

Womack, B. (1996) "Vietnam in 1995: Successes in Peace," *Asian Survey* 36(1): 73–82.

Woodward, B. (1987) *Veil: The Secret Wars of the CIA, 1981–1987*, New York: Simon & Schuster.

—— (1991) *The Commanders*, New York: Simon & Schuster.

—— (2002) *Bush at War*, New York: Simon & Schuster.

—— (2004) *Plan of Attack*, New York: Simon & Schuster.

—— (2006) *State of Denial: Bush at War*, Part III, New York: Simon & Schuster.

Wright, D.P. and Reese, T.R. (2008) *On Point II: Transition to the New Campaign, The United States Army in Operation IRAQI FREEDOM, May 2003–January 2005*, Fort Leavenworth, KS: Combat Studies Institute Press, U.S. Army Combined Arms Center.

Yaqub, S. (2002) "Imperious Doctrines: U.S.-Arab Relations from Dwight D. Eisenhower to George W. Bush," *Diplomatic History* 26(4): 571–591.

Yergin, D. (1978) *Shattered Peace: The Origins of the Cold War and the National Security State*, Boston: Houghton Mifflin.

Zakaria, F. (2008) *The Post-American World*, New York: W.W. Norton.

Zimmermann, W. (2002) *First Great Triumph: How Five Americans Made Their Country a World Power*, New York: Farrar, Straus and Giroux.

Zorzi, A. (2004) "The 'Material Constitution' of the Florentine Dominion," in W.J. Connell and A. Zorzi (eds) *Florentine Tuscany: Structures and Practices of Power*, Cambridge: Cambridge University Press.

Zoubir, Y.H. (2002) "Libya in US Foreign Policy: From Rogue State to Good Fellow?" *Third World Quarterly* 23(1): 31–53.

Zunes, S. (2003) "The US Invasion of Grenada: A Twenty Year Retrospective," *Foreign Policy in Focus*, October. Online. Available: http://www.globalpolicy.org/empire/history/2003/10grenada. htm (accessed 6 April 2005).

Document collections

FRUS (U.S. Department of State, *Foreign Relations of the United States*, Washington, DC: Government Printing Office)

FRUS 1910, 1915.

FRUS 1927, vol. 3, 1942.

FRUS 1931, vol. 3, 1946.

FRUS Japan: 1931–41, 2 vols., 1943.

FRUS 1933, vol. 2: *The British Commonwealth, Europe, Near East and Africa*, 1949.

FRUS 1937, vol. 5: *The American Republics*, 1954.

FRUS 1940, vol. 4: *The Far East*, 1955.

FRUS: The Conferences at Washington and Quebec, 1943, 1970.

FRUS: The Conference at Quebec, 1944, 1972.

FRUS: The Conferences at Malta and Yalta, 1945, 1955.

FRUS: The Conference of Berlin (The Potsdam Conference), 1945, 2 vols., 1960.

FRUS 1945, vol. 6: *The British Commonwealth; The Far East*, 1969.

FRUS 1945–50, Emergence of the Intelligence Establishment, 1996.

FRUS 1946, vol. 7: *The Far East*, 1971.

FRUS 1947, vol. 3: *The British Commonwealth; Europe*, 1972.

FRUS 1948, vol. 3: *Western Europe*, 1974.

FRUS 1948, vol. 5: *The Near East, South Asia, and Africa*, 1976.

FRUS 1949, vol. 6: *The Near East, South Asia, and Africa*, 1977.

FRUS 1950, vol. 6: *Asia and the Pacific*, 1976.

FRUS 1950, vol. 7: *Korea*, 1976.

FRUS 1951, vol. 6: *Asia and the Pacific*, 1977.

FRUS 1951, vol. 7, pt. 1: *Korea and China*, 1983.

FRUS 1952–54, vol. 4: *The American Republics*, 1983. Guatemala Compilation rereleased 2003 online: http://www.state.gov/r/pa/ho/frus/ike/iv/

FRUS 1952–54, vol. 9: *The Near and Middle East*, 1986.

FRUS 1952–54, vol. 13, 2 pts.: *Indochina*, 1982.

FRUS 1952–54, vol. 15, 2 pts.: *Korea*, 1984.

FRUS 1952–54, Guatemala, 2003.

FRUS 1955–57, vol. 13: *Near East: Jordan–Yemen*, 1989.

FRUS 1955–57, vol. 22: *Southeast Asia*, 1989.

FRUS 1958–60, vol. 4: *Foreign Economic Policy*, 1992.

FRUS 1958–60, vol. 6: *Cuba*, 1991.

FRUS 1958–60, vol. 7, pt. 1: *Western European Integration and Security; Canada*, 1993.

FRUS 1958–60, vol. 10, pt. 2: *Eastern Europe Region; Poland; Greece; Turkey; Yugoslavia*, 1994.

FRUS 1958–60, vol. 11: *Lebanon and Jordan*, 1992.

FRUS 1958–60, vol. 15: *South and Southeast Asia*, 1992.

FRUS 1958–60, vol. 17: *Indonesia*, 1994.

FRUS 1958–60, vol. 18: *Japan and Korea*, 1994.

FRUS 1961–63, vol. 1: *Vietnam, 1961*, 1988.

FRUS 1961–63, vol. 4: *Vietnam, August–December 1963*, 1991.

FRUS 1961–63, vol. 8: *National Security Policy*, 1996.

FRUS 1961–63, vol. 9: *Foreign Economic Policy*, 1995.

FRUS 1961–63, vol. 10: *Cuba 1961–62*, 1997.

FRUS 1961–63, vol. 11: *Cuban Missile Crisis and Aftermath*, 1996.

FRUS 1961–63, vol. 12: *American Republics*, 1996.

FRUS 1961–63, vol. 22: *China; Korea; Japan*, 1996.

FRUS 1961–63, vol. 23: *Southeast Asia*, 1994.

FRUS 1961–63, vol. 24: *Laos Crisis*, 1994.

FRUS 1964–68, vol. 1: *Vietnam, 1964*, 1992.

FRUS 1964–68, vol. 2: *Vietnam, January–June 1965*, 1996.

FRUS 1964–68, vol. 3: *Vietnam, June–December 1965*, 1996.

FRUS 1964–68, vol. 6: *Vietnam, January–August 1968*, 2002.

FRUS 1964–68, vol. 12: *Western Europe*, 2001.

FRUS 1964–68, vol. 14: *Soviet Union*, 2001.

FRUS 1964–68, vol. 16: *Cyprus; Greece; Turkey*, 2002.

FRUS 1964–1968, vol. 24: *Africa*, 1999.

FRUS 1964–1968, vol. 26: *Indonesia; Malaysia-Singapore; Philippines*, 2001.

FRUS 1964–1968, vol. 28: *Laos*, 1998.

FRUS 1964–1968, vol. 29, pt. 2: *Japan*, 2006.

FRUS 1964–1968, vol. 31: *South and Central America; Mexico*, 2004.

FRUS 1964–1968, vol. 32: *Dominican Republic; Cuba; Haiti; Guyana*, 2005.

FRUS 1969–1976, vol. 17: *China, 1969–1972*, 2006.

FRUS 1969–1976, vol. E-4: *Documents on Iran and Iraq, 1969–1972*, 2006.

Other collections

Baker, R.S. and Dodd, W.E. (eds) (1926) *The Public Papers of Woodrow Wilson*, vol. 1: *The New Democracy*, New York and London: Harper & Brothers.

Byrne, M. (ed.) (2002) "The 1956 Hungarian Revolution: A History in Documents," *National Security Archive Electronic Briefing Book No. 76*, 4 November. Online. Available: http://www.gwu.edu/%7Ensarchiv/NSAEBB/NSAEBB76/ (accessed 9 January 2006).

Cambone, S. (2001) Notes from Meetings with Rumsfeld, 11 September. Online. Available: http://flickr.com/photos/66726692@N00/sets/72057594065491946/ (accessed 21 September 2006).

Federation of American Scientists (ed.) (2001) "Military Analysis Network, NATO Expansion." Online. Available: http://www.fas.org/man/nato/ (accessed 13 April 2005).

—— (2003) "NSDD – National Security Decision Directives, Reagan Administration," Intelligence Resource Program, 25 February. Online. Available: http://www.fas.org/irp/offdocs/nsdd/index.html (accessed 25 August 2005).

Gerald R. Ford Library (2000) "The Vietnam War Declassification Project," April. Online. Available: http://www.ford.utexas.edu/library/exhibits/vietnam/vietnam.htm (accessed 11 October 2005).

John F. Kennedy Library (2006) "National Security Action Memoranda," 16 March. Online. Available: http://www.jfklibrary.net/nsam.htm (accessed 20 April 2006).

Kornbluh, P. (ed.) (1998) "Chile and the United States: Declassified Documents Relating to the Military Coup, September 11, 1973," *National Security Archive Electronic Briefing Book No. 8*, September. Online. Available: http://www.gwu.edu/~nsarchiv/NSAEBB/NSAEBB8/nsaebb8i.htm (accessed 10 May 2005).

—— (ed.) (2002) "Conflicting Missions: Secret Cuban Documents on History of Africa Involvement," *National Security Archive Electronic Briefing Book 67*, 1 April. Online. Available: http://www.gwu.edu/~nsarchiv/NSAEBB/NSAEBB67/ (accessed 26 April 2006).

Link, A.S. (ed.) (1979) *The Papers of Woodrow Wilson*, vol. 29: *December 2, 1913 – May 5, 1914*, Princeton, NJ: Princeton University Press.

Mary Ferrell Foundation (2006) "Castro Assassination Plots." Online. Available: http://www.maryferrell.org/wiki/index.php/Castro_Assassination_Plots (accessed 9 April 2006).

National Security Archive (2001) "Bay of Pigs 40 Years After," 22–24 March. Online. Available: http://www.gwu.edu/~nsarchiv/bayofpigs/index.html (accessed 9 April 2006).

Pentagon Papers (1971) *The Pentagon Papers: The Senator Gravel Edition: The Defense Department History of United States Decisionmaking on Vietnam*, Boston, MA: Beacon Press.

ProQuest (2005) *Digital National Security Archive*. Online. Available: http://nsarchive.chadwyck.com/ (accessed 8 September 2005).

Simpson, B. (ed.) (2004) "Indonesia's 1969 Takeover of West Papua not by 'Free Choice,'" *The Indonesia/East Timor Documentation Project*, 9 July. Online. Available: http://www.gwu.edu/~nsarchiv/NSAEBB/NSAEBB128/index.htm (accessed 31 March 2005).

Truman Presidential Museum and Library (2003) "Week by Week Accounts and Official Documents," *The Korean War*. Online. Available: http://www.trumanlibrary.org/whistlestop/study_collections/korea/large/index.htm (accessed 20 August 2005).

U.S. Central Intelligence Agency (2006) Electronic Reading Room. Online. Available: http://www.foia.cia.gov/ (accessed 23 February 2006).

U.S. Department of State (1949) *United States Relations with China, with Special Reference to the Period 1944–1949*, Publication 3573, Far Eastern Series 30.

Government and international documents

African Development Bank (2005) "Bank Group's 2004 Approvals." Online. Available: http://www.afdb.org/BK_2004_APPROVALS.xls (accessed 14 June 2005).

Angolan Government and UNITA (1994) *Lusaka Protocol*, 15 November. Online. Available: http://www.c-r.org/accord/ang/accord15/c09x.shtml (accessed 25 April 2006).

Asian Development Bank (2005) *Asian Development Bank Annual Report 2004*. Online. Available: http://www.adb.org/Documents/Reports/Annual_Report/2004/default.asp (accessed 14 June 2005).

Australia Department of Defence (2004) "Department of Defence Submission," Joint Standing Committee [Parliament] on Foreign Affairs, Defence and Trade Inquiry into Australia-United

States Defence Relations, Submission No. 6, February. Online. Available: http://www.aph.gov.au/house/committee/jfadt/usrelations/subs/ussub6.pdf (accessed 3 June 2005).

Canada Department of Foreign Affairs and International Trade (2002) *Canada and the World: A History. 1939–1945: The World at War*, October. Online. Available: http://www.dfait-maeci.gc.ca/department/history/canada6-en.asp (accessed 14 April 2005).

Canada Department of National Defence (1994) Policy Group, *1994 White Paper on Defence*. Online. Available: http://www.forces.gc.ca/admpol/eng/doc/white_e.htm (accessed 3 June 2005).

—— (2005) DND/CF, Canada-US Relations, "Interoperability," 12 May. Online. Available HTTP: http://www.forces.gc.ca/site/focus/canada-us/backgrounder_e.asp (accessed 3 June 2005).

Council of Europe (2007) Parliamentary Assembly, *Secret Detentions and Illegal Transfers of Detainees Involving Council of Europe Member States: Second Report*, Doc. 11302 rev., 11 June. Online. Available: http://assembly.coe.int/Documents/WorkingDocs/Doc07/edoc11302.pdf (accessed 27 March 2008).

European Bank for Reconstruction and Development (2005) Countries and Sectors: Signed Projects. Online. Available: http://www.ebrd.com/country/index.htm (accessed 14 June 2005).

Export.gov (2008) "U.S. Free Trade Agreements." Online. Available: http://www.export.gov/fta/index.asp (accessed 17 August 2008).

Inter-American Development Bank (2005a) *Annual Report 2004*. Online. Available: http://www.iadb.org/exr/ar2004/pdf_files.cfm?language = english (accessed 13 June 2005).

—— (2005b) *Approved Loans by Country and Fund*, May. Online. Available: http://services.iadb.org/imp_aboutus/frames.cfm?lg = EN&module = 02 (accessed 11 May 2005).

International Monetary Fund (2008) World Economic Outlook Database, April. Online. Available HTTP: http://www.imf.org/external/pubs/ft/weo/2007/01/data/index.aspx (accessed 28 August 2008).

National Security Presidential Directive 1, *Organization of the National Security Council System*, 13 February 2001. Online. Available: http://www.fas.org/irp/offdocs/nspd/nspd-1.htm (accessed 10 November 2004).

North Atlantic Treaty Organization (2005) *Ministerial Communiqués*, 21 April. Online. Available: http://www.nato.int/docu/comm.htm (accessed 29 May 2005).

Organisation for Economic Co-operation and Development (2005a) *Geographical Distribution of Financial Flows to Aid Recipients 1999–2003: Disbursements, Commitments, Country Indicators*, Paris. Online. Available: http://juno.sourceocde.org/vl = 3523069/cl = 103/nw = 1/rpsv/cgi-bin/fulltextew.pl?prpsv = /ij/oecdthemes/99980215/v2005n1/s1/p1l.idx (accessed 27 May 2005).

—— (2005b) *Final Official Development Assistance (ODA) Data for 2003*, 31 January. Online. Available: http://www.oecd.org/dataoecd/19/52/34352584.pdf (accessed 27 May 2005).

U.K. Foreign and Commonwealth Office (2004) *Foreign and Commonwealth Office Facts and Figures*. Online. Available: http://www.fco.gov.uk/servlet/Front?pagename = OpenMarket/Xcelerate/ShowPage&c = Page&cid = 1067970621009 (accessed 19 February 2005).

UN Department of Peacekeeping Operations (2003) "UN Mission's [sic] Contributions by Country," 31 October. Online. Available: http://www.un.org/Depts/dpko/dpko/contributors/2003/October2003_5.pdf (accessed 5 June 2005).

U.S. Agency for International Development (2004a) *USAID Organization Chart*, 6 January. Online. Available: http://www.usaid.gov/about_usaid/orgchart.html (accessed 7 October 2004).

—— (2004b) *Congressional Budget Justification FY 2005: Latin America and the Caribbean: Bolivia*, 24 May. Online: Available: http://www.usaid.gov/policy/budget/cbj2005/lac/bo.html (accessed 15 October 2004).

—— (2005) *U.S. Overseas Loans and Grants: Obligations and Loan Authorizations (The Greenbook)*. Online. Available: http://qesdb.cdie.org/gbk/ (accessed 31 March 2005).

U.S. Central Intelligence Agency (2000) "Subject: CIA Activities in Chile," 19 September. Online. Available: http://www.gwu.edu/~nsarchiv/news/20000919/01–01.htm (accessed 27 September 2005).

—— (2003) Electronic Reading Room, *Guatemala*. Online. Available: http://www.foia.cia.gov/guatemala.asp (accessed 16 May 2005).

—— (2004) *Diagram of Director of Central Intelligence Command Responsibilities.* Online. Available: http://www.cia.gov/cia/publications/facttell/dci_responsibilities.html (accessed 7 October 2004).

—— (2005) *The World Factbook.* Online. Available: http://www.cia.gov/cia/publications/factbook (accessed 14 June 2005).

U.S. Congress, House (1974) *United States Aid to Indochina,* Report of a Staff Survey Team to South Vietnam, Cambodia, and Laos, Committee on Foreign Affairs, July. 93rd Cong., 2d sess.

—— (1976) *Final Report,* Select Committee on Intelligence, January. 94th Cong., 2d sess. Publ. as *CIA: The Pike Report,* Nottingham, U.K.: Spokesman Books, 1977.

—— (2004a) "Testimony of General James T. Hill, United States Army, Commander, United States Southern Command," Armed Services Committee, 24 March. 108th Cong., 2d sess. Online. Available: http://www.house.gov/hasc/openingstatementsandpressreleases/108thcongres s/04-03-24hill.html (accessed 9 August 2005).

—— (2004b) *The Situation in Haiti,* Hearing Before the Subcommittee on the Western Hemisphere, Committee on International Relations, 3 March. 108th Cong., 2d sess., Serial No. 108–193.

—— (2008a) Submitted Testimony of Robert M. Gates, Secretary of Defense, Armed Services Committee, 15 April. 110th Cong., 2d sess. Online. Available: http://armedservices.house.gov/ pdfs/FC041508/GatesTestimony041508.pdf (accessed 20 May 2008).

—— (2008b) Statement for the Record of Dr. Thomas Fingar, Deputy Director of National Intelligence for Analysis and Chairman of the National Intelligence Council, Permanent Select Committee on Intelligence/Select Committee on Energy Independence and Global Warming, 25 June. 110th Cong., 2d sess.

U.S. Congress, Joint Committee on the Investigation of the Pearl Harbor Attack (1946) *Report,* Doc. No. 244, 20 July. 79th Cong., 2nd sess.

U.S. Congress, Senate (1971) *Laos: April 1971,* Staff Report, Subcommittee on U.S. Security Agreements and Commitments Abroad, Committee on Foreign Relations, 3 August. 92nd Cong., 1st sess.

—— (1973) *Thailand, Laos, Cambodia, and Vietnam: April 1973,* Staff Report, Subcommittee on U.S. Security Agreements and Commitments Abroad, Committee on Foreign Relations, 11 June. 93rd Cong., 1st sess.

—— (1975a) *Supplemental Assistance for Cambodia,* Report, with Minority Views, Committee on Foreign Relations, 21 March. 94th Cong., 1st sess., S. Rep. 94–54.

—— (1975b) *Alleged Assassination Plots Involving Foreign Leaders,* Interim Report of the Select Committee to Study Governmental Operations with Respect to Intelligence Activities, 20 November. 94th Cong., 1st sess., S. Rep. 94–465.

—— (1975c) *Covert Action in Chile 1963–1973,* Staff Report of the Select Committee to Study Governmental Operations with Respect to Intelligence Activities, 18 December. 94th Cong., 1st sess.

—— (1976) *Final Report of the Select Committee to Study Governmental Operations with Respect to Intelligence Activities,* 23 April. 94th Cong., 2d sess., S. Rep. 94–755.

U.S. Defense Institute of Security Assistance Management (2005) *DISAM's Online Green Book: The Management of Security Assistance,* 5 January. Online. Available: http://www.disam.dsca. mil/pubs/DR/greenbook.htm (accessed 18 February 2005).

U.S. Defense Intelligence Agency (2002) "The Defense Attaches," *History: 40 Years of DIA,* 22 November. Online. Available: http://www.dia.mil/History/Histories/attaches.html (accessed 18 February 2005).

U.S. Defense Security Cooperation Agency (2004) *Foreign Military Sales, Foreign Military Construction Sales and Military Assistance Facts, as of September 30, 2003,* 4 October. Online. Available: http://www.dsca.mil/programs/biz-ops/2003_facts/Facts_Book_2003_Oct04_FINAL. pdf (accessed 23 November 2004).

—— (2005) *36(b) Arms Sales Notifications.* Online. Available: http://www.dsca.osd.mil/PressRel eases/36-b/36b_index.htm (accessed 3 June 2005).

U.S. Department of Defense (1992) *Conduct of the Persian Gulf War: Final Report to Congress*, April. Online. Available: http://www.ndu.edu/library/epubs/cpgw.pdf (accessed 27 March 2008).

—— (1999) *DoD Directive 5111.1: Under Secretary of Defense for Policy (USD(P))*, 8 December. Online. Available: http://www.dtic.mil/whs/directives/corres/pdf/d51111_120899/d51111p.pdf (accessed 23 November 2004).

—— (2003) *DISAM's [Defense Institute of Security Assistance Management] Online Green Book: The Management of Security Assistance*, 23d edn. 30 December. Online. Available: http://www.disam.dsca.mil/pubs/DR/greenbook.htm (accessed 14 October 2004).

—— (2004a) Directorate for Information Operations and Reports, Statistical Information Analysis Division, Work Force Publications, *Monthly Report of Federal Civilian Employment. Report for: Office of the Secretary of Defense, Report Month: 200409*. Online. Available: http://www.dior.whs.mil/mmid/civilian/fy2004/July2004/osdd.pdf (accessed 11 November 2004).

—— (2004b) Office of the Under Secretary of Defense for Policy, International Security Affairs, *Responsibilities and Functions*. Online. Available: http://www.dod.gov/policy/isa/about.html (accessed 11 November 2004).

—— (2004c) *Unified Command Plan*, 10 November. Online. Available: http://www.dod.gov/specials/unifiedcommand/ (accessed 29 November 2004).

—— (2004d) Office of the Deputy Under Secretary of Defense (Installations and Environment), *Base Structure Report (A Summary of DoD's Real Property Inventory): Fiscal Year 2004 Baseline*, 10 September. Online. Available: http://www.defenselink.mil/pubs/20040910_2004BaseStructureReport.pdf (accessed 29 March 2005).

—— (2004e) Washington Headquarters Services, Information Technology Management Division, *Worldwide Manpower Distribution by Geographical Area*, 30 September. Online. Available: http://web1.whs.osd.mil/mmid/M05/m05sep04.pdf (accessed 29 March 2005).

U.S. Department of Defense and U.S. Department of State (2004) *Joint Report to Congress: Foreign Military Training in Fiscal Years 2003 and 2004, Volume 1*, June. Online. Available: http://www.state.gov/t/pm/rls/rpt/fmtrpt/2004/ (accessed 31 March 2005).

U.S. Department of State (1991) "Vietnam: The Road Ahead, Statement by Assistant Secretary of State Richard H. Solomon to the Senate Subcommittee on East Asian and Pacific Affairs, 25 April 1991," *Dispatch* 2,18 (6 May). Online. Available: http://dosfan.lib.uic.edu/erc/briefing/dispatch/1991/html/Dispatchv2no18.html (accessed 25 September 2006).

—— (2003) *International Narcotics and Law Enforcement: FY 2004 Budget Justification: Andean Counterdrug Initiative*. Online. Available: http://www.state.gov/g/inl/rls/rpt/cbj/fy2004/21881.htm (accessed 11 October 2004).

—— (2004a) *Department Organization*. Online. Available: http://www.state.gov/r/pa/ei/rls/dos/436.htm (accessed 5 October 2004).

—— (2004b) *Key Officers of Foreign Service Posts*. Online. Available: http://foia.state.gov/mms/koh/keyoffcity.asp (accessed 11 October 2004).

—— (2004c) *Treaties in Force: A List of Treaties and Other International Agreements of the United States in Force on January 1, 2004*. Online. Available: http://www.state.gov/s/l/38294.htm (accessed 20 February 2005).

—— (2004d) Bureau of Near Eastern Affairs, *Background Note: Qatar*, November. Online. Available: http://www.state.gov/r/pa/ei/bgn/5437.htm (accessed 29 March 2005).

—— (2004e) Bureau of Near Eastern Affairs, *Background Note: Kuwait*, August. Online. Available: http://www.state.gov/r/pa/ei/bgn/35876.htm (accessed 16 April 2005).

—— (2004f) Bureau of East Asian and Pacific Affairs, *Background Note: New Zealand*, September. Online. Available: http://www.state.gov/r/pa/ei/bgn/35852.htm (accessed 31 March 2005).

—— (2004g) Bureau of Western Hemisphere Affairs, *Background Note: Suriname*, August. Online. Available: http://www.state.gov/r/pa/ei/bgn/1893.htm (accessed 31 March 2005).

—— (2004h) Bureau of European and Eurasian Affairs, *Background Note: Macedonia*, December. Online. Available: http://www.state.gov/r/pa/ei/bgn/26759.htm (accessed 10 April 2005).

—— (2004i) Bureau of Western Hemisphere Affairs, *Background Note: The Bahamas*, August. Online. Available: http://www.state.gov/r/pa/ei/bgn/1857.htm (accessed 23 April 2005).

—— (2005a) *Fiscal Year 2006 Budget Request: International Affairs Function 150: Summary and Highlights*. Online. Available: http://www.state.gov/documents/organization/41913.pdf (accessed 18 February 2005).

—— (2005b) *Congressional Budget Justification: Foreign Operations, Fiscal Year 2006*. Online. Available: http://www.state.gov/documents/organization/42258.pdf (accessed 20 February 2005).

—— (2005c) *The Budget in Brief: Fiscal Year 2006 Budget Request*. Online. Available: http://www.state.gov/documents/organization/41676.pdf (accessed 20 February 2005).

—— (2005d) Bureau of African Affairs, *Background Note: Ethiopia*, March. Online. Available: http://www.state.gov/r/pa/ei/bgn/2859.htm (accessed 31 March 2005).

—— (2005e) Bureau of European and Eurasian Affairs, *Background Note: Poland*, February. Online. Available: http://www.state.gov/r/pa/ei/bgn/2875.htm (accessed 13 April 2005).

—— (2008) *Congressional Budget Justification: Foreign Operations, Fiscal Year 2009*, 29 February. Online. Available: http://www.usaid.gov/policy/budget/cbj2009/ (accessed 20 May 2008).

U.S. Department of the Army (1994) *Noncombatant Evacuation Operations*, FM 90–29, 17 October. Online. Available: http://www.globalsecurity.org/military/library/policy/army/fm/90–29/index.html (accessed 10 October 2004).

U.S. Department of the Treasury (2004) *Treasury Organization Chart*, February. Online. Available HTTP: http://www.treasury.gov/organization/org-chart-2004.pdf (accessed 7 October 2004).

—— (2005) Office of International Affairs, *ESF Credit Arrangements, 1936–1972; ESF Credit Arrangements, 1972–2002*. Online. Available: http://www.treas.gov/offices/international-affairs/esf/history/credits.pdf (accessed 26 June 2005).

U.S. Department of War (1900) *Annual Reports of the War Department for the Fiscal Year Ended June 30, 1900, Report of the Lieutenant-General Commanding the Army in Seven Parts*, vol. 1, Washington, DC: U.S. Government Printing Office.

U.S. Drug Enforcement Administration (2004a) *DEA Domestic Office Locations*. Online. Available: http://www.dea.gov/agency/domestic.htm (accessed 11 October 2004).

U.S. Embassy La Paz (2004) *Principal Officers*. Online. Available: http://lapaz.usembassy.gov/english/officers.htm (accessed 11 October 2004).

U.S. Export-Import Bank (2004) *2004 Annual Report*, Washington: GPO. Online. Available: http://www.exim.gov/about/reports/ar/ar2004/index.html (accessed 8 May 2005).

—— (2007) *Annual Report 2007*, Washington: GPO. Online. Available: http://www.exim.gov/about/reports/ar/ar2007/Financial-Report_IR.html (accessed 27 March 2008).

U.S. General Accounting Office (1996) Report to the Chairman, Committee on Banking and Financial Services, House of Representatives, *Mexico's Financial Crisis: Origins, Awareness, Assistance, and Initial Efforts to Recover*, GAO/GGD-95-56, February. Online. Available: http://www.gao.gov/archive/1996/gg96056.pdf (accessed 26 June 2005).

U.S. Government Accountability Office (2008) Report to Congressional Requesters, *Combating Terrorism: The United States Lacks Comprehensive Plan to Destroy the Terrorist Threat and Close the Safe Haven in Pakistan's Federally Administered Tribal Areas*, GAO-08-622, April. Online. Available: http://www.gao.gov/new.items/d08622.pdf (accessed 18 April 2008).

U.S. Library of Congress (1994) Federal Research Division, *Laos: A Country Study*, 1 July. Online. Available: http://countrystudies.us/laos/ (accessed 26 April 2005).

U.S. National Commission on Terrorist Attacks Upon the United States (2004) *9/11 Commission Report: Final Report*, New York: Barnes and Noble Books.

U.S. National Intelligence Council (2005) "Estimative Products on Vietnam, 1948–75," 20 September. Online. Available: http://www.cia.gov/nic/NIC_foia_vietnam.html (accessed 15 October 2005).

U.S. Office of Management and Budget (2004) *Budget of the United States Government: Fiscal Year 2005*. Online. Available: http://www.whitehouse.gov/omb/budget/fy2005/budget.html (accessed 5 October 2004).

—— (2005) *Budget of the United States Government: Fiscal Year 2006: Historical Tables.* Online. Available: http://www.whitehouse.gov/omb/budget/fy2006/pdf/hist.pdf (accessed 17 June 2005).

U.S. Special Operations Command (2002) *History: 15th Anniversary,* History and Research Office, MacDill Air Force Base, FL. Online. Available: http://www.socom.mil/Docs/15th_aniversary_history.pdf (accessed 9 September 2005).

Wassenaar Arrangement (2004) *Guidelines and Procedures, Including the Initial Elements,* amended and updated, Wassenaar Arrangement Secretariat, Vienna, July. Online. Available: http://www.wassenaar.org/2003Plenary/initial_elements2003.htm (accessed 27 May 2005).

World Bank (2002) *Haiti: Country Assistance Evaluation,* Report No. 23637, Operations Evaluation Department, 12 February.

—— (2004a) *World Bank Group Historical Chronology,* April. Online. Available: http://siteresources.worldbank.org/EXTARCHIVES/Resources/World_Bank_historical_chronology.pdf (accessed 9 May 2005).

—— (2004b) *The World Bank's First Loan: May 9, 1947.* Online. Available: http://web.worldbank.org/WBSITE/EXTERNAL/EXTABOUTUS/EXTARCHIVES/0,contentMDK:20035704~menuPK:56273~pagePK:36726~piPK:36092~theSitePK:29506,00.html (accessed 9 May 2005).

—— (2004c) *The World Bank Annual Report 2004,* vol. 2, September. Online. Available: http://www.worldbank.org/annualreport/2004/Vol_2/PDF/WB%20Annual%20Report%202004.pdf (accessed 13 June 2005).

—— (2005) *Projects Database by Country/Area,* May. Online. Available: http://web.worldbank.org/external/projects/main?category = country&menuPK = 51559&pagePK = 221246&piPK = 95913&theSitePK = 40941 (accessed 11 May 2005).

—— (2008) World Development Indicators. Online. Available: http://web.worldbank.org/WBSITE/EXTERNAL/DATASTATISTICS/0,contentMDK:21725423~hlPK:1365919~isCURL:Y~menuPK:64133159~pagePK:64133150~piPK:64133175~theSitePK:239419,00.html (accessed 28 August 2008).

Index

9/11 attacks: 15–16, 212, 216, 218, 229

Abu Ghraib prison: 86
Acheson. D.: 56, 133–34, 149, 205
acquisition contexts *see* client acquisitions
ACRI (African Crisis Response Initiative): 241
Adams, J.: 3
Adams, J.Q.: 250, 253n8
Ad hoc vs. programmatic interactions
  see macro-continuity
Afghanistan 1, 13–14, 61, 72, 89, 93–94;
  acquisition as client 44, 260n14; as enemy
  54; emergency covert political assistance
  119; life-preserver intervention 135 36,
  147, 225, 227–28, 232, 245, 249, 252;
  combat operations alongside local
  insurgent forces 211–12, 213, 216;
  overthrow of Khalq-PDPA regime 221;
  see Soviet Union
AFL-CIO: 69–70
Africa: 21, 30, 32, 55, 81, 105–6, 232
African Command: 55
African Development Bank: establishment 79
African Union: 94, 237
AID *see* U.S. Agency for International
  Development
aid to internal armed opposition forces (node
  19) 195–99; Indonesia 195; Iraq (Kurds)
  195–96; Vietnam (Cambodia) 196, 205,
  283n42; Soviet Union (Afghanistan) 196,
  205, 211, 283n42; Cuba (Angola) 21,
  196–98, 205; Somalia 199, 283n42;
  Pakistan 199
"A" Mandates *see* client states and indirect
  rule
Albania *see* Soviet Union
Algeria: 52
Allende, S.: 118, 170–71
alliances: formal 55; not imply client status
  55–58; military bases 58
Al Qaeda: 13–14, 135–36, 199, 212, 213, 216,
  217, 229
Angola 21, 52, 178; *see* Cuba

annexed territories 6, 247–49, 258n49;
  administration of 247; citizenship 247;
  unincorporated 247; incorporation of
  248; halted 248–49, 251; restriction of
  franchise 249
Anti-Communist National Salvation Army
  (NSA): 192–94
anti-drug operations: 23, 28, 84, 128, 136,
  257n29, 257n30
ANZUS Pact: 55, 57, 63, 92–93, 259n7,
  262n58
Aquino, B.: 119
Aquino, C: 119–20
Arab-Israeli War of 1973: 225
Arbenz, J.: 164–66, 168
Argentina 58, 63–64, 96, 172, 233; acquisition
  as client 61
argumentative nature of foreign policy: 10,
  11, 254n20
Aristide, J.-B.: 166–67, 168
arms sales 91–92, 98, 102–6; trends in 101; by
  wealthier clients 95–96; *see* military
  instruments; *see* military assistance
Army of the Republic of Vietnam (ARVN)
  130–32, 150; *see* South Vietnam
Asia: 15, 18, 30, 32, 55, 75, 83, 227, 232
Asian Development Bank: establishment 79
assassination 213–14; not type of intervention
  214; possibility of institutionalized capacity
  214
at-hand availability 255n26;
  see meso-continuity
Australia 57, 79, 90, 92, 93, 96, 278n11;
  acquisition as client 63, 262n58;
  intervention as junior partner 94;
  see ANZUS Pact
Austria: acquisition as client 44
Austria-Hungary: 177, 230
Axis: 58–59, 61

Ba'ath party: 185, 188, 217
Bahamas: acquisition as client 70
Bahrain: acquisition as client 64